MACRO-QUANTITATIVE ANALYSIS

Conflict, Development, and Democratization

John V. Gillespie, *Indiana University*
Betty A. Nesvold, *San Diego State College*

SAGE PUBLICATIONS

Copyright © 1971 by Sage Publications, Inc.

Printed in the United States of America

All rights reserved. No part of this book may be reproduced or utilized in any form or by any means, electronic or mechanical, including photocopying, recording, or by any information storage and retrieval system, without permission in writing from the Publisher.

> *For information address:*
> SAGE PUBLICATIONS, INC.
> 275 South Beverly Drive
> Beverly Hills, California 90212

International Standard Book Number: 0-8039-0054-6 (C)   0-8039-0055-4 (P)

Library of Congress Catalog Card Number: 74-103013

FIRST PRINTING

EDITORS' PREFACE TO THE SERIES

This volume is part of a new series in social science that is devoted to cross-national research. Although cross-national research is of relatively new concern to social scientists, it has become an exciting area of social exploration. Its surface has only been scratched, and the variety of conceptual problems that can be fruitfully explored, cross-nationally, has only begun to be realized. Cross-national research raises numerous problems in the logic of social inquiry—the methods of data collection and analysis—and imposes a basic challenge to conventional study of foreign political and social systems.

Cross-national research involves social scientists from all disciplines, and their reports of significant research findings are in a variety of journals, research monographs, and proceedings of conferences. Cross-national research is international in focus and is not strictly an American or even West European academic enterprise. Because of the interdisciplinary and international dimensions to cross-national research, this series is provided to bring together the work of social scientists for both increased communication and productive use in the advanced classroom.

The series editors are grateful to the contributors for their cooperation, to those who aided in the direction of this series, and to those who did much of the mundane work always necessary in the production of a new series.

John V. Gillespie
Betty A. Nesvold

FOREWORD

Scholarship in the social sciences today is in an exciting period of change and expansion. New areas of research interests are being developed, areas of long standing concern are being scrutinized from new perspectives that rely on recently developed techniques, while the boundaries of each of the social sciences are increasingly overlapping each other. Many of the earlier innovations were developed by scholars of American societal phenomena: economists testing theories of economic growth, or sociologists and political scientists analyzing social and political behavior. Accumulated research in these areas enabled us to develop well tested generalizations about a variety of phenomena. The obvious question that has arisen is, are we explaining phenomena and testing propositions only in the American context or is our knowledge more widely applicable? In the last half-decade or so there has been a rapidly growing body of cross-national research; research which attempts to go beyond the American context. However, very little of this research has been pulled together and published in convenient, readily available form. The findings have been scattered through various professional journals and presented as papers at professional meetings. The political scientist who finds himself unable to examine journals and professional papers of economists, sociologists, psychologists and mass communications specialists is likely to be unaware of research in progress that is highly relevant to his own area of interest. It was this concern that led us to launch this series of volumes in cross-national research.

This present volume, which is the first one in our series, contains articles by political scientists, sociologists, economists, psychologists, and mass communications scholars. They all use aggregate data to analyze phenomena as they occur in several or many nations in the world. None are written, however, by people who consider themselves methodologists or data analysts per se. They are all written by scholars who have substantive concerns in their respective fields of interest and rely on macro-quantitative analysis to generate knowledge on the phenomena of interest. By bringing these articles together in a single volume, we feel that the interested scholar can consider some of the most important work that has been done recently on conflict, development and democratization.

Future volumes will bring together cross-national research on other phenomena. None of the research on public opinion or on socialization studies has been included in this volume. This is the intended focus of the second volume which will be edited by John Pierce of Tulane University and Richard Pride of Vanderbilt University. Subsequent volumes are planned with the same general parameters. We hope, thus, to provide collections of materials that inform the student and provide scholars in the field with current findings that constitute refinement and increasingly precise knowledge of cross-national research.

Many people have been generous with their support and comments. We would particularly like to acknowledge the assistance of David L. Carr, James C. Holmberg, and Kay Staub.

John V. Gillespie
Betty A. Nesvold

January, 1970

CONTENTS

Editors' Preface to the Series   5

Foreword   7

Part I. An Introduction to Macro-Cross-National Research
                JOHN V. GILLESPIE   13

Part II. Studies in Domestic Conflict

1. Introduction: Studies in Domestic Conflict
                BETTY A. NESVOLD   31

2. Dimensions of Conflict Behavior Within Nations, 1946–59
                RUDOLPH J. RUMMEL   39

3. Dimensions of Conflict Behavior Within and Between Nations
                RUDOLPH J. RUMMEL   49

4. Dimensions of Conflict Behavior Within and Between Nations, 1958–60
                RAYMOND TANTER   85

5. Political Instability in Latin America: The Cross-Cultural Test of a Causal Model
                DOUGLAS P. BWY   113

6. Aggressive Behaviors Within Polities, 1948–62: A Cross-National Study
        IVO K. FEIERABEND *and* ROSALIND L. FEIERABEND   141

7. Scalogram Analysis of Political Violence
                BETTY A. NESVOLD   167

8. The Conditions of Civil Violence: First Tests of a Causal Model
     TED ROBERT GURR *with* CHARLES RUTTENBERG   187

9. A Causal Model of Civil Strife: A Comparative Analysis using New Indices
                TED ROBERT GURR   217

10. Problems in Causal Analysis of Aggregate Data with Applications to Political Instability
     F. GERALD KLINE, KURT KENT, *and* DENNIS DAVIS   251

Part III. Studies in Political Development

11. Introduction: Studies in Political Development
    BETTY A. NESVOLD   283
12. Dimensions of Political Systems: Factor Analysis of *A Cross-Polity Survey*
    PHILLIP M. GREGG *and* ARTHUR S. BANKS   289
13. Grouping Political Systems: Q-Factor Analysis of *A Cross-Polity Survey*
    ARTHUR S. BANKS *and* PHILLIP M. GREGG   311
14. A Scalogram Analysis of Political Development
    PETER G. SNOW   321
15. A Factor Analysis of the Interrelationship Between Social and Political Variables and per capita Gross National Product
    IRMA ADELMAN *and* CYNTHIA TAFT MORRIS   331
16. Communism and Economic Development
    ROGER W. BENJAMIN *and* JOHN H. KAUTSKY   353

Part IV. Studies on Democratization

17. Introduction: Studies on Democratization
    JOHN V. GILLESPIE   375
18. Measuring Democratic Change in Latin America
    RUSSELL H. FITZGIBBON   383
19. The Relationship of Systemic Frustration, Political Coercion, and Political Instability: A Cross-National Analysis
    IVO K. FEIERABEND *and* ROSALIND L. FEIERABEND   417
20. Patterns of Political Development and Democratization: A Quantitative Analysis
    WILLIAM FLANIGAN *and* EDWIN FOGELMAN   441
21. Patterns of Democratic Development: An Historical Comparative Analysis
    WILLIAM FLANIGAN *and* EDWIN FOGELMAN   475
22. Toward a Communications Theory of Democratic Political Development: A Causal Model
    DONALD J. MCCRONE *and* CHARLES F. CNUDDE   499
23. Inequality: A Cross-National Analysis
    PHILLIPS CUTRIGHT   513
24. Political Structure, Economic Development, and National Social Security Programs
    PHILLIPS CUTRIGHT   539

Selective Bibliography   557

About the Contributors   565

Indexes   569

Part I

**AN INTRODUCTION TO
MACRO-CROSS-NATIONAL
RESEARCH**

An Introduction to
Macro-Cross-National Research

JOHN V. GILLESPIE

This book is a report of current efforts in macro-cross-national research. It attempts to bring together in a single volume a series of studies which involve the use of data on whole political systems and analyses of these data across national boundaries. The studies have been grouped according to the major thrust of the research: political development, domestic conflict, or democratization. None of these three headings is independent of the others, and there are many interesting interrelationships which remain to be analyzed. But in viewing the macro-cross-national literature, the studies seem to fall into these three basic groupings. Hopefully, a compilation of studies of this sort will point to several deficiencies, new areas for analysis, topics yet to be explored, the need for new measures, new data sources, and methodological advancement. By bringing together in one volume many of the current studies in macro-cross-national research, many of the problems of quantitative analysis across national boundaries could be brought to the fore. Such is the goal and purpose of this volume.

Cross-national research is still in its infancy as an approach to comparative politics. Growing out of the early efforts of Karl Deutsch (1961), Phillips Cutright (1963), the Yale Political Data Program, and similar rigorous efforts to collect and archive data on political systems, cross-national research has relatively few practitioners today.[1] As with any new approach to a given subject, there are numerous problems that arise. Early analyses provide for some speculation on the potentialities of cross-national research approach, and begin to uncover the varieties of methodological problems, which have to be faced and resolved.[2] Although such speculation may be optimistic, the methodological problems of analyzing data drawn from a large number of political systems are almost overwhelming. This volume reports the state-of-the-art, with all its present methodological and theoretical problems, as well as its potential for providing a fruitful approach to comparative political analysis.

The Cross-National Approach and the Configurative Approach in Macro-Comparative Analysis

Political and social scientists are interested in the conditions under which a given unit-of-analysis exhibits certain attributes. Social research has the responsibility of testing hypotheses to determine the nature of the relationships between conditions and the attributes of the unit-of-analysis set. In macro-cross-national research, the concern is for formulating empirical generalizations about whole political systems. Such empirical generalizations relate conditions to attributes of the political system—the unit-of-analysis. Regardless of whether the research deals with some specified subset of the unit-of-analysis set, such as Communist political systems or industrializing political systems, the effort is to link conditions with the attributes of political systems and to describe that linkage.

In comparative politics, the configurative approach has been by far the most frequently employed for the task of linking conditions with attributes of political systems.[3] In the configurative approach, data from each political system are analyzed separately, noting the relationships between conditions and attributes of a given political system. Hence, comparative analysts using the same conceptual scheme would analyze data on country A, country B, and so on. In each case, the relationships between the variables are noted. By application of the same conceptual scheme to several instances, the same hypothesis is tested over and over again, noting the discrete differences from political system A to political system B, and so on. In the configurative approach, a complex cluster of conditions and attributes of political systems is studied in each political system, and subsequent comparisons are made among political systems.

The cross-national approach differs significantly from the configurative approach in that political systems are analyzed simultaneously. That is, each political system is perceived as a case of the universe of political systems, and data from some samples or from all political systems are analyzed together, rather than each system being analyzed separately. Whereas, in the configurative approach a profile is constructed for each country, in the cross-national approach a given relationship is analyzed using data drawn from several political systems.

The differences between the cross-national and the configurative approaches can be seen by examining Figure 1.[4] In the configurative approach (vertical arrows), a political system is analyzed across a set of variables ($x_1, x_2, \ldots, x_m$). The variables $x_1, x_2, \ldots, x_m$ for the ith political system are analyzed separately from the variables for the jth political system. In the cross-national approach (horizontal arrows), the set of variables x_1 is analyzed across the set of political systems (A, B, ..., N). That is, in the cross-national approach, the attempt is to explain an attribute of the political system by using several cases, rather than to explain a variety of attributes in a specific political system.

An Introduction to Macro-Cross-National Research

Both approaches have methodological weaknesses. Using the configurative approach, it is difficult to make empirical generalizations that hold for the entire set of political systems (A, B, ..., N). For example, from an examination of some system A, we cannot make a generalization for the entire set of political systems. However, in the configurative approach, the variables (x_1, x_2, ..., x_m) have all been considered. After the configurative approach, the analyst attempts to make a set of statements about relationships between sets of conditions and a number of attributes of a given political system, without formulating generalizations that apply to more than one case. Generalizations are only formulated after analyses have been completed on several political systems.

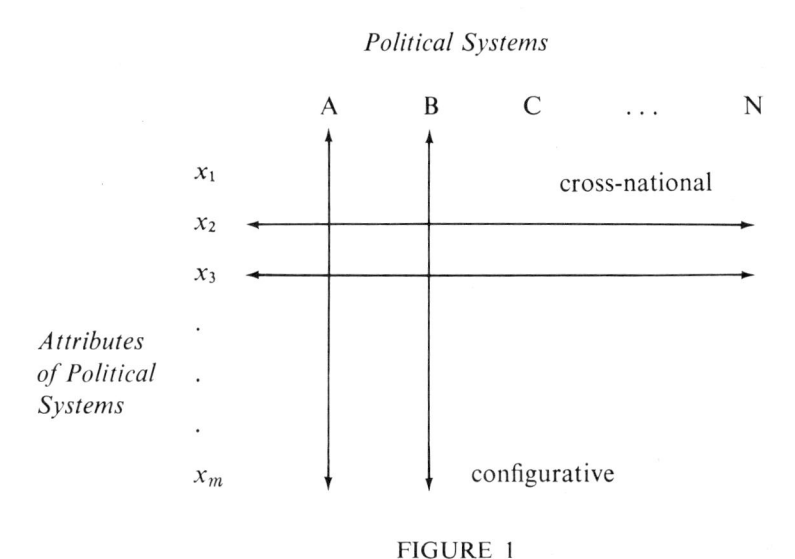

Political Systems

```
                    A    B    C   ...   N
           x₁       ↑    ↑
                    |    |        cross-national
           x₂   ←───┼────┼─────────────────→
           x₃   ←───┼────┼─────────────────→
Attributes      .
of Political    .
Systems         .
           xₘ       ↓    ↓        configurative
```

FIGURE 1

DIFFERENCES BETWEEN THE CROSS-NATIONAL AND CONFIGURATIVE APPROACHES

In the cross-national approach, generalizations are made about the relationships between a set of conditions and a set of given attributes of political systems. The attempt is to explain the attributes of political systems across all nations or some subset of nations using data drawn from several cases rather than from a single case. However, in the cross-national approach, consideration is not given to the vast number of x-variables as in the configurative approach. Whereas the configurative approach does not have the capacity of immediate empirical generalization, since it is an example of single-case analysis, the cross-national approach loses much of the indepth analysis of the configurative approach, but it provides for empirical generalization. Using the configurative approach until several analyses have been completed, the analyst has no sense of the degree to which a proposition holds true for a universe of political systems. Using the cross-national approach, the researcher cannot provide the depth of analysis achieved in the configurative approach, but he can arrive at empirical generalizations relating conditions of political systems to their attributes. Hence, the major drawback of the configurative approach is the lack of empirical generalization; the major limitation of the cross-national approach is the lack of depth analysis.

The differences between the configurative and cross-national approaches are rooted in differences between paradigms of the political system. Whereas, in the configurative approach, the variables ($x_1, x_2, \ldots, x_m$) are perceived as being highly interrelated, and hence must be analyzed together, in the cross-national approach the perception is that these variables are analytically separable. In the configurative approach, the paradigm stipulates that attributes of political systems are complexly interrelated, and an analysis of the conditions of some subset of attributes of political systems is not appropriate and theoretically feasible, given this complexity of interrelationships. In the cross-national approach, the paradigm stipulates that subsets of the entire set of attributes are not interrelated in such a way as to prohibit decomposition, and that the complexity of interrelationships stipulated in the configurative approach only holds for certain subsets. Whereas, in the configurative approach a complex set of relationships are postulated, in the cross-national approach, the postulated relationships allow the researchers to deal with something less than the whole political system. *The political system for the configurative approach cannot be divided, in any theoretically meaningful way, into component parts with respect to its attributes. In the cross-national approach, the political system can be divided into meaningful subsets of attributes* and furthermore, this decomposition implies that not all x-variables must be considered.

Although the distinction between paradigms might seem quite artificial at first glance, it is highly significant for making statements about the conditions under which political systems exhibit certain attributes. If the political system is to be thought of in terms of a highly interdependent set of variables which prohibit decomposition, the configurative approach would seem to yield the best way to proceed in the analysis of political systems. On the other hand, if the paradigm of the political system is to be divisible into related but independent subsets of attributes, the cross-national approach would seem more appropriate. Furthermore, there are epistemological ramifications to the differences between these approaches. The configurative approach offers an *emergentist explanation* (the whole is not divisible); the cross-national approach offers a *reductionist explanation* (the whole is divisible).[5] Since systems are aggregations of parts, the analyst, using the configurative approach with its emergentist viewpoint, would argue that new attributes are produced by this aggregation not definable in terms of parts of systems. Using the reductionist explanation found in the cross-national approach, he would argue that the attributes of the aggregation of parts are reducible to the component parts and the relations among the component parts. It follows that subsets of attributes of the political system may be theoretically decomposed and analyzed separately because of this reduction. In the emergentist viewpoint, subsets of attributes cannot be analyzed because of new nonreducible attributes that are produced by the aggregation of the component parts. That is, political systems for the emergentist have a complex nature not definable in terms of the component parts and relations among the component parts. Hence, the analyst must consider the entire political system because of the new emergentist phenomena, and he cannot separate some parts from other parts. On the other hand, if system attributes are reducible to parts and relations among parts, the entire political system does not have to be considered, but only certain highly related attributes of it analyzed in order to make meaningful generalizations.

This difference between emergentist and reductionist explanations is exemplified in the types of evidence that are used in the cross-national approach as opposed to the configurative approach. Often in the configurative approach, political scientists hope to describe the performance of a set of functions by the political system. The attempt is to provide some description of how the political system as a whole functions, or satisfies certain prerequisites for its continuance. Since the performance of a function is a complex attribute of political systems that emerges only in the aggregation of parts, each political system must be profiled before comparisons can be made across political systems. The evidence brought to bear on this emergentist explanatory scheme is drawn from a vast number of variables and phenomena. In the configurative approach following the emergentist viewpoint, the evidence must be drawn from a wide variety of structures and phenomena, since the functioning of the whole system is not reducible to relations between component parts.

In the cross-national approach, on the other hand, the attributes of the political systems are defined in a reductionist framework—by the relations between component parts and the attributes of these parts. Often in the cross-national approach, researchers hope to describe the conditions under which a political system exhibits instability. Instability in the cross-national approach may be defined in terms of behaviors such as people rioting against their government, governments instituting martial law, and similar extreme behaviors. Such an approach stipulates the reduction of the system attributes to component parts and the relations between the component parts. Hence, political instability may be considered divorced from other characteristics such as political development because development is defined in terms of other attributes of components and relations. This is not to say that political development and instability are not related. It is to say that there is no *necessary* relationship between political development and instability.

Although there is some disagreement among philosophers of science, it is generally thought that reductionist explanations are preferable to emergentist explanations. This is because the variables in reductionist explanations are defined in terms of observable and measurable attributes, whereas in the emergentist approach, the variables are related to complex composites of variables, and these clusters are not totally reducible to measurable phenomena.[6]

The configurative approach is more widely practiced in comparative politics than is the cross-national approach. Although both operate from different paradigmatic premises and different methodological positions, in a practical sense the two need each other. The cross-national researcher needs the area specialist to provide him with the necessary information and refinement of data from the variety of political systems in today's world. Those who follow the configurative approach need the cross-national researcher to provide the generalizations about the attributes of political systems.

Data and Data Problems in Macro-Cross-National Research

In macro-cross-national research, the central concern is to determine the relationships between conditions and attributes of political systems. In this regard, cross-national researchers are interested in measuring system attributes. Such attributes as stability, integration, democratization, and development are among the attributes in which cross-national researchers at the macro-level have shown interest. Such conditions as economic and social development, and social and cultural homogeneity-heterogeneity have commonly been used as the basis for determining the attributes of political systems. In measuring attributes and conditions, a variety of data is used. These data are aggregate data—data aggregated from component parts of the political system—generally coming from United Nations sources, encyclopedia sources such as *Facts on File, Deadline Data on World Affairs*, or the *New York Times Index*. Indicators such as government expenditures in differing policy areas, economic data on the standards of living, vital statistics, political events, and the like can be obtained from these and similar sources.

Several problems are involved in using these macro-indicators of attributes and conditions. First, the data must be reliable, or the degree of reliability must be assessed. If the data are reliable, then they can be said to be accurate and to report properly the phenomena of interest. For example, if the gross national product (GNP) per capita is to be used as an indicator of economic development, then the actual figures that the researcher uses in his analysis must report accurately the GNPs of the countries involved. For data to be reliable, the numbers used must provide an accurate and realistic account of the phenomena of interest.

Data reliability is obviously a central problem in cross-national research. Much of the data relies upon secondary sources whose information is open to questions of reliabliity. Hence some estimation of the reliability error is often necessary in cross-national research. To establish an estimate of error in data, there are several procedures which can be employed: (1) reference to alternative sources for collection of information on the variable of interest, (2) reference to other research using the variable of interest, and (3) examination of the procedures used in the original data collection. Regarding the first procedure, with some types of cross-national data, this is a clear option. For example, when research focuses on attributes of political events, concise chronicles and historical accounts can be used to establish agreement on the information reported. For research on political structures, there are a variety of encyclopedic summaries as well as area and case studies reporting the desired information in detail. If research requires the use of aggregate social and economic data, national records as well as United Nations sources can both be used to establish data reliability. Only in rare instances are there no alternative sources for collecting data. By using alternative sources, the degree of reliability can be established so that researchers may have greater confidence in the data.

A second procedure which can be used to establish the reliability of data is by reference to other research. As indicated by the studies in this volume, measures can be compared from one research effort to the next to locate the sources from which questions in data reliability arise. Once the unreliable numbers are isolated, a variety of procedures can be pursued which compensate for error. Hence, by comparing studies which use similar measures of a given phenomenon, cross-national researchers can begin to resolve the questions of data reliability.

A third procedure which can be used to resolve reliability problems is the examination of the accounting procedures used to generate the data. Whether one is using newspaper accounts, United Nations statistical reports, or scholarly case studies, the accounting procedure used to generate the data must be examined. Then, the researcher can come to some assessment as to how reliable the generated data happen to be. Accounting procedures that are highly suspect inform the researcher that the data must be further examined to make their use in cross-national analyses meaningful with respect to the conceptual problem under investigation.

Examination of data following any or all of the above procedures provides the information necessary for making reliability estimates. Evaluations of data based on impressionistic notions and preconceptions are not sufficient, for although often empirically based, they may be incomplete, inexact, and biased by subjection to partial information. The question of data reliability is not absolute, but relative to alternative procedures and estimates. In cross-national research, or for that matter in any social research, the attempt is to use the most reliable data—we can never claim that a given datum is totally without question. In macro-cross-national research, where systematic efforts to collect data are just beginning to develop, approximate solutions to the question of data reliability will only be solved by further systematic exploration of alternative data sources and collection and coding of this alternative information.

As we have seen, there are several procedures which can be used to assess the degree of data reliability. Among these procedures are a variety of methods attempting to evaluate reliability using alternative data sources. Also some assessment of data reliability can be achieved by providing internal checks. Although there are no set procedures for examining reliability by internal checks—comparing a given indicator over time, comparing indicators cross-sectionally, or by interpolation—some evidence, although not entirely convincing, can be obtained to point to particular numbers that might be unreliable. Thus far in cross-national research, too little effort has been made in attempting to assess the degree of reliability of current archived data. One of the more important tasks is to attempt to examine the reliability of data now used, and to examine systematically the accounting procedures for generating the data employed in macro-cross-national analysis.

A second attribute which macro-cross-national data must satisfy is *comparability*. If the data are comparable, then the procedures used for accounting in one political system are identical to the procedures used for accounting in other political systems. By comparability, we mean that the procedures used for generating data are rigorously employed in every case, and hence, meaningful comparisons can be drawn among political systems. If, for example, we are interested in the degree of political instability exhibited in political systems, a riot or coup d'etat in one political system must be equivalent to a riot or coup d'etat in another political system. Or, if we are interested in determining the level of economic development as a condition for some set of attributes, it is necessary that the accounting procedures used to generate numbers for one political system are comparable to those for another political system.

Data comparability is an especially difficult problem in cross-national research. Given that cross-national data are drawn from a variety of sources in which a number of standards and procedures have been employed for generating data, and given that cross-national data are reported and collected by a large number of individuals and are often reported by governments, questions concerning the comparability of the data from one political system to another are especially acute. Comparability cannot be achieved simply by using identical indicators from each political system. If, for example, a particular researcher is interested in analyzing the relationship between cultural heterogeneity and attributes of the political system, a variety of cultural differences must be examined as a source for cultural heterogeneity. In some cases, cultural differences may be tied to religious differences; in other cases, heterogeneity may be tied to linguistic, racial, or ethnic differences. Hence, a false comparability would be achieved by looking only at one of these sources of cultural heterogeneity, and some assessment must be made in the analysis as to what are the bases of cultural heterogeneity in each individual case. Comparability of data involves not only comparability of the procedures for generating data, but also the achievement of comparable indicators from one case to another which may not contain identical indicators.

Data reliability and data comparability are basic methodological problems in cross-national research. Even though macro-cross-national data do not have the properties of perfect reliability and comparability, it does not follow that such data should be avoided in political and social analyses. What does follow is that analyses using these data should be viewed as tentative. That is, no single research can be viewed as conclusive given the variety of methodological problems that arise in any analysis, but only upon replication, with analyses using differing data sources and analyses using differing methods, can more conclusive findings be generated. In macro-cross-national research, only preliminary findings are being produced, and many further analyses are necessary before any notion of valid empirical generalizations and scientific laws about political systems can be established.

Measurement and Measurement Problems in Macro-Cross-National Research

The term "measurement" is often misused by analysts. Measurement means the placing of data into a given format for analysis. We measure the height of an object by using the standard of a ruler. The ruler is calibrated to allow height to be transformed into some set of numbers. The set of numbers is only meaningful with respect to the measuring instrument and its acceptance as a standard for converting observations into some particular format—in this case, an interval scale. Measurement is the application of a standard to a given set of observations to transform the observations into a format compatible with data analysis. In macro-cross-national research, the measurement problems are not as simple as measuring height with a ruler. There are few, if any, standard instruments for transforming observations into numbers. The difficulties of measurement in macro-cross-national research may be put into two large categories: (1) problems in selection of indicators and (2) problems in reduction of multiple indicators to single measures.

The first problem in the selection of indicators can be exemplified in macro-cross-national research by using the example of measuring political instability. There are a variety of events one might look for in assessing the level of political instability of a given political system. Such indicators might include political riots, demonstrations, boycotts, falls of cabinets, cabinet reshufflings, political resignations, civil wars, guerrilla warfare, political rebellions, and revolutions. As with almost any variable in macro-cross-national research, there are a number of indicators applicable to the given variable. The problem, however, is not only that there are multiple indicators, but there are indicators that can be expressed in a variety of ways. For example, we can count the number of riots, demonstrations, and so on that occur in a given political system over a particular time. But we can also express the phenomena of rioting, demonstrating, and the like in terms of the number of people involved, the number of people injured, or the duration of the event. Which of these possibilities is to be used? How is the researcher to select the variety of formats in which a given phenomenon can be represented? In part, the answer to these questions involves the definition of the term "political instability." In a practical way, the availability of data has much to do with the selection of a given format for representing the data.

A series of research decisions must be made to select clearly and consistently the most meaningful representation of the data. The most meaningful representation is that which most closely approximates the theoretical problem being investigated. Hence, part of the problem of measurement is the problem of refining theoretical and operational meanings of variables to the degree that particular representation of the data will be opted. Simply, vague theoretical and operational definitions yield measurement problems.

In macro-cross-national research, the problem of indicator selection is especially acute. This is generally because the concepts and variables that interest cross-national researchers are not usually precise enough for them to determine the types of data representations to be used. Further, much of the problem of indicator selection can be solved only by repeated exploration, using a variety of differing representations of data, to establish the most appropriate attributes for a given analysis problem.

The second problem of measurement is data reduction. Data reduction refers to the combining of a variety of indicators into a single measure. With multiple indicators for a given variable, some set of procedures must be employed to reduce these indicators to single measures. There are a number of standard procedures for accomplishing data reduction, including simple indexing with or without weights, scaling, cluster analysis, factor analysis (with its variety of possible formats), and canonical analysis. With each of these techniques, the multiple indicators are reduced to a single score of the variable being measured. Each technique for data reduction employs differing assumptions and differing operations on the data. The problem that the cross-national researcher must face is to select the technique most clearly approximating the theoretical problem under investigation. Once again, the variables and their hypothesized relationship must be defined clearly to allow the researcher to select a given routine or combination of routines for measurement purposes. Much of the appropriateness of a technique depends upon the attributes of the data. But the procedure to be employed to reduce data does have an effect on the findings of a given analysis. Therefore, it is important that the measurement techniques used are compatible with the problem under investigation, and that conclusions reached by the analysis are not artifacts of the technique, but meaningful statements of relationship among sets of variables.

As with the problems of macro-cross-national data, the problems of measurement require experimentation, using a variety of formats and techniques. Only with replication of research will cross-national researchers become fully aware of the implications in using certain measurement options and how they affect data analysis.

Longitudinal and Cross-Sectional Designs in Macro-Cross-National Research

There are a variety of types of research designs that can be employed in cross-national research. Two distinctive designs are the cross-sectional and the longitudinal. In the cross-sectional design, attributes of political systems and their conditions are analyzed across national boundaries during a given period. In the longitudinal design, the same political system is analyzed through time, and then the longitudinal analysis is compared across national boundaries.[7] The longitudinal design accounts for development over time, whereas the cross-sectional design accounts for development by the use of a number of political systems at differing developmental stages. In the longitudinal design, the effort is to describe the differences and similarities within political systems over time, and then to compare these descriptions. In the cross-sectional design, the effort is to provide a description of the differences and similarities among political systems.

Obviously, the longitudinal design provides for a deeper analysis than the cross-sectional design. The added dimension of time, and hence development to the longitudinal design, allows for greater variety and depth in the data. The difficulty so far is that little longitudinal data have been collected and systematically archived. Collecting longitudinal data is not an easy project. Efforts to evaluate the reliability and comparability of data are very difficult in longitudinal archiving. Often in collecting historical data, gross estimates must be used, and it is extremely difficult to establish the accuracy of these estimates.

Although longitudinal designs have special advantages over cross-sectional designs, we have to be satisfied with cross-sectional designs for many theoretical problems because of the lack of historical data, especially when pre-World War II data are to be used. Further, by performing a cross-sectional analysis before longitudinal data are to be collected, much can be learned that can be valuable in the collection of historical data. In macro-cross-national research, greater effort is needed to collect and archive historical data systematically for longitudinal analysis.

Sampling and Independence Problems in Macro-Cross-National Research

In macro-cross-national research, it is insufficient just to describe relationships between variables either cross-sectionally or longitudinally. It is, however, necessary to give concern to sampling and independence of units-of-analysis problems. Since the effort of cross-national research is to determine under what conditions political systems exhibit certain attributes, the goal is to construct generalizations that hold true across national boundaries. In attempting to construct generalizations about political systems, data are drawn from a number of political systems. Rarely is there extensive enough data in any given analysis to say that every case has been used. In cross-sectional designs, data are often lacking on many African and Asian countries. Hence, working with something less than the world, cross-national researchers face sampling problems.

If generalizations are to be applied to the universe of political systems, or to some subset of the universe of political systems, such as authoritarian political systems or developing political systems, the political systems used in the analysis must be representative of the universe. Given the difficulty of unavailable data on many political systems, the analysis in macro-cross-national research is often skewed because of missing items. Further, cross-national researchers cannot arbitrarily select certain countries for analysis. The selection of countries for analysis must be performed in such a way as to allow generalizations to be made from those selected to the universe under consideration.

Many of the sampling problems in cross-national research will only be solved by filling in the gaps of missing data. However, greater concern and care for constructing representative samples is necessary so findings would not be so badly skewed from unavailability of data.

Another problem in macro-cross-national research related to the problem of sampling is independence of elements in the unit-of-analysis set. This problem is often referred to as Galton's problem.[8] The unit-of-analysis set is the collection of political systems used in a given analysis. To describe relationships between attributes and conditions of political systems, theoretically, the probability of a given system to have certain attributes must be equal to the probability of any other system to have the same attributes. What cross-national researchers attempt to do is to defy these probabilities, hence noting relationships between conditions and attributes of political systems. We cannot, however, assume that one political system is independent of others because in the international system countries do interact. Historically, the relations between nations can be important for determining their attributes. Hence, some controls must be exercised in cross-national research for isolating the variance in system attributes from the interactions of political systems both in the historical and contemporary international system. That is, attributes of the international system and relations between nations must be considered among the determining factors for attributes of the political system. In macro-cross-national research, we must separate the variables that are the product of historical interaction of political systems from those that might be hypothesized as the internal conditions producing a given system attribute.

As yet, in macro-cross-national research, little effort has been made to control the effects of historical interaction and the contemporary international system. As more research develops, one of the problems to be tackled is the systematic control of these effects upon the attributes of political systems.

We have sketched only a few of the major methodological problems associated with macro-cross-national research. There are others, such as the multi-colinearity often found between macro-indicators, the problems asssociated with the theoretical significance of cross-national analysis, and the problems in using specific statistical techniques which are present in cross-national as well as in many other areas of political and social analysis. This cataloging of problems points to much of the necessary focus for further research. Although cross-national research is well on its way toward establishing itself as a legitimate area of comparative politics, there are numerous tasks yet be performed.

The research reports that follow are examples of much of the current variety in macro-cross-national research. Nevertheless, they do have methodological deficiencies—they do have theoretical problems—they do exhibit many of the problems mentioned. But, they also report much of the potentiality and excitement in this new approach to comparative political analysis.

NOTES

1. For some early research on macro-cross-national research by Karl W. Deutsch, see Deutsch (1961). Also important in the early development of macro-cross-national research are the works of Cutright (1963), Lipset (1959), Shannon (1958, 1959, and 1961), and Kuznets (1957–63). Often overlooked in the development of macro-cross-national research are the works of Raymond Cattell (1949 and 1950) and his early attempts to factor analyze cross-national data.

The Human Relation Area Files, under the direction of George P. Murdock and his associates, have also contributed to the development of cross-national research in political science; see Murdock (1940, 1957, and 1963).

For a report on the Yale Political Data Program and other programs in cross-national research, see Merritt and Rokkan (1966). The most recent works of the Yale data is reported in Bruce M. Russett's forthcoming *World Handbook of Social and Political Indicators*, 2nd ed. See also Feierabend and Feierabend (1965) and Banks and Textor (1963).

2. For some discussion of the potentialities and problems of macro-cross-national research, see Alker (1966), Retzlaff (1965), and Deutsch (1960).

3. For discussions of the configurative approach, see Eckstein (1963) and Hecksher (1958). For some examples of the use of the configurative approach in comparative politics, see Holt and Turner (1966), Almond and Coleman (1960) and their numerous attempts to apply functionalist categories and vocabularies.

4. I am indebted to Alfred Diamant for suggesting to me this particular way for displaying the differences between the configurative and cross-national approaches.

5. For discussions of the problems of emergentist and reductionist explanations, see Gellner (1969), Watkins (1969), and Brodbeck (1969).

6. See Brodbeck (1969).

7. For examples of longitudinal analyses in macro-cross-national research, see "Pattern of political development and democratization: a quantitative analysis" by William Flanigan and Edwin Fogelman in this volume, Chapter 20.

8. For description and solutions to Galton's problem, see Naroll (1961, 1962, 1963, 1964, 1965, and 1969).

REFERENCES

ALKER, H.R. (1966) "The comparison of aggregate political and social data: potentialities and problems." *Social Science Information:* 63–80.

ALMOND, G.A. and J.S. COLEMAN, Eds. (1960) *The Politics of the Developing Areas.* Princeton: Princeton University Press.

BANKS, A.S. and R.B. TEXTOR (1963) *A Cross-Polity Survey.* Cambridge: MIT Press.

BRODBECK, M. (1969) "Methodological individualism: definitions and reductions." Pp. 254–303 in M. Brodbeck, Ed., *Readings in the Philosophy of the Social Sciences.* New York: Macmillan.

CATTELL, R. (1950) "The principle culture patterns discoverable in the syntal dimensions of existing nations." *Journal of Social Psychology:* 215–253.

— (1949) "The dimensions of culture patterns by factorization of national characteristics." *Journal of Abnormal and Social Psychology:* 443–469.

CUTRIGHT, P. (1963) "National political development: measurement and analysis." *American Sociological Review:* 253–264.

DEUTSCH, K.W. (1961) "Social mobilization and political development." *American Political Science Review:* 493–514.

— (1960) "Toward an inventory of basic trends and patterns in comparative and international politics." *American Political Science Review:* 34–57.

ECKSTEIN, H. (1963) "Perspective on comparative politics, past and present." Pp. 3–32 in H. Eckstein and D.E. Apter, Eds., *Comparative Politics.* New York: Free Press.

FEIERABEND, I.K., R.L. FEIERABEND et al. (1965) *Cross-National Data Bank of Political Instability Events.* San Diego: Public Affairs Research Institute.

GELLNER, E. (1969) "Holism versus individualism." Pp. 245–268 in M. Brodbeck, Ed., *Readings in the Philosophy of the Social Sciences.* New York: Macmillan.

HECKSHER, G. (1958) *The Study of Comparative Government and Politics.* London: Allen and Unwin; New York: Macmillan.

HOLT, R.T. and J.E. TURNER (1966) *The Political Basis of Economic Development.* Princeton: Van Nostrand.

KUZNETS, S. (1957–63) Series of articles in Economic Development and Cultural Change.

LIPSET, S.M. (1959) "Some political requisites for democracy, economic development and political legitimacy." *American Political Science Review:* 69–109.

MERRITT, R.L. and S. ROKKAN, Eds. (1966) *Comparing Nations.* New Haven: Yale University Press.

MURDOCK, G.P. et al. (1963) *An Outline of World Cultures*, 4th ed. New Haven: Human Relations Area Files Press.

— (1957) "World ethnographic sample." *American Anthropologist:* 664–687.

— (1940) "The cross-cultural survey." *American Sociological Review:* 361–370.

NAROLL, R. (1969) "Some thoughts on the comparative method in cultural anthropology." Pp. 236–277 in H. and A. Blalock, Eds., *Methodology in Social Research.* New York: McGraw-Hill.

— (1965) "Galton's Problem: the logic of cross-cultural research." *Social Research:* 428–451.

— (1964) "A fifth solution to Galton's Problem." *American Anthropologist:* 863–867.

— (1963) "Two further solutions to Galton's Problem." *American Anthropologist:* 1053–1067.
— (1962) *Data Quality Control.* New York: Free Press.
— (1961) "Two solutions to Galton's Problem." *Philosophy of Science:* 15–39.
RETZLAFF, R.H. (1965) "The use of aggregate data in comparative political analysis." *Journal of Politics:* 797–817.
RUSSETT, B.M. et al. (forthcoming) *World Handbook of Social and Political Indicators*, 2nd ed. New Haven: Yale University Press.
SHANNON, L. (1961) "The statistical measurement of urbanization and economic development." *Land Economics:* 229–245.
— (1959) "Socio-economic development and political status." *Social Problems:* 157–169.
— (1958) "Is the level of development related to capacity for self-government?" *American Journal of Economics and Sociology:* 367–381.
WATKINS, J.W.N. (1969) "Methodological individualism and social tendencies." Pp. 269–279 in M. Brodbeck, Ed., *Readings in the Philosophy of the Social Sciences.* New York: Macmillan.

Part II

STUDIES IN DOMESTIC CONFLICT

1 Introduction: Studies in Domestic Conflict

BETTY A. NESVOLD

Empirical investigation of political questions across a group of nations demands a classification scheme that provides objective criteria for evaluating conditions despite widely diverse national circumstances. Such criteria can be developed empirically or theoretically. The studies included in this section have utilized both approaches to measure and compare the level of conflict behavior within nations.

Clearly, it would be an unmanageable research task to record, code, and analyze all instances of conflict within all nations. In the following studies, focus is upon *social conflict*, i.e., that which involves society generally. Thus, personal affairs, whether conducted in a harmonious or an aggressive manner, are eliminated. Also eliminated from the research interest are conflicts over administrative matters involving internal institutions (e.g., educational institutions, business firms, church organizations, etc.). Therefore, the conflict behaviors that are of interest to the researchers are those having a direct or potential effect on the political stability of the nation. Thus, underlying the data collections of Rummel, Tanter, Gurr, Bwy, the Feierabends, and Nesvold is the assumption of systemic effects of conflict on politics.

Although different techniques are employed by the authors in this section to measure the extent of domestic conflict within the nations of the world, the data on which they rely are quite similar. Broad patterns of regularity of conflict are sought in cross-national analysis, employing such indicators as instances of revolution, guerrilla warfare, riot, and assassination, as well as less violent conflict behavior such as governmental crisis. All of the investigators attempt to discriminate among different types of conflict so as to reflect the intensity of conflicts and the strain they place on the polity.

The following research reports are addressed to the task of isolating systemic similarities in domestic conflict by cross-national study. Furthermore, these research efforts attempt to account for domestic conflict by using a variety of social, economic and cultural variables. The task is not only to build comparable measures of domestic conflict, but to explain the conditions which give rise to political instability.

Measurement of the Dependent Variable

One of the inductive techniques to cluster a set of variables into a smaller number of dimensions is factor analysis.[1] By the use of factor analysis, events of domestic conflict can be grouped together according to the likelihood they will co-occur. Thus, Rummel finds that strikes, demonstrations and riots cluster, i.e., occur in limited time periods within single nations. He found two additional clusterings in his conflict data bank, but in a replication of Rummel's design, Tanter found that these two were combined. Rummel had collected data for nations for the period 1955-57, while Tanter collected data for the same nations on the same variables for the period 1958-60. During the earlier period variables that indicated *subversion* and *revolutionary* dimensions of conflict formed into distinct clusters. During the latter period, they tended to co-occur.

It is all too rare that we see a deliberate attempt to replicate another researcher's findings in the social sciences. This is certainly a common practice in the physical sciences; the need is even greater in the social sciences. Precise rules are extraordinarily difficult to develop in any design in which coding of qualitative, verbal material is a central part of the data collection. Judgmental coder decisions must often be accepted as a methodological price one pays if one wants to deal directly with such materials. If a second researcher can apply the coding criteria independently, the two research efforts can be compared, and one can evaluate the objectivity of the exercise with this replication technique. The strikingly similar results in the two analyses, despite the obvious probability that empirical events differed in the two periods, lends credence to the hypothesis that there are empirical dimensions in conflict behavior. If a nation experiences riots, then it is also likely to experience other *turmoil* behaviors. This was a finding of the Rummel study, but the confidence one has in accepting this finding is raised considerably with the Tanter replication.

In a similar enterprise, looking at Latin American data, Bwy clusters nine variables into three dimensions; and the Feierabends, using a much larger set of variables, reduce thirty variables to nine factors. The reason for this data reduction is that a smaller number of variables is more easily manipulated than a larger number. More importantly, with a small number of variables the attachment of theoretical interpretation to clusterings makes the formulation of predictive models more feasible. Rummel, for example, discovers that his three factors could be theoretically interpreted as containing: (1) turmoil events, (2) revolutionary activity events, and (3) subversive events. Although Rummel and Tanter do not seek the correlates of each type of conflict behavior, these clusterings are far more suggestive of theoretical models than the original nine variables. Likewise, Bwy finds that his first two factors are interpretable as measuring: (1) organized violence, and (2) anomic violence.

Rummel's, Tanter's and Bwy's uses of factor analysis point both to the utility of this technique and its limitations. Factor analysis is a statistical tool to reduce large sets of variables to smaller numbers of dimensions solely on the basis of how frequently the variables occur together. Unless theoretical interpretation can be given to the clusterings of variables, no guidelines for developing an explanatory model will be generated. For example, in Bwy's analysis no theoretical meaning can be attached to the clusterings of variables on his third factor. Even though Bwy can attach meaning to the first two factors in his analysis, the factor analysis does not reveal any meaningful interpretation for the residual third category.

Whereas Rummel, Tanter, and Bwy are attempting to distinguish among types of domestic conflict, the Feierabends present a different procedure for measuring domestic conflict. The Feierabends employ a single measuring instrument which weights for differing degrees of political instability and which can be used to score *all* conflict events. Thus, while Bwy examines a nation's scores on organized violence or on anomic violence, and Rummel calculates separate scores for nations on turmoil or revolutionary activity, the Feierabends establish a score that supposedly reflects the level of *all* domestic conflict rather than within types of domestic conflict. The Feierabends devise a seven-point scale that is operationally defined in terms of specific events representing differing degrees of stability and instability. Each conflict event can be given a scale value according to criteria specified in the measuring instrument. The underlying guide for these criteria is that each of the seven scale positions reflects increasing amounts and intensity of aggressive behavior. Obviously, this technique for developing a measuring instrument differs radically from the factor analysis approach. The factor analysis approach is purely empirical and relies upon the analyst to bring theoretical significance to the results. The Feierabend approach is developed on the basis of some conceptual grounding in the notion of political instability. However, whereas the factor analysis approach has theoretical limitations, the Feierabend indexing approach also has limitations. We could ask why the weights selected were used; by what criteria the authors determined differences between the thirty events; and if the weights reflect an accurate accounting of political instability. Furthermore, some form of a validity test would seem desirable to further justify the Feierabend index. Such a validity test is provided in the Nesvold research report.

Nesvold, using the same thirty variables as the Feierabends, randomizes their order and asks an independent group of political scientists to order them on a scale indicating the intensity of political instability denoted by each variable. When the Feierabend scale and the scale generated from Nesvold's independent group of political scientists are correlated, the evidence demonstrates that there is a high degree of agreement between the Nesvold and Feierabend results. The Nesvold validation of the Feierabend scale is generally referred to as a consensual validation exercise wherein the test is to determine whether or not individuals have a common frame of reference for interpretation. What the Nesvold validation demonstrates is that political scientists generally view the same events as indicating extremely high levels of conflict, moderate levels, etc.

Nesvold also develops an alternative measuring instrument of domestic conflict. The twelve more intensive variables from the Feierabend analysis are grouped into four clusters. These four clusters are then submitted to a scalogram analysis to determine if the occurrence of events in the most extreme cluster is accompanied by events in all of the clusters denoting less extreme behaviors.[2] As the Nesvold analysis demonstrates, the twelve variables scale with a high coefficient of reproducibility, showing that there is a unidimensional feature to the development of political instability. While the Nesvold scalogram analysis only uses a portion of the data incorporated into the Feierabend scale, nevertheless the scores generated from the Nesvold analysis show a high degree of correlation with the Feierabend scale, providing further validation of the original Feierabend scale.

Gurr presents a slightly different measure of domestic conflict. He reasons that a measure of domestic conflict should reflect three basic attributes of a conflict situation: (1) the proportion of the population involved, (2) the duration of the event, and (3) the destructiveness of the actions. The basis of Gurr's measuring instrument is similar to that of the Feierabends. His criteria for sorting events, however, constitutes a different strategy. Whereas the Feierabends do not precisely specify the criteria for scoring, Gurr provides such criteria, thus eliminating the problem of the coder's judgmental responsibilities. Whereas with the Gurr approach coders are specifically given the information necessary to place variables into given categories, with the Feierabend approach the criteria are not explicitly stated. However, with the Feierabend approach, a greater variety of contextual aspects of the event is reflected in the scale value, whereas with the Gurr approach the limitation is to the specifically stated criteria.

In reviewing the strategies of measurement employed by the researchers represented in this section, one obvious point emerges. There is no single best measure of the complex variable of domestic conflict. The specific research interest of the authors is paramount in the development of measuring instruments. However, a variety of measuring instruments must be tried, reapplied and reformulated if there is to be some effective way of selecting measures of political instability. The measurement instruments must be compared, and the scores generated from each strategy must be intercorrelated so as to assess the degree of agreement between the instruments. The measures of political instability reported here are only a beginning toward a more fully developed and refined notion of political instability and its indicators.

Development of Explanatory Variables

In searching for explanations as to why some nations experience greater levels of domestic conflict than others, varying approaches are used in the studies included in this section. Gurr, Ruttenberg, and the Feierabends attempt to operationalize a conceptual model, while Bwy and Nesvold engage in a more inductive search for the correlates of conflict. Which strategy is most likely to generate a satisfactory explanation is hardly resolved in these studies, however. Both approaches are somewhat limited by the availability of data. Both approaches are limited by their reliance upon measures of covariance as a base for explanation. Both approaches are limited by crude measurement techniques and questions of data reliability and validity.

As Gurr, Ruttenberg, and the Feierabends point out, their measures are only crude approximations of the theoretical scheme which they are attempting to operationalize. Both Gurr and the Feierabends rely upon frustration-aggression theory for the development of hypotheses. Thus, the authors are interested in measuring such notions as "want formation," "frustration," and "want satisfaction." In the Feierabend research, eight indicators of modernization are combined into an index of "modernity," and a ratio of six of these indicators presumed to measure "want satisfaction" to two indicating "want formation" yields an index which is assumed to measure frustration. This index of frustration is to represent the independent variable in the Feierabends' test of the frustration-aggression hypothesis. The data do not clearly delineate the want satisfaction and want formation components of social frustration. Literacy, one component of want formation, may instigate aspirations for a wide range of goods and services that were not present prior to the acquisition of this skill; yet literacy may also be hypothesized as providing satisfaction itself.

The Feierabends, Gurr, and Ruttenberg are interested in the relationship between modernization and the propensity for a political system to exhibit instability. Gurr attempts to elaborate a set of variables postulated in his conceptual scheme by using a more extensive set of data than in the Feierabend design. However, in Gurr's elaboration—and limitations of data availability are again apparent—his measures can only be considered extremely crude indicators of his variables, not direct and refined measures. To some extent, both Gurr and the Feierabends are using inductive techniques in their search for an explanation of domestic conflict. This is especially apparent in Gurr's step-wise regression analysis in which variables are selected with respect to the proportion of variance explained in the dependent variable. In the Feierabend analysis the inductive aspects are demonstrated in the dichotomization of the contingency tables so as to identify empirically levels of political instability. Although in both the Feierabend and Gurr analyses original selection of variables is guided by the theoretical framework, in the final analysis the researchers relied upon inductive techniques for making distinctions among variables.

In the introductory comments to this volume, it was pointed out that the sampling problem presents researchers of cross-national politics with methodological difficulties. The units of analysis (in this case nations) are selected on the basis of data availability rather than as a purposive sample or the complete universe of units in the population. Gurr and Ruttenberg attempted a complete enumeration of all nations that met their definitional criteria, but, in their data analysis, problems of missing data forced them to drop many of their cases. There is unquestionably a systematic effect of these missing data on their analysis. Traditional nations simply fail to collect data; other nations fail to collect data on some variables for political reasons.

Kline, Kent, and Davis develop a technique for estimating missing data in order to solve this problem. The underlying rationale for the approach is simply, if we know some of the attributes of a nation, to match it with other nations of similar attributes. Then the probability is high that the unmeasured attributes will also be similar. For one familiar with the use of typologies in political analysis, the utility of the statistical approach developed by Kline and his associates becomes apparent. Their present analysis was exploratory, and the application of their technique to analyses of substantive concerns was somewhat ambiguous, in that the explained variance in domestic conflict was actually not as high as in some of the previous analyses in this section. However, the patterned relationships are strong enough to encourage further work in this area. Kline's effort used only a few variables in a causal model predicting domestic conflict. The Kline analysis probably oversimplifies the complexities in this social phenomenon, but the analysis clearly demonstrates the potential utility of interpolative techniques in solving the missing data problem that plagues macro-cross-national research efforts.

One final methodological point can be made with regard to this research. All the authors are relying upon aggregated data of national political systems. There may be intrinsic limitations in this type of data precluding fully satisfactory explanations. The dependent variable is a set of *behaviors*, the independent variables are indicators of *conditions* hypothesized to lead to these behaviors. We do not know whether those who engage in these behaviors actually experience the hypothesized conditions. In other words, even in nations where we feel the data clearly indicate that there should be an imbalance in expectations and forthcoming gratifications, we have no data to show whether the *persons* who engage in the conflict behaviors are persons experiencing this frustrating situation. We do not even have the data whereby we could test whether hypothetically deprived *strata* of the population are those who engage in conflict behavior. Data, however, indicate that there is strong presumptive evidence that this is the case. The consistency of the findings from independent research in this direction cannot be dismissed.

Yet at this high system level it is not trivial to point out that we must realize that a sizable portion of unexplained variance will plague us despite increasingly sophisticated techniques of data analysis and increasingly broad and reliable sets of data collections. Furthermore, it is claimed that cross-national analysis of large numbers of nations can never explain more than a modest level of variance in complex social phenomena since it does not take into account unique circumstances and national cultures. It is precisely because of this fact, however, that a general understanding of these phenomena can be developed.

NOTES

1. For explication of the factor analysis technique, see Rummel (1967), Fruchter (1954), Kerlinger (1964: 650–689). For the reader with a technical background, see Harman (1960).

2. The best single explanation of the scalogram technique is found in Guttman (1950: 60–90).

REFERENCES

FRUCHTER, BENJAMIN (1954) *Introduction to Factor Analysis.* Princeton: Van Nostrand.

GUTTMAN, LOUIS (1950) "The basis for scalogram analysis." In S.A. Stouffer et al., Eds., *Studies in Social Psychology in World War II*, Volume IV of *Measurement and Prediction.* Princeton: Princeton University Press.

HARMAN, HARRY H. (1960) *Modern Factor Analysis.* Chicago: University of Chicago Press.

KERLINGER, FRED N. (1964) *Foundations of Behavioral Research.* New York: Holt, Rinehart & Winston.

RUMMEL, RUDOLPH J. (1967) "Understanding factor analysis." *Journal of Conflict Resolution* 11: 444–480.

2 Dimensions of Conflict Behavior Within Nations, 1946–59

R. J. RUMMEL

Conflict behavior within nations may take a number of forms. There may be riots, demonstrations, coups, social revolutions, guerrilla warfare, assassinations, general strikes, and so on. Any one of these forms may occur by itself or in conjunction with others. When a number of conflict acts take place together within a nation, such as riots, demonstrations, and general strikes, we can speak of a cluster of conflict behavior. If such behavior is generally found to cluster together for all nations, then we might speak of a *dimension* of conflict behavior.

The identification of such dimensions within an empirical domain constitutes one of the first stages of scientific analysis. To discover dimensions helps to reduce a large number of phenomena to major patterns of covariation—to suggest labels by which such phenomena can be parsimoniously conceptualized, and to provide handles by which they might be analyzed and manipulated. Within the social sciences, research has been pursued for decades by those interested in identifying empirical dimensions in their domains. The primary tool of these investigations has been factor analysis,[1] a method for determining the major clusters of variation—dimensions—among phenomena of concern.

The goal of this paper is to apply this method to conflict behavior within countries from 1946 to 1959 in an attempt to delineate their major dimensions and to compare the results with those of similar studies.

Author's Note: Prepared in connection with research supported by the National Science Foundation, contracts NSF-G24827 and NSF-GS-536. I am indebted to Richard Chadwick, Raymond Tanter, and Dina Zinnes for comments on a prior draft.

Editors' Note: An extended version of this paper has been deposited with the American Documentation Institute. Order Document No. 8691 from the Chief, Photoduplication Service, Library of Congress, Washington, D.C. 20025, Auxiliary Publication Project, remitting $1.75 for microfilm (35mm) or $2.50 for photocopies.

Reprinted from the *Journal of Conflict Resolution*, Volume 10, pages 65–73, by permission of the author and the publisher. Copyright © 1966 by The University of Michigan.

Methodology

The data used were collected by Harry Eckstein (1962) from the *New York Times Index* on twelve kinds (measures) of domestic conflict for 113 countries for 1946-59: internal warfare, turmoil, rioting, large-scale terrorism, small-scale terrorism, mutinies, coups, plots, administrative actions, quasi-private violence, total number of unequivocal acts of violence (UE), and total number of unequivocal plus equivocal acts of violence ($UE+E$). A thirteenth measure, extended violence, derived from his tables was also used. (See Appendix for definitions.)

The data generally have negative exponential distributions, with more than a majority of nations for each measure having zero values. UE and $UE+E$ measures were normally distributed.

To test for the effect and existence of systematic data error on the analysis, a preliminary correlation matrix and factor analysis through oblique (biquartimin) rotation was computed for Eckstein's *raw* data on thirteen measures of conflict behavior in addition to three measures of error.[2] The results, along with a discussion of the error measures, are filed with the American Documentation Institute (see Editors' Note).

This preliminary error analysis of the data indicated that sources of systematic error in the Eckstein data, as indexed in the above measures, generally would have only a random error effect, *if any*, on the results of correlating and factoring the data (Rummel, 1965a). They might cause the correlations among the data to be lower than they should be, but they would not create distortion of the factor structure.

Results

The subsequent *substantive* analysis was carried out on the thirteen conflict behavior measures with all, except the normally distributed UE and $UE+E$ data, log transformed.[3] The correlation matrix is on file in the extended version of this paper (see Editors' Note). The unrotated and rotated factors are given here in Table 1. Orthogonal and oblique factor matrices are shown for comparison.[4]

A comparison of the orthogonal and oblique factor rotations in Table 1 shows little difference in loadings between them and no change in interpretation. That such should be expected is indicated by the low correlation (given in footnote d of the table) between the oblique factors. This low correlation and absence of change in interpretation from orthogonal to oblique rotations argues that we are dealing here with relationships that have an orthogonal structure—that is, dimensions which are *independent* of one another.

Turning to an interpretation of these independent dimensions based on the orthogonally rotated matrix given in Table, 1, the first factor is seen to delineate a cluster of relationships among mutinies (.73),[5] coups (.85), and plots (.83). The UE (.55) and $UE+E$ (.61) measures and administrative

Dimensions of Conflict Behavior within Nations, 1946–59

TABLE 1
FACTOR MATRICES OF 1946–59 CONFLICT BEHAVIOR TRANSFORMED DATA[a]

Variable	Unrotated factors[b]				Orthogonally rotated factors[c]			Oblique factors, P matrix[d]		
	1	2	3	h²	1	2	3	1	2	3
1. UE	(.94)	.11	−.15	.92	(.55)	.25	(−.75)	(.76)	(.52)	.21
2. Warfare	.41	(.61)	.35	.67	.22	(.78)	−.12	.16	.19	(.77)
3. Turmoil	.36	.21	−.36	.31	−.02	.11	(−.54)	(.55)	−.05	.11
4. Riots	(.82)	.01	−.27	.74	.44	.08	(−.74)	(.74)	.41	.05
5. Large-scale terrorism	(.55)	.40	−.03	.46	.21	.46	−.45	.47	.17	.45
6. Small-scale terrorism	(.75)	.05	−.22	.61	.41	.12	(−.66)	(.66)	.37	.09
7. Mutinies	(.61)	−.09	.47	.60	(.73)	.26	−.03	.04	(.72)	.21
8. Coups	(.63)	−.31	.49	.73	(.85)	.07	.01	−.01	(.85)	.01
9. Plots	(.75)	−.36	.25	.75	(.83)	−.04	−.25	.24	(.83)	−.10
10. Admin. actions	(.56)	−.41	−.03	.49	(.57)	−.25	−.31	.30	(.57)	−.29
11. Quasi-private	.15	.05	(−.65)	.45	−.26	−.20	(−.59)	(.58)	−.28	−.18
12. Extended violence	.06	(.81)	.25	.72	−.18	(.83)	−.01	.05	−.20	(.84)
13. UE + E	(.96)	.01	−.16	.94	(.61)	.15	(−.74)	(.75)	(.57)	.11
Percent common variance:	40.7	12.6	11.0	64.3	26.8	13.7	23.8			
Sum of squares:								3.14	3.33	1.74

[a] Loadings ⩾|.50| are given in parentheses.

[b] N = 113. Principal components technique with unities in the principal diagonal of the correlation matrix. Calculations of unrotated and orthogonally rotated factor matrices carried out on the Northwestern University IBM 709, using the University of Chicago Mesa 2 factor analysis program.

[c] Kaiser's varimax criterion employed for the rotation and only factors with eigenvalues ⩾1.0 rotated.

[d] Factor pattern matrix of the biquartimin criterion. Factor correlations (cosines) are $r_{12} = .05$, $r_{13} = -.05$, $r_{23} = .10$. Computations carried out on the Indiana University IBM 709, using a revised version of John Carroll's "IBM 709-7090 Program for Generalized Analytic Rotation Solution in Factor Analysis." The biquartimin solution reported here took 60 major cycles at a precision level for the criterion of 0.1×10^{-4}, and 308 iterations at an iteration accuracy of 0.1×10^{-5}.

actions (.57) have lesser loadings. The nature of the highly loaded variables suggests that this is a *revolution* dimension, involving rebellion, planned or carried out, against government authority. Although administrative action is not very highly loaded on this factor (a loading of .57 means that the factor accounts for 32.5 percent of its variance), it has its highest loading of the three factors on the *revolution* factor.

Revolutionary conflict behavior takes place independently of the relationships evidenced by factor 2. Warfare, or guerrilla warfare (see definitions in Appendix), and extended violence (.78 and .83, respectively) mainly define this factor. Large-scale terrorism (.46) has a low but still appreciable loading. The nature of this factor seems to be one of *subversion*, that is, attempts to undermine the strength of the government and to cause defection of the people through unconventional warfare and terrorism. This conflict behavior for 113 countries, 1946–59, takes place independently of revolution—of direct attempts to overthrow the government.

The *revolution* and *subversion* dimensions represent planned conflict behavior. The third dimension, on the other hand, delimits a kind of spontaneous conflict behavior. Riots (−.74), turmoil (−.54), small-scale terrorism (−.66), quasi-private violence (−.59), and the two summation measures, UE (−.75) and $UE+E$ (−.74), are the variables mainly involved in this cluster.[6] Such conflict behavior appears to represent a *turmoil* dimension, a dimension of unplanned, uncoordinated violence which generally occurs unrelated to revolutionary and subversive behavior.

Comparison with Other Studies

The delineation of these three dimensions does not suffice. They must be compared with the results of other analyses—linked with similar studies so that our convergence upon reliable dimensions of domestic conflict behavior may be assessed.

Two similar studies have been done of domestic conflict behavior.[7] The first (Rummel, 1963 [reprinted in this volume, Chapter 3]) factored, and rotated orthogonally, 1955–57 domestic conflict behavior data for 77 nations[8] on nine measures: assassinations, general strikes, guerrilla warfare, major government crises, purges, riots, revolution, demonstrations, and number killed in all domestic conflict. (See Appendix I of the Tanter study, this volume, Chapter 4, for their definitions.) Most of the data came from the *New York Times Index*, although *Facts on File, Keesing's Contemporary Archives, Britannica Book of the Year*, and *New International Yearbook* were also consulted. Systematic error from censorship or lack of interest of the press in a nation was checked by including two measures of this error in a factor analysis of the data. They were found to have low correlations with the data and to load highly on a factor by themselves.

The orthogonal rotation of the 1955–57 data resulted in three dimensions, which—in terms of overlapping definitions—have the same meaning as those found in the Eckstein data. They too were labelled *revolution, subversion*, and *turmoil* dimensions.

A second study (Tanter, 1964a; and see Tanter's study, this volume, Chapter 4) involved replicating the analysis of the 1955–57 conflict behavior data. The factor analysis and rotation of Tanter's 1958–60 data delineated the same *turmoil* dimension as found in the 1946–59 and 1955–57 data. The revolution and subversion dimensions of these earlier data, however, were found by Tanter to merge into one dimension—an *internal war* dimension. Nonetheless, the distinction between planned behavior (*revolutionary* and *subversive* behavior) and spontaneous, uncoordinated behavior (*turmoil*) was found to hold.

The three findings for the three sets of data, 1946–59, 1955–57, and 1958–60, are given in Table 2. The measures used are reordered and combined according to similarity in definitions.[9] Tanter's unpublished three-factor rotations are shown for better comparison rather than the two dimensions included in his 1964a study.

TABLE 2
COMPARISON OF THE OBLIQUE FACTOR MATRICES FOR THE ECKSTEIN, RUMMEL, AND TANTER DATA[a]

Eckstein variables	Rummel–Tanter variables	Oblique P factor matrices[b]								
		E_1	R_1	T_1	E_2	R_2	T_3	E_3	R_a	T_2
1. UE		(76)			(52)					
	9. Killed		32			(80)			43	(72)
13. UE + E		(75)			(57)					
2. Warfare								(77)		
12. External violence	3. Guerrilla war						35	(84)	(91)	(91)
5. Large-scale terrorism				47					45	
6. Small-scale terrorism	1. Assassinations	(66)	(63)	(52)	37				(65)	32
3. Riots		(74)			41					
	6. Riots		(82)	(87)			36			
4. Turmoil		(55)								
7. Mutinies					(72)					
8. Coups	7. Revolution				(85)	(87)	32			(82)
9. Plots					(83)					
10. Admin. actions	5. Purges		30	38	(57)	(73)	(87)			
11. Quasi-private	—	(58)								
	2. Gen. strikes				(57)	(70)		(63)–31		
	4. Major govt. crises				(62)	32				(60)
	8. Demonstrations				(88)	(90)				

100 × (sum of squares/number of variables): 24.0, 31.0, 27.8; 25.6, 29.7, 12.2; 13.4, 16.5, 28.2

Factor (cosines) correlations: $E_{12} = .05$, $R_{12} = -.12$, $T_{13} = .03$
$E_{13} = -.05$, $R_{13} = -.03$, $T_{12} = .35$
$E_{23} = .10$, $R_{23} = -.09$, $T_{23} = .17$

[a] Only loadings $\geq |.30|$ are given. Those $\geq |.50|$ are shown in parentheses.
[b] E = Eckstein data factors given in Table 1. R = previously unpublished biquartimin solution for factors published in Rummel (1963). Major cycles for the R-factors were 20; iterations were 1,131. T = factors taken from computer output graciously made available to the author by Raymond Tanter. Analysis was on 1958–60 data for 83 nations. Major cycles were 10; iterations were 199. The R and T oblique factors were calculated on the Indiana University 709 using the same program employed for the Eckstein data oblique factors and the same precision levels.

The first set of similar factors in Table 2 are the *turmoil* dimensions, E_1, R_1, and T_1. The very close congruence between the high loadings of R_1 and T_1 can be seen. Their congruence with E_1 is also apparent although it is less evident because of the different measures being used. Considering the set of three factors, riots (.74) and turmoil (.55) are loaded on E_1, riots on R_1 and T_1 (.82 and .87, respectively). Small-scale terrorism has a high loading on E_1 (.66) and assassinations on R_1 (.63) and T_1 (.52). None of the three has a high loading for revolutions, purges, or guerrilla war-like measures. *UE* and *UE+E*, on the other hand, have high loadings (.76 and .75, respectively), while domestic killed has no loadings $\geq |.50|$ for R_1 and T_1. If one considers the cells defined by the vertical and horizontal lines in Table 2, and the presence or absence of loadings $\geq|.50|$ within each cell, then for the six cells in which loadings can appear for all three factors, the correlation (loadings $<|.50| = 0$, loadings $\geq|.50| = 1$)[10] between E_1 and R_1 and between E_1 and T_1 is .78 in both cases. For the nine measures for which mutual loadings can occur for both R and T, the correlation between R_1 and T_1 is .80. Consequently, one can conclude that the same *turmoil* dimension has been extracted from the three sets of data.

Considering the second set of factors in Table 2, the E_2 and R_2 factors are the *revolution* dimensions previously discussed. The congruence between the two is quite high; their correlation coefficient, calculated in the same manner as those above, is 1.0—a perfect correlation. T_3, however, is a dissimilar dimension. Its correlation with E_2 is .45; with R_2 it is .30.

The third set of factors constitutes the *subversion* dimension for E_3 and R_3. The congruence between E_3 and R_3 is not as close as for the *revolution* dimensions, but still quite close, with a correlation of .63. In this set of factors, again, the T dimension has the least congruence. The correlation of T_2 with E_3 is .45; with R_3 it is .06.

These low correlations of T_3 and T_2 with the *revolution* and *subversion* dimensions is due to the fact that T_2 combines elements of both, and to the specificity of T_3 to purges (.87). Note the much lower percent (12.2) of sum of squares for T_3 compared to those for E_2 and R_2 (25.6 and 29.7, respectively). Tanter quite rightly points out in his study that a two-factor rotation is, accordingly, the correct one for his data. The *internal war* dimension he found, in addition to the *turmoil* dimension, was essentially a combination of the T_2 and T_3 factors given in Table 2. The greater congruence of this 1958–60 *internal war* dimension with a combination of the *revolution* and *subversion* dimensions for 1946–59 and 1955–57 can be seen by combining the $E_2 - E_3$, $R_2 - R_3$, and $T_3 - T_2$ loadings.[11] The correlation between $E_2 - E_3$ and $T_3 - T_2$ is then 1.0; between $R_2 - R_3$ and $T_3 - T_2$ it is .32—an overall improvement over the separate correlations of T_3 and T_2 with the E and R dimensions.

Conclusions and Propositions

Before tying together the results of the last section, it should be noted, first, that the three studies compared involved data collected independently of each other. Secondly, while Eckstein's data were collected from one source, *The New York Times Index*, the 1955–57 data were collected from several additional sources, such as *Facts on File*, and the 1958–60 data were collected from yet an additional source, *Deadline Data*. Thirdly, it might be mentioned that although there is about a 20 percent overlap in years between the Eckstein data for 1946–59 and the 1955–57 and 1958–60 sets of data, the latter two sets are for quite different periods. The overlap with the Eckstein data still allows considerable room for different correlations and a different factor structure to appear as a result of the relations among the 80 percent of non-overlapping data, *were the relations different*. Finally, evaluation of the results should take cognizance of the tests for systematic error that were made on *each* set. In no case were measures of *censorship* or *world interest in a nation* related to the findings in a way indicating possible distortion of the dimensions delineated.

Considering these points with regard to the comparisons of the three studies, the conclusion is that insofar as post-World War II domestic conflict behavior is concerned, *turmoil* is a major dimension—one that should be taken into account in a typology or empirical study of domestic conflict.

Moreover, it also appears clear that the kind of spontaneous behavior represented by *turmoil* has little relationship to the organized, cooperative kind of behavior represented by the *revolution–subversion* or the *internal war* dimensions. This spontaneous–planned distinction is clear in the results also. The independence between the two argues that different sufficient conditions or causes must be sought for *turmoil*, on the one hand, and *revolution* and *subversion*, on the other.[12]

What is not unambiguous is whether the planned conflict behavior constitutes two dimensions, as found in the 1946–59 and 1955–57 data, or one as found for 1958–60. Tanter has explored this ambiguity by doing a factor analysis (Tanter, 1964b) of the combined 1955–60 data. In this study, the *turmoil* and *internal war* dimensions were extracted also, further emphasizing the independence between spontaneous and planned behavior, but underlining the ambiguity as to whether the planned behavior constitutes one or two dimensions. Further research on different sets of data is certainly needed to approach a decision on this question.[13]

Some propositions are suggested on the basis of the results given and comparisons made above.

(1) Domestic conflict behavior is highly structured in terms of independent clusters of activities.

(2) A spontaneous kind of conflict behavior, or *turmoil*, is a major dimension of domestic conflict behavior.

(3) Independently of a turmoil dimension, domestic conflict behavior also involves planned behavior represented by *revolution* and *subversion* dimensions, or their combination into one *internal war* dimension.

APPENDIX. DEFINITIONS OF 1946–59 ECKSTEIN CONFLICT BEHAVIOR MEASURES

(1) *UE:* This is the total number of incidents of unequivocal violence which occurred during 1946–59.

(2) *Warfare:* "This category includes both civil and guerrilla warfare, which have not been separately counted because of the frequent inadequacy of the source. Like external wars, both are characterized by a high degree

of organization of the opponents, the continuity of fighting, the presence of operational planning, and the existence of territorial control, extended or discontinuous, by the insurgents."

(3) *Turmoil:* "Simultaneous, continuous rioting of considerable duration in two or more distinct geographic areas."

(4) *Rioting:* "Relatively unorganized and spontaneous short-term incidents, typically involving police contingents and an unintegrated mass whose objectives are somewhat modest. Frequently, however, the actual instigators are highly organized extremist groups."

(5) *Large-Scale (L.S.) Terrorism:* "Large-scale terrorism (L.S.) is the systematic use of intimidation and harassment by assassination and/or sabotage by relatively small but cohesive groups."

(6) *Small-Scale (S.S.) Terrorism:* "Small-scale (S.S.) terrorism distinguishes the above from the more undisciplined and discontinuous use of terror, and includes the occasional assassination or bomb-plant."

(7) *Mutiny:* "Violence on the established order by groups which are part of its own instruments of force, such as the police, military, etc."

(8) *Coup:* "Violence or the threat of it by one or more parts of the power elite against other parts, i.e., Lasswell and Kaplan's 'palace revolution'."

(9) *Equivocal Plots:* "These are equivocal either because they are exposed while in an early conspiratorial stage (and thus are not violent), or because the alleged plot may be only a pretext by which the government seeks to eliminate its political competitors."

(10) *Administrative Action:* "The removal of political opposition through the use of the formal administrative apparatus, as in Soviet-type purges, police round-ups or raids."

(11) *Quasi-Private:* "Cases which are equivocal internal wars because the violence was not initially directed at the government, or which appear not to be anti-government because of insufficient information. The Index gave a very high number of such cases for South Africa, but these so-called inter-tribal disputes are very often genuine internal wars."

(12) *Extended Violence:* This measure is derived from Harry Eckstein's indication of the existence of extended violence, such as a prolonged civil war, through a double asterisk attached to the particular nation in his data table.

(13) $UE+E$: This is the total number of incidents of unequivocal (UE) and equivocal violence which occurred during 1946-59. "The equivocal–unequivocal distinction is one between cases of clear-cut internal wars and cases which are ambiguous for these reasons: 1) effective countermeasures by the incumbent power holders minimized or precluded actual violence, e.g., abortive insurrections or coups; 2) cases for which the Times Index coverage was so inadequate that the presence of violence was difficult to determine; 3) cases which took the form of police or administrative actions which may or may not have involved outright violence, e.g., police roundups of political

opponents, or Soviet-type purges; 4) the violence was apparently not directed at the incumbents in the first instance, and cases of intertribal disputes."

All quotes are from Eckstein (1962, Appendix I).

NOTES

1. For an overview of methodological and empirical factor analysis studies, see the bibliography contained in Harman (1960).

2. See Rummel (1965a) for a methodological discussion of assessing error in this fashion. For other applications of the methodology, see Rummel (1963 [reprinted in this volume, Chapter 3]) and Tanter (1964a).

3. With negative exponential distributions, the problem was to pull in extreme values at the right tail.

4. The biquartimin criteria were used for the oblique rotation. As a check, the covarimin and quartimin solutions were also calculated. Although these different oblique solutions resulted in small changes in loadings, the interpretation of the factor patterns remained the same in each case.

5. Since we are discussing the orthogonal results, the loadings given in parentheses may be considered as the *correlation* of the particular measure with the dimension.

6. The author is indebted to Raymond Tanter and Richard Chadwick for independently pointing out that UE and $UE+E$ are necessarily related to each other. Tanter further suggested that since they are summary measures, they are necessarily related to riots as well. As a consequence of this large shared variance, they might result in spurious factors; such would most likely be the case with the factor being discussed. To check the possibility of spurious factors, the author reanalyzed the data for all except the UE and $UE+E$ measures. The new factor structure came out largely the same with each factor maintaining the identical interpretation.

7. Other studies (Tanter, 1964b; Rummel, 1965a) have been completed, but too late for their results to be included. The findings, however, further confirm the conclusions of this paper. See note 11 below.

8. Only nations that exchanged ambassadors and had a population greater than 750,000 were included.

9. Table 4 of the extended version of this paper, on file with the ADI (see Editors' Note), similarly orders and compares the results of the orthogonal solutions.

10. Calculating the correlation between loadings dichotomized into high and low avoids the problem of misleading pattern correlation which may result from correlating the loadings themselves. For example, while the magnitude of the loadings on one factor may be quite high and those on the other factor quite low, if their patterns of loadings are the same the correlation between them may be perfect.

11. For example, for purposes of calculating the correlation, the two E_2 and E_3 dimensions are combined into one E_2-E_3 dimension in this fashion: if either (or both) has a high loading $\geqslant |.50|$, the combined dimension is given a high loading; if both have a low loading, the combined dimension is given a low loading.

12. The findings indicate, for example, that the correlation between *turmoil* and *revolution* dimensions is near zero. Consequently, if any variable x correlates near 1.0 with either *turmoil* or *revolution* dimensions, then its correlation with the other dimensions will be near zero.

13. The Rummel (1965b) study compared twelve factor analyses of data that included some measures of domestic conflict. Using Ahmnavaara's transformation method of factor comparison, it was found that *turmoil* appeared by itself unambiguously in all studies. Although not always distinct from each other as dimensions, *subversion* also appeared in all studies and *revolution* in eleven out of twelve.

REFERENCES

ECKSTEIN, H. (1962) "The incidence of internal wars, 1946–59." Appendix I of *Internal War: The Problem of Anticipation*. A report submitted to the Research Group in Psychology and the Social Sciences, Smithsonian Institution, Washington, D.C., January 15.

HARMAN, H. (1960) *Modern Factor Analysis*. Chicago: University of Chicago Press.

RUMMEL, R.J. (1965a) "Dimensions of error in cross-national data in the mid-1950s." Dimensionality of Nations Project, Yale University (mimeo.).

— (1965b) "A field theory of social action and of political conflict within nations." *General Systems Yearbook 10*.

— (1963) "Dimensions of conflict behavior within and between nations." Pp. 1–50 in *General Systems Yearbook 8*. Reprinted in this volume, Chapter 3.

TANTER, R. (1965) "Dimensions of conflict behavior within and between nations, 1955–60." *Peace Research Society Papers 3*.

— (1964a) Dimensions of Conflict Behavior Within and Between Nations, 1958–60. Ph.D. dissertation, Indiana University.

— (1964b) "Dimensions of conflict behavior within nations, 1955–60: turmoil and internal war." Prepared for delivery before the Peace Research Conference, University of Chicago, November 16–17.

3 Dimensions of Conflict Behavior Within and Between Nations

RUDOLPH J. RUMMEL

This study has three goals: first, to find the dimensions of variation among nations with respect to their domestic and foreign conflict behavior during a period of contemporary history; second, to determine the approximate position of each nation along these dimensions; and third, to ascertain what relationship exists between the dimensions of foreign conflict behavior on the one hand, and the domestic conflict behavior dimensions on the other.

Data have been collected on 22 measures of foreign and domestic conflict behavior for 77 nations for the years 1955, 1956, and 1957. These data will be intercorrelated and factor-analyzed. Factor scores for each country will be calculated to determine the position of each nation along the foreign and domestic conflict dimensions found. These scores will then be used in a multiple regression analysis of the relationship between domestic and foreign conflict behavior.

Although factor analysis has been formulated and developed within the discipline of psychology,[1] as a purely statistical method for determining the patterns of relationships among a collection of variables, the method is of great potential value outside of psychology. This can be seen from its increasingly wide use. Factor analysis has been applied to the value scores of foreign students to determine the factor patterns of the values of Americans, Indians, Japanese, Chinese, and Norwegians (Morris, 1956) to locate the dimensions of interaction among people within groups (Borgatta, et al., 1955, 1956), to test an hypothesis about the voting behavior of justices of the Supreme Court (Schubert, 1962), to study the factors making for the success of thirty-two businesses (Godfrey, et al., 1959), to determine the dimensions of eighty-eight community (county) systems (Jonassen and Peres, 1960) and the dimensions of American local governments (Wood, 1961), to determine the

---

Reprinted (in a slightly edited version) from *General Systems Yearbook 8*, pages 1–50, by permission of the author and the publisher. Copyright © 1963 Society for General Systems Research.

factors of cerebral disease (Bechtoldt, et al., 1962), and for determining the weights to apply to indices that might be used to predict the course of a stock market (Rhodes, 1937).

But, so far, the method has found little use in trying to make sense out of the innumerable and ever-shifting constellations of variables with which the student of cross-national behavior is confronted. I know of only three scholars who have published applications of factor analysis to such subject matter. The most encompassing of them is Raymond Cattell's set of three articles (1951, 1949, 1950) that were published within a space of three years, and that were the result of factor analyses of 72 variables. The first of these studies (1949) involved a population of 69 countries, which because of difficulties with his data, he later reduced in his more "refined" study (1951) to forty countries.[2] His other study (1950) was an attempt to group nations according to similar cultural patterns as derived from his 72 variable, 69 nation analysis. With the possible exception of Hofstaetter (1951), who did his factor analysis using American states as his population, there is apparently no published research whose aim has been to follow up and replicate Cattell's work.[3]

Another application of factor analysis to cross-national variables has been made separately by Brian Berry (1960, 1961) who, using Norton Ginsberg's data (1961), did a factor analysis of 43 variables on a population of 95 countries. His analysis resulted in the variation between nations on his variables being accounted for by four factors: technology, demographic, contrast in income and external relations, and large vs. small nations. The only other published factor analysis of cross-national variables that I know about is Leo Schnore's (1961) analysis of 11 variables in an effort to see if urbanization forms a cluster with indices to economic development. A factor common to urbanization and economic development emerged from his study.

The research here, then, certainly is beating no new path in applying factor analysis to nonpsychological data, nor is it essentially unique in using the method on cross-national data. What is different about this study, however, is that it is trying to apply factor analysis for the first time to delineate the dimensions of internation and intranation conflict behavior.

CONFLICT BEHAVIOR AND ITS MEASURES

Conflict Behavior

Interpersonal and intergroup conflict have variously been defined as "a test of power between antagonistic parties" (Coser, 1956: 137), the existence of "incompatible or mutually exclusive goals or aims or values espoused by human beings" (Bernard, 1957: 38), "opposition among social entities directed against one another . . ." (Wright, 1954: 146), or "an adjustment process in which, as opposing energy-systems meet, the energies of each are directed against the other to remove, dominate, or destroy it" (Carr, italics omitted, 1946: 301). The common components of these and other definitions of conflict appear to be that of *a situation* in which *two or more* parties direct their energies *at each other* in order *to achieve goals* that can only be *gained at each others' expense.*

The key to identifying a conflict situation, therefore, may be to look for the *actions* which those involved in conflict are directing toward each other. Since "conflictful behaviors are those designed to destroy, injure, thwart, or otherwise control another party or other parties . . ." (Mack and Snyder, italics omitted, 1957: 218), one should be able to measure such conflict behavior in terms of specific acts (e.g., assassinations, threats), or occurrences reflecting an aggregation of such acts (e.g., revolution, war).

Measures of Conflict Behavior

With respect to the methods and goals of this study, any act or occurrence chosen to index conflict behavior must:

(1) be capable of empirical delimitation;

(2) be an act or occurrence of sufficient interest to be generally reported—that is, data must be available;

(3) be applicable to all countries (e.g., "colonial violence" if made a measure, would not be applicable to those countries without colonies) if spurious factors are not to result;

(4) be as diverse as possible to cover the greatest possible range of conflict behavior;

(5) be an act of or within, or an occurrence with respect to, seven or more countries (this is to prevent the correlations from being dependent on too few such happenings and, therefore, to reduce the role of aberrations on what are meant to be general conclusions).

On the basis of these criteria, nine measures of domestic and thirteen measures of foreign conflict were chosen for this study.[4] The domestic conflict measures and a brief definition of the conflict act or occurrence are as follows:

(1) *Number of assassinations:* any politically motivated murder or attempted murder of a high government official or politician.

(2) *Number of general strikes:* any strike of 1,000 or more industrial or service workers that involves more than one employer and that is aimed at national government policies or authority.

(3) *Presence or absence of guerrilla warfare:* any armed activity, sabotage, or bombings carried on by independent bands or citizens or irregular forces and aimed at the overthrow of the present regime.

(4) *Number of major government crises:* any rapidly developing situation that threatens to bring the downfall of the present regime—excluding situations of revolt aimed at such an overthrow.

(5) *Number of purges:* any systematic elimination by jailing or execution of political opposition within the ranks of the regime or the opposition.

(6) *Number of riots:* any violent demonstration or clash of more than 100 citizens involving the use of physical force.

(7) *Number of revolutions:* any illegal or forced change in the top governmental elite, any attempt at such a change, or any successful or unsuccessful armed rebellion whose aim is independence from the central government.

(8) *Number of antigovernment demonstrations:* any peaceful public gathering of at least 100 people for the primary purpose of displaying or voicing their opposition to government policies or authority, excluding those demonstrations of a distinctly antiforeign nature.

(9) *Number of people killed in all forms of domestic violence:* any deaths resulting directly from violence of an intergroup nature, thus excluding deaths by murder and execution.

And the measures of foreign conflict and definitions are as follows:

(1) *Number of antiforeign demonstrations:* any demonstration or riot by more than 100 people directed at a particular foreign country (or group of countries) or its policies.

(2) *Number of negative sanctions:* any nonviolent act against another country—such as boycott, withdrawal of aid—the purpose of which is to punish or threaten that country.

(3) *Number of protests:* any official diplomatic communication or governmental statement, the purpose of which is to complain about or object to the policies of another country.

(4) *Number of countries with which diplomatic relations severed:* the complete withdrawal from all official contact with a particular country.

(5) *Number of ambassadors expelled or recalled:* any expelling of an ambassador from, or recalling for other than administrative reasons an ambassador to, a particular country—this does not involve expulsion or recall resulting from the severance of diplomatic relations.

(6) *Number of diplomatic officials of lesser than ambassador's rank expelled or recalled:* replace "ambassador" by "officials of lesser . . . rank" in above definition.

(7) *Number of threats:* any official diplomatic communication or governmental statement asserting that if a particular country does or does not do a particular thing it will incur negative sanctions.

(8) *Presence or absence of military action:* any military clash of a particular country with another and involving gunfire, but short of war as defined below.

(9) *Number of wars:* any military clash for a particular country with another and in which more than .02 percent of its population are militarily involved in the clash.

(10) *Number of troop movements:* any rapid movement of large bodies of troops, naval units, or air squadrons to a particular area for the purpose of deterring the military action of another country, gaining concessions, or as a show of strength.

(11) *Number of mobilizations:* any rapid increase in military strength through the calling up of reserves, activation of additional military units, or the demothballing of military equipment.

(12) *Number of accusations:* any official diplomatic or governmental statement involving charges and allegations of a derogatory nature against another country.

(13) *Number of people killed in all forms of foreign conflict behavior:* the total number of deaths resulting directly from any violent interchange between countries.

In order to avoid logically necessary correlations and factors, each of these measures is defined in a way to make them mutually exclusive and each datum is used only once. A logical connection might be made between threats and accusations, for example, if threats were defined as "any accusations that contained an implied or stated sanction that would result from the recipient doing or not doing a certain thing," then accusations would be a necessary condition for the occurrence of threats, and the two would be found correlated together in the results of the analysis.

Sources of Data

Five sources, *The New York Times Index*, *New International Yearbook*, *Keesing's Contemporary Archives*,[5] *Facts on File*, and *Britannica Book of The Year*, were combed for data with respect to these measures. Each datum was recorded on a separate card, some 3,500 cards in all being collected; where the sources differed with respect to an event—say, the number of killed or number of riots—the mean value between them was used.

Measures of Error

Random Error. The kinds of error that might affect the results of this study can be divided into two types: random error and systematic error. If random error were present, it would mean that there was an equal probability that the values on a particular measure for a certain country are under or overstated—that the direction of error as well as its magnitude is not correlated with any attributes of the countries of concern, nor with the other measures for which data are taken.

Some random error resulting from clerical mistakes and ambiguous descriptions in the sources probably exists in the data of this study. Assuming for the moment that the data are highly affected by such error, what would be its influence upon the results? Its effect on the correlations between the measures would be to reduce the value of the correlations below what they would be without such error. That is, a significant correlation between data that one suspects have a lot of random "noise" can be considered even more significant than if one were dealing with uncontaminated data.[6] And the impact of such error on the results of the factor analysis would apparently be to lower somewhat the loadings that the variables have on the factors,[7] but not to distort the factor structure as a whole. With or without random error, one would likely extract the same factors, but with slightly lower loadings if random error were present.[8] The possible existence of random error, then, should not unduly affect one's confidence in the results. But the situation is different with respect to systematic error.

Systematic Error. Errors which cause the data to consistently over or understate that being measured and which are correlated with the other measures of concern may bias the analysis to a degree that the outcome is highly distorted. That is, the result may be overly high or low correlations, and factors with little existential validity.

It would be unwise to assume that such errors do not exist in the data. In fact, the contrary assumption that such errors contaminate the data to a high degree appears more plausible. Also warranted appears to be the assumption that this systematic error is in the direction of causing the data to understate consistently the actual occurrence of conflict behavior. Except in the case of random error, I cannot imagine any influence that would cause a country systematically to be reported as having more riots, more troop movements, more assassinations, etc., than it really does have.

Three elements may influence the systematic understating of conflict behavior for a particular country. Censorship may prevent news of such behavior from being disseminated. Or if such news is disseminated, it may not get into the sources used because the country of concern is of little interest to the world at large (e.g., a demonstration in Nepal or Uruguay), or the news goes unreported because it happened concurrently with an occurrence considered important enough to be reported in great depth. Two measures will be used to index the possibility that systematic error in the form of censorship and/or lack of world interest is influencing the results.

The first measure will be a three point censorship scale based on data from a 1955 Associated Press survey of the world's press (*New York Times*, January 9, 1955) and from the *Worldmark Encyclopedia of Nations* (1960). World interest in a particular nation will be measured by the number of countries with foreign embassies and legations in that nation.[9] The assumption here, of course, is that the number of resident embassies and legations in a country reflects the interest the world has in that nation's affairs.

The correlation between each of these systematic error measures and each of the domestic and foreign conflict behavior measures will be assessed, and these measures will also be included in the factor analysis of the conflict measures. If there is no correlation between the measures of systematic error and the measures of conflict behavior, then one can conclude that systematic errors as tapped by the two measures are not seriously affecting the results. The same conclusion will be valid if high positive correlations between the two measures and other measures are found. This is because we can assume the direction of systematic error to be under rather than overstatement. For example, if censorship is positively correlated with riots and if censorship is acting to suppress information about the actual number of riots, then even in the case that the actual number of riots were known, such knowledge would not alter the rank of this nation relative to other nations on this measure sufficiently to distort the correlations. Censorship would then act much like random error—making the correlations lower than they really are. If, however, these two measures are negatively correlated with others then the interpretation of the results should be made with the utmost care. For then the suppression of information, for example, could cause a nation's rank relative to others to be completely reversed on the measures.

In the event that there is no correlation between the measures of systematic error and the data on conflict behavior, however, there is still no certainty that such errors have not affected the conclusions—as is true in any scientific study. Only replication and independent confirmation can give one confidence enough to assert that the effect of systematic error is nil. As Sidman (1960: 70) suggests, the "soundest empirical test of the reliability of data is provided by replication," and as McClelland (1961: 24) counsels, as "independent studies continue to confirm the general hypothesis, it becomes less and less likely that some nonrandom error of measurement could have created the relationship under investigation."

Population

Data have been collected on all nations for the period 1955, 1956, and 1957 which meet the following criteria:

(1) sovereign statehood for at least two years,[10] as evidenced by diplomatic relations with other countries and the existence of a foreign ministry or its equivalent;[11]

(2) a minimum population of 800,000, which eliminates aberrations within the nation-state system like Monaco and Liechtenstein.

The number of nations thus considered is seventy-seven.

Each measure used in this study is a summation of the data for the three years, 1955–57. The years were chosen with future studies in mind, some of which will attempt to relate factors resulting from a factor analysis of the structural characteristics and nonconflict behavior of nations to the dimensions of conflict behavior resulting from this study.

Stability of the Data

Since the data were collected for only three years, one might justifiably ask whether the data are unique to this period, and whether or not generalizations thus derived are only specific to this particular span of history. After all, during this period the Mid-East War and the Hungarian Revolution occurred.

The stability of the data—how well the data reflect general conflict behavior over extended periods of time—was checked in three ways. First, the data on three measures—war, war and military action, and number of people killed in all foreign conflict—were checked for their correlation with Lewis F. Richardson's (1961) data on war from 1825–1945 inclusive. The results are given in Table 1. These are extremely high correlations and imply that the frequency of war for each of the thirty nations is predictive of the amount of war each will have from 1955 to 1957. Of the thirty, those countries that depart most from this prediction are the U.S.S.R., which had far more war (Hungary), and China, which had far more military action (Formosa), than could be predicted on the basis of their past history of warfare.

TABLE 1

CORRELATIONS OF 1955–57 DATA WITH RICHARDSON'S DATA

Richardson's data[b]	1955–57 Conflict data		
	War	War and military action	$\log_{10}$ (No. killed)
War, 1825–1945	.86[a]	.81[a]	.83[a]

[a] Product moment Γ, $p < .01$ (nonnormal distributions); N = 30.

[b] Lewis Fry Richardson, *Statistics of Deadly Quarrels*, 1961. This is a count of the number of wars in which a nation was involved which resulted in more than 3,163 deaths, i.e., more than $\log_{10}$ (deaths) = 3.5.

TABLE 2

CORRELATIONS OF 1955–57 DATA WITH ECKSTEIN'S DATA

1946–59[c]	No. killed in domestic violence	Total violence[b]	Guerrilla war and revolution	Rioting
Total violence[b]	.55[a] (.52)[d]	.71[a] (.70)[d]		
Internal warfare and coup			.50[a] (.52)[d]	
Rioting				.67[a] (.66)[d]

[a] Product moment Γ, $p < .01$ (nonnormal distributions); N = 70.

[b] Derived by summing all occurrences of domestic conflict behavior.

[c] Harry Eckstein, "The incidence of internal wars, 1946–1959," Appendix I of *Internal War: The Problem of Anticipation*, a report submitted to the Research Group in Psychology and the Social Sciences, Smithsonian Institution, Washington, D.C., January 15, 1962.

[d] Partial correlation, holding 1955 population constant.

Second, the data on domestic conflict were compared with data collected by Harry Eckstein (1962) for similar measures for seventy nations for 1945–59.[12] The product moment correlations are given in Table 2. Since the number of riots and other forms of domestic violence may be a function, in part, of the number of people there are that can be involved in such violence, the correlations were calculated a second time holding population constant.

Third, the correlations between Raymond Cattell's (1949) five measures of conflict behavior, which he included in his factor analysis of 72 variables for 69 countries, were calculated from his unrotated factor structure and compared with the intercorrelations among similar measures for the 1955–57 data of this study. Table 3 shows the results. A comparison of ten intercorrelations shows that only one for the 1955–57 data differs significantly from that for the 1837–1937 data. As a matter of fact, the correlations from the different data for war-revolution, revolution-foreign clashes, and foreign clashes-assassinations are surprisingly close.

These three comparisons—with the Richardson (1961) and with the Eckstein (1962) data, and with the Cattell (1949) correlations—point to the conclusion that the 1955–57 data are probably not unique, but instead may mirror the long run conflict behavior within and between nations.

TABLE 3

COMPARISON OF CORRELATIONS BETWEEN 1955–57 DATA AND CORRELATIONS BETWEEN CATTELL'S DATA

Measures[b]	Cattell's correlations[d] 1837–1937	Conflict data correlations 1955–57
1. War-revolution	.06	−.04[a]
2. War-riots	.41	.12[a]
3. War-foreign clashes	.58	.38[a]
4. War-assassinations	.08	.19[a]
5. Revolution-riots	.14	.32[a]
6. Revolution-foreign clashes	.13	.12[a]
7. Revolution-assassinations	.06	.19[a]
8. Riots-foreign clashes	.54	.08[c]
9. Riots-assassinations	.36	.45[a]
10. Foreign clashes-assassinations	.14	.15[a]

[a] Correlations are not significantly different from Cattell's, $p > .05$.

[b] Cattell defines foreign clashes as "fighting incidents and political clashes not accompanied by or immediately followed by war."

[c] Correlations significantly different, $p = .002$.

[d] Calculated from Cattell's unrotated factor structure, "The Dimensions of Culture Patterns of Factorization of National Characters," *Journal of Abnormal and Social Psychology*, 44 (1949), pp. 443–469.

Transformations

In order to reduce the effect on the correlations of aberrant data—data, say, with a standard score of ten or twenty—transformations were applied to most nondichotomous distributions. In the case of the two number-of-killed measures and the accusations measure, a log transformation was used. For the other measures, where generally one, and not more than two digits values are present, data were grouped on a 0, 1–3, 4–7, 8–15, ..., basis with the common ratio of the geometric progression after zero being two.

FACTOR ANALYSIS
The Method
Factor analysis seems ideally suited to determining the nature of interrelationships between a large number of variables. Applied to a collection of variables, factor analysis delineates those which cluster together—which covary more with each other than they do with any of the other variables included in the analysis.[13] If, for example, one were to factor analyze an aggregation of cross-national variables, like GNP, number of vehicles, electrical production, number of religious groups, size of country, population, and trade, it would probably be found that GNP, vehicles, and electricity covary together quite closely in comparison with the other variables—that is, they are a dimension of variation among all those cross-national variables.

Principal Components
One may choose among many factor *techniques* for determining the clusters of relationships—the dimensions—among the conflict behavior measures.[14] The technique chosen here is called principal components (or principal factor), and is chosen from among competing techniques because it yields a mathematically unique solution and because the first factor extracts the maximum of variance from the original data while each succeeding factor extracts the maximum of remaining variance.

Assumptions. The application of factor analysis to any set of data assumes certain characteristics of the data that should be made explicit.[15] First, the data for each country are assumed to be of equal importance, and are thus given equal weight. That is, the number of riots for the United States is considered just as important as the number of riots for Yemen and each is thus given equal weight in the results. For a study like this, which is trying to determine the general characteristics of conflict for all countries, such an assumption appears warranted.

A second assumption is that all the interrelationships between the variables are linear. "The one scale condition which destroys the effectiveness of factorization is that in which true curvilinear relations exist in the correlation plots" (Cattell, 1952: 328). As a check on this assumption, the 24 transformed measures were plotted against each other, with the result that no significant curvilinear relationships were found.

If one wishes to test the significance of the correlations each of the measures has on the factors extracted, then a third assumption is that the data are distributed normally. However, the data used here do not meet this assumption, and because often more than half the nations are tied at the minimum value, the distributions are generally such that they cannot be transformed to a normal distribution. No tests of significance will be made, therefore, of the relationships between the variables and the factors. With respect to the factors themselves, however, the same basic factors most probably would emerge regardless of the underlying distribution of the data.[16]

Problem of the Correlation Coefficient. For assessing the intercorrelation among the measures, there are several correlation coefficients one can choose, such as the product moment, rank, tetrachoric, and phi-over-phi-max. Since the factors are extracted on the basis of the interrelationships among the data determined by the correlation coefficient, the choice of the coefficient is basic to the analysis. Because the distributions of the conflict data are non-normal, generally J distributions, and because some of the data are dichotomous, thought was given to which correlation coefficient would give the most meaningful results.[17] The rank correlation coefficient was ruled out because of the large number of tied ranks (about 80 percent of the nations tied for the minimum rank for some of the measures). Tetrachoric and phi-over-phi-max were ruled out because of the extreme splits on some of the measures (the most extreme being a 91–9 percent split in the case of the war measure), and because of the continuous nature of many of the distributions. The product moment coefficient (which becomes the phi coefficient where dichotomous data are concerned) on the other hand, is applicable to both continuous and dichotomous data. Moreover, not only does it appear to make more use of the information in the data and to give more meaningful and less distorted results than the other coefficients, but it is also the coefficient upon which the factor analytic model is based. The product moment, therefore, was chosen for this study.

Problem of Communality. A further problem confronts the factor analyst with regard to what value to put in the principal diagonal of the correlation matrix to be factor analyzed. This value determines the portion of the total variance of the measures that will be factored.

If one wants to analyze only the variance common to more than one of the measures, then one might insert in the diagonal for that measure its squared multiple correlations with all the other measures—squared multiple correlation thus being inserted for all the measures. If one is concerned with reliable variance, including that unique to single measures, then reliabilities may be inserted (if they are available), and if one wants to analyze all the variance—common, specific, and error—then unities are appropriate (see Fruchter, 1954: 51–52).

In this study I am interested in accounting for as much of the total variance of my measures as possible, and in having an indication of how much of this total variance has been extracted by the factors. Unities, therefore, will be inserted in the principal diagonal.

Problem of Number of Significant Factors. Regardless of what is put in the principal diagonal, there is still the problem of determining the number of factors that will be extracted. For, if all the factors possible were extracted, one would end up with as many factors as there are measures—hardly a parsimonious solution. One possibility is to specify the minimum amount of variance a factor must account for in order to be extracted, which specification can be made on the basis of an estimate as to the amount of error the data contain. Since the actual amount of error in my data is a large unknown and will largely be indicated by the results of the factor analysis itself, possibly a more analytic solution is called for. The one that will be used here is that suggested by Kaiser (1960: 146), who says,

> allow me to suggest a "best" answer to the question of the number of factors: it is the number of latent roots greater than one of the observed correlation matrix. This conclusion is based on the relatively independent criteria of algebraic necessity, psychometric reliability, and psychological meaningfulness.

Rotation

Whatever the factor technique chosen, the factor analyst is faced with the problem of whether he will be satisfied with the factor solution as given, or whether he wishes to *rotate* the factors to a more desirous solution. The difficulty with an unrotated factor solution is that the correlations of the measures with the factors are dependent on the whole set of measures included in the analysis, and will thus vary from analysis to analysis as new measures are included or old ones omitted (Cattell, 1952: 249). If one wants to delimit the dimensions that reflect recurring patterns of relationships among the measures, that is, to be able to identify recurring factors in subsequent studies, then rotation is necessary.

Problem of the Criteria of Rotation. The decision to rotate presents one with numerous alternatives. The factors can be rotated to an a priori solution by making the first factor colinear with a particular measure. For example, if one were interested in what kind of factors would emerge independent of a war factor and how the other measures would correlate with this dimension, then the first factor might be rotated to make it perfectly correlated—colinear—with the war measure.

Another possibility is to rotate to an oblique solution, where the factors can be correlated with each other and thus may give the best possible fit to the clusters of measures. This is the solution most favored by Cattell (1952: 116–117, 123). If one, however, is exploring a field for the first time, it may be best to rotate to a solution in which the factors give the best possible orthogonal fit to the clusters. This gives one a parsimonious solution with which to work. And, if after visual inspection of the orthogonally rotated solution a more meaningful oblique solution appears feasible, such can then be done.

A decision to use orthogonal rotation, at least initially, still does not exhaust the alternatives. There are several possible criteria for orthogonal rotation which could be used (see Harman, 1960: Chapter 14). The one chosen for use here is an analytic criterion that has gained wide recognition for yielding a meaningful and invariant solution—Thurstone's (1947: Chapter 14) simple structure criterion as determined by Kaiser's (1959) Varimax analytic solution.[18]

RESULTS

Domestic Conflict Behavior Measures

Table 4 gives the unrotated and orthogonally rotated factor matrices for the domestic conflict measures. The triangular correlation matrix is given in the upper left portion of Table 9 below. The unrotated matrix shows the typical principal component general dimension, and two bipolar dimensions. That a general dimension should come out with as high loadings as it has (the lowest loading is .48 for guerrilla warfare) and accounting for as much of the common variance—65 percent—and total variance—45.8 percent—is a good indication that the domestic conflict measures used are reflecting a general conflict situation, or the existence of domestic conflict societies, one might say.[19] One might note the high communalities (h^2) for the measures and the fact that 70.8 percent of the total variance of the measures is being accounted for by the three factors. This implies that there is a great deal of relationship among all the measures and that the dimensions are reflecting a good deal of meaning. If the data were infused with considerable *random* error and arbitrariness due to ambiguous and meaningless definitions, the communalities should be quite low.

TABLE 4

FACTOR ANALYSIS OF DOMESTIC CONFLICT MEASURES[c]

Measures	Factor matrix[a] D_1	D_2	D_3	Orthogonally rotated factor matrix[a] Turmoil	Revolutionary[b]	Subversive[b]	h^2
1. Assassinations	(62)	17	(61)	(59)	−03	(66)	78
2. General strikes	(75)	05	−24	(52)	(60)	05	63
3. Guerrilla warfare	48	(−57)	(59)	−04	28	(90)	90
4. Major government crisis	(52)	35	−10	(60)	21	−04	41
5. Purges	(67)	−14	−34	32	(71)	03	60
6. Riots	(76)	38	−03	(79)	31	09	73
7. Revolutions	(66)	−43	−36	09	(85)	13	75
8. Antigovernment demonstrations	(74)	46	14	(85)	17	19	79
9. Domestic number killed	(80)	−40	−05	23	(75)	42	79
% Common variance	65.0	18.0	16.0	39.0	37.6	23.4	100.0
% Total variance	45.8	13.3	11.7	27.7	26.7	16.6	70.8

[a] Parentheses indicate loadings ≥.50.
[b] Signs reversed.
[c] Decimals omitted from loadings.

When the dimensions are rotated to a more invariant position, the first rotated dimension comes out as a nonorganizational, spontaneous conflict behavior dimension—a turmoil dimension.[20] Antigovernment demonstrations, riots, and major government crises, are highest on this dimension with assassinations and general strikes having lower but respectable loadings. Assassinations and general strikes, which are not always of a spontaneous nature, and general strikes, which generally are organized, are not wholly of this dimension. General strikes have a high correlation with the second dimension, and assassinations are also higher on the third dimension.

The second and third dimensions appear to represent organized conflict behavior, i.e., behavior that is planned with definite objectives and methods in mind. This type of behavior is the most violent, as shown by the high correlations of number killed with these two dimensions. Since revolutions, purges, and general strikes are highly correlated with the second dimension while the correlation of assassinations and guerrilla warfare is low, the second dimension might be an overt, organized conflict behavior dimension—or for short, a *revolutionary* dimension.[21] The third dimension, which is also specific to guerrilla war, and which also has assassinations highly correlated with it, is a kind of covert, organized conflict behavior dimension—a *subversion* dimension.

Hence, one can divide domestic conflict into three independent continua: a disorganized, spontaneous conflict behavior, a *turmoil* dimension; an overt, organized conflict behavior, or *revolutionary* dimension; and a covert, organized conflict behavior, or subversion dimension. In terms of accounting for the relationships among the measures, the turmoil and revolutionary dimensions, respectively, account for 29 percent and 27.6 percent of the common variance, as opposed to 23.4 percent for the subversive dimension, and, therefore, may be considered the most important dimensions of domestic conflict behavior.

Foreign Conflict Behavior Measures

Table 5 shows the unrotated and rotated factor matrices of the foreign conflict behavior measures, and the bottom right of Table 9 gives the triangular correlation matrix. The unrotated general dimension in the case of foreign conflict behavior is not as strong as is the general dimension for domestic behavior. Expulsion or recall of ambassadors is quite low on the general dimension; severance of diplomatic relations has a much higher loading but still below the lowest on the general domestic conflict behavior dimension.

The first dimension accounts for a high 69.2 percent of common and 46 percent of total variance, with the amount of variance being extracted by the second dimension dropping off sharply. Like the domestic dimensions, the first foreign conflict behavior dimension is accounting for most of the conflict behavior. The communalities are also generally high, and in conjunction with the high variance being accounted for, imply that here also something of meaning is being extracted.

TABLE 5

Factor Analysis of Foreign Conflict Measures[c]

Measures	Factor matrix[a] F_1[b]	F_2	F_3	Orthogonally rotated factor matrix[a] F_1[b]	F_2	F_3	h^2
1. Antiforeign demonstrations	(59)	14	48	13	42	(63)	60
2. Negative sanctions	(65)	11	44	20	41	(64)	62
3. Protests	(78)	22	−13	(62)	49	22	67
4. Severance of diplomatic relations	45	−46	(54)	13	−17	(82)	71
5. Expulsions or recalls—ambassadors	10	(67)	12	−16	(66)	−08	47
6. Expulsions or recalls—lesser officials	(53)	44	−06	33	(60)	08	48
7. Threats	(91)	07	05	(65)	43	48	84
8. Military action	(73)	−48	04	(65)	−14	(57)	77
9. Wars	(65)	−04	(−57)	(85)	15	−10	57
10. Troop movements	(73)	33	01	47	(59)	28	64
11. Mobilizations	(61)	−34	−10	(60)	−08	35	49
12. Accusations	(89)	01	−05	(70)	35	41	79
13. Number killed—foreign	(80)	−19	−36	(87)	10	19	80
% Common variance	69.2	16.6	14.2	46.2	24.6	29.1	100.0
% Total variance	46.0	11.0	9.4	30.7	16.3	19.3	66.4

[a] Parentheses indicate loadings, $\geq .50$.
[b] Signs reversed.
[c] Decimals omitted from loadings.

The first dimension of the rotated factor matrix defines a cluster containing war, number killed, mobilizations, accusations, threats, military action, and protests. When one disregards those measures which are also highly correlated ±.4 or better with other dimensions, mobilizations, war, and number killed remain. These are measures which represent the preparation for war, the actual act of war, and the consequences of war. Therefore, it appears reasonable to call the first rotated dimension a *war* dimension. As can be seen from Table 6, this dimension accounts for much more of the relationship among foreign conflict behavior—46.2 percent of common variance—than either of the other dimensions. That a war continuum accounting for the most variance in conflict behavior should emerge may not perhaps appear strange to students of international relations, who look upon war as a prime mechanism through which the international system adjusts to changes within the system (see Millis, 1961).

The second dimension appears to represent a nonviolent form of foreign conflict behavior. The measures that are mainly correlated with this dimension—expelling or recalling ambassadors, expelling or recalling officials of lesser than ambassadorial rank, and troop movements—are forms of nonviolent behavior—military action, war, and number killed have very low loadings. Consequently, this dimension seems to pull together that conflict behavior which stops short of violence—which may only be designed as diplomatic moves or counters with respect to minor or ephemeral issues. The second factor might, therefore, be named a diplomatic dimension.

The third dimension apparently characterizes an actively hostile mood represented by the tendency to sever diplomatic relations, antiforeign demonstrations, military action of a limited nature, and negative sanctions, and may accordingly be called a *belligerency* dimension. The extraction of a belligerency dimension independent from war and a diplomatic dimension is not unreasonable. War and diplomatic conflict behavior both may be calculated coldly rational at one time and at another be underlain with considerable belligerency. The emergence of the cluster of measures defined by the third dimension indicates, however, that there are kinds of foreign conflict behavior that one may identify as being particularly of a belligerent nature.

Three independent continua of foreign conflict behavior can now be identified: a *war* dimension; a nonviolent foreign conflict behavior, diplomatic dimension; and an actively hostile, belligerent dimension.

TABLE 6

CORRELATIONS OF THREATS AND ACCUSATIONS WITH OTHER FOREIGN CONFLICT MEASURES

Foreign conflict measures	Number of threats	Number of accusations
1. No. of antiforeign demonstrations	.50[a]	.46[a]
2. No. of negative sanctions	.64[a]	.48[a]
3. No. of protests	.66[a]	.69[a]
4. No. of countries with which relations severed	.38[a]	.39[a]
5. No. of ambassadors expelled or recalled	.12[b]	.11[b]
6. No. of non-ambassador officials expelled or recalled	.50[a]	.45[a]
7. No. of threats	—	.81[a]
8. Presence or absence of military action	.62[a]	.65[a]
9. No. of wars	.55[a]	.56[a]
10. No. of troop movements	.68[a]	.62[a]
11. No. of mobilizations	.55[a]	.46[a]
12. No. of accusations	.81[a]	—
13. No. of people killed in all foreign conflict	.63[a]	.70[a]

[a] $p < .01$ (nonnormal distributions); N = 77.
[b] $p > .05$ (nonnormal distributions); N = 77.

Other information also can be extracted from this factor analysis. If one looks at the rotated domestic conflict dimensions, it can be seen that no one measure has loadings greater than ±.35 for all three dimensions—that is, no one measure is general to these continua. However, for the foreign conflict behavior rotated factor matrix, one notices that "threats" (.65; .43; .48) and "accusations" (.70; .35; .41) are such general measures. This reflects their high values on the first unrotated dimension (.91 and .89 respectively), which in turn reflects their high correlations with all the other measures. These product moment correlations are shown in Table 6 and imply that threats, and to a slightly lesser extent, accusations are fairly good indices to the existence of general foreign conflict behavior. This suggests that a simple summation of standard scores for threats and accusations may be an index to the state of relations between countries—a sort of thermometer for measuring the extent of their conflict behavior or the severity of a crisis.

Factor Scores

With respect to this study, the factor scores are the values each country has on each of the dimensions extracted. They indicate, for instance, whether a country is high or low on the *turmoil war* dimensions. The nations with standard scores on each dimension equal to or greater than 1.0 are given in Table 7. Due to the skewness of the factor score distributions, there are no standardized negative factor scores less than or equal to −1.00.

The factor scores for each dimension are calculated by adding together the standard scores for those measures on the particular dimension which have a correlation greater or equal to .50, and no correlation on another dimension within the matrix equal to or greater than .40. Hence, the factor score is a composite of those measures which are most strongly associated with that dimension.

RELATIONSHIP BETWEEN DOMESTIC AND FOREIGN CONFLICT BEHAVIOR

Two approaches will be used here in determining what relationship exists between domestic and foreign conflict behavior. First, a factor analysis of domestic and foreign conflict behavior measures together will be calculated. This should help determine whether there are any common conflict behavior dimensions general to both the domestic and foreign domains, e.g., whether the turmoil dimension extends into international behavior or is specific to domestic relations; whether the war or belligerency dimensions will merge with the subversion dimension.

And, secondly, a multiple regression analysis will be done to see how well each of the foreign conflict behavior dimensions separately can be predicted by all the domestic conflict behavior dimensions, and vice versa. While the

TABLE 7
Standardized Factor Scores by Rank

Domestic dimensions			Foreign dimensions		
Turmoil	Revolutionary	Subversive	War	Diplomatic	Belligerent
France (3.16)	Argentina (4.07)	Cuba (4.08)	Israel (3.20)	U.S.S.R. (3.85)	Egypt (3.80)
Argentina (3.00)	China (2.69)	Burma (4.08)	Egypt (3.19)	U.S. (2.73)	Jordan (3.80)
India (2.25)	India (2.69)	Philippines (4.08)	France (3.18)	Dominican R. (2.65)	Pakistan (3.80)
Pakistan (.172)	Guatemala (2.16)	Argentina (2.61)	U.K. (3.18)	Argentina (2.31)	Afghanistan (1.71)
Guatemala (1.71)	Brazil (1.85)	Indonesia (2.61)	Hungary (2.27)	Venezuela (2.31)	Chile (1.71)
Haiti (1.71)	Paraguay (1.85)	Columbia (1.14)	U.S.S.R. (2.27)	Hungary (1.61)	Rep. of China (1.71)
U. of S. Africa (1.68)	Hungary (1.62)	Costa Rica (1.14)	Syria (2.24)	Sweden (1.61)	West Germany (1.71)
Iraq (1.54)	Syria (1.62)	India (1.14)	Yemen (1.31)	Iraq (1.19)	India (1.71)
Italy (1.44)	Haiti (1.54)	Lebanon (1.14)	Nicaragua (1.09)	Yugoslavia (1.19)	Iraq (1.71)
Jordan (1.44)	Egypt (1.09)				Peru (1.71)
Cuba (1.41)	Burma (1.00)				Syria (1.71)
Indonesia (1.30)	Honduras (1.00)				
Poland (1.14)	Indonesia (1.00)				
Chile (1.11)					

[a] Only countries with standardized factor score $\geq \pm 1.00$ are shown; where countries are tied for the same rank, they are ranked in alphabetical order.

factor analysis should tell us how specific the domestic and foreign conflict behavior dimensions are to their respective domains, the multiple regression should tell us to what degree foreign (or domestic) conflict behavior can be predicted from such domestic (or foreign) behavior.

Domestic and Foreign Conflict Measures

The results of factor analyzing the domestic and foreign conflict measures together are given in Table 8. The upper right block of Table 9 gives the correlation between the domestic and foreign measures. The first thing one might note from Table 8 is that the first unrotated dimension is not general to all the measures, thus indicating a lack of commonness among them. What this lack of commonness might be is suggested by the rotated dimensions, which show the clear separation of domestic and foreign conflict into distinct dimensions. This suggests that there may be little relationship between domestic and foreign conflict behavior. More precise evidence of this lack of relationship is given below with the results of the multiple regression.

The first rotated dimension, accounting for 31.2 percent of the common and 22 percent of the total variance, appears strongly as an *aggressive dimension*, delimiting a cluster of measures including those of a violent (war, .83; number killed in foreign conflict, .89; military action, .70; menacing threats, .78; mobilizations, .63; troop movements, .62) and assertive (protests, .69; accusations, .80) nature. The second dimension, in contrast, is wholly a domestic conflict behavior continuum, with high correlations for all domestic measures, excepting guerrilla war and assassinations. On this dimension one finds a merging of those measures which previously had delimited the turmoil and revolutionary dimensions, and one might, therefore, call this continuum an *instability* dimension—representing a general conflict atmosphere reflected by a wide range of conflict behavior.

The third dimension represents the two error measures (which intercorrelate .28), and may be called an error dimension. The reason that these error measures formed an independent dimension can be seen from the correlations of these measures with the conflict behavior measures as shown along the margin of Table 9. The highest correlation of censorship with any of the conflict behavior measures is $-.27$, with most of the other correlations being very nearly zero. The correlations for the other measure of error are higher, but with the highest being .34, and with many of the correlations being also close to zero. The lowness of these correlations and the extraction of an error dimension are good evidence that systematic error *as tapped by these measures*, has little effect on the results.

The fourth dimension—expulsion or recall of ambassador (.72)—is like the diplomatic dimension extracted from the factor analysis of the foreign conflict behavior measures. And the fifth dimension—guerrilla warfare (.73) and assassinations (.72)—is similar to the *subversion* dimension found in the domestic analysis.

The sixth dimension, with severance of diplomatic relations (.75), anti-foreign demonstrations (.59), and military action (.41) correlated with it, is much the same dimension found in the separate factor analysis of the foreign conflict measures—the *belligerent* dimension.[22]

When domestic and foreign conflict behavior measures, then, are factor analyzed together, foreign and domestic conflict behavior per se retain their distinctiveness, but the results of the separate analyses are altered slightly. The domestic turmoil and revolutionary dimensions combine into a more general instability dimension. And the war dimension changes into the more

TABLE 8
Factor Analysis of Domestic and Foreign Conflict Measures[c]

Measures	Factor matrix[a]					
	F_1	F_2	F_3	F_4	F_5	F_6
1. Assassinations	38	−48	20	30	(−51)	−16
2. General strikes	25	(−72)	−05	03	25	17
3. Guerrilla war	01	(−57)	−04	−03	−49	−35
4. Major government crisis	32	−41	13	45	20	21
5. Purges	(50)	−49	−31	−07	15	06
6. Riots	45	(−61)	20	06	13	11
7. Revolutions	19	(−66)	−31	−04	01	13
8. Antigovernment demonstrations	(59)	(−51)	28	01	06	04
9. No. killed—domestic	33	(−73)	−20	−33	−11	03
10. Antiforeign demonstrations	(62)	−04	20	17	22	−26
11. Negative sanctions	(63)	17	31	26	07	−32
12. Protests	(71)	35	18	−15	05	11
13. Severed diplomatic relations	44	06	−33	45	45	−22
14. Expelled/recalled ambassadors	19	−28	20	(−50)	−01	−42
15. Expelled/recalled lesser officials	(52)	17	20	−44	30	13
16. Threats	(86)	32	01	−05	−02	−13
17. Military action	(66)	25	−43	30	−09	−04
18. Wars	(61)	24	−04	−10	−35	46
19. Troop movements	(69)	25	11	−33	−01	−15
20. Mobilizations	(54)	31	−12	24	−29	−07
21. Accusations	(84)	24	−15	−07	−02	−05
22. No. killed—foreign	(77)	19	−30	−03	−25	28
23. Censorship	−19	−02	(51)	44	−18	17
24. Embassies and legations	31	02	(74)	−05	−01	20
% Common variance	40.9	23.1	11.5	9.9	7.9	6.6
% Total variance	28.2	16.0	8.0	6.8	5.5	4.6

[a] Parenthesis indicates loadings $\geq .50$.

[b] Signs reversed.

[c] Decimals omitted from all loadings, and orthogonally rotated factor matrix follows.

TABLE 8 (CONTINUED)

Measures	Orthogonally rotated factor matrix[a]							
	F_1	F_2[b]	F_3	F_4[b]	F_5[b]	F_6[b]	h^2
1. Assassinations	19	35	30	00	(72)	13	78
2. General strikes	−11	(81)	04	00	00	07	67
3. Guerrilla war	−12	28	−09	21	(73)	−10	69
4. Major government crisis	02	(54)	30	−29	02	32	57
5. Purges	24	(70)	−21	10	02	14	62
6. Riots	06	(72)	29	11	09	17	66
7. Revolutions	−02	(71)	−22	−03	17	−09	59
8. Antigovernment demonstrations	21	(63)	36	22	13	21	69
9. No. killed—domestic	09	(76)	−16	30	26	−19	81
10. Antiforeign demonstrations	29	21	20	22	02	(59)	57
11. Negative sanctions	38	−04	32	19	10	(64)	70
12. Protests	(69)	−01	25	23	−25	20	70
13. Severed diplomatic relations	19	19	−27	−20	−15	(75)	76
14. Expelled/recalled ambassadors	−05	17	01	(72)	16	01	58
15. Expelled/recalled lesser officials	41	14	18	44	−46	06	63
16. Threats	(78)	01	06	27	−05	41	86
17. Military action	(70)	06	−27	−22	09	41	78
18. Wars	(83)	09	17	−10	−04	−21	78
19. Troop movements	(62)	−01	08	49	−09	20	68
20. Mobilizations	(63)	−13	−01	−11	21	27	55
21. Accusations	(80)	12	−06	20	−06	33	80
22. No. killed—foreign	(89)	20	−09	−08	01	02	85
23. Censorship	−20	−13	(59)	−33	18	01	55
24. Embassies and legations	17	05	(78)	21	−09	02	69
% Common variance	31.2	23.3	11.5	10.6	9.7	13.5	100.0
% Total variance	22.0	16.1	8.0	7.3	6.7	9.3	69.0

[a] Parenthesis indicates loadings ≥.50.
[b] Signs reversed.

TABLE 9
Correlation Matrix[a]

	1	2	3	4	5	6	7	8	9	10	11	12	13	14	15	16	17	18	19	20	21	22	23	24
1. Ass.		28	45	35	31	45	19	51	33	23	28	01	03	16	−09	15	15	19	06	28	20	18	08	21
2. Gen. strikes			24	29	46	56	50	57	51	20	−01	−01	14	13	07	−04	01	−01	−10	−09	07	04	−03	00
3. Guerrilla war				09	17	13	33	20	52	00	−00	−23	−08	17	−11	−10	−10	−10	−11	−11	−09	−04	05	−07
4. Major govt. crisis					30	36	38	41	20	21	29	10	28	−01	05	09	11	09	−05	05	11	13	05	22
5. Purges						42	49	36	57	24	13	08	32	18	24	26	30	17	24	13	27	34	−21	03
6. Riots							32	69	53	36	16	19	18	26	08	15	08	12	13	02	21	19	05	19
7. Revolutions								23	62	05	−04	−11	03	12	−11	−04	12	−04	07	−12	04	12	−08	−06
8. Demonstrations									45	38	26	29	14	26	28	36	16	20	23	21	35	21	−07	30
9. Domestic killed										16	−04	−00	−03	25	16	05	02	07	14	−06	12	22	−22	−01
10. Antiforeign demonstrations											53	39	36	14	29	50	33	25	39	22	46	35	05	18
11. Negative sanctions												47	33	05	33	64	35	24	45	38	49	30	03	33
12. Protests													19	09	47	66	39	51	63	46	69	52	−10	29
13. Severed diplomatic relations														−08	12	38	54	07	15	23	39	31	−15	−08
14. Expelled/recalled ambassadors															10	12	−08	01	24	−10	11	02	−14	13
15. Expelled/recalled lesser officials																50	13	33	43	15	45	32	−23	34
16. Threats																	62	55	68	55	81	63	−19	25
17. Military action																		38	45	54	65	72	−09	07
18. War																			32	37	56	77	−10	20
19. Troop movements																				30	62	53	−13	33
20. Mobilizations																					46	41	−17	07
21. Accusations																						70	−27	09
22. Foreign killed																							−16	08
23. Censorship																								28
24. Embassies and legations																								

[a] Correlations rounded off and multiplied by 100.

Dimensions of Conflict Behavior Within and Between Nations 71

general aggressive dimensions. The subversive, diplomatic, and belligerent dimensions, however, retain their identity. It is not surprising that the first dimensions of the separate analysis should thus be changed when all the measures are combined. Amalgamating the measures has the effect of making what factors emerge more relevant to general conflict behavior. One might expect, therefore, that factors specific to a particular area of conflict behavior would become broader in interpretation when other kinds of behavior are brought into comparison. What is surprising is the virtually complete specificity of the dimensions extracted from the separate factor analysis. When all the measures are analyzed together no two domestic and foreign conflict measures have correlations greater than $\pm.46$ with the same factor. That is, the dimensions remain common to their domains.

The dimensions that have been extracted from the merged analysis are orthogonal to each other—an orthogonality which is forced on the dimensions by the varimax criteria used for rotation. This separation of foreign and domestic conflict behavior on the most general first two dimensions, therefore, may be an artifact of the forced independence of the dimensions. Figure 1 displays the result of manually rotating the previously rotated first factors to a better fitting oblique solution. The war dimension is rotated to α_1, and the turmoil dimension to α_2. The result is little different. The correlation between the two dimensions is increased from .00 to .16, a very low correlation, and an indication that the orthogonal results are hardly artifactual.

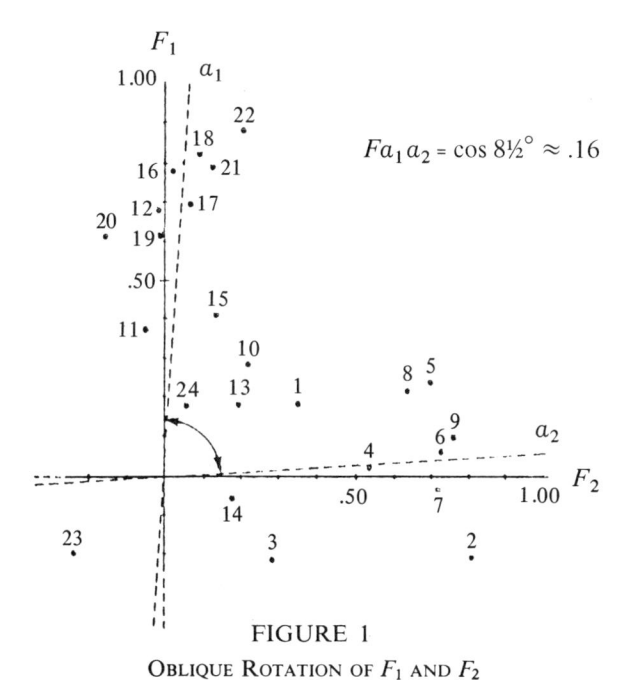

FIGURE 1

OBLIQUE ROTATION OF F_1 AND F_2

Multiple Regression

The results of the factor analysis of the amalgamated domestic and foreign conflict measures, where the domestic and conflict measures were separated into different dimensions, suggests that there may be no relationship between the two domains. This lack of relationship can be more precisely investigated through the use of multiple regression.

Factor analysis is relevant when one is concerned with determining the nature of the interrelationships among a collection of measures, or when prior to multiple regression one wants to reduce a set of highly related measures to a smaller number of uncorrelated dimensions that can serve as independent variables in the multiple regression. If highly interrelated variables are used as independent variables in a multiple regression, the reliability of the regression coefficients is decreased considerably (Ezekiel and Fox, 1959: 295-298) and the results may accordingly be distorted. Therefore, in the case that one suspects high intercorrelations among his independent variables, a two step approach might be warranted—factor analysis of the measures to get uncorrelated dimensions, and the use of such dimensions in place of the measures in the multiple regression.[23]

Table 10 gives the most relevant results of multiple regression of the three domestic conflict behavior dimensions on each of the three foreign conflict behavior dimensions separately.

TABLE 10

PREDICTIONS OF FOREIGN CONFLICT BEHAVIOR INDEPENDENT VARIABLES: TURMOIL; REVOLUTIONARY; SUBVERSION

Dependent variable	Standard deviation	Standard error	Multiple R	Prop. variable R^2
War	2.40	2.36	.26[a]	.07
Diplomacy	1.49	1.46	.26[a]	.07
Belligerency	1.00	.97	.31[a]	.10

[a] $p > .05$ (nonnormal distributions); N = 77.

An important thing to note in the table is that domestic conflict behavior accounts for very little of the variance R of foreign conflict behavior along the three foreign dimensions. This is reflected in the very small change from standard deviation to standard error. The standard error is the standard deviation of the residuals—the difference between the value predicted on the basis of the multiple regression and the actual value for a country on the dependent variable. The standard error indicates the degree to which the prediction equation fits the dependent variable. The slight change between the standard deviation of the dependent variable and the standard error shows that the variation in the dependent variable is not being predicted by the independent variables.

Therefore, multiple regression of the domestic dimensions on each of the foreign conflict behavior dimensions, in turn, leads to the conclusion that domestic conflict cannot predict foreign conflict behavior.

The foreign conflict dimensions together, however, might still predict the position of a country on any one of the domestic conflict behavior dimensions. The results of checking this possibility are given in Table 11.

TABLE 11

PREDICTIONS OF FOREIGN CONFLICT BEHAVIOR INDEPENDENT VARIABLES:
WAR; DIPLOMACY; BELLIGERENCY

Dependent variable	Standard deviation	Standard error	Multiple R	Prop. variable R^2
Turmoil	2.43	2.31	.37[b]	.14
Revolutionary	1.73	1.70	.27[a]	.07
Subversive	1.00	1.01	.14[a]	.02

[a] $p > .05$ (nonnormal distributions); N = 77.
[b] $.01 < p < .05$ (nonnormal distribution).

Here, also, the lack of relationship appears, with the possible exception of the prediction of turmoil, which would be significant at the .05 level if the factor scores for the dimensions involved had been distributed normally. Since the distributions are not distributed normally, however, one cannot gauge the precise significance of the correlation. Nevertheless, one can still see from R that all but a small part—14 percent—of the variance of turmoil is unaccounted for by the foreign conflict behavior dimensions and that the standard error (2.31) of the prediction of turmoil by these dimensions is only slightly different from the standard deviation (2.43).

As suggested strongly by the merged factor analysis, and reinforced by the multiple regressions, then, foreign and domestic conflict behavior are not generally related to and generally cannot be predictors of each other. This finding is justified in regard to conflict behavior as tapped by my measures, and in regard to sovereign nations for the middle 1950s.[24] This is not to say that there are no particular cases in which domestic and foreign conflict behavior are related. There well may be situations in which the domestic political elite of a nation will foment foreign conflict as a means of quieting internal squabbling.[25] Moreover, if one were to take a longitudinal slice out of the history of many nations, a very close relation in the fluctuations of domestic and foreign conflict behavior might be found. What the conclusion as a whole does say, however, is that taking sovereign nations as a whole for the same period of time, foreign and domestic conflict behavior generally vary independently of each other.

POSSIBLE ERRORS OF COMMISSION OR OMISSION

No one is closer to a particular piece of research than the one who actually has done the investigation and analysis. And although the more methodologically sophisticated might point out many errors of commission or omission and the substantively oriented many assumptions, factual errors, sources not considered, and data omitted, the researcher is in a position to know many possible errors of commission or omission in his own work.

Possible Errors of Commission

Nontheoretical Choice of Measures. The measures used here were chosen on definitional, practical, and statistical criteria. Theoretical relevance within the context of conflict theory was not made a criterion. Possibly, if such were done, the over-all results would be more theoretically relevant, and would help to choose between competing theories of conflict. Such a criterion is not used here, however, because of my belief that such comprehensive theories of conflict *capable of test* do not yet exist.

Number of Years. Resources did not permit collecting data on more than three years. The evident stability of the 1955–57 data notwithstanding, the collection of data for a longer period would have considerably added to the methodological soundness of this study and the persuasiveness of its conclusions. If data had been collected for a longer period, say ten years, many of the distributions probably would have lost their J shapes and would have been normal or capable of normalization—thus allowing the use of many statistical tests and increasing the reliability of the conclusions.

Static Approach. This study does not take change into consideration. The findings, therefore, are relevant only to the *absolute* amount of conflict behavior. It is possible, for example, that a high rate of increase in domestic conflict behavior may be strongly related to the increase in amount of foreign conflict behavior. Such a relationship, however, would be missed by this study. The static rather than dynamic approach was used as a "best" first step to map the relationships between the amount of conflict behavior. Later, it was thought these findings could be used as stepping stones for moving into the far more complex area of change.

Correlation Coefficient. The product-moment coefficient has been used here, and was chosen over several other possible coefficients. The question as to which coefficients are best under given conditions is still moot. Possibly, although not likely, the use of another coefficient, such as the tetrachoric, might have given more reliable and invariant results. An approach to an answer to this question could be made by doing the factor analysis using different coefficients, but such is beyond the resources of this study.

Reliability Test. No direct test of the reliability of the definitions was made. Indirectly, however, their reliability was indicated by the high correlations by others and by the high communalities of the measures in the factor analyses. If the definitions were unreliable, then considerable random error should contaminate the data, lowering considerably or making nonsignificant their correlations with data from other studies and also reducing the amount of common variance that will be associated with the other measures included in the factor analyses.

Measures of Error. Two measures of error were used to get at systematic bias. Neither of these measures, however, indexes the possibility of conflict behavior news being squeezed out of our sources by the occurrence of events of great importance and interest. Hence, a good deal of systematic error from this source, as well as other unknown sources, may have contaminated the results without one knowing it. Only replication may lessen the probability of this having happened.

Factor Scores. The factor scores were calculated by adding the standard scores of each nation on those measures high on the particular dimension and low on the others. The result is probably a very close approximation to the actual factor scores a country would have if one were to use more precise techniques involving the data, correlation, and factor matrices. The additional accuracy one would thus gain, however, did not seem worth the expenditure in time and resources.

Possible Errors of Omission

Lack of Cooperation Measures. Conceptually, conflict is generally considered as one end of a cooperation-conflict continuum. The dimensions of conflict behavior found here might very well, then, be only parts of continua which would also involve cooperation behavior. As implied by Richardson (1960), for example, war and trade might well form a bipolar dimension. It would be interesting and important, therefore, to find out whether and what cooperation measures lie at the opposite ends of the various dimensions of conflict extracted. This possibility was recognized from the beginning, but a decision had to be made as to whether to limit the collection of data to half of the conflict behavior measures in order to collect data on an equal number of cooperation measures, or try to cover the conflict behavior field as best as possible first. Because the former approach would assume knowledge about the relationships among conflict behavior data—the very knowledge the study was supposed to uncover—in order to decide which measures to omit, the latter approach, as a first step, was thought advisable.

Pairs of Nations. The results of this study are a comparison of each nation with all other nations. It might have been more relevant, however, to have done the analysis with respect to pairs of nations. An analysis across pairs of nations, for example, would have yielded information on the relationship between the measures of conflict behavior of Syria and Israel, and the U.S. and U.S.S.R., with such relationships generalized across all possible pairs. Such information might be of more immediate foreign policy import than that resulting from a comparison of each nation with all others. It was felt, however, as in the case of the static versus the dynamic alternative, that the approach used here should come first, as a necessary prior step, and that the information derived from this study can then be used in a future study of these dyadic relationships.

Oblique Rotation. Some factor analysts, such as Raymond Cattell, argue that oblique rotation is to be preferred over the orthogonal solution this study employs. Quite possibly he is right, but these things should be judged relevant to the area of concern. In a field where little prior factor exploration has taken place to serve as a guide as to what to expect, the more parsimonious and conceptually simpler solution might be better as a first approximation. This was the reasoning behind the orthogonal rotation decided upon, although others might weigh the alternatives differently.

Political, Economic, Sociological Measures. No multiple regression of nonconflict measures on the conflict-behavior factors has been done. Certainly, this is a most important step and will enable us to get some leverage on some of the significant conditions underlying both domestic and foreign conflict behavior. Rather than use measures like size of population, GNP, extent of party competition, and so forth, it was felt that a more reliable study of the conditions underlying conflict could be made later using the results to come out of the Dimensionality of Nations Project, which is attempting to determine the dimensions of the political, economic, social cultural, and value characteristics and behavior of nations around 1955. The orthogonal factors resulting from the Project's analysis of such data may then be used as independent variables in a multiple regression study of conflict behavior.

DISCUSSION, SUMMARY, AND PROPOSITIONS

Discussion

One of the significant findings of this study is perhaps the apparent lack of relationship between domestic and foreign conflict behavior. That they vary independently of each other was brought out both by the factor analysis and the multiple regression. This lack of relationship between them may be seen in the results of two other studies.

In Cattell's 72 variable, 69 nation study (1949), three domestic conflict variables and two foreign conflict variables remained separated both in the unrotated and oblique rotation cases. His rotation leads to equivocal results, however, since the two foreign conflict variables load highly on a factor correlated $-.44$ with the factor upon which two of the domestic conflict variables are highly loaded. What would happen in the case of orthogonal rotation is not clear. Still, the unrotated matrix, the continual separation of the variables on different factors after rotation, and the fact that his data are taken from the period 1837–1937, point to a certain historical generality to the lack of relationship between domestic and foreign conflict.

Richardson (1952) also found a difference between domestic and foreign conflict behavior, but of a different kind. He found that domestic violence occurred less often in comparison to foreign violence than one should expect—that there must be some kind of "pacifying" influence at work in domestic affairs. Although Richardson felt he had proved the existence of a pacifier, he could not determine its nature. For some reason, as one crosses from the domestic to the international system the frequency of violent conflict behavior increases—as though we were crossing between two worlds.

The general independence between domestic and foreign conflict behavior indicates that different necessary and sufficient conditions for both must be sought—that rapid industrialization, or underdevelopment, or dictatorships, or unstable political systems, or technological changes cannot be general conditions of both domestic and foreign conflict behavior as is often asserted. This is not to say that such conditions may not be generally *necessary*—producing the required atmosphere for conflict behavior—but that the general condition setting off the behavior must differ between the two worlds.

Also indicated by the general independence between foreign and domestic conflict behavior is the conclusion that foreign conflict behavior is not a necessary and sufficient condition of domestic peace. The idea that brothers will squabble unless faced by a common enemy appeals to common sense and is enshrined in public mythology. The results of this study, however, show that domestic conflict behavior and domestic peace occur whether or not foreign conflict is present. Throwing this lack of relationship between domestic and foreign conflict into sharp relief is the fact that within the domestic and foreign domains conflict behavior is highly related. These high within-domain correlations can be seen from the intercorrelations of the domestic measures given in the upper left triangular matrix and the intercorrelation of the foreign measures in the lower right matrix in Table 10 above.

Another finding of interest emerging from the 1955–57 data is the great significance of threats and accusations, which were found highly related to almost all the measures of foreign conflict. With regard to this study, one may only conjecture about the mechanism at work here. Perhaps threats and accusations are a form of communication which takes place only after a certain threshold of unfriendliness has been passed. Protests, a communication measure which was found not so generally related to international conflict behavior, may operate above or below this threshold. A country may protest routinely to another about some incident, but probably will not openly charge another with an unfriendly act or threaten that country unless strained relations already exist. Then, accusations may function to state the case, both domestically and internationally, and threats to draw the line and make explicit the commitment or the consequences.

While serving as communications devices, threats and accusations may also feed back into the conflict situation, acting strongly to increase tension and stimulate greater involvement. A charge-countercharge, threat-counterthreat nexus may occur, feeding on itself, and transcending the original issue. This is speculation, of course, but the possibility is strongly suggested by threats and accusations being the most highly correlated among the foreign conflict behavior measures with the general dimension of the unrotated factor matrix in Table 5.

If such be the case, it poses a dilemma for the student of deterrence. Threats appear necessary to state the conditions under which nuclear weapons will be used—to prevent miscalculation on the part of the enemy. Threats, however, must be repeated to show that national resolve has not slipped and to reinforce the deterrent ability of one's weapons. Yet, the use of such threats by both sides—their reiteration and accentuation—might escalate a current crisis beyond control.

Whether or not such a dilemma exists in reality, whether or not threats do act as both stimulus and response, threats and accusations together may enable the systematically oriented student of international conflict to get some purchase on measuring crisis. An index that is a linear composite of threats and accusations may well serve as a thermometer for measuring and comparing the heat—the intensity—of crises so that hypotheses about crisis may be both tested and generated.

While threats and accusations are generally related to international conflict, war is not. Accounting for 46.2 percent of the common variance, the war dimension is the most important of the international conflict dimensions. Still, the occurrence or nonoccurrence of many kinds of conflict behavior seem to operate independently of war. This is reflected by the other orthogonal dimensions, the diplomacy and belligerent, which account for low, but still respectable amounts of variance. International conflict behavior is not, therefore, unidimensional—a sort of Guttman scale of behavior, with each act becoming more severe until war is reached—but tridimensional. This multidimensional quality of international conflict behavior has been noted elsewhere. With respect to tensions and disputes Morgenthau (1954: 404) says, for example, that: "Between two nations there is sometimes no tension at all, yet there are disputes. Or sometimes, despite the existence of a tension, the dispute has no relation to the tension."

A particular conflict act, then, need not presage war. It may instead be an almost automatic diplomatic reaction to a relatively minor situation—expelling an official for spying, applying pressure on a country by recalling one's ambassador, or discontinuing aid shipments, and so forth. Or a conflict act may be evidence of contained hostility—enmity sufficient to bring the people to the streets condemning the other country, to cause diplomatic relations to be severed, boycotts to be imposed, and perhaps frequent and spontaneous border clashes—but "contained" hostility in that mobilization does not occur, war is not declared, and the lid is kept on. War may indeed escalate out of such situations, but the finding here is that war generally occurs independently of them.

In addition to the three foreign conflict behavior and three domestic conflict behavior dimensions, five dimensions of domestic and foreign conflict behavior taken together have also been extracted. The main value of this merged analysis is in indicating the lack of relationship between the measures of domestic and foreign conflict behavior and the relationship of systematic error to the measures. Since the measures are so generally unrelated across domestic and foreign domains, the dimensions resulting from the separate factor analyses should be used as input into future research.

These three domestic and three foreign dimensions of conflict behavior may now serve as independent variables in other studies or, in particular, they can be used to test various propositions as to the causes of conflict behavior. As dimensions of conflict behavior, they may also serve as guides for constructing the conflict component of computer or human simulations of international relations. Less obvious, perhaps, is their value in pointing out the measures upon which one might concentrate data collection. If several measures are highly correlated with the same dimension, then one need only collect data on possibly one or two of them in order to represent the dimensions with respect to the period of concern.

Summary

The goals of this study were to determine the dimensions of variation in the domestic and foreign conflict behavior of nations, to locate the position of each nation on these dimensions, and to use these dimensions to ascertain the relationship between domestic conflict behavior and that in the international area.

Data were collected for 77 nations of 9 measures of domestic conflict behavior and 13 measures of foreign conflict behavior for the years 1955, 1956, and 1957. The data were intercorrelated using the product moment coefficient, and with unities in the diagonal of the correlation matrix, a principal component factor analysis was calculated separately for the domestic and for the foreign conflict behavior data.

Factors whose foreign values were greater than unity were extracted and these solutions were rotated orthogonally to simple structure using the varimax criterion. In this manner, three dimensions of domestic conflict behavior—*turmoil, revolutionary,* and *subversive* dimensions—and three dimensions of foreign conflict—*war, diplomatic,* and *belligerent* dimensions—were determined. Factor scores for each of the 77 nations were computed to locate these nations on the 6 dimensions.

The relationship between domestic and foreign conflict behavior was investigated in two ways. First, a factor analysis along the above lines was calculated for all the conflict behavior measures together. The result was that the measures of domestic conflict behavior completely separated themselves onto dimensions different from those upon which the foreign conflict measures were loaded, thus indicating a general lack of relationship across the two domains of conflict behavior within them. This lack of relationship was defined further by doing a multiple regression analysis of the domestic conflict behavior dimensions on each of the dimensions of foreign conflict behavior in turn, and, similarly, by doing a multiple regression of the foreign conflict behavior dimensions on each of the domestic ones.

The stability of the data was checked by assessing their correlation with similar domestic data for 1946–59 collected by Harry Eckstein (1962), with war data for 1825–1945 collected by Lewis F. Richardson (1961), and by comparing the intercorrelations among the 1955–57 data with intercorrelations calculated by Raymond Cattell (1949) for similar data on five like measures, 1837–1937. As a consequence, the data were found highly stable. The possibility of systematic error distorting the results was tested by including in the factor analysis measures relating to the amount of censorship in and world importance of a country. An independent error factor was extracted and is a good indication that systematic error as tapped by these measures of error did not unduly affect the results.

Propositions

With respect to a comparison across nations for the same period of time, the following propositions emerge from this study:[26]

(1) The domestic conflict behavior of nations varies along three uncorrelated dimensions: *turmoil, revolutionary, subversive*.

(2) The foreign conflict behavior of nations varies along three uncorrelated dimensions: *war, diplomatic, belligerent*.

(3) A *war* dimension is more important than any other dimension of foreign conflict behavior in accounting for the variation in conflict behavior between nations.

(4) The variation in acts or occurrences of domestic conflict behavior are generally highly related to each other.

(5) The variation in acts or occurrences of foreign conflict behavior are generally highly related to each other.

(6) Foreign conflict behavior is generally completely unrelated to domestic conflict behavior.

(7) Foreign conflict behavior is not a necessary and sufficient condition for domestic peace.

(8) The acts or occurrences of conflict behavior within and between nations are not sporadic—unpredictable—but are patterned and can be predicted on the basis of their history of such conflict behavior.

(9) General international conflict behavior and the intensity of the underlying conflict may be indexed through a summation of the standard scores of the number of threats and number of accusations made.

(10) Systematic error resulting from censorship or the lack of interest in a nation will not unduly affect the conclusions derived from domestic and foreign conflict behavior data.

NOTES

1. For a concise but clear history of factor analysis, see Harman (1960: 3-6).

2. The factors he extracted from his two studies differ slightly. From each he got twelve factors, which, with respect to the more refined work, are enlightened affluence vs. narrow poverty, vigorous order vs. unadopted rigidity; cultural pressure and complexity vs. direct ergic expression, size, emancipated rationalism vs. unchanged stability, classical patriarchalism vs. uncontrolled ferment, oriental pattern, metropolitan laxity vs. rural austerity, bourgeois philistinism vs. improvident bohemianism, mechanics culture, morality vs. poor integration and morale, and a residual factor.

3. One of the primary aims of the National Science Foundation's Dimensionality of Nations Project at Northwestern University, and under which data for this study were collected, is to do such a replication of Cattell's work. [The Project is now located at the University of Hawaii, Department of Political Science—Ed.]

4. Data have been collected on more measures than are used in the study. These measures—number of disputes, number of civil wars, number of social revolutions, number of demands, number of reprisals, presence or absence of banditry, presence or absence of colonial violence, presence or absence of political strife—did not conform to one or another of the criteria above. The occurrence of civil war and social revolution were too infrequent for criterion five and were consequently merged with data on palace revolutions into a more general measure called "number of revolutions." And data on reprisals were merged with the data on boycotts into a measure called "number of negative sanctions," since the two categories could not be kept empirically distinct.

5. *Keesing's Contemporary Archives* was found least productive of data, and, therefore, was used only in the very beginning of the data collection.

6. See Ezekiel and Fox (1959: Chapter 18) on the effect of random error.

7. When the factors are uncorrelated (orthogonal) among themselves, a "loading" is the correlation of each measure with each factor.

8. See Mosier's experimental findings on this point (1939) and Cattell's comments (1952: 293).

9. I had thought originally of using the number of AP and UP reporters in a particular country as an index to interest in its affairs, but research in the library, contact with the Journalism Department, and communication with AP and UP have convinced me that the idea is impractical. Each wire service, evidently, has a large number of part-time employees of the nationality of the country in which its bureau is located. The number of such employees is increased or decreased according to current events within the country, and the records as to the number of such employees at any time are kept only by each foreign bureau.

10. The time period of two years is to allow domestic behavior to adjust to independence after what may have been a period of nationalistic and, perhaps, violent agitation for independence.

11. This is similar to the definition employed by Haas and Whiting (1956: 61,

n. 3)—"the pro forma capacity to enter into diplomatic relations with other states through the existence of a foreign ministry, regardless of whether the ministry is *in fact* able to make independent policy."

12. Since his data are not broken down into separate years, a reliability check of my data against his data for 1955-57 cannot be made.

13. For a conceptual introduction to the nature of factor analysis, see Fruchter (1954: 1-11). For a discussion of many of the nontechnical methodological aspects of factor analysis, see Henrysson (1957: 56).

14. See Harman (1960: 115) for a tabular breakdown of the different factor techniques, their assumptions and properties and distinguishing characteristics.

15. For an outline of the assumptions concerning the nature of the data, see Henrysson (1957: 29-30).

16. This point is strongly made by Cattell (1952: 328); with less vehemence by Thurstone (1947: 66-67).

17. On this point, see also Cattell (1952: 326), Fruchter (1954: 201), and Carroll's article (1961). For a comparison of the results using the tetrachoric, phi-over-phi max, and the phi coefficient on the same dichotomous data, see Comrey and Levonian (1958).

18. One, however, should not accept unqualifiedly the Varimax solution. Hurley and Cattell (1962: 260) warn that "the extreme facility of application of Varimax, plus a lack of forewarnings in its publication, has led to a great number of man hours of research ending in nothing—or worse—when the factor analytically unqualified psychologist or editor *accepts*, as uniquely meaningful, the machine given answer." To avoid this danger, the Varimax solution will be checked manually to make sure that orthogonal simple structure is compatible with the data.

19. This is also evidenced by all the correlations between the measures being positive.

20. There are possibly two approaches to naming a factor or dimension. One may try to label a factor with what one considers the underlying source of the clustering of measures (or variables). Hence, I might call the first rotated factor a "rapid industrial growth factor," implying that in those countries in which rapid economic growth is taking place, one finds many riots, demonstrations, etc. This I call source labeling, and it is with respect to source labeling that the term "factor" appears to me most appropriate. On the other hand, one might label the factor in terms of the measures entering into the cluster and what they may represent in terms of a typology. This kind of labeling I call *type* labeling, and it is the approach used here. I prefer to leave source labeling to the future, when systematic analysis of the relationship between the dimensions of this study and such things as rapid industrial growth, technological change, political system, and so forth, will indicate some of the possible sources of such a cluster of conflict behavior as indicated by the turmoil dimension. When type labeling is used, "dimension" may more aptly describe the different types emerging from the factor analysis. The methodology of factor analysis, however, is so deeply infused with the term "factor" as to require its use in describing the operations performed.

21. The name "revolutionary" is chosen over "revolution," since the latter implies an event or act, whereas the former stands more for a situation or atmosphere. This is more in accord with purges and general strikes being highly correlated with this dimension.

22. "Belligerency" implies both attitude and action—an attitude of hostility, enmity, or hatred, and overt acts following such hostility. "Aggressive," in terms of which the first dimension is named, implies only overt action. A nation may have assertive, non-passive foreign policies, which may or may not have their sources in hostility, hatred, or the balancing of alternatives.

23. See Buchatzsch (1947) as a research example of such an approach.

24. Although the above test of stability of the measures would argue that the findings are valid for a much longer period.

25. As Haas and Whiting (1956: 62) suggest, "groups seeking self-preservation and no more may be driven to a foreign policy of conflict—if not open war—in order to defend themselves against the onslaught of domestic rather than foreign enemies. In times of extreme domestic tension among elites, a policy of uniting a badly divided nation against some real or alleged outside threat frequently seems useful to a ruling group."

26. It is important to note that because these propositions were derived from a spatial study across nations, they are not relevant to the conflict behavior and relationship between such behaviors of a nation over a period of time.

REFERENCES

BECHTOLDT, H.P., A.L. BENTON and M.L. FOGEL (1962) "An application of factor analysis in neuropsychology." *Psychological Record* 12: 147–156.

BERNARD, J. (1957) "The sociological study of conflict." UNESCO: 33–117.

BERRY, B.J.L. (1961) "Basic patterns of economic development." Pp. 110–119 in N. Ginsberg, Ed., *Atlas of Economic Development*. Chicago: University of Chicago Press.

— (1960) "An inductive approach to the regionalization of economic development." In N. Ginsberg, Ed., *Essays of Geography and Economic Development*. Chicago: University of Chicago Press.

BORGATTA, E.F. and L.S. COTTRELL, JR. (1955) "On the classification of groups." *Sociometry* 18: 665–678.

BUCHATZSCH, E.J. (1947) "The influence of social conditions on mortality rates." *Population Studies* 1: 229–248.

CARR, L.J. (1946) "A situational approach to conflict and war." *Social Forces* 24: 300–303.

CARROLL, J.B. (1961) "The nature of the data, or how to choose a correlation coefficient." *Psychometrika* 26: 347–371.

CATTELL, R. (1952) *Factor Analysis*. New York: Harper.

— (1950) "The principal culture patterns discoverable in the syntal dimensions of existing nations." *Journal of Social Psychology* 32: 215–253.

— (1949) "The dimensions of culture patterns of factorization of national characters." *Journal of Abnormal and Social Psychology* 44: 443–469.

CATTELL, R., H. BREUL and H.P. HARTMAN (1951) "An attempt at a more refined definition of the cultural dimensions of syntality in modern nations." *American Sociological Review* 17: 408–421.

COSER, L.A. (1956) *The Functions of Social Conflict*. New York: Free Press.

ECKSTEIN, H. (1962) *Internal War: The Problem of Anticipation*. A report submitted to the Research Group in Psychology and the Social Sciences, Smithsonian Institution, Washington, D.C.

EZEKIEL, M. and K.A. FOX (1959) *Methods of Correlation and Regression Analysis*, 3rd ed. New York: John Wiley.
FRUCHTER, B. (1954) *Introduction to Factor Analysis*. New York: D. Van Nostrand.
GINSBERG, N. (1961) *Atlas of Economic Development*. Chicago: University of Chicago Press.
GODFREY, E.P., F.E. FIEDLER and D.M. HALL (1959) *Boards, Management and Company Success*. Danville, Ill.: Interstate Printers and Publishers.
HAAS, E.B. and A.S. WHITING (1956) *Dynamics of International Relations*. New York: McGraw-Hill.
HARMAN, H.H. (1960) *Modern Factor Analysis*. Chicago: University of Chicago Press.
HOFSTAETTER, P.R. (1951) "A factorial study of culture patterns in the U.S." *Journal of Psychology* 32: 99–113.
HURLEY, J.R. and R.B. CATTELL (1962) "The procrustes program: producing direct rotation to test a hypothesized factor structure." *Behavioral Science* 7: 258–261.
JONASSEN, C.T. and S.H. PERES (1960) *Interrelationships of Dimensions of Community Systems*. Columbus: Ohio State University Press.
KAISER, H.F. (1960) "The application of electronic computers to factor analysis." *Educational and Psychological Measurement* 19: 413–420.
MACK, R.W. and R.C. SNYDER (1957) "The analysis of social conflict—toward an overview and synthesis." *Journal of Conflict Resolution* 1: 212–248.
MCCLELLAND, D.C. (1961) *The Achieving Society*. Princeton: D. Van Nostrand.
MILLIS, W. (1961) "A world without war." Pp. 53–106 in Millis, et al., *A World Without War*. New York: Washington Square Press.
MORGENTHAU, H. (1954) *Politics Among Nations: The Struggle for Power and Peace*, 2nd ed. New York: Alfred A. Knopf.
MORRIS, C. (1956) *Varieties of Human Value*. Chicago: University of Chicago Press.
MOSIER, C.I. (1939) "Influence of chance error on simple structure: an empirical investigation of the effect of chance error and estimated communalities on simple structure in factorial analysis." *Psychometrika* 4: 33–44.
RHODES, E.C. (1937) "Construction of an index of business activity." *Journal of Royal Statistical Society* 100: 18–39.
RICHARDSON, L.F. (1960) *Arms and Insecurity*. Pittsburgh: Boxwood Press.
— (1952) "Contiguity and deadly quarrels: the local pacifying influence." *Journal of the Royal Statistical Society* A 115: 219–231.
SCHNORE, L.F. (1961) "The statistical measurement of urbanization and economic development." *Land Economics* 37: 229–245.
SCHUBERT, G. (1962) "The 1960 term of the Supreme Court: a psychological analysis." *American Political Science Review* 56: 90–113.
SIDMAN, M. (1960) *Tactics of Scientific Research*. New York: Basic Books.
THURSTONE, L.L. (1947) *Multiple-Factor Analysis*. Chicago: University of Chicago Press.
WOOD, R.C. (1961) *1400 Governments*. Cambridge: Harvard University Press.
WRIGHT, Q. (1954) *Problems of Stability and Progress in International Relations*. Berkeley: University of California Press.

4 Dimensions of Conflict Behavior Within and Between Nations, 1958-60

RAYMOND TANTER

This is a replication of a study by Rudolph J. Rummel (1963b [reprinted in this volume, Chapter 3]). The goals of that study were to determine the dimensions of variation in the domestic and foreign conflict behavior of nations, to locate nations on these dimensions, and to employ these dimensions in order to discover the relationship between both forms of conflict behavior. The goals of the replication are to obtain additional evidence relative to the dimensions of conflict behavior and the relationship between domestic and foreign conflict behavior. Data have been collected across eighty-three nations for 1958, 1959, and 1960 on the same twenty-two measures of conflict behavior used in the previous study. Similarly, these data are to be intercorrelated and factor analyzed, and multiple regression is to be used to examine the relationship between domestic and foreign conflict behavior.

Theory

Many of the generalizations about international conflict behavior have been discovered through the use of historical analysis. For example, Richard

---

Author's Note: Prepared in connection with research supported by the National Science Foundation, Grant NSF-GS224. The data were collected as part of the Dimensionality of Nations Project supported by that foundation, the Carnegie Seminar supported by the Carnegie Corporation, and the International Development Research Center (IDRC) at Indiana University, supported by the Ford Foundation.

The author wishes to thank Fred Riggs, formerly acting director of the IDRC, and Rudolph Rummel, principal investigator of the Dimensionality of Nations Project, University of Hawaii, for making this study possible. Professor Rummel has aided in the preparation of the research design phase of this study in order to assure continuity from his study (Rummel, 1963b [this volume, Chapter 3]) to the present one. I am also quite grateful for his comments on my interpretation of the results, and in reading earlier drafts; any errors, however, are mine. In addition, I am grateful to Milton Hobbs, Harold Guetzkow, J. David Singer, and Dean Pruitt for their comments, and to the Indiana and Northwestern University Research Computing Centers for the generous provision of their facilities.

Reprinted from the *Journal of Conflict Resolution*, Volume 10, pages 41-64, by permission of the author and the publisher. Copyright © 1966 by The University of Michigan.

Rosecrance concludes that through time there is a tendency for international instability to be associated with the domestic insecurity of elites (Rosecrance, 1963: 304). Two other students of international relations, Ernst Haas and Allen Whiting, suggest an explanation for the relationship between internal and external conflict behavior. They contend that groups seeking self-preservation may be driven to a foreign policy of conflict. The authors reason that the elites become fearful of losing their domestic positions during periods of rapid industrialization and widespread social change; they then try to displace the attention of the disaffected population onto some outside target. But the authors suggest that this form of self-preservation rarely leads to war (Haas and Whiting, 1956: 61–62).

In addition to Rosecrance and Haas and Whiting, Quincy Wright suggests that there is a general relationship between internal and external conflict behavior. Interspersed in his two volumes of *A Study of War* (1942) are propositions such as the following:

> By creating and perpetuating in the community both a fear of invasion and a hope of expansion, obedience to a ruler may be guaranteed. A system of world politics resting upon a balance of power contributes to the integration of each power by maintaining among the peoples the fear of war as well as the hope of dominance [Vol. II, p. 1016]. Rulers have forestalled internal sedition by starting external wars [Vol. I, p. 140]. There is no nation in which war or preparations of war have not to some degree or at some time been used as an instrument of national stability and order [Vol. I, p. 254]. In later stages of the Napoleonic Wars, Napoleon began to appreciate the value of war as an instrument of internal solidarity [Vol. II, p. 725]. Governments have often started war because it apeared to them a necessary or convenient means of establishing, maintaining, or expanding the power of the government, party, or class within the nation [Vol. II, p. 727].

Hopefully, this study will provide a systematic examination of the propositions of such theorists as Rosecrance, Haas and Whiting, and Wright. From a systematic examination and a series of *replications*, it may be possible to construct a general theory of intra- and internation conflict behavior.

Replication

Increasing the number of observations or trials in a particular design is referred to in the literature on the logic of experimentation as increasing the replications. Increasing the replications generally increases the confidence that the findings are not the result of chance factors (Edwards, 1954: 273). One frequently comes across references to the need for replication in the literature on research methods. For example, Katz asserts that the history of social psychology shows the significance of the replication of findings in that many of the original propositions have not been confirmed by later studies (Katz, 1953: 64). Moreover, Sidman contends that the most appropriate empirical test of the reliability of data is provided by replication (Sidman, 1960: 70).

Replication is especially suggested when there is disagreement with a well-established finding, the number of replications warranted being a function of the extent to which the previous findings were firmly established (Sidman, 1960: 78). As regards quantitative studies, the finding that there is very little relationship between domestic and foreign conflict behavior (Sorokin, 1937; Rummel, 1963b [this volume, Chapter 3]) contrasts with other findings of a negative relationship (Huntington, 1962) and a positive relationship (McKenna, 1962). On the other hand, most of the nonquantitative works support the hypothesis of a positive relationship (Hass and Whiting, 1956; Rosecrance, 1963).[1] The quantitative studies where the generalization was not based on the collected data (such as Wright, 1942) also support the finding of a positive relationship.

The quantitative studies where the generalization was based on the data meet a minimum criterion for replication, e.g., the standardization of the specifications for data. And as Katz points out, "Only when we attain the level of standardizing our specifications for data can we see the extent to which reported findings are true generalizations" (Katz, 1953: 64). Moreover, the ability to replicate scientific inquiry depends largely upon an explicit statement of the research design decisions such as data collection and analysis procedures.

Population

To be included in this study, nations had to be sovereign for at least two years and have a population equal to or greater than 800,000 in 1958. As a result of more nations being able to meet these criteria for 1958 than for 1955, the population size increased to eighty-three from the seventy-seven in the 1955–57 study (see Appendix II for the list of nations). Intragroup replication would entail the use of the exact sample employed in the prior study. As with the Rummel study, however, the total *population* is being used. Consequently, sampling restrictions of this sort are not applicable.[2]

Data Sources and Coding Reliability

The New York Times Index, *Deadline Data on World Affairs*, *Britannica Book of the Year*, and *Facts on File* were used as sources of data for the twenty-two conflict behavior measures. The first two sources, however, proved to be far more productive of data than the others. Consequently, most of the data reported in this study were derived from *The New York Times Index* and *Deadline Data*, the others being consulted for an overview.

It may be argued that the cross-reference system of one of the primary data sources, *The New York Times Index*, is such that any reliability tests would have to be conducted over *all* the nations by two or more coders in order to test for the agreement between coders for a subset of nations. That position, however, is valid only as regards foreign conflict behavior measures. That is, when there is conflict between two countries, parts of the conflict behavior are recorded under each country involved as well as in other places. For example, as regards the United States, the bulk of its international activity is recorded under topic headings other than "United States." Although some of these cross-references are given in the *Index*, a large part of them are not. Consequently, only by going through all the nations can one be confident that he is obtaining most of the information on foreign conflict as regards a subset of the countries. For domestic conflict, however, the information is generally contained under the country heading. With these caveats in mind, reliability tests were conducted on the domestic measures. To assure maximum continuity in the codings for the 1955–57 and 1958–60 data, to discover the consistency of the author's codings at different points in time, and to ascertain the extent to which other coders would agree with the author's codings, three partial reliability tests were conducted.

A random sample of five nations from the 1955–57 data reported by Rummel were recoded by the author as regards the nine measures of internal conflict behavior. Agreement ranged from 85 to 100 percent, with purges and major government crises being the variables on which there was least agreement. Since the author did the large portion of the 1958–60 coding, he recoded a random sample of ten nations three months after the initial codings were made. In only two cases were there discrepancies. A third reliability test consists of the author recoding the five nations for 1958–60 that were initially coded by two assistants. Perfect agreement was found for these five. Although these partial reliability tests indicate that *some* of the data are reliable, there may be coding errors in the data which might bias the conclusions.

Systematic Error in the Data Sources

Censorship may result in a systematic understatement of the conflict behavior of a given country in the sources. Accordingly, a three point censorship scale for 1958 is derived from the Inter-American Press Survey of 1958[3] and the Survey of the World's Press by the International Press Institute,[4] and for 1959[5] and 1960[6] from Associated Press Surveys of World Press Freedom. Values for each year were then summed across the three years for each nation so that those with high censorship had low scores.

Lack of world interest in a country may also result in an understatement of its conflict behavior. World interest may be operationalized as the number of embassies or legations *in* each country for 1959. The assumption is that this value for each nation reflects world interest in that nation. Although there are obvious exceptions to this assumption, such as the values for East Germany and China, the assumption appears to be valid for most other nations. A second measure of world interest is derived from one of the data sources— *Deadline Data on World Affairs*. It is the number of index cards per country in the card file itself.

Dimensions of Conflict Behavior, 1958–60

These three error measures are included in the correlation and factor analysis. If censorship has no correlation with the conflict behavior measures, then systematic bias as tapped by the censorship measure does not distort the conclusions. Negative correlation of censorship and the conflict behavior measures is not crucial because one can assume the direction of systematic bias to be under- instead of overstatement. Aside from possible exaggeration by the press, one would not expect nations to overstate the number of riots and revolutions it has. So if censorship is negatively correlated with riots, it might be inferred that the correlations between riots and the other conflict behavior measures would undergo little change even if censorship were suppressing knowledge of such incidents. Positive correlations between the censorship and the conflict behavior measures indicate that censorship in a nation could be distorting the results; positive correlation, however, is a necessary but not sufficient condition for such systematic error to distort the results of this study.

A high positive correlation between the world interest measures and the conflict behavior measures might mean that lack of world interest in some countries could be causing their conflict behavior to go unreported. Positive correlation, however, is a necessary but not sufficient condition for such systematic error to distort the conclusions. (In the Rummel study [1963b, this volume, Chapter 3] the direction of the correlation between the world interest measure and the conflict behavior measures was inadvertently stated as negative for systematic error to distort the results.)

Results

In order to determine how well the 1958–60 data[7] reflect a longer period, the data were compared and correlated with Rummel's 1955–57 data.[8] Table 1 contains the correlations of the 22 measures of conflict behavior for both 1955–57 and 1958–60. In the upper left hand corner of the matrix the domestic variables are intercorrelated with themselves; the values to the left are the 1958–60 correlations. The fact that all the correlations for each period are positive indicates a remarkable degree of similarity in the direction of the relationships. Out of a total of 36 correlations for each period there are 10 which are greater than or equal to .50. In other words, 28 percent of the domestic correlations for each period are ⩾.50.

This stability of the ratio of high correlations to the total for the domestic variables, however, is not found for the foreign variables. (The foreign variables for each period are located in the bottom right hand side of the matrix; the 1955–57 values are to the right of the diagonal while 1958–60 values are to the left.) Out of a total of 78 correlations 23, or 29 percent, are ⩾.50 for the 1955–57 period, while only nine, or 12 percent, are ⩾.50 for the 1958–60 period. The direction of the relationships, however, argues for similarity between the periods. There are only two negatives for 1958–60 and three for 1955–57.

TABLE 1
Correlation Matrix, 1955–57 and 1958–60[a]

Measures[b]	1	2	3	4	5	6	7	8	9	10	11	12	13	14	15	16	17	18	19	20	21	22	23	24	25
1. Assass		28	45	35	31	45	19	(51)	33	23	28	01	03	16	−09	15	15	19	06	28	20	18	29	08	21
2. Strike	38		24	29	46	(56)	(50)	(57)	(51)	20	−01	−01	14	13	07	−04	01	−01	−10	−09	07	04	03	−03	00
3. Gu-War	49	36		09	17	13	33	20	(52)	00	00	−23	−08	17	−11	−10	−10	−10	−11	−11	−09	−04	06	05	−07
4. Gvtcrs	43	42	(55)		30	36	38	41	20	21	29	10	28	−01	05	09	11	09	−05	05	11	13	12	05	22
5. Purges	29	04	25	24		42	49	36	(57)	24	13	08	32	18	24	26	30	17	24	13	27	34	12	−21	03
6. Riots	(51)	(55)	34	41	25		32	(69)	(53)	36	16	19	18	26	08	15	08	12	13	02	21	19	29	05	19
7. Revolu	31	20	(65)	42	(51)	30		23	(62)	05	−04	−11	03	12	−11	−04	12	−04	07	−12	04	12	−02	−08	−06
8. Demons	46	(54)	32	44	19	(73)	19		45	38	26	29	14	26	28	36	16	20	23	21	35	21	47	−07	30
9. D-Kill	(51)	33	(67)	46	41	47	(69)	39		16	−04	00	−03	25	16	05	02	07	14	−06	12	22	18	−22	−01
10. F-Dmst	29	28	27	12	17	38	26	22	31		(53)	39	36	14	29	(50)	33	25	39	22	46	35	42	05	18
11. Negsan	23	00	20	14	20	17	10	13	13	21		47	33	05	33	(64)	35	24	45	38	48	30	(57)	03	33
12. Protst	04	15	05	−01	07	29	−01	24	04	27	39		19	09	47	(66)	39	(51)	(63)	46	(69)	(52)	(60)	−10	29
13. Sevdip	08	19	27	28	05	23	19	21	11	22	20	02		−08	12	38	(54)	07	15	23	39	31	04	−15	−08
14. Er-Amb	05	27	08	10	−03	16	−13	18	−08	19	36	(54)	09		10	12	−08	01	24	−10	11	02	24	−14	13
15. Er-Les	27	11	10	08	11	17	−01	15	04	16	32	20	13	25		(50)	13	33	43	15	45	32	42	−23	34
16. Threat	10	01	07	−08	06	20	−05	18	07	42	(55)	(59)	13	42	22		(62)	(55)	(68)	(55)	(81)	(63)	(72)	−19	25
17. Milact	05	03	05	06	19	12	06	10	12	17	30	39	05	28	07	47		38	45	(54)	(65)	(72)	19	−09	07
18. War	00	−06	−05	01	03	01	−02	02	07	−06	21	22	08	25	−09	24	(51)		32	37	(56)	(77)	(51)	−10	20
19. Trpmvt	14	01	01	−07	19	40	02	24	11	30	24	49	11	23	22	42	26	22		30	(62)	(53)	(74)	−13	33
20. Mobili	00	04	07	00	31	05	04	03	14	25	30	36	16	38	04	48	43	41	37		(46)	41	19	−17	07
21. Accusa	18	−07	17	07	32	19	16	18	12	25	47	(64)	12	40	29	(62)	49	38	39	44		(70)	(63)	−27	09
22. F-Kill	34	06	30	21	25	24	23	15	27	25	40	30	13	22	05	39	(60)	(52)	46	38	(51)		44	−16	08
23. Cards	03	10	05	−02	12	30	−05	31	09	28	35	(77)	−02	(53)	22	(67)	38	23	(55)	43	(63)	33		00	28
24. Censor	−03	19	−09	02	−28	17	−16	13	−13	21	−27	00	14	07	−18	−16	−37	−22	06	−09	−41	−26	00		
25. D-Emby	01	34	04	06	−08	44	−17	40	−02	22	02	(52)	−02	37	21	21	06	01	34	15	14	−08	(57)	39	

[a] To the right of the principal diagonal of the matrix are the 1955–57 correlations, $N = 77$; to the left are the 1958–60 correlations, $N = 83$. Parenthesis indicates correlations $\geq .50$. Correlations are rounded off and multiplied by 100. Product moment coefficients of correlation are used throughout this study unless otherwise specified. No significance tests are given throughout this study because the entire universe under investigation is being analyzed.
[b] See Appendix I for full names of the variables as well as their definitions.

The other portions of the matrix, the correlations of domestic with foreign variables for both periods, are much more similar, although the negative range is greater in the earlier period. (The domestic–foreign intercorrelations for 1955–57 are in the upper right hand corner of the matrix, while those for 1958–60 are in the lower left hand corner.) An analysis of the percentage of correlations falling within certain intervals argues for a similarity across both periods. This type of analysis does not tell one *which* variables have similar intercorrelations over both periods. An example of correlations between intra- and international characteristics that are similar across periods is furnished by "riots" and "anti-foreign demonstrations." The 1955–57 correlation is .36, and for 1958–60 it is .38. One of the most similar correlations across both periods, at the international level, is that between accusations and mobilizations, which is .46 for 1955–57 and .44 for 1958–60; one of the least stable is the correlation at the intranational level between purges and general strikes: .46 in 1955–57 and .04 in 1958–60.

The variability in Table 1 in the correlation of purges with general strikes might be partially explained by the very low correlation of 1955–57 purges with 1958–60 purges in Table 2. Out of 22 correlations, eight (36 percent) are $\geqslant .50$. The variables which have the most similar intercorrelations generally appear to be those that happen most often, or those in which coding is not much of a problem (e.g., accusations, threats, riots).

TABLE 2
CORRELATIONS BETWEEN 1955–57 AND 1958–60 DATA[a]

Measures	Correlations[b]	Measures	Correlations[b]
1. Assass	24	12. Protst	(57)
2. Strike	33	13. Sevdip	08
3. Gu-War	(65)	14. Er-Amb	14
4. Gvtcrs	36	15. Er-Les	38
5. Purges	05	16. Threat	(66)
6. Riots	(69)	17. Milact	43
7. Revolu	(55)	18. War	41
8. Demons	44	19. Trpmvt	(58)
9. D-Kill	(55)	20. Mobili	15
		21. Accusa	(71)
10. F-Dmst	38	22. F-Kill	48
11. Negsan	47		

[a] Each value for a 1955–57 measure is correlated with the corresponding values for 1958–60; $N = 74$. Parenthesis indicates correlations $\geqslant .50$.
[b] Egypt, Syria, and Yemen were originally included in the 1955–57 study but were excluded, along with the UAR for 1958–60, in the calculations of these correlations.

Dimensions of Foreign Conflict Behavior

Table 3 gives the results of the factor analyses of the foreign conflict behavior measures for 1955–57, 1958–60. The orthogonally rotated matrix is given.[9]

In the orthogonally rotated solution of the 1958–60 data, a *diplomatic* dimension emerges first.[10] It is defined by the variables with high loadings,

TABLE 3[d]
FACTOR ANALYSIS OF FOREIGN CONFLICT MEASURES[a]: ORTHOGONALLY ROTATED FACTOR MATRIX, 1955–57 DATA WITH 1958–60 DATA[b]

Measures	Diplomatic T_1	Diplomatic R_2	War T_2[c]	War R_1[c]	Belligerency T_3	Belligerency R_3	Communality (h^2) T	Communality (h^2) R
1. F-Dmst	34	42	03	13	(64)	(63)	52	60
2. Negsan	(58)	41	22	20	26	(64)	46	62
3. Protst	(79)	49	26	(62)	−06	22	70	67
4. Sevdip	−06	−17	09	13	(82)	(82)	68	71
5. Er-Amb	(67)	(66)	18	−16	−05	−08	49	47
6. Er-Les	(59)	(60)	−29	33	21	08	47	48
7. Threat	(70)	43	35	(65)	23	48	66	84
8. Milact	28	−14	(74)	(65)	02	(57)	63	77
9. War	02	15	(83)	(85)	−09	−10	70	75
10. Trpmvt	46	(59)	32	47	26	28	38	64
11. Mobili	34	−08	(58)	(60)	19	35	48	49
12. Accusa	(67)	35	46	(70)	09	41	66	79
13. F-Kill	21	10	(76)	(87)	23	19	67	80
% Common variance	43.3	24.6	37.7	46.2	18.9	29.1	100.0	100.0
% Total variance	25.2	16.3	21.8	30.7	10.1	19.3	57.9	66.4
Intraclass correlation coefficient	.68		.67		.67			

[a] Parenthesis indicates loadings ⩾.50.
[b] Decimals omitted from all loadings.
[c] Signs reversed.
[d] Factors labelled "T" are Tanter's 1958–60 orthogonally rotated factors. Factors labelled "R" are Rummel's 1955–57 orthogonally rotated factors (Rummel, 1963, p. 13).

such as protests, threats, and accusations. (The higher the loading, the more the variable is associated with the factor, e.g., a set of highly related variables. The range of the loading is from +1.00 to −1.00, as is the range for the product moment correlation coefficients if the univariate distributions are similar.) This dimension represents a nonviolent type of foreign conflict behavior similar to that which emerged as the second factor in the 1955–57 study. The 1955–57 measures that are mainly correlated with the *diplomatic* dimension are expelling or recalling ambassadors, expulsion of lesser officials, and troop movements. The *diplomatic* dimensions from both periods pull together rationally calculated activities of a nonviolent nature, that is, diplomatic moves short of the use of force which are intended to influence other nations.

The second orthogonally rotated factor of the 1958–60 data is a *war* dimension. The variables with high loadings are war, military action, foreign killed, and mobilization. This dimension is comparable to the first factor which emerged from the 1955–57 data. Mobilization, war, and number killed best define the 1955–57 *war* dimension. The *war* dimensions in both periods pull together activities which index the preparation for war, war itself, and its consequences.

The third rotated factor of the 1958–60 data has antiforeign demonstrations and severance of diplomatic relations as the only high loadings. This factor might be labeled a *belligerency* dimension which is similar to the third factor of the earlier period. The 1955–57 *belligerency* dimension is defined by a cluster containing severance of diplomatic relations, antiforeign demonstrations, military action of a limited nature, and negative sanctions. Some of the activities on the *belligerency* dimension in both periods are of an "emotional" nature as opposed to the "rational" nature characteristic of the activities on the *diplomatic* dimension.

Three dimensions of foreign conflict behavior describe both the 1955–57 and the 1958–60 data: *war*, *diplomatic*, and *belligerency* dimensions. (The degree of similarity—intraclass correlations—between the equivalent dimensions for each period is discussed in the section on *Comparisons of Dimensions from 1955–57 and 1958–60*.)

DIMENSIONS OF DOMESTIC CONFLICT BEHAVIOR

Table 4 gives the results of the factor analysis of the domestic conflict behavior measures for 1955–57 and 1958–60. The orthogonally rotated solution is given.[11] Upon orthogonally rotating the two factors for 1958–60 to a more stable solution, two distinct dimensions emerge, the first of which might be

TABLE 4[d]

Factor Analysis of Domestic Conflict Measures[a]: Orthogonally Rotated Factor Matrix, 1955–57 Data with 1958–60 Data[b]

Measures	Turmoil T₁	Turmoil R₁	Revolutionary R₂[c]	Internal war T₂	Subversive R₃[c]	Communality (h^2) T	Communality (h^2) R
1. Assass	(59)	(59)	–03	41	(66)	52	78
2. Strike	(79)	(52)	(60)	06	05	63	63
3. Gu-War	35	–04	28	(74)	(90)	66	90
4. Gvtcrs	(53)	(60)	21	47	–04	50	41
5. Purges	01	32	(71)	(68)	03	46	60
6. Riots	(83)	(79)	31	21	09	73	73
7. Revolu	09	09	(85)	(89)	13	80	75
8. Demons	(86)	(85)	17	10	19	75	79
9. D-Kill	37	23	(75)	(78)	42	74	79
% Common variance	50.8	39.0	37.6	49.2	23.4	100.0	100.0
% Total variance	32.7	27.7	26.7	31.7	16.6	64.4	70.8
Intraclass correlation coefficient	.74		.45		.12		

[a] Parenthesis indicates loadings ⩾.50.
[b] Decimals omitted from all loadings.
[c] Signs reversed.
[d] Factors labelled "T" are Tanter's 1958–60 orthogonally rotated factors. Factors labelled "R" are Rummel's 1955–57 orthogonally rotated factors (Rummel, 1963, p. 12).

called a *turmoil* dimension. Demonstrations, riots, strikes, assassinations, and crises have high loadings and thus define the dimension. A similar dimension can be found in the rotated matrix of the 1955–57 data. The *turmoil* dimension for the earlier period is also defined by demonstrations, riots, crises, assassinations, and strikes.

The second 1958–60 orthogonally rotated factor pulls together a cluster of activities such as revolutions, domestic killed, guerrilla war, and purges. These activities are generally associated with organized conflict behavior of a highly violent nature. This factor might thus be labeled an *internal war* dimension. The *internal war* dimension of the 1958–60 data subsumes the *revolutionary* and *subversive* dimensions of 1955–57. The *revolutionary* dimension pulled together overt, organized conflict behavior, while the *subversive* dimension was defined by activities of a covert organized nature.

Domestic conflict behavior for 1958–60 may thus be separated into two independent scales—a disorganized spontaneous *turmoil* dimension and an organized violent *internal war* dimension. Since both dimensions account for almost equal amounts of the total variance in the rotated solution, they may be considered equally important in describing domestic conflict behavior during the 1958–60 period.[12]

TABLE 5
CORRELATIONS OF 1955–57 AND 1958–60 DIMENSIONS AND REPRESENTATIVE VARIABLES[d]

Dimensions correlated	Intraclass correlation coefficient	Representative variables correlated	Product moment correlation coefficient
Foreign:[a]		Foreign:[c]	
1955–57 *War* with		1955–57 F-Kill[e] with	
1958–60 *War*	.67	1958–60 War	.64
1955–57 *Diplomatic* with		1955–57 Er-Amb with	
1958–60 *Diplomatic*	.68	1958–60 Protst	.21
1955–57 *Belligerency* with		1955–57 Sevdip with	
1958–60 *Belligerency*	.67	1958–60 Sevdip	.08
Domestic:[b]		Domestic:[c]	
1955–57 *Subversion* with		1955–57 Gu-War with	
1958–60 *Internal War*	.12	1958–60 Gu-War	.65
1955–57 *Revolutionary* with		1955–57 Revolu with	
1958–60 *Internal War*	.45	1958–60 Gu-War	.38
1955–57 *Turmoil* with		1955–57 Demons with	
1958–60 *Turmoil*	.74	1958–60 Demons	.44

[a] $n = 13$ variables loaded on orthogonally rotated factors.
[b] $n = 9$ variables loaded on orthogonally rotated factors.
[c] $N = 74$ nations.
[d] A representative variable is one which has the highest loading on a particular factor and the lowest loadings with the remaining factors in the matrix.
[e] See Appendix I for full names of the variables as well as their definitions.

Comparison of Dimensions from 1955–57 and 1958–60

In order to obtain a more precise description of the degree of similarity between the dimensions which emerge from the two time periods, the intraclass coefficient of correlation is calculated (cf. Robinson, 1959: 25). Since the product moment coefficient converts raw data to standard scores, it does not take into account differences in origins, means, and variances; for the variance of a variable in standard form is unity, while the mean is zero. Consequently, the product moment only measures *changes* in one variable which are associated with *changes* in another variable. The intraclass coefficient, however, is sensitive to differences in origins, means, and variances; and as these differences increase, the coefficient decreases (Haggard, 1958: 30).

Table 5 compares the foreign and domestic dimensions between the two time periods; also given are the correlations between representative variables which index the dimensions for each period. The correlations for the representative variables indicate that the two war measures are the most similar forms of foreign conflict behavior across the whole 1955–60 time span ($r = .64$). The most similar of the domestic representative variables is guerrilla war ($r = .65$). In terms of dimensions, however, the *turmoil* dimension is the most similar for the two periods. Moreover, the *internal war* dimension of 1958–60 is more similar to the 1955–57 *revolutionary* dimension than it is to the 1955–57 *subversive* dimension.

Relationship between Domestic and Foreign Conflict Behavior

The relationship between domestic and foreign conflict behavior is discovered by first factor analyzing all the conflict behavior measures together and then by regressing upon one another the variables which best index both forms of conflict behavior. Table 6 contains the results of the merged factor analysis; the obliquely rotated solution is given.[13] Upon rotation to the more invariant oblique solution, domestic and foreign conflict behavior become clearly separate. In no case do any domestic measures have pattern values $\geqslant .50$ on the same factor on which a foreign measure is $\geqslant .50$.

The first factor in the oblique matrix is the *turmoil* dimension. The second factor is the *diplomatic* dimension and is defined by the communications variables as well as expulsion of ambassadors. In addition to these measures of diplomatic activity, however, the two error measures of world interest also help to define this dimension.

As previously mentioned, negative correlation or lack of correlation between censorship and the conflict behavior measures is no cause for alarm. A second error measure—cards per nation in *Deadline Data*—has to be analyzed in a different manner. There is a high positive pattern value of cards (.82) on the *diplomatic* dimension, where protests also show a value of .82 and expulsion of ambassadors .72; and there are high positive correlations of cards with protests (.77) and cards with expulsion of ambassadors (.55).

TABLE 6[c]

FACTOR ANALYSIS OF DOMESTIC AND FOREIGN CONFLICT MEASURES[a]: SEVEN FACTOR SOLUTION

	Measures	F_1 Turmoil	F_2 Diplomatic	F_3 Int. War	F_4 War	F_5	F_6	F_7
1.	Assass	(64)	−31	18	12	31	02	18
2.	Strike	(70)	18	07	−02	−09	09	−23
3.	Gu-War	28	01	(66)	−08	07	20	−24
4.	Gvtcrs	(53)	−03	37	08	03	11	−40
5.	Purges	−05	09	(76)	−02	02	−19	06
6.	Riots	(77)	09	14	07	−02	−01	28
7.	Revolu	05	−07	(91)	−10	−12	06	−08
8.	Demons	(81)	14	06	09	02	−09	05
9.	D-Kill	35	−07	(76)	05	−13	−03	02
10.	F-Dmst	04	11	22	−14	03	(53)	(52)
11.	Negsan	−08	19	03	16	(62)	25	−01
12.	Protst	05	(82)	03	09	14	−13	04
13.	Sevdip	01	−15	−03	06	10	(83)	05
14.	Er-Amb	08	(72)	−16	11	22	12	−34
15.	Er-Les	13	14	−11	−27	(82)	01	−07
16.	Threat	−14	46	−04	22	34	22	27
17.	Milact	04	21	01	(74)	02	−08	01
18.	War	06	06	−16	(91)	−21	−02	−04
19.	Trpmvt	14	22	−06	25	01	05	(68)
20.	Mobili	−27	47	22	36	−15	22	07
21.	Accusa	−11	49	22	31	38	−09	02
22.	F-Kill	17	−10	08	(79)	04	12	27
23.	Cards	06	(82)	04	11	10	−17	13
24.	Censor	20	09	−28	−33	−45	42	30
25.	D-Emby	41	(73)	−15	−20	−13	17	03

[a] Parenthesis indicates pattern values $\geq .50$.
[b] Decimals omitted from all loadings. The oblique rotation is a part of the Mesa 3 computer program. It consists of the class of analytical solutions called *oblimin*, developed by John B. Carroll at Harvard. The *biquartimin* solution is selected over the *quartimin* or *covarimin* because the quartimin solution is generally biased toward factor axes which are too highly correlated, while the covarimin is almost invariably biased toward factor axes which are too orthogonal (cf. Harmon, pp. 324–34).
[c] Correlations between factors for oblique rotation are cosines of the angles between the factors rather than the intraclass correlations based upon the pattern values. Correlations $>.25$ are: $r_{F_1F_6} = .26$; $r_{F_2F_7} = .28$; $r_{F_3F_4} = .26$; $r_{F_3F_5} = .26$; $r_{F_4F_5} = .27$.

This indicates that the level of world interest in a nation is associated with the tendency for its protests and expulsions of ambassadors to be reported.

The high correlation and mutually high pattern values of protests and the "cards" measure of world interest is likewise found for the other measure of world interest—the number of embassies or legations in a country. The latter measure has a .52 correlation with protests and a pattern value of .73 on the *diplomatic* dimension (see Tables 1 and 6).

The similar manner in which the world interest measures act with the protest variable indicates that the two world interest measures are tapping the same thing. The small difference between the two may come from the fact that the cards in *Deadline Data* measure the extent of interest that the *editors* manifest in particular nations, while the number of embassies or legations in a country may reflect the degree of interest other *nations* have in that country.

On the basis of the relationships between protests and expulsion of ambassadors on the one hand, and the world interest error measures on the other, propositions about these conflict measures should be qualified to this extent: the data of nations in which there is little interest *may not* be included in the correlations from which the propositions are inferred. But an alternative explanation is also plausible. The correlation of the cards measure of world interest with diplomatic behavior *may* be due to increased interest when there is diplomatic conflict. Also, the more important nations have more interactions with other nations, and this may give them more opportunities for protest as well as more foreign newspapers in which their activities are reported.

Besides the *turmoil* and *diplomatic* dimensions, other factors in the oblique matrix of Table 6 may be interpreted. These are *internal war* (factor 3) and *international war* (factor 4). The merged factor analysis seems to show a lack of relationship between domestic and foreign conflict behavior. This relationship may be investigated more precisely by using multiple regression.

Multiple Regression

Both forms of conflict behavior for 1958–60 are regressed upon one another[14] to discover the relationship between them at one cross section in time. In addition, the 1958–60 data are regressed on the 1955–57 data in order to discover the relationship between domestic and foreign conflict behavior with a time lag.

The independent foreign variables for the 1955–57 study are the *war*, *diplomatic*, and *belligerency* dimensions. The values of the variables used in regression in the Rummel study are the factor scores each nation has on each of the six factors extracted. These scores were estimated by adding together the standard scores of variables which have a loading $\geqslant .50$ on a particular dimension and no loading $\geqslant .40$ on another dimension within the matrix (Rummel, 1963b: 15–16 [this volume, Chapter 3]).

The variables used in the prediction of domestic conflict behavior for 1958–60 are measures of conflict behavior which measure the dimensions,

TABLE 7
PREDICTIONS OF 1955–1957 FOREIGN CONFLICT BEHAVIOR[a]: INDEPENDENT VARIABLES—TURMOIL, REVOLUTIONARY, SUBVERSION

Dependent variable	Year	Standard deviation	Standard error	Multiple R	R^2
War	1955–57	2.40	2.36	.26	.07
Diplomacy	1955–57	1.49	1.46	.26	.07
Belligerency	1955–57	1.00	.97	.31	.10

[a] $N = 77$ (Rummel, 1963, p. 20).

rather than the dimensions themselves. These measures are called representative variables. They are selected on the basis of having the highest loading on the orthogonally rotated dimensions, but no other high loadings in the matrix.

Thus the variables for the 1958–60 domestic dimensions are antigovernment demonstrations and revolutions, which measure the *turmoil* and *internal war* dimensions respectively. The representative variables for the foreign dimensions are war, protests, and severance of diplomatic relations, which measure the *war*, *diplomatic*, and *belligerency* dimensions respectively.

In the time lag regressions of 1958–60 data on 1955–57 data, representative variables rather than factor scores for 1955–57 were employed as independent variables. Thus, the representative variables for the 1955–57 domestic dimensions are anti-government demonstrations, revolutions, and guerrilla warfare, which index the *turmoil, revolutionary*, and *subversive* dimensions respectively. The representative variables for the 1955–57 foreign dimensions are foreign killed, expulsion or recall of ambassadors, and severance of diplomatic relations, which measure the *war*, *diplomatic*, and *belligerency* dimensions respectively.

Representative variables were selected rather than factor scores because the substantive meaning of the variable is clear, whereas the meaning of factor scores is not so readily apparent. In addition, the theoretical significance of the representative variables can be readily discovered through a series of replications. But it is considerably more difficult to ascertain the theoretical significance of dimensions because the exact composition of the dimension is unique to each study.

Table 7 gives the results of the predictions of 1955–57 foreign from 1955–57 domestic conflict behavior dimensions carried out by Rummel (1963b: 20 [this volume, Chapter 3]). Only eight percent of the total variance in foreign conflict behavior is explained by domestic conflict behavior.[15] The small difference in the values for the standard deviation and the standard error indicates the failure of the domestic dimensions to predict changes in the foreign dimensions.

Table 8 contains the results of the prediction of the 1958–60 foreign from the 1958–60 domestic conflict behavior variables. Only about four percent of the total variance in foreign conflict behavior is explained by the domestic measures for 1958–60, which is somewhat lower than the eight percent found for the 1955–57 data.

Table 9 gives the results of the prediction of the 1955–57 domestic from the 1955–57 foreign conflict behavior dimensions. Almost eight percent of the total variance in the domestic dimensions is explained by the foreign dimensions. This is remarkably similar to the seven percent of the total variance in the 1958–60 domestic which is predicted by the 1958–60 foreign basic variables. Table 10 contains these results.

From the two sets of regressions for the 1955–57 and 1958–60 cross sections, there appears to be only a small relationship between domestic and

TABLE 8

PREDICTIONS OF 1958–60 FOREIGN CONFLICT BEHAVIOR[a]: INDEPENDENT VARIABLES—ANTI-GOVERNMENT DEMONSTRATIONS AND REVOLUTIONS

Dependent variable	Year	Standard deviation	Standard error	Multiple R	R^2
Wars	1958–60	.75	.76	.03	.00
Severance of diplomatic relations	1958–60	.15	.15	.26	.07
Protests	1958–60	.35	.35	.24	.06

[a] $N = 83$.

foreign conflict behavior. This apparent lack of relationship at one point in time may be investigated further by means of time lag regressions.

Time Lag Regressions

The 1955–57 foreign predicts 22.3 percent of the variance in the foreign variables for 1958–60 (Table 11). But only half as much variance (11.7 percent) in the 1958–60 foreign is explained by the 1955–57 domestic (Table 12).

Table 13 contains the results of the prediction of 1958–60 domestic by 1955–57 domestic variables. The domestic conflict behavior of the 1955–57 period explains 27.5 percent of the total variance of the 1958–60 domestic.

The 1955–57 foreign, however, cannot predict the 1958–60 domestic variables. The results in Table 14 show that only 8.5 percent of the variance in the 1958–60 domestic is explained by the 1955–57 foreign variables.

From the time lag regressions one may conclude that there is a *moderate relationship* between domestic conflict behavior at one time and the same behavior at a later point in time. Similarly, there is a *moderate relationship* between foreign conflict behavior at the two points in time. In the absence of the time lag, only seven percent and 4.3 percent of the variance are explained by the 1958–60 foreign and domestic measures respectively. With the introduction of the lag, the explained variance increases to 8.5 and 11.7 percent. Although this is still a very small amount of variance on which to make a generalization, there seems to be some relationship between domestic and foreign conflict behavior with a time lag.[16]

TABLE 9

PREDICTIONS OF 1955–57 DOMESTIC CONFLICT BEHAVIOR[a]: INDEPENDENT VARIABLES—WAR, DIPLOMACY, BELLIGERENCY

Dependent variable	Year	Standard deviation	Standard error	Multiple R	R^2
Turmoil	1955–57	2.43	2.31	.37	.14
Revolutionary	1955–57	1.73	1.70	.27	.07
Subversive	1955–57	1.00	1.01	.14	.02

[a] See Rummel, 1963, p. 20. $N = 77$.

TABLE 10
PREDICTIONS OF 1958–60 DOMESTIC CONFLICT BEHAVIOR[a]: INDEPENDENT VARIABLES—WAR, PROTESTS, AND SEVERANCE OF DIPLOMATIC RELATIONS

Dependent variable	Year	Standard deviation	Standard error	Multiple R	R^2
Anti-government demonstrations	1958–60	.36	.35	.32	.10
Revolutions	1958–60	.27	.27	.20	.04

[a] $N = 83$.

Discussion and Summary

DIMENSIONS OF DOMESTIC CONFLICT BEHAVIOR

One finding that appears to emerge from the 1958–60 data is that the structure of domestic conflict behavior is slightly different from that found in 1955–57. The internal war dimension combines the 1955–57 *subversion* and *revolutionary* dimensions; the *turmoil* dimension, however, is found in both periods.

The correlation matrix of Table 1 illustrates the changes in shared variance that revolutions and guerrilla war have which may result in their separation in the 1955–57 study and their merger in this study. The correlation of the two for the 1955–57 data is only .33, while for 1958–60 it is .65. In addition to the fact of an increase in shared variance from the 1955–57 period, the absolute magnitudes and means for revolutions and guerrilla war have also increased. During 1955–57 ($N = 77$) there were 17 codings for the presence of guerrilla warfare and 44 revolutions with means of .21 and .57 respectively; on the other hand, during 1958–60 ($N = 83$), there were 58 codings for the presence of guerrilla warfare and 83 revolutions with means of .70 and 1.00 respectively.

TABLE 11
PREDICTIONS OF 1958–60 FOREIGN CONFLICT BEHAVIOR: INDEPENDENT VARIABLES—1955–57 NUMBER KILLED IN FOREIGN CONFLICT BEHAVIOR, EXPULSION OR RECALL OF AMBASSADORS, AND SEVERANCE OF DIPLOMATIC RELATIONS[a]

1958–60 Dependent variable	Standard deviation	Standard error	Multiple R	R^2
Protest	.35	.33	.40	.16
War	.68	.52	.66	.43
Severance of diplomatic relations	.16	.15	.28	.08

[a] The independent variables are representative variables from the 1955–57 study (Rummel, 1963, p. 13). $N = 74$.

TABLE 12
PREDICTIONS OF 1958–60 FOREIGN CONFLICT BEHAVIOR: INDEPENDENT VARIABLES—1955–57 ANTI-GOVERNMENT DEMONSTRATIONS, REVOLUTIONS, AND GUERRILLA WARFARE[a]

1958–60 Dependent variable	Standard deviation	Standard error	Multiple R	R^2
Protest	.35	.32	.42	.18
War	.68	.69	.12	.01
Severance of diplomatic relations	.16	.14	.40	.16

[a] These independent variables are representative variables from the 1955–57 study (Rummel, 1963, p. 13). $N = 74$.

TABLE 13
PREDICTIONS OF 1958–60 DOMESTIC CONFLICT BEHAVIOR: INDEPENDENT VARIABLES—1955–57 ANTI-GOVERNMENT DEMONSTRATIONS, REVOLUTIONS, AND GUERRILLA WARFARE[a]

1958–60 Dependent variable	Standard deviation	Standard error	Multiple R	R^2
Anti-government demonstrations	.38	.34	.44	.19
Revolutions	.26	.22	.60	.36

[a] These independent variables are representative variables from the 1955–57 study (Rummel, 1963, p. 12). $N = 74$.

TABLE 14
PREDICTIONS OF 1958–60 DOMESTIC CONFLICT BEHAVIOR: INDEPENDENT VARIABLES—1955–57 FOREIGN KILLED, EXPULSION OR RECALL OF AMBASSADORS, AND SEVERANCE OF DIPLOMATIC RELATIONS[a]

1958–60 Dependent variable	Standard deviation	Standard error	Multiple R	R^2
Anti-government demonstrations	.38	.38	.16	.03
Revolutions	.26	.25	.37	.14

[a] These independent variables are representative variables from the 1955–57 study (Rummel, 1963, p. 12). $N = 74$.

Although 1958–60 domestic conflict behavior has a slightly different structure in comparison with the earlier period, foreign conflict behavior bears a remarkable similarity across the two points in time.

DIMENSIONS OF FOREIGN CONFLICT BEHAVIOR

The dimensions of 1958–60 foreign conflict behavior appear to reflect a strong similarity of structure with the 1955–57 dimensions with respect to the *type* of variables which define the clusters as well as to the magnitude and *pattern* of the loadings themselves. For example, the *war*, *diplomatic*, and *belligerency* dimensions do emerge from the 1958–60 data and the intraclass correlations are relatively high (see Table 7).

The previously mentioned change in the ratio of high to total correlations among the foreign measures in Table 1 might account for the slightly weaker loadings and consequent smaller amount of explained variance for the 1958–60 data. Not only are the correlations among the foreign variables lower than in the earlier period; the intensity of conflict behavior appears to have decreased also. The most extreme change can be seen in one of the measures of intensity—number killed due to foreign conflict behavior. The total for 1955–57 is 51,123 with a mean value of 664, while for 1958–60 the total is 974 with a mean of 11.74.

Hence, foreign conflict behavior appears to be slightly less correlated and somewhat less intense during the 1958–60 period, but nonetheless it compares quite well with the earlier period as regards the dimensions of conflict behavior.

RELATIONS BETWEEN DOMESTIC AND FOREIGN CONFLICT BEHAVIOR

The merged factor analysis and the regression of both forms of conflict behavior on one another suggest only a small relationship between the two. A stronger relationship was expected on the basis of the theories of scholars such as Lewis Coser and Georg Simmel:

(1) The unity of a group is frequently lost when it does not have an opponent (Simmel, 1955: 97).

(2) Hostilities preclude the group boundaries from disappearing and they are frequently consciously cultivated to guarantee existing conditions (Simmel, 1955: 97).

(3) If a group with basic consensus regarding its preservation engages in outside conflict, internal cohesion is likely to be increased (Coser, 1956: 92–93).

(4) Groups may look for enemies to help maintain and/or increase internal cohesion (Coser, 1956: 104).

(5) Exaggeration of the danger of an enemy serves to maintain group structure when it is threatened by internal dissension (Coser, 1956: 106).

Whereas Simmel and Coser agree as to the tendency for between-group relations to be largely a result of within-group relations, the experimental data of Muzafer Sherif and his colleagues suggest otherwise. Their general thesis is that inter-group attitudes and behavior are determined *primarily* by the nature of relations between groups and *not primarily* by the pattern of relations and attitudes within groups themselves (Sherif et al., 1961: 38; italics in original). They conclude, however, that when friendliness already characterizes between-group relations, harmonious in-group relations probably contribute to solutions of mutual problems between groups (Sherif et al., 1961: 200).

The theories and findings of Coser, Simmel, and Sherif are based upon small groups. Thus, expectations at the national and international levels on the basis of their propositions should be qualified. The finding in this study of a small relationship between domestic and foreign conflict behavior, especially with a time lag, can be viewed more clearly in the perspective of other empirical studies at the national and international levels.

Another theorist, Samuel Huntington, contends that a decrease in the frequency of interstate conflict is likely to increase the frequency of domestic violence.[17] He thus admits that some relationship exists between the internal and external conflict behavior of nations, but he asserts that it does not follow that external peace stimulates internal conflict or that there is any *necessary* relationship between the two. Furthermore, he admits that in this century the data appear to suggest a general relation between the inhibition of external war and the prevalence of internal war (Huntington, 1962: 40–41). This agrees with Rummel's cross-sectional finding of a small inverse relationship between subversion and foreign conflict behavior (Rummel, 1963: 47); but little evidence is provided for Huntington's hypothesis in the present study.

Rummel also found a consistently positive relationship between domestic conflict behavior other than subversion and the *diplomatic* and *belligerency* dimensions. In the cross-sectional correlations of Table 1 the highest correlations between domestic and foreign variables are between riots and troop movements (.40), and riots and anti-foreign demonstrations (.38). Since anti-foreign demonstrations help to define the *belligerency* dimension, and the riots variable does not appear on the *internal war* dimension, this study provides evidence in favor of a small positive relationship between domestic conflict behavior other than *subversion* and one of the variables which helps to define the *belligerency* dimension.

Another facet of the relationship between the *diplomatic* dimension and domestic conflict behavior is suggested by Joseph McKenna (1962). McKenna suggests some internal effects of diplomatic behavior. He contends that diplomatic protests may function to assure domestic interests that the government is active on their problems and to provide propaganda for home consumption so that the general public may become aroused in support of the official policy toward the state to whom the protest is directed. More generally, he contends that the purpose of foreign policy is to influence external events so that domestic values are maintained and furthered (McKenna, 1962: 20, 26). Three of his findings bear directly on the theme of this study. He finds that the nations to whom United States protests were directed most frequently were characterized by revolution and other forms of domestic turmoil. Secondly, protest to major powers was less likely than to minor powers because the internal stability of the former probably minimized the number of offensive incidents directed at United States citizens. Thirdly, resistance to American demands was motivated by the domestic politics of the recipient (McKenna, 1962: 20, 38–40, 201). The first two propositions suggest a positive relationship between domestic and foreign conflict behavior. Thus, he suggests a positive relationship between protests, on the *diplomatic* dimension, and revolution and/or turmoil. But, in the present study, the highest correlation between protests and a domestic variable is that with riots (.29), and in the oblique biquartimin matrix of the merged factor analysis, riots and revolutions appear on factors different from protests (cf. Tables 1 and 6).

The studies of Sorokin (1937) and Richardson (1960) may also be relevant to interpreting the findings in the present study. Sorokin visually examines data through seventeen centuries, 525 A.D. to 1925, and finds a small association between unsuccessful external wars and internal disturbances. As with the present study, he concludes that the presence or absence of general war and internal disturbances are fairly independent of one another (Sorokin, 1937: 487, 492).

From 1820 to 1945, Richardson finds 112 mainly internal as compared with 137 mainly external fatal quarrels (Richardson, 1960: 186).[18] Even though he is primarily interested in the relationship between deadly quarrels and such variables as the rate of armaments increase, trade, language differences, contiguity, and other nonconflict variables, he does allude to the possible relationship between intranation solidarity and external threats (Richardson, 1960: 156). But a proposition about such a relationship does not emerge from his data, nor does he subject one to systematic test.

IMPLICATIONS OF FINDINGS FOR THEORY CONSTRUCTION

The principal finding of a small relationship between domestic and foreign conflict behavior may have implications for theory-building. There may be no "simple" relationship between domestic and foreign conflict behavior, but there may be a causal relationship which is being obscured by other phenomena. That is, the relationship may be mediated by a third variable such as the personality characteristics of the national decision-makers as is suggested by Haas and Whiting (1956: 61–62).

Evidence against the "third variable" interpretation for *aggregate* data, however, is provided by the Dimensionality of Nations Project of which the present work is a substudy. The 22 domestic and foreign conflict behavior measures were included in a factor analysis of 236 national and international characteristics across 82 nations. A domestic and a foreign conflict behavior dimension came out *separate* from one another as well as from economic development, political orientation, and Catholic culture dimensions. The fact that domestic and foreign conflict behavior dimensions remain separate within the larger context adds evidence that they are unrelated to other aggregate data at one point in time. Thus, having *controlled* for such things as the level of development, political orientation, and Catholic culture, the domestic and foreign conflict behavior dimensions remain separated. (Cf. Rummel, Guetzkow, Sawyer, and Tanter, *Dimensions of Nations*, forthcoming.)

The "third variable" interpretation, however, may be valid for individual level characteristics as distinct from aggregate data. It may prove theoretically useful to inquire into the nature of the decision-maker's characteristics in order to see whether the relationship between domestic and foreign conflict behavior would increase. For example, the decision-making scheme presented by Richard Snyder and Glenn Paige (1958) might be relevant for suggesting third variables that mediate between the domestic and foreign conflict behavior relationship.

SUMMARY

The goal of this study was to replicate an earlier work (Rummel, 1963b [this volume, Chapter 3]) in order to obtain additional evidence relative to the dimensions of conflict behavior and the relationship between domestic and foreign conflict behavior. Data were collected across eighty-three nations on nine domestic and thirteen foreign measures of conflict behavior for 1958, 1959, and 1960. From a factor analysis of these data there emerged two domestic dimensions—*turmoil*, and *internal war*—and three foreign dimensions—*war*, *diplomatic*, and *belligerency*.

The *turmoil* dimension compares favorably with a similar dimension derived from the 1955–57 data, while the *internal war* dimension subsumes the *revolutionary* and *subversive* dimensions from the 1955–57 study. The three 1958–60 foreign dimensions are quite similar to the three derived from the 1955–57 foreign measures.

Dimensions of Conflict Behavior, 1958–60

From a factor analysis of domestic and foreign conflict behavior, the domestic measures separated themselves from the foreign variables, implying only a small relationship between the two. This relationship was investigated still further with multiple regression. Representative variables were selected on the basis of high correlation with the dimensions. Representative variables which indexed domestic and foreign dimensions were regressed upon each other to discover the relationship between domestic and foreign conflict behavior. The regression yielded a small relationship between domestic and foreign conflict behavior that increased with a time lag.

Three error variables were used to discover the extent to which systematic bias might distort the conclusions. Two of these, number of cards per nation in *Deadline Data* and number of embassies or legations in a country, were found to correlate highly with the protest variable and also to have high pattern values on the *diplomatic* dimension. It was concluded that the level of world interest in a nation is related to the tendency for a nation's protests and (to a lesser extent) its expulsion of ambassadors to be reported. Hence, propositions about these two conflict measures should be qualified to the extent that the data of nations in which little interest is expressed *may not* be included in the correlations from which the propositions are inferred.

PROPOSITIONS

The following generalizations are offered on the basis of an analysis of domestic and foreign conflict behavior for 1958–60:

(1) The 1958–60 domestic conflict behavior of nations varies along two uncorrelated dimensions of equal importance—*turmoil* and *internal war*. The *turmoil* dimension is quite similar to the 1955–57 *turmoil* dimension, and the *internal war* dimension subsumes the 1955–57 *revolutionary* and *subversive* dimensions.

(2) The 1958–60 foreign conflict behavior of nations varies along three uncorrelated dimensions of the following order of importance: *diplomatic*, *war*, and *belligerency*, which compares favorably with the 1955–57 foreign dimensions.

(3) The variation in acts or occurrences of 1958–60 domestic conflict behavior are generally highly related in a manner similar to that for 1955–57.

(4) The variation in acts or occurrences of 1958–60 foreign conflict behavior are generally highly related, but not as highly related as that for 1955–57.

(5) There is a small relationship between 1958–60 domestic and foreign conflict behavior which increases with a time lag.

(6) Five representative variables measure the dimensions of domestic and foreign conflict behavior for 1958–60: anti-government demonstrations (*turmoil*); revolutions (*internal war*); protest (*diplomatic*); war (*war*); and severance of diplomatic relations (*belligerency*). These compare favorably with the representative variables for 1955–57: anti-government demonstrations

(*turmoil*); revolutions (*revolutionary*); guerrilla warfare (*subversion*); foreign killed (*war*); expulsion or recall of ambassadors (*diplomatic*); and severance of diplomatic relations (*belligerency*).

(7) Level of world interest in a nation is associated with the tendency for its protests and expulsions of ambassadors to be reported.

APPENDIX I. DEFINITIONS OF CONFLICT BEHAVIOR MEASURES

The criteria by which the conflict behavior measures were chosen and brief definitions of the measures themselves are the same as those used in the 1955–57 study.

Measures of Conflict Behavior

With respect to the methods and goals of this study, any act or occurrence chosen to index conflict behavior must: (1) be capable of empirical delimitation; (2) be an act or occurrence of sufficient interest to be generally reported—that is, data must be available; (3) be applicable to all countries (e.g., "colonial violence," if made a measure, would not be applicable to those countries without colonies) if spurious factors are not to result; (4) be as diverse as possible to cover the greatest possible range of conflict behavior; and (5) be an act of or within, or an occurrence with respect to, seven or more countries (this is to prevent the correlations from being dependent on too few such happenings and, therefore, to reduce the role of aberrations on what are meant to be general conclusions).

On the basis of these criteria, nine measures of domestic and thirteen measures of foreign conflict were chosen for this study. The domestic conflict measures and a brief definition of the conflict act or occurrence are as follows:

    1. *Number of assassinations:* any politically motivated murder or attempted murder of a high government official or politician.

    2. *Number of general strikes:* any strike of 1,000 or more industrial or service workers that involves more than one employer and that is aimed at national government policies or authority.

    3. *Presence or absence of guerrilla warfare:* any armed activity, sabotage, or bombings carried on by independent bands of citizens or irregular forces and aimed at the overthrow of the present regime.

    4. *Number of major government crises:* any rapidly developing situation that threatens to bring the downfall of the present regime—excluding situations of revolt aimed at such an overthrow.

    5. *Number of purges:* any systematic elimination by jailing or execution of political opposition within the ranks of the regime or the opposition.

    6. *Number of riots:* any violent demonstration or clash of more than 100 citizens involving the use of physical force.

7. *Number of revolutions:* any illegal or forced change in the top government elite, any attempt at such a change, or any successful or unsuccessful armed rebellion whose aim is independence from the central government.

8. *Number of anti-government demonstrations:* any peaceful public gathering of at least 100 people for the primary purpose of displaying or voicing their opposition to government policies or authority, excluding those demonstrations of a distinctly anti-foreign nature.

9. *Number of people killed in all forms of domestic violence:* any deaths resulting directly from violence of an intergroup nature, thus excluding deaths by murder and execution.

The measures of foreign conflict definitions are as follows:

1. *Number of anti-foreign demonstrations:* any demonstration or riot by more than 100 people directed at a particular foreign country (or group of countries) or its policies.

2. *Number of negative sanctions:* any non-violent act against another country—such as boycott, withdrawal of aid—the purpose of which is to punish or threaten that country.

3. *Number of protests:* any official diplomatic communication or governmental statement, the purpose of which is to complain about or object to the policies of another country.

4. *Number of countries with which diplomatic relations severed:* the complete withdrawal from all official contact with a particular country.

5. *Number of ambassadors expelled or recalled:* any expelling of an ambassador from, or recalling for other than administrative reasons an ambassador to, a particular country—this does not involve expulsion or recall resulting from the severance of diplomatic relations.

6. *Number of diplomatic officials of less than ambassador's rank expelled or recalled:* replace "ambassador" by "officials of lesser . . . rank" in above definition.

7. *Number of threats:* any official diplomatic communication or governmental statement asserting that if a particular country does or does not do a particular thing it will incur negative sanctions.

8. *Presence or absence of military action:* any military clash of a particular country with another and involving gunfire, but short of war as defined below.

9. *Number of wars:* any military clash for a particular country with another and in which more than .02 percent of its population are militarily involved in the clash.

10. *Number of troop movements:* any rapid movement of large bodies of troops, naval units, or air squadrons to a particular area for the purpose of deterring the military action of another country, gaining concessions, or as a show of strength.

11. *Number of mobilizations:* any rapid increase in military strength through the calling up of reserves, activation of additional military units, or the demothballing of military equipment.

12. *Number of accusations:* any official diplomatic or governmental statement involving charges and allegations of a derogatory nature against another country.

13. *Number of people killed in all forms of foreign conflict behavior:* the total number of deaths resulting directly from any violent interchange between countries.

See Appendix I in the 1955–57 study (Rummel, 1963b) for more extensive definitions.

APPENDIX II. LIST OF NATIONS

Afghanistan	Dominican Rep.	Jordan	Saudi Arabia
Albania	Ecuador	Korea (Dem. Rep.)	Spain
Argentina	El Salvador	Korea (Rep. of)	Sweden
Australia	Ethiopia	Lebanon	Switzerland
Austria	Finland	Liberia	Thailand
Belgium	France	Libya	Turkey
Bolivia	Germany (DDR)	Mexico	U. of South Africa
Brazil	Germany (Fed. R.)	Nepal	U.S.S.R.
Bulgaria	Greece	Netherlands	U.K.
Burma	Guatemala	New Zealand	U.S.A.
Cambodia	Haiti	Nicaragua	Uruguay
Canada	Honduras	Norway	Venezuela
Ceylon	Hungary	Outer Mongolia	Yugoslavia
Chile	India	Pakistan	Laos
China	Indonesia	Panama	North Vietnam
Rep. of China	Iran	Paraguay	South Vietnam
Colombia	Iraq	Peru	Morocco
Costa Rica	Irish Republic	Philippines	Sudan
Cuba	Israel	Poland	Tunisia
Czechoslovakia	Italy	Portugal	U.A.R.
Denmark	Japan	Rumania	

NOTES

1. The way some propositions are stated, however, makes it almost possible to interpret them as suggesting a negative relationship. This interpretation, though, does not fit in with the context in which the propositions appear. With the introduction of a time lag between the occurrence of domestic and foreign conflict behavior, the theories of Coser (1956) and Simmel (1955) suggest a negative relationship.

2. See Sidman (1960: 73) regarding intragroup and intergroup replication, and (1960: 46 ff.) as regards the concept of generality.

3. *New York Times*, March 29, 1959.

4. *New York Times*, April 13, 1959.

5. *New York Times*, January 3, 1960.
6. *New York Times*, January 1, 1961.
7. Biomedical (BIMD) Computer Program 24 was used to test for outliers, and a visual test of linearity from the cross tabulation of each variable with every other. Outliers greater than three standard scores from the mean were "brought in" through transformation. No curvilinearity was found which might distort the conclusions.
8. In addition, Richardson's data (1960) on war for thirty nations from 1825–1945 were correlated with 1958–60 data on war, war and military action, and number killed due to all foreign conflict; Harry Eckstein's data (Eckstein, 1962) for 1946–59 on total violence, internal warfare, and a coup are correlated with 1958–60 measures for seventy nations; and Raymond Cattell's correlations (Cattell, 1949) for five measures of conflict behavior were compared with similar correlations from 1958–60. The results indicate that the 1958–60 data are not unique to that period and appear to be moderately general to longer time periods.
9. Mesa 3 computer program is used for the factor analysis. Principal components technique is used with unities in the diagonal of the correlation matrix (see Rummel, 1963b [this volume, Chapter 3] for a detailed discussion of the research design decisions). Since the eigenvalue (sum of squares) of the unrotated fourth factor of the 1958–60 data is equal to only .95, only three factors are extracted and rotated orthogonally and obliquely. The criterion for the *number of significant factors* to extract and to which rotation is to be started is the same for the 1955–57 and 1958–60 studies. This criterion is the number of factors whose eigenvalues are ⩾1.00. An eigenvalue is the root of a characteristic equation.

Rotation is carried out in order to obtain a more stable solution, e.g., one that is not entirely dependent upon each particular variable in the analysis.

Orthogonal rotation is the fitting of factors to variables with the restriction that the correlation between the factors is zero. Hence, independence among the factors is forced on the data. The varimax criterion (Kaiser, 1958) is used to rotate orthogonally to simple structure, e.g., the maximization of low loadings.

Oblique rotation allows the factors to become correlated if such correlations actually exist among the factors.

The criterion for accepting either rotation is the extent to which simple structure is achieved. The number of variable loadings in the ±.10 hyperplane is used to indicate the degree of simple structure. Hence, the solution which has the largest number of near-zero loadings will be accepted.

Loadings are correlations with factors for the unrotated and orthogonally rotated solutions. The values in the oblique matrices are pattern values which are coordinates rather than correlations.

The *communality*, h^2, of a variable is the sum of the squares of the loadings across the factors for the unrotated and orthogonally rotated solutions.

Percent of Total Variance under each column in the factor matrix is that portion of the variance in all the variables which that factor extracts. It is the sum of the squares in the factor column divided by the total number of variables.

Percent of Common Variance is the percent of variance that a factor has divided by the total variance extracted by all factors.

10. The orthogonally rotated solution is selected over the oblique because the former meets more adequately the simple structure criterion. (The ±.10 hyperplane

of the orthogonal solution contains more low variable loadings than the oblique solution has low pattern values.)

11. Since the eigenvalue of the third factor of the 1958–60 data is only .84, only two factors are extracted and rotated orthogonally and obliquely. The orthogonal solution is selected over the oblique because the number of loadings and pattern values in the $\pm.10$ hyperplane for each solution is the same (4). And since the orthogonal solution is the simplest, it is selected.

12. The inference as to degree of organization was based upon an inspection of background information on the conflict events in question. This tentative distinction should not lead us to ignore facts such as that some of the riots were highly organized. A further study is planned where the degree of organization will be coded systematically to see whether organization varies with type of conflict behavior.

13. Seven factors are extracted in contrast with the six-factor solution of the 1955–57 study because the eigenvalue of the seventh factor of the present work is 1.002 (see note 10). The oblique is selected over the orthogonal solution on the basis of simple structure criteria. The $\pm.10$ hyperplane contains sixteen more loadings in the oblique than are found in the orthogonal solution.

14. Multiple regression is a method by which the variation in a single dependent variable is related to the variation in several independent variables. Whereas factor analysis is the appropriate method for ascertaining the *interdependency* among variables, multiple regression is appropriate for discovering *independence–dependence* relationships. The rationale for factor analyzing prior to the regression analysis is to select conflict behavior variables for regression which best index the dimensions and which are relatively independent of one another. For example, one text asserts that, "The more highly the independent variables are interrelated among themselves, the less reliably can the net regression of X_1 upon any of them be determined" (Ezekiel and Fox, 1959: 283–284).

15. The percent of total variance for the dependent variables is calculated by summing down the R^2 column, dividing the result by the number of dependent variables, and multiplying by 100 (Rummel, 1963b: 20 [this volume, Chapter 3]).

16. The range of the multiple R is $\geqslant 0 \leqslant +1.0$. Thus R cannot be negative. In order to see whether the time lag resulted in any negative relationships between domestic and foreign conflict behavior, reference was made to the zero order correlations. None of the negative correlations was greater than $r = -.08$.

17. Although Huntington's hypotheses deal with the relationship between internal and external conflict behavior, he appears to have the international system as the unit of focus rather than the individual nations. In order for the propositions from the 1955–57 and 1958–60 studies to be comparable to Huntington's, one would have to sum each variable across all the nations and then examine the relationship between domestic and foreign conflict behavior at the *system* level. The design of this study, however, uses the *nation* as the unit, and examines the internal and external relationship across each nation.

18. A fatal quarrel is a war in which a nation was involved which resulted in more than 3,163 deaths, e.g., more than $\log_{10}$ (deaths) = 3.5. Richardson contends that there is ambiguity as regards the classification of some forms of fatal quarrels; consequently, he categorizes them in three groups: mainly internal, mixed, and mainly external (1960: 186–187).

REFERENCES

CARROLL, J.B. (1957) "Biquartimin criterion for rotation to oblique simple structure in factor analysis." *Science* 126 (November): 1114–1115.

CATTELL, R. (1960) "The culture patterns discoverable in the syntal dimensions of existing nations." *Journal of Social Psychology* 32: 215–253.

— (1949) "The dimensions of cultural patterns of factorization of national characters." *Journal of Abnormal and Social Psychology* 44: 443–469.

—, et al. (1951) "An attempt at more refined definition of the cultural dimensions of syntality in modern nations." *American Sociological Review* 17: 408–421.

COSER, L.A. (1956) *The Functions of Social Conflict*. New York: Free Press.

ECKSTEIN, H. (1962) "The incidence of internal wars, 1946–59." Appendix I of H. Eckstein, *Internal War: The Problem of Anticipation*. Report submitted to Research Group in Psychology and the Social Sciences, Smithsonian Institution, January 15.

—, Ed. (1964) *Internal War*. New York: Free Press.

EDWARDS, A.L. (1954) "Experiments: their planning and execution." Pp. 259–288 in G. Lindzey, Ed., *Handbook of Social Psychology*. Cambridge: Addison Wesley.

EZEKIEL, M. and K.A. FOX (1959) *Methods of Correlation and Regression Analysis*. New York: John Wiley.

HAAS, E.R. and A.S. WHITING (1956) *Dynamics of International Relations*. New York: McGraw-Hill.

HAGGARD, E.A. (1958) *Intraclass Correlation and the Analysis of Variance*. New York: Dryden Press.

HARMAN, H. (1960) *Modern Factor Analysis*. Chicago: University of Chicago Press.

HUNTINGTON, S.P. (1962) "Patterns of violence in world politics." In S.P. Huntington, Ed., *Changing Patterns of Military Politics*. New York: Free Press.

KAISER, H.F. (1959) "The applications of electronic computers to factor analysis." *Educational and Psychological Measurement* 19: 413–420.

— (1958) "The varimax criterion for analytic rotation in factor analysis." *Psychometrika* 23 (September): 187–200.

KATZ, D. (1953) "Field studies." Pp. 56–97 in H. Festinger and D. Katz, Eds., *Research Methods in the Behavioral Sciences*. New York: Dryden Press.

MCKENNA, J.C. (1962) *Diplomatic Protest in Foreign Policy*. Chicago: Loyola University Press.

RICHARDSON, L.F. (1960) *Statistics of Deadly Quarrels*. Pittsburgh: Boxwood Press.

ROBINSON, E.A. (1959) *An Introduction to Infinitely Many Variates*. New York: Hafner.

ROSECRANCE, R.N. (1963) *Action and Reaction in World Politics*. Boston: Little, Brown.

RUMMEL, R.J. (forthcoming) "Dimensions of international relations in the mid-1950s."

— (1963a) "Testing some possible predictors of conflict behavior within and between nations." *Proceedings of the Peace Research Conference*, November 18–19.

— (1963b) "The dimensions of conflict behavior within and between nations." Pp. 1–50 in *General Systems Yearbook 8*. Reprinted in this volume, Chapter 3.

RUMMEL, R.J., H. GUETZKOW, J. SAWYER and R. TANTER (forthcoming) *Dimensions of Nations*.

SHERIF, M. et al. (1961) *Intergroup Conflict and Cooperation: The Robbers Cave Experiment.* Norman: University of Oklahoma Institute of Group Relations.

SIDMAN, M. (1960) *Tactics of Scientific Research.* New York: Basic Books.

SIMMEL, G. (1955) *Conflict* and *The Web of Intergroup Affiliations.* New York: Free Press.

SNYDER, R. and G. PAIGE (1958) "The United States decision to resist aggression in Korea: the application of an analytical scheme." *Administrative Science Quarterly* 3: 341–378.

SOROKIN, P. (1937) *Social and Cultural Dynamics.* New York: American Books.

WRIGHT, Q. (1951) "The nature of conflict." *Western Political Quarterly* 4 (June): 193–209.

— (1942) *A Study of War.* Chicago: University of Chicago Press.

5 Political Instability in Latin America: The Cross-Cultural Test of a Causal Model

DOUGLAS P. BWY

II. POLITICAL INSTABILITY: DEFINING THE DOMAIN AND SYSTEMATICALLY MEASURING IT

Political instability has meant many things to many researchers, and the primary purpose of this article will not only be to define the concept, but to indicate how political instability might best be systematically measured among the twenty republics of Latin America.

Merle Kling (1956: 21) seems to have summarized at least three of its distinguishing features, when he noted that (i) it is chronic, (ii) that it frequently is accompanied by *limited* violence, and (iii) that it generally produces no basic shifts in economic, social, or political policies. William Stokes (1952: 445) notes further, that "violence seems to be institutionalized in the organization, maintenance, and changing of governments in Latin America." And Kalman Silvert (1961: 20) comments that indeed "... some types of revolutionary disturbances do not indicate instability."[1] "To treat violence and the military coup as aberrations," concludes James Payne (1965: 363), "places one in the awkward position of insisting that practically all significant

---

Author's Note: Acknowledgments are due to the National Science Foundation, which partially supported (GS-789) the research for the paper. Special thanks are also due to Professors R.J. Rummel and Raymond Tanter for the use of their (1955-64) conflict data; to Professor Russell Fitzgibbon for the use of his "democratic attainment" ratings across the 20 Latin American republics for 5 time periods since 1945; to Professor Phillips Cutright for making available his individual data (1940-61) from which he composed the "Political Representativeness Index"; and to Professor George Blanksten for guidance and encouragement.

This is an abridged version, reprinted from the *Latin American Research Review*, Volume III, Number 2 (Spring, 1968) pages 17–66, by permission of the author and the publisher (copyright holder). Section I, pages 17–34 and related footnotes, are omitted, but summarized briefly in Section IV.

political events in the past half century are deviations." That these deviations do not represent basic alterations in the ongoing systems, is a point driven home by George Blanksten (1960: 497) when he observes that "if the term is used precisely, true revolution—a basic change in the political system, a recasting of the social order—is surprisingly infrequent in Latin America. Indeed, revolutions are at least as rare there as anywhere else in the world." Phillips Cutright (1963: 260–261) seems to offer some empirical validation of Blanksten's observations, when he calculates the residuals for a multiple regression equation which predicts to what he terms "political development." Concludes Cutright: "Our common stereotype of Latin American political instability is subject to some re-evaluation when seen from the world perspective. Far from being unstable, the prediction equation suggests that they are not only relatively stable but relatively more developed than comparable nations around the world."[2]

The word "revolution," it has been noted, is generally employed loosely and imprecisely, and this especially so in Latin America. This one word, according to Blanksten (1958: 119) has been used to refer to a number of different types of social and political phenomena. The phenomena, of course, range from the Chilean "revolution" of 1924—when, in the throes of a continuous cycle of cabinet instability (16 fell within a period of 4 years), Arturo Alessandri resigned leaving Chile with no government—to the rather violent removal of Porfirio Díaz, or Jorge Ubico, or Enrique Peñaranda, and the installation of the kinds of socio-economic uprooting which took place in Mexico during 1911 and after, in Guatemala during 1945 and after, and in Bolivia in 1943 and in 1952. "Revolutions" have taken place after the central decision-maker has spent as little as 28 hours in office—as was the case when the Perón revolution, led by a clique of GOU officers, "installed" General Arturo Rawson as president—or as many as 44 years, as in the case of Mexico's Porfirio Díaz, or 28 years in the case of Venezuela's Juan Vicente Gómez. They have been as brutal and bloody as that recently taking place in Cuba, and as peaceful as the kind of "musical chairs" game which is played out year after year in Paraguay. Revolutions have been pulled off by men in support of the governments they overthrew. Venezuelan Colonel Corlos Delgado Chalbaud, for example, was very much in favor of Medina Angarita's policies; the "revolution," however, was called to prevent the apparent "succession" to the presidency of López Contreras, with whom Chalbaud most stoutly disagreed. And, they have even been directed by, of all things, political parties, as when a coalition of parties overthrew Chile's Carlos Ibañez in 1931.

Imposición, candidato único, and *continuismo*, have also been at times referred to as "revolutions." To be sure, these are outwardly peaceful methods of obtaining and maintaining power. But, according to Stokes (1952: 445) "... they rest upon a foundation of force." Merle Kling (1956: 22) further notes that "... obscured by data of these kinds, is the presence of 'concealed instability.'" Revolutions by *continuismo* have a history in many Latin American republics, but perhaps the most consistent is Haiti. The classic example of the practice seems to have been offered by Dr. Francois Duvalier, Haiti's self-proclaimed president-for-life. An excellent example of *candidato único* (single candidate), according to Stokes (1952: 464) was that of General Manuel Odría of Peru, who obtained power by *cuartelazo* (barracks revolt) in October 1948, and then developed his position so strongly that he was able to run for the presidency on July 2, 1950, without opposition. Paraguay, which in a 32-year period went through 22 presidents—21 of them coming to office by an "election" which featured only one candidate, seems to offer the best illustration of a country in which this form of office acquisition has indeed become institutionalized. *Imposición* (in which the candidate is "imposed" on the electorate in a rigged election) was very much of a problem in the latter years of the Mexican Revolution, when a type of "succession crises" accompanied by revolts ensued in Mexico in 1923, 1927, and 1929—since "the candidate of the incumbent regime always wins." But perhaps the clearest illustration of it was when Colonel Carlos Castillo Armas was "elected" by *imposición* in October 1954, following his June revolutionary invasion from Honduras, to rid Guatemala of what he saw as Arbenz's communist-run government.

On occasion, the populace itself acts as an autonomous agent of the "revolution." The few instances in which this exists seem to be, as well, empirical illustrations of the "general will." Describing the capitulation of General Maximiliano Hernández Martínez, who ruled El Salvador from 1931 to 1944, Alberto de Mestas (1950) notes that "the people carried out a general shutdown, private and public offices closed, railroads and busses stopped running. Everything stopped. The government searched for the leaders to capture them and end the revolution. But there were no leaders. The University started it; but, after that, it was all the people spontaneously." More often, however, revolutions are events designated by limited involvement, heavy elite participation, and things of precision and planning. The recent *golpe militar* in Argentina, which saw Arturo Illia's government fall prey to the militarism of General Juan Carlos Onganía, seems to be more the mode of "revolutionary" action. Fulgencio Batista's April 1952 *cuartelazo*, also known as the "*golpe de Madruga*," and the civilian-military coup d'etat which shanghaied Argentina's Arturo Frondizi March 29, 1962, also offer clear examples of this modal pattern.

A resurgence of a very old variety of "revolution" in Latin America appears to be that of guerrilla, or unconventional, warfare. The most dramatic of the recent occurrences, of course, is Fidel Castro's 26th of July Movement against the Batista regime from 1956 to 1959. Examples of guerrilla activities go back to the nineteenth century, and before. An early illustration would be Antonio Conselheiro's guerrilla rebellion against the Brazilian government in the northeastern sectors of the country at the end of the nineteenth century.

More recent examples, though on a less grandiose scale, are the guerrilla activities in Bolivia, Guatemala, and Venezuela.

Perhaps the one clear revelation which emerges from the foregoing discussion is a picture of the rather eclectic nature of governmental instability in Latin America. How, then, is one to pick from such a myriad of possible measures of "extra-legal" aggression, the most meaningful and valid measure? One approach would be to consider the variants of the expression of social conflict one at a time, as they relate separately to different independent or "casual" agents. A rather simple notion would be the proposition hypothesizing a casual relationship existing between (1) modal psycho-social dissatisfaction, a people's concomitant popular expression of such dissatisfaction in a civil revolt, and a resulting abrupt change in government. No such necessary connection need exist between (ii) modal psycho-social dissatisfaction and other abrupt changes in governments, such as a resignation, assassination, or a coup d'etat. There exists, no doubt, a casual connection in the first instance in the full-scale Venezuelan uprising on January 22, 1958, which brought Peréz Jiménez's tearful capitulation; or the now famous *huelga de los brazos caidos* (the strike of the fallen arms) which brought down the Guatemalan dictator-president Jorge Ubico; or Columbia's *bogotazo*—the 1948 explosive "social vomiting" which cost the lives of over 5,000 Bogotá residents within less than a week. On the other hand, one would be hard put to argue a necessary connection between popular social dissatisfaction with Brazil's Jânio Quadros (who was swept into office with a large electoral plurality), and his abrupt resignation in August 1961. Equally difficult to argue would be Argentina's "Children's Revolution" of September 6, 1930, in which the commandant of a military secondary school, José Uriburo, led his cadets, with dummy drill rifles in hand, down the avenida to the *Casa Rosada*, taking it by force.

But, treating the various manifestations of violence separately places one in the burdensome position of creating classification schemes of impossible proportions. The question becomes, how then, to bring some order to this area, while at the same time developing inclusive classifications in a reasonable human-free manner. Of the number of techniques available for isolating clusters of empirically correlated characteristics, Factor Analysis seems to offer the most advantages. The developer of this statistical technique, L. L. Thurstone (1960: 55–56) encouragingly notes that "a factor problem starts with the hope or conviction that a certain domain is not so chaotic as it looks."[3] Basically the analysis takes a large number of *operational indices* (such as demonstrations, riots, *machetismos*, golpes militares, coup d'etats, cuartelazos, and so on) and reduces these to a smaller number of *conceptual variables*, or common factors. Underlying the use of factor analysis is the notion that if we have a number of indices which are intercorrelated, these interrelationships may be due to the presence of one or more underlying factors. By various operations (consisting essentially of matrix inversion) on a matrix of correlation coefficients, one may identify a set of factors which accounts for practically all of the intercorrelations, with a number often substantially smaller than the original set of variables.[4] Regardless of what computation methods are used, the first factors have the property of being statistically independent of each other.[5] Perhaps the most commonly used technique, for determining clusters of underlying relationships from a matrix of correlation coefficients, is the "principal-axes," or "principal-components" method. It was chosen here because it provides a solution in which each factor has extracted the maximum amount of variance[6] and leaves the smallest possible residual variance. In short, the correlation matrix is condensed into the smallest number of orthogonal, or independent, factors by this method.[7]

TABLE I

Correlation Coefficients for Nine Indices of Domestic Violence (1958–60)

	1	2	3	4	5	6	7	8	9
1. Assassinations	1.000								
2. Strikes	—.053	1.000							
3. Guerrilla War	.218	.225	1.000						
4. Gov't Crises	.226	.399	.602	1.000					
5. Purges	.213	.159	.522	.619	1.000				
6. Riots	.181	.275	.154	.070	.299	1.000			
7. Demonstrations	.354	.401	.097	.189	.310	.582	1.000		
8. Revolutions	—.133	.366	.611	.559	.430	.364	.211	1.000	
9. Domestic Killed	.167	.141	.417	.567	.928	.122	.209	.330	1.000

[1] Any politically motivated murder or attempted murder of a high government official or politician.

[2] Any strike of 1,000 or more industrial or service workers that involves more than one employer and that is aimed at national government policies or authority.

[3] Any armed activity, sabotage, or bombings carried on by independent bands or citizens or regular forces aimed at the overthrow of the present regime.

[4] All rapidly developing situations that threaten to bring the downfall of the present regime, excluding situations of revolt aimed at such overthrow.

[5] Systematic elimination by jailing or execution of political opposition within the ranks of the regime or the opposition.

[6] Any violent demonstration or clash of more than 100 citizens, involving the use of physical force.

[7] All peaceful, public gatherings of at least 100 people for the primary purpose of displaying or voicing their opposition to government policies or authority, excluding those demonstrations of a distinctly anti-foreign nature.

[8] Any illegal or forced change in the top government elite; any attempt at such change; or any successful armed rebellion whose aim is independence from the central government.

[9] Deaths resulting directly from violence of an inter-group nature, thus excluding deaths by murder and execution.

A second stage in the factor analysis may be selected, which consists of "rotating" or transforming the set of orthogonal factors into another set (not necessarily independent of each other) which in Thurstone's terms meet the criteria of "simple structure." Its aim is to establish a set of factors which has the property that any given factor will be fairly highly correlated with some of the original indices but uncorrelated with the rest. Each factor can then be identified with one of these clusters of original indices. Once these linear weighted sums (or rotated factors) of the original indices have been obtained, they can be identified and interpreted through the use of factor loadings (that is, by observing the highest correlations between an index and a given factor). In addition, the usefulness and strength of any factor will be determined by the percent of total variance which it explains.

Nine indices were selected[8] to measure different types of domestic aggressive actions against Latin American governments. The definitions of these indicators, and the results from correlating them with each other, appear in Table I, above. Note that although one can begin to get a notion of the clustering effect among these nine indices, the pattern is not entirely obvious. The higher coefficients (those at the .50 and above level) seem to show that guerrilla activity is moderately associated with governmental crises (.60), purges (.52), and revolutions (.61). Governmental crises, as well, seem to be correlated with revolutions (.59) and with the number of persons killed in domestic violence (.56). On the other hand, events of a more sporadic nature, such as demonstrations and riots, seem to correlate among themselves more highly than among the other indices (.58).

In order to determine whether or not the clustering effect among these indices would warrant the use of a smaller set of conceptual variables, the matrix of correlation coefficients in Table I was factor analyzed.[9] To obtain that set of factors maximizing high and low loadings, the extracted factors were then rotated and a new set of factors obtained, which are presented in Table II, below.

TABLE II

ROTATED FACTOR MATRIX

	Factor I	Factor II	Factor III	h^2
1. Number of Assassinations	.202	.291	−.759	.702
2. Number of General Strikes	.213	.580	.476	.609
3. Presence or Absence of Guerilla Warfare	.761	.096	.160	.613
4. Number of Major Governmental Crises	.829	.130	.124	.720
5. Number of Purges	[.878]	.174	−.215	.847
6. Number of Riots	.081	.827	−.025	.691
7. Number of Anti-Government Demonstrations	.113	.865	−.225	.812
8. Number of Revolutions	.606	.321	.547	.770
9. Number of People Killed in Domestic Violence	.849	.029	−.233	.776
Percent of Common Variance	56.8	23.6	19.7	100.0

The values within the table are the correlation coefficients between the original nine indices and the three rotated factors—what were referred to as "factor loadings" previously. By looking at the highest factor loadings, the clustering effects suggested by the correlation matrix are now considerably clarified. The first of the rotated factors, then, is related to five of the indices, namely: guerrilla war, governmental crises, purges, revolutions, and deaths from domestic violence, and unrelated to the rest. The second factor is related to strikes, riots, and demonstrations, but not to the remaining indices. With the exception of two factor loadings with any weight, the third factor appears quite weak in terms of "defining" aggressive activity, and seems to be defined more by high negative loadings, and might, therefore, be interpreted as a "lack of conflict" dimension.[10]

The communalities (h^2) indicate the proportion of variation in each index explained by the three factors. The variance of each coefficient can be computed simply by squaring it, and since the factors are independent of each other, the communality of the index represents nothing more than the sum of these squared coefficients. In terms of the fifth index, for example, the three factors explain over 84 percent of the variance about the occurrence of purges. Furthermore, the three rotated factors explain a very high percentage of the variation in all of the indices.

Before discussing the merits of these findings in terms of substantiating criteria from the conflict literature in Latin America and from other factor solutions of conflict data, a word about the factors themselves. Demonstrations and riots, and to a certain extent, strikes, represent a kind of sporadic, unorganized conflict dimension in Latin America. To Almond and Coleman (1960: 34) "spontaneous breakthroughs into the political system, such as riots and demonstrations" were conceptualized as interest articulation by Anomic Groups. To use their name for such a cluster, Factor 2 reflects the degree of *Anomic violence* among the nation-units. The first factor, on the other hand, displays high loadings on guerrilla warfare, revolutions, governmental crises, and deaths from domestic violence—most of which seem to represent illustrations of aggressive actions defined more by an underlying organization and planning. This dimension, therefore, appears to be referencing an *Organized violence* factor, and will be identified as such. The last index (deaths from domestic group violence), in associating more strongly with Organized violence, indicates that this dimension (at the nation-unit level of analysis) is by far the more violent.

In comparing the results here to other factor analytic studies of domestic conflict, one has a host of publications from which to choose. Since, however, the data from which the specific matrix of correlation coefficients were derived in Table I came from the study conducted by Raymond Tanter, it seems more appropriate that the regional results for Latin America be contrasted to those derived from the study of the universe of independent nations for the same time period.

Upon orthogonally rotating his factors for the 1958–60 conflict data, Tanter discovered two dimensions emerged,[11] the first of which he called a "turmoil" dimension, and which consisted of: demonstrations, riots, strikes, governmental crises, and assassinations. Notice that this dimension favorably compares with that extracted for the Latin American data, with the exception that in Latin America assassinations do not load heavily on any of the factors and the additional fact that governmental crises load on the first factor and not the second. The second orthogonally rotated factor which emerged from Tanter's study clustered such activities as: revolutions, domestic killed, guerrilla war, and purges. Once again, with the exception of the appearance of governmental crises among the first rotated factor extracted for the Latin American data, the comparison between the two is most favorable.

Now that we have a better idea of the strength of the empirical determination of domestic conflict into two domains of violence—one an Organized component, and the other an Anomic component—can we find any such "validation" among the more subjective literature on typologies? Two analysts have described typologies which correspond quite closely to the factor solution presented in Table II. The first, a general comparative political scientist and long-time student of domestic conflict, Harry Eckstein (1962: 104) sees emerging from these schemes:

> ... a sort of composite typology, distinguishing between relatively unorganized and spontaneous riots by crowds with low capabilities for violence and modest aims, coups d'etat by members of the elite against other members of the elite, full-scale political revolutions to achieve important constitutional changes, social revolutions to achieve large-scale socio-economic as well as constitutional changes, and wars of independence to achieve sovereignty in a previously dependent territory.

Without doing too much injustice to Eckstein, it seems fair to conclude that he views "internal wars" in two basic parts: (i) a disorganized, spontaneous component, and (ii) a component defined by underlying organization, with longer-term goals in mind, whether these involve insurrections aimed at socio-economic changes within the system or attempts to free oneself from foreign domination. Notice how these two phenomena emerged from the empirically derived factors, listed in Table II. Demonstrations, riots, and strikes (in that order) define the spontaneous component. All of these appear to be, in Eckstein's terms, measuring unorganized instabilities with low capacity for violence and with modest aims. Factor I, on the other hand, represents the empirical counterpart to Eckstein's second basic component. At this juncture, note how the variable weightings (see note 16)—established on the basis of the factor solution presented in Table II—emphasize the planned nature of this continuum: guerrilla wars = .65, governmental crises = .57, revolutions = .31, and domestic killed (the variable with the least theoretical ties to planned violence) only receives an empirical weighting of .0008.

The second analyst, a political scientist and long-time student of Latin American political processes, Kalman Silvert (1961) in discussing types of revolutions and their incidence, notes two "families" of violence. The first was categorized by: the simple and the complicated barracks revolt, the peasant revolt, the regional revolt, the civilian political revolt, and the social revolution. All appear to be phenomena defined by an underlying organization.[12] Within Silvert's second "family" of violence (isolated under the heading of "unstructured violence") were: the street riots or *manifestaciones* (which Silvert sees more as anti-government demonstrations[13]) and *Bogotazos* (which in terms of the variables used in the present analysis, would find their counterpart in the category of riots). By further denoting these occurrences to be "undirected"—a kind of "social vomiting," as he puts it—Silvert's classification very closely approximates the empirical resolution of the conflict domain which emerges as Factor 2 in Table II.

In addition to the substantive discovery of the two basic dimensions of conflict in Latin America, the factors themselves may be used as criteria for the construction of indices of Organized and Anomic violence. The factor solution, therefore, goes beyond just providing an empirical assessment of the clusterings of original indices on basic underlying variables. Through factor loadings, it allows the analyst to "weight" each of the variables composing the index. The indices of Organized and Anomic conflict, therefore, can be weighted according to their loadings, or correlations, with the Organized violence factor, and then with the Anomic violence factor. In this manner, the resulting indices are in effect weighted according to the strength of their intercorrelations with the other indices, rather than arbitrarily. And since the new indices are based on orthogonal factors, they too remain independent.[14]

Four of the original nine indicators of domestic conflict behavior were used to form an index of the first, or Organized violence, factor. Although the variable "the number of purges," came out on this dimension, the decision was made to exclude it from the index on the basis that such occurrences represent more a governmental activity—often, for example, a governmental response to aggressive activity on the part of the populace—and therefore should not appear among variables ultimately destined for the dependent side of the model.[15] From the preceding review of the literature, then, it is not an unwarranted assumption that guerrilla warfare, governmental crises, revolutions, and people killed in domestic group violence, are best measuring in combination Organized violence. And likewise, that strikes, riots, and demonstrations are measuring Anomic violence best in combination. In discussing the construction of indices of this type, Hagood and Price noted that it has been demonstrated that if we wish to use these items to form an index of each factor, we should weight the items (in standard score form) in proportion to their correlations with each factor. (See Wilks, 1938: 24–43.) The items, then, most highly correlated with Organized violence should receive the higher weights on this index, and those more highly correlated with

Anomic violence should receive the higher weights on this index. With these criteria in mind, a formula for computation of the two basic indices to be used in this study was followed, and is footnoted below. It appears first in basic form, using the Anomic Violence Index as an example, and then in converted form for both the Organized as well as the Anomic Violence Index.[16]

Indices were calculated for the 20 Latin American republics for the three time periods for which data were available: 1955–57 (3 years) (Rummel, 1963 [reprinted in this volume, Chapter 3]), 1958–60 (3 years) (Tanter, 1964: 71–74, Appendix II), and 1962–64 (2 years) (Rummel, 1965: iii–viii). Since these indices, as computed, did not allow comparisons across the three time periods (the last period resulting from a coding of conflict only for a two-year period), and since the value for any one country on any index told nothing about its position in relation to the other Latin American republics, the indices were standardized. These standard, or z-scores, appear in Table III, below.

Both the Organized and Anomic violence indices appear to be accurate reflections of historical developments, which can be briefly illustrated by the 1958–60 data. The rather high *negative* z-score of −.525 for the Dominican Republic, for example, seems to correspond to theoretical notions which point

TABLE III

z-SCORES OF ORGANIZED AND ANOMIC VIOLENCE ACROSS THREE TIME PERIODS

	1955–57 Organized	1955–57 Anomic	1958–60 Organized	1958–60 Anomic	1962–64 Organized	1962–64 Anomic
Argentina	+3.832	+2.664	+ .934	+1.455	+1.585	+ .212
Bolivia	− .167	− .472	+ .542	− .405	− .119	+ .309
Brazil	+ .539	− .381	−1.027	− .405	+ .884	+2.713
Chile	− .021	− .218	− .919	− .538	− .711	+ .021
Colombia	+ .140	+ .582	+ .251	− .672	+2.192	+1.236
Costa Rica	− .113	− .716	− .886	−1.072	− .998	− .874
Cuba	+ .708	+2.559	+2.994	+ .731	+2.046	− .139
Dominican Republic	− .685	− .716	+ .320	− .525	− .034	+1.745
Ecuador	− .500	− .333	− .904	+ .262	− .197	+1.171
El Salvador	− .685	− .716	− .784	− .605	− .998	− .874
Guatemala	+ .357	+ .705	− .122	+ .022	− .404	− .874
Haiti	+ .741	+1.065	+ .419	− .378	+ .453	− .874
Honduras	− .115	− .520	− .053	− .912	− .328	− .874
Mexico	− .672	− .569	−1.158	+2.533	− .990	− .139
Nicaragua	− .685	− .528	+ .482	− .725	− .996	− .683
Panama	− .685	− .618	− .477	+ .277	− .998	− .683
Paraguay	− .128	− .667	+ .457	+ .170	− .415	− .874
Peru	− .501	− .308	− .292	− .525	+ .629	+ .468
Uruguay	− .685	− .716	−1.167	− .965	− .998	− .874
Venezuela	− .675	− .096	+1.391	+2.278	+ .395	− .109

to the tight association between a central decision-maker's total control, and the occurrence of Anomic violence. Through one of the grandest schemes of kinship and elite patronage, Trujillo managed to sustain his reign over his half of Hispañola for thirty years, the second longest dictatorship in the history of the Americas since independence. Rambo (1964: 175) observes, for example, that "an understanding of the magnitude of official terrorism under Trujillo is necessary to the understanding of the political apathy [what the Anomic Violence Index would be picking up as a lack of strikes, demonstrations, or riots] exhibited by most Dominicans." In short, for this period we would expect (as the Index reflects) very little in the way of anomic breakthroughs; while quite the contrary might be predicted with the demise of such a system, as is reflected by the Index of the following time period (Trujillo was assassinated in 1961), which jumps to +1.745.

Certainly in terms of the country whose z-score remains close to that for the Dominican Republic, and which can likewise be "explained" in terms of high penalties for the expression of Anomic-type acts, would be Haiti. Under Duvalier (1957 to the present), Haiti began to take on similar totalitarian qualities (1958–60 Anomic Violence Index: —.378), until today it is as much of a totalitarian state as the underdeveloped technology at Duvalier's disposal makes possible (Anomic Index: —.874).

Bolivia, although sustaining low instances of Anomic violence (with a z-score value of —.405), probably did so during the 1958–60 time period for entirely different reasons than did Haiti or the Dominican Republic. The years following the National Revolution (April, 1952) saw the total incorporation of the Indians into full citizenship status, granting them the vote, land, and arms. The major tin mines were nationalized. Land was redistributed on a grand scale, which has since prompted observers to note that "whatever the economic results of agrarian reform, its political impact has been highly significant. It has been largely responsible for the fact that the Indians have been overwhelmingly in favor of the Revolutionary regime, and upon various occasions when it has been threatened have rallied to its defense. The result has been that Bolivia since 1952 has enjoyed the most stable government in a very long time, one the of most stable in the hemisphere." Things, of course, changed considerably since Alexander (1964: 329) commented in this way, and the Anomic Violence Index, once again, clearly reflects the shift. Anomic Violence Indices for Bolivia during the 1955–57 time period are low (—.472), as they are during the 1958–60 time period (—.405), but take a .714 shift toward the direction of increased Anomic violence (to +.309) during the 1962–64 time period. In December 1964, following a series of strikes, demonstrations, and riots, Victor Paz Estenssoro was overthrown and a military government under the direction of Air Force General René Barrientos was established. The Index reflects these qualitative changes.

Just as fear of punishment inhibits aggressive actions (Dominican Republic, Haiti), then, so also can relative systemic satisfactions. System access (as illustrated by Bolivia) may very well be a negative correlate of anomic breakthroughs. Such a mechanism points to a rather nice "explanation" for the high negative scores, and therefore the low level of Anomic violence taking place in either Costa Rica or Uruguay, which sit at the extreme ends of the scale. Three of these countries—Uruguay, Costa Rica, and Chile— have been known to rate low on both Anomic as well as Organized violence, and their negative z-scores for these values across the three time periods (in Table III) validate these conclusions.

III. TESTING THE CAUSAL MODEL

The linkages between the three independent variables and each of the dependent variables of Anomic and Organized violence will be tested through the use of zero-order correlational analysis. In addition, whenever the strengths of the coefficients warrant it, the scatter plots will be presented, thereby allowing us to identify the exact position of any of the twenty republics in comparison to any of the others. But high correlations between phenomena do not give conclusive evidence about causation. Such evidence is more closely approximated from the results of the systematic application of "cross-lagged panel correlations." This design model is based on the premise that the "effect" should correlate higher with a prior "cause" than with subsequent "cause," i.e., $r_{C_1 E_2} > r_{C_2 E_1}$ (Campbell and Stanley, 1963:239). Campbell (1963) and others have used this design in an effort to discover causation by noticing the direction of the temporal lag which maximizes the correlation.[17] The coefficients calculated for a number of different operationalizations of the variable "legitimacy," and presented in Table IV,[18] below, offer empirical evidence of the validity of the direction of the relationship postulated in the earlier theoretical discussion of the model. In illustration, the 1955 Fitzgibbon rating of system "openness" correlates $-.504$ with the occurrence of Organized violence in 1958–60. That is, as the openness (or legitimacy) of the system (in 1955) goes up, instances of Organized violence go down. Ratings of system "openness" in 1960, however, have little or no relationship (.14) to organized violence taking place four to five years earlier. Summarizing these findings according to the causal model, we have: $-.51_{c_1 E_2} > .14_{c_2 E_1}$.

With reasonable assurance that the correct time sequence had indeed been specified among the variables in the model, each of the explanatory variables was correlated with each of the effect variables. The first of these appears in a scatter plot (Figure 1) of the relationship between Satisfaction and Organized violence, where Satisfaction is measured by the Annual Growth of GNP per capita.

The association between satisfaction and Organized violence clearly emerges as both linear and negative ($-.63$) in the scatter plot displayed in Figure 2. Satisfaction doesn't, however, appear to yield the same strong inverse relationship when correlated with Anomic violence. Here the coefficient drops to $-.33$. As a check on these findings, a separate correlation was

TABLE IV

Legitimacy	1955-57 Organized Violence (Z-scored)	1955-57 Anomic Violence (Z-scored)	1958-60 Organized Violence (Z-scored)	1958-60 Anomic Violence (Z-scored)	1962-64 Organized Violence (Z-scored)	1962-64 Anomic Violence (Z-scored)
Change in PRI (1955-1950)	—.245	—.442	—.453	—.219	—.615	—.213
Change in PRI (1960-1955)	.111	.003	.073	—.074	.385	.190
Change in FITZ (1955-1950)			—.714	—.138		
Change in FITZ (1960-1955)	.230	.176				
Fitzgibbon Index (1955)			—.504	—.065		
Fitzgibbon Index (1960)	.114	.004				
LEGITIMACY (1955)[a]			—.384	—.041		
LEGITIMACY (1960)[b]	.085	—.067				

[a] 1950+1955 Fitzgibbon ratings.
[b] 1960+1965 Fitzgibbon ratings.

run between another index of satisfaction (the Per Cent of the Central Government's Expenditures on Public Health and Welfare in 1958) and Organized violence, which yielded a negative correlation of —.51. Here too, the coefficient between Anomic violence and governmental inputs into public welfare seems to be somewhat lower: —.30. From Figure 1, note the apparent explanatory power the change concept of increase or decrease in GNP per capita has over its static counterpart. For example, although Argentina was still the country with the third highest GNP per capita in 1957, this seems of little consequence in explaining the high incidence of planned violence during this time period. Over the years prior to the violence (recorded in Figure 1[19]), it seems particularly significant to note that Argentinians were steadily getting smaller shares than they had before, of the total goods and services produced by their economy.

It is of special significance that *both* the Organized and Anomic violence measures do yield negative relationships when correlated with the variable "change in GNP per capita." And, although satisfaction has a stronger impact on Organized than on Anomic violence, violence in general goes down as satisfaction goes up.

The form of the relationship between "force" and "aggressive acts against government" was specified as curvilinear. Given the continuing problem of "militarism" in Latin America, however, "force" (as measured by "expenditures on defense," "number of military personnel as a percentage of the population," and so on) cannot be analyzed in the role of inhibiting aggression, simply because the inhibiting agent itself may, and often does, aggress against the government. In short, no independence can be maintained between the present operationalizations at the nation-unit level. Certainly the military often contributes to "governmental crises" (rapidly developing situations that threaten to bring the downfall of the regime) as well as to "revolutions" (extra-legal or forced change in the top government elite, or any successful armed rebellion whose aim is independence from the central government). Such contributions are being picked up by the Organized violence dimension (in Table II), and are often witnessed in the form of golpes

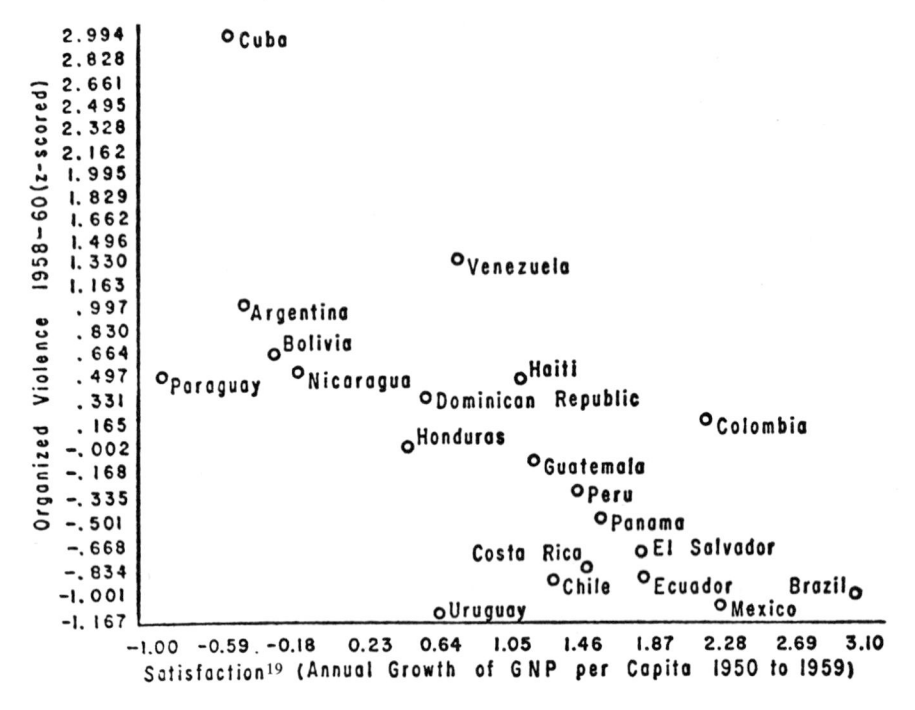

FIGURE 1

SATISFACTION AND ORGANIZED VIOLENCE

militares, military coups, cuartelazos, and so on. To be sure, in some cases the opposition, usually being without the necessary tools for toppling a government, goads the military into performing this function. This technique was used by the mid-leftist, Belaúnde, who when a three-way tie emerged in 1962 Peruvian elections (with no one getting the necessary 33 percent of the vote), called fraud. He demanded a "tribunal of honor" to recount the vote, and if he didn't get it, threatened to overthrow the government. The Army stepped in and annulled the elections. As an indication of the kind of impartial role the Peruvian military plays in these circumstances, just before this they deposed conservative Manuel Prado. The point to be made, therefore, is that no adequate test of the relationship between "force" and "violence" (as generally conceived and when measured at the nation-unit level) can be made. On the other hand, this does not appear to be the case when Anomic violence is being considered. Here the population can be reasonably sure that the military force will most likely be brought to bear on anomic breakthroughs, regardless of their origin. As an illustration, the same military establishment which carried out the two golpes discussed above is credited by Payne, who notes: ". . . when *demonstrations* and *riots* reach excessive proportions, it is the Army which contains and disperses the mobs" (Payne, 1965: 369. Italics added).

As hypothesized, the scatter diagram displayed as Figure 2, below, reveals the rather strong curvilinear relationship which emerges from an association of Force with Anomic Violence. Countries which input high levels of force (and it might be added, most of those on the right side of this continuum consistently do so) are: the Dominican Republic (in this 1958-60 time period, still under the rule of Trujillo), Haiti (under Duvalier), and Paraguay (under Stroessner). These same countries maintained low levels of Anomic violence during the same time period. Peru is not normally thought of as falling within the same category as the nations just mentioned—and to be sure, if any long-term analysis were being displayed, Peru would undoubtedly move toward the middle of the Force continuum. During the years in question, however, it should be recalled that Peru was ruled by a most conservative member of the "Forty-family" elite, General Manuel Prado.[20]

At the other end of the continuum, such countries as Costa Rica, Uruguay, and Chile consistently maintain open systems, and during the years in question, force inputs also continued to be minimal. The Army in Bolivia, following the 1952 National Revolution, was abolished. The period in question in Figure 2[21] saw it reorganized, but along very reduced as well as achievement-oriented lines (many Indians, for example, were recruited into its ranks). Although Nicaragua, El Salvador, and Honduras seem to be strange bedfellows for this end of the Force continuum, the "force index" is plotting them accurately in terms of defense expenditures.

It is clear from the plot, that it is the middle-range internal force countries which are the ones experiencing most of the anomic breakthroughs. Mexico, in many respects, is a very explainable deviant case. During the end of the Ruiz Cortines and beginning of the López Mateos administrations, Mexico was fraught with demonstrations, strikes, and riots, not at all typical of other periods, which tended to be more negative than not on Anomic violence (see Table III). These data are suggestive of the fact that Mexico (like Costa Rica, Uruguay, and the other "open" systems) does not counter anomic breakthroughs with only force. Venezuela, Argentina, Ecuador, Cuba, Panama, and Guatemala, however, appear to have also sustained high amounts of anomic violence; and, as hypothesized, lie toward the center of the Force continuum. The case of Cuba offers what seems to be the perfectly ambivalent situation:[22] with Batista's efforts at force being countered by guerrilla efforts, the perceptions of force would indeed be anything but clear. To be sure, a more sensitive interpretation of defense figures for this period, would be to assume that defense allocations were more a function of the amount of Organized violence being waged by Castro guerrillas. For the same period, the z-score for Cuba's Organized Violence Index was $+2.994$ (against the Anomic violence z-score of $+.731$ presently under consideration).

```
                    oMexico
                                    oVenezuela


                                         oArgentina


                        oCuba

                         oPanama          oEcuador
                                            oParaguay
                    oGuatemala

                 oBolivia     oChile    oBrazil    oHaiti
             Nicaragua  oEl Salvador                     oPeru
                     oColombia         Dominican Republico
               Uruguayo  oHonduras
             oCosta Rica
```

Anomic Violence 1958-60 (z-scored) vs. Force[21] (Expenditure on Defense as a Percentage of GNP, 1959-60)

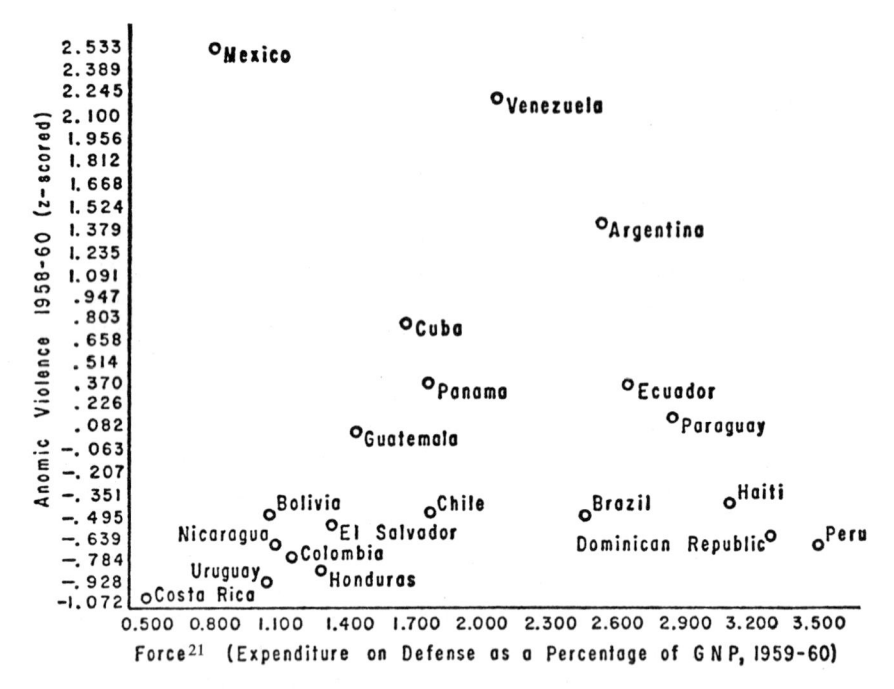

FIGURE 2

THE CURVILINEAR RELATIONSHIP BETWEEN FORCE AND ANOMIC VIOLENCE

The most evident manifestations of Anomic violence, of course, are Venezuela and Argentina. As was noted in the earlier discussion of Venezuela's z-score, the population has tended to remain relatively uninvolved and apathetic (which would appear to account for the middle-range input into defense), and that with the overthrow of Pérez Jiménez in 1958, the ensuing years were particularly volatile. Although Juan Perón was ousted from Argentina in 1955, it seems a reasonable assumption that the Frondizi government (whose position with respect to the Peronistas was at times unclear) internal force capability was not sufficient to contain the anomic breakthroughs which occurred throughout succeeding years.

When the same Force data (Expenditure on Defense as a Percentage of GNP) was plotted against Organized violence for the same 1958–60 time period, as hypothesized, no relationship emerged, and the data points distributed themselves randomly about the plot area. Organized violence was, however, hypothesized to be both linear and positive, when related to Force in an inverted time sequence; in other words, when Organized violence was the independent variable. Simply stated, high incidences of planned violence should bring about comparable inputs of force on the part of the government. When the 1958–60 Organized violence data was correlated with a *change*-in-defense measure[23] from 1958 to 1963, the correlation coefficient was +.416; the same calculations for Anomic violence yielded a coefficient of .005, indicating no relationship.

Political Legitimacy was conceived in both static as well as dynamic terms. Although several measures were selected to represent this concept, the "weighted" Fitzgibbon ratings were used in the scatter plot for Figure 3,[24] below. When a change in Legitimacy (from 1950 to 1955) was correlated with Organized violence taking place in the following three years, the form of the relationship was discovered to be linear, and the strength of the Pearson coefficient was a high, negative −.71. The same negative, linear relationship emerged from a cross tabulation of the static Fitzgibbon ratings for the 20 republics in 1955 with the same Organized violence data for 1958–60.[25]

While high, negative associations emerged from the relationship between measures of Legitimacy and Organized violence, no such negative associations were discovered among these measures and Anomic Violence. Furthermore, these findings do not seem to be a function of the 1958–60 conflict data represented in the plot in Figure 3. Reference to Table IV will reveal that, with but one exception, all measures of Legitimacy (PRI as well as Fitzgibbon; static as well as dynamic) show little or no association with Anomic violence. The impact of such a finding is obvious. Aggressive activities defined more by an underlying planning and organization (such as guerrilla activities—those most heavily emphasized by the Organized Violence Index[26]) appear to be challenging the legitimacy of the political system; whereas no such challenges exist among aggressive activities of an anomic nature (such as demonstrations, strikes, and riots). To be sure, anomic breakthroughs may be more an indication of "political development," than not. The fact that no strong *negative* associations were found between Legitimacy and Anomic violence seems highly suggestive of Lipset's (1959: 92) remark that: "... the existence of a moderate state of conflict [and it would be reasonable to interpret his reference to "conflict" as including such things as demonstrations, strikes, and riots] is an inherent aspect of a legitimate democratic system, and is in fact another way of defining it. ..."

The same negative, linear relationship emerged when Organized violence was correlated with the static Fitzgibbon ratings for 1955. In fact, with but few exceptions, the countries which were high on Legitimacy in 1955 (Uruguay, Mexico, Costa Rica, Chile, and Brazil) tended to be the same countries increasing on Legitimacy from 1950 to 1955 (see Figure 3). In both instances, they fell at the negative end of the Organized violence axis. This finding seems also to hold for nations on the low end of the Legitimacy continuum; and it was Cuba, Venezuela, Argentina, Nicaragua, Paraguay, and Guatemala in 1955 which also made the lowest gains in Legitimacy from 1950 to 1955. These were the countries plagued with the largest amounts of Organized violence during 1958 to 1960. With respect to Cuba, the country experiencing the

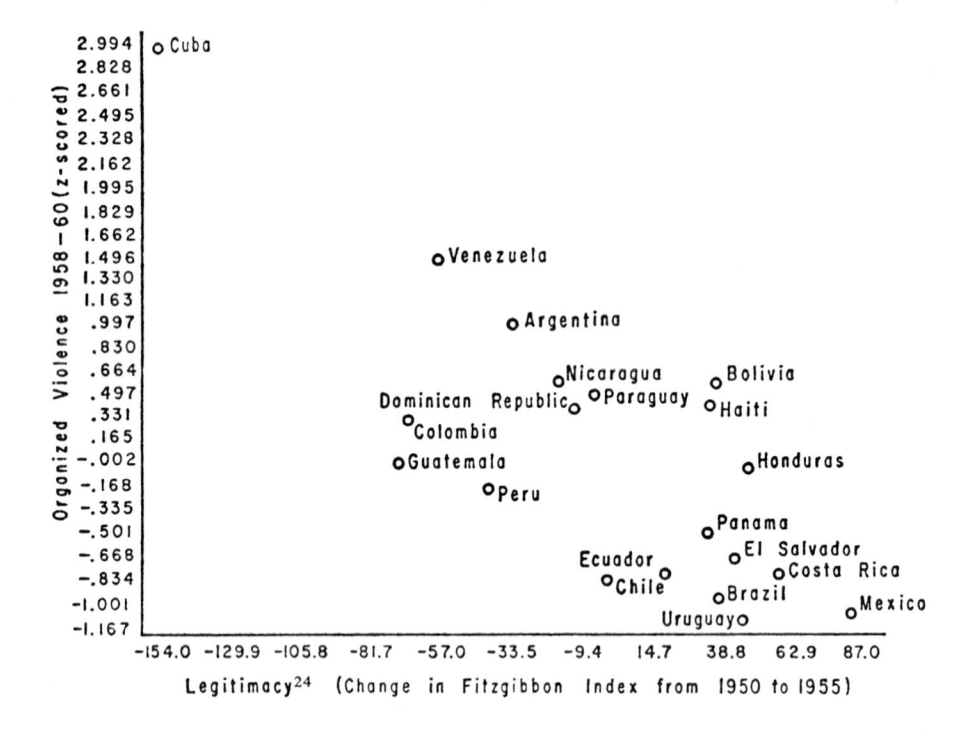

FIGURE 3

THE NEGATIVE LINEAR RELATIONSHIP BETWEEN LEGITIMACY AND ORGANIZED VIOLENCE

highest Organized violence, the Legitimacy measure cannot be considered deviant. Ratings for the change measure took place in 1950 and 1955. As has been pointed out, Fidel Castro's revolutionary invasion didn't take place until 1956 (the attack on the Moncada barracks, however, did take place in 1953). In the case of the latter, it should be remembered that it wasn't until after the consummation of the revolution, that this "symbolic" gesture of defiance gained in stature. While one must always be wary of subjectivity in judgmental codings such as those involved in the Fitzgibbon Index, it seems clear that the high rating of "illegitimacy" fell to Batista's last regime (1952–58), rather than to Castro's.

IV. SUMMARY AND CONCLUSIONS

In pointing to the preconditions of political instability, both in Latin America and elsewhere, much of the recent theory and research on domestic conflict appears to have concentrated on three basic independent variables: (i) systemic discontent, (ii) political legitimacy, and (iii) anticipated retribution (Section I).

But if it is generally agreed that these "causal" variables may lead to the presence or absence of political instability, there is no such agreement on the type of political instability they may bring about. Indeed, since it is quite conceivable that different styles of violent activity may each have its own set of correlates, the decision as to how political instability is conceived and operationalized becomes crucial. In Section II ("Political Instability: Defining the Domain and Systematically Measuring It"), the many individual types of domestic conflict were discussed. Treating each of these various types of political aggression separately, however, places one in the burdensome position of creating classification schemes of impossible proportions. While the Rummel-Tanter data operationally reduced the Latin American conflict domain to a series of basic indices (assassinations, strikes, guerrilla warfare, governmental crises, purges, riots, anti-government demonstrations, revolutions, and the number of people killed in domestic group violence), it still left us essentially with nine dependent variables. The statistical technique of Factor Analysis provided the means for reducing these nine operational indices to a smaller set of conceptual variables. The results of the factor analysis revealed (i) that political instability in Latin America is highly structured in terms of independent clusters of activities, and (ii) reduces to two basic dimensions of conflict behavior, (iii) a non-organized (or disorganized), spontaneous, or Anomic factor (indexed by such things as riots, strikes, and demonstrations), which is independent of (iv) an Organized factor (indexing, among other things, guerrilla warfare, governmental crises, revolutions, armed rebellions), defined more by an underlying planning and organization.

Factor scores, the value each nation has on each of the two basic conflict dimensions, were computed by taking each country's individual conflict score (in standard score form) and weighting it by the factor loadings participating on each of the conflict dimensions (Table II). Upon standardizing these, six distributions of Anomic and Organized violence scores for the twenty Latin American republics were available across three separate time periods (Table III). By placing each of the three independent or "causal" variables (systemic discontent, political legitimacy, and anticipated retribution) in the proper time sequence, separate tests of their impact on each of the two dependent or "effect" variables (Anomic and Organized violence) were made, and the following general conclusions emerged:

1. Systemic Satisfaction (as measured by *change* in gross national product

per capita) is negatively associated with political instability. Both the theoretical orientation and empirical findings discussed in the opening section of the paper suggested that societies past a "traditional-transitional threshold" should experience a decrease in domestic conflict as they experience an increase in wealth. This was decidedly the case with respect to Latin America, and the finding does not appear to be a function of the measures used. When Satisfaction was operationalized differently (i.e., the percent of the central government's expenditure on public health and welfare), the same negative, linear association emerged. When the dimensions of political instability were controlled for, however, the stronger correlate of discontent was discovered to be Organized violence activity (see Figure 1).

2. The form of the relationship between the inhibition of political aggression through the use of force, was specified to be curvilinear. Under this model, the application of both extreme amounts of force (e.g., restrictive systems), as well as little or no force (permissive systems), was predicted to yield similar results—low levels of political instability. Intermediate levels of force, on the other hand, neither sufficient to inhibit political aggression and in many cases acting as an additional frustration, would be accompanied by high levels of political instability. Arguing from the premise that (military) force can almost always be counted on to disperse demonstrations and riots of serious proportions (that is, support of this nature is given, often irrespective of the loyalty of such force to the regime in power), a test of the inhibitive effects of the use of Force (as measured by expenditures on defense as a percent of gross national product) on Anomic violence revealed that the curvilinear model does indeed apply to Latin America (see Figure 2).

Correlating the same Force data with Organized violence, on the other hand, yielded no association. Two suggestive interpretations can be offered. The first involves two critical conditions not met by these data: (i) independence between the measures of Force (military expenditures) and the measures of Organized violence (primarily the variable "revolutions," which may involve military coups) cannot be maintained, and (ii) the allegiance of the forces (a condition of their impact as inhibitors of political aggression) has not been measured. The first conclusion, therefore, would be that no reasonable interpretation can be given to the correlation (in this case, lack of correlation) between Force and Organized violence. If it can be assumed that the contamination is negligible and that the punitive forces are generally allegiant, however, the lack of relationship between the extent of Force and Organized violence would lead to conclusions that guerrilla warfare, terrorism, and sabotage (the highest loading variables in the Organized violence factor score formula), as well as armed rebellions, occur and continue irrespective of the extent and quality of governmental force. That is, they may break out just as readily among militarily strong as militarily weak regimes; and they may continue in the face of what would appear to be overwhelmingly adverse inhibiting power. Knowing the Force level, then, doesn't appear to help in explaining the occurrence of Organized violent activity, but it is decidedly a factor in understanding the strength and form of Anomic violence.

3. Political legitimacy was conceived of as the amount of positive affect toward the political system (and the government) held by the populace. It was recognized that (i) feelings of allegiance can and are ascribed to non-competitive (unitary, hierarchically organized) as well as competitive (polyarchic, participant) structures, (ii) that such feelings are the products of, among other things, "politicization," or socialization over time, and (iii) that while feelings of legitimacy toward a political system can be separated analytically from those feelings developed as a result of the system's ability in satisfying demands, the two are most likely closely interrelated sub-systems of phenomena. It was equally clear, however, that people like political systems (legitimacy) not only because "this is the way it has always been" (traditional legitimacy), and because of gratifications received from the system, but also because they had a hand in making it the way it is. In short, the ability to participate in a system leads directly to the building of positive affect toward it. While this mechanism is not at work in all political systems (there is evidence, for example, to indicate that it may not function at all in semi-authoritarian structures—which may lead to serious reservations about applying it to some of the Latin American nations), Almond and Verba (1963) did find that participation led to positive affect in Mexico, Great Britain, and the United States.

On the assumption that systems moving toward higher "democratic attainment" over time would be providing greater opportunities to participate, legitimacy was operationalized as the amount of change from one period to the next measured by the Fitzgibbon Index (see Figure 3). In this, and the many other operationalizations of the concept (see Table IV), legitimacy proved to be the strong negative correlate of Organized violence. In all cases, as political legitimacy decreased Organized violence increased. When the effect of political legitimacy on Anomic violence was tested, however, in every case, the association was proved to be very weak or non-existent. That is, systems that were high on political legitimacy were just as likely to experience Anomic activity as those which were low on political legitimacy. Once again, by referring to the formulas for the computation of the factor scores used to distribute nations on Organized violence, one can see that activities such as guerrilla warfare, terrorism, sabotage, armed rebellion, and so on, break out in far greater proportions at times of low political legitimacy (e.g., when the Fitzgibbon index of "democratic attainment" is negative—lower at t_2 than it was at t_1). In short (if we can dismiss the pitfalls of ecological correlations for the moment), the participants in Organized violent activity seem to be challenging the legitimacy of the political systems involved, while no such connection can be drawn from the roles of participants in Anomic violence.

In summary, then, what can be said of these two styles of political instability in Latin America? Anomic violence finds its strongest correlate (curvilinear) in forces of retribution. When force (punishment) is both very permissive as well as very restrictive, Anomic violence is negligible. Punishment in the mid-levels of intensity (apparently acting as a frustrator) elicits high levels of Anomic violence. Positive effect, or the amount of legitimacy ascribed to a political system, however, cannot be used in any way to determine the occurrence and intensity of riots, strikes, and demonstrations—they break out just as frequently in highly legitimate as poorly legitimate systems. Systemic discontent, on the other hand, is linearly correlated to the outbreak of Anomic violence, but at a much lower level than with Organized violence. When systemic dissatisfaction is measured in terms of negative or positive changes in per capita gross national product, one can more accurately predict the occurrence of (i) guerrilla warfare, governmental crises, and armed rebellions, than (ii) riots and demonstrations. Guerrilla insurrections and armed rebellions, on the other hand, cannot be predicted on the basis of knowing the amount of punishment (force) the government might be able to apply—that is, Organized violent activity that breaks out in Latin America at the system-level appears to have little or nothing to do with the fear of retribution for such action. It does, however, appear to be strongly related to the open or closed nature of the system, and if systems are slipping into more closed patterns (i.e., losing Fitzgibbon points on "democratic attainment"), the mechanism of participation feeding positive affect closes off this avenue of legitimacy formations. And, as legitimacy formations decrease, Organized violent activity can be observed to increase in a strong, linear pattern.

NOTES

1. "If the normal way of life of rotating the executive in a given country is by revolution," continues Silvert, "and if there have been a hundred such changes in a century, then it is not being facetious to remark that revolutions are a sign of stability—that events are marching along as they always have." See Silvert (1961: 20).

2. Cutright (1963: 260-261). The basis for Cutright's jump from notions of political development to those of instability is not precisely clear. This is especially true when one realizes that his measure of political development consists of a rating across all countries in terms of the quality of (i) minority party representation within the legislative body, and (ii) nations ruled by chief executives elected in open and competitive election. While such things *may be* the negative correlate of "political instability"—as we have suggested in Section I, "Psycho-Social Dissatisfaction," which *re-interprets* both the Cutright and Lipset work—such interpretations can only be made after the linkages between "competition for equal power sharing" ("democracy") and political stability or instability are "established," and then only with extreme caution.

3. Thurston further notes that "the exploratory nature of factor analysis is often not understood. Factor analysis has its principal usefulness at the border line of science. It is naturally superseded by rational formulations in terms of the science involved. Factor analysis is useful, especially in those domains where basic and fruitful concepts are essentially lacking and where crucial experiments have been difficult to conceive."

4. The underlying assumptions involved in the use of factor analysis are (i) the

variables used in the analysis are linear, (ii) the data for each observation are assumed to be of equal importance and are thus given equal weight (in terms of the present study, therefore, the number of demonstrations in the Dominican Republic are considered equally important as those occurring in Argentina), and (iii) the assumption that the data are distributed normally. Since the Pearson Product Moment Correlation Coefficient is used as input into the factor analysis, the data will have to meet the assumptions underlying this statistic (two of which appear above) as well.

5. This property of independence becomes quite useful when delimiting domain of numerous variables into a manageable one with few, uncorrelated, or independent, variables. Independence, or orthogonality, between factors will be of prime importance in the analysis section of this paper, when we try to establish the variants of inter-group aggression against government into separate dimensions.

6. That is, the sum of squares (the sum of the squared deviations from the mean) of factor loadings is maximized on each factor.

7. The method also has the advantage of providing a mathematically unique, or least squares, solution for the matrix of correlation coefficients.

8. The nine basic variables used in this part of the analysis were those selected and used in a study of conflict behavior within and between nations, conducted by R. J. Rummel in 1963 and published in *General Systems Yearbook 8* (1963: 1–50 [reprinted in this volume, Chapter 3]). See also Rummel (1963).

The Rummel data (gathered for the years 1955–57, for 78 nations) were richly supplemented by Raymond Tanter, when he replicated the Rummel study after gathering similar (see Chapter 4, this volume) data for the following three-year period (1958–60) across 83 nations. It is the Tanter data which were factor analyzed, and are presented in Tables I and II.

9. The computer program which monitored these calculations was MESA 1, a 95 × 95 Factor Analytic Program with Varimax Rotation. Special thanks are due Northwestern University's Vogelback Computing Center for their generous allowance of computing time.

The lower limit for eigenvalues (i.e., a proportion of variance which may vary from near zero to *n*, where *n* is the number of variables entering a factor matrix) to be included in rotation was 1.00. Rotation is carried out in order to obtain a solution which is not entirely dependent upon each particular variable in the analysis. Orthogonal rotation is the fitting of factors to clusters of variables with the restriction that the correlation between factors is zero. The *varimax* criterion is used to rotate orthogonally to "simple structure," that is, the maximization of high and low loadings. Thus, this form of rotation continues to maintain independence among the factors.

10. One possible way to test this assumption would be to compute the factor scores for each of the 20 republics on this third dimension. If the assumption is accurate, nations experiencing *low* levels of conflict (e.g. Uruguay and Costa Rica) should come out *high* on such a distribution.

11. One less dimension than emerged for similar data gathered over the 1955–57 time period by Rudolph Rummel. For a detailed discussion of these dimensions, and a comparison of them to both the earlier Rummel study, as well as to the basic dimensions extracted from an analysis of connflict data (1946–59) gathered by Eckstein, see R. J. Rummel (1966 [reprinted in this volume, Chapter 2]) and R. Tanter (1966 [reprinted in this volume, Chapter 4]).

12. With the possible exception of "peasant revolt," which is generally referred to as *machetismo* (a sporadic outbreak, generally in rural areas, by peasants or peons, primarily involved in agriculture economies), and which is probably measuring violence more of an anomic nature.

13. Of street riots, Silvert says "... they usually take place to protest governmental actions, such as a rise in bus fares or the arrest of political or labor leaders. University students are very prone to this kind of violence" (Silvert, 1961: 20-33).

14. A common term for indices which take all loadings into account is "factor scores," which represent the country's overall score (in standard score form) weighted by the factor loadings for each of the indices in the analysis. Such scores are automatically computed for both unrotated and rotated factor solutions by Mesal, but were not used here because a more discriminating index was desired. For a description of some formulas for calculating these "factor" or "component" scores, see Fruchter and Jennings (1962: 260-262); Kaiser (1962: 83-88).

15. Purges, for example, might be one of the component parts of a factor which allows a population to perceive a government as repressive, and therefore, should appear as an intervening variable (perhaps helping "cause" potential aggressors to temper feelings of hostility with notions of possible reprisal for "deviant" behavior).

16. The computation formulas for both the Organized and Anomic Violence Indices are:

$$\text{Anomic Index} = .508 \left[\frac{X_1 - \bar{X}_1}{s_1}\right] + .827 \left[\frac{X_2 - \bar{X}_2}{s_2}\right] + .865 \left[\frac{X_3 - \bar{X}_3}{s_3}\right]$$

$$\text{Anomic Index Computation Formula} = \frac{.508}{s_1}X_1 + \frac{.827}{s_2}X_2 + \frac{.865}{s_3}X_3 - \left[\frac{.508}{s_1}\bar{X}_1 + \frac{.827}{s_2}X_2 + \frac{.865}{s_3}\bar{X}_3\right]$$

$$\frac{.761\,(\text{GU-WAR})}{1.164} + \frac{.829\,(\text{GVTCRS})}{1.446} + \frac{.606\,(\text{REVOLU})}{1.905} + \frac{.849\,(\text{D-KILL})}{995.901} -$$

$$\left[\frac{.761}{1.164}(1.250) + \frac{.829}{1.446}(1.750) + \frac{.606}{1.905}(2.050) + \frac{.849}{995.901}(311.400)\right]$$

$$\text{Organized Violence} = \frac{\text{GU-WAR}}{.6537 X_1} + \frac{\text{GVTCRS}}{.5733 X_2} + \frac{\text{REVOLU}}{.3181 X_3} + \frac{\text{D-KILL}}{.0008 X_4} - 2.7216$$

$$\frac{.508\,(\text{STRIKE})}{2.762} + \frac{.827\,(\text{RIOTS})}{6.018} + \frac{.865\,(\text{DEMONS})}{1.638} -$$

$$\left[\frac{.508}{2.762}(1.450) + \frac{.827}{6.018}(5.700) + \frac{.865}{1.638}(1.500)\right]$$

$$\text{Anomic Violence} = \frac{\text{STRIKE}}{.1839\,Y_1} + \frac{\text{RIOTS}}{.1374\,Y_2} + \frac{\text{DEMONS}}{.5280\,Y_3} - 1.8419$$

17. See Campbell (1963: 212-242). The *panel* correlation, originally designed for use with survey research data, where the same respondent was interviewed at more than one point in time, seems directly applicable here, where data for the same nation is also analyzed at more than one point in time.

18. Although coefficients were available for all of the data points within the matrix (as, for example, those appearing in all the cells of the first variable, "Change in PRI"), correlations only appear which test the causal model: $r_{c_1 E_2} > r_{c_2 E_1}$.

19. Satisfaction: "Annual Growth of G.N.P. per Capita," data for 13 of the

Latin American republics from the *World Handbook of Political and Social Indicators* (Russett, 1964: 160–161); data for the remaining nations (including the corrected calculation for Venezuela) were computed from GNP per capita statistics from the following sources: 1952 GNP per capita—Harold Davis, *Government and Politics in Latin America*, p. 64 (most of these figures came from the *1955 Statistical Abstract of Latin America*); 1957 (58) GNP per capita—figures here came from two sources: *The World Handbook of Political and Social Indicators*, pp. 155–157, and the *1960 Statistical Abstract of Latin America*, p. 30; the difference between the 1952 and 1957 (58) figures was taken, and divided by the number of years involved, to obtain the annual growth figure.

Pearson Product Moment Correlation = $-.63$.

20. The high value of 3.5 percent of GNP allocated to defense expenditures during 1959–60, does not appear to be a data-quality error. When checked against similar data gathered by Bruce Russett for the 1959 period, the Peruvian statistics placed at 3.0 percent.

21. Force: data directly from John D. Powell, "Military Assistance and Militarism in Latin America," *Western Political Quarterly*, 18 (June 1965), p. 384. Supplemental data for Uruguay and Cuba taken from: Bruce M. Russett, "Measures of Military Effort," *American Behavioral Scientist*, 7 (February 1964), pp. 26, 28.

Data presented in raw form; when Y variable transformed to $\log_{10}$, the curve is smoother and more accentuated; kept in raw score form, here, for comparative purposes.

22. It should be recalled that it was ambivalence, in terms of a permissive and then a coercive colonial policy, which LeVine (1959) postulated gave rise to anti-European conflict in Africa.

23. The resulting coefficient, while in the same direction as hypothesized, can only be considered a suggestive test of the relationship. For various reasons, it was felt that the strength of the coefficient would be considerably boosted with more sensitive data; for example, if the change-in-defense data were available between 1960 to 1963, the period immediately following the 1958–60 Organized violence data.

Data for the calculation of the change measure was gathered from the following sources: "1958–59 per cent of central government expenditure on defense"—*1960 Statistical Abstract of Latin America*, p. 32; *1961 Statistical Abstract of Latin America*, p. 35. "1962–63 per cent of central government expenditure on defense" —*1962 Statistical Abstract of Latin America*, p. 66; *1963 Statistical Abstract*, p. 76; *1964 Statistical Abstract*, p. 104.

24. Legitimacy: Change scores calculated from data published by Russell Fitzgibbon and Kenneth Johnson (1961: 518).

Data presented in raw form; when Y variable is transformed to $\log_{10}$, the negative correlation coefficient of $-.71$ (for the relationship in Figure 2) is strengthened.

25. The $\log_{10}$ transformation was used, which increased the $-.50$ relationship found among the raw data to $-.67$.

26. It will be recalled that the Organized Violence Index, constructed on the basis of the empirical evidence from the factor analysis of conflict activity, weights guerrilla activities .65, governmental crisis .57, and revolutions .31. It is not surprising, therefore, that Cuba and Venezuela, which have experienced considerable guerrilla-type activity during the period 1958–60, should come out highest on Organized violence in the scatter plot in Figures 1 and 3.

REFERENCES

ALEXANDER, R.J. (1964) "Bolivia: the national revolution." In M.C. Needler, Ed., *Political Systems of Latin America.* New York: D. Van Nostrand.
ALMOND G. and J. COLEMAN, Eds. (1960) *The Politics of the Developing Areas.* Princeton: Princeton University Press.
ALMOND, G.A. and S. VERBA (1963) *The Civic Culture.* Boston: Little, Brown.
BLANKSTEN, G.I. (1960) "The politics of Latin America." In G. Almond and J. Coleman, Eds., *The Politics of the Developing Areas.* Princeton: Princeton University Press.
— (1958) "Revolutions." In H.E. Davis, Ed., *Government and Politics in Latin America.* New York: Ronald Press.
CAMPBELL, D.T. (1963) "From description to experimentation: interpreting trends as quasi-experiments." Pp. 212–242 in C.W. Harris, Ed., *Problems in Measuring Change.* Madison: University of Wisconsin Press.
CAMPBELL, D.T. and J.C. STANLEY (1963) "Experimental and quasi-experimental designs for research on teaching." In N.L. Gage, Ed., *Handbook of Research on Teaching.* New York: Rand McNally.
CUTRIGHT, P. (1963) "National political development: measurement and analysis." *American Sociological Review* 28 (April): 253–264.
DE MESTAS, A. (1950) *El Salvador: País de Lagos y Volcanos.* Madrid: Editorial Cultura Hispánica.
ECKSTEIN, H. (1962) "Internal war: the problem of anticipation." In I. de Sola Pool et al., *Social Science Research and National Security.* Washington, D.C.: Smithsonian Institution.
FITZGIBBON, R. and K. JOHNSON (1961) "Measurement of Latin American political change." *American Political Science Review* 55 (September).
FRUCHTER, B. and E. JENNINGS (1962) "Factor analysis." In H. Borko, Ed., *Computer Applications in the Behavioral Sciences.* Englewood Cliffs: Prentice-Hall.
HOTELLING, H. (1933) "Analysis of a complex of statistical variables into principal components." *Journal of Educational Psychology* 24: 417–441, 488, 520.
KAISER, H. (1962) "Formulas for component scores." *Psychometrika* 27: 83–88.
KLING, M. (1956) "Toward a theory of power and political instability in Latin America." *Western Political Quarterly* 9 (March).
LEVINE, R.A. (1959) "Anti-European violence in Africa." *Journal of Conflict Resolution* 3 (December): 420–429.
LIPSET, S.M. (1959) "Some social requisites of democracy: economic development and political legitimacy." *American Political Science Review* 53 (March).
PAYNE, J. (1965) "Peru: the politics of structured violence." *Journal of Politics* 27 (May).
RAMBO, A.T. (1964) "The Dominican Republic." In M.C. Needler, Ed., *Political Systems of Latin America.* New York: D. Van Nostrand.
RUMMEL, R.J. (1966) "Dimensions of conflict behavior within nations, 1946–59." *Journal of Conflict Resolution* 10 (March): 65–73. Reprinted in this volume, Chapter 2.
— (1965) "A field theory of social action and of political conflict within nations." *General Systems Yearbook 10.*
— (1963) Dimensions of Conflict Behavior Within and Between Nations. Paper

prepared in connection with research supported by the National Science Foundation, under Contract G24827, June, 108 pp. Abridged, revised and reprinted in this volume, Chapter 2.

RUSSETT, B.M. (1964) *World Handbook of Political and Social Indicators*. New Haven: Yale University Press.

SILVERT, K. (1961) *The Conflict Society: Reaction and Resolution in Latin America*. New Orleans: The Hauser Press.

STOKES, W. (1952) "Violence as a power factor in Latin American politics." *Western Political Quarterly* (September).

TANTER, R. (1964) *Dimensions of conflict behavior within and between nations, 1958–60*. Evanston, Ill.: Monograph prepared from research under National Science Foundation Contract NSF-GS 224.

THURSTONE, L.L. (1960) *Multiple Factor Analysis*. Chicago: University of Chicago Press.

WILKS, S.S. (1938) "Weighting systems for linear functions of concealed variables when there is no independent variable." *Psychometrika* 3 (March): 24–43.

6 Aggressive Behaviors within Polities, 1948-62: A Cross-National Study

IVO K. FEIERABEND and ROSALIND L. FEIERABEND

A recent trend in behavioral research is the systematic and empirical analysis of conflict behaviors both within and among nations. External conflict behaviors among nations are typified by wars, embargoes, interruption of diplomatic relations, and other behaviors indicative of aggression between national political systems. Internal conflict behaviors within nations, on the other hand, consist of such events as demonstrations, riots, coups d'état, guerrilla warfare, and others denoting the relative instability of political systems.

There are a few studies which have attempted systematic empirical analyses of internal conflict, more or less broadly based in cross-national studies (Kling, 1959; LeVine, 1959; Davies, 1962; Eckstein, 1962, 1964; Feierabend, Feierabend, and Nesvold, 1963; Haas, 1964; Russett, 1964; Nesvold, 1964; Hoole, 1964; Conroe, 1965; Walton, 1965). Furthermore, cross-national inquiry, as a method, is being used by many researchers (Cattell, 1949, 1950, 1952; Rokkan, 1955; Lerner, 1957, 1958; Lipset, 1959, 1960; Inkeles, 1960; Deutsch, 1960, 1961; Deutsch and Eckstein, 1961; Fitzgibbon and Johnson, 1961; McClelland, 1961; Cantril and Free, 1962; Cantril, 1963, 1965; Banks and Textor, 1963; Almond and Verba, 1963; Russett et al., 1964; Gregg and Banks, 1965 [reprinted in this volume, Chapter 12]; Merritt and Rokkan, 1966; Singer and Small, 1966; Rokkan, forthcoming). All of these efforts have in common an interest in abstracting relevant dimensions on which to compare large numbers of nations. Some (McClelland, 1961; Cantril and Free, 1962; Cantril, 1963, 1965; Almond and Verba, 1963) are

---

Authors' Note: This research was partially supported by a grant from the San Diego State College Foundation. A paper based on this article was delivered at the Annual Meeting of the American Psychological Association in Chicago, Illinois, September 1965 (Feierabend and Feierabend, 1965b).

Reprinted from the *Journal of Conflict Resolution*, Volume 10, pages 249-271, by permission of the authors and the publisher. Copyright © 1966 by The University of Michigan.

concerned with measuring psychological dimensions. Others (especially Banks and Textor, 1963; Russett et al., 1964) are directed toward a large-scale empirical assessment of the interrelationships among all available ecological variables—political, economic, and societal. A very few (Rummel, 1963 [reprinted in this volume, Chapter 3], 1965, 1966 [reprinted in this volume, Chapter 2]; Tanter, 1964, 1966 [reprinted in this volume, Chapter 4]; Hoole, 1964; Feierabend, Feierabend, and Litell, 1966) attempt to discover the structure of the complex universe of internal or external conflict behavior through factor analysis.

The studies here described are directly concerned with the measurement of political instability and, furthermore, with a search for the correlates of internal conflict behaviors. As a first step, a theoretical framework is adopted to aid in the analysis of the problem.

Theoretical Framework

Although political instability is a concept that can be explicated in more than one way, the definition used in this analysis limits its meaning to aggressive, politically relevant behaviors. Specifically, it is defined as the degree or the amount of aggression directed by individuals or groups within the political system against other groups or against the complex of officeholders and individuals and groups associated with them. Or, conversely, it is the amount of aggression directed by these officeholders against other individuals, groups, or officeholders within the polity.

Once this meaning is ascribed, the theoretical insights and elaborations of frustration–aggression theory become available (Dollard et al., 1939; Maier, 1949; McNeil, 1959; Buss, 1961; Berkowitz, 1962). Perhaps the most basic and generalized postulate of the theory maintains that "aggression is always the result of frustration" (Dollard et al., 1939: 3), while frustration may lead to other modes of behavior, such as constructive solutions to problems. Furthermore, aggression is not likely to occur if aggressive behavior is inhibited through devices associated with the notion of punishment. Or it may be displaced onto objects other than those perceived as the frustrating agents.[1]

The utility of these few concepts is obvious. Political instability is identified as aggressive behavior. It should then result from situations of unrelieved, socially experienced frustration. Such situations may be typified as those in which levels of social expectations, aspirations, and needs are raised for many people for significant periods of time, and yet remain unmatched by equivalent levels of satisfactions. The notation:

$$\frac{\text{social want satisfaction}}{\text{social want formation}} = \text{systemic frustration}$$

indicates this relationship. Two types of situations which are apt to produce high levels of systemic frustration are investigated in this research, although certainly many other possibilities are open to study.

In applying the frustration–aggression framework to the political sphere, the concept of punishment may be identified with the notion of coerciveness of political regimes. And the constructive solution of problems is related to the political as well as the administrative, entrepreneurial, and other capabilities available in the environment of politics. The notion of displacement may furthermore be associated with the occurrence of scapegoating against minority groups or aggression in the international sphere or in individual behaviors.

The following general hypotheses are yielded by applying frustration–aggression theory to the problem of political stability:

1. Under a situation of relative lack of systemic frustration, political stability is to be expected.
2. If systemic frustration is present, political stability still may be predicted, given the following considerations:
    a. It is a nonparticipant society. Politically relevant strata capable of organized action are largely lacking.
    b. It is a participant society in which constructive solutions to frustrating situations are available or anticipated. (The effectiveness of government and also the legitimacy of regimes will be relevant factors.)
    c. If a sufficiently coercive government is capable of preventing overt acts of hostility against itself, then a relatively stable polity may be anticipated.
    d. If, as a result of the coerciveness of government, the aggressive impulse is vented or displaced in aggression against minority groups and/or
    e. against other nations, then stability can be predicted.
    f. If individual acts of aggression are sufficiently abundant to provide an outlet, stability may occur in the face of systemic frustration.
3. However, in the relative absence of these qualifying conditions, aggressive behavior in the form of political instability is predicted to be the consequence of systemic frustration.

A more refined set of hypotheses concerning socially aggressive behaviors and frustration can be achieved by interpreting the frustration–aggression hypothesis within the framework of theories of social and political action and political systems (Merton, 1949; Parsons and Shils, 1951; Lasswell, 1951; Almond and Coleman, 1960; Parsons et al., 1961; Deutsch, 1963; Easton, 1965a, 1965b; Gurr, 1965).

Methodology

The methodology of the studies is indicated by the scope of the problem. Concern is not with the dynamics underlying stability in any one particular country but with the determinants of stability within all national political systems. As many cases as possible, or at least an appropriate sample of cases, must be analyzed. Thus the present studies are cross-national endeavors in which data are collected and analyzed for as many as eighty-four polities. (The eighty-four nations are listed in Table 1.) The cross-national method is here conceived in similar terms as the cross-cultural studies of anthropology (Whiting and Child, 1953; Murdock, 1957; Feierabend, 1962).

A crucial aspect of the research is the collection of relevant cross-national data. Although data are available on ecological variables of political systems through the Yale Political Data Program, the Dimensionality of Nations Project, and the Cross-Polity Survey, data collections on the political stability dimension are scarcer.

In order to carry out the research, data on internal conflict behaviors were collected for eighty-four nations for a fifteen-year period, 1948–62. The data derive from two sources: *Deadline Data on World Affairs* and the *Encyclopaedia Britannica Yearbooks*. They are organized into a particular format in which each instability event is characterized according to country in which it occurs, date, persons involved, presence or absence of violence, and other pertinent characteristics (Feierabend and Feierabend, 1965a). The data are on IBM cards, creating a storage bank of some 5,000 events.[2]

Study 1. The Analysis of the Dependent Variable: Political Stability

WITH BETTY A. NESVOLD, FRANCIS W. HOOLE, AND NORMAN G. LITELL

In order to evaluate the political stability–instability continuum, data collected on internal conflict behavior were scaled. The ordering of specific instability events into a scale was approached from the viewpoint of both construct validity and consensual validation (Nesvold, 1964).

A seven-point instrument was devised, ranging from 0 (denoting extreme stability) through 6 (denoting extreme instability). Each point of the scale was observationally defined in terms of specific events representing differing degrees of stability or instability. An illustration may be given of one item typical of each position on the scale. Thus, for example, a general election is an item associated with a 0 position on the rating instructions. Resignation of a cabinet official falls into the 1 position on the scale; peaceful demonstrations into the 2 position; assassination of a significant political figure into the 3 position; mass arrests into the 4 position; coups d'état into the 5 position; and civil war into the 6 position.

Consensual validation for this intensity scale was obtained by asking judges to sort the same events along the same continuum. The level of agreement among judges on the distribution of the items was fairly high (Pearson $r = .87$). Other checks performed on the reliability of the method were a comparison of the assignment of items to positions on the scale by two independent raters. Their level of agreement for the task, involving data from eighty-four countries for a seven-year time period, was very high (Pearson $r = .935$).

Using this scaling instrument, stability profiles for the sample of eighty-four nations were ascertained for the seven-year period, 1955–61. Countries were assigned to groups on the basis of the most unstable event which they experienced during this seven-year period. Thus countries which experienced a civil war were placed in group 6; countries which were prey to a coup d'état were placed in group 5; countries with mass arrests were assigned to group 4, and so on. The purpose of this assignment was to weight intensity (or quality) of instability events equally with the frequency (or quantity) of events.

Following the allotment to groups, a sum total of each country's stability ratings was calculated. Countries were then rank-ordered within groups on the basis of this frequency sum total. The results of the ratings are given in Table 1.[3]

In this table, it may be seen first of all that the distribution is skewed. Instability is more prevalent than stability within the sample of nations, and the largest proportion of countries are those experiencing an instability event with a scale weighting of 4. Furthermore, there is an interesting combination of countries at each scale position. The most stable scale positions, by and large, include modern nations but also a sprinkling of markedly underdeveloped polities and some nations from the Communist bloc. Again, the small group of extremely unstable countries at scale position 6 comprise nations from Latin America, Asia, and the Communist bloc. The United States, contrary perhaps to ethnocentric expectations, is not at scale position 1 although it is on the stable side of the scale.

Another approach to the ordering of internal conflict behavior was based upon frequency alone (Hoole, 1964).[4] The frequency of occurrence of thirty types of internal conflict behaviors was determined for the eighty-four countries for the time period, 1948–62. Analysis in terms of frequency was used in three different ways:

(1) A global instability profile for all types of events, for all countries, was drawn to show changes in world level of instability during the time period under study. As may be seen in Figure 1, instability has been on the increase in recent years, reaching one peak in the late 1950s and an even higher level in the early 1960s.

(2) Frequencies of particular types of instability behaviors were compared for the entire sample of countries. The range of frequencies was from 18 (execution of significant persons) to 403 (acquisition of office). When the events were rank-ordered in terms of frequency of occurrence and the rank-ordering divided into quartiles, the first quartile, with the highest frequency of occurrence (1,555 occurrences) included events denoting routine governmental change (such as acquisition of office, vacation of office, elections, and significant changes of laws). The second quartile (704 occurrences) appeared to be one of unrest, including such events as large-scale demonstrations, general strikes, arrests, and martial law. The third quartile (333 occurrences) indicated serious societal disturbance, in the form of coups d'etat, terrorism and sabotage, guerrilla warfare, and exile. And the fourth quartile

TABLE 1
FREQUENCY DISTRIBUTION OF COUNTRIES IN TERMS OF THEIR DEGREE OF RELATIVE POLITICAL STABILITY, 1955–1961
(STABILITY SCORE SHOWN FOR EACH COUNTRY)

0	1	2	3	4	5	6
				France 499		
				U. of S. Africa 495		
				Haiti 478		
				Poland 465		
				Spain 463		
				Dom. Rep. 463		
				Iran 459		
				Ceylon 454		
				Japan 453		
				Thailand 451		
				Mexico 451		
				Ghana 451		
				Jordan 448		
				Sudan 445		
				Morocco 443		
				Egypt 438		
				Pakistan 437		
				Italy 433		
				Belgium 432		
				Paraguay 431		
				USSR 430		
			Tunisia 328	Nicaragua 430		
			Gr. Britain 325	Chile 427		
			Portugal 323	Burma 427	India 599	
			Uruguay 318	Yugoslavia 422	Argentina 599	
			Israel 317	Panama 422	Korea 596	
			Canada 317	Ecuador 422	Venezuela 584	
	Norway 104		U. S. 316	China 422	Turkey 583	
	Netherlands 104		Taiwan 314	El Salvador 421	Lebanon 581	
	Cambodia 104	W. Germany 217	Libya 309		Iraq 579	
	Sweden 103		Austria 309	Liberia 415	Bolivia 556	
	Saudi Ar. 103	Czech. 212	E. Germany 307	Malaya 413	Syria 554	
	Iceland 103	Finland 211	Ethiopia 307	Albania 412	Peru 552	Indonesia 699
	Philippines 101	Romania 206	Denmark 306	Greece 409	Guatemala 546	Cuba 699
	Luxembourg 101	Ireland 202	Australia 306	Bulgaria 407	Brazil 541	Colombia 681
N. Zea. 000		Costa Rica 202	Switzer. 303	Afghanistan 404	Honduras 535	Laos 652
					Cyprus 526	Hungary 652

STABILITY ←――――――――――――――――――――――→ INSTABILITY

(150 occurrences) consisted primarily of events connoting violence: executions, severe riots, civil war. Thus an inverse relationship was revealed between the frequency of occurrence of an event and the intensity of violence which it denotes.

(3) Finally, countries were compared for the relative frequency of occurrence of all thirty instability behaviors during this time period. The range was from 136 events (France) to one event (Switzerland). The median of this distribution was represented by Laos and Burma, with 28 and 26 events, respectively.

An additional refinement in the understanding of political instability is achieved by factor analysis, which reduces the large number of observed variables to a smaller number of underlying dimensions. Four previous factor analyses of internal conflict behaviors have been performed. Rummel (1963 [this volume, Chapter 3]), factor analyzing nine types of internal conflict behaviors for a three-year time period (1955–57), emerged with three underlying dimensions: turmoil, revolution, and subversion. Tanter (1964, 1966 [this volume, Chapter 4]), replicating the Rummel variables for the years 1958–60, found a two-factor solution: turmoil and internal war. Recently, Rummel (1966 [this volume, Chapter 2]) factor-analyzed thirteen variables obtained from Eckstein's collection of internal conflict behaviors (Eckstein, 1962) for the time period 1946–50. This factor analysis again yielded three dimensions, which Rummel identifies with the three dimensions of the 1963 factor solution (see Rummel, 1963 [this volume, Chapter 3]) namely, revolution, subversion, and turmoil. Hoole (1964) factor-analyzed thirty variables

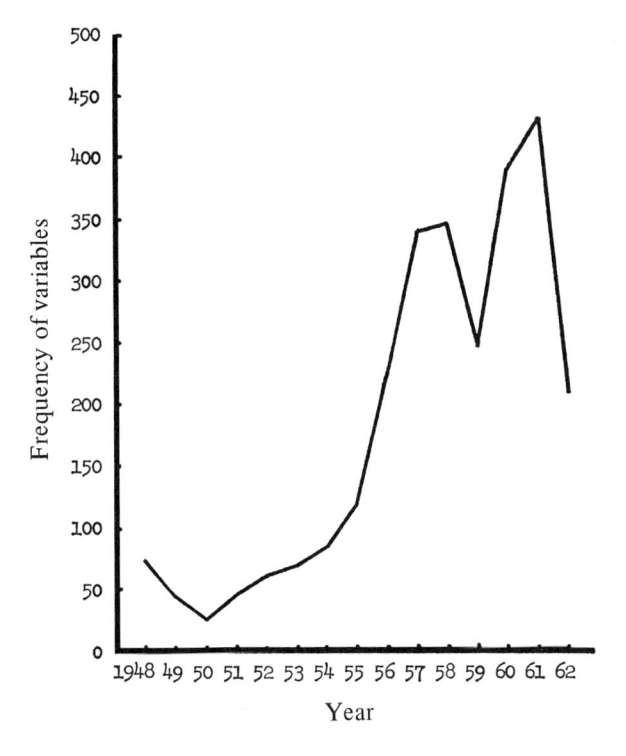

FIGURE 1

FREQUENCY OF VARIABLES BY YEAR, 1948–62

collected over a fifteen-year time span, 1948–62, from a single source (see note 2), and emerged with five major and five minor factors. The five major factors were labeled: demonstrations, change of officeholder, riots, guerrilla warfare, and strikes.

Most recently, Feierabend, Feierabend, and Litell (1966), using Hoole's thirty variables for the fifteen-year period 1948–62 and the complete data bank derived from two sources, performed a factor analysis with a principal components solution and an orthogonal Varimax rotation. (See Table 2

TABLE 2
Rotated Factor Matrix of Domestic Conflict Measures

Variables	Mass partic-ipation —Tur-moil	Palace revo-lution —Re-volt	Power strug-gle— Purge	Riot	Elec-tion	Dem-on-stra-tion	Im-pris-on-ment	Civil war	Guer-rilla war-fare
1. Elections	29	−02	09	−18	70*	−10	−17	−05	−23
2. Vacation of office	38	08	74*	−14	20	−11	−15	−25	09
3. Significant change of laws	38	41	41	−01	31	15	−16	−23	−11
4. Acquisition of office	29	06	75*	−19	15	−04	−25	−19	22
5. Crisis within a nongovernmental organization	40	13	12	−21	04	−09	62*	07	−23
6. Organization of opposition party	08	10	−02	02	56*	36	19	−39	−10
7. Repressive action against specific groups	46	61*	27	01	−03	16	12	04	12
8. Micro strikes	67*	00	−15	−26	−16	05	12	03	23
9. General strikes	73*	13	04	−42	09	−06	03	08	−18
10. Macro strikes	43	−22	−11	−35	15	−17	−33	−12	−19
11. Micro demonstrations	61*	19	−02	02	20	59*	10	03	02
12. Macro demonstrations	73*	−01	00	26	06	19	18	−21	03
13. Micro riots	46	11	−06	68*	27	−03	−03	−15	11
14. Macro riots	69*	28	−04	33	20	02	04	−08	−05
15. Severe macro riots	64*	−03	−04	53*	11	−19	−02	−20	14
16. Arrests of significant persons	09	64*	54*	07	−14	−06	23	−10	−01
17. Imprisonment of significant persons	−14	12	49	17	−05	16	38	−33	−22
18. Arrests of few insignificant persons	42	09	05	−08	07	75*	07	07	21
19. Mass arrests of insignificant persons	52*	33	14	54*	−12	−02	−01	05	01
20. Imprisonment of insignificant persons	26	−08	09	08	−12	34	64*	−03	−14
21. Assassination	17	40	23	06	24	23	−07	−10	56*
22. Martial law	11	71*	03	03	15	09	−27	−06	−08
23. Execution of significant persons	−08	01	54*	31	−26	14	−04	31	05
24. Execution of insignificant persons	01	−10	63*	32	−07	12	−02	47	−02
25. Terrorism and sabotage	62*	28	12	−21	13	−01	10	07	38
26. Guerrilla warfare	04	42	07	−19	19	−35	25	21	55*
27. Civil war	−14	25	31	14	45	08	−08	60*	02
28. *Coup d'état*	03	69*	07	01	−02	12	−40	07	−32
29. Revolts	06	75*	−01	11	07	−01	−10	32	16
30. Exile	−09	40	00	03	−36	32	−19	−13	04
Percentage of common variance	23.37	16.30	13.20	9.67	8.33	8.00	7.99	6.76	6.40 = 100.0
Percentage of total variance	23.33	11.11	7.52	6.77	5.89	5.32	4.18	3.82	3.62 = 71.46

* Asterisks indicate loadings >.50. Decimals omitted from loadings.

for the rotated factor matrix.) Nine factors emerged. The first three of these, ranked according to importance in terms of the amount of variance accounted for after rotation, were labelled, first, a turmoil dimension (characterized by violence and mass participation); second, a palace-revolution–revolt dimension (distinguished by a marked lack of mass support); and, third, a power-struggle–purge dimension (connoting violent upheavals and changes of office within regimes). It will be noted that there is definite correspondence between the first two factors revealed in this analysis and the factors discovered by both Rummel and Tanter.

Looking at the variables with the highest loadings on each factor, we see that the first factor comprises strikes of all types; demonstrations and riots, large and small, violent and severe; and also mass arrests and terrorism. One could say that it denotes serious, widespread disturbance, anomie, popular mass participation, and some governmental retaliation.

The second factor presents a sharp contrast to this mass turmoil dimension. It encompasses revolts, coups d'état, martial law, arrests of politically prominent leaders, and governmental action against specific groups. These events do not connote mass participation but rather extreme instability created by highly organized and conspiratorial elites and cliques. And the third factor presents yet another divergent pattern, including acquisition and loss of office, arrests and executions of politically significant figures, and some punitive action. Mass turmoil is not evident, as on the first factor; neither is the situation one of revolt and coup d'état. This is an instability dimension of violent internal power struggles, purges, depositions, and changes within ruling parties and cliques, which nevertheless remain in power.

The nine factors in combination account for 71.5 percent of the total variance. After rotation the three first factors combined account for over half of the common variance (53 percent). The remaining six factors, accounting in combination for less than half of the common variance, seem to reveal the following patterns: a specific riot dimension; an election dimension; two factors connoting mild, limited unrest; and, finally, two separate dimensions of civil war and guerrilla warfare, respectively, the extreme forms of political instability.

Study 2. The Relation of Social Frustration and Modernity to Political Stability

WITH BETTY A. NESVOLD

Once the data for the dependent variable, political stability, were collected, factor-analyzed, and scaled, the major step of seeking correlates of instability became feasible. In this attempt, two generalized and related hypotheses were investigated. (1) *The higher (lower) the social want formation in any given society and the lower (higher) the social want satisfaction, the greater (the less) the systemic frustration and the greater (the less) the impulse to political instability.* (2) *The highest and the lowest points of the modernity continuum in any given society will tend to produce maximum stability in the political order, while a medium position on the continuum will produce maximum instability* (Nesvold, 1964).

These hypotheses embody the basic propositions of the frustration–aggression theory, as well as insights gained from the literature on processes of modernization (Lerner, 1958; Deutsch, 1961; Cutright, 1963). In the first hypothesis, the discrepancy between social wants and social satisfactions is postulated to be the index of systemic frustration. The relationship is represented as follows:

$$\frac{\text{want satisfaction low}}{\text{want formation high}} = \text{high frustration}$$

$$\frac{\text{want satisfaction low}}{\text{want formation low}} = \text{low frustration}$$

$$\frac{\text{want satisfaction high}}{\text{want formation high}} = \text{low frustration}$$

A variety of social conditions may satisfy or leave unsatisfied the social wants of different strata of the population within social systems. In our present century the process of modernization is certain to create new wants and aspirations, as well as to lead in the long run to their satisfaction.

The notion of modernity denotes a very complex set of social phenomena. It includes the aspiration and capacity in a society to produce and consume a wide range and quantity of goods and services. It includes high development in science, technology, and education, and high attainment in scores of specialized skills. It includes, moreover, new structures of social organization and participation, new sets of aspirations, attitudes, and ideologies. Modern affluent nations, with their complex of economic, political, and social systems, serve best as models of modernity to nations emerging from traditional society. In these transitional nations, the growing, politically relevant strata of the population are all participants in modern life. Lerner (1957), for one, states categorically that once traditional societies are exposed to the modern way of life, without exception they desire benefits associated with modernity.

The acquisition of modern goals, although an integral aspect of modernity, is hardly synonymous with their attainment. The notion of "the revolution of rising expectations" (Lerner, 1958), also termed "the revolution of rising frustrations," points to the essentially frustrating nature of the modernization process. The arousal of an underdeveloped society to awareness of complex modern patterns of behavior and organization brings with it a desire to emulate and achieve the same high level of satisfaction. But there is an inevitable lag between aspiration and achievement which varies in length with the specific condition of the country. Furthermore, it may be postulated that the peak discrepancy between systemic goals and their satisfaction, and hence the maximum frustration, should come somewhere in the middle of the transitional phase between traditional society and the achievement of modernity. It is at this middle stage that awareness of modernity and exposure to modern patterns should be complete, that is, at a theoretical ceiling, whereas achievement levels would still be lagging far behind. Prior to this theoretical middle stage, exposure and achievement would both be lower. After the middle stage, exposure can no longer increase, since it already amounts to complete awareness, but achievement will continue to progress, thus carrying the nation eventually into the stage of modernity. Thus, in contrast to transitional societies, it may be postulated that traditional and modern societies will be less frustrated and therefore will tend to be more stable than transitional societies.

The most direct way to ascertain systemic frustration is through field work in the many countries, administering questionnaires (see Inkeles, 1960; Doob, 1960; Cantril, 1963, 1965; Almond and Verba, 1963). For the purpose of this study, an inexpensive and very indirect method was adopted.

The highly theoretical notions of want satisfaction and want formation were translated into observable definitions. For this purpose, available collections of cross-national statistical data were consulted and a few statistical items were chosen as appropriate indicators. The following selection of indicators was made. GNP and caloric intake per capita, physicians and telephones per unit of population were singled out as indices of satisfaction. Newspapers and radios per unit of population were also included. Many other indicators denoting material or other satisfactions could have served the purpose. The selection was guided by parsimony as well as availability of data.

The indicators, of course, have different significance in referring to the satisfaction of different wants. Furthermore, their significance may vary at different levels of relative abundance or scarcity. A great deal of theorizing is necessary to select and use the indicators wisely. For example, it is possible that a country with many physicians and telephones may still be starving. Or, beyond a certain point, caloric intake cannot measure the satisfaction of some other less basic needs than hunger, while GNP per capita may do so.

For want formation, literacy and urbanization were chosen as indicators. This selection was influenced by the notion of exposure to modernity (Lerner, 1958; Deutsch, 1961). Exposure to modernity was judged a good mechanism for the formation of new wants, and literacy and city life were taken as the two agents most likely to bring about such exposure.

These eight indices (GNP, caloric intake, telephones, physicians, newspapers, radios, literacy, and urbanization) were used to construct both a frustration index and a modernity index. The modernity index was formed by combining scores on all of the eight indicators. Raw scores were first transformed into standard scores and then a mean standard score was calculated for each of the eighty-four countries on the basis of the available data. The frustration index was a ratio. A country's combined coded score on the six satisfaction indices (GNP, caloric intake, telephones, physicians, newspapers, and radios) was divided by either the country's coded literacy or coded urbanization score, whichever was higher.[5]

The data on the independent variables were collected for the years 1948–55 whereas the stability ratings were made for the years 1955–61. It was assumed that some lag would occur before social frustrations would make themselves felt in political aggressions, that is, political instabilities.

Results

The main finding of the study is that the higher the level of systemic frustration, as measured by the indices selected, the greater the political instability. The results are shown in Table 3. The stable countries are those which experience the least amount of measured systemic frustration. Conversely, the countries beset by political instability also suffer a high level of systemic frustration, although certain interesting exceptions occur.

TABLE 3
RELATIONSHIP BETWEEN LEVEL OF SYSTEMIC FRUSTRATION AND DEGREE OF POLITICAL STABILITY*

DEGREE OF POLITICAL STABILITY	INDEX OF SYSTEMIC FRUSTRATION RATIO OF WANT FORMATION TO WANT SATISFACTION			Total
	High systemic frustration		Low systemic frustration	
Unstable	Bolivia Brazil Bulgaria Ceylon Chile Colombia Cuba Cyprus Dom. Republic Ecuador Egypt El Salvador Greece Guatemala Haiti India Indonesia	Iran Iraq Italy Japan Korea Mexico Nicaragua Pakistan Panama Paraguay Peru Spain Syria Thailand Turkey Venezuela Yugoslavia	Argentina Belgium France Lebanon Morocco Union of South Africa	40
	34		6	
	2		20	
Stable	Philippines Tunisia		Australia Austria Canada Costa Rica Czech. Denmark Finland West Germany Great Britain Iceland Ireland Israel Netherlands New Zealand Norway Portugal Sweden Switzerland United States Uruguay	22
Total	36		26	62

Chi square** = 30.5, $p = <.001$ Yule's $Q = .9653$

* The number of cases in this and the following tables varies with the data available in the UN statistical sources. This table includes only those countries with data on all eight indices.
** All chi squares in this and the following tables are corrected for continuity in view of the small frequencies in the nonconfirming cells.

Each indicator of want formation and satisfaction is also significantly related to political stability. The relationships between each indicator and stability are presented in Table 4. Another finding of interest in this table is that all eight indicators do not predict degree of stability with equal efficiency. Level of literacy is the best single predictor, as seen by the .90 degree of relationship (Yule's Q) between literacy and stability. Comparatively, GNP is one of the weaker predictors, along with percent of urbanization, population per physician, and caloric intake per capita per day.

These data on the predictors of political stability also determine empirical threshold values for each indicator. Above these values, countries are predominantly stable; below them, countries are predominantly unstable. The cutting point for each of the indicators was selected so as to reveal the maximum difference between stable and unstable countries.

From these empirical thresholds, a composite picture of the stable country emerges. It is a society which is 90 percent or more literate; with 65 or more radios and 120 or more newspapers per 1,000 population; with two percent or more of the population having telephones; with 2,525 or more calories per day per person; with not more than 1,900 persons per physician; with a GNP of 300 dollars or more per person per year; and with 45 percent or more of the population living in urban centers. If all of these threshold values are attained by a society, there is an extremely high probability that the country will achieve relative political stability. Conversely, if gratifications are less than these threshold values, the more they fail to meet these levels, the greater the likelihood of political instability.

In order to investigate the relationship between modernity and stability, countries were rank-ordered on the modernity index and the distribution was broken into three groups representing modern countries, transitional countries, and traditional countries. The cutting points for these three groups were to some extent arbitrary: the twenty-four countries which were highest on the modernity index were selected as the modern group. The traditional group was chosen to be equal in size to the modern group, while ranking at the opposite end of the modernity continuum. The remaining countries, falling between the modern and traditional groups, were designated transitional. The difficulty in determining the true state of the countries lies not so much in finding the cutting point for the modern group as in selecting the traditional one. Truly traditional countries do not report data and hence have no way of being included in the study. The countries designated traditional are simply less modern than those classed as transitional, but they have nonetheless been exposed to modernity.[6]

A mean stability score was calculated for each group of countries. The differences between the mean stability scores for the three groups were then estimated. According to the hypothesis, the difference in mean stability score should be greatest between the transitional group and either of the other two groups. The difference in mean stability score between modern and

TABLE 4
Relationships Between the Eight Indicators of Systemic Frustration and Degree of Political Stability

A. Literacy:

| | % Literate | | |
	Low (below 90%)	High (above 90%)	Total
Unstable	48	5	53
Stable	10	19	29
Total	58	24	82

Chi square = 25.83; $p = <.001$
Yule's Q = .90

B. Radios:

| | per 1,000 population | | |
	Low (below 65)	High (above 65)	Total
Unstable	45	6	51
Stable	9	20	29
Total	54	26	80

Chi square = 25.02; $p = <.001$
Yule's Q = .887

C. Newspapers:

| | per 1,000 population | | |
	Low (below 120)	High (above 120)	Total
Unstable	48	5	53
Stable	6	10	16
Total	54	15	69

Chi square = 17.34; $p = <.001$
Yule's Q = .88

D. Telephones:

| | % of population owning telephones | | |
	Low (below 2%)	High (above 2%)	Total
Unstable	35	6	41
Stable	7	18	25
Total	42	24	66

Chi square = 19.68; $p = <.001$
Yule's Q = .875

E. Calories:

| | per capita per day | | |
	Low (below 2,525)	High (above 2,525)	Total
Unstable	39	10	49
Stable	8	20	28
Total	47	30	77

Chi square = 17.42; $p = <.001$
Yule's Q = .81

F. Physicians:

| | people per physician | | |
	Low (above 1,900)	High (below 1,900)	Total
Unstable	40	13	53
Stable	6	19	25
Total	46	32	78

Chi square = 11.41; $p = <.001$
Yule's Q = .81

G. GNP:

| | per capita (in US dollars) | | |
	Low (below 300)	High (above 300)	Total
Unstable	36	8	44
Stable	9	18	27
Total	45	26	71

Chi square = 14.92; $p = <.001$
Yule's Q = .80

H. Urbanization:

| | % of population living in urban centers | | |
	Low (below 45%)	High (above 45%)	Total
Unstable	38	6	44
Stable	11	15	26
Total	49	21	70

Chi square = 13.08; $p = <.001$
Yule's Q = .79

traditional countries should not be significant. The results are given in Table 5.

As may be seen in the table, the predicted difference between the stability level of modern and of transitional countries emerges as highly significant. The difference between modern and traditional countries is less but nonetheless also significant. And the difference between traditional and transitional countries does not reach significance. The difficulty in obtaining data on truly traditional countries undoubtedly contributes to the lack of significant difference between countries labelled in this sample as transitional and traditional.

In view of the lack of support in these eighty-four nations for the hypothesized curvilinear relationship between modernity and stability, the assumption may be made that all of the countries have been exposed to modernity. Hence want formation should be at a relatively high level throughout the sample.

TABLE 5
RELATIONSHIP BETWEEN MODERNITY AND STABILITY

Modernity level	N	Mean stability score	t	p*	t	p*
Modern countries	24	268	6.18	<.001	3.71	<.01
Transitional countries	37	472	1.53	>.05		
Traditional countries	23	420				

* Probability levels are two-tailed.

One might hypothesize that want formation reaches an early maximum with exposure to modernity, after which further awareness of the modern world can no longer increase desire for modernity. Under these conditions, the modernity index is also in fact a frustration index, indicating the extent to which these measured economic satisfactions are present within a society which may be presumed to have already been exposed to modernity.

To compare the relative efficacy of these two frustration indices, product-moment correlations were calculated between each index and stability. The results show that while both indices are significantly correlated with stability, the correlation between the so-called modernity index and stability is the higher of the two. The product-moment correlation between modernity and stability is .625; the correlation between the so-called frustration index and stability is .499. An *eta* calculated between the modernity index and the stability index, to show curvilinearity of relationship, is $\eta = .667$, which is not significantly different from the Pearson r of .625. Thus again the hypothesis of curvilinearity between modernity and stability is not supported.

Study 3. The Prediction of Changes in Political Stability Over Time

WITH WALLACE R. CONROE

In the previous study, stability, modernity, and the frustration index were all calculated as static measures. Each variable was represented by a single score, indicating an overall estimate of the level of the variable during the time period under study. The question raised in this study concerns the effect of relative rates of change over time in the ecological variables. It seeks to uncover dynamic relationships which would supplement the static ones.

The assumptions made in this study of dynamic trends are based on a view of change as essentially disruptive in character. The process of transition toward modernity, discussed in the previous study, is one during which, almost inevitably, goals and demands will exceed achievements. It is also a process during which former patterns of behavior, outdated technologies, established roles, statuses and norms, must all give way to new, unfamiliar patterns. The transitional personality is frustrated by his breakoff from the past and the uncertainty of the present.

To this picture of a society in ferment is now added the notion of the relevance of time. Insofar as the transitional process is a gradual one, there is a possibility that new patterns may be adopted and adjusted to before old ones are completely abandoned. There is also the further possibility that achievements may begin to approximate the level at which aspirations are set, before aspirations move even further ahead. Where the transitional process is rapid, however, the effect will be to decrease the possibility of adaptation, thus increasing the probability of disruption, chaos, and feelings of personal discontent. Furthermore, the more rapid the process of change, the greater the likelihood of opening new perspectives of modernity, that is, of creating higher and higher levels of aspiration, thus inevitably increasing the gap between aspiration and achievement, at least in the early stages.

Thus the hypothesis promulgated in this study is that: *the faster (the slower) the rate of change in the modernization process within any given society, the higher (the lower) the level of political instability within that society* (Conroe, 1965).

As a first step in investigating this hypothesis, yearly changes in instability pattern for each of the eighty-four countries were calculated for the time period under study, 1948-62. From the evidence accumulated on the global frequency of occurrence of instability events (Figure 1), it was clear that the world instability level increased sharply during the fifteen years, reaching its highest peak in the last six years. In order to compare countries as to their relative position on the instability continuum over time, the period was split in half and country instability scores were calculated for each seven-year period separately. The country scores for the second period tended to be higher than for the first one. A rank-order correlation between stability levels in the two seven-year periods for the eighty-four countries showed a moderate degree of relationship (Spearman $r = .43$). Not only was the instability level generally on the increase, but there was a tendency for countries to maintain their relatively stable or unstable positions over time.

As a further, more refined method of analyzing the stability–instability continuum over time, stability scores for the eighty-four nations were calculated on a year-by-year basis and plotted as a function of time. To characterize the time function, at least two measures were necessary: the slope of a best-fit line, indicating the average instability trend, over the fifteen-year period; and amplitude of change from year to year, as estimated by variance.

A calculation of the relationship between these two measures showed them to be independent and unrelated dimensions (Spearman $r = .06$). Of the two, only amplitude was related to static stability level as measured by the intensity scale (Spearman $r = .64$). This indicates that the meaning of instability as empirically ascertained in these studies is identified with the fluctuation of instability rather than with the average trend over time. Furthermore, it is the measure of amplitude and not the average trend over time which is directly related to rate of change in the independent variables. The average instability trend over time (increases or decreases) is related to the ecological variables only when combined with the data on yearly fluctuations in stability levels.

Turning to the predictors of instability, interest was in the effect of changes in levels of ecological variables upon changes in stability. The general hypothesis of this study was that rapid change will be experienced as an unsettling, frustrating societal condition and hence will be associated with a high level of internal conflict. To test the hypothesis, nine predictor indices were selected for study: caloric intake, literacy, primary and postprimary education, national income, cost of living, infant mortality, urbanization, and radios per thousand population. Data for these indices were collected for a 28-year period from 1935 through 1962. Plotting of the data revealed a consistent trend for substantially all countries in the sample to improve their position on all indices over time. Hence a yearly percent rate of change was calculated for each indicator.[7] These indicators are not identical to those of the previous study, although there is overlap. The new choice was determined by the availability of data for as many years as possible and for a maximum number of countries in the sample.

To summarize the results of the interrelationship between rates of change in the independent indices and rate of change in stability, it may be said that the higher the rate of change on the indices, the greater the increase in instability. A contingency table showing the relationship between mean rate of change on six or more of the nine indices and instability, as measured only by variation in pattern (amplitude), is given in Table 6.

As may be seen from the table, the countries experiencing a highly erratic instability pattern are those also undergoing a rapid rate of change in the

TABLE 6
Relationship Between Mean Rate of Change on Ecological Variables and Rate of Change in Stability

MEAN RATE OF CHANGE ON ECOLOGICAL VARIABLES (PERCENT)	CHANGE IN STABILITY — AMPLITUDE OF FLUCTUATIONS IN YEARLY STABILITY SCORES			TOTAL
	Low change (amplitude)		High change (amplitude)	
Low change	Argentina Australia Austria Bulgaria Canada Chile Denmark Ecuador Finland France Guatemala Iceland Ireland Israel Italy Luxembourg	Mexico Netherlands New Zealand Norway Pakistan Philippines Spain Sweden Switzerland Taiwan Un. of S. Africa United Kingdom United States Uruguay West Germany	Belgium Cuba Greece Hungary Paraguay	36
	31		5	
High change	Ceylon Ghana India Syria Turkey	Bolivia Brazil Burma Cambodia Colombia Costa Rica Dom. Republic Egypt El Salvador Haiti Honduras Indonesia Iraq	Japan Korea Malaya Morocco Panama Peru Poland Portugal Thailand Tunisia USSR Venezuela Yugoslavia	31
	5		26	
Total	36		31	67*

Chi square = 30.0; p = <.001.

* The N on this and some of the following tables is reduced to include only those countries with data on six or more indices, from which to calculate the mean rate of change score.

ecological variables selected for study. On the other hand, countries experiencing political stability in the sense of a steady pattern are the static countries in which ecological change proceeds at a slower pace.

Furthermore, the rate at which modernization occurred from 1935 to 1962 is correlated with static stability level in the 1955–61 time period (as measured in Study 1). A Pearson r of .647 was found between rate of change (calculated as a combined measure on six or more of the nine indices) and static stability score. Relationships were also calculated between rates of change on each of the nine independent indices taken separately and instability level, measured both as a static score and as a dynamic fluctuation (variance measure) for the 1948–62 period (see Table 7).

The pattern is somewhat the same for both sets of calculations, indicating primary education to be the best single predictor of instability and literacy the worst.[8] The most interesting finding is the inverse relationship revealed between rate of change in national income and instability. In the case of this indicator, the higher the rate of change, the greater the likelihood of stability. This finding may be understood when one contrasts the pattern of rate of change on national income to that for the nine indices taken together (see Tables 8 and 9).

TABLE 7

Rank-Order Correlations (rho) Between Rate of Change on Ecological Variables and Two Measures of Stability, 1948–1962

	N	Static stability	Dynamic stability (amplitude)
Primary education	70	.61	.57
Calories per capita per day	39	.49	.35
Postprimary education	30	.36	.41
Cost of living	72	.36	.21
Radios	82	.34	.31
Infant mortality rate	60	.33	.36
Urbanization	69	.17	.14
Literacy	82	.03	.01
National income	70	−.34	−.45

From Table 8 it is clear that all countries except the modern show a high rate of change on ecological variables. (This again confirms the point made earlier that no truly traditional countries are included in the sample. By definition, a traditional country should be characterized by lack of change.) The modern countries are those undergoing the least amount of change, They are also those experiencing the least amount of instability.

In Table 9, however, we find the situation reversed for growth in national income. On this indicator, it is the modern countries which show the highest rate of change over time. National income may be viewed as a variable with no intrinsic ceiling and one on which marked improvement will not occur until a country is well advanced toward modernity and has achieved a relatively high standard on other ecological variables, such as literacy, education, caloric intake, and infant mortality. Thus again it is the modern countries which are the most stable and which show the greatest growth rate in national income.

A final comparison between rate of change in modernization and instability level was made by grouping countries on instability in terms of both amplitude of yearly fluctuations and general trend in instability over time (variance and slope). Three groups of countries were distinguished: stable countries (in which yearly fluctuations are low and the trend over time is either stationary or improving); unstable countries (in which yearly

TABLE 8
RELATIONSHIP BETWEEN MODERNITY LEVEL AND MEAN RATE OF CHANGE ON ECOLOGICAL VARIABLES

MEAN RATE OF CHANGE (PERCENT)	MODERNITY LEVEL				Total
	Traditional countries	Transitional countries	Modern countries		
Low change	Pakistan Philippines Taiwan	Bulgaria Chile Cuba Guatemala Hungary Italy Mexico Paraguay Spain Union of South Africa	Argentina Australia Austria Belgium Canada Denmark Finland France Iceland Ireland Israel	Luxembourg Netherlands New Zealand Norway Sweden Switzerland United Kingdom United States Uruguay W. Germany	34
	3	10	21		
High change	Bolivia Burma Cambodia Ghana Haiti India Indonesia Iraq Malaya Morocco	Brazil Ceylon Colombia Costa Rica Dom. Rep. Ecuador Egypt El Salvador Greece Honduras Japan	Korea Panama Peru Poland Portugal Syria Thailand Tunisia Turkey Venezuela Yugoslavia	USSR	33
	10	22	1		
Total	13	32	22		67

Chi square = 31.0; p = <.001.

fluctuations are high and the trend over time is either stationary or worsening); and indeterminate countries which represent conflicting combinations of trend and fluctuation. Four levels of rate of change were also distinguished. With these refinements, the relationship between rate of modernization and instability level over time appears more clearly (see Table 10).

The countries with the lowest rate of change are predominantly stable, as measured both by a low level of yearly fluctuations in instability and by a lack of any worsening trend toward instability over time. Conversely, the countries with the highest rate of change on the ecological variables are beset by instability, as measured both by yearly fluctuations in instability levels and the absence of evidence of any improvement in trend toward stability over time. Furthermore, countries experiencing intermediate rates of change toward modernization are also intermediate in instability, showing some conflicting combination of fluctuation and trend over time.

In conclusion, one might speak of a syndrome which is exemplified by the modern group of nations. With interesting exceptions, they are relatively satisfied economically and relatively stable politically, no longer changing

TABLE 9

RELATIONSHIP BETWEEN MODERNITY LEVEL AND RATE OF CHANGE IN NATIONAL INCOME

RATE OF CHANGE IN NATIONAL INCOME (PERCENT)	MODERNITY LEVEL			Total
	Traditional countries	Transitional countries	Modern countries	
Low change	Burma Cambodia China Ghana Haiti India Iraq Jordan	Indonesia Malaya Morocco Pakistan Philippines Sudan	Bulgaria Colombia Costa Rica Dom. Rep. Ecuador Egypt El Salvador Guatemala	Honduras Lebanon Panama Poland Portugal Syria Tunisia Venezuela	E. Germany Ireland Switzerland USSR United Kingdom	35
		14	16	5	
High change	Taiwan	Brazil Chile Ceylon Cuba Greece Hungary Italy Japan Korea	Mexico Paraguay Peru Spain Thailand Turkey Un. of So. Africa Yugoslavia	Argentina Australia Austria Belgium Canada Denmark Finland France Iceland Israel	Luxembourg Netherlands New Zealand Norway Sweden United States W. Germany	35
	1	17	17	
Total	15	33	22	70

Chi square = 17.8; $p = <.001$.

rapidly on many economic dimensions, although making sizable gains in national income. In contrast are the transitional nations, some moving more rapidly toward modernity than others but, by and large, all characterized by relative economic deprivation, a high rate of change on many economic dimensions but a low rate of growth on national income, and a strong tendency to political instability, finding overt expression in many diverse events such as strikes, demonstrations, riots, coups d'etat, and even civil war.

The results of these studies are an encouraging indication that cross-national, correlational, and scaling methods can profitably be applied to complex areas such as the analysis of internal conflict behaviors. The scaling,

TABLE 10

RELATIONSHIP BETWEEN MEAN RATE OF CHANGE ON ECOLOGICAL VARIABLES AND CHANGE IN STABILITY AS MEASURED BY VARIANCE AND SLOPE

MEAN RATE OF CHANGE ON ECOLOGICAL VARIABLES	STABLE — Low variance and either negative slope or zero slope	INDETERMINATE — Low variance/positive slope or high variance/negative slope	UNSTABLE — High variance and either positive slope or zero slope	Total
Low change	Norway / New Zealand / W. Germany / Australia / Denmark / Iceland / Israel United States / Canada / Sweden / Switzerland / Netherlands / Luxembourg	Great Britain / Austria	Belgium	16
	13	2	1	
Moderately low change	Ireland / Guatemala / Bulgaria / Taiwan Finland / Italy / Chile / Philippines	France / Un. S. Africa / Mexico / Pakistan / Greece Argentina / Uruguay / Spain / Ecuador	Cuba / Paraguay / Hungary	20
	8	9	3	
Moderately high change		Thailand / Colombia / Egypt / Ceylon / Poland Costa Rica / Ghana / Turkey / India	Peru / Portugal / Panama / Brazil / Haiti / Iraq Japan / Yugoslavia / Tunisia / Burma / USSR	20
	0	9	11	
High change	Syria	Korea / Malaya	El Salvador / Bolivia / Venezuela / Dom. Rep. Cambodia / Morocco / Honduras / Indonesia	11
	1	2	8	
Totals	22	22	23	67

as well as the identification of the dimensions of internal conflict behavior, show that these events can be classified and disentangled.

Furthermore, the results of the studies provide empirical corroboration for many current notions regarding the determinants of political instability. The fact that change may lead to unrest has been suggested. By applying postulates drawn from the frustration–aggression model to this area of internal conflict behavior, and by subjecting the area to empirical analysis, new insights are also obtained. On the basis of these findings, it may be suggested that one compelling reason for the greater stability of modern countries lies in their greater ability to satisfy the wants of their citizens. The less advanced countries are characterized by greater instability because of the aggressive responses to systemic frustration evoked in the populace. It could be argued simply that the increase in instability resulting from a change in ecological conditions is due to the disruptive effect of change. But it is also possible that the satisfaction of wants has a feedback effect, adding to the strength of the drive for more satisfactions. As wants start to be satisfied, the few satisfactions which are achieved increase the drive for more satisfactions, thus in effect adding to the sense of systemic frustration. It is only when a high enough level of satisfaction has been reached that a country will tend toward stability rather than instability.

Although exploratory in nature, the findings are sufficiently striking and persuasive to argue for continuing with additional designs. A large-scale series of studies utilizing a wider scope of ecological, psychological, and political variables, an inventory of other, complementary aggressive behaviors, and a longer time period should lead to more refined results.

NOTES

1. More recent analyses of aggression have placed increasing emphasis on the role of the stimulus in eliciting an aggressive response. (For a discussion of recent approaches, see Berkowitz, 1965.)

2. The data bank of political instability events, including the *Code Index* to the bank, instructions to raters, etc., is available through the Inter-University Consortium for Political Research, Box 1248, Ann Arbor, Michigan.

3. These stability profiles correlate with the ordering of the same countries based on Eckstein's index, "Deaths from domestic group violence per 1,000,000 population, 1950-1962." The rank-order correlation between these two indices is Spearman $r = .69$. On the other hand, only a low correlation exists with Russett's index, "Executive stability: number of years independent/number of chief executives, 1945-1961." The rank-order correlation between these two indices is Spearman $r = .38$.

4. The data used in Hoole's 1964 study were gathered from a single source, *Deadline Data on World Affairs*. The data bank as presently constituted comprises two sources, *Deadline Data on World Affairs* and *The Encyclopaedia Britannica Yearbooks*.

5. The difficulty of dividing these highly correlated indicators should be noted. Each contains some error component due to the unreliable reporting of cross-national data. For an estimate of error in cross-national data, see Russett (1964) and Rummel (1963 [reprinted in this volume, Chapter 3]).

6. This modernity ranking, based on eight indices, is highly comparable to that of Russett et al. (1964) based on GNP alone. A Spearman r calculated between the two rank-orderings is .92.

7. The yearly percent rate of change on the ecological variables was calculated by subtracting the lowest value of the variable in the 28-year period from the highest value attained, dividing by the lowest value to convert to a percentage change, and then dividing by the number of years spanned to obtain the yearly percentage change.

8. This finding is in contrast to the high level of relationship obtained between literacy and static stability level reported in Study 1. The explanation may lie in the observed inconsistency in the literacy data reported over the longer time period in various sources.

REFERENCES

ALMOND, G. and J.S. COLEMAN, Eds. (1960) *The Politics of the Developing Areas.* Princeton: Princeton University Press.

ALMOND, G.S. and S. VERBA (1963) *The Civic Culture.* Princeton: Princeton University Press.

BANKS, A.S. and R.B. TEXTOR (1963) *A Cross-Polity Survey.* Cambridge: MIT Press.

BERKOWITZ, L. (1965) "The concept of aggressive drive: some additional considerations." In L. Berkowitz, Ed., *Advances in Experimental Social Psychology.* Vol. 2. New York: Academic Press.

— (1962) *Aggression: A Social Psychological Analysis.* New York: McGraw-Hill.

BUSS, A.H. (1961) *The Psychology of Aggression.* New York: John Wiley.

CANTRIL, H. (1965) *The Pattern of Human Concerns.* New Brunswick: Rutgers University Press.

— (1963) "A study of aspirations." *Scientific American* (February) 41–45.

CANTRIL, H. and L.A. FREE (1962) "Hopes and fears for self and country." *American Behavioral Scientist* 6 (October): 3–30.

CATTELL, R. (1952) *Factor Analysis.* New York: Harper & Bros.

— (1950) "The principal culture patterns discoverable in the syntal dimensions of existing nations." *Journal of Social Psychology:* 215–253.

— (1949) "The dimensions of culture patterns of factorization of national characters." *Journal of Abnormal and Social Psychology:* 443–469.

CATTELL, R., H. BREUL, and H.P. HARTMAN (1951) "An attempt at more refined definition of the cultural dimensions of syntality in modern nations." *American Sociological Review* 16: 408–421.

CONROE, W.R. (1965) A Cross-National Analysis of the Impact of Modernization upon Political Stability. Master's thesis, San Diego State College.

CUTRIGHT, P. (1963) "National political development: measurement and analysis." *American Sociological Review* 28 (April): 253–264.

DAVIES, J.C. (1962) "Toward a theory of revolution." *American Sociological Review* 27 (January): 5–19.

DEUTSCH, K.W. (1963) *The Nerves of Government.* New York: Free Press.

— (1961) "Social mobilization and political development." *American Political Science Review* 55 (September): 493–514.

— (1960) "Toward an inventory of basic trends and patterns in comparative and international politics." *American Political Science Review* 54 (March): 34–57.

DOLLARD, J. et al. (1939) *Frustration and Aggression.* New Haven: Yale University Press.

DOOB, L.W. (1960) *Becoming More Civilized: A Psychological Exploration.* New Haven: Yale University Press.

EASTON, D. (1965a) *A Framework for Political Analysis.* Englewood Cliffs: Prentice-Hall.

— (1965b) *A Systems Analysis of Political Life.* New York: John Wiley.

ECKSTEIN, H., Ed. (1964) *Internal War.* New York: Free Press.

— (1962) Internal War: The Problem of Anticipation. A Report submitted to the Research Group in Psychology and the Social Sciences, Smithsonian Institution, Washington, D.C., January 15.

FEIERABEND, I.K. (1962) "Exploring political stability: a note on the comparative method." *Western Political Quarterly* (Supplement) 15 (September): 18–19.
FEIERABEND, I.K. and R.L. FEIERABEND (1965a) *Cross-National Data Bank of Political Instability Events* (Code Index). Public Affairs Research Institute, San Diego State College, January.
— (1965b) "Aggressive behaviors within polities: a cross-national study." Paper delivered at the Annual Meeting of the American Psychological Association, Chicago, September.
FEIERABEND, I.K., R.L. FEIERABEND, and N.G. LITELL (1966) "Dimensions of political unrest: a factor analysis of cross-national data." Paper delivered at the annual meeting of the Western Political Science Association, Reno, March.
FEIERABEND, I.K., R.L. FEIERABEND, and B.A. NESVOLD (1963) "Correlates of political stability." Paper delivered at the Annual Meeting of the American Political Science Association, New York City, September.
FITZGIBBON, R.H. and K. JOHNSON (1961) "Measurement of Latin American political change." *American Political Science Review* 55 (September).
GREGG, P.M. and A.S. BANKS (1965) "Dimensions of political systems: factor analysis of *A Cross-Polity Survey*." *American Political Science Review* 59: 602–614. Reprinted in this volume, Chapter 12.
GURR, T. (1965) The Genesis of Violence: A Multivariate Theory of the Preconditions of Civil Strife. Ph.D. dissertation, New York University.
HAAS, M. (1964) *Some Societal Correlates of International Political Behavior*. Stanford: Studies in International Conflict and Integration, Stanford University.
HOOLE, F.W. (1964) Political Stability and Instability within Nations: A Cross-National Study. Master's thesis, San Diego State College.
INKELES, A. (1960) "Industrial man: the relation of status to experience, perception and value." *American Journal of Sociology* (July): 1–31.
KLING, M. (1959) "Taxes on the 'external' sector: an index of political behavior in Latin America." *Midwest Journal of Political Science* (May): 127–150.
LASSWELL, H.D. (1951) *The Political Writings of Harold D. Lasswell*. Glencoe: Free Press.
LERNER, D. (1958) *The Passing of Traditional Society*. Glencoe: Free Press.
— (1957) "Communication systems and social systems: a statistical exploration in history and policy." *Behavioral Science* 2 (October): 266–275.
LeVINE, R.A. (1959) "Anti-European violence in Africa: a comparative analysis." *Journal of Conflict Resolution* 3 (December): 420–429.
LIPSET, S.M. (1960) *Political Man*. Garden City: Doubleday.
— (1959) "Some social requisites of democracy." *American Political Science Review* 53 (March): 69–105.
MAIER, N.R.F. (1949) *Frustration: The Study of Behavior without a Goal*. New York: McGraw-Hill.
McCLELLAND, D. (1961) *The Achieving Society*. Princeton: Van Nostrand.
McNEIL, E.B. (1959) "Psychology and aggression." *Journal of Conflict Resolution* 3 (September): 195–293.
MERRITT, R.L. and S. ROKKAN (1966) *Comparing Nations: The Uses of Quantitative Data in Cross National Research*. New Haven: Yale University Press.
MERTON, R.K. (1949) *Social Theory and Social Structure*. New York: Free Press.

MURDOCK, G.P. (1957) "Anthropology as a comparative science." *Behavioral Science* 2 (October): 249–254.

NESVOLD, B.A. (1964) Modernity, Social Frustration, and the Stability of Political Systems: A Cross-National Study. Master's thesis, San Diego State College.

PARSONS, T. and E.A. SHILS (1951) *Toward a General Theory of Action*. Cambridge: Harvard University Press.

PARSONS, T., E.A. SHILS, K. NAEGELE, and J. PITTS (1961) *Theories of Society*. New York: Free Press.

ROKKAN, S., Ed. (forthcoming) *Comparative Research across Cultures and Nations*.

— (1955) "Comparative cross-national research: II. bibliography." *International Social Science Bulletin:* 622–641.

RUMMEL, R.J. (1966) "Dimensions of conflict behavior within nations, 1946–59." *Journal of Conflict Resolution* 10: 65–74. Reprinted in this volume, Chapter 2.

— (1965) "A field theory of social action and political conflict within nations." *General Systems Yearbook 10.*

— (1963) "Dimensions of conflict behavior within and between nations." Pp. 1–50 in *General Systems Yearbook 8*. Reprinted in this volume, Chapter 3.

RUSSETT, B.M. (1964) "Inequality and instability: the relation of land tenure and politics." *World Politics* 16 (April): 442–454.

RUSSETT, B.M. et al. (1964) *World Handbook of Social and Economic Indicators*. New Haven: Yale University Press.

SINGER, J.D. and M. SMALL (1966) "The composition and status ordering of the international system: 1815–1940." *World Politics* 18 (January): 236–282.

TANTER, R. (1964) *Dimensions of Conflict Behavior Within and Between Nations, 1958–1960*. Monograph prepared in connection with research supported by National Science Foundation Contract NSF-GS 224.

— (1966) "Dimensions of conflict behavior within and between nations, 1958–60." *Journal of Conflict Resolution* 10 (March): 41–65. Reprinted in this volume, Chapter 4.

WALTON, J.G. (1965) Correlates of Coerciveness and Permissiveness of National Political Systems: A Cross-National Study. Master's thesis, San Diego State College.

WHITING, J.W. and I.L. CHILD (1953) *Child Training and Personality: A Cross-Cultural Study*. New Haven: Yale University Press.

7 Scalogram Analysis of Political Violence

BETTY A. NESVOLD

This is a cross-national analysis of political violence as it occurred in eighty-two nations during the period 1948–61. It is also a study that relies upon statistical techniques of analysis; data had to be quantified, and we relied extensively on using coded categories of behavior. We have operationalized our concept of political violence in this study, used both intuitive and inductive techniques to form a scale on which the eighty-two nations can be rated for this variable, and sought correlates of this type of political instability. The research has been in progress for some five years, and in a sense this constitutes a progress report. Some of the findings have been extensively tested and found highly reliable. Some of the data analysis that we present reports only tentative findings. The potential scope of the research is so large, though, that it seems desirable to publish findings and seek criticism and suggestions.

The problem has been conceived of as one of measuring the amounts of social unrest in a nation—including both violent events and those that were potentially violent. All events that indicated this type of activity were recorded for these eighty-two nations. Coding decisions were made so that the data could be put into a form amenable to machine analysis (Feierabend and Feierabend, 1965). Clearly, the first responsibility was to develop an instrument for weighting these various types of events so that those occurring in a single country could be combined into a weighted score of political instability. The first set of analyses used events that denoted nonviolent political instability as well as the more turbulent aspects of it. With this broad set of data,

---

Author's Note: This is a revised version of a paper originally prepared for delivery at the 1967 Annual Meeting of the American Political Science Association in Chicago. The data used in this study were collected at San Diego State College while working with Ivo K. and Rosalind L. Feierabend. Grateful acknowledgment is made for the encouragement and stimulation they provided. Funds were made available through the San Diego State College Research Foundation and the National Science Foundation. The suggestions and criticisms of William Flanigan, University of Minnesota, have been most helpful.

Reprinted from *Comparative Political Studies*, Volume II, pages 172–194, by permission. Copyright © 1969 Sage Publications, Inc.

an intuitive seven-point scale was developed and subjected to some initial tests of validity.[1] The scale proved fruitful for subsequent analyses, but it seemed essential to devote a concentrated effort to building a validated scale of political instability in order to feel we were on firm ground in future analyses.

In the first instance, forty-six graduate students, enrolled in a seminar on Quantitative Analysis in Political Science at the Interuniversity Consortium for Political Analysis in the summer of 1966, were given a list of these coded events, which were ordered in random fashion. Those participating in this exercise were given a "thermometer" that was calibrated from zero to one hundred. They were asked to place events on the thermometer so as to give the highest scores to the indicators of most extreme instability, and the lowest scores to the events denoting stability. Events in each country were then scored on the basis of the mean value suggested by the members of this class. These scores were summed for each country, and the resulting value was considered that nation's instability score.[2]

A third exercise was to subject these data to Guttman scaling—a statistical technique designed for ordering data. Since this technique tests scalar properties of a *single* underlying dimension, only those events that denoted incipient or overt violence were used in this exercise. They were grouped into four classes that denoted increasing amounts of violence. Essentially, one has a Guttman scale if occurrence of events in class four is accompanied by events in classes three, two, and one, and if there are no events in class four but there are events in class three, then they are accompanied by events in classes two and one, and so on. A perfect scale would be perfectly reproducible from the knowledge of the most extreme event on that scale, i.e., knowledge that a class-two event was the most extreme one would also convey the knowledge that class-one events are present—but none in classes three and four. Perfect scales are unlikely to be found in empirical data. Guttman acknowledged this and suggested that one could test for reasonable empirical approximation of a perfect scale by counting "errors" and calculating a coefficient of reproducibility. If 90 percent of the behaviors are scalable and only 10 percent or less constitute errors, then one could use scaling techniques to order data and as a basis for assigning weights (Guttman, 1950). The advantage of using scaling as a basis for analyzing data is the methodological assumption that data will not scale unless they contain unidimensionality. That is, there must be a single underlying attribute that objectively verifies using statements of "more" or "less" on qualitative variables. For example, a set of questions on racial tolerance will form a Guttman scale, if, when extreme questions elicit a "yes," the less extreme questions must also elicit a "yes." In this instance one has an empirically verified instrument with which one can rate respondents as being more or less racially intolerant. In our own study violence is the underlying dimension. Since these events do scale, if a nation experiences extreme violence, it also experiences less extreme violence. It makes sense

Scalogram Analysis of Political Violence

empirically to assess nations as being more or less violent, and it also provides justification for assigning weights to events as they fall into the scaled categories.

One contribution of this inductive technique was to provide a basis for scoring a type of political instability that could be used in a validity matrix with the other techniques for assigning this value. This is not the only finding of interest, and the Guttman scaling project is described in more detail below. For the present, however, attention is directed to Table 1. Scores were assigned to each event on the basis of weights assigned by the three independent techniques: (1) the Guttman scaling exercise, (2) the initial intuitive scale, and (3) consensual validation exercise at the University of Michigan.

TABLE 1

VALIDITY MATRIX OF INSTABILITY SCORES[a]

	1	2	3
1. Sum of scores based on Guttman scales	—	.948	.940
2. Sum of scores based on intuitive scales	.948	—	.986
3. Sum of scores based on consensual validation exercise (n = 82)	.940	.986	—

[a] Scores were logged and intercorrelations recalculated to see if these extremely high coefficients could have been the result of a few extreme values having an overriding effect on the results. The new coefficients were substantially the same as those reported above.

The scores were summed for each country in each of the three exercises, and the resulting values constituted an instability rating for each country. Their correlation coefficients are presented on this table. The first rating scale used only the data on violent events while the other two used more comprehensive data, yet the intercorrelations are extremely high among all three measures.

Empirical Scales of Political Violence

In analyzing the country-by-country scalar patterns, one is confronted with a dilemma as to whether the entire fourteen years (1948–61) should be considered a single scale or whether this should be divided into segments. Table 2 lists the events that are classified under each of the four scale positions.

As one notes, the events contain increasing amounts of violence as one moves from Position 1 to Position 4. As mentioned above, these events are considered scalable if a nation experiencing events under Position 4 also experiences events under Positions 3, 2, and 1. If a nation has no class-four events, but does have class-three events, then it must also have those coded two and one. In order to determine the presence or absence of these scalar patterns, however, one must select a time period during which it is hypothesized that the patterns will be revealed. There seemed no objective basis on

TABLE 2
Scaling Political Violence

Position 1	Position 2	Position 3	Position 4
Riots and demonstrations	Martial law	Guerrilla warfare	Politically motivated executions
Boycotts against the government	Coup d'etat	Politically motivated assassinations	Civil war
Politically motivated arrests	Revolt		
Government action against specific groups			
Sabotage			

which this decision could be made; thus, one calendar year was arbitrarily selected as a reasonable basis on which to sort the data. Of course, one hazard here is that if a pattern of events started in, say, December and carried into the early part of the next year, then its true scalability might not be revealed and an error mistakenly accorded to this pattern. This situation would serve to reduce the pattern of reproducibility and increase assigned errors. However, a contrary problem was confronted in that if a few countries scaled perfectly, the accumulation of fourteen perfect scales (one for each year) for each of these countries would unrealistically inflate the "correct" pattern and concomitantly inflate the coefficient of reproducibility. In order to control for such an effect, time periods were collapsed to see if this had any significant effect on the coefficient of reproducibility. These ranged from a high of .97 to a low of .94—any one of which is a highly satisfactory level for validating the scales. It was noticed, however, that the Communist countries

TABLE 3
Coefficients of Reproducibility for Various Time Segments

Time segment	Entire sample	Non-Communist countries	Communist countries
One year	.97	.97	.95
Two years	.96	.96	.92
Three years (1948–50, 1951–53, 1954–56, 1957–59, 1960–61)	.95	.96	.90
Four years (1948–51, 1952–55, 1956–59, 1960–61)	.95	.96	.89
Five years (1948–52, 1953–57, 1958–61)	.95	.96	.87
Seven years (1948–54, 1955–61)	.94	.96	.84
Fourteen years (1948–61)	.94	.97	.77
	(n = 82)	(n = 71)	(n = 11)

had a high proportion of error. Feeling that there might be some systematic error in these eleven nations that was not present in the remaining seventy-one nations, they were sorted out and new coefficients calculated. The three sets of coefficients are presented on Table 3.

Thus, the scalable countries tend to inflate slightly the coefficient of reproducibility when one treats the entire sample of nations on a year by year analysis. Any systematic error persists, and as the coded categories decrease by collapsing years, this persistent error exerts more statistical influence. This is dramatically revealed in the column listing these coefficients for the Communist nations, and slightly revealed in the column for the entire sample. However, when the column for the non-Communist countries is examined this

TABLE 4

SCALAR PATTERNS—ALBANIA

Year	1	2	3	4	Years	1	2	3	4	Years	1	2	3	4
1948	+	—	—	+	1948–49	+	—	—	+	1948–51	+	+	—	+
1949	+	—	—	—	1950–51	+	+	—	+	1952–55	—	—	—	+
1950	+	—	—	—	1952–53	—	—	—	—	1956–59	—	—	—	—
1951	+	+	—	+	1954–55	—	—	—	+	1960–61	+	—	—	+
1952	—	—	—	—	1956–57	—	—	—	—					
1953	—	—	—	—	1958–59	—	—	—	—					
1954	—	—	—	+	1960–61	+	—	—	+	1948–52	+	+	—	+
1955	—	—	—	—						1953–57	—	—	—	+
1956	—	—	—	—						1958–61	+	—	—	+
1957	—	—	—	—	1948–50	+	—	—	+					
1958	—	—	—	—	1951–53	+	+	—	+					
1959	—	—	—	—	1954–56	—	—	—	+	1948–54	+	+	—	+
1960	—	—	—	—	1957–59	—	—	—	—	1955–61	+	—	—	+
1961	+	—	—	+	1960–61	+	—	—	+					
										1948–61	+	+	—	+

effect is entirely absent. Thus, the scale can be considered an efficient instrument for describing political violence in these seventy-one countries, but it cannot be so assessed for the Communist nations.

Examination of the data revealed that the "errors" in the Communist countries were a result of coding politically motivated executions under Position 4. In all other nations this seems to be associated with civil war or incipient civil war, and where this is present there are also the behaviors under Positions 3, 2, and 1. However, this seems to be a much more routine event in Communist countries and represents a systematic departure from the pattern found in all other nations. We can examine the scale pattern in Albania presented in Table 4 as an example. Scales are presented for the year-by-year analysis and as they appear when these years are combined.

One can note the persistence of the error pattern that looms larger proportionately as the longer time spans provide fewer coding categories.

This pattern revealed on Table 4 demonstrates why it is not efficient to use this scale to describe the patterns of political violence in Communist countries. If a nation scales well, it is a parsimonious way of conveying a great deal of information to say in 1948 (or any combination that forms a scale pattern) Albania had a level four of political violence (overt or incipient civil war as well as events in all the less serious levels). Albania simply did not have a level-four political violence pattern. Although that nation experienced events under Position 1, there were none under Positions 2 and 3. This is what is meant when we say that the pattern does *not* scale. If it does, then the scale is an efficient, parsimonious device for summarizing complex data; since it did not in Albania, the application of the notion is misleading.

Each of the Communist nations conforms generally to the scalar pattern of Albania. That is, there are errors in each of the nations because of occurrence of politically motivated executions without the accompanying experiences of guerrilla war, assassinations, revolt, etc. A new grouping of data is needed if one is to represent the political violence in these nations with a Guttman scale.

TABLE 5

Scalar Pattern—Australia

Year	1	2	3	4	Year	1	2	3	4
1948	—	—	—	—	1955	—	—	—	—
1949	+	—	—	—	1956	+	—	—	—
1950	+	—	—	—	1957	—	—	—	—
1951	—	—	—	—	1958	—	—	—	—
1952	—	—	—	—	1959	—	—	—	—
1953	—	—	—	—	1960	—	—	—	—
1954	—	—	—	—	1961	+	—	—	—

We can contrast this pattern with some representative ones from the seventy-one nations that do scale. Table 5 shows the year-by-year pattern of Australia which is representative of the industrialized, western nations. Australia's pattern is typical of this group of nations in that any instances of political violence are almost always of the type grouped under column 1. While these are experiences that any nation might wish to avoid, they do comprise a category that denotes much less violence than any other on the scale. Riots, boycotts, political arrests, etc. are coded under this category. Since there are no errors, they certainly cannot increase by collapsing years—this would only serve to decrease the number of categories in which it was *possible* for errors to appear. Thus, the effect of Australia's zero-error pattern on the entire analysis is reduced when the years are collapsed. It is conceivable that a handful of zero patterns could inflate the coefficient of reproducibility when this year-by-year scaling is used. If that were the case, however, the coefficients would have been reduced for these seventy-one nations in a similar fashion to the reduction in the case of the Communist nations. If it does not occur, one has evidence that the errors are randomly distributed. The fact that a .96 to .97 coefficient of reproducibility consistently emerged is powerful evidence of the underlying scalability and unidimensionality in occurrence of political violence.

TABLE 6

SCALAR PATTERNS—LEBANON

Year	1	2	3	4	Years	1	2	3	4	Years	1	2	3	4
1948	—	+	—	—	1948–49	+	+	+	+	1948–51	+	+	+	+
1949	+	—	+	+	1950–51	+	—	+	—	1952–55	+	—	—	—
1950	—	—	—	—	1952–53	+	—	—	—	1956–59	+	+	+	+
1951	+	—	+	—	1954–55	+	—	—	—	1960–61	+	+	—	—
1952	+	—	—	—	1956–57	+	+	—	—					
1953	—	—	—	—	1958–59	+	+	+	+	1948–52	+	+	+	+
1954	+	—	—	—	1960–61	+	+	—	—	1953–57	+	+	—	—
1955	—	—	—	—						1958–61	+	+	+	+
1956	+	+	—	—										
1957	+	+	—	—	1948–50	+	+	+	+					
1958	+	+	+	+	1951–53	+	—	+	—					
1959	—	—	+	—	1954–56	+	+	—	—	1948–54	+	+	+	+
1960	+	—	—	—	1957–59	+	+	+	+	1955–61	+	+	+	+
1961	—	+	—	—	1960–61	+	+	—	—					
										1948–61	+	+	+	+

In some nations we find occasional errors that are reduced or eliminated as one collapses years. The pattern of Lebanon, presented on Table 6, demonstrates this. One can see that in contrast to Albania's pattern, the errors in the Lebanese data disappear as the years are collapsed.

There are non-Communist nations whose scalar patterns do not combine so as to entirely eliminate error—as did Lebanon's. If this had not been the case there would have been a perfect coefficient of reproducibility when we collapsed years. However, when these errors are examined, there is no discernible theoretical basis on which to eliminate them—as there was with the Communist nations. It may be an error of measurement. We certainly do not claim to have identified the universe of behaviors that would qualify for rating under one of the theoretical scale positions. The goal was to select and record behaviors that were conceivably universal, i.e., could occur in any nation and were not identifiable as an idiosyncratic cultural phenomenon.

Indeed, one expected benefit of the development of a cross-national scale of political violence is that theoretical concepts that have been validated in such a large number of nations can prove useful for the more detailed examination of any single nation within which it is presumed that idiosyncratic behaviors are amenable to broader theoretical interpretation. If such use does prove feasible, then clearly we will have generated an instrument that contributes significantly to scientific explanation of these phenomena.

The Political Violence and Data Analysis

With these scales to determine the weights for various events, scores for political violence were calculated for the nations examined. This gives us a summary measure to test with postulated independent variables. Table 7 presents these scores.

TABLE 7

POLITICAL VIOLENCE SCORES, SUMMARY MEASURE, 1948–61—
NON-COMMUNIST COUNTRIES (n = 71)

Country	Score	Country	Score	Country	Score
Luxembourg	0	Ecuador	21	Turkey	47
Ireland	1	United Kingdom	21	Peru	48
Netherlands	1	Greece	22	Burma	50
Saudi Arabia	1	Malaya	22	Thailand	54
Denmark	3	Costa Rica	24	Paraguay	57
Iceland	3	Philippines	26	Sudan	57
Norway	4	Honduras	27	Spain	58
Sweden	4	Japan	27	Iran	59
Afghanistan	5	Brazil	28	Morocco	60
Australia	5	Portugal	29	Haiti	61
Austria	5	El Salvador	30	Syria	66
Israel	5	United States	30	Guatemala	68
New Zealand	5	Laos	31	Lebanon	68
China (Taiwan)	6	Dominican Republic	32	Iraq	74
Finland	6	Italy	32	India	76
Switzerland	6	Jordan	34	Korea	77
Canada	7	Mexico	36	Venezuela	78
West Germany	8	Panama	37	Bolivia	79
Ethiopia	10	Tunisia	38	Colombia	80
Liberia	12	Chile	40	Union of S. Africa	83
Cambodia	13	Egypt	40	France	97
Belgium	14	Ceylon	43	Argentina	109
Libya	14	Nicaragua	44	Indonesia	113
Uruguay	18	Pakistan	46		

This particular grouping of data did not scale for the Communist countries; therefore, any summary scale using the above technique probably does not efficiently describe the pattern of violence in those countries. For this reason they will not be included in much of the subsequent data analysis. However, for purposes of comparison with the nations on Table 7, Table 8 reports the scores.

TABLE 8

Political Violence Scores, Summary Measure, 1948-61—
Communist Countries (n = 11)

Country	Score	Country	Score	Country	Score
Bulgaria	15	Albania	27	Poland	41
East Germany	21	China	29	Hungary	46
Yugoslavia	21	Czechoslovakia	29	Cuba	89
Romania	23	U.S.S.R.	29		

With this quantification of the dependent variable, we can turn attention to the problem of isolating factors in societies that lead to high and low positions on the violence continuum. Perusal of Table 7 will show that those nations that experience the least violence tend to be the modern, industrial countries and that less-industrialized nations tend to have the higher scores. This is certainly not a perfect relationship. Saudi Arabia, Afghanistan, Ethiopia, and Liberia are among the most traditional nations in the world and are also among the most peaceful. The United States and the United Kingdom are near the middle of this continuum and France has experienced extreme amounts of violent activity. These three nations can certainly be considered among the most developed and industrialized in the world. However, there is clearly the tendency for the most industrialized nations to be the most peaceful nations. This finding is certainly anticipated in the literature on developing nations in which the "demonstration effect" of modernization is hypothesized to have an impact on the aspirations of large numbers of people who, until quite recently, were politically uninvolved participants of a traditional society. As nations embark on the path to industrialization, it is postulated, large numbers of persons are attracted away from their traditional environments to form a pool of labor for the developing factory system, as well as to engage in service trades that serve the growing urban centers. If these people find frustration and poverty rather than some of the gratifications of modernized society, one can expect to find a core of discontented persons who are living in close enough proximity so that collective expressions of this discontent are all too likely to occur. Furthermore, there is speculation in the literature that the paternalistic aspect of traditional society causes these new participants in modernity to look to the government as the agency with the power to dispense or withhold these sought-after benefits.

If this model does fit empirical reality well, it should be testable cross-nationally with our political violence data. Ideally, one would like to have data about the individual participants in these outbreaks of political violence. One would like to know to what extent expectations have been raised and then frustrated in the population of each nation, and whether it is indeed such persons who participate in riots, guerrilla war, etc. These data are not available, and the cost of their collection would be enormously high even if research efforts were focused on only a few countries. To collect such data from all eighty-two nations would be prohibitive. With the presently available data, hypotheses can be tested on only the broadest level.

The general model suggests that as a nation modernizes, benefits will be difficult to achieve. It is much easier to paint a glowing picture of the economic and social benefits that will be acquired through industrialization than it is to actually achieve these benefits. The gap between expectations and actual progress should be quite wide in the early stages and gradually narrower as modernization proceeds. Thus, we hypothesize the following: the higher the level of economic and social development, the lower the level of political violence. We have selected four indicators of the independent variable to test this relationship. The percentage of the labor force that is engaged in agricultural occupations was selected as an indicator of economic development. The daily newspaper circulation per 1,000 population was used as an indicator of mass media development. Life expectancy indicates health and social development, and the percentage of the population voting in national elections is broadly an indicator of political development. Since these variables were presumed to measure different aspects of development, in addition to simple correlations, multiple correlations were calculated to determine whether one can significantly increase the explanatory power by combining two of these indicators. Table 9 presents this analysis.

TABLE 9

Relationships Among Selected Predictor Variables and Instability

Simple correlations	Multiple correlations	
$r_{12} = .42$	$r_{1.23} = .57$	$r_{1.24} = .68$
$r_{13} = -.47$	$r_{1.34} = .52$	$r_{1.25} = .44$
$r_{14} = -.52$	$r_{1.45} = .52$	$r_{1.35} = .47$
$r_{15} = -.30$		

KEY: 1. Summary score of political violence
2. Percentage of labor force in agriculture (economic development)
3. Daily newspaper circulation (mass media development)
4. Life expectancy (health, social development)
5. Percentage of population voting in national elections (political development)

The simple correlations show that only a modest amount of the variance in the political violence scale can be explained by using a single predictor variable. The highest coefficient is between the violence scale and life expectancy, in which 27 percent of the variance is accounted for. The indicator of political development is probably not a very good one, but it was used because of a dearth of quantified material on political variables. It was hoped that by combining it with other types of indicators this one would account for significant portions of the variance beyond that accounted for by indicators of economic or social development. As one can see, the inclusion of variable 5 in the multiple correlations provides little or no gain over the use of a single variable. When it is combined with life expectancy, the coefficient is no higher than that gained by using variable 4 alone. There are two significant increases in predictive power—the combination of 2 and 4 raise the amount of explained variance from 27 percent (the r^2 of life expectancy and political violence) to 46 percent (the r^2 when the percentage of the labor force in agriculture is added as a predictor variable). A gain is also achieved when one combines the percentage of the labor force in agriculture with the daily newspaper circulation. The better predictor here accounts for 22 percent of the variance; the combination accounts for 32 percent of the variance.

In order to make use of existing theories of the effect of political development on the political behavior of citizens, the Almond and Coleman typology was used on which nations are classified and sorted as to the type of political structure they have. Forty-five of our seventy-one non-Communist nations are rated under either Latin American or Asian and African types of systems. These ratings are based on an analysis that identifies the functional roles of the political structure in each of these nations. They suggest that the greater the functional specificity of political structures in a society, the more democratic it can be considered. The most authoritarian nations are those in which a single structure performs most of the requisite functions (Almond and Coleman, 1960). This is certainly one assessment of political development. In addition to the forty-five nations in our study that were rated by Almond and Coleman as different types of developing polities, we have added twenty-three nations that can be considered developed nations. Table 10 examines the median political violence score[3] for these sixty-eight nations[4] as well as including median levels of economic development (as indicated by GNP per capita) and social development (as indicated by the percentage of literate persons in the nation).[5] The data present a striking pattern of linear changes in indicators of social and economic development along with a curvilinear pattern in the political violence experienced at each level. The greatest amount of violence occurs at the middle levels of development. Those groups of nations with the highest and lowest GNP per capita and the highest and lowest literacy rates are the most nonviolent groups on Table 10.

From these data one can infer that as there is growth in the economic and social sectors of a society the political system changes also. Concomitantly

TABLE 10

Economic and Social Development, Political Violence, and the Political System (n = 68)

Political system	GNP per capita median score	Percentage literate median score	Political violence median score
Developed and/or European (n = 23)	$943	98.5	6
Latin American competitive (n = 5)	379	80.1	28
Latin American semicompetitive (n = 5)	262	55.7	37
Asia and Africa political democracy (n = 7)	220	47.5	43
Latin American authoritarian (n = 9)	189	39.4	57
Asia and Africa tutelary democracy (n = 4)	136	17.5	55
Asia and Africa modernizing oligarchy (n = 6)	119	16.4	56
Asia and Africa conservative oligarchy (n = 6)	99	16.2	22
Asia and Africa traditional oligarchy (n = 3)	92	2.5	5

with these changes there is an increasing amount of manifest conflict in the society. Once, however, the system approaches full modernization (as indicated by almost universal adult literacy) and its economy can be classified as a high mass-consumption level (as indicated by a GNP per capita that is well above the subsistence level), then political stability tends to reemerge as characteristic.

These data do not conclusively verify the hypothesis that political violence is curvilinearly related to political, economic, and social development. At best they verify a curvilinear pattern of relationships among those nations that are *presently* at different levels of development. It would require time series data to establish this pattern of relationships in any single country or in any set of countries. One can speculate that this phenomenon may not have been so clearly manifested in the past. Modern electronic communications may be a crucial variable in that these are extremely efficient mechanisms for stimulating the aspirations of large numbers of persons. These communications are a modern phenomenon. They are also fundamental to the many analyses of political behavior in the developing world. It is doubtful that there was a similar agent for raising mass aspirations in the past. One could, however, test this pattern for selected countries in the future. We would have to be alerted for technological innovations that would have a significant effect on these variables, but the general hypothesis holds promise for use as an explanatory model of development.

METHODOLOGICAL APPENDIX

Cross-national studies generated by other researchers have been used to test some properties of our measures. Some of the work constructs variables that can be conceived of as predictors of political violence. One research endeavor that deals with data highly similar to those used in our own dependent variable is Rudolph Rummel's factor analysis of conflict data for seventy-seven nations during the years 1955-57 (Rummel, 1963 [reprinted in this volume, Chapter 3]).[6] He isolated three major factors of internal conflict, which he labeled: turmoil, revolution, and subversion. Rummel's description of these three variables is strikingly similar to the traits isolated by our own scale Positions 1, 2, and 3. It was felt that one could profitably use the Rummel findings to test validation of these three types of violence as separate measures. Such categorization of our data would convey a different type of information from that conveyed by the summary measure. There was a dilemma, however, in determining whether these scale positions should be quantified on the basis of frequency of events in each category or on the basis of the number of years a country had this score as the highest scale position. Both measures were tested against Rummel's scores. For each nation a value was assigned by the two respective techniques and correlated with the factor score that nation received on each of the three Rummel factors.

These findings are presented in Table 11, in what can be called a multitrait-multimethod matrix for testing convergent and discriminant validation. This technique of presenting data was developed by Campbell and Fiske (1959).

The italicized correlation coefficients are the validity diagonals on the matrix. Thus, Rummel's Factor 1 (turmoil) correlates at a level of .35 with the number of years at scale Position 1 (turmoil on our scale also) and .78 with frequency of scale Position 1. On trait 1 we see clear evidence that we are tapping Rummel's variable more efficiently when we use frequency of position rather than the number of years where this was the highest score. With the other traits, it doesn't seem to matter which technique we use for quantifying the scale. His Factor 2 (revolution) correlates .56 with the number of years at scale Position 2, and .59 with the frequency of scale Position 2. The trait of subversion, which Rummel measures in Factor 3, correlates .62 with the number of years at scale Position 3 and .66 with the frequency of scale Position 3.

Obviously, the higher the correlation coefficient on the validity diagonal, the stronger the evidence that one has developed efficient techniques for quantifying this trait. This is known as *convergent* validation—a confirmation by independent measurement procedures. The relatively high coefficients

TABLE 11

MULTITRAIT-MULTIMETHOD MATRIX OF VALIDATION

	Method 1 (Rummel)			Method 2 (Number of years at a given scale position)			Method 3 (Frequency at a given scale position)		
(Traits):	1	2	3	1	2	3	1	2	3
Method 1									
Trait 1 (Turmoil)	—								
Trait 2 (Revolution)	.55	—							
Trait 3 (Subversion)	.09	.40	—						
Method 2									
Trait 1	.35	−.06	−.21	—					
Trait 2	.40	.56	.12	−.17	—				
Trait 3	.15	.24	.62	−.18	.09	—			
Method 3									
Trait 1	.78	.36	.10	.59	.32	.20	—		
Trait 2	.44	.59	.22	−.23	.91	.25	.35	—	
Trait 3	.15	.21	.66	−.18	.08	.87	.18	.27	—

would seem to meet the requirements here. However, the matrix presented in this fashion can also give information on *discriminant* validation. That is, the validity diagonals should be higher than the correlations obtained between that variable and any variables having a different trait, as well as between that variable and any other variable having neither trait nor method in common. If those triangles enclosed by the solid lines (the heterotrait-monomethod triangles) have high correlation coefficients, this would indicate that the method was failing to discriminate the traits, that cases examined by this method generally had highly associated scores despite the attempt to distinguish separate traits. These heterotrait-monomethod triangles generally have low correlations—all of them much lower than those on the validity diagonal except for the association between Rummel's Factor 1 and Factor 2. It is significantly higher than the association between Rummel's Factor 1 and the number of years at scale Position 1, and almost equal to the correlation between Rummel's Factor 2 and the number of years at scale Position 2. The remaining correlations in the triangles enclosed by solid lines give quite satisfactory evidence of discriminant validation.

The heterotrait-heteromethod triangles (those enclosed by broken lines) contain the second set of evidence one needs for discriminant validation. They should be significantly lower than the correlations on the main diagonal. Again, the correlation between Rummel's Factor 1 and the number of years at scale Position 1 is the only departure from this pattern. In all other cases the evidence is overwhelming in its support of discriminant validation.

On the basis of the findings presented on this matrix, one can conclude that the number of years at scale Position 1 is not a good method for measuring that trait. Since Rummel's data and our data seem to be measuring the same traits, it would seem better to use frequency of scale position rather than the number of years at the scale position to develop these separate measures of political violence.

Several other cross-national analyses seemed to offer interesting comparisons with our findings. This first study is based on the data collected by Banks and Textor (1963). A Q-Factor analysis of these data reported in the *American Behavioral Scientist* grouped the nations of the world on five major factors. These were: (1) polyarchic, on which the nations with the highest loadings were western industrial nations; (2) elitist, with African nations predominating on the high loadings; (3) centrist, predominately a Communist nation factor; (4) personalist, dominated by the Latin American nations; and (5) traditional, primarily nations that are very low on development indices (Banks and Gregg, 1965 [reprinted in this volume, Chapter 12]).

A second index which we compare with our own is Phillips Cutright's quantification of national political development. He scored seventy-one nations on the existence of democratic political institution, i.e., a representative, competitive, and participant legislative branch of government and a chief executive selected in open election in which he faced competition. The scoring was done on a year-by-year basis from 1940–61—a period closely similar to that covered by our index of political violence (Cutright, 1963.)

The third measure was developed by David McClelland and was used to quantify a psychological variable hypothesized to be a prerequisite to economic development. He called this variable need-achievement and associated it with a strong motivation to succeed. McClelland postulated that those societies that became rapidly industrialized contained a pervasive norm that valued success highly. In contrast, those societies that were slow in developing promoted other types of social norms, such as duty or patient acceptance of life as one finds it. He measured need-achievement in several different ways, but the technique used to quantify it across forty nations was based on an examination of children's readers for story content. These readers were rated for the number of times the success motive was prominent in them (McClelland, 1961).

Table 12 reports the correlation coefficients between the McClelland, Cutright, and Banks and Gregg indexes and the different scales of political violence. It also shows the relationship between the indexes and aggregate data

TABLE 12

RELATIONSHIPS AMONG CROSS-NATIONAL QUANTIFIED VARIABLES

	Banks and Gregg factor scores					Cutright Index	McClelland Need-achievement
	Polyarchy	Elitist	Centrist	Personalist	Traditional		
Summary score of violence	-.480	.396	.135	.509	.150	-.294	.462
Frequency of violence type 1	-.147	.108	.090	.210	.059	-.096	.406
Frequency of violence type 2	-.453	.227	.078	.691	.023	-.220	.436
Frequency of violence type 3	-.368	.573	.095	.104	.108	-.277	.182
Frequency of violence type 4	-.494	.386	.118	.372	.318	-.317	.221
Percentage of labor in agriculture	-.801	.616	.431	.538	.386	-.702	.226
Newspaper circulation	.787	-.610	-.454	-.500	-.427	.715	-.304
Life expectancy	.775	-.663	-.232	-.608	-.384	.552	-.259
Percentage voting	.663	-.269	-.573	-.331	-.414	.506	-.109

Scalogram Analysis of Political Violence

on economic and social development,[7] thus enabling one to compare these relationships with those reported on Table 9 for the political violence index.

In looking over the correlations between the Banks and Gregg factor scores and the several types of political violence scores, one notes some interesting relationships. Polyarchy is consistently negatively related to political violence—regardless of whether it is the summary score or one of the separate types. As one would expect, this relationship is less clear in the frequency of type 1 violence. We discovered in our earlier analysis that the more highly developed a nation is, the less likely it is to experience violence, but if such events of violence do occur, they are almost exclusively confined to type 1 events. It is clear that polyarchy is associated with economic and social development by strong positive relationships between this factor and standard of living indicators. The elitist factor has a positive relationship with type 3 events—guerrilla warfare and political assassinations. There is a strong negative relationship between the elitist factor and standard of living indicators—bearing out the postulated nature of this factor.

The centrist factor bears no relationship, either positive or negative, to the measures of political violence. This may be due to our removal of the Communist countries from the analysis, since they were the ones on which this factor loaded highest. There is a negative relationship between this factor and standard of living data, even with the Communist countries removed, but the magnitude of these values is not as great as it was with the elitist factor. On the personalist factor, we find a stronger positive relationship with the summary score of political violence than with any other factor. An even stronger relationship can be seen as existing between scores on this factor and the type 2 events. This factor is dominated by Latin American nations, and it is not unexpected that type 2 events—coup d'état, martial law, revolt—would correlate highly with this factor. The traditional factor shows no relationship with political violence except for a modest positive relationship with the frequency of type 4 events—civil war and political executions. Fairly weak relationships are also seen with standard of living data although one would have predicted a strong negative pattern.

When we examine the correlations of political violence with the Cutright index of national political development, we find an unexpectedly low magnitude of relationship. The direction is as one would predict: a negative association between violence and development, but the values are far too low to use this index as an efficient explanation of political violence. In order to see if there is a tendency toward a curvilinear relationship, the Cutright index was trichotomized, and a mean score for violence was calculated. However, linearity was suggested by the results. The mean violence score of the group Cutright rated as most highly developed was 18.2, for the middle level development it was 38.6, and for the lowest level of development it was 47.6. Thus, the correlation coefficients are probably accurate descriptions of the magnitude of relationship—a disappointing finding.

A very surprising finding was that McClelland's need-achievement index correlated positively with political violence and correlated negatively with standard of living data. McClelland found a positive correlation between his index and economic development by using national income and kilowatt-hours of electricity per capita as his indicators. We find a contrary relationship in the four indicators that we have used. The magnitude of the correlation coefficients is not very high in this matrix, but all four of them are consistently in the same direction.

In order to compare the correlations of the separate components of the violence summary score with the other findings on the matrix, the coefficients between frequency at each scale position (as well as the summary score) and the standard of living data are presented on Table 13.

TABLE 13

RELATIONSHIPS AMONG THE SEPARATE TYPES OF POLITICAL VIOLENCE AND STANDARD OF LIVING DATA

	1	Frequency at scale 2	3	4	Summary score
Percentage of labor in agriculture	−.087	.438	.373	.373	.418
Newspaper circulation	−.218	−.438	−.371	−.328	−.474
Life expectancy	−.204	−.594	−.425	−.354	−.521
Percentage voting	−.259	−.212	.033	−.327	−.299

On the whole, type 2 events—coup d'etat, martial law, revolt—are more easily predicted than any of the other component scales of political violence. In other words, the lower the standard of living, the greater the likelihood of experiencing these events. On the basis of our scalogram analysis we know that nations experiencing these events may not have those rated under type 3 or type 4, but they will surely have type 1 events. Other countries that have *only* the less violent type 1 events interfere with this type 1 component scale, having very high correlation coefficients. It will be recalled that if highly industrialized nations do experience political violence, it is almost exclusively of type 1—turmoil rather than any of the more widespread and more serious types of violence. But nations experiencing *any* of the more serious types of violence also have these less serious (turmoil) events. Thus, it was an expected finding that any use of the type 1 events exclusive of the others would give more ambiguous results with possible predictor variables than the other types of violence. What was unexpected was that type 2 events show a greater magnitude of relationship with the predictor variables than any other component type. These data indicate that we cannot predict the scalar position by standard of living data. Although it follows from this and other tests that the higher the standard of living, the lower the likelihood of political violence, it does *not* follow that the higher scale positions can be predicted by such data. Apparently, there are other causal variables involved when type 3 or type 4 events erupt. We can say with some confidence, though, that nations containing a low level of living for their populace can be expected to experience type 2 and type 1 events.

One variable that does not tend to follow this pattern is the political one. The percentage of the population voting has its strongest relationship with events of type 4. More analysis needs to be done with political variables to clarify this relationship. It is this very point that led us to attach this appendix to the main part of the research report. Standard of living data can be used directly from census reports and collections of cross-national statistics. These, however, are only a portion of the data needed to understand the complex setting in which political behavior occurs. In recent years, social scientists have made a heavy investment in time and talent to understand, operationalize, and quantify some of these other variables. The McClelland, Cutright, and Banks and Gregg analyses are representative of some of the most interesting of these efforts. Others are surely forthcoming. This extension of quantified variables promises the laboring behavioralist the data with which to extend his knowledge and improve his explanations of behavior—including political violence.

NOTES

1. For a description of this scale, the initial tests for validity, and data analysis in which it was used as a dependent variable, see Feierabend, Feierabend, and Nesvold (1963) and Feierabend and Feierabend (1966 [reprinted in this volume, Chapter 6]).

2. Appreciation is certainly acknowledged for Donald E. Stokes' kind permission to conduct this test in his class, and to Joseph Massey for his assistance.

3. Median rather than mean scores were used because the N is small in many groups, and one extreme value can distort the central tendency indication conveyed by mean values.

4. Korea, Taiwan, and the Union of South Africa were not included in this analysis.

5. These indicators were used rather than the ones on Table 9 because data are available for all countries and because they are such commonly used indicators of these variables.

6. See also Tanter (1964). This is a replication, a retest of the Rummel analysis in which data for a later period were collected for analysis.

7. Note that a *negative* relationship between the percentage of the labor force in agriculture is expected when the variable is associated with a high standard of living. In all other indicators of social and economic development, the same relationship is identified by a *positive* sign.

REFERENCES

ALMOND, GABRIEL A. and JAMES S. COLEMAN, Eds. (1960) *The Politics of Developing Areas*. Princeton: Princeton University Press.

BANKS, ARTHUR S. and PHILLIP M. GREGG (1965) "Grouping political systems: Q-factor analysis of 'A Cross-Polity Survey.'" *The American Behavioral Scientist* 9 (November): 3-6. Reprinted in this volume, Chapter 12.

BANKS, ARTHUR S. and ROBERT B. TEXTOR (1963) *A Cross-Polity Survey*. Cambridge: MIT Press.

CAMPBELL, DONALD T. and DONALD W. FISKE (1959) "Convergent and discriminant validation by the multitrait-multimethod matrix." *Psychological Bulletin* 56 (March): 81-105.

CUTRIGHT, PHILLIPS (1963) "National political development: measurement and analysis." *American Sociological Review* 28: 253-264.

FEIERABEND, IVO K. and ROSALIND L. FEIERABEND (1966) "Aggressive behaviors within polities, 1948-1962: a cross-national study." *Journal of Conflict Resolution* 10 (September): 249-271. Reprinted in this volume, Chapter 6.

— (1965) *Cross-National Data Bank of Political Instability Events* (Code Index). San Diego: Public Affairs Research Institute.

FEIERABEND, IVO K., ROSALIND L. FEIERABEND, and BETTY A. NESVOLD (1963) "Correlates of political stability." Paper delivered at the American Political Science Convention, September, New York.

GUTTMAN, LOUIS (1950) "The basis for scalogram analysis." Pp. 60-90 in Samuel A. Stouffer et al. *Studies in Social Psychology in World War Two*. Vol. 4, *Measurement and Prediction*. Princeton: Princeton University Press.

MCCLELLAND, DAVID C. (1961) *The Achieving Society*. Princeton: D. Van Nostrand.

RUMMEL, RUDOLPH J. (1963) *Dimensions of Conflict Behavior Within and Between Nations*. Evanston, Ill.: Report of research under National Science Foundation Contract NSF-F 24827. Reprinted in this volume, Chapter 3.

TANTER, RAYMOND (1964) *Dimensions of Conflict Behavior Within and Between Nations*. Evanston, Ill.: Monograph prepared from research under National Science Foundation Contract NSF-GS 224.

8 The Conditions of Civil Violence: First Tests of a Causal Model

TED ROBERT GURR with CHARLES RUTTENBERG

It seems evident that most riots and revolutions are made by angry men, not dispassionate ones, and that the more intense their anger, the more destructive their actions are likely to be. Nonetheless, this characteristic of strife has received no significant attention in most recent theoretical inquiries into the causes of violent conflict within nations.[1] This monograph reports research designed to evaluate a theoretical model that specifically attempts to account for the sources and consequences of collective anger. It is assumed that frustration-induced anger is the common denominator of participants in acts of civil violence, that anger is the principal characteristic distinguishing them from participants in other forms of collective behavior, and that it constitutes a drive that disposes them to the general character of their behavior, namely, violent attacks on those they hold responsible for their frustration.

Generalization of the frustration-aggression variables to the collectivity is neither reification nor mere statement of isomorphism. The violence (defined below) can be usefully treated by reference to the distribution of relevant properties of individual behavior among collectivities. This approach also recognizes the relevance of aspects of social structure and process. Our supposition is that theory about civil violence can fruitfully be based on systematic knowledge about those properties of men which determine how they react to certain characteristics of their societies. Generalization to the collectivity thus is facilitated by the development of some additional concepts.

The central premise of the theory is that the necessary precondition for violent civil conflict is *relative deprivation*, defined as actors' perception of discrepancy between their *value expectations* and their environment's *value capabilities*. Value expectations are the goods and conditions of life to which

---

Editors' Note: An abridgement of Research Monograph No. 28, Center of International Studies, Woodrow Wilson School of Public and International Affairs, Princeton University, April 1967.
Reprinted by arrangement with the author and publisher.

people believe they are justifiably entitled. The referents of value capabilities are to be found largely in the social and physical environment: they are conditions that determine people's chances for getting or keeping the values they legitimately expect to attain. This definition of relative deprivation varies from that of sociologists, who denote by the term an objective discrepancy between an individual's positions on several status or value dimensions.[2] Our definition is narrower, insofar as it is restricted to discrepancies that are both perceived and regarded as unjustifiable, and broader in that it recognizes that such perceived discrepancies can arise in a wide variety of ways, e.g., through changes in expectation levels alone, by comparison with one's own past condition, by abrupt political or economic change, and so forth.

Relative deprivation can be related to the frustration concept by extending Yate's (1962: 175-178) distinction between the frustrating situation and the frustrated organism. A frustrating situation can be defined as one in which an actor is, judged by objective standards, thwarted by some social or physical barrier in attempts to attain or continue enjoyment of a value. The actor can be said to be frustrated, however, only when he is aware of the interference. The awareness of interference is equivalent to the concept of relative deprivation as defined above; discontent or anger is the emotional reaction to that awareness.

A further distinction is necessary between those deprivations that are personal and those that are group or category experiences.[3] For given groups, and for some classes of societies, one can identify events and patterns of conditions that are likely to be widely seen as unjust deprivation. Such events may occur more or less abruptly—for example, the suppression of a political party or the onset of economic depression—or slowly, like the decline of the *Bürgertum*'s status relative to other social classes in Weimar Germany. Such conditions are called here *societal frustrations*. The empirical research reported here focuses on conditions inferred to be societally frustrating. Other research strategies, notably survey techniques, permit direct assessment of relative deprivation.[4]

Choosing the cross-sectional alternative required one final decision: which class of ecological units to use. Several arguments supported the use of the polity as the basic unit. In political science there is intrinsically more theoretical interest in variations of levels of strife among polities than among regions of a given nation. Moreover, single occurrences of strife often encompass several or all regions of a polity; the polity is thus the minimal unit that avoids interdependence of cases. The total universe of contemporary polities—between 110 and 150, depending on one's definition—is adequate for most statistical purposes, and, more important, it is possible to include the entire universe, a strategy that avoids some problems of the representativeness of a sample. A distinct operational advantage is the fact that quantitative, comparative data that can be used in correlational analysis are more often available for national than for subnational units. Finally, several quantitative studies of cross-national correlates of civil strife have been previously undertaken; their results bear comparison with those reported here (Feierabend and Feierabend, this volume, Chapter 19; Russett, 1964; Rummel, 1963; Russett et al., 1964: 272, 317-321; Bwy, 1966; Midlarsky and Tanter, 1967: 209-227).

The Universe of Analysis and Index Stability

Quantitative, cross-national comparison has limitations as well as advantages. It is suited to gross discrimination among nations but not to the microanalysis that would account more precisely for the forms, timing, and targets of specific occurrences of civil strife. Since our immediate concern is the relevance of the theory for the most general case, however, this characteristic is less a limitation than microanalysts might argue.

More serious is the problem of index instability: that is, the likelihood that a given event, condition, or measure varies in significance, both for actors and with reference to the theoretical questions at hand, from one cultural or political context to another. Some index instability problems can be resolved by choosing or devising indicators that are more stable, and by care in the theoretical interpretation of what common property is denoted by a particular index. Voting turnout is a poor measure of "democracy" in its common range of scholarly usage, but one can less easily quarrel with its use as a comparative measure of level of *formal* political participation.

The likelihood remains, as Russett et al. (1964: 323) observe, that "relationships between variables will be different for data from different geographic or cultural contexts." To recognize the likelihood is not to invoke the fact of geographic or cultural regionalism as a sufficient explanation. The high incidence of civil strife in Latin America is insufficiently accounted for by statements that it is "an inherent aspect of Latin American political culture." It is more adequately interpreted as the result of a particular constellation of positions on universal variables—e.g., persistent discrepancies between the ideals and practice of political leadership, low socioeconomic mobility, low valuation of cooperative collective endeavor, and so forth, the judgments of "high" and "low" being made with reference to other, non-Latin American polities.

The research design here presented incorporates a method of controlling for systematic variation of this sort: division of the total universe of polities into "clusters," the polities of each of which are relatively homogeneous with respect to some constellation of political or socioeconomic conditions. Once such clusters are distinguished, separate multiple correlation analyses can be made for each one, a procedure that constitutes a partial control for those variables on the basis of which they are discriminated. The total universe of polities, and the components of each cluster, are identified in Table 1.

TABLE 1

THE UNIVERSE OF POLITIES AND COMPONENT CLUSTERS OF POLITICALLY,
SOCIOECONOMICALLY, AND ECOLOGICALLY HOMOGENEOUS POLITIES[a]

Polity	Political rule characteristics[a]	Sociocultural characteristics[b]	Technological development level	Size of population and productivity
Afghanistan	Centrist	Asian[b]	Very low	Moderate
Albania	Centrist	E. European	Medium[b]	Small
Algeria	Centrist	Asian	Medium	Moderate
Angola	Centrist	African	Very low	Small
Argentina	Personalist	Latin[b]	High	Dominant
Australia	Polyarchic	Anglo-Saxon	High	Dominant
Austria	Polyarchic	W. European	High	Moderate
Belgium	Polyarchic	W. European	High	Dominant
Bolivia	Polyarchic	Latin	Low	Small
Brazil	Polyarchic	Latin	Medium	Dominant
Bulgaria	Centrist	E. European	Medium	Moderate
Burma	Elitist	Asian	Low	Moderate
Burundi	Elitist	African	Very low[b]	Very small
Cambodia	Elitist	Asian[b]	Low[b]	Small
Cameroun	Elitist	African	Low[b]	Small
Canada	Polyarchic	Anglo-Saxon	High	Dominant
Central African R.	Elitist	African	Very low	Very small
Ceylon	Polyarchic	Asian	Medium	Moderate
Chad	Elitist	African	Very low	Very small
Chile	Polyarchic	Latin	Medium	Moderate
China—Peking	Centrist	E. European	Low	Dominant
China—Taiwan	Centrist[b]	Asian[b]	Medium	Moderate
Colombia	Polyarchic	Latin	Medium	Moderate
Congo—Léopoldville	Elitist	African	Low	Moderate
Costa Rica	Polyarchic	Latin	Medium	Very small
Cuba	Centrist	Latin	Medium	Small
Czechoslovakia	Centrist	E. European	High	Dominant
Dahomey	Elitist	African	Very low[b]	Very small
Denmark	Polyarchic	W. European	High	Moderate
Dominican Rep.	Personalist[c]	Latin	Low	Small
Ecuador	Personalist	Latin	Low	Small
El Salvador	Personalist	Latin	Medium	Small
Ethiopia	Centralist	African	Very low	Moderate
Finland	Polyarchic	Anglo-Saxon[d]	High	Moderate
France	Polyarchic	W. European	High	Dominant
Germany—East	Centrist	E. European	High	Dominant
Germany—West	Polyarchic	W. European	High	Dominant
Ghana	Elitist	African	Low	Small
Greece	Polyarchic	W. European	Medium	Moderate
Guatemala	Personalist	Latin	Low	Small
Guinea	Elitist	African	Low[b]	Very small

TABLE 1 (CONTINUED)

Polity	Political rule characteristics[a]	Sociocultural characteristics[b]	Technological development level	Size of population and productivity
Haiti	Personalist	Asian	Very low	Very small
Honduras	Personalist	Latin	Low	Very small
Hong Kong	Centrist[b]	Asian[b]	Medium	Small
Hungary	Centrist	E. European	High	Moderate
India	Polyarchic	Asian	Medium	Dominant
Indonesia	Elitist	Asian	Low	Dominant
Iran	Centrist[c]	Asian	Low	Dominant
Iraq	Personalist	Asian	Medium	Moderate
Ireland	Polyarchic	W. European	High	Small
Israel	Polyarchic	W. European	Medium	Small
Italy	Polyarchic	W. European	High	Dominant
Ivory Coast	Elitist	African	Low[b]	Very small
Jamaica	Polyarchic	Asian	Medium[b]	Very small
Japan	Polyarchic	W. European	High	Dominant
Jordan	Centrist	Asian	Very low	Very small
Kenya	Elitist[b]	African	Low[b]	Small
Korea—North	Centrist	E. European[b]	Very low[b]	Moderate
Korea—South	Personalist	Asian	Low	Moderate
Laos	Elitist[c]	Asian[b]	Low	Very small
Lebanon	Personalist	W. European	Medium	Small
Liberia	Centrist	African	Very low	Very small
Libya	Polyarchic	Asian[b]	Very low	Very small
Malagasy	Elitist	African	Low	Small
Malaya	Polyarchic	Asian	Medium	Small
Mali	Elitist	African	Very low[b]	Very small
Mexico	Polyarchic	Latin	High	Dominant
Mongolia	Centrist	E. European[b]	Low[b]	Very small
Morocco	Polyarchic	Asian	Medium	Moderate
Mozambique	Centrist[b]	African	Very low	Small
Nepal	Centrist	Asian	Very low[b]	Small
Netherlands	Polyarchic	W. European	High	Dominant
New Zealand	Polyarchic	Anglo-Saxon	High	Small
Nicaragua	Personalist	Latin	Low	Very small
Niger	Elitist	African	Very low[b]	Very small
Nigeria	Elitist[c]	African	Low	Moderate
N. Rhodesia	Elitist[b]	African	Low[b]	Small
Norway	Polyarchic	Anglo-Saxon[d]	High	Moderate
Nyasaland	Elitist	African	Very low[b]	Very small
Pakistan	Elitist	Asian	Low	Dominant
Panama	Personalist	Latin	Low	Very small
Papua-New Guinea	Centrist[b]	Asian[b]	Very low[b]	Very small
Paraguay	Personalist	Latin	Very low	Very small
Peru	Personalist	Latin	Medium	Moderate

TABLE 1 (Continued)

Polity	Political rule characteristics[a]	Sociocultural characteristics[b]	Technological development level	Size of population and productivity
Philippines	Polyarchic	Asian[b]	Medium	Moderate
Poland	Centrist	E. European	High	Dominant
Portugal	Centrist	W. European	Medium	Moderate
Puerto Rico	Polyarchic	W. European	High[b]	Small
Rumania	Centrist	E. European	Medium	Dominant
Rwanda	Elitist	African	Very low[b]	Very small
Saudi Arabia	Centrist	Asian[b]	Very low[b]	Moderate
Senegal	Elitist	African	Low[b]	Very small
Sierra Leone	Elitist	African	Very low	Very small
Singapore	Polyarchic[b]	Asian[b]	Medium[b]	Very small
Somalia	Elitist	African	Very low[b]	Very small
South Africa	Centrist[c]	Anglo-Saxon	High	Dominant
S. Rhodesia	Centrist[b]	Anglo-Saxon[b]	Medium[b]	Small
Spain	Centrist	W. European	High	Dominant
Sudan	Elitist	African	Very low	Small
Sweden	Polyarchic	Anglo-Saxon[d]	High	Moderate
Switzerland	Polyarchic	W. European	High	Moderate
Syria	Personalist	Asian	Low	Small
Tanganyika	Elitist	African	Very low[b]	Small
Thailand	Personalist	Asian	Low	Moderate
Togo	Elitist	African	Very low[b]	Very small
Tunisia	Elitist	Asian	Low	Small
Turkey	Polyarchic	Asian	Moderate	Dominant
Uganda	Elitist	African	Low[b]	Small
U.A.R.	Centrist	W. European[b]	Moderate	Dominant
United Kingdom	Polyarchic	W. European	High	Dominant
United States	Polyarchic	Anglo-Saxon	High	Dominant
U.S.S.R.	Centrist	E. European	High	Dominant
Uruguay	Polyarchic	Latin	Moderate	Small
Venezuela	Polyarchic	Latin	High	Dominant
Vietnam—North	Centrist	E. European[b]	Very low[b]	Moderate
Vietnam—South	Elitist	Asian[b]	Very low	Moderate
Voltaic Republic	Elitist	African	Very low[b]	Very small
Yemen	Elitist[c]	Asian[b]	Very low[b]	Very small
Yugoslavia	Centrist	E. European	Moderate	Dominant

[a] See text and text notes for sources and procedures used in determining the polities for inclusion in the universe and in the various clusters. Another revised set of clusters is reported in Gurr (1969b). The sociocultural regions are somewhat differently defined and three rather than four technological development levels are distinguished.

[b] Not included or unclassifiable in source; assigned to cluster on judgmental grounds or by use of comparable data.

[c] Assigned to another cluster in source; reassigned here on judgmental grounds.

[d] "Anglo-Saxon" may be a misnomer for a cluster that includes three of the four Scandinavian countries but not the United Kingdom. Whatever the label, however, the analysis clearly distinguishes this cluster from the "Western European" cluster.

Universe of Analysis. The universe consists of all distinct national and colonial entities that had populations of one million or more in 1962, a total of 119, comprising 99 percent of the world's entire population. Polities with smaller populations were excluded because data for them tend to be of low quality, because of the minute fraction of the world's population that they represent, and because of questions about the advisability of comparative generalizations that give equal weight to very large and very small nations. We included colonies—excluded from some cross-polity studies—on the ground that if colonial status is a significant variable affecting internal political behavior it should be treated as such, i.e., as an independent variable, not as a limitation on the selection of cases.

Political Clusters. The background conditions for civil strife ought to vary markedly from one type of political system to another, suggesting that polities be grouped on the basis of their political rule characteristics. Banks and Gregg have undertaken a Q-factor analysis of 68 specifically political variables for 115 nations. Their analysis distinguishes five classes of nations, each characterized by rather distinct constellations of political behavior and rule patterns. The authors label them *polyarchic*, comprising 42 nations that approximate Western democratic political structures and processes; *elitist*, 30 recently independent, predominantly African states with relatively small, modernizing elites; *centrist*, 24 communist and other non-Latin authoritarian regimes; *personalist*, 15 predominantly Latin regimes characterized by a high degree of political personalism; and *traditional*, four nations such as Yemen. We reclassified polities from the traditional class to others, because the N of 4 is too small for most statistical purposes, and judgmentally assigned polities included in our universe but excluded by Banks and Gregg to the remaining four classes. This procedure gave us four politically distinct subsets of polities, each of which is subject to separate multiple correlation analysis. The clusters are not necessarily those that might be made by reference to some current conceptual schemes; they do, however, take full account of a large number of political variables of theoretical relevance.[5]

Sociocultural Clusters. Patterns of strife, deprivation, social control, and other theoretically relevant system characteristics ought to vary systematically with respect to sociocultural patterns as well as type of political rule. Russett has used factor analysis of 54 socioeconomic and cultural variables first to discriminate five basic dimensions along which polities vary, and then to partition 82 nations into five, essentially regional, clusters according to their degree of sociocultural homogeneity with respect to these dimensions. Sub-Saharan African Polities are not included in the Russett analysis for want of sufficient data, but they may be said to constitute a distinct region on geographic and cultural grounds. Polities in our set not classified by these procedures were judgmentally assigned to the six sets identified. The clusters, and the numbers of polities included in each, are *Asian* (31, including the Islamic states); *Eastern European* (13, including Asian Communist states);

African (29); *Latin* (19); *Anglo-Saxon* (9); and *Western European* (18). These clusters are not identical with those identifiable on solely geographic or cultural criteria, but again have the advantage of representing constellations of polities determined with reference to a large number of relevant variables.[6]

Technological Development Clusters. The vastly different economic structures of contemporary polities, and the frequent empirical association of civil strife with the social changes contingent on stages of economic development, strongly suggest differential significance of the independent variables among polities according to their level of development. Berry's factor analysis of 43 economic and demographic variables for 95 polities resolves the variables into a single major "technological scale" dimension. Since technological development is essentially unidimensional, we can identify clusters of polities by dividing country scores on this scale into four equal-sized groups.[7] The resultant four clusters are arbitrary—we could as well divide the scale values into thirds or fifths, or judgmentally select other cutting points—in contrast with the multidimensionally defined political and sociocultural clusters, but they serve a comparable function: they discriminate among groups of polities having rather distinct economic characteristics by taking into account a large number of variables.

Ecological Size Clusters. It is plausible to suspect that the population size and related characteristics of nations systematically affect the types, and perhaps the likelihood and intensity, of civil strife. Moreover, of all the factor-analytically identified dimensions on which countries vary, Rummel has found a "size" or "power bases" dimension to be one of the strongest. Three measures that are closely associated with this dimension are total population, total GNP, and total energy production. We obtained data for each of these "marker" variables for each polity in our universe, rank-ordered the polities on each variable, averaged their ranks, and then ranked the average rankings. The final step in this ad hoc procedure was to divide the polities into four equal-sized groups on the basis of the combined ranking.[8] The polities in each cluster are thus more or less homogeneous with respect not to geographic size but to what might be called ecological size. The cluster containing the most populous and productive polities is labeled Dominant, the others Moderate, Small, and Very Small.

Overlapping Clusters. There is substantial overlapping among some of the clusters. The Personalist political rule cluster includes more than half the states in the Latin cluster. The Elitist cluster includes most of the polities in the Very Small size cluster, all of those in the African cluster, and many of those in the Very Low technological development cluster. All of the Eastern European polities are included among the Centrist polities. Almost all the Anglo-Saxon and Western European polities are included in the Polyarchic cluster. Such overlapping suggests that a smaller number of clusters might equally well control for systematic interregional variation; in the present analyses, however, it facilitates validation and interpretation of the results for some of the clusters.

Magnitude of Civil Violence

A consideration of frustration-aggression theory suggests that no single measure of quantity of aggression is in itself sufficient. If we assume for the moment the validity of the basic frustration-aggression postulate that the greater the strength of anger, the greater the quantity of violence, it seems likely that strong anger can be satisfied either by inflicting severe immediate damage on the source of frustration or by prolonged but less severe aggression, and that either of these means can probably substitute for the other. Which alternative is taken may very well be a function of opportunity, and while opportunities can be controlled in an experimental situation, in civil violence they are situationally determined. Hence, neither severity nor duration alone is likely to be adequate as an indicator of modal strength of collective anger or as a measure of the quantity of civil violence.

Moreover, there are evidently individual differences—presumably normally distributed—in the strength of anger needed to precipitate overt aggression. Hence the *proportion* of a population that participates in collective violence ought to vary with the modal strength of anger; discontent will motivate few to violence, anger will push more across the threshold, rage is likely to galvanize large segments of a collectivity into action.

This line of argument suggests that at least these three aspects of civil violence be taken into account in specifying its intensity: (1) the extent of participation by the affected population—in this research design, the population of each polity; (2) the length of time they persist in the violent action; and (3) the destructiveness of their actions. In devising operational measures of these characteristics we have followed Sorokin (1937: 383–407) who, on more ad hoc grounds, chose to construct a "magnitude of social disturbances" scale based on component measures of social area, duration, and intensity of civil disorder. In modifying and extending Sorokin's approach, we asked the following operational question about each polity for each year: How many participants, encompassing what social area, caused how many casualties and how much property damage over what period of time? Data on the first two of these variables provided the basis for a composite measure of extent of participation, or *pervasiveness*; estimates of casualties and damage provided a measure of destructiveness, or *intensity*. These composite measures were combined with the *duration* measure to provide a summary measure of the *magnitude of civil violence*.

Measures of Civil Violence

The five Basic Measures of civil violence are defined and scaled as follows:

BM1: Number of Participants. Participants are all those reported to have been members of the group(s) engaging in violence, excluding the punitive forces opposing them. Police, army, and other regime personnel are counted if acting in a capacity other than that of agent of the regime. This is a derived measure, weighted by total population: 100,000 rioters in a country with a population of one million represent proportionally greater strife for that country than the same number of rioters in a country of ten million. The measure is the number of participants per 100,000 population.

$P_1 = 1$–50 $\qquad P_3 = 151$–500
$P_2 = 51$–150 $\qquad P = 501+$

BM2: Social Area. The extent of the polity affected by the most widespread strife event of the year.

$a_1 =$ single urban or rural location
$a_2 =$ several urban and/or rural locations
$a_3 =$ major area or section of polity (province, state)
$a_4 =$ most or all of polity

BM3: Number of Casualties. This is the total number of deaths and injuries reported as direct consequences of civil violence. The measure is the proportion of casualties per 1,000 participants.

$c_1 = 1$–20 $\qquad c_3 = 51$–150
$c_2 = 21$–50 $\qquad c_4 = 151+$

BM4: Property Damage. This measure, having no direct relationship to monetary value, is intended to reflect the amount of damage relative to the scope of action indicated by the preceding Basic Measures.

$d_1 =$ slight (objects thrown, windows broken)
$d_2 =$ moderate (vehicles, buildings damaged or destroyed)
$d_3 =$ extensive (widespread arson, other complete destruction, widespread looting and pillaging)

BM5: Duration. The total amount of time encompassed by all occurrences of civil violence during any one calendar year.

$t_1 =$ one week or less $\qquad t_3 =$ one month to six months
$t_2 =$ one week to one month $\qquad t_4 =$ six months to one year

The five Basic Measures were combined to produce four Composite Scales of amount of civil violence. Each Composite Scale is an ordinal scale derived by weighted combinations of two or more of the Basic Measure ordinal scales. Each of the Basic Measures relates to the concept operationally defined by the corresponding Composite Scale. The rules for producing the Composite Scales are defined below, and the scales themselves are found in their entirety in Table 2. Table 3 below shows schematically how all the measures of civil violence are interrelated.

TABLE 2
THE COMPOSITE SCALES

Pervasiveness[a]			Intensity[b]			Amplitude[c]		
P_1	$p_1a_1 =$	1	I_1	$c_1d_1 =$	1	A_1	$P_1I_1 =$	1.0
	$p_1a_2 =$	2		$c_1d_2 =$	2	A_2	P_1I_2	
	$p_2a_1 =$	3		$c_2d_1 =$	3		$P_2I_1 =$	2.5
	$p_1a_3 =$	4	I_2	$c_1d_3 =$	4	A_3	P_3I_1	
P_2	$p_2a_2 =$	5		$c_2d_2 =$	5		$P_1I_3 =$	4.5
	$p_1a_4 =$	6		$c_3d_1 =$	6	A_4	P_1I_4	
	$p_3a_1 =$	7	I_3	$c_2d_3 =$	7		P_2I_2	
	$p_2a_3 =$	8		$c_3d_2 =$	8		$P_4I_1 =$	7.0
P_3	$p_3a_2 =$	9		$c_4d_1 =$	9	A_5	P_2I_3	
	$p_2a_4 =$	10	I_4	$c_3d_3 =$	10		$P_3I_2 =$	9.5
	$p_4a_1 =$	11		$c_4d_2 =$	11	A_2	P_2I_4	
	$p_3a_3 =$	12		$c_4d_3 =$	12		$P_4I_2 =$	11.5
P_4	$p_4a_2 =$	13				A_7	$P_3I_3 =$	13.0
	$p_3a_4 =$	14				A_8	P_3I_4	
	$p_4a_3 =$	15					$P_4I_3 =$	14.5
	$p_4a_4 =$	16				A_9	$P_4I_4 =$	16.0

Magnitude of Civil Violence (MCV)[d]

MCV_1 $A_1t_1 =$ 1.0	MCV_{13} $A_4t_2 =$ 23.0	MCV_{25} $A_7t_2 =$ 48.0
MCV_2 $A_1t_2 =$ 2.0	MCV_{14} $A_3t_4 =$ 25.5	MCV_{26} $A_6t_4 =$ 49.5
MCV_3 $A_2t_1 =$ 3.5	MCV_{15} $A_5t_1 =$ 27.5	MCV_{27} $A_8t_1 =$ 51.5
MCV_4 $A_1t_3 =$ 5.0	MCV_{16} $A_4t_3 =$ 30.0	MCV_{28} $A_7t_3 =$ 53.0
MCV_5 $A_2t_2 =$ 6.5	MCV_{17} $A_5t_2 =$ 32.5	MCV_{29} $A_8t_2 =$ 54.5
MCV_6 $A_1t_4 =$ 8.0	MCV_{18} $A_4t_4 =$ 35.0	MCV_{30} $A_7t_4 =$ 56.0
MCV_7 $A_3t_1 =$ 9.5	MCV_{19} $A_6t_1 =$ 37.5	MCV_{31} $A_9t_1 =$ 57.0
MCV_8 $A_2t_3 =$ 11.5	MCV_{20} $A_5t_3 =$ 39.5	MCV_{32} $A_8t_3 =$ 58.5
MCV_9 $A_3t_2 =$ 13.5	MCV_{21} $A_6t_2 =$ 41.5	MCV_{33} $A_9t_2 =$ 60.0
MCV_{10} $A_2t_4 =$ 15.5	MCV_{22} $A_5t_4 =$ 43.5	MCV_{34} $A_8t_4 =$ 61.5
MCV_{11} $A_4t_1 =$ 18.0	MCV_{23} $A_7t_1 =$ 45.0	MCV_{35} $A_9t_3 =$ 63.0
MCV_{12} $A_3t_3 =$ 20.5	MCV_{24} $A_6t_3 =$ 46.5	MCV_{36} $A_9t_4 =$ 64.0

[a] A combination of scaled scores of Participants (p) and Social Area (a), weighted as shown.
[b] A combination of scaled scores of Casualties (c) and Property Damage (d), weighted as shown.
[c] A weighted combination of Pervasiveness (P) and Intensity (I) scores.
[d] A weighted combination of Amplitude (A) and Duration (t) scores.

CS1: Pervasiveness. This scale combines BM1, Number of Participants, and BM2, Area, to obtain a measure of the extent to which civil violence is diffused throughout the polity. The composite ranking gives more weight to participants than to area, according to the following rule: the rank on the BM1 scale determines the composite ranking except when the corresponding rank on the BM2 scale differs from it by at least two levels. This scale runs from 1 to 16.

CS2: Intensity. This scale combines BM3, Number of Casualties, and BM4, Property Damage, to index the relative degree of violence resulting from civil strife. The composite ranking gives more weight to casualties than to damage. The rank on the BM3 scale determines the composite ranking *except* when the corresponding rank on the BM4 scale differs from it by at least two levels. The Intensity scale runs from 1 to 12.

CS3: Amplitude. This scale combines Pervasiveness and Intensity by equal weighting, a procedure that accounts for ties in the composite ranking. Before being combined, the Pervasiveness and Intensity scales are collapsed into four ranks each. The Amplitude scale runs from 1 to 16.

CS4: Magnitude of Civil Violence. This scale is the final weighted combination of all five Basic Measures. Amplitude is combined with Duration according to a rule that gives greater weight to Amplitude: the rank on the Amplitude scale determines the composite rank except when the rank on the Duration scale differs from it by at least two levels. Ties result because allowance is made for each possible Amplitude score. The magnitude of Violence scale for each year runs from 1 to 64; the score for 1961-63 is the sum of all three years.

The Basic Measures contributing to each Composite Scale are unequally weighted, as noted above. Given the analytic methods employed, weighting is necessary because behavior—in the present case, civil strife behavior—is intrinsically partially ordered. When we compare polity A and polity B on various characteristics of civil violence, we see that As strife is more pervasive than Bs but Bs is more intensive than As. Which polity has a greater amplitude of violence? There is no necessary or unique single order to be obtained by collapsing the natural partial order of our data. We have mapped a multidimensional *space* into several *lines* because the larger data analysis model (multiple regression) requires that such decisions be made. The decision functions for converting natural multidimensional traits into necessary, though "unnatural," lines involve assumptions about weighting that are not, and cannot be, absolutely "valid." There are bound to be arguments about the particular decision functions used. But as Coombs (1964: 284–291) points out in this context, "The problem is not to eliminate (differences of opinion) but to resolve (them) without creating havoc and disruption." This has been accomplished by making the decision functions explicit.

Scope of the Data and Their Sources

The universe under consideration is composed of the 119 polities that in 1962 had populations exceeding one million. The time period examined for the dependent variables is 1961 through 1963. Specifically, the following sources were searched for evidence of civil violence; they are listed in the order of their contribution to the final data set: the *New York Times* (via its Index), *Newsyear* (the annual volumes of *Facts on File*), *The Annual Register of World Events* (based on *The Times* of London), and, providing as a group the least amount of useful data, *Asian Recorder: Weekly Digest of Asian*

Events, Africa Diary: Weekly Record of Events in Africa, Africa Digest, Africa Report, East Europe: A Monthly Review of Eastern European Affairs, and *Eastern Europe.*

In spite of the use of sources that promise some degree of comprehensiveness, it is clear that some acts of civil violence are not reported. We can be quite sure that all large-scale events—successful coups d'état and major guerrilla wars—are identified by our procedures. We are equally certain that only a small percentage of less widespread or internationally less important events, such as brief riots and localized rural strife, are reported in that portion of the world press upon which we rely.[9]

Our use of multiple and intensive sources may be compared to the sources used by others in developing quantitative measures of collective civil violence. Eckstein used only the Index to the *New York Times*; the Feierabends used only *Deadline Data on World Affairs*; Russett, Rummel, and Tanter used somewhat more comprehensive sources—the *New York Times* Index, *New International Yearbook*, *Facts on File*, and *Britannica Book of the Year*. It should be noted that, with the exception of the Feierabends, these authors' data-collection interests coincided with ours only to the extent of determining the number killed in civil violence and/or the number of different events that took place. However, we have found that, with the partial exception of *Facts on File*, these sources are of limited value for deriving the more detailed descriptions of events necessary for our analysis.

A test for the inter-coder reliability of the data on the five Basic Measures was made for a random sample of six different polities for each year, i.e., 5 percent of the total number of polity-years.[10] The level of agreement was .75—high, considering that one of the coders had had no prior experience with either the scales or the sources. Another factor affecting the level of reliability our data display is the often diffuse nature both of the events and of the observations of them upon which we rely. This study is one in which the goal of precise data on the dependent variable is elusive indeed.

The five Basic Measures were constructed, then, in an attempt to compensate for the lack of quantitative precision found in sources that are, for the most part, journalistic in treatment. It should be noted, however, in fairness to reporters covering tumultuous events like riots and revolutions, that the use of even the most precise and objective observational techniques would not be likely to obtain the data in their theoretically most desirable form.

As an example of the scoring procedure, reports on a hypothetical polity that experienced four violent events in one year might yield information on the number of participants such as this: Event 1—7,000; Event 2—"few thousand"; Event 3—10,000; Event 4—"very many." A coder is expected to "sum" these "numbers," weight them for polity population, and place the result into one of the four categories of BM1, Number of Participants. Sophisticated judgment is necessary in order to estimate, for example, the value of "very many" from the context of the report. Thus, though the conceptualization of the Basic Measures suggests an interval scale, data are not always presented in numerical form, and when they are, the numbers are usually qualified by such words as "about" and "approximately."

Another reason for tolerating gross discriminations is that missing data would otherwise have presented us with an unnecessarily severe obstacle in this initial state of analysis. We have overcome this problem by eliminating it. That is, we rely on the coder's considered judgment to supply values for missing data. For example, when a report of a riot gives no hint at all about the amount of area involved or the amount of damage resulting, the coder estimates these levels on the basis of the information on the number of participants and casualties, and on the duration of the event.

These considerations account for the ordinal nature of the Basic Measures and the Composite Scales. This strategy of measurement was adopted because, quite simply, we have more confidence in our ability to say that Event 1 involves more participants than Event 2 and fewer than Event 3 than we would have in our saying that Event 1, for instance, involves 451 more people than Event 2 and 1,111 fewer than Event 3. (For certain kinds of events we could sometimes make such strong statements—for example, in small and well-organized coups—but over the entire range of strife events such precision is quite impossible.)

Final Measures of Civil Violence

The final set of dependent measures of violent civil strife, as outlined in Table 3, consists of one Basic Measure, Duration,[11] and the four Composite Scales, Pervasiveness, Intensity, Amplitude, and Magnitude of Civil Violence. All were used, in addition to the dichotomous measures, in the multivariate regression analysis; for most analyses, however, Magnitude of Civil Violence was used as the most representative measure. The data, by polity, are summarized in Table 4, which gives cumulative scores for each polity for the three-year period.

Each of the Final Measures displays a highly skewed distribution, with each showing a high percentage of polities with low or zero scores, tailing off rapidly to a small percentage of polities with extremely high scores. (It should be noted that we could technically have converted ordinal scales to interval scales if we could assume normal distribution [Coombs, 1964: 284].) However, a transformation of $\log(X = 1)$ was performed on each Final Measure in order to bring it somewhat more in line with the requirements of the statistics of regression analysis. This made a reduction in the effect of extreme variances on the calculation of correlation coefficients. Table 5 gives the correlation matrix for the transformed Final Measures.

It is clear why the intercorrelations are high. Except for the first three correlations in the left-hand column (which are themselves quite high, indicating, not unexpectedly, that the longer violence persists, the more pervasive

TABLE 3

ALL MEASURES OF CIVIL VIOLENCE[a]

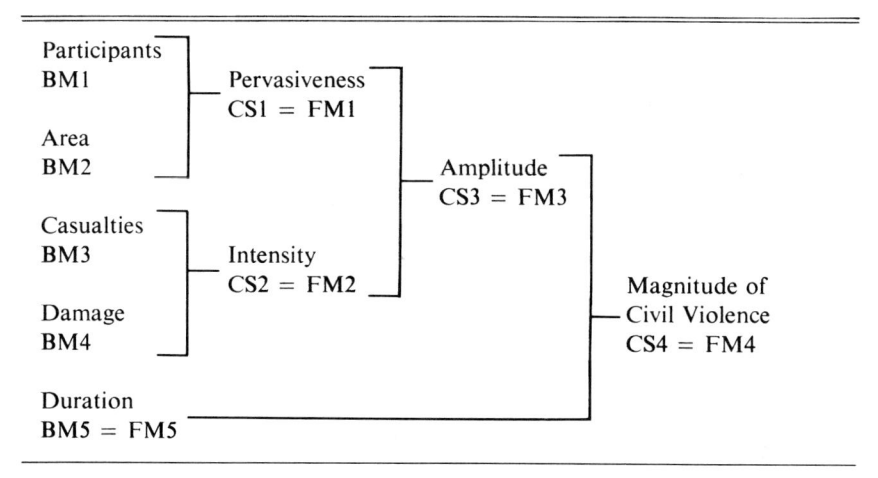

```
Participants ─┐
BM1           │
              ├─ Pervasiveness ─┐
Area          │   CS1 = FM1     │
BM2          ─┘                 │
                                ├─ Amplitude ──┐
Casualties   ─┐                 │   CS3 = FM3  │
BM3           │                 │              │
              ├─ Intensity     ─┘              ├─ Magnitude of
              │   CS2 = FM2                    │  Civil Violence
Damage        │                                │  CS4 = FM4
BM4          ─┘                                │
                                               │
Duration                                       │
BM5 = FM5 ─────────────────────────────────────┘
```

[a] BMs (Basic Measures) and CSs (Composite Scales) are ordinal. FMs (Final Measures) are ordinal scales treated as if they were interval.

and intense it is likely to be), all correlations in this table are between two Final Measures that have at least one common component.

It will be seen that Basic Measure 5 and the four Composite Scales have, in becoming Final Measures, jumped one level of measurement. Ordinal scales are treated as if they were interval scales. What argument can we submit as justification for this? Why have we used scales that violate the assumptions of the regression model as inputs to that model?

We have synthesized a line of decision and endowed it with assumptions appropriate only to an interval scale for the following reason: The price we pay for lack of rigorous adherence to measurement models is more than compensated for by the advantages gained from using the power of regression analysis. Without an intervally scaled dependent variable, we would not have been able to make any significant decisions about the joint effects of the predictor variables in determining the characteristics of civil violence. Our basic argument, then, is for the instrumental value of the methodology. We justify the relaxation of the requirements of a model, particularly during the exploratory phases of analysis, if it helps us to answer our substantive questions, or more usually, to rephrase our initial questions on the basis of preliminary findings.

TABLE 4
Cumulative Final Measurements for 1961–63

Polity	Duration	Pervasive-ness	Intensity	Amplitude	Total magnitude of civil violence (TMCV)[a]	Turmoil	Conspiracy	Internal war	CV 0/1
Congo-Leopoldville	240	42	36	48.0	192.0	0	1	1	1
Laos	240	48	34	48.0	192.0	0	0	1	1
Vietnam—South	240	48	36	48.0	192.0	1	1	1	1
Angola	240	40	34	46.5	189.5	1	0	1	1
Algeria	190	36	29	42.0	172.0	1	1	1	1
Dominican Republic	65	40	18	39.0	154.0	1	1	1	1
Colombia	240	14	35	30.0	134.0	0	0	1	1
Venezuela	111	28	18	33.0	127.0	1	1	1	1
Rwanda	40	32	23	33.0	125.0	1	0	1	1
Iraq	161	35	18	27.5	108.5	0	1	1	1
Cuba	90	16	24	24.0	98.0	1	0	1	1
Indonesia	115	22	16	23.5	97.5	1	1	1	1
Guatemala	36	23	20	26.5	96.5	1	1	1	1
Yemen	60	19	15	23.0	93.0	0	1	1	1
N. Rhodesia	11	25	17	28.5	92.5	1	0	0	1
S. Rhodesia	82	30	10	23.5	80.5	1	0	1	1
Philippines	115	20	13	18.0	75.0	1	0	1	1
Uganda	40	15	13	17.5	64.5	1	0	1	1
Nepal	85	14	11	15.5	62.5	1	0	1	1
Argentina	11	29	8	18.5	55.5	1	1	0	1

Country								
Ethiopia	5	12	10	14.5	54.5	0		
Tunisia	5	15	7	14.5	54.5	1	1	1
Kenya	111	14	10	10.5	46.5	1	1	1
Belgium	7	16	13	16.5	45.5	1	0	1
Burma	7	8	25	16.5	44.5	1	0	1
Ghana	5	5	12	11.5	41.5	1	1	1
Brazil	7	11	14	13.5	40.5	1	0	1
Iran	61	12	14	9.5	35.5	1	1	1
Syria	7	13	14	12.5	33.5	1	1	1
Honduras	2	9	9	10.5	28.5	1	0	1
Somalia[a]	7	12	9	10.5	27.5	1	0	1
India	61	12	12	7.5	26.5	1	1	1
South Africa	7	12	14	10.5	25.5	1	0	1
Sudan	31	13	3	5.5	21.5	1	1	1
Malaya	30	2	7	4.5	20.5	0	1	1
Italy	15	12	11	7.5	19.5	1	1	1
Pakistan	7	12	11	9.5	19.5	1	0	1
Greece	2	16	2	8.0	19.0	1	0	1
Spain	11	8	12	7.5	16.5	1	0	1
Israel	7	14	4	6.5	15.5	1	1	1
France	15	14	7	6.0	15.0	1	0	1
United States	90	6	3	3.0	15.0	1	0	1
Nicaragua	3	16	8	8.0	14.0	1	0	1
Turkey	3	10	13	8.0	14.0	1	1	1
United Kingdom	10	8	8	5.0	13.0	1	1	1
Chile	2	4	10	5.5	10.5	1	0	1
Paraguay	2	12	2	5.5	10.5	1	0	1
Germany—West	2	2	8	5.5	10.5	1	0	1
Haiti	10	15	6	7.0	10.0	1	1	1

TABLE 4 (CONTINUED)

Polity	Duration	Pervasiveness	Intensity	Amplitude	Total magnitude of civil violence (TMCV)[a]	Turmoil	Conspiracy	Internal war	CV 0/1
Jordan	1	11	1	4.5	9.5	1	0	0	1
Liberia	1	11	1	4.5	9.5	1	0	0	1
Canada	10	2	6	3.5	8.5	1	0	1	1
Ecuador	7	9	6	4.5	8.5	1	1	0	1
Peru	3	6	7	6.0	8.0	1	0	1	1
Portugal	3	6	9	6.0	8.0	1	1	0	1
U.S.S.R.	5	2	4	2.5	6.5	1	0	0	1
Bolivia	3	6	8	4.5	5.5	1	0	0	1
Jamaica	2	2	7	3.5	4.5	1	0	0	1
Poland	2	3	6	3.5	4.5	1	0	0	1
Puerto Rico	2	4	6	3.5	4.5	1	0	0	1
U.A.R.	1	1	4	2.5	3.5	1	0	0	1
Mexico	2	8	4	4.5	3.5	1	0	0	1
Panama	1	1	4	2.5	3.5	1	0	0	1
Papua-New Guinea	1	8	3	2.5	3.5	1	0	0	1
Singapore	1	1	6	2.5	3.5	1	0	0	1
Uruguay	1	3	4	2.5	3.5	1	0	0	1
Bulgaria	3	3	6	3.0	3.0	1	0	0	1
Japan	3	4	5	3.0	3.0	1	0	0	1
Mali	6	3	2	2.0	3.0	1	0	1	1
Korea—South	6	2	3	2.0	3.0	1	0	0	1
Thailand	6	6	4	2.0	3.0	1	1	1	1

The Conditions of Civil Violence: First Tests of a Causal Model

China—Peking	2	4	4	2.0	2.0	1	0	1
Czechoslovakia	2	2	2	2.0	2.0	1	0	1
Lebanon	2	3	3	2.0	2.0	1	1	1
Nigeria	2	2	2	2.0	2.0	1	0	1
Cameroun	1	1	1	1.0	1.0	1	0	1
Ceylon	1	1	1	1.0	1.0	1	0	1
Chad	1	1	1	1.0	1.0	1	0	1
Dahomey	1	1	1	1.0	1.0	1	1	1
Germany—East	1	1	1	1.0	1.0	0	0	1
El Salvador	1	1	1	1.0	1.0	1	1	1
Hong Kong	1	3	3	1.0	1.0	0	0	1
Niger	1	1	1	1.0	1.0	1	0	1
Nyasaland	1	3	3	1.0	1.0	1	1	1
Senegal	1	3	3	1.0	1.0	1	0	1
Togo	1	1	1	1.0	1.0	1	0	1
Afghanistan	0	0	0	0.0	0.0	0	0	0
Albania	0	0	0	0.0	0.0	0	0	0
Australia	0	0	0	0.0	0.0	0	0	0
Austria[c]	0	0	0	0.0	0.0	0	0	0
Burundi[c]	0	0	0	0.0	0.0	0	0	0
Cambodia	0	0	0	0.0	0.0	0	0	0
Central African Rep.	0	0	0	0.0	0.0	0	0	0
Costa Rica	0	0	0	0.0	0.0	0	0	0
Denmark	0	0	0	0.0	0.0	0	0	0
Finland	0	0	0	0.0	0.0	0	0	0
Guinea[c]	0	0	0	0.0	0.0	0	0	0
Hungary	0	0	0	0.0	0.0	0	0	0
Ireland	0	0	0	0.0	0.0	0	0	0
Ivory Coast	0	0	0	0.0	0.0	0	0	0

TABLE 4 (CONTINUED)

Polity	Components of violence[a]					Forms of violence[b]		
	Duration	Pervasiveness	Intensity	Amplitude	Total magnitude of civil violence (TMCV)[a]	Turmoil	Conspiracy	Internal war	CV 0/1
Libya	0	0	0	0.0	0.0	0	0	0	0
Malagasy	0	0	0	0.0	0.0	0	0	0	0
Mongolia	0	0	0	0.0	0.0	0	0	0	0
Morocco	0	0	0	0.0	0.0	0	0	0	0
Mozambique[c]	0	0	0	0.0	0.0	0	0	0	0
Netherlands	0	0	0	0.0	0.0	0	0	0	0
New Zealand	0	0	0	0.0	0.0	0	0	0	0
Korea—North	0	0	0	0.0	0.0	0	0	0	0
Vietnam—North	0	0	0	0.0	0.0	0	0	0	0
Norway	0	0	0	0.0	0.0	0	0	0	0
Rumania	0	0	0	0.0	0.0	0	0	0	0
Saudi Arabia	0	0	0	0.0	0.0	0	0	0	0
Sierra Leone	0	0	0	0.0	0.0	0	0	0	0
Sweden	0	0	0	0.0	0.0	0	0	0	0
Switzerland	0	0	0	0.0	0.0	0	0	0	0
China—Taiwan	0	0	0	0.0	0.0	0	0	0	0
Tanganyika	0	0	0	0.0	0.0	0	0	0	0
Voltaic Rep.	0	0	0	0.0	0.0	0	0	0	0
Yugoslavia	0	0	0	0.0	0.0	0	0	0	0

[a] Scores for Duration, Pervasiveness, Intensity, and Amplitude are the sums of annual scores for the three-year period 1961–63. The Total magnitude of civil violence scores were computed separately for each year, by procedures outlined in the text, and summed to give the totals listed here.

[b] Each polity is coded "1" for the presence and "0" for the absence of each of these generic forms of civil violence during the three-year period 1961–63.

[c] Subsequent data collection indicates the occurrence of small-scale strife events in these polities in 1961–63.

[d] The Somalia score is inaccurate because of an incorrect coding decision that border hostilities with Ethiopia constituted internal war.

Table 6: Explanatory Variables in 27 Analyses

The results of 27 step-wise regression analyses are summarized in Table 6. In the step-wise regression procedure, the computer program used selects from the set of 29 independent variables the one most closely correlated with the dependent variable, determines how much variance it accounts for, performs tests of statistical significance, and makes a residual analysis—i.e., determines the extent to which each case is predicted by that variable. This constitutes a "step." In the next step, the program selects from the remaining independent variables the one that accounts for the largest amount of unexplained variance (i.e., the one that makes the greatest reduction in error sum of squares), enters it in a two-variable regression equation with the previously selected variable, calculates significance levels, and makes another residual analysis. This procedure is repeated until either all variables are entered or until the unentered variables fall below some specified significance level.

TABLE 5

Correlation Matrix for Transformed Final Measures ($N = 119$)

	Duration	Pervasiveness	Intensity	Amplitude	Magnitude of civil violence
Duration (FM5)					
Pervasiveness (FM1)	86				
Intensity (FM2)	85	90			
Amplitude (FM3)	88	96	96		
Magnitude of civil violence (FM4)	91	95	94	99	

At each step the program also computes partial coefficients for each variable that has entered the equation. Each such coefficient represents the proportion of otherwise unexplained variation accounted for by that specific variable, i.e., the variation it explains after all the other entered variables have accounted for their shares. Partials thus permit judgments about the relative importance of each variable in an equation. Partials are listed in Table 6 for each variable that entered each analysis through the last "significant" step. Our criterion for determining the last significant step is that the last variable to enter be statistically significant by the F test at the .10 level. In a few cases the significance of the partial of a previously entered variable dropped below the .10 level at the final step; such partials are parenthesized.

TABLE 6
Explaining Civil Violence: Results of Analyses

Independent variables and partial r's[b]	TMCV raw scores	TMCV logged scores	TMCV logged scores by year 1961	1962	1963	CV 0/1	Turmoil 0/1	Conspiracy 0/1	Internal war 0/1
Relative deprivation									
I.11 Group discrimination[c]	+23	+21	+19	+26	+22	+			+27
I.12 Potential separatism[c]		+17		+22	+17	+			+
I.13 Migrants to cities									
I.14 Higher-school leavers[c]						−26	−17		
I.15 Elite access[d]				+21					
Value expectations[e]									
I.21 School attendance 1960						+30[g]			−
I.22 School attendance 1950[c]			+16						−
I.23 Annual school change	+	+	+				+19		
I.31 Per expectant capita $[c]									
I.32 Expectant $ growth	−						+23	−	−
I.33 Underemployment 1960									
I.34 Underemployment 1950									
Value capabilities									
I.41 Per capita $ 1962[c]	−								−
I.42 Per capita $ 1958[c]									−
I.43 Economic growth rates									
I.44 Economic fluctuations	−13						(−12)		
I.51 Government $ per capita[c]	−	+21[g]				−			−
I.52 Government $ growth rates							−22		
I.53 Government Budget/GDP[c]		−39	−21	−	−20	−30	−		−20
I.54 Political modernization						−			
I.55 Executive stability[c]		−	−			−	(−10)		−
Social control									
M.11 Military/10,000[c]	+24	+24		+17	+30				+20
M.12 Military loyalty[d]	−25	−25	−18	−26	−29	−22		−52	−30
M.13 Police/10,000[c]	−25				−18				−20
M.21 Nonviolent protest[c]		+23	+21	+26	+	+33	+39	+16	
M.31 Unionization[c]	−	−	−	−	−	−	−	−	−
M.32 Party stability[d]	−17	−20	−	−	−27	−22	−15	−	−
Social Facilitation									
M.51 Physical access[c]	−	−				−19			−18
M.52 Urbanization[c]	−	−17			−				−
Correlation at last R	51	64	43	53	63	61	51	56	56
significant step[f] R^2	26	41	19	28	40	37	26	32	31

Civil violence measures for all polities[a]
Dichotomous measures

FOR ALL 119 POLITIES AND FOR CLUSTERS OF POLITIES

Political rule				Technical development				Size					Sociocultural region					
Centrist (32)	Polyarchic (38)	Personalist (16)	Elitist (33)	High (29)	Medium (30)	Low (30)	Very low (30)	Dominant (29)	Moderate (30)	Small (30)	Very small (30)	Asian (30)	E. European (14)	African (29)	Latin (19)	Anglo-Saxon (9)	W. European (18)	
		+52			+	+44		+58	+				+57		+94			I.11
		+33		+54	+			+					+42		+			I.12
		−53																I.13
	+36					−37				−48					−			I.14
						+73		+55							−53−			I.15
		+41		−				−							−			I.21
+		+			−				−							−			I.22
				+						+49			+63					I.23
+													+		+49			I.32
													+78		−		+53	I.32
										+71								I.33
		−50				−55		−		−								I.34
		+51						−		+53			+		+57	−			I.41
													+					I.42
																		I.43
										−65								I.44
+46ᵍ				−				−		−						−			I.51
	−40														−50			I.52
−70	−|		−47		−|	−|	−67	−|	−71	−62	−38	−38				I.53
−|									−39			+37			−|		I.54
−45	−					−37		−		−		−			+59			I.55
−			+		(+29)		+62			+48	+58					−	(+39)	M.11
	−		−41		−		−51		−		−		(−24)						M.12
−56			+		−48	−43												M.13
		+52		+62	+58	(+33)	+64		+				+		+		+76	M.21
		−				−67			+50ᵍ		−42			−43	−			M.31
−36				−67		−		−66	−		−64	−42			−72−			M.32
+44ᵍ	−			−		−												M.51
−51						−38			−		−63					−		M.52
84	60	63	84	85	55	87	78	84	86	75	83	62	85	81	82	94	83	
71	37	40	70	72	30	76	61	70	74	57	68	39	72	65	67	88	69	

Footnotes to this table on following page

Footnotes to Table 6

[a] The measures of the dependent variable used in each analysis are as follows:
(1) TMCV raw scores: the total magnitude of civil violence scores given for each polity for the three-year period in Table 4.
(2) TMCV logged scores: logarithmic transformation of the above scores.
(3) Scores by year: logarithmic transformation of the total magnitude of civil violence scores for each year.
(4) Dichotomous measures: "yes-no" measures of the presence or absence of any kind of violent strife (CV 0/1); of turmoil (0/1); of conspiracy (0/1); and of internal war (0/1), as shown in Table 4.
The number of cases for each of these analyses is 119.

[b] Partial correlation coefficients are shown for each variable that enters the equation through the last significant step, as defined in footnote e. Coefficients in parentheses fail to meet a .10 level of significance test using the two-tailed t test. Each partial represents the amount of otherwise unaccounted for variance explained by this variable alone.

The signs + and — indicate that these variables have correlations with the dependent variable measure that are significant at the .10 level but do not enter the equation, their variance being largely or entirely accounted for by the variables that are entered.

[c] Measures so footnoted were subject to log transformations before analysis. All civil violence measures except for the initial "raw score" analysis and the dichotomous (0/1) analyses were so transformed.

[d] These are dichotomous measures.

[e] These indices were devised to measure aspects of value expectations; interpretation of the results can be found in the unabridged monograph, pp. 71–87, not reprinted in this selection.

[f] Multiple correlation coefficients obtained in step-wise multiple regression analyses. R^2 constitutes the percentage of variation in civil violence scores that is statistically explained or predicted by the equation. Our criterion for determining the last significant step is that the last variable to enter the equation be statistically significant by the F test at the .10 level. For a few analyses, inspection suggested a .05 criterion; in a few others, variables at the .20 level of significance are included because they apparently serve as control variables, allowing variables in successive steps to enter with .01 or .05 significance levels.

[g] In these instances, the correlation matrix for this set of polities showed this measure to be negatively associated with the dependent variable. After the more important variables were controlled—by entering in the first several steps of step-wise regression analysis—the correlations of this measure, with the residual variance *reversed*, were sufficiently strong to enter the regression equation at greater than the prescribed .10 level of significance. Causal or substantive interpretations of such sign reversal, especially when it occurs after a number of variables have entered the equation, are difficult.

[h] The bases on which clusters of polities are discriminated are summarized in pp. 189–195. The number of cases, or countries, in each analysis is given in parentheses in the column heading.

Variables marked + or − are significantly related to the civil violence measure (r significant at the .10 level), but do not enter the equation. Their potential contribution is largely or entirely accounted for by the variables that are entered.

The Western European cluster analysis, the last column on the right in Table 6, provides an illustration. Eighteen nations are included in the analysis; the dependent variable is total magnitude of civil violence, logarithmically transformed (logTMCV). Reading down the column, four partial correlation coefficients are listed. The most important explanatory variable is M.21, nonviolent protest 1948–62 (partial $r = +.76$). I.32 and I.52 are somewhat less important but also significant ($r = +.53, −.50$). The size of the military establishment, M.11, was related closely enough to enter the equation in one of the first steps, but at the final step its contribution was significant at less than the .10 level. The four independent variables taken together account for 69 percent of the total variation in magnitude of civil violence ($R^2 = .69$). None of the other 25 independent variables was significantly correlated with logTMCV in this cluster. Examination of the adjacent Anglo-Saxon cluster analysis shows quite a different pattern; no fewer than 15 independent variables correlate significantly with variation in strife levels among these nine nations, but one, discrimination, is very highly correlated with logTMCV, $r = +.94$. In this instance, no other variable enters; the unexplained variance is little more than that of a single case; hence, no other variable can make a significant contribution.

The nine analyses on the left side of Table 6 comprise all 119 polities but different measures of civil strife. Amounts of variation explained are relatively low, the multiple correlation coefficients ranging from $R^2 = .19$ to $R^2 = .41$. Analyses were also made for three of the component measures of TMCV: Duration ($R^2 = .32$), Pervasiveness ($R^2 = .39$), and Intensity ($R^2 = .36$), all of which were logarithmically transformed. Essentially the same independent variables contributed to each as to logTMCV; hence, they are not reported in detail.

In addition to being the most comprehensive measure of levels of civil strife, logTMCV proved to be the best-explained in the all-polity analyses and was used as the dependent variable in the 18 cluster analyses summarized on the right side of Table 6.[12] Within these smaller, relatively homogeneous groups of polities, levels of strife are substantially better accounted for, typically by fewer variables. The proportions of variation explained range from 30 percent to 88 percent, with an average of 63 percent. In other words, the regression equations account on the average for nearly two-thirds of the variation in levels of civil violence in the clusters, compared with 41 percent when all polities are taken together.

The Predictive Equations: All Polities

When all polities are analyzed together, the variations in relative levels of civil violence are not well explained, as Table 6 demonstrates. The best-explained dependent variable is the total magnitude of violence 1961–63, when logarithmically transformed to minimize the effects of its skewed distribution: the R^2 obtained for logTMCV with the nine most closely related independent variables is .41, i.e., 41 percent of the variation is accounted for. By contrast, only 19 percent of civil violence in 1961 is accounted for by the five variables that contribute significantly to its explanation. The regression equations for the all-polity analyses are given in Table 7, below.

The effect of transforming the raw TMCV scores is evident: the R^2 increases from .26 to .41. The increase in explanatory capacity in each succes-

TABLE 7

MULTIPLE REGRESSION EQUATIONS FOR ALL-POLITY ANALYSES[a]

Dependent variable	Constant	b-Coefficients	R^2
TMCV =	70.2	−1.5(I.44)[b] + 14.8(logI.11) + 22.7(logM.11) − 26.7(M.12) −46.4(logM.13) − 17.3(M.32)	.259
logTMCV =	1.51	+.45(logI.51) − 1.22(logI.53) + .20(logI.11) +.15(logI.12) + .49(logM.21) + .33(logM.11) −.39(M.12) − .31(M.32) − .45(logM.52)	.412
logTMCV 1961 =	0.53	−.48(logI.53) + .23(logI.22) + .16(logI.11) + .42(logM.21) −.25(M.12)	.187
logTMCV 1962 =	−0.29	+.21(logI.11) + .18(logI.12) + .23(I.15) + .50(logM.21) +.16(logM.11) − .35(M.12)	.282
logTMCV 1963 =	1.18	−.39(logI.53) + .17(logI.11) + .13(logI.12) + .34(M.11) −.37(M.12) + .40(logM.13) − .32(M.32)	.399
CV 0/1[c] =	1.34	−.45(logI.53) + .0068(I.21) − .34(logI.14) +.44(logM.21) − .21(M.12) − .19(M.32) − .19(logM.51)	.372
Turmoil 0/1[c] =	0.48	−.021(I.52) − .15(logI.55)[b] + .085(I.23) + .026(I.32) −.25(I.14) + .62(logM.21) − .14(M.32)	.262
Conspiracy 0/1[c] =	0.40	−.011(I.44)[b] + .18(logM.21) − .46(M.12)	.315
Internal War 0/1[c] =	1.25	+.33(logI.53) + .16(logI.11) + .18(logM.11) − .30(M.12) −.36(logM.13) − .15(logM.51)	.313

[a] Cases number 119 in all analyses. Summary lists of the independent variables appear in Tables 6 and 7. The dependent variables are described, and data for the most important of them presented, in pp. 196–206. Independent variables are listed neither in the order in which they entered the regression equation nor in order of their contributions to R^2, but in the order of the initial master listing of variables.

[b] These variables contribute to the equation at less than the .10 significance level according to the two-tailed t test.

[c] These are dichotomous measures, indicating respectively the presence or absence of any kind of civil violence; of turmoil; of conspiracy; and of internal war. See pp. 196–206 for definitions and data.

sive single-year analysis, from $R^2 = .19$ in 1961 to .28 in 1962 and .40 in 1963, was unexpected, but may be evidence of some general time-lag effects. The fact that logTMCV for all three years is better accounted for than any of its single-year components reflects the continuity of most of the conditions indexed; discrimination, for example, is a persisting condition, perhaps not likely in the short run to result in violence, but highly likely to do so over a longer period. Three analyses not reported in Table 6 were made of the component measures of TMCV: Duration, Pervasiveness, and Intensity. As noted these measures are highly inter-correlated, and not unexpectedly the same variables contributed to each in the regression analysis. The "explained" variation was in each analysis less than that of logTMCV, however: the R^2 values were, respectively, Duration, .32; Pervasiveness, .39, and Intensity, .36. This suggests again that logTMCV is the most representative of the civil strife measures devised for this study.

Essentially the same independent variables contribute to the explanation of the TMCV scores and their component measures, however they are scaled and whatever their period of reference. There is one notable exception to this generalization: the three measures of retribution are better predictors of strife in 1963 than in 1962, and better in 1962 than in 1961. The data in these indices represent varying years in the early 1960s, which precludes any causal inferences but suggests further analyses. The contribution of such variables as per capita government expenditures (I.51), 1950 school enrollment ratios (I.22), and elite access (I.15) to one TMCV analysis only, without significant relation to others, raises the possibility that the relationships are spurious. The indices regularly associated with levels of strife are rather evenly divided between direct measures of deprivation and the mediating variables—those classes of variables that we would expect to have the greatest index stability.

NOTES

1. For example, Smelser (1963: Chapters 8 and 10); Parsons (1964: 33–70); Johnson (1966); and Zolberg (1968: 70–87). These works, among many others, implicitly or explicitly regard civil strife as a calculated response to objective social conditions. Little or no attention is given motivational considerations that might explain men's differential responses to the stipulated conditions. For an attempt at a more balanced analysis see Gurr (1969a).

2. For a brief review of the concept of and research on status deprivation, see Adams (1965: 268–272). A tabular summary of findings and a bibliography appear in Galtung (1964: 116–118).

3. This distinction is made by David F. Aberle in Thrupp (1962: 210).

4. This approach is exemplified by Cantril (1965).

5. See Banks and Gregg (1965 [reprinted in this volume, Chapter 13]). All 68 variables included in the factor analysis are ordinally or dichotomously scaled. Some are descriptive, e.g., those relating to geographical grouping and colonial tutelage (if any); others are judgmental and relate to the degree or nature of such charac-

teristics as ideological orientation, interest articulation, power distribution, role of the military, and many others. The raw and processed indices are given in Banks and Textor (1963).

6. Results of this factor analysis are reported in Russett (1965). The data analyzed are selected from variables in *World Handbook* (Russett, 1964). All the data are intervally scaled and include, as examples, GNP, Communist votes as a percentage of all votes, population density, inequality of farm land distribution, Roman Catholics as a percentage of population, and a number of others.

7. Results of this factor analysis are reported in Berry (1960: 78–108). The canonical variate values on the basis of which we discriminate clusters appear on (Berry, 1960) page 84. To obtain estimated values for polities not included in the Berry analysis, we made use of an index of per capita income in U.S. dollars for 1958. Each "unknown" polity was matched with three to ten "known" polities of approximately the same per capita income, the canonical variate values of the "known" polities were averaged, and the average value was assigned to the "unknown" polity. On completion of this procedure, the set was divided into quartiles denoted "high," "medium," "low," and "very low."

8. The factor analysis is reported in Rummel (1964). We are indebted to the author for calling to our attention the desirability of controlling for size effects, but absolve him of responsibility for the procedure we devised for doing so.

9. George Lichtheim (1965: 33–46) has written incisively, if somewhat stridently, of the *New York Times*'s preoccupation with international events to the extent of allowing seriously inadequate coverage of intranational news.

10. $R = 2(C_{1,2})/(C_1 + C_2)$. This formula is taken from North et al. (1963: 49).

11. BM5 is transformed into FM5 by multiplying the midpoints of the BM5 intervals (measured in weeks) by two to indicate the four points of the Final Measure of Duration; thus, $t_1 = 1$; $t_2 = 5$; $t_3 = 30$; $t_4 = 80$.

12. A 19th analysis was made combining the Anglo-Saxon and Western European sociocultural clusters, with results not sharply different from those of the two clusters separately ($R^2 = .76$).

REFERENCES

ABERLE, D.F. (1962) "A note on relative deprivation theory." In S.L. Thrupp, Ed., *Millenial Dreams in Action: Essays in Comparative Study*. The Hague: Mouton.

ADAMS, J.S. (1965) "Inequity in social exchange." Pp. 268–272 in L. Berkowitz, Ed., *Advances in Experimental Social Psychology*. Vol. II. New York: Academic Press.

BANKS, A.S. and P.M. GREGG (1965) "Grouping political systems: Q-factor analysis of *A Cross-Polity Survey*." *American Behavioral Scientist* 9: 3–6. Reprinted in this volume, Chapter 13.

BANKS, A.S. and R.B. TEXTOR (1963) *A Cross-Polity Survey*. Cambridge: MIT Press.

BERRY, B.J.L. (1960) "An inductive approach to the regionalization of economic development." Pp. 78–108 in N. Ginsberg, Ed., *Essays on Geography and Economic Development*. Chicago: University of Chicago Press.

BWY, D. (1966) "Governmental instability in Latin America: the preliminary test of a causal model of the impulse to 'extra-legal' change." Paper presented to the Annual Meeting of the American Psychological Association, New York, September 2–6.

CANTRIL, H. (1965) *The Pattern of Human Concerns.* New Brunswick: Rutgers University Press.
COOMBS, C.H. (1964) *A Theory of Data.* New York: John Wiley.
GALTUNG, J. (1964) "A structural theory of aggression." *Journal of Peace Research* 2: 116–118.
GURR, T.R. (1969a) *Why Men Rebel.* Princeton: Princeton University Press.
— (1969b) "A contemporary survey of civil strife." Pp. 489–491 in H.D. Graham and T.R. Gurr, Eds., *Violence in America: Historical and Comparative Perspectives.* Washington, D.C.: U.S. Government Printing Office.
JOHNSON, C. (1966) *Revolutionary Change.* Boston: Little, Brown.
LICHTHEIM, G. (1965) "All the news that's fit to print—reflections on the *New York Times.*" *Commentary* 60 (September): 33–46.
MIDLARSKY, M. and R. TANTER (1967) "Toward a theory of political instability in Latin America." *Journal of Peace Research* 3: 209–227.
NORTH, R.C. et al. (1963) *Content Analysis.* Evanston: Northwestern University Press.
PARSONS, T. (1964) "Some reflections on the place of force in social process." Pp. 33–70 in H. Eckstein, Ed., *Internal War: Problems and Approaches.* New York: Free Press.
RUMMEL, R.J. (1964) "Dimensionality of nations project: orthogonally rotated factor tables for 236 variables." Department of Political Science, Yale University (mimeo.).
— (1963) "Testing some possible predictors of conflict behavior within and between nations." *Proceedings of the Peace Research Society* 1.
RUSSETT, B.M. (1965) "International regions and international integration: homogeneous regions." Department of Political Science, Yale University (mimeo.).
— (1964) "Inequality and instability: the relation of land tenure to politics." *World Politics* 16 (April): 442–454.
RUSSETT, B.M. et al. (1964) *World Handbook of Political and Social Indicators.* New Haven: Yale University Press.
SMELSER, N. (1963) *Theory of Collective Behavior.* New York: Free Press.
SOROKIN, P. (1937) *Social and Cultural Dynamics,* Vol. III: *Fluctuations of Social Relationships, War and Revolutions.* New York: American Book Co.
YATES, A.J. (1962) *Frustration and Conflict.* New York: John Wiley.
ZOLBERG, A.R. (1968) "The structure of political conflict in the new states of tropical Africa." *American Poliiical Science Review* 62 (March): 70–87.

9 A Causal Model of Civil Strife: A Comparative Analysis using New Indices

TED ROBERT GURR

This article describes some results of a successful attempt to assess and refine a causal model of the general conditions of several forms of civil strife, using cross-sectional analyses of data collected for 114 polities. The theoretical argument, which is discussed in detail elsewhere, stipulates a set of variables said to determine the likelihood and magnitude of civil strife (Gurr, 1968a). Considerable effort was given here to devising indices that represent the theoretical variables more closely than the readily available aggregate indices often used in quantitative cross-national research. One consequence is an unusually high degree of statistical explanation: measures of five independent variables jointly account for two-thirds of the variance among nations in magnitude of civil strife ($R = .80$, $R^2 = .64$).

It should be noted at the outset that this study does not attempt to isolate the set of conditions that leads specifically to "revolution," nor to assess the social or political impact of any given act of strife except as that impact is

---

Author's Note: This is a revised version of a paper read at the 1967 Annual Meeting of the American Political Science Association, Chicago, September 5–9. The research was supported in part by the Center for Research in Social Systems (formerly SORO), the American University, and by the Advanced Research Projects Agency of the Department of Defense. This support implies neither sponsor approval of this article and its conclusions nor the author's approval of policies of the U.S. government toward civil strife. The assistance of Charles Ruttenberg throughout the process of research design, data collection, and analysis is gratefully acknowledged. Substantial portions of the data were collected by Joel Prager and Lois Wasserspring. The author owes special thanks to Harry Eckstein for his advice and encouragement. Bruce M. Russett and Raymond Tanter provided useful criticisms of the paper in draft form. Research was carried out at the Center of International Studies, Princeton University.

Reprinted from *The American Political Science Review*, Volume LXII, pages 1104–1124, by permission of the author and the publisher. Copyright © 1968 The American Political Science Association.

reflected in measures of "magnitude" of strife. The relevance of this kind of research to the classic concern of political scholarship with revolution is its attempt at identification and systematic analysis of conditions that dispose men to strife generally, revolution included.

THEORETICAL CONSIDERATIONS

The basic theoretical proposition is that a psychological variable, relative deprivation, is the basic precondition for civil strife of any kind, and that the more widespread and intense deprivation is among members of a population, the greater is the magnitude of strife in one or another form. Relative deprivation is defined as actors' perceptions of discrepancy between their value expectations (the goods and conditions of the life to which they believe they are justifiably entitled) and their value capabilities (the amounts of those goods and conditions that they think they are able to get and keep). The underlying causal mechanism is derived from psychological theory and evidence to the effect that one innate response to perceived deprivation is discontent or anger, and that anger is a motivating state for which aggression is an inherently satisfying response. The term relative deprivation is used below to denote the perceived discrepancy; the term discontent to denote the motivating state which is the postulated response to it. The relationship between discontent and participation in strife is, however, mediated by a number of intervening social conditions. The initial theoretical model stipulated three such societal variables that are explored here, namely coercive potential, institutionalization, and social facilitation.[1] Results of a previous attempt to operationalize some of these variables and relate them to strife suggested that a fourth variable whose effects should be controlled is the legitimacy of the political regime in which strife occurs (Gurr and Ruttenberg, 1967 [reprinted in this volume, Chapter 8]).

The initial model, sketched in simplified form in Figure 1, specified no hierarchical or causal interactions among the mediating variables. Each was assumed to have an independent effect on the fundamental relationship between deprivation and strife. The theoretical arguments with reference to each variable are briefly stated here.

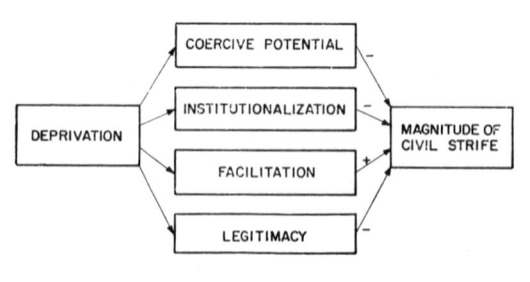

FIGURE 1

Great importance is attributed in psychological theory and, equally, in theoretical and empirical studies of revolutionary behavior, to the inhibiting effects of punishment or coercion, actual or threatened, on the outcome of deprivation. The relationship is not necessarily a linear one whereby increasing levels of coercion are associated with declining levels of violence. Psychological evidence suggests that if an aggressive response to deprivation is thwarted by fear of punishment, this interference is itself a deprivation and increases the instigation to aggression. Comparative studies of civil strife suggest a curvilinear relationship whereby medium levels of coercion, indexed, for example, by military participation ratios or ratings of regime repressiveness, are associated with the highest magnitudes of strife. Only very high levels of coercion appear to limit effectively the extent of strife. (See Bwy, 1966; Walton, 1965; Gurr and Ruttenberg, 1967: 81-84.) No systematic comparative study has examined whether the curvilinear relationship also holds for levels of coercion actually applied. Comparative studies have, however, emphasized the importance of the loyalty of coercive forces to the regime as a factor of equal or greater importance than the size of those forces in deterring strife, and this relationship is almost certainly linear, i.e., the greater the loyalty of coercive forces, the more effective they are, *ceteris paribus*, in deterring strife. (See, for example, Johnson, 1964: 14-20.) Two measures of coercion are used in this study: *coercive force size*, which is hypothesized to vary curvilinearly with levels of strife, and coercive force size weighted for the degree of loyalty of coercive forces to the regime, referred to throughout as *coercive potential*, which is expected to have a linear relationship with strife.

The second intervening variable is *institutionalization*, i.e., the extent to which societal structures beyond the primary level are broad in scope, command substantial resources or personnel, and are stable and persisting. Representative of the diverse arguments about the role of associational structures in minimizing strife are Huntington (1965) on the necessity of political institutionalization for political stability, Kornhauser (1959) on the need for structures intervening between mass and elite to minimize mass movements, and a variety of authors on the long-range tendencies of labor organizations to minimize violent economically based conflict (for example, Ross and Hartmann, 1960). Two underlying psychological processes are likely to affect the intensity of and responses to discontent. One is that the existence of such structures increases men's value opportunities, i.e., their repertory of alternative ways to attain value satisfaction. A complementary function is that of displacement: labor unions, political parties, and a range of other associations may provide the discontented with routinized and typically nonviolent means for expressing their discontents (Gurr, 1968a). The proposed relationship is linear: the greater the institutionalization, the lower the magnitude of strife is likely to be.

Given the existence of widespread discontent in a population, a great number of social and environmental conditions may be present that facilitate the outbreak and persistence of strife. They may be categorized according to their inferred psychological effects—for example, according to whether they facilitate interaction among the discontented, or provide the discontented with a sense that violent responses to deprivation are justified, or give them the means to make such responses with maximum effect, or shelter them from retribution (Gurr, 1968a). Two aspects of facilitation are treated separately in this study: *past levels of civil strife* and *social and structural facilitation* per se. The theoretical basis for the first of these variables is that populations in which strife is chronic tend to develop, by an interaction process, a set of beliefs justifying violent responses to deprivation; the French tradition of urban "revolution" is a striking example. Social and structural facilitation (referred to below simply as "facilitation") comprises aspects of organizational and environmental facilitation of strife, and the provision of external assistance. The operational hypotheses are that the greater the levels of past strife, and of social and structural facilitation, the greater is the magnitude of strife.

Two considerations suggested the incorporation of the fourth intervening variable examined in this study, *legitimacy of the regime*. A study of strife for the years 1961–63 identified a number of nations that had less strife than might be expected on the basis of characteristics they shared with more strife-ridden polities (Gurr and Ruttenberg, 1967: 100–106). One apparent common denominator among them was a high degree of popular support for the regime. This appeared consistent with Merelman's recently proposed learning-theory rationale for legitimacy, to the effect that people comply with directives of the regime in order to gain both the symbolic rewards of governmental action and the actual rewards with which government first associated itself, an argument that applies equally well to acceptance of deprivation and is compatible with experimental findings, in work on the frustration–aggression relationship, that people are less aggressive when they perceive frustration to be reasonable or justifiable. (See also the work of Pastore and of Kregarman and Worchel, reviewed in Berkowitz, 1962.) The proposed relationship of legitimacy as an intervening variable is linear: the greater is regime legitimacy at a given level of deprivation, the less the magnitude of consequent strife.

OPERATIONAL MEASURES

The universe of analysis chosen for evaluating the model comprised 114 distinct national and colonial political entities, each of which had a population of one million or more in 1962.[2] Data on civil strife were collected for 1961 through 1965. Cross-sectional multiple and partial correlation techniques were used. The use of product-moment correlation coefficients was justified on grounds of their necessity for multiple regression, although not all the indicators formally meet the order-of-measurement requirements of the techniques used.

Because of the very considerable difficulties of operationalizing a number of the variables, and the fact that most of the indicators constructed are new, this article gives relatively close attention to the data collection and scaling procedures.

With the exception of magnitude of strife and its components, the underlying variables examined in this study are unmeasured and must be inferred from indicators. In most instances they are in fact unmeasurable by aggregate data, since they relate in the instance of deprivation-induced discontent to a state of mind, and in the case of the intervening variables to conditions that have their effect only insofar as the discontented perceive them, and moreover perceive them as relevant to their response to deprivation. Following Blalock's recommendation that *"when dealing with unmeasured variables it will usually be advisable to make use of more than one indicator for each underlying variable,"* each of the summary measures used in this study is derived by combining two to seven indicators of the underlying variable. This procedure has not only the advantage Blalock attributes to it, namely of minimizing the effects of confounding variables, but also facilitates incorporation of various empirically discrete conditions that have theoretically identical effects (Blalock, 1964: 166-167).

Magnitude of Civil Strife

The dependent variable of the theoretical model is magnitude of civil strife. Civil strife is defined as all collective, nongovernmental attacks on persons or property that occur within the boundaries of an autonomous or colonial political unit. By "nongovernmental" is meant acts by subjects and citizens who are not employees or agents of the regime, as well as acts of such employees or agents contrary to role norms, such as mutinies and coups d'état. Operationally the definition is qualified by the inclusion of symbolic demonstrative attacks on political persons or policies, e.g., political demonstrations, and by the exclusion of turmoil and internal war events in which less than 100 persons take part.

A threefold typology of civil strife is also employed, based on an empirical typology of civil strife events identified by Rummel, Tanter, and others in a series of factor analyses. The general categories, and representative subcategories, are

(1) *Turmoil:* relatively spontaneous, unstructured mass strife, including demonstrations, political strikes, riots, political clashes, and localized rebellions.

(2) *Conspiracy:* intensively organized, relatively small-scale civil strife, including political assassinations, small-scale terrorism, small-scale guerrilla wars, coups, mutinies, and plots and purges, the last two on grounds that they are evidence of planned strife.

(3) *Internal war:* large-scale, organized, focused civil strife, almost always accompanied by extensive violence, including large-scale terrorism and guerrilla wars, civil wars, private wars, and large-scale revolts.[3]

Various measures of the relative extent of civil strife have been used in recent literature, among them counts by country of number of strife events of various types, factor scores derived from such typologies, number of deaths from violent strife, man-days of participation in strife, and scaling procedures that take account of both number of events and their severity. (See, for example, Rummel, 1965; Tanter, 1965; Russett, 1964; Tilly and Rule, 1965; Feierabend and Feierabend, 1966.) One can infer from frustration–aggression theory that no single measure of magnitude of aggression, individual or collective, is likely to be sufficient. It is likely that high levels of discontent may be expressed either in intense, short-lived violence or in more protracted but less severe strife. Moreover, the proportion of a collectivity that participates in civil strife ought to vary with the modal intensity of discontent: mild discontent will motivate few to participate, whereas rage is likely to galvanize large segments of a collectivity into action.

Three aspects of civil strife thus ought to be taken into account in specifying its magnitude:

(1) *Pervasiveness:* the extent of participation by the affected population, operationally defined for this study as the sum of the estimated number of participants in all acts of strife as a proportion of the total population of each polity, expressed in terms of participants per 100,000 population.

(2) *Duration:* the persistence of strife, indexed here by the sum of the spans of time of all strife events in each polity, whatever the relative scale of the events, expressed in days.

(3) *Intensity:* the human cost of strife, indexed here by the total estimated casualties, dead and injured, in all strife events in each polity as a proportion of the total population, expressed as casualties per 10,000,000 population.

To approximate these requirements an extensive data collection and estimation effort was undertaken. Coding sheets and a coding manual were devised for recording a variety of information about any strife event, and a large number of sources scanned and coded to get as full as possible a representation of the strife events that occurred in the 144 polities in the 1961–65 period. Three sources were systematically searched for data: the *New York Times* (via its *Index*), *Newsyear* (the annual volumes of *Facts on File*), and *Africa Digest*. This information was supplemented from a variety of other sources, among them *The Annual Register of World Events, Africa Diary: Weekly Record of Events in Africa, Hispanic-American Report*, and country and case studies. Some 1,100 strife events were thus identified, coded, and the data punched onto IBM cards.[4] Many small-scale strife events, and some larger ones, probably went unreported in these sources and hence are not included in this civil strife data bank. Moreover, much reported and estimated data is in varying degrees inaccurate. However, neither random nor systematic error seem sufficient to affect in any substantial way the analyses or conclusions reported here; the data are adequate for the purposes to which they are put.[5]

Data estimation procedures were used to circumvent the substantial missing-data problem. Methods for determining number of initiators serve as examples. The coding sheet itself contained two "number of initiator" scales. The first was a modified geometric progression of two used to record proximate estimates of initiators, its first interval being 1 to 40, its highest 55,001 to 110,000; for purposes of summing such estimates to obtain total number of initiators, the midpoint of each interval was used. The second scale was used for recording rough estimates, sometimes coder estimates, of number of initiators, ranging from "less than 100" (set equal to 40 for purposes of computing totals) to "10,001 to 100,000" (set equal to 40,000). Data for events for which no estimate could be made were supplied by calculating and inserting means for the appropriate subcategory of event, e.g., if a riot was coded "no basis for judging" for number of initiators, it was assigned the average number of initiators of all riots for which estimates were available.

"Duration" posed little difficulty, being coded on a geometric progression whose first two intervals were "one-half day or less" and "one-half to one day," and whose upper intervals were four to nine months, nine to fifteen months, etc. No event was assigned a duration of more than five years, though some began before and/or persisted after the 1961–65 period.

Casualties were coded similarly to number of initiators, the principal missing-data component being estimates of injuries. The ratio of injuries to deaths was calculated for all events of each subcategory for which both data were available—the general ratio for all well-reported strife being 12:1—and was used to estimate injuries for all such events for which "deaths" but not injuries estimates were given.[6]

Strife events occurred in 104 of the 114 polities during the 1961–65 period. Pervasiveness, Duration, and Intensity scores were calculated separately, following the guidelines specified above, for turmoil, conspiracy, and internal war for each country, and for all strife taken together for each polity. All the distributions were highly skewed, hence were subjected to a log $(X+1)$ transformation. To obtain combined magnitude scores for turmoil, conspiracy, internal war, and all strife, the three component logged scores were added, divided by eight to obtain their eighth root, and the anti-log used as the polity magnitude-of-strife score. The distributions remained skewed, but substantially so only in the case of internal war, which by our definitions occurred in only 25 of the 114 polities.[7]

Measures of Deprivation

A very large number of conditions are likely to impose some degree of relative deprivation on some proportion of a nation's citizens. Similarly, all men are likely to be discontented about some of their conditions of life at some time. On the basis of prior theoretical and empirical work, however, it was possible to construct, and subsequently to combine, a set of cross-nationally comparable indices of conditions that by inference cause pervasive and intense types of deprivation, relying in part on aggregate data and in part on indices constructed by coding narrative and historical material. In the initial stages of data collection, a large number of measures were constructed, some of them representing short-term and some persisting conditions, some of each relating to economic, political, and sociocultural deprivation. Whenever possible, separate measures were included of the intensity of inferred deprivation and of its pervasiveness, i.e., of the proportion of the population presumably affected, plus a third measure combining the two elements. A correlation matrix for 48 such measures and a variety of strife measures was generated, and 13 representative deprivation measures selected for combination.[8] The general rationale for the two general types of measures, short-term and persisting deprivation, and the measures finally selected, are summarized.

TABLE 1

(1) *Economic discrimination* is defined as systematic exclusion of social groups from higher economic value positions on ascriptive bases. For each polity the proportion of population so discriminated against, if any, was specified to the nearest .05, and the intensity of deprivation coded on a four-point scale (see below). The proportion and the intensity score were multiplied to obtain a polity score.

(2) *Political discrimination* is similarly defined in terms of systematic limitation in form, norm, or practice of social groups' opportunities to participate in political activities or to attain elite positions on the basis of ascribed characteristics. Proportionality and intensity scores were determined and combined in the same manner as economic discrimination scores. The intensity scales were defined as follows:

Intensity score	*Economic discrimination*	*Political discrimination*
1	Most higher economic value positions, *or* some specific classes of economic activity, are closed to the group.	Some significant political elite positions are closed to the group, *or* some participatory activities (party membership, voting, etc.).
2	Most higher and some medium economic value positions are closed, *or* many specific classes of economic activity.	Most or all political elite positions are closed *or* most participatory activities, *or* some of both.
3	Most higher and most medium economic value positions are closed.	Most or all political elite positions and some participatory activities are closed.
4	Almost all higher, medium, and some lower economic value positions are closed.	Most or all political elite positions and most or all participatory activities are closed.

(3) *Potential separatism* was indexed by multiplying the proportional size of historically-separatist regional or ethnic groups by a four-point intensity measure.[a] The intensity of separatist deprivation was scored as follows:

TABLE 1 (CONTINUED)

Intensity score — *Type of inferred separatism*

1. The separatist region or group was incorporated in the polity by its own request or mutual agreement.
2. The separatist region or group was assigned to the polity by international agreement or by fiat of a former colonial or governing power, except when (3) or (4) below holds.
3. The separatist region or group was forcibly assimilated into the polity prior to the twentieth century, *or* was forcibly conquered by a former colonial power prior to the twentieth century.
4. The separatist region or group was forcibly assimilated into the polity during the twentieth century, *or* was forcibly reassimilated in the twentieth century after a period of autonomy due to rebellion or other circumstance.

(4) *Dependence on private foreign capital*, indexed by negative net factor payments abroad as a percentage of gross domestic product in the late 1950s, is assumed to be a chronic source of dissatisfaction in an era characterized by economic nationalism. The greater the proportion of national product that accrues to foreign suppliers of goods or capital, the greater the inferred intensity of deprivation; the extent of such deprivation was assumed equal to the proportion of population engaged in the monetary economy. The polity score is the extent score multiplied by the intensity score.[b]

(5) *Religious cleavages* are a chronic source of deprivation-inducing conflict. The scale for intensity of religious cleavage takes account both of number of organized religious groups with two percent or more of total population (the major Christian and Muslim subdivisions are counted as separate groups) and of the duration of their coexistence, the greater that duration the less the inferred intensity. The extent measure is the proportion of the population belonging to any organized religious group. The polity score is the product of the two scores.

(6) *Lack of educational opportunity* was indexed, in proportionality terms only, by subtracting primary plus secondary school enrollment ratios ca. 1960 from 100. Education is so widely regarded as an essential first step for individual socio-economic advancement that one can infer deprivation among the uneducated, and among the parents of children who cannot attend school if not yet among the children themselves.

[a] Coding judgments for both discrimination indices and for separatism were made on the basis of country studies. The proportionality measures are versions of indices reported in Ted Gurr, 1966 (67–90).

[b] A crude measure of the proportion of each polity's population engaged in the monetary economy, to the nearest .10, was constructed for the purpose of weighting this and some other measures. The measure was based primarily on labor census data.

Persisting Deprivation. In the very long run, men's expectations about the goods and conditions of life to which they are entitled tend to adjust to what they are capable of attaining. In the shorter span, however, some groups may persistently demand and expect values, such as greater economic opportunity, political autonomy, or freedom of religious expression, that their societies will not or cannot provide. Six indicators of persisting deprivation were combined to obtain a single long-run deprivation measure (Table 1).

These six measures all had distributions approaching normality, and correlations with several strife measures ranging from .09 to .27. To combine them, they were weighted to bring their means into approximate correspondence, and each polity's scores added and then averaged to circumvent the missing data problem.

TABLE 2

(1) *Short-term trends in trade value, 1957–60 compared with 1950–57:* The percentage change of trade value, exports and imports, for 1957–60 was compared with the rate for 1950–57, and any relative decrease in the later period was treated as an indicator of short-term economic deprivation. Decreases were scaled so that polities with lower rates of increase in the earlier period received greater deprivation scores than those with high rates.

(2) *Short-term trends in trade value, 1960–63 compared with 1950–60:* Procedures identical with (1), above, were used. Both measures were incorporated in the final analysis because both were markedly correlated with strife measures but had a relatively low intercorrelation of .18.[a]

(3) *Inflation 1960–63 compared with 1958–61:* Data on cost-of-living indices were scaled and combined in such a way that the highest deprivation scores were assigned to polities with substantial and worsening inflation in the 1958–63 period, the lowest scores (0) to polities with stable or declining costs-of-living throughout the period.

(4) *1960–63 GNP growth rates compared with 1950s growth rate:* Economic growth rate data were scaled so that polities having low rates in the 1950s and even lower rates in the early 1960s received the highest deprivation scores; those with moderate rates in the 1950s but substantial relative decline in the early 1960s received somewhat lower deprivation scores; and those with steadily high, or moderate but steadily increasing, rates received zero deprivation scores.

(5) *Adverse economic conditions 1960–63:* To supplement aggregate data indicators of economic deprivation, several summary news sources were searched for evaluative statements about adverse internal economic conditions such as crop failures, unemployment, export market slumps, drought, etc. Each such description was coded on the following intensity and extent scales:

Severity (intensity) scores		*Proportion affected (extent) scores*	
Moderate	= 1	One region or city, *or* a small economic sector	= 0.2
Substantial, *or* moderate and persisting for more than one year	= 2	Several regions or cities, *or* several economic sectors	= 0.5
Severe, *or* substantial and persisting for more than one year	= 3	Much of country, *or* several major or one dominant economic sector	= 0.7
Severe *and* persisting for more than one year	= 4	Whole country, *or* all economic sectors	= 1.0

A Causal Model of Civil Strife: A Comparative Analysis

TABLE 2 (CONTINUED)

The score for each such condition is the product of the extent and intensity scores; the score for each polity for each year is the sum of the "condition" scores; and the score used for the summary index is the sum of annual scores for 1960 through 1963.[b]

(6) *New restrictions on political participation and representation by the regime* were coded from the same sources for the same years. Seventeen types of action were defined on *a priori* grounds as value-depriving political restrictions, including harassment and banning of parties of various sizes, banning of political activity, and improper dismissal of elected assemblies and executives. These were ranked on a nine-point intensity scale.[c] The extent measure was the politically-participatory proportion of the population, crudely estimated to the nearest .10 on the basis of voting participation levels and, in lieu of voting data, on the basis of urbanization and literacy levels. The score for each action identified is the product of the intensity and extent scores; the annual polity score the sum of "action" scores; and the summary index the sum of annual scores for 1960-63.

(7) *New value-depriving policies of governments 1960-63* were defined as any new programs or actions that appeared to take away some significant proportion of attained values from a numerically or socially significant group, for example land reform, tax increases, restrictions on trade, limitations of civil liberties, restrictive actions against ethnic, religious, or economic groups, and so forth. Two aspects of such policies were taken into account in scaling for intensity: the degree of deprivation imposed, and their equality of application. The "degree of deprivation" scale values are: small = 1, moderate = 2, substantial = 3, most or all = 4. The "equality of application" scale values are: uniform = 1, discriminatory = 2. The intensity score is the product of values on these two scales. The most intensely depriving policies are assumed to be those intentionally discriminatory and designed to deprive the affected group of most or all the relevant value, e.g. seizure of all property of absentee landlords without compensation (score = 8). Deprivation is inferred to be least intense if the policy is uniformly applicable to all the affected class of citizens and deprives them of only a small part of the value, e.g. a five percent increase in corporation tax rates (score = 1). The extent measure is a crude estimate of the proportion of the adult population likely to be directly affected, the permissible values being .01, .02, .05, .10, .20, .40, .60, .80 and 1.00. The score for each policy identified is the product of the intensity and extent scores; the annual polity score the sum of "policy" scores; and the summary index the sum of annual scores for 1960-63. The sources are the same as for (6) and (7).[d]

[a] The two measures will be used in subsequent analyses to examine time-lag relationships between short-term economic deprivation and strife. The trade data, obtained primarily from United Nations sources, were converted to U.S. currency when necessary to maintain comparability over time.

[b] The sources used were the *Hispanic-American Report*, which is much more comprehensive a source than the other, the *Annual Register* of other polities; hence the mean deprivation scores for Latin America were much higher than those for other polities. As a crude adjustment, the Latin American polity scores were divided by a constant so that their mean approximated that of other polities. The same procedure was followed for indices 6 and 7, below. Analyses of regional clusters of polities, not reported here, provide a check on the adequacy of the procedure.

[c] Types of restrictive actions, and their scale values, are as follows:
1 Amalgamation of splinter party with larger party
1 Restriction or harassment of splinter party

TABLE 2 (Continued)

2 Banning of splinter party
2 Amalgamation of minority party with larger party
2 Restriction or harassment of minority party
3 Banning of minority party
3 Amalgamation of a major party with another major party
3 Restriction or harassment of major party
4 Banning of major party
4 Improper dismissal of regional representative body
4 Improper dismissal of elected regional executive
5 Ban on party activities, parties allowed to continue their organizational existence
5 Improper dismissal of national legislature, with provision for calling new one within a year
5 Improper dismissal of elected chief executive, with provision for replacement within a year
6 Dissolution of all parties, ban on all political activity
6 Improper dismissal of national legislature, no short-term provision for reestablishment
6 Improper dismissal of elected chief executive, no short-term provision for reelection

[d] The annual scores for (5), (6), and (7) are being used in a series of time-lagged and cross-panel correlation analyses, not reported here, in further tests of causal relationships.

Short-Term Deprivation. Any sharp increase in peoples' expectations that is unaccompanied by the perception of an increase in value capabilities, or any abrupt limitation on what they have or can hope to obtain, constitute relative deprivation. We inferred that short-term, relative declines in system economic and political performance were likely to be perceived as increased deprivation for substantial numbers of people. Indices were devised of five kinds of short-term economic deprivation and two of political deprivation (Table 2).

Three summary short-term deprivation scores were calculated for each polity from these seven indices. The five economic variables were multiplied by constants so that their means were approximately equal and averaged to circumvent the missing-data problem. This is the "short-term economic deprivation" index referred to below. The summary measures of politically related deprivation were similarly combined to obtain a summary "short-term political deprivation" measure. The two measures were then added to comprise a single short-term deprivation measure for the purposes of some subsequent analyses.

Measures of the Mediating Variables

Coercive Potential and Size of Coercive Forces. A composite index was contructed to take into account four aspects of the regime's apparent potential for controlling strife. Two of the component indices represent the manpower resources available to the regime, namely military and internal security forces' participation ratios, i.e., military personnel per 10,000 adults about 1960 (N = 112), and internal security forces per 10,000 adults (N = 102). The two distributions were normalized and their means brought into correspondence by rescaling them using ten-interval geometric progressions. The other two component indices deal respectively with the degree of *past loyalty of coercive forces to the regime*, and the extent of *illicit coercive-force participation in strife in the 1960–65 period*.

The rationale for the five-point coercive-force loyalty scale, below, is that the more recently coercive forces had attacked the regime, the less efficacious they would be perceived to be by those who might initiate strife—and the more likely they might be to do so again themselves. Countries were scored on the basis of information from a variety of historical sources.

Loyalty score	Regime status and military attempts to seize control of the regime
5	As of 1960 the polity or its metropolitan power had been autonomous for 25 years or more and had experienced no military intervention since 1910.
4	As of 1960 the polity or its metropolitan power had been autonomous for 5 to 24 years and had experienced no military intervention during that period; *or* had been autonomous for a longer period but experienced military intervention between 1910 and 1934.
3	The polity last experienced military intervention between 1935 and 1950, inclusive.
2	The polity last experienced military intervention between 1951 and 1957, inclusive.
1	The polity last experienced military intervention between 1958 and 1960, inclusive.

For 28 polities that became independent after 1957, no loyalty score was assigned unless the military or police did in fact intervene between independence and the end of 1960. For purposes of calculating the summary score, below, a military loyalty score for these polities was derived from the legitimacy score.

Insofar as the military or police themselves illicitly initiated strife in the 1961–65 period, they lost all deterrent effect. To quantify the extent of such involvement, all military or police participation in strife was determined from the data bank of 1,100 events, and for each polity a coercive forces' strife participation score calculated, by weighting each involvement in a mutiny or a turmoil event as one and each involvement in any other event (typically coups and civil wars) as two, and summing for each country.

All four of the coercive potential measures were correlated in the predicted direction with several preliminary measures of strife levels. The participation ratios had low but consistently negative correlations with strife; the loyalty and strife participation indices had correlations of the order of -40 and $+40$ with strife respectively.[9] The composite coercive potential score was calculated by the following formula:

$$\text{Coercive potential} = 10 \cdot \sqrt{\frac{L[2(\text{Hi}R) + 1(\text{lo}R)]}{1+P}}$$

where L = loyalty score, $\text{Hi}R$ = the higher of the scaled military and security forces participation ratios,[10] $\text{lo}R$ = the lower of the participation ratios, and P = coercive forces' strife participation score.

The effect of the formula is to give the highest coercive potential scores to countries with large coercive forces characterized by both historical and concurrent loyalty to the regime. The more recently and extensively such forces have been involved in strife, however, the lower their coercive potential score.

A second coercion measure was included in the final analysis to permit a further test of the curvilinearity hypothesis. The measure used is the expression in brackets in the coercive potential formula above, i.e., a weighted measure of the relative sizes of military and internal security forces (*coercive force size*).

Institutionalization. Indices of institutional strength and stability which I found in previous analyses to be negatively associated with strife are the *ratio of labor union membership to nonagricultural employment*, *central government budgeted expenditure as a percentage of gross domestic product, about 1962*, and the *stability of the political party system*.[11] A ten-interval geometric progression was used to normalize the first of these indices; the second was multiplied by 100 and rounded to the nearest 10. To index characteristics of party systems, two scales were used, one relating to the number of parties, the other to party system stability per se:

No. of parties score — *Characteristics*

0   no parties, or all parties illegal or ineffective
1   one or several parties, membership sharply restricted on ascriptive bases (typically along ethnic lines) to less than twenty percent of the population
2   one party with no formal or substantial informal restrictions on memberships
3   one party dominant
4   two-party (reasonable expectation of party rotation)
5   multi-party

Party system stability score — *Party system characteristics*

0   no parties, or membership restricted on ascriptive bases to less than twenty percent of population
1   unstable
2   all parties relatively new (founded after 1945), long-range stability not yet ascertainable
3   moderately stable
4   stable

Scores on these two scales were combined on an eight-point scale using party stability as the primary indicator of institutionalization but giving highest scores at each stability level to systems with larger numbers of party structures.

The summary institutionalization measure was constructed using this formula:

$$\text{Institutionalization} = 3(\text{hi}I) + 2(\text{mid}I) + \text{lo}I$$

where $\text{hi}I$ = the highest of the three institutionalization scores, and so on. This procedure gives greatest weight to the most institutionalized sector of society on the assumption that high institutionalization in one sector compensates for lower levels in others. The highest scores are attained by the Eastern European Communist states, while the scores of the Western European democracies are slightly lower. The lowest scoring polities are Ethiopia, Haiti, Nepal, and Yemen.

Facilitation. Two aspects of facilitation were indexed separately: *past levels of civil strife* and *"social and structural facilitation"* per se. The past levels of strife measure was derived from the Eckstein data on frequency of internal wars of various types in the period 1946–59; although its reliability is only moderate, it covers a longer period and a larger number of polities than other available data (Eckstein, 1963). Data were collected for those of the 114 polities not included in the Eckstein tabulation, using the same procedure (a *New York Times Index* count) and re-collected for a few others. Weights were assigned to events in various categories, e.g., riots = 1, coups = 5, and a summary score for each polity calculated. The distribution was normalized with a log $(X+1)$ transformation.

The terrain and transportation network of a country constitute a basic structural limitation on the capabilities of insurgents for maintaining a durable insurrection. A complex inaccessibility index was constructed, taking account of the extent of transportation networks related to area, population density, and the extent of waste, forest, and mountainous terrain; the highest inaccessibility scores were received by polities like Bolivia, Sudan, and Yemen, which have limited transportation networks and large portions of rugged terrain.[12]

A crucial social variable that facilitates strife is the extent to which the discontented can and do organize for collective action. The relative strength of Communist Party organizations was used as a partial index, taking into account both the number of party members per 10,000 population and the status of the party. Unfortunately, no comparable data could be obtained for extremist parties of the right. Party membership ratios were rescaled to an eleven-point scale based on a geometric progression of two. The party status scale, below, is based on the premise that illegal parties are more facilitative of strife because their membership is likely, because of the exigencies of repression, to be more dedicated, better organized, and committed to the more violent forms of conflict. Factionalized parties are assumed to be more facilitative because they offer more numerous organizational foci for action.

Score	Communist party status and characteristics
0	In power or nonexistent.
1	Out of power; no serious factionalization or multiple organization; party permitted to participate in electoral activities.
2	Out of power; multiple factions or organizations; party permitted to participate in electoral activities.
3	Out of power; party excluded from electoral activities but other party activities tolerated.
4	Out of power; no serious factionalization or multiple organization; party illegal and/or actively suppressed.
5	Out of power; multiple factions or organizations; party illegal and/or actively suppressed.

The score for each polity is the scaled membership ratio times the party status score.

The third measure of facilitation is the extent of external support for initiators of strife in the 1961–65 period. Each strife event in the 1,100-event data bank was coded for the degree of support for initiators (if any) and for the number of nations supporting the initiators in any of these ways. The scale points for degree of support are provision of arms and supplies ($= 1$), refuge ($= 2$), facilities and training ($= 3$), military advisors and mercenaries ($= 4$), and large (1,000+) military units ($= 5$). The event support score is the degree score times the number of nations score, these scores then being summed for all events for each polity to obtain a polity score. This measure alone has a relatively high correlation with strife-level measures, ranging from .3 to .4; its two extreme outliers, South Vietnam and the Congo, are also among the three extreme outliers on the total magnitude of strife distribution.

The three social and structural facilitation measures were weighted to bring their means into approximate correspondence, several missing-data items estimated, and the weighted measures added to obtain the composite index.

Legitimacy. The legitimacy of a regime can be defined behaviorally in terms of popular compliance, and psychologically by reference to the extent to which its directives are regarded by its citizens as properly made and worthy of obedience. In lieu of evidence on compliance or allegiance necessary to operationalize the concept directly, I combined one indicator of an inferred cause of legitimacy, the circumstances under which the regime attained its present form, with an indicator of an inferred effect, the durability of the regime. The character of the regime was scored on a seven-point scale.

Character score	Origins of national political institutions
7	Institutions are wholly or primarily accretive and autochthonous; reformations, if any, had indigenous roots (although limited foreign elements may have been assimilated into indigenous institutions).

6   Institutions are a mixture of substantial autochthonous and foreign elements, e.g. polities with externally derived parliamentary and/or bureaucratic systems grafted to a traditional monarchy.

5   Institutions are primarily foreign in origin, were deliberately chosen by indigenous leaders, and have been adapted over time to indigenous political conditions. (By adaptation is meant either the modification of regime institutions themselves or development of intermediate institutions to incorporate politically the bulk of the population.)

4   Institutions are primarily foreign in origin, have been adapted over time to indigenous political conditions, but were inculcated under the tutelage of a foreign power rather than chosen by indigenous leaders of their own volition.

3   Institutions are primarily foreign in origin, were deliberately chosen by indigenous leaders, but have *not* been adapted over time to indigenous political conditions.

2   Institutions are primarily foreign in origin, were inculcated under the tutelage of a foreign power, and have not been adapted to indigenous political conditions.

1   Institutions are imposed by, and maintained under threat of sanctions by, foreign powers (including polities under colonial rule as of 1965).

A similar scale, based on the number of generations the regime had persisted as of 1960 without substantial, abrupt reformation, was constructed for durability.

Durability
score   *Last major reformation of institutions before 1960*

7   More than eight generations before 1960 (before 1800).
6   Four to eight generations (1801–80).
5   Two to four generations (1881–1920).
4   One to two generations (1921–40).
3   One-half to one generation (1941–50).
2   One-quarter to one-half generation (1951–55).
1   Institutions originated between 1956 and 1960, or were in 1960 in the process of transition.

Examples of coding decisions about major reformations are that France experienced such a change in 1957; that most French tropical African polities date their basic institutional structures from the 1946 reforms, not the year of formal independence; that the Canadian regime dates from 1867, when dominion status was attained; and that many Latin American regimes, despite performance of musical chairs at the executive level, attained their basic institutional structures at various (historically specified and coded) points in the middle or late nineteenth century.

The summary legitimacy index was constructed by summing and rescaling the character and durability scores.[13]

RESULTS OF CORRELATION AND REGRESSION ANALYSIS

The results of four multiple-regression analyses are discussed in this paper, one of them in detail. The dependent variables in the four analyses are, respectively, total magnitude of civil strife, magnitude of conspiracy, magnitude of internal war, and magnitude of turmoil. The correlations between the ten summary independent variables and these four strife measures are given in Table 3. The independent variables all correlate with the dependent variables

TABLE 3

Correlates of Civil Strife[a]

Variable[b]	1	2	3	4	5	6	7	8	9	10	11	12	13	14
1 Economic deprivation (+)		48	83	−02	−17	−16	−36	−09	26	32	34	31	25	44
2 Political deprivation (+)			88	08	−18	03	−37	−20	33	27	44	18	30	38
3 Short-term deprivation (+)[c]				04	−20	−07	−42	−17	34	34	46	28	32	48
4 Persisting deprivation (+)					−04	−21	−14	−37	−04	17	29	26	27	36
5 Legitimacy (−)						25	48	02	−05	−15	−29	−23	−29	−37
6 Coercive force size (±)							53	27	31	04	−23	−11	−01	−14
7 Coercive potential (−)								41	−14	−37	−44	−39	−35	−51
8 Institutionalization (−)									−19	−40	−35	−23	−26	−33
9 Past strife levels (+)										41	24	16	30	30
10 Facilitation (+)											42	57	30	67
11 Magnitude of conspiracy												30	32	59
12 Magnitude of internal war													17	79
13 Magnitude of turmoil														61
14 Total magnitude of strife														

[a] Product moment correlation coefficients, multiplied by 100. Underlined r's are significant, for $n = 114$, at the .01 level. Correlations between 18 and 23, inclusive, are significant at the .05 level.

[b] The proposed relationships between the independent variables, nos. 1 to 10, and the strife measures are shown in parentheses, the ± for coercive force size signifying a proposed curvilinear relationship. Examination of the r's between the independent and dependent variables, in the box, shows that all are in the predicted direction with the anticipated exception of coercive force size, and that all but one are significant at the .05 level.

[c] Short-term deprivation is the sum of scores on the short-term economic and short-term political deprivation measures. The separate short-term deprivation measures were used in the regression analyses reported below; the summary measure was used in the causal inference analysis.

in the predicted direction, with the exception of coercive force size. The r's for the remaining nine independent variables are significant at the .01 level, except for four correlates of internal war, three of which are significant at the .05 level.

The hypothetical curvilinear relationship between coercive force size and total magnitude of strife (TMCS) is examined graphically in Figures 2 and 3, each of which is a smoothed curve of deciles of the independent variable plotted against TMCS. Figure 2, based on all 114 polities, suggests an apparent tendency, among countries with relatively small forces, for strife to increase with the size of those forces, and also a slight increase in TMCS at very high levels of coercive forces.[14] It is quite likely that countries with protracted political violence expand their coercive forces to meet it. It also seems likely that armies in countries facing foreign threats cause less dissatisfaction —by their presence or actions—than armies in states not significantly involved in international conflict. Both factors might contaminate the proposed curvilinear relationship, so countries with either or both characteristics were removed and the relationship plotted for the remaining 69 countries; the results, in Figure 3, show curvilinearity even more distinctly. Figure 4 indicates that the measure of coercive force potential, in which size is weighted for military loyalty to the regime, is essentially linear, as predicted. The latter measure is used in the multiple regression analyses, below.

Eight of the ten independent variables (excluding coercive force size and short-term deprivation, the sum of the two specific short-term deprivation measures) are included in the multiple regression analyses summarized in Table 4. The variables yield considerable and significant multiple correlation coefficients (R), including a high R of .806 for total magnitude of strife ($R^2 = .650$); a moderately high R for conspiracy of .630 ($R^2 = .397$); a similar R for internal war of .648 ($R^2 = .420$); and a somewhat lower R for turmoil for .533 ($R^2 = .284$).[15] There are several possible explanations for the finding that total magnitude of strife is accounted for nearly twice as well as the several forms of strife. One technical factor is that all the class-of-strife measures have greater distributional irregularities than does TMCS, hence TMCS should be somewhat better explained. It is also possible that the categorization employed has less empirical merit than other work has suggested, i.e., that conspiracy, internal war, and turmoil are not sharply distinct forms of civil strife. To qualify this possibility, the correlation matrix in Table 3 suggests that the forms of strife are only weakly related in magnitude— the highest r among the three is .32—but it may still be that they are more strongly related in likelihood, and hence that the universe of strife is more homogeneous than the typology suggests. The least-predicted class of strife— turmoil—might be better accounted for if turmoil events in the context of internal wars, e.g., riots and localized rebellions in such polities as the Congo and South Vietnam, were categorized as aspects of the internal wars in these countries rather than turmoil per se. The most likely substantive interpretation of the relatively low predictability of turmoil, however, is that much turmoil is a response to a variety of locally incident deprivations and social conditions of a sort not represented in the indices used in this study.

The multiple regression equation for total magnitude of strife was used to calculate predicted magnitude of strife scores. Only ten polities have

TABLE 4

MULTIPLE LINEAR REGRESSION RESULTS:
SIMPLE CORRELATIONS, PARTIAL CORRELATIONS, AND STANDARD WEIGHTS[a]

Dependent Variables	Independent Variables								
	Econ. Dep.	Pol. Dep.	Per. Dep.	Coerce	Instit.	Past CS	SS Facil.	Legit.	R, R²
Total Magnitude of Strife:									
Simple r's	44	38	36	−51	−33	30	67	−37	
Partial r's	24	(09)	39	−17	(07)	(04)	55	−26	R = .806
Constant	− 3.11								
Weights	.177	.066	.271	− .140	.056	.024	.481	− .184	R² = .650
Magnitude of Conspiracy:									
Simple r's	34	44	29	−44	−35	24	42	−29	
Partial r's	(10)	24	22	(−11)	(−09)	(03)	19	(−15)	R = .630
Constant	1.10								
Weights	.094	.238	.194	− .120	− .088	.026	.181	− .135	R² = .397
Magnitude of Internal War:									
Simple r's	31	18	26	−39	−23	16	57	−23	
Partial r's	(14)	(−08)	22	−17	(11)	(−07)	48	(−07)	R = .648
Constant	− 3.66								
Weights	.128	− .073	.186	− .179	.102	− .066	.513	− .063	R² = .420
Magnitude of Turmoil:									
Simple r's	25	30	27	−35	−26	30	30	−29	
Partial r's	(07)	(08)	23	(−09)	(−05)	21	(04)	−19	R = .533
Constant	1.37								
Weights	.072	.085	.223	− .102	− .056	.205	.043	− .192	R² = .284

[a] Simple correlations from Table 1 are repeated here to facilitate comparisons. Partial correlations in parentheses have standard (beta) weights that are significant at less than the .05 level, using the one-tailed T test with n = 114. Since this analysis is concerned with what is, effectively, the entire universe of polities, all the correlations are in one sense "significant," but those in parentheses are of substantially less consequence than the others. The weights are reported to facilitate comparisons of the relative importance of the independent variables; because of the use of a variety of scaling and combination procedures for both independent and dependent variables, the weights do not permit direct interpretations, for example, of the effects of a one-unit decrease in intensity of economic discrimination on extent of turmoil.

predicted scores that differ from their actual scores by more than one standard deviation (7.70 units of TMCS). These polities, and three others that have discrepancies approaching one standard deviation, are listed in Table 5.

In five of the thirteen polities—the Congo, Indonesia, Zambia, Rwanda, and Yemen—there is probably systematic error from data-estimation procedures. All of these countries had intense but inadequately reported civil

```
                    17.0
                    15.0
                    13.0
    TOTAL           11.0
    MAGNITUDE        9.0
    OF CIVIL
    STRIFE           7.0
                     5.0
                     3.0
                     1.0
                        2                    27
                    DECILES OF COERCIVE FORCE SIZE, n = 114
```

FIGURE 2

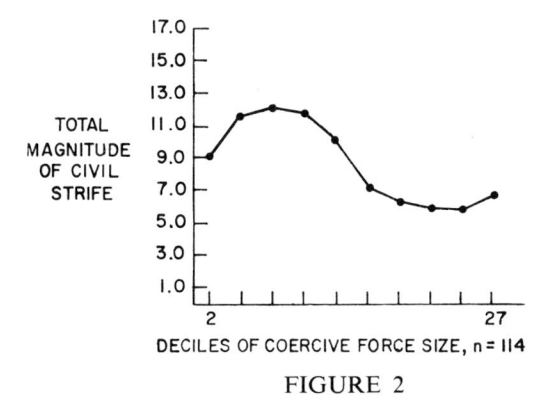

MAGNITUDE OF CIVIL STRIFE AND COERCIVE FORCE SIZE, 114 POLITIES

violence for which only rough and quite possibly exaggerated estimates of deaths were available. When estimates of wounded were added to deaths estimates, using a ratio of about twelve to one based on better reported but smaller scale events (see above), the result was almost certainly a gross inflation of actual casualties, and hence inflation of TMCS scores. The high actual TMCS score for Israel is the result of a questionable coding judgment about the extent and duration of extremist Orthodox religious conflict. More substantive questions are raised by some of the countries. Paraguay, Argentina, Ecuador, and Volta all could be argued to have had an unrealized potential for strife: in fact both Argentina and Ecuador experienced coups in the mid-1960s that, according to their initiators, were preventive or

TABLE 5

POLITIES WITH LEAST-PREDICTED TOTAL MAGNITUDE OF CIVIL STRIFE[a]

Polity	Predicted TMCS	Actual TMCS[b]	Residual	Polity	Predicted TMCS	Actual TMCS[b]	Residual
Congo-Kinshasa	31.6	48.7	+17.1	Belgium	2.4	10.5	+ 8.1
Rwanda	12.7	28.2	+15.5	Zambia	8.1	15.5	+ 7.4
Yemen	9.4	23.6	+14.2	Israel	6.9	14.0	+ 7.1
Indonesia	23.8	33.7	+ 9.9	Argentina	20.5	13.2	− 7.3
Dominican Republic	12.1	21.9	+ 9.8	Ecuador	18.6	10.1	− 8.5
Italy	3.1	12.3	+ 9.2	Volta	9.3	0.0	− 9.3
				Paraguay	17.2	5.0	−12.2

[a] See text. A negative residual indicates that a polity had less strife than would be predicted on the basis of the characteristics it shares with other polities; a positive residual indicates more than predicted strife.

[b] Corrected scores. See note 15.

protective in nature, and early in 1966 the government of Volta succumbed to rioting followed by a coup. In the Dominican Republic, the Congo, and Rwanda, the unexpectedly high levels of violence followed the collapse of rigid, authoritarian regimes; one can infer a time-lag effect from the deprivation incurred under the old regimes. These are special explanations rather than general ones, however. The lack of apparent substantive similarities among the thirteen poorly predicted polities suggests that the analysis has included measures of most if not all the general determinants of magnitudes of civil strife.

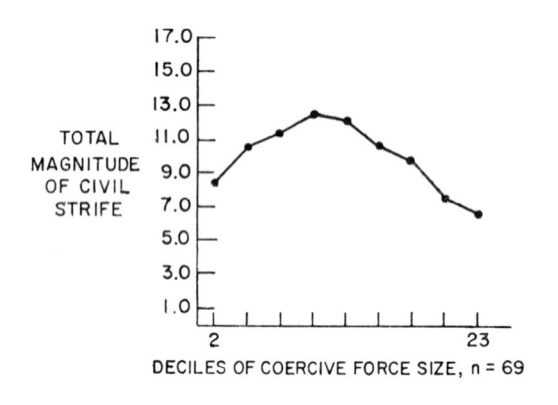

FIGURE 3

MAGNITUDE OF CIVIL STRIFE AND COERCIVE FORCE SIZE, 69 LOW-CONFLICT POLITIES

A REVISED CAUSAL MODEL

One striking result of the regression analyses is that the partial correlations of several of the variables tend to disappear when the other variables are introduced (see Table 4). The short-term deprivation measures consistently decline in consequence, in most instances falling below the .05 level of significance. Institutionalization is in all analyses controlled for by the other variables. One or the other of the two facilitation variables declines to zero in each analysis, "past levels of strife" vanishing in three of the four. Coercive potential and legitimacy also decline rather sharply in their relation to strife. The only variable that is consistently unaffected by the introduction of the control variables specified by the model is persisting deprivation. A preliminary analysis of the behavior of first- and second-order partials suggests what causal interactions and sequences may be involved in these results. The causal path analysis is concerned principally with the sources of the total magnitude of strife, examining the causal sequences of the specific forms of strife only when they appear to deviate from that of all strife.

A basic supposition for the evaluation of causal models is that, if X_1 is an indirect cause of X_3 whose effects are mediated by an intervening variable X_2, then if X_2's effects are controlled, the resulting partial correlation between X_1 and X_3 should be approximately zero. Similarly, if several intervening variables are specified, controlling for all of them or for the last in a causal chain should, if the causal model is not to be falsified, result in a partial correlation not significantly different from zero.[16]

The initial model of the causes of civil strife (Figure 1) postulated that all the mediating variables intervened separately and simultaneously between deprivation and strife. The results indicate that this supposition is only partly

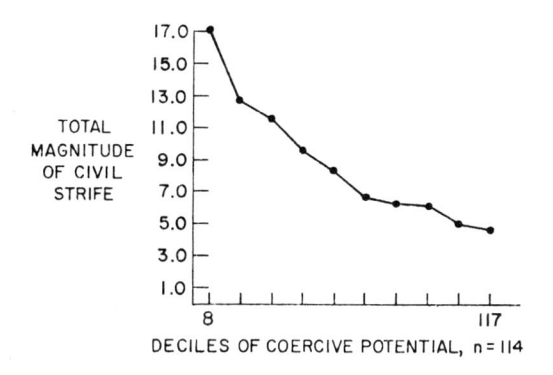

FIGURE 4

MAGNITUDE OF CIVIL STRIFE AND COERCIVE POTENTIAL

Note: The vertical axes in Figures 2, 3 and 4 give the average magnitude of civil strife scores for deciles of countries with coercive forces of increasing size (Figures 2 and 3) and for deciles of countries with increasingly large coercive forces relative to their loyalty. The range of TMCS scores for the 114 polities is 0.0 to 48.7, their mean 9.0, and their standard deviation 7.7. Units on the horizontal axes represent numbers of cases, not proportional increases in force size/loyalty; the figures represent the scores of the extreme cases. Eleven rather than ten groupings of cases were used in computations for Figures 2 and 4; the curves of all three figures were smoothed by averaging successive pairs of decile scores.

correct; none of the mediating variables appear to affect the relationship between *persisting deprivation* and strife, i.e., there is a certain inevitability about the association between such deprivation and strife. Persisting deprivation is moreover equally potent as a source of conspiracy, internal war, and turmoil. With the partial and weak exception of institutionalization, no patterns of societal arrangements nor coercive potential that are included in the model have any consistent effect on its impact.

The effects of short-term deprivation on strife are substantially different— and, it should be added, uncorrelated with persisting deprivation. The intervening variables do tend to control for short-term deprivation's effects. To determine which one or ones exercise primary control, first-order partials were calculated for the several postulated intervening variables, with these results.

(1) The simple r between short-term deprivation and strife = .48[17]
(2) The partial r between short-

term deprivation and strife is:	when the control variable is:
.46	institutionalization
.45	legitimacy
.42	past strife
.36	facilitation
.34	coercive potential

Only the last two constitute a significant reduction, and moreover when they are combined, the second-order partial, $r_{dS \cdot fc}$, = .27, i.e., *coercive potential* and *facilitation* are the only consequential intervening variables affecting the outcome of short-term deprivation. Short-term deprivation taken alone accounts for $(.48)^2 = .23$ of the magnitude of strife; controlling for coercive potential and facilitation reduces the proportion of strife directly accounted for to $(.27)^2 = .07$, a relatively small but still significant amount.

The same controlling effects of coercive potential and facilitation on short-term deprivation occur among the three generic forms of strife. It is worth noting that when the mediating variables are controlled, short-term economic deprivation still accounts directly for a portion of strife, internal war in particular, while political deprivation contributes significantly to conspiracy. These relationships may reflect contamination of the independent and dependent variables because of their partial temporal overlap. Some short-term economic deprivation in the early 1960s may be attributable to protracted internal wars, and successful conspirators may impose politically depriving policies once they are in power. The relationship between short-term deprivation of both types and the magnitude of turmoil, however, is effectively mediated or controlled by characteristics of the society and its response to strife.

The relationships among the mediating variables remain to be examined. Institutionalization has no significant relation to any measure of strife when the other variables are controlled, and in the case of magnitude of total strife and of internal war a weak positive relationship emerges, i.e., there is a slight though not statistically significant tendency for high institutionalization to be associated with higher levels of strife. A computation of partials between institutionalization and the other three mediating variables indicates that institutionalization has a preceding or causal relationship both to coercive potential and to the facilitation variables, as shown in the revised model in Figure 3. Polities with high levels of institutionalization tend to have high coercive potential and to have few of the conditions that facilitate strife.

Legitimacy apparently has a causal relationship with strife independent either of deprivation or the other intervening variables. About half of the

A Causal Model of Civil Strife: A Comparative Analysis 241

initial correlation between legitimacy and strife is accounted for by the apparent causal relation between legitimacy and coercive potential, i.e., legitimate regimes tend to have large and, most importantly, loyal military and police establishments. Separately from this, however, high legitimacy is significantly associated with low levels of strife, a finding consistent with the postulate that political legitimacy itself is a desired value, one whose absence constitutes a deprivation that incites men to take violent action against their regimes. The relationship is relatively strongest for total magnitude of strife, less so for turmoil and conspiracy, and inconsequential for internal war.

Coercive potential appears in several respects to be a crucial variable in the revised causal model: it is evidently attributable in part to both levels of institutionalization and of legitimacy, and has a major mediating effect on short-term deprivation. Nonetheless, when all variables are controlled (see Table 7), the partial r between coercive potential and strife is sharply reduced, in two instances below the .05 level of significance. This is in part due to the effects of legitimacy, which is causally linked to both strife and coercive potential.[18] The other major intervening variable is facilitation ($r_{cs} = -.52$; $r_{cs \cdot f} = -.40$, where c = coercive potential, s = strife, and f = social and structural facilitation), i.e., whether or not facilitative conditions exist for civil strife is partly dependent upon the coercive potential of the regime, and thus indirectly dependent upon legitimacy as well. (The relationship is evidently between coercive potential on the one hand and the "Communist

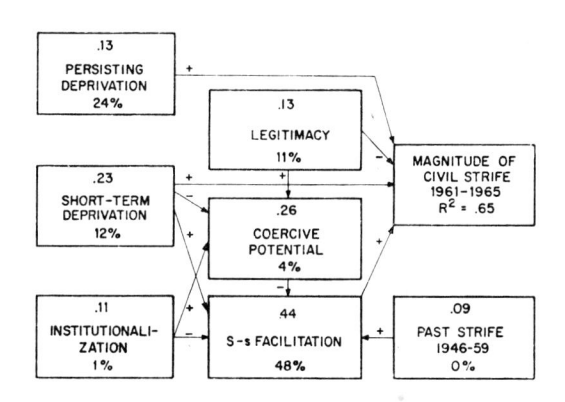

FIGURE 5

REVISED CAUSAL MODEL OF THE DETERMINANTS OF MAGNITUDE OF CIVIL STRIFE

Note: The proportion at the top of each cell is the simple r^2 between the variable and civil strife, i.e. the proportion of strife accounted for by each variable separately. The percentages are the proportion of explained variance accounted for by each variable when the effects of all others are controlled, determined by squaring each partial r, summing the squares, and expressing each as a percentage of the sum. The explained variance, R^2, is .65.

party status" and the "external support for initiators" components of facilitation on the other; coercive potential cannot have any consequential effects on "physical inaccessibility.")

This completes the revision of the causal model with the exception of the second component of facilitation, *past strife levels*. This variable has a consistently lower relationship with strife than other variables, with the exception of the turmoil analysis. Moreover its partial correlation is reduced to zero in these analyses, with the same exception, the sole significant controlling variable being *social and structural facilitation*. Among the causes of turmoil, however, social and structural facilitation is controlled for by several variables —principally past strife, coercive potential, and institutionalization— whereas past strife remains significant when other effects are partialled out. Both findings support the theoretical argument that suggested the past strife measure: a history of chronic strife apparently reflects, and contributes to, attitudes that directly facilitate future turmoil, and indirectly acts to facilitate general levels of strife.

The revised model, with proportional weights inserted, is sketched in Figure 5. The most proximate and potent variable is social and structural facilitation, which accounts for nearly half the explained variance. The deprivation variables account directly for over one-third the magnitude of strife; legitimacy and institutionalization for one-eighth. But these proportions refer only to direct effects, and in the case of both coercive potential and facilitation part of that direct effect, i.e., the illicit participation of the military in strife and the provision of foreign support for initiators, can be determined only from the characteristics of strife itself.[19] The more remote causes of strife, namely deprivation, institutionalization, legitimacy, and prior strife, are the more fundamental and persisting ones. Some additional regression analyses provide some comparisons. Four of the independent variables relate to inferred states of mind: the two short-term deprivation measures, persisting deprivation, and legitimacy. The R based on these variables is .65, compared with .81 when the remaining four variables are added. The R based on the three deprivation variables alone is .60. These analyses show that all "states of mind" conditions contribute significantly to magnitude of strife, but that long-term deprivation has a partial controlling effect on political deprivation. The inference is that short-term political deprivation, as indexed in this study, is most likely to lead to strife if it summates with conditions of persisting deprivation.

We can also ask, and answer, the question, to what extent do the remaining four mediating conditions alone account for magnitude of strife? The variables coercive potential, facilitation, institutionalization, and past strife give a multiple R of .73, with almost all the explained variance accounted for by the first two variables. This result should provide aid and comfort to those concerned with "levels of analysis" problems: research of this sort can focus on aggregative, societal characteristics—which the mediating variables represent—and the (inferred) psychological level can be ignored with relatively little loss of statistical explanatory power. Why these variables are strongly operative and others, like levels of development and type of political system, are relatively weak still needs answering; the answer may be to treat psychological variables as unoperationalized assumptions, or to replace them with variables whose rationale is strictly in terms of effects of social structure or processes on stability.

A further problem is identification of the set of variables that provides the most parsimonious account of magnitude of civil strife. As one approach to the answer, Figure 5 implies that three variables can be eliminated: coercive potential, institutionalization, and past strife, all of which have no consequential direct effects on TMCS. The remaining five variables—the state of mind variables and facilitation—give an R of .80 and R^2 of .64, results almost identical to those obtained when all eight variables are included.[20] Four of the five variables included contribute substantially to the regression equation; as expected, the effects of short-term deprivation, political deprivation in particular, are partially controlled. One important observation is that *social and structural facilitation*, though it is substantially the strongest explanatory variable,[21] has here, as in Figure 5, only a moderate direct controlling effect on short-term deprivation. One interpretation is that some of the effects of facilitation on TMCS are independent of deprivation. Two of its three component measures, Communist party status and external support for initiators, have in common a "tactical" element, i.e., one can infer that underlying them are calculations about gains to be achieved through the employment of strife. This tactical element is not wholly independent of deprivation, inasmuch as three of the four correlations between facilitation and deprivation measures are significant, ranging from .17 to .34 (see Table 3). The basic proposition of this study, that relative deprivation is a necessary precondition for strife, is not challenged by these observations. They do, however, suggest that tactical motives for civil strife are of sufficient importance that they deserve separate operational attention comparable to the conceptual attention given them by conflict theorists. (See, for example, Boulding, 1962; Coser, 1956; Schelling, 1960.)

A number of additional causal inference analyses can be made which might lead to modifications of these conclusions, and of the causal model in Figure 5. Other articles will report the results of causal analyses of various subsets of the universe of polities, and of the causal sequences that can be identified for the several forms of strife.[22]

SUMMARY AND CONCLUSION

Quantitative comparative research cannot flourish in a theoretical vacuum, even if it makes use of an armamentarium of techniques of causal inference. This article may not be proof of that assertion, but it should suggest the usefulness of beginning with a theoretical model based on previous substantive work. The theoretical model of the causes of civil strife employed here dictated the construction of a number of aggregate indicators of not-easily-operationalized variables for 114 polities. Eight summary indicators proved to account jointly for two-thirds of the variance among nations in relative magnitudes of civil strife during 1961–65 ($R^2 = .65$). Of greater theoretical consequence, the initial analysis of partial correlation coefficients makes possible a number of more precise statements about the causal interactions among the theoretical variables.

The fundamental proposition that strife varies directly in magnitude with the intensity of relative deprivation is strongly supported; the three deprivation variables alone provide an R of .60 ($R^2 = .36$), and when a fourth state of mind variable, legitimacy, is added the R^2 increases to .43. One criticism of this research, and of other cross-national studies of strife that make inferences about collective manifestations of psychological variables, is that the results are not a direct test of the relevance of such variables, since the indices of psychological variables are derived from aggregate data rather than being obtained, for example, from cross-national surveys. It is unquestionably necessary to test all hypotheses, including psychological ones, in a variety of ways, for example, to determine whether the inferentially deprived groups are those most likely to engage in strife, and to ask highly frustrated individuals whether they would, or have, taken part in collective violence. No scientific proposition is ever *directly* confirmed or disconfirmed, but some tests are less indirect than others. However, there is only one scientifically acceptable alternative to regarding the results reported here as strong indirect evidence for the psychological propositions relating deprivation and legitimacy to civil violence. That is to provide some reasonably parsimonious, alternative explanations (substantive or technical) of the fact that indices of inferred collective states of mind account for two-thirds of the explained variance (43 percent compared with 65 percent for all variables) in total magnitude of strife.

The effects of the intervening or mediating variables on the disposition to civil violence proved considerably more complex than those of the deprivation variables. Regime legitimacy apparently has no consequential mediating effect on deprivation but acts much as deprivation itself does; low levels of legitimacy, or, by inference, feelings of illegitimacy apparently motivate men to collective violence. Levels of institutionalization, as reflected in high levels of unionization, party system stability, and large public sectors, have no direct mediating effect on deprivation; they are however important determinants of coercive potential and of social facilitation, variables which in turn crucially affect the outcome of short-term deprivation. Social and structural facilitation is the most potent of the intervening variables and appears to have some independent effect on magnitudes of strife. One inference is that the index of this variable reflects tactical decisions to engage in strife as a means of goal attainment. The measure of past levels of strife, 1946–59, provides a partial test of what might be called the null hypotheses of human conflict, that the best predictor of future conflict is the level of past conflict.[23] The measure has relatively weak relationships with magnitude of strife measures for 1961–65 and is an important mediating variable only among the causes of turmoil.

One striking finding is that nations' levels of persisting deprivation are consistently and directly related to their levels of strife. Deprivation attributable to such conditions as discrimination, political separatism, economic dependence, and religious cleavages tends to contribute at a relatively moderate but constant rate to civil strife, whatever may be done to encourage, deter, or divert it, short only of removing its underlying conditions. One other result has important implications for theory, and also for policy, if it is supported by further research. The relation between coercive force size (the relative size of military and internal security forces) and the magnitude of civil violence is distinctly curvilinear; as the level of resources devoted to coercive forces increases, the magnitude of violence also tends to increase up to a certain point, and only at relatively high levels of coercive force does strife tend to decline. Moreover, at the outer limit the relationship again tends to change direction: countries with the very largest coercive forces tend to have more strife than those with somewhat smaller forces. When one eliminates from analysis the countries that have experienced protracted internal or external conflict, the basic curvilinear relationship remains. The adage that force solves nothing seems supported; in fact, force may make things worse.

NOTES

1. Coercive potential is labelled "retribution" in Gurr (1968a). The theoretical model also stipulates a set of variables that determines the intensity of deprivation. In the research reported in the present article, deprivation was operationalized directly rather than by reference to its component variables. The causal mechanism of the theory is the frustration–aggression relationship, which the author has attempted to modify and apply to collective strife in the light of recent empirical and theoretical work. For example, Berkowitz (1962); Yates (1962).

2. Five polities meeting these criteria were excluded: Laos, on grounds that at no time in the 1960s did it have even the forms of a unified regime, and Albania, Mongolia, North Korea, and North Vietnam for lack of sufficient reliable data. The universe nonetheless includes polities with more than 98 percent of the world's population.

3. In each of a number of analyses by Rummel and others a set of domestic conflict measures was factor analyzed. Turmoil, indexed by riots and demonstrations, is found to be a distinct dimension in all the analyses; two other factors, labelled by Rummel "revolution" and "subversion," are in some cases separate and in others combined. Principal components of the revolution dimension are coups, palace revolutions, plots, and purges; the category is labelled here conspiracy.

Guerrilla war and terrorism are major components of the subversion dimension, here labelled internal war. See Rummel (1965); Tanter (1965). The subcategories used here are adapted, with their operational definitions, from Rummel (1963).

4. Information coded, in addition to that required for the three measures specified, included the socioeconomic class(es) of the initiators, the social context in which they acted, the category of events, the targets and apparent motives of the action, the number and role of coercive forces, and the extent and types of external support for initiators and regime, if any. Although no formal reliability tests were undertaken, the four coders did extensive practice coding on the same set of materials prior to coding and reviewed points of disagreement, and the author reviewed all coding sheets for internal consistency and, where necessary, recoding or search for additional information. It should be noted that the 1,100 events include many cumulated reports, e.g., civil rights demonstrations in the United States were treated as a single set of events, all European-OAS terrorism in Algeria as a single event, and so on.

5. It has been suggested that strife in countries with press restrictions is underreported. As a check on this type of systematic error, a nine-point measure of press freedom was incorporated in initial analyses; the measure is from Nixon (1965). The correlations of this measure, in which high scores reflect low press freedom, with some measures of strife are: duration, +19; intensity, +17; pervasiveness, −16; total magnitude of strife, +11. The first two are significant at the .05 level, the third at .10. In effect, *more* strife tends to be reported from polities with low press freedom, not less, as might be expected. The results almost certainly reflect the association of high levels of economic development and press freedom in the Western nations, which tend to have less strife than the developing nations.

6. The missing-data procedures gave implausibly high estimates for initiators and casualties for a number of events. In subsequent and comparable analysis, it seems advisable to rely on estimates of deaths alone, rather than casualties, and to insert means derived from comparable events *in comparable countries* rather than such events in all countries.

7. Tables are available on request from the author listing the 114 countries, their strife scores, the summary measures of deprivation, and mediating conditions discussed below, and the data sources.

8. The 48 deprivation measures, with only one statistically significant exception, were positively associated with strife, most of them at a relatively low level. The thirteen were selected with regard to their representativeness, relatively high correlations with the dependent variables, and low intercorrelations.

9. These are product-moment correlation coefficients, the strife measures of duration, pervasiveness, intensity, and total magnitude of strife for 1961–65. The last two strife measures are defined differently from those employed in the present analysis, but are derived from the same 1,100-event data bank.

10. If one or the other ratio was missing, it was assumed equal to the known ratio. Internal security force ratios for 94 polities are reported in Gurr (1966): 111–126.

11. The first two indices are reported in Gurr (1966): 33–66; 91–110. Correlations among all three and strife measures are reported in Gurr and Ruttenberg (1967). The party characteristics are recoded from Banks and Textor (1963): raw characteristics 41 and 43.

12. Inaccessibility appears to be an almost-but-not-quite necessary condition for protracted internal wars. With one exception, all such internal wars in the post-1945 period occurred in polities with high or very high scores on this index; the exception, a notable one, is Cuba.

13. The following rescaling was used, the sum of the "durability" and "character" scores being given on the upper line, the final legitimacy score on the lower:

Sum: 3,4 5 6 7 8 9 10 11 12 13,14
Legitimacy: 0 1 2 3 4 5 6 7 8 9

14. The S shape of this relationship is considerably more pronounced when coercive-force size is related to total magnitude of turmoil; see Gurr (1968a).

15. Significant computational errors in internal wars and TMCS scores of several countries were identified and corrected after completion of the analyses reported here. Robert van den Helm of Princeton University has analyzed the corrected data, using the combined short-term deprivation measure in lieu of the two separate measures, with these multiple regression results: for TMCS, $R^2 = .638$; conspiracy, $R^2 = .391$; internal war, $R^2 = .472$; and turmoil, $R^2 = .284$. The significant increase in the degree of explanation for internal war is the result of increased correlations between magnitude of internal war and short-term deprivation (from .28 in Table 1 to .34); facilitation (from .57 to .61); and legitimacy (from $-.23$ to $-.26$). The r between magnitudes of turmoil and internal war increases from .17 to .23, the r between TMCS and internal war from .79 to .86. No other results of the analyses reported here are significantly affected by the reanalysis. The actual TMCS scores shown in Table 5 are corrected ones.

16. These and other fundamental arguments about causal inference are well summarized in Blalock (1964): Chapters 2 and 3. A partial correlation coefficient can be most easily regarded as the correlation between X and Z after the portions of X and Z that are accounted for by Y are removed, or held constant. The results discussed below are based on the use of only one of a variety of related causal inference techniques and are open to further, more refined analysis and interpretation. For other applicable approaches, see, e.g. Alker (1965): Chapters 5 and 6.

17. To simplify evaluation of the effects of the control variables, the summary short-term deprivation variable was employed rather than its economic and political components separately.

18. Analysis of the correlation coefficients does not indicate definitively that legitimacy contributes to coercive potential rather than vice versa; nor would it be impossible to argue, on the basis of the partial r's alone, that short-term deprivation is a weak intervening variable between coercive potential and facilitation, on the one hand, and strife on the other. It is the plausibility of the theoretical arguments, in each case, that gives deciding force to the interpretation proposed. For a comparable argument, see Forbes and Tufte (1968).

19. Tanter (1967) has examined time-lag effects between a number of measures of foreign economic and military assistance for the regime and magnitude of civil violence in 1961-63 for Latin American nations and finds generally weak relationships. The only consequential positive relationship, an indirect one, is between levels of U.S. military assistance and subsequent strife.

20. In a reanalysis using corrected data (see note 15), four variables—the combined short-term deprivation measure, persisting deprivation, legitimacy, and facilitation—given an R^2 of .629.

21. The partial *r*'s for these five variables are: economic deprivation, .27; political deprivation, .13; persisting deprivation, .39; legitimacy, .36; facilitation, .61.

22. See Gurr (1968a) for a causal inference analysis of the sources of turmoil. The turmoil model differs principally in that "past strife levels" has the primary mediating role that facilitation has in the TMCS model.

23. The test is less than precise because the measures are not comparable; the past strife measure is based on an arbitrary weighting of counts of number of events, whereas the magnitude of strife measures reflects levels of participation, duration, and intensity.

REFERENCES

ALKER, HAYWARD R., JR. (1965) *Mathematics and Politics.* New York: Macmillan.
BANKS, ARTHUR S. and ROBERT B. TEXTOR (1963) *A Cross-Polity Survey.* Cambridge: MIT Press.
BERKOWITZ, LEONARD (1962) *Aggression: A Social Psychological Analysis.* New York: McGraw-Hill.
BLALOCK, HUBERT M., JR. (1964) *Causal Inferences in Nonexperimental Research.* Chapel Hill: University of North Carolina Press.
BOULDING, KENNETH E. (1962) *Conflict and Defense: A General Theory.* New York: Harper & Row.
BWY, DOUGLAS (1966) "Government instability in Latin America: the preliminary test of a causal model of the impulse to 'extra-legal' change." Paper presented to the American Psychological Association. New York. (September 2-6).
COSER, LEWIS (1956) *The Functions of Social Conflict.* New York: Free Press.
ECKSTEIN, HARRY (1963) "Internal war: the problem of anticipation." In Ithiel de Sola Pool et al., Eds., *Social Science Research and National Security.* Washington, D.C.: Smithsonian Institute. (March 5).
FEIERABEND, IVO K. and ROSALIND L. FEIERABEND (1966) "Aggressive behaviors within polities, 1948-1962: a cross-national study." *Journal of Conflict Resolution* 10 (September): 249-271. Reprinted in this volume, Chapter 6.
FORBES, HUGH D. and EDWARD R. TUFTE (1968) "A note of caution in causal modelling." *American Political Science Review* 62 (December).
GURR, TED (1968a) "Psychological factors in civil violence." *World Politics* 20 (January): 245-278.
— (1968b) "Why urban disorder? Perspectives from the comparative study of civil strife." *American Behavioral Scientist* 10 (March-April).
— (1966) *New Error-Compensated Measures for Comparing Nations.* Princeton: Princeton University Center of International Studies.
— and CHARLES RUTTENBERG (1967) *The Conditions of Civil Violence: First Tests of a Causal Model.* Research Monograph 28 (April). Princeton: Princeton University. Reprinted in this volume, Chapter 8.
HUNTINGTON, SAMUEL P. (1965) "Political development and political decay." *World Politics* 17 (April): 386-430.
JOHNSON, CHALMERS (1964) *Revolution and the Social System.* Stanford: The Hoover Institution on War, Revolution and Peace.

KORNHAUSER, WILLIAM (1959) *The Politics of Mass Society*. New York: Free Press.
MERELMAN, RICHARD M. (1966) "Learning and legitimacy." *American Political Science Review* (September).
NIXON, RAYMOND B. (1965) "Freedom in the world's press: a fresh appraisal with new data." *Journalism Quarterly*. (Winter): 3–14.
ROSS, ARTHUR M. and GEORGE W. HARTMANN (1960) *Changing Patterns of Industrial Conflict*. New York: John Wiley.
RUMMEL, RUDOLPH J. (1965) "A field theory of social action with application to conflict within nations." *Yearbook of the Society for General Systems Research* 10: 189–195.
— (1963) "Dimensions of conflict behavior within and between nations." *Yearbook of the Society for General Systems Research* 8: 25–26. Reprinted in this volume, Chapter 3.
RUSSETT, BRUCE M. (1964) "Inequality and instability: the relation of land tenure to politics." *World Politics* 16 (April): 442–454.
SCHELLING, THOMAS C. (1960) *The Strategy of Conflict*. Cambridge: Harvard University Press.
TANTER, RAYMOND (1967) "Toward a theory of conflict behavior in Latin America." Paper presented to the International Political Science Association. Brussels. (September).
— (1965) "Dimensions of conflict behavior within nations, 1955–1960: turmoil and internal war." *Peace Research Society Papers* 3: 159–183.
TILLY, CHARLES and JAMES RULE (1965) *Measuring Political Upheaval*. Princeton: Princeton University Center of International Studies.
WALTON, JENNIFER (1965) "Correlates of coerciveness and permissiveness of national political systems: a cross-national study." M.A. thesis. San Diego: San Diego State College.
YATES, AUBREY J. (1962) *Frustration and Conflict*. New York: John Wiley.

10 Problems in Causal Analysis of Aggregate Data with Applications to Political Instability

F. GERALD KLINE, KURT KENT, and DENNIS DAVIS

One of the many research strategies for the study of political instability is that of causal modeling. This technique found recent application to this topic, for example, in the work of D. P. Bwy (1968) on Latin America.

A number of theoretical and methodological problems connected with causal modeling have yet to be investigated, however. In this paper, some of these topics are examined with reference to a specific model of political instability. This treatment will probably serve as both a methodological and a pedagogical device, in addition to illustrating a particular method of approaching the question of instability.

The choice of the level of analysis utilized in this paper, the nation, was suggested by the topic of interest, political instability, and by the extremely difficult problem of finding, or even hypothesizing, adequate composition laws relating to the behavior of units of various less macroscopic sizes to the behavior of nations.[1] "Nation" is defined in this study as "an independent or quasi-independent state," operationalized as follows.

Nations were chosen for analysis if they appeared on lists of such units from two of the following sources: (1) U.S. Department of State (1967) *Status of the World's Nations*, (2) UNESCO (1966) *Statistical Yearbook 1963*, and (3) Nixon (1965) Press Freedom Survey. Some nations to which quasi-independence was attributed were not included because of their small population.

Authors' Note: This work was supported by the Office of International Programs, the University Computing Center, and the School of Journalism and Mass Communication at the University of Minnesota. The authors also wish to acknowledge the assistance of Robert Ellis of the University of Minnesota and Arthur Stevens of the University of Michigan.

This paper was originally prepared for presentation to the International Association for Mass Communication Research, Ljubljana, Yugoslavia, September, 1968. It is published here, for the first time, by arrangement with the authors. Copyright © 1970 Sage Publications, Inc.

In addition, the basis for inclusion was the status of the unit in 1963, the current year the data were analyzed. Total number of nations meeting these criteria was 135 (a complete list appears in Appendix A—Units of Analysis).

A number of the problems connected with causal modeling discussed below follow from this choice of a unit of analysis for which most data are in the form of aggregations. It should be noted that many of these problems would also be present in studies using different group-level units of analysis and aggregate data.

The model chosen for analysis was the Lerner model of communication and development, as explicated by McCrone and Cnudde (1967 [reprinted in this volume, Chapter 22]), Alker (n.d.), and Alker (1965), with the substitution of political instability for political participation. The availability of other studies using a similar model opens possibilities for comparisons of methodological interest. This model is conceived as an example of the structure of the theory presented in natural language form in the work of Lerner (1958) and others.[2] This viewpoint of the model follows that of Colby (1967). It is further explicated in Black (1962) but disputed by Brodbeck (1968b).

The substitution is suggested by the later work of Lerner (1963) and is endorsed by Bwy (1968: 20–21 [reprinted in this volume, Chapter 5]). The model may be represented schematically in its untested form, as follows:

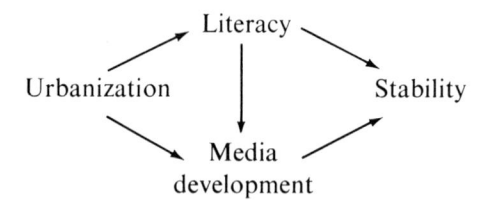

```
              Literacy
            ↗    │    ↘
Urbanization     │     Stability
            ↘    ↓    ↗
               Media
            development
```

That is, urbanization causes both an increase in literacy and media development; rising literacy causes further media development; and rising literacy and media development cause an increasing political stability (or, equivalently, decreasing instability). It is assumed, of course, that these relationships, stated in a form which appears to imply reification, are effected through processes involving individuals.

As a system of general propositions, this scheme presents the researcher with a number of problems. First, the system is meant to be dynamic; this requirement is embodied in the notion of "cause" as a temporally asymmetric process (Feigl, 1953).[3] Available data did not allow such investigation, however, and a static analysis was therefore undertaken. Further efforts will be devoted to dynamic analysis; the a fortiori treatment presented below also has bearing on the problem of stages vs. levels.

Second, the notion of "cause," although calling for intransitivity with respect to time over a given period, still allows circularity of causation over a number of periods. This topic will also be investigated later.[4]

Third, as general propositions, these statements would apply to all units of analysis at all times, in at least a statistical, if not a deterministic, sense (Brodbeck, 1968c). Again, the appropriate data are not available, nor are data available for a random sample of all units. Indeed, given the difficulty with the notion of "nation," it would seem a major task simply to list all appropriate units of analysis for all times in the past, or for a number of different times, even given a procedure such as used in this study.[5] Thus the results of this analysis must be considered as applying only to the particular units analyzed, for the particular point in time for which the data were gathered.

The next step in the analysis was locating data for the variables in the model and preparing these data for the analysis. This work is summarized in the following section, and then various techniques of analysis are presented and discussed.

DATA PREPARATION

Data for analysis of the model were taken from published sources. They were then subjected to a technique of estimation of missing values, after the resulting distributions were normalized. Some implications of measurement were investigated.

Data Sources. The aggregate data from three sources were combined to yield the raw data analyzed in the present study. These sources were the Yale Political Data Bank (see Merritt and Rokkan, 1964; Russett et al., 1964), the Banks and Textor (1963) Cross-Polity Data Bank, and the Cross-National Data Bank of Political Instability Events (see Feierabend and Feierabend, 1965; Feierabend and Feierabend, 1966; Nesvold, 1967).

The Yale Political Data Bank includes data on 60 variables collected from 140 countries and colonies. Sources of the data include

> the United Nations and its numerous agencies, the official statistical publications of national governments, various special studies like those prepared in recent years under the auspices of the United States Congress, and a considerable number of monographs and other works from nongovernmental research organizations and individual scholars [Merritt and Rokkan, 1964: 88].

Variables were selected for this data bank on the basis of two criteria. First, their usefulness to and relevance for studies in such fields as "political modernization and democratization, of nationalism and large-scale political integration, of political culture and socialization, of administration, of political development in non-Western countries, and of the international political system" was weighed. Second, variables were selected according to the twin criteria of accuracy and availability (Merritt and Rokkan, 1964: 84). Those variables for which data were judged to be inaccurate on the basis of a preliminary analysis were discarded. If data was not available for more than

30 countries on a particular variable, that variable was omitted (Russett, 1964: 2). Polities were selected for analysis on the basis of their significance for comparative or international politics (Merritt and Rokkan, 1964: 86).

The Banks and Textor Data Bank represents a rating of 115 separate political entities on 57 different political and social characteristics. Some of the basic characteristics measured were "hard" quantifiable items such as literacy or national income; others were "soft" judgmental variables such as interest articulation or the political role of the police. In addition, Banks and Textor chose to dichotomize their variables for analysis. In some cases this was the only reasonable procedure; it was not possible to draw fine distinctions in the political importance of police from country to country. At other times this meant the loss of important information, as in the case of literacy or national income, where more precise measurement was possible (Russett et al., 1964: 8). The authors characterize their grouping of polities into classes as being highly relativistic for many variables. Particular polities were placed into particular classes on the basis of the range of characteristics these polities exhibited in relation to other polities in that class and to polities in other classes of these variables. Reliability of coding was evaluated through checks against material published by area experts and through consultation with such experts in the Boston area. Lack of funds made more formal reliability assessments unfeasible. Nations were included in this analysis on the basis of their status as independent polities (Banks and Textor, 1963: 9–10).

The Cross-National Data Bank of Political Instability Events contains data compiled for 84 nations for the seventeen-year period 1948–65. The sources used in the collection of the data were *Deadline Data on World Affairs* and the *Encyclopedia Britannica Yearbooks*. Each political instability event which occurred was characterized on a separate tab card, using multiple categories. In one type of instability coding, each event was coded on a seven-point scale of intensity level of aggressive behavior in instability events. A zero scale value stood for an absence of instability, while scale point six indicated extreme instability. A formal check on the reliability of this coding scheme was made. Consensual validation for the intensity scale was obtained by asking judges to sort the same events along the same continuum. The level of agreement among judges on the distribution of the items was quite high (Pearson $r = .87$). Another check performed was a comparison of the assignment of items to positions on the scale by two independent raters. Their (Feierabend and Feierabend, 1966: 252 [reprinted in this volume, Chapter 6]) agreement for the task, involving data from 84 countries for a seven-year time period, was also high (Pearson $r = .935$).

It should be pointed out here that there is an inherent problem with the Instability Data that will affect our analysis. The data sources reflect, to a considerable extent, reliance upon newspaper accounts of event happenings. In those countries where there is high media development one can expect a greater number of events to receive publicity than in those countries where media development has lagged. As a consequence we would expect large numbers of events, scoring low on the zero to six point scale, to be correlated with media development whereas only those events which have a high instability score would have a high probability of receiving publicity in those countries where media development is low. Taking this into account we can expect an attenuation in the level of our effect measures between media development and instability. That is, if we find that as media development goes up stability goes up then the measure of this effect will be less than it should be as a consequence of this bias.

Measurement Error. Measurement error, an endemic disability in social science research, has not received great attention in causal modeling publications. While this topic may be crucial for all causal modeling approaches, only one line of thought in causal modeling has yet been investigated by the present authors for measurement error implications. Further research along this line is planned.[6]

The approach investigated is the Simon-Blalock partial correlation tradition (Simon, 1957; Blalock, 1964). Although some types of measurement error are discussed and possible corrections given (Blalock, 1964), the case of random errors would appear amenable to solutions beyond those suggested (Blalock, 1964).

One means of approaching such error is through correction formulas suggested by Tucker, Myers and Terwilliger (n.d.). When these corrections were applied to the data of McCrone and Cnudde (1967), and of Alker (n.d.; 1965), conclusions different from those of these authors concerning plausible causal models were obtained in both cases. Thus considerable caution must be exercised in the application of this type of causal analysis to fallibly measured data.

Data Normalization. The next step in the data preparation process was to seek transformations which would complement the assumptions inherent in our parametric model. The use of the transformations served two primary functions: (1) they operated to relax the constraints imposed by the assumption of additivity and linearity in our regression equations and (2) to limit the range of variations between the actual and expected values for all levels of our independent variables. Thus by choosing appropriate transformations we achieve the two necessary goals of normalization and reduction of variance for levels of aggregation in the estimation process. See Frank (1966).

The Yale Political Data Bank chose to make a logarithmic transformation for variables that appeared to be highly skewed, to meet the general requirements of parametric analysis. It was our feeling, however, that transformations other than some logarithm would achieve a more normal distribution. Our criteria were minimal skewness and kurtosis as well as a visual display of the distributions. Table 1 indicates the kinds of transformations that were optimal for the variables in the present analysis.

Missing Data Estimation. In much of the analysis done with nation-level aggregate data, investigators relied upon available data only, not including those polities for which data were missing. This is a particularly crucial shortcoming when the goal of the analysis is to relate differential effects of various independent and dependent variables through causal models in the context of "national development."[7] It is exactly those nations that have not developed sufficiently to undertake the task of social bookkeeping which must be included in these analytic models of development. To attempt to alleviate this problem and to highlight the difficulties encountered in using a complete set of data which includes estimations, missing values were estimated for those nations for which data on various variables were not available to the sources cited above. Three different "aggregating variables" were chosen. These were areal grouping, date the nation gained independence, and political modernization as defined in the Banks and Textor (1963) Cross-Polity Survey.

TABLE 1

Optimal Transformations

Variable	No transformation	Square root	Cube root	Logarithm$_{10}$
Urbanization		X		
Literacy	X			
Newspaper circulation			X	
Radio sets				X
Cinema seats		X		
Political stability			X	

For each level of each of these three aggregating variables mean scores were computed on all analysis variables. These mean scores are the best estimates of actual scores obtainable. Thus for each nation for which data were not reported, three estimates of actual scores were obtained. In the present paper, then, we will indicate how our analysis looked for the three sets of data, for all countries, and the differential results that accompany the different estimates that are a byproduct of using different aggregating variables. But first let us indicate how we dealt with some of the major mathematical pitfalls associated with the estimation of aggregate data.

For the purpose of this paper we will only deal with those variables that are used in the analysis of the model outline above. We did attempt to estimate missing data for all of the quantifiable variables originally chosen, succeeding in doing so for all but population, television sets per thousand, GNP and GNP per capita. The reason for our lack of success with these four variables will be outlined below.

Robinson (1959) pointed out that statistical association for aggregated populations can differ in degree and sign from the statistical association

Problems in Causal Analysis of Aggregate Data

that can be computed from individual members of the population. Following Alker's (1966) typology of ecological fallacies, let us notationally outline the covariance theorems that are pertinent to this analysis. We shall define our variables X and Y for a universe of N units i which can be divided into subsets or disjoint regions r. We will be dealing with only one point in time, $t = 1$. Each observation Xir, Yir, etc., will be associated with the ith unit in region r. In this particular analysis a unit will be defined as a "nation" and various regions (r's) will be used.

Using a "dot" notation to indicate averages over nations and regions we can decompose the universal deviation into an individual or "unit" one and a region or "ecological" one:

$$(Xir - X..) = (Xir - X.r) + (X.r - X..) \quad (1)$$

From this beginning, we can generate other equations dealing with covariation. For example, the universal covariance of X and Y for all i units is:

$$Cxy_i = 1/N \sum_{i=1}^{N} (Xir - X..)(Yir - Y..) \quad (2)$$

And the variance for all i units is:

$$Cxx_i = 1/N \sum_{i=1}^{N} (Xir - X..)^2 \quad (3)$$

Following this, we can see that equations (4) and (5) define the covariance within-region and between-regional respectively:

$$WCxy_i = 1/N \sum (Xir - X.r)(Yir - Y.r) \quad (4)$$

$$ECxy_i = 1/N \sum (X.r - X..)(Y.r - Y..) \quad (5)$$

Using equation (1) we can multiply corresponding expressions for $(Xir - X.r)$ and $(Yir - Y.r)$ and average them over $i = 1, \ldots, N$ so that it can be shown that:

$$Cxy_i = WCxy_i + ECxy_i \quad (6)$$

This equation, (6), indicates how the covariance of X and Y for N individuals i can be partitioned into the within-region and between-region covariance. If we were to divide equation (6) by $\sqrt{Cxx_i Cyy_i}$, we would obtain the same formulation that Robinson (1959) used to make his point about the problem of ecological fallacy.

$$Rxy = \frac{WCxy_i + ECxy_i}{\sqrt{Cxx_i Cyy_i}} \quad (7)$$

For our purposes we are concerned with the problems that associate with the choice of levels of aggregation when we wish to make estimates of missing data. Using equation (6), we can see that if we do not want to fall prey to the ecological trap of having high between-region covariance we must be careful to choose levels of aggregation that have equivalent variances, or relatively so, when we make our estimates. Thus as $ECxy_i$ approaches zero, the more confident we are that the universal covariance is equivalent to the within-region covariance. For missing data estimation, we would be considering the situation where

$$Cxx_i = WCxx_i + ECxx_i \tag{8}$$

and $ECxx_i$ should be minimized. As a rule of thumb, we used the ratio of 6:1 as a determinant. If the range of variance from level to level was greater than 6:1, we readjusted the level. For the variables of population, television sets per thousand, GNP, and GNP per capita, it was not possible to choose levels that met this criterion.

The methodological aim of this paper prompted us to choose three variables for aggregation purposes so that we might compare the grand means and variances of the three missing data estimations. That is, we decided that three different methods of data estimation should be examined to see what effect there would be on the analysis portion of the project. At the outset, we used all possible levels of the aggregating variables, operating on the assumption that the greater the number of levels the more refined the data estimation would be across the whole population. This procedure had to be changed, however, because of the wide range of variances. Subsequently, we chose six levels of areal grouping, four levels of date of independence and three levels of political modernization. Tables 2a, 2b, and 2c indicate the levels of aggregation for selected variables along with the means and variances.

DATA ANALYSIS

Study of problems of causal relations between pertinent variables has been an active area of late in the fields of sociology, psychology, and political science. For example, the early works of Simon (1957) and Wold and Jureen (1953) were explicated and expanded upon by Blalock (1964) to provide sociologists, with models for causal analysis. Alker (n.d.) and McCrone and Cnudde (1967 [this volume, Chapter 22]) applied these models to political data. In a similar vein, but starting in a different tradition, Boudon (1965) and Duncan (1966) drew upon the work of Wright (1934) to obtain more powerful insights with regard to causal structures using the path coefficient method.

In a more restrictive way, Campbell (1963) attempted to deal with the problem of two-variable causal relations using the technique of cross-lagged correlations. A requirement for this two-variable model, unnecessary for the more extended causal structure we will be using, is collection of data at two or more points in time. This model grew out of early work done by Lazarsfeld (1948)[8] on 16-fold turnover tables. Pelz and Andrews (1964) arrived at the same model independently and Yee and Gage (n.d.) and Rozelle (1965) have attempted to implement it. It should be noted here that recent work by

TABLE 2a
MISSING DATA ESTIMATES BY POLITICAL MODERNIZATION

		Modernized	Mid-transitional	Early transitional
1. Urbanization	N	58	16	30
	$\bar{X}$	16.74	12.00	8.81
	Var.	18.56	21.46	37.45
2. Literacy	N	58	17	30
	$\bar{X}$	72.45	45.55	27.42
	Var.	9807.4	6119.7	5779.7
3. Newspapers	N	58	17	30
	$\bar{X}$	4.64	2.82	1.77
	Var.	3.73	1.22	2.08
4. Radio	N	58	17	30
	$\bar{X}$	2.60	1.94	1.67
	Var.	.45	.46	.66
5. Cinema	N	58	17	30
	$\bar{X}$	3.65	2.94	2.02
	Var.	1.13	2.05	1.25
6. Stability	N	54	15	11
	$\bar{X}$	31.7	31.9	29.4
	Var.	144.7	83.7	83.9

TABLE 2b
MISSING DATA ESTIMATES BY DATE OF INDEPENDENCE

		Before 19th century	1800–1913	1914–45	1945
1. Urbanization	N	21	29	13	37
	$\bar{X}$	15.96	15.03	14.60	10.50
	Var.	34.27	28.35	26.57	34.15
2. Literacy	N	21	29	13	37
	$\bar{X}$	71.22	62.87	62.27	31.9
	Var.	13669.5	6812.3	15607.3	5589.2
3. Newspapers	N	21	29	13	37
	$\bar{X}$	4.68	3.93	4.53	1.78
	Var.	5.43	2.41	3.59	1.80
4. Radios	N	21	29	13	37
	$\bar{X}$	2.60	2.44	2.67	1.61
	Var.	.59	.35	.28	.63
5. Cinema	N	21	29	13	37
	$\bar{X}$	3.80	3.50	4.07	2.06
	Var.	.80	1.21	1.06	1.40
6. Stability	N	19	30	11	18
	$\bar{X}$	32.2	34.8	29.6	30.5
	Var.	197.5	114.9	71.0	65.7

TABLE 2c
Missing Data Estimates by Areal Grouping

		Australasia and S.E. Asia	North and Central America, Carribean	South America	Africa and Middle East	West Europe and Scandinavia	East Europe
1. Urbanization	N	18	13	9	38	18	8
	$\bar{X}$	12.18	14.14	16.80	9.84	17.70	17.4
	Var.	34.39	28.89	17.95	32.46	12.15	16.16
2. Literacy	N	18	13	9	38	18	8
	$\bar{X}$	42.4	57.33	68.08	25.85	76.19	88.02
	Var.	955.83	560.22	514.24	467.64	1443.83	132.66[a]
3. Newspapers	N	18	13	9	18	18	8
	$\bar{X}$	2.92	3.57	4.30	1.82	4.96	5.78
	Var.	4.03	2.12	2.23	1.93	5.06	.78[a]
4. Radio	N	18	13	9	38	18	8
	$\bar{X}$	1.78	2.07	2.70	1.70	2.65	2.78
	Var.	.49	.24	.25	.61	.31	.17
5. Cinema	N	18	13	9	38	18	8
	$\bar{X}$	2.67	2.79	3.40	2.36	3.74	4.33
	Var.	1.72	1.70	.54	1.87	1.54	.56
6. Stability	N	13	12	10	24	17	8
	$\bar{X}$	33.7	34.3	39.7	30.8	29.0	29.8
	Var.	101.2	141.6	105.3	61.7	120.0	85.5

[a] The 6:1 ratio of variances across groups did not hold for this level. However, we did not have to make estimates for Eastern European countries because we had full data on these variables.

Rozelle and Campbell (n.d.) and Kline[9] has indicated that there are inherent difficulties associated with the cross-lagged correlation technique which debilitates it as a model for analysis. Applications of the model by Schramm and Ruggels (1967) and Bwy (1968 [this volume, Chapter 5]) did not take these difficulties into account in their analysis. Coleman postulates a different approach to the two-variable causal relationship (1964) which may alleviate the difficulties associated with the cross-lagged model if the assumptions of his model are appropriate to the data at hand. Our data analysis relies totally on the path coefficient method noted above.

All Nations Analysis. Using Lerner's own words we can see where the model indicated above came from: "... increasing urbanization has tended to raise literacy; rising literacy has tended to increase media exposure; increasing media exposure has 'gone with' wider economic participation (per capita income) and political participation (voting)." See Lerner (1958: 46). This mode, as diagrammed above, can then be mathematized as follows (where urbanization $= X_1$; literacy $= X_2$; media development $= X_3$; and political participation $= X_4$):

Problems in Causal Analysis of Aggregate Data

$$X_2 = b_{20}X_0 + b_{21}X_1 + e_1 \tag{9}$$
$$X_3 = b_{30}X_0 + b_{31}X_1 + b_{32}X_2 + e_2 \tag{10}$$
$$X_4 = b_{40}X_0 + b_{42}X_2 + b_{43}X_3 + e_4 \tag{11}$$

This hierarchical model can be solved in a standardized form to delete the intercept coefficients and thus give this set of equations:

$$X_2 = B_{21}X_1 + e_1 \tag{12}$$
$$X_3 = B_{31}X_1 + B_{32}X_2 + e_2 \tag{13}$$
$$X_4 = B_{42}X_2 + B_{43}X_3 + e_3 \tag{14}$$

The standardized regression coefficients (B_{ij}'s) are equivalent to path coefficients in Wright's (1934) formulations. Using available data Alker tested this model with data drawn from sources similar to those used in this paper and determined the following weights for each of the links in the diagrammed model. See Table 1 and Alker (n.d.).

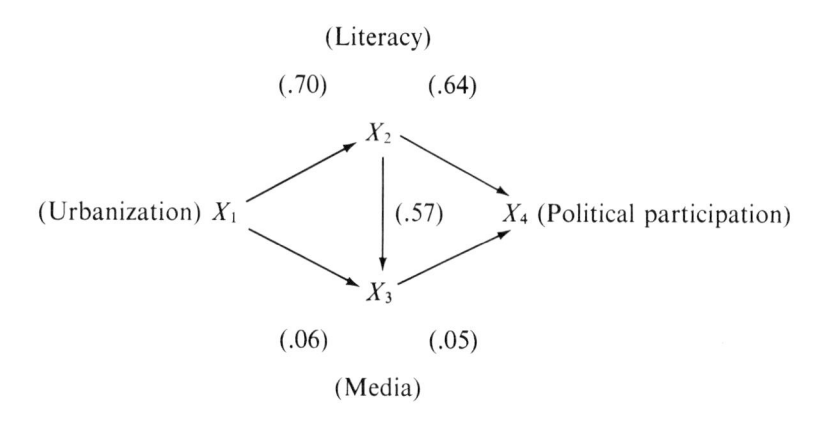

(Literacy)

(.70)   (.64)

X_2

(Urbanization) X_1 (.57) X_4 (Political participation)

X_3

(.06)   (.05)

(Media)

This finding downgrades the Lerner formulation. He would not predict the very weak link between media and political participation (Alker, n.d.). The amount of variance explained by the Alker analysis amounts to 20 percent, which means about 80 percent is being explained outside of the model by exogenous factors.

It was our intent to examine a similar model to see what effect the variables of urbanization, literacy, and media would have on political stability. One would expect that where there was wide political participation (reasonably well predicted by the three other variables according to Lerner), there would be a large degree of political stability. Aside from the Lerner formulation one would expect that widespread literacy and media information would have an effect on the root causes of political instability. We were not, however, willing to delete any links in the four variable model (Lerner did not consider the direct link between urbanization and political participation to be important) a priori. Thus, in diagrammatic fashion, the model looked like this:

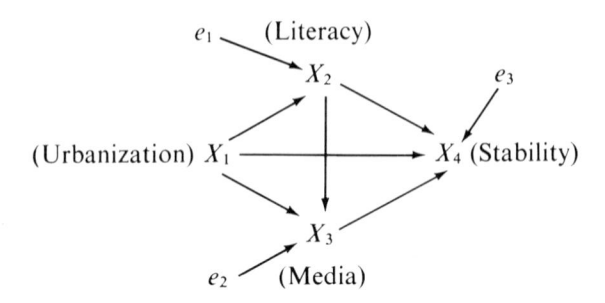

[Diagram: Urbanization (X_1) → Literacy (X_2), Media (X_3), Stability (X_4); with errors e_1, e_2, e_3]

And mathematically, it looked like this in standardized form:

$$X_2 = B_{21}X_1 + B_{2e}e_1 \tag{15}$$

$$X_3 = B_{31}X_1 + B_{32}X_2 + B_{3e}e_2 \tag{16}$$

$$X_4 = B_{41}X_1 + B_{42}X_2 + B_{43}X_3 + B_{4e}e_3 \tag{17}$$

Because of our interest in newspaper circulation, radio sets, and cinema seats (you will recall that we could not estimate missing data scores for television and thus it cannot be included here), we treated each medium development separately to evolve this model:

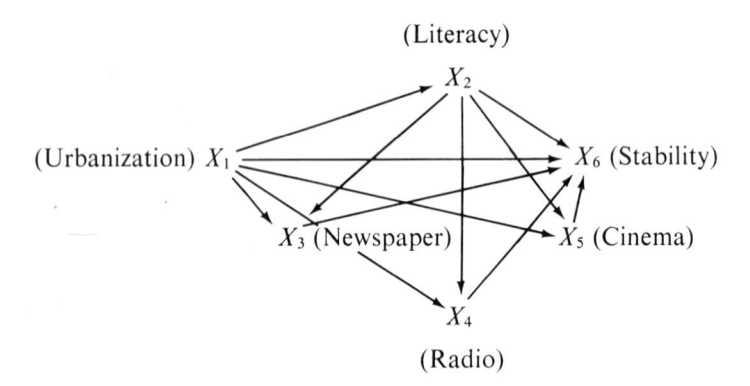

[Diagram: Urbanization (X_1) linked to Literacy (X_2), Newspaper (X_3), Radio (X_4), Cinema (X_5), Stability (X_6)]

The next step in our analysis was to obtain the regression coefficients for each link in the model, delete those that did not meet a criterion level,[10] and recompute. This recomputation procedure, as pointed out by Duncan (1966: 6-7), eliminates the tedious search procedure recommended by Blalock. Table 3 indicates the regression coefficients for the final model by type of aggregation for missing data estimation.

TABLE 3
Standardized Regression Coefficients for all Nations by Type of Aggregation for Missing Data Estimation

Link	Date of independence	Areal grouping	Political modernization
Urbanization → Literacy	.73	.77	.76
Urbanization → Stability	−.28	−.36	−.30
Urbanization → Newspaper	.26	.26	.22
Urbanization → Radio	—	—	.24
Urbanization → Cinema	—	—	—
Literacy → Newspaper	.71	.71	.73
Literacy → Radio	—	—	.58
Literacy → Cinema	—	—	—
Literacy → Stability	—	—	—
Newspaper → Stability	.27	.40	.39
Radio → Stability	—	—	−.21
Cinema → Stability	—	—	—

One can see from Table 3 that there is a good deal of similarity in the coefficients between estimation by date of independence and areal grouping. The discrepancy in the model, when estimates made by political modernization is used, may not be as great as would be indicated here. The criterion cutoff level used was just below the −.21 regression coefficient found for the link from radio → stability. If the cutoff was raised by .02, the models would be identical and would have similar interpretations. They would all look like this:

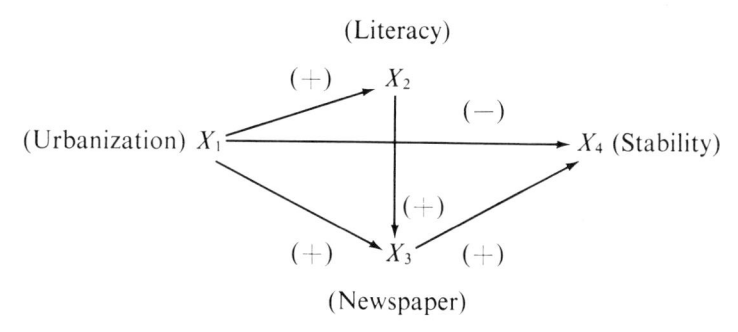

```
                    (Literacy)
             (+)    X₂
                 ↗  │  (−)
(Urbanization) X₁───┼────────→ X₄ (Stability)
                 ↘  │(+)      ↗
             (+)   X₃    (+)
                (Newspaper)
```

and one could see immediately that there seems to be a decrease in stability with an increase in urbanization and an increase in stability with an increase in newspaper circulation.

To this point in the analysis, it would seem that the type of variable chosen for aggregation and missing data estimation has little substantive effect on the interpretation of the results. We will pursue this point in the next section.

The similarity of results for the models was also found in explanation of variance. For date of independence estimation, the model explained only 6 percent of the variance; for areal grouping the model accounted for only 8 percent; and for the more complicated political modernization estimation model it accounted for only 6 percent. It would seem that our original notions concerning a macro-model of political stability had left out either one or more important exogenous variables, or clusters of variables, or both. Two of the advantages of using the path coefficient method of analysis are that we can examine the residual effect on each of the variables in our model, estimate these regression coefficients, and we can determine what the correlations might be between the residuals for each variable.

In equations (15), (16), and (17) the regression coefficients attached to e_1, e_2, and e_3 represent the effect the residuals have on the variables. In most standard representations of regression equations, these combinations of terms would be combined to represent the error variation that is unexplained by the independent variables. Following Duncan's exposition of path analysis (Duncan, 1966), the basic theorem of the technique can be written in the general form:

$$r_{ij} = \sum_q B_{iq} r_{jq} \qquad (18)$$

"where i and j denote two variables in the system and the index q runs over all variables from which paths (links) lead directly to X_i." (See Duncan 1966.) Taking into account the correlation of unity for one variable with itself, and the crucial assumption of no correlation between the residual of one variable and the immediately preceding variable,[11] we may manipulate formula (18) in such a way as to allow determination of the regression coefficients associated with the residual:

$$r_{ii} = 1 = \sum B_{iq} r_{iq} \qquad (19)$$

Using the information from Table 3 and knowing the correlations among all of the variables prior to the calculation of the path coefficients, we calculated the correlation matrices for the three residuals as well as the regression coefficients for the residuals. They are shown in Tables 4 and 5.

TABLE 4

STANDARDIZED RESIDUAL REGRESSION COEFFICIENTS FOR ALL COUNTRIES BY TYPE OF AGGREGATION FOR MISSING DATA ESTIMATION

Link	Date of independence	Areal grouping	Political modernization
Residual → Literacy	.67	.64	.65
Residual → Newspaper	.65	.89	.64
Residual → Radio	—	—	.78
Residual → Stability	.99	1.00	1.00

TABLE 5

CORRELATION MATRIX FOR RESIDUALS FOR ALL COUNTRIES BY AGGREGATION FOR MISSING DATA ESTIMATION

	Date of independence		
	(1)	(2)	(3)
Literacy residual (1)	1.00		
Newspaper residual (2)	−.12	1.00	
Stability residual (3)	−.32	−.34	1.00

	Areal grouping		
	(1)	(2)	(3)
Literacy residual (1)	1.00		
Newspaper residual (2)	−.12	1.00	
Stability residual (3)	−.46	−.40	1.00

	Political modernization			
	(1)	(2)	(3)	(4)
Literacy residual (1)	1.00			
Newspaper residual (2)	.08	1.00		
Radio residual (3)	.28	.58	1.00	
Stability residual (4)	−.28	−.50	−.05	1.00

The information provided in these tables once again illustrates the similarity of findings across type of data estimation. Apparently the exogenous effects on literacy are uncorrelated with those affecting newspaper circulation, where there is a moderate correlation between the residuals attached to literacy and radio set penetration under one type of estimation (.28). The fairly large negative correlation between the residuals for literacy and stability and for newspapers and stability would seem to point to patterns of relationships which could be systematically sought to obtain clearer insights into the exogenous effects outside our model of political instability.

So far we have found that there are similarities in our findings across the three types of estimations made; extremely little explanation of the variation in political instability with our model; and residual regression coefficients and residual correlations which seem to indicate patterns of relationships which are exogenous to our model. It is possible that this set of circumstances is due to counteracting influences across our whole roster of countries. Perhaps our model is more applicable in specific areas? For example, in Alker's (n.d.) analysis it is pointed out that the Lerner model is not applicable to the American scene, due to high male political participation prior to high media development and economic development, and that this model makes much more sense in European and Afro-Asian contexts. To pursue a possibility similar to this with our model, we chose, in an a fortiori fashion, those nations that we deemed to be politically stable and unstable. Our criterion was intuitive and based on what seemed to us to have been politically unstable parts of the world during the period our data were collected. This criterion was not based in any way on the political instability scores we assembled, but we did expect a correlation with these scores. Our next section deals with application of the original full link model to a set of stable and unstable nations for the three types of estimation of missing data.

Stable and Unstable Nations Analysis. In beginning this analysis we were guided by two points: Alker's reference to the Lerner-type model being more relevant for European and Afro-Asian areas, and our own concern for the difference between stages and levels. Our choice of the "stable" and "unstable" nations, in effect, selected those areas which were at different stages of development due to the correlation between political instability and economic and political development. If Alker is correct, we should arrive at similar interrelationships, whereas if the levels vs. stages notion is correct there should be obvious differences between the stable and unstable areas we have chosen.

Our selection of stable nations included those in North America, Western Europe and Scandinavia. Those deemed unstable came from the Middle East and Southeast Asia. Table 6 indicates the regression coefficients that were calculated for both groups and by all three types of aggregation for missing data estimation. It becomes immediately apparent that no clear pattern emerges either to support or reject the two contentions above. There does seem to be a modicum of similarity across the three stable groups but the variance explanation, although a great deal higher than across all nations taken together, fluctuates considerably. There is very little similarity across the three unstable groups. This brings into question our technique of estimating for missing data.

Because most of the data we had to estimate pertained to underdeveloped nations, it becomes apparent that our estimations, which did not seem to vary much across all countries when one examined the means and standard deviations, vary considerably when we select our subsets for analysis (see Appendix B). It is not clear, however, whether the data estimation itself, that is the uniqueness associated with a particular choice of aggregation variable, is the culprit, or whether we have fallen into an ecological trap.

If you will recall, equation (6) showed how the total covariation could be divided into the within-group covariance and the between-group covariance. Using this as a point of departure we can continue expanding equation (7) by dividing the $WCxy_1$ and $ECxy_1$ by the relevant standard deviations. This will give us the equation

$$Rxy = \frac{WCxy}{\sqrt{Wcxx \cdot WCyy}} \cdot \sqrt{\frac{WCxx \cdot Wcyy}{Cxx \cdot Cyy}} + \frac{ECxy}{\sqrt{ECxx \cdot ECyy}} \cdot \sqrt{\frac{ECxx \cdot Ecyy}{Cxx \cdot Cyy}}$$

(19)

TABLE 6
STANDARDIZED REGRESSION COEFFICIENTS FOR STABLE AND UNSTABLE COUNTRIES BY TYPE OF AGGREGATION FOR MISSING DATA ESTIMATION

Link	Date of independence Stable	Date of independence Unstable	Areal group Stable	Areal group Unstable	Political modernization Stable	Political modernization Unstable
Urb → Lit	.71	.43	.72	.45	.77	.44
Urb → Stab	—	−.36	−.21	—	−.25	−.35
Urb → News	—	—	—	—	—	—
Urb → Rad	—	—	—	—	—	—
Urb → Cin	—	—	—	—	—	—
Lit → News	.77	.56	.69	—	.85	—
Lit → Rad	—	—	—	—	—	—
Lit → Cin	—	.30	—	.32	—	—
Lit → Stab	−.37	.44	—	.39	−.29	.37
News → Stab	.70	−.24	.69	—	.86	—
Rad → Stab	—	—	—	—	—	—
Cin → Stab	—	.27	—	−.34	—	—
Variance explained	20%	20%	36%	19%	28%	15%

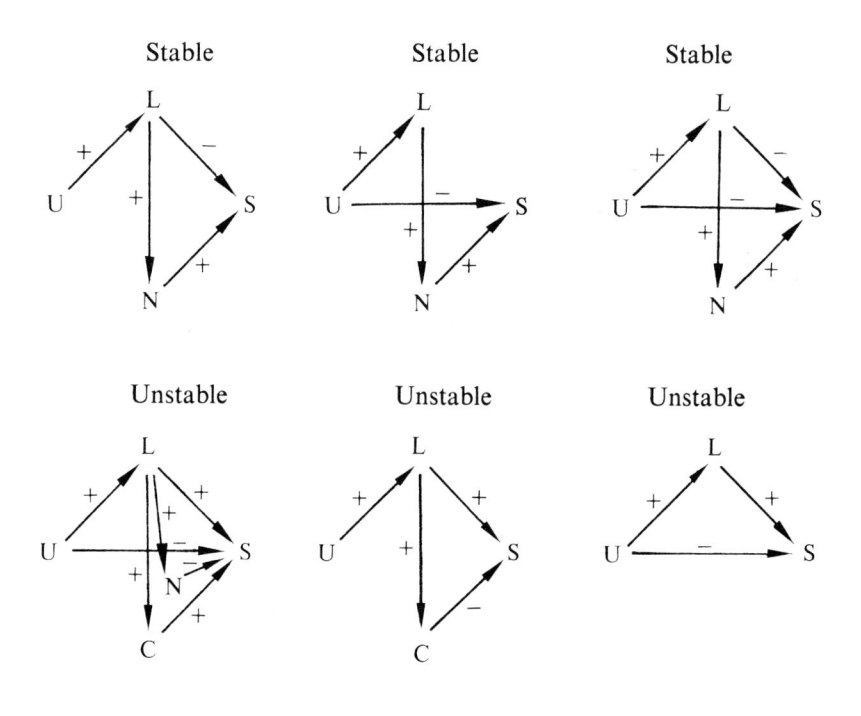

which can be simplified by substituting R_w (within correlation) and R_{ec} (ecological correlation) for their formulae above and by converting the expressions under the second and fourth square root signs to correlation ratios.[12] Making these substitutions gives us the following equation:

$$R = R_w \cdot \sqrt{1-E_{xr}^2} \cdot \sqrt{1-E_{yr}^2} + R_{ec} \cdot (E_{xr}) \cdot (E_{yr}) \qquad (20)$$

If the correlation ratios for each of the variables being analyzed are low, the amount of covariation and thus the size of the ecological correlations between variables will be low. If the correlation ratios are large, however, we must be wary of the fallacy of making cross-level inferences from subsamples to universally true relationships. When the subsamples are randomly drawn, only the problems associated with statistical inference are present. But if subsamples are selected purposefully, as we have done, there is the possibility of confounding grouping with universal relationships.

For example, if the correlation ratio E_{xr}^2 was .1 and E_{yr}^2 was .2 then we would have an equation as follows:

$$R = R_w(.95)(.89) + R_{ec}(.31)(.44)$$

Solving this equation, we can see that a factor of .14 is associated with the ecological correlation and a factor of .84 is associated with the within correlation. As the E_{xr}^2's become larger the greater is the factor associated with R_{ec} and thus the more hazardous it is to make inferences from the findings within groups to universal relationships. As E_{xr}^2 approaches zero the less risky the inference. Table 7 indicates the correlation ratios for each of our variables and for each type of aggregation for missing data estimation.

Inspection of Table 7 indicates that the previous analysis is one that can only be related to the countries in each of the stable and unstable groups and that no cross-level inferences should be hazarded. The low correlation

TABLE 7

CORRELATION RATIOS FOR STABLE VS. UNSTABLE ANALYSIS
BY TYPE OF AGGREGATION FOR MISSING DATA ESTIMATION

	Date of independence	Areal grouping	Political modernization
Urbanization	.35	.44	.38
Literacy	.58	.64	.59
Newspaper circulation	.57	.67	.62
Radio sets	.41	.48	.49
Cinema seats	.13	.33	.29
Stability	−.02[a]	−.02[a]	.05

[a] Rounding error in the computing routine caused a very small negative ecological variance here. It would be safe to assume that there is no ecological correlation in these two types.

ratio found for stability would seem to indicate that our choice of countries was indeed highly correlated with the actual stability scores used in this paper.

Dummy Variable Analysis. The previous analysis provided some information concerning relationships between a set of variables in a causal model with political stability as the dependent variable. One drawback that emerged with this type of analysis was the difficulty in interpreting why one medium would remain in the model in one instance, but drop out in another. It was also difficult to determine why one medium would stay in a model in one instance while another medium would not be included. It seems possible that the combination of media development in a particular nation might cause such a situation to exist. To investigate how the media combine in different patterns in different nations, we decided to array our data for the four media (we could include television sets here because of the data reduction process used) to determine median cuts for each of them. Using this criterion we then assigned "dummy variable" (Johnston, 1963; Suits, 1957) scores to each country for each medium. A score of zero meant the nation was in the lower fiftieth percentile on a particular medium and a score of one meant it was in the upper fiftieth percentile. Thus a pattern of 0000, 1000, 1100, 1110, or another of the permutations (16 in all) could be assigned to each nation. Upon examination across all three of the aggregations for missing data estimation, it was found that empty cells for certain patterns and unreliably low numbers of nations in other cells mitigated against use of a dummy variable regression analysis. Three predominant and two subsidiary patterns emerged. These major patterns and the frequencies across our three aggregations are shown in Table 8.

TABLE 8

Frequency of Patterns of Media Development with Median Cut Criterion for all Countries by Type of Aggregation for Missing Data Estimation

Pattern[a]	Date of independence	Areal grouping	Political modernization
0000	59	69	76
1111	25	24	24
1110	16	11	13
1000	5	14	3
1010	7	5	7

[a] The order of media in the patterns is Newspaper, Radio, Cinema, and Television.

Conjoint Measurement Analysis. Another approach that seemed appropriate for getting at the relationships for a combined media score in the original all link model was to determine some way in which the median cut scores could be utilized to provide a single interval-level measure which would be appropriate for regression analysis. It was decided to explore the possibility of using a conjoint measurement model[13] to achieve this goal.

If we consider a matrix of X of elements x_{ij} such that the matrix is additive, in the conjoint measurement sense, there exists a real valued function f, g, and h such that (1) $h(x_{ij}) = f(i)+g(j)$ for all i and j, and (2) h is monotone. This is equivalent to saying that the "row" and "column" effects in a two-way analysis of variance combine additively with no interaction. The difference between analysis of variance and conjoint measure matrices is that the latter requires only ranking of cell entries and thus does not have to meet the parametric assumptions associated with analysis of variance. Consider, for example, a matrix whose (i,j) element is the product of a positive factor for the ith row and a positive factor for the jth column, say $x_{ij} = c_i d_j$. Taking logarithms yields $\log x_{ij} = \log c_i + \log d_j$, meeting the first condition noted above. Since the logarithm function is monotone, the second condition is also met. Thus such a matrix is "additive" in the conjoint sense (McFarland, 1968).

In this paper we sought an additive respresentation by constructing two matrices with the rows of both equivalent to patterns of media development (where row 1 equated countries which were high on 3 or 4 media; row 2 those countries high on 1 or 2 media; and row 3 those countries low on all media), columns equivalent to 3 levels of linguistic and religious homogeneity respectively, and cell scores equivalent to the average GNP/capita for all countries falling in each ij cell. Table 9 indicates what the two matrices looked like.

The bonus-feature to be gained by arraying the data in manner similar to Table 9 is that when an additive representation is found (Lingoes, 1967: 501–502) the row and column scores that are generated to provide a best fit for the original data are interval scale scores that then can be used in our parametric regression model. For our data we found that across all three aggregations for missing data estimation and over the two types of homogeneity used for column variables we obtained almost exactly identical scores for our media combinations. Nations high on 3 or 4 media received a score of 1.5, nations high on 1 or 2 received a score of 1.0 and nations high on no media, using our median cut as a criterion, also received a score of 1.0. The scores given to the linguistic and religious homogeneity levels were identical across all categories.

It was satisfying to obtain clean solutions across all aggregations and for the two homogeneity column variables, but it became apparent as we went along that this particular technique has serious drawbacks. The average GNP per capita score assigned to each cell was an effort on our part to obtain a media development score that reflected the available resources that a person could allot to media purchases—and thus aid media development. However, had we assigned any other variable to the cells, or had we used any other variable for column variables we would have had a different solution. This means that the score that one assigns to media development, in this particular case, is unique only to this combination of three variables. Replacement of one or both of the column and cell variables would have given a different

TABLE 9

Two Conjoint Matrices used to Generate Combined Media Scale Scores

Religious homogeneity

		Homogeneous	Heterogeneous	Ambiguous
	High on 3 or 4 media	$\bar{X}$ for GNP/capita		
Media development	High on 1 or 2 media			
	High on no media			

Linguistic homogeneity

		Homogeneous	Heterogeneous	Ambiguous
	High on 3 or 4 media	$\bar{X}$ for GNP/capita		
Media development	High on 1 or 2 media			
	High on no media			

score to the different levels of media development—and thus a different solution to the model than the one shown below.

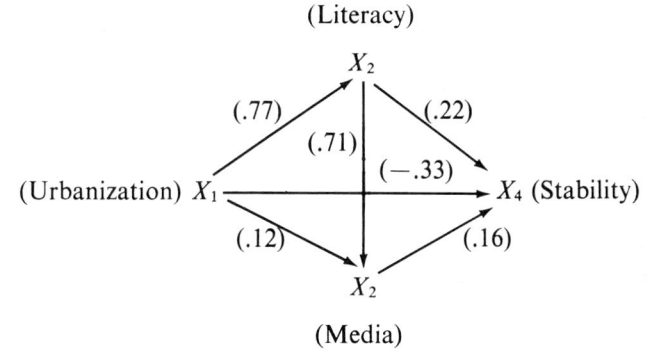

(Literacy)

X_2

(Urbanization) X_1 — (.77) (.71) (.22) (−.33) — X_4 (Stability)

(.12) (.16)

X_2

(Media)

The regression coefficients shown here represent only analysis for areal grouping estimation. The problems associated with using the conjoint technique did not warrant analysis of all three types of data estimation. For this particular analysis we would have deleted the urb → media and media → stability links had we maintained our .20 criterion for including regression links.

CONCLUSIONS

It is difficult to draw unambiguous conclusions from the analysis presented above—particularly at the substantive level. A fairly stable model was defined over three types of aggregation for missing data estimations but the variance accounted for was so low as to reject the model as a useful explanation for political stability. The analysis of exogenous patterns seems to indicate that this is an area for fruitful enquiry. The relatively high correlations between patterns of residuals makes this an interesting possibility for future research in this area. At a less substantive level the paper explicated some of the necessary steps that need to be taken in the way of data preparation and care in analysis of aggregate data. It appears that the choice of how to estimate missing data has less consequences when total populations of units are being analyzed. When finer analysis is undertaken, however, as in our choice of isolating in an a fortiori manner stable and unstable nations, the problems of cross-level inference become increasingly important. The problems of correlation between the aggregation variable and the kinds of subsets chosen for analysis, and ecological difficulties associated with non-random grouping, need to be carefully scrutinized.

The attempts undertaken to look at combinations of media development, such as dummy variable regressions and the use of conjoint measurement, provide techniques not normally associated with aggregate data analysis such as this. These attempts, however, were in vain in this instance. The problem of null and low frequency cells ruled out use of the dummy variable regressions. The uniqueness problem associated with the analyst's choice of variables for achieving media scale scores via the conjoint measurement model seems to be a stumbling block that may be overcome only in very special instances.

Also present throughout the analysis is the problem of coping with the measurement error associated with the variables being studied. This topic, and the ramifications it has for the resulting calculations, must be pursued to a much greater extent than was done in this paper.

FOR FURTHER STUDY

With few other techniques of data analysis are the intimate connections among substantive theory, methodological theory, and methodological technique as clear as with causal modeling. As should be apparent upon reading this paper, there are a number of areas related to causal analysis within these broad fields that promise to bear fruit for the investigator interested in subjecting theoretical propositions to empirical test.

A number of these areas are related to the notion of "cause." Among these are the problem of circularity of causation, which may be approached through the analysis of overtime data for a sample of the population of units of analysis, as suggested in note 4. Along with this goes the problem of the type of law intended, be it a statistical law or some form of deterministic law, in the theory under investigation, and the specificity with which the propositions of the theory are stated, especially with respect to the time periods with which events are to be taken as "causes" and "effects." This, in turn, is connected to the problem of definition of the units of analysis to which the propositions are meant to apply (especially difficult for macroscopic social units over time), and the "stages" vs. "levels" controversies over certain well-known social science theories. As well as studying these questions as they relate to causal modeling in general, it would seem that the payoff would be high from study of these topics in relation to specific social science theories with bearing on political instability.

In addition to these fairly wide questions, on a more technical level study of the effect of measurement error on conclusions drawn from causal modeling procedures should take high priority. Preliminary investigations, discussed under Data Preparation, demonstrated the importance of this topic. Another technical subject that bears promise is the importance of the statistical assumptions underlying the various techniques of causal modeling to the conclusions which are drawn. Some straightforward applications could be made of other work in this tradition.[15] These works deal with assumed shapes of distributions, levels of measurements, cell frequencies, and other such topics.

A topic which partakes especially of both technical and wider questions is the subject of the type of unit to which the data under analysis pertains, in relation to the level of unit of analysis. For example, in this study literacy is obviously an aggregate variable, pertaining to the unit of the individual, although the unit of analysis is that nation. Political instability, as measured by the source from which the data used in this study were taken, seems to pertain directly to nations, however. What would be the empirical effect of various possible distributions of literacy within nations on relationships found between an aggregate measure of literacy and a nation-level measure of political stability? Might other theories, dealing directly with nation-level measures, be more appropriate? Would causal modeling techniques not be sensitive to such mixing of units? Such questions are of deepest importance to the further development of this field of study.

APPENDIX A. UNITS OF ANALYSIS

Afghanistan	Guatemala	Peru
Albania	Guinea	Philippines
Algeria	Haiti	Poland
Andora	Honduras	Portugal
Argentina	Hungary	Puerto Rico
Australia	Iceland	Qatar
Austria	India	Rumania
Bahrein	Indonesia	Rwanda
Belgium	Iran	San Marino
Bhutan	Iraq	Saudi Arabia
Bolivia	Ireland	Senegal
Brazil	Israel	Sierra Leone
Brunei	Italy	Sikkim
Bulgaria	Ivory Coast	Somalia
Burma	Jamaica	South Africa
Burundi	Japan	Spain
Cambodia	Jordan	Sudan
Cameroon	Kenya	Sweden
Canada	Korea (North)	Switzerland
Central African Republic	Korea (South)	Syria
Ceylon	Kuwait	Tanganyika
Chad	Laos	Thailand
Chile	Lebanon	Togo
China (Mainland)	Liberia	Tonga
China (Nationalist-Taiwan)	Libya	Trinidad and Tobago
Colombia	Liechtenstein	Trucial States
Congo (Brazzaville)	Luxembourg	Tunisia
Congo (Leopoldville)	Malagasy Republic	Turkey
Costa Rica	Malaya	Uganda
Cuba	Mali	United Arab Republic
Cyprus	Mauritania	(Egypt)
Czechoslovakia	Mexico	United Kingdom
Dahomey	Monaco	U.S.S.R.
Denmark	Mongolia	United States
Dominican Republic	Morocco	Upper Volta
Ecuador	Muscat and Oman	Uruguay
El Salvador	Nepal	Vatican City
Ethiopia	Netherlands	Venezuela
Finland	New Zealand	Vietnam (North)
France	Nicaragua	Vietnam (South)
Gabon	Niger	Western Samoa
Gambia	Nigeria	Yemen
Germany (East)	Norway	Yugoslavia
Germany (West)	Pakistan	Zanzibar
Ghana	Panama	
Greece	Paraguay	

APPENDIX B. MEANS AND STANDARD DEVIATIONS

MEANS AND STANDARD DEVIATIONS FOR ALL NATIONS BY
TYPE OF AGGREGATION FOR MISSING DATA ESTIMATION

	Date of independence		Areal grouping		Political modernizations	
	Mean	S.D.	Mean	S.D.	Mean	S.D.
Urbanization	13.4	5.5	13.3	5.4	12.9	5.7
Literacy	52.2	31.7	51.0	32.7	49.9	32.2
Newspapers	3.3	2.0	3.3	2.0	3.2	2.0
Radios	2.1	.77	2.1	.7	2.1	.75
Cinema	3.0	1.3	3.0	1.3	2.9	1.2
Stability	32.0	8.7	32.0	8.2	30.9	8.3
	(N = 130)		(N = 132)		(N = 135)	

MEANS AND STANDARD DEVIATIONS FOR STABLE NATIONS
BY TYPE OF AGGREGATION FOR MISSING DATA ESTIMATION

	Date of independence		Areal grouping		Political modernizations	
	Mean	S.D.	Mean	S.D.	Mean	S.D.
Urbanization	18.7	3.4	18.8	3.3	18.4	3.7
Literacy	88.4	16.9	90.0	15.4	86.2	19.2
Newspapers	5.7	1.3	5.9	1.1	5.6	1.4
Radios	2.9	.4	2.8	.4	2.8	.4
Cinema	4.0	.7	4.1	.7	3.9	.7
Stability	31.4	11.4	30.3	9.9	30.8	9.9
	(N = 28)		(N = 29)		(N = 29)	

MEANS AND STANDARD DEVIATIONS FOR UNSTABLE NATIONS
BY TYPE OF AGGREGATION FOR MISSING DATA ESTIMATION

	Date of independence		Areal grouping		Political modernizations	
	Mean	S.D.	Mean	S.D.	Mean	S.D.
Urbanization	12.7	4.7	12.2	4.1	11.8	4.6
Literacy	38.6	24.9	36.3	23.8	34.7	22.9
Newspapers	2.8	1.3	2.6	1.1	2.4	1.1
Radios	2.0	.7	1.9	.6	1.9	.5
Cinema	3.1	1.3	2.5	1.4	2.6	1.3
Stability	30.7	9.2	30.9	9.1	29.6	8.8
	(N = 30)		(N = 31)		(N = 33)	

NOTES

1. On composition laws in social science, see Brodbeck (1968a).
2. See also Lerner (1958, 1963, and 1967) and Schramm and Ruggels (1967).
3. This is the common view taken in "causal modeling." See, e.g. Campbell and Stanley (1966) and Pelz and Andrews (1964). This avoids the notion of "forcing" found, among other places, in Blalock, Jr. (1964).
4. Such an investigation would include drawing a sample of countries randomly from our list and collecting data pertinent to our hypotheses over an extended period. Once the variables and the time periods have been established, models similar to those explicated by Wright (1960) and Turner and Stevens (1959) may be used.
5. Concerning the notion of "nation" with implications for overtime analysis, see Emerson (1966: 157–173).
6. Corrections to be applied include those suggested by Wolins (1967).
7. All of the analyses cited above—those undertaken by Lerner, Nixon, McCrone and Cnudde, Alker, and Schramm and Ruggels—used only available data. These data, then, pertained only to those countries that were developed highly enough to have the expertise necessary for the data collection process.
8. See also Zeizel (1957: chapter X).
9. In an unpublished memo, I have established that at least three points in time are necessary if the analyst is to be able to control for the possibility of differential auto-correlation between the two time series associated with each of the two variables being studied.
10. We chose to delete links that had a regression coefficient less than .20. This was an attempt on our part to take into account measurement error that would affect low estimates.
11. This assumption is necessary if we are to meet the specifications of the hierarchical causal model and solution of the regression equations.
12. The correlation ratio is $E_{xr}^2 = ECxx/Cxx$.
13. See, e.g. Luce and Tukey (1964), Krantz (1964), and Tversky (1964).
14. These two variables are defined by Banks and Textor (1963: 71–75).
15. See Baker, Hardyck, and Petrinovich (1966), Labovitz (1967), Collier, Jr., Baker, and Mandeville (1967), and Collier, et al. (1967).

REFERENCES

ALKER, H.R., JR. (1965) "Causal inference and political analysis." Pp. 7–43 in J.L. Bernd, Ed., *Mathematical Applications in Political Science*. Dallas: Southern Methodist University Press.
— (1966) "A typology of ecological fallacies: problems of spurious associations in cross-level inferences." Paper presented at the Symposium on Quantitative Ecological Analysis in the Social Sciences, Evian, France, 12–16 September.
— (n.d.) "Causal inference and political analysis."
BAKER, B.E., C.D. HARDYCK, and L.F. PETRINOVICH (1966) "Weak measurement vs. strong statistics: an empirical critique of S.S. Stevens' proscriptions on statistics." *Educational and Psychological Measurement* 26: 291–309.
BANKS, A. and R.B. TEXTOR (1963) *A Cross-Polity Survey*. Cambridge: MIT Press.

BLACK, M. (1962) *Models and Metaphors.* New York: Cornell University Press.
BLALOCK, H.M., JR. (1964) *Causal Inferences in Nonexperimental Research.* Chapel Hill: University of North Carolina Press.
BOUDON, R. (1965) "A method of linear causal analysis: dependence analysis." *American Sociological Review* 30: 365–374.
BRODBECK, M. (1968a) "Methodological individualism: definition and reduction." Pp. 280–303 in M. Brodbeck, Ed., *Readings in the Philosophy of the Social Sciences.* New York: Macmillan.
— (1968b) "Models, meanings, and theories," and "General introduction." Pp. 579–600 and 1–11, respectively, in M. Brodbeck, Ed., *Readings in the Philosophy of the Social Sciences.* New York: Macmillan.
— (1968c) "Explanation, prediction, and 'imperfect' knowledge." Pp. 363–398 in M. Brodbeck, Ed., *Readings in the Philosophy of the Social Sciences.* New York: Macmillan.
BWY, D.P. (1968) "Political instability in Latin America: the cross-cultural test of a causal model." *Latin American Research Review* 3: 17–66. Reprinted in this volume, Chapter 5.
CAMPBELL, D.T. (1963) "From description to experimentation: interpreting trends as quasi-experiments." Pp. 212–242 in C. Harris, Ed., *Problems in Measuring Change.* Madison: University of Wisconsin Press.
— and J.C. STANLEY (1966) *Experimental and Quasi-Experimental Designs for Research.* Chicago: Rand McNally.
COLBY, K.M. (1967) "Computer simulation of change in personal belief systems." *Behavioral Science* 12: 248–253.
COLEMAN, J.S. (1964) *Introduction to Mathematical Sociology.* New York: Free Press.
COLLIER, R.O., JR. et al. (1967) "Estimates of test size for several test procedures based on conventional variance ratios in the repeated measures design." *Psychometrika* 32: 339–353.
COLLIER, R.O., JR., F.B. BAKER, and G.K. MANDEVILLE (1967) "Tests of hypothesis in a repeated measures design from a permutation viewpoint." *Psychometrika* 32: 15–24.
DUNCAN, O.D. (1966) "Path analysis: sociological examples." *American Journal of Sociology* 72: 1–16.
EMERSON, R. (1966) "Nationalism and political development." Pp. 157–173 in J.L. Finkle and R.W. Gable, Eds., *Political Development and Social Change.* New York: John Wiley.
FEIERABEND, I.K. and R.L. FEIERABEND (1965) *Cross-National Data Bank of Political Instability Events* (Code Index). San Diego: Public Affairs Research Institute.
— (1966) "Aggressive behavior within polities, 1948–1962: a cross-national study." *Journal of Conflict Resolution* 10: 249–271. Reprinted in this volume, Chapter 6.
FEIGL, H. (1953) "Notes on causality." Pp. 408–418 in H. Feigl and M. Brodbeck, Eds., *Readings in the Philosophy of Science.* New York: Appleton-Century-Crofts.
FRANK, R.E. (1966) "Use of transformations." *Journal of Marketing Research* 3: 247–253.
JOHNSTON, J. (1963) *Econometric Methods.* New York: McGraw-Hill.
KRANTZ, D.H. (1964) "Conjoint measurement: The Luce-Tukey Axiomatization and some extensions." *Journal of Mathematical Psychology* 1: 248–277.

LABOVITZ, S. (1967) "Some observations on measurement and statistics." *Social Forces* 46: 151–160.
LAZARSFELD, P.F. (1948) "Mutual effects of statistical variables." Unpublished report of the Bureau of Applied Social Research, Columbia University.
LERNER, D. (1958) *The Passing of Traditional Society*. New York: Free Press.
— (1963) "Toward a communication theory of modernization: a set of considerations." Pp. 327–350 in L.W. Pye, Ed., *Communications and Political Development*. Princeton: Princeton University Press.
— (1967) "International cooperation and communication in national development." Pp. 103–125 of D. Lerner and W. Schramm, Eds., *Communication and Change in the Developing Countries*. Honolulu: East-West Center Press.
LINGOES, J.C. (1967) "An IBM-7090 program for Guttman-Lingoes Conjoint Measurement—I." *Behavioral Science* 12: 501–502.
LUCE, D.R. and J.W. TUKEY (1964) "Conjoint measurement: a new type of fundamental measurement." *Journal of Mathematical Psychology* 1: 1–27.
MCCRONE, D.J. and C.F. CNUDDE (1967) 'Toward a communications theory of democratic political development: a causal model." *American Political Science Review* 61: 72–79. Reprinted in this volume, Chapter 22.
MCFARLAND, D.D. (1968) "An extension of conjoint measurement to test the theory of quasi-perfect mobility." *Michigan Studies in Mathematical Sociology*, Paper 3: 10.
MERRITT, R.L. and S. ROKKAN, Eds. (1964) *Comparing Nations*. New Haven: Yale University Press.
NESVOLD, B.A. (1967) "Scalogram analysis of political violence: a cross-national study." Paper delivered at the 1967 Annual Meeting of the American Political Science Association, Chicago.
NIXON, R.B. (1965) "Freedom in the world's press: a fresh appraisal with new data." *Journalism Quarterly* 62: 3–14.
PELZ, D.C. and F.M. ANDREWS (1964) "Detecting causal priorities in panel study data." *American Sociological Review* 29: 836.
ROBINSON, W.S. (1959) "Ecological correlation and the behavior of individuals." *American Sociological Review* 15: 351–357.
ROZELLE, R.M. (1965) "An exploration of two quasi-experimental designs: the cross-lagged panel correlation and the multiple time series." Unpublished manuscript, Dept. of Psychology, Northwestern University.
ROZELLE, R.M. and D.T. CAMPBELL (n.d.) "More plausible rival hypotheses in cross-lagged panel correlation and the multiple time series." Unpublished manuscript, Dept. of Psychology, Northwestern University.
RUSSETT, B.M. et al. (1964) *World Handbook of Political and Social Indicators*. New Haven: Yale University Press.
SCHRAMM, W. and L. RUGGELS (1967) "How mass media systems grow." Pp. 57–75 in D. Lerner and W. Schramm, Eds., *Communication and Change in the Developing Countries*. Honolulu: East-West Center Press.
SIMON, H.A. (1957) *Models of Man*. New York: John Wiley.
SUITS, D.B. (1957) "Use of dummy variables in regression equations." *Journal of the American Statistical Association* 52: 548–551.
TUCKER, L.R., A.E. MYERS, and J.S. TERWILLIGER (n.d.) "Comments on partial correlation involving fallible measures."

TURNER, M.E. and C.D. STEVENS (1959) "The regression of causal paths." *Biometrics* 15: 236–258.

TVERSKY, A. (1964) Additive choice structures. Ph.D. dissertation, University of Michigan.

UNESCO (1966) *Statistical Yearbook 1963*. Paris: UNESCO.

UNITED STATES DEPARTMENT OF STATE (1967) *Status of the World's Nations*. Washington, D.C.: U.S. Government Printing Office.

WOLD, H. and L. JUREEN (1953) *Demand Analysis*. New York: John Wiley.

WOLINS, L. (1967) "The use of multiple regression procedures when the predictor variables are psychological tests." *Educational and Psychological Measurement* 27: 821–827.

WRIGHT, S. (1934) "The method of path coefficients." *Annals of Mathematical Statistics* 5: 161–215.

— (1954) "The interpretation of multivariate systems." Chapter II in O. Kempthorne et al., Eds., *Statistics and Mathematics in Biology*. Ames: Iowa State College Press.

— (1960) "Path coefficients and path regressions: alternate or complementary concepts?" *Biometrics* 16: 189–202.

— (1960) "The treatment of reciprocal interaction, with or without lag, in path analysis." *Biometrics* 16: 423–445.

YEE, A.H. and N.L. GAGE (n.d.) "Techniques for determining causal relationships between interpersonal attitudes." Unpublished.

ZEIZEL, H. (1957) *Say It with Figures*. New York: Harper & Row.

Part III

STUDIES IN POLITICAL DEVELOPMENT

11 Introduction: Studies in Political Development

BETTY A. NESVOLD

Political scientists often use the terms "political development," "social development," and "economic development" interchangeably. Implicit in the interchangeable use of these terms has been the assumption that social and economic development accompany political development. The status of this assumption is, however, empirically questionable. If political development is something different from social and economic development, analyses of the empirical relationships among these variables are important for understanding the processes involved in political change. In order to submit the relationships among social and economic development and political development to empirical tests, the differences among these terms must be clearly defined.

In a broad sense, economic development is a concept readily operationalized. Commonly such indicators as gross national product or gross national product per capita are used in measuring economic development. To be sure, such indicators distort the common sense concept of economic development when applied to a few nonindustrialized but mineral-rich nations such as Kuwait, which happens to rank first among the world's nations on gross national product per capita. But to insist upon some more refined measure, such as level of industrialization, also brings forth anomalies such as placing Denmark, with an agricultural base to its economy, as one of the nations in a transitional stage of economic development. Thus, many cross-national researchers have relied upon either a single broad measure, generally gross national product (GNP), or a combination of indicators indexed by some particular statistical technique.

If the concept of economic development and its operationalization have been used imprecisely, the use of the concept of political development has been thoroughly muddled. In early analyses, cross-national researchers often made the hypothesis and conclusion, which for some became a kind of natural law of politics, that economic development leads to pluralistic, competitive political structures. The difficulty with this naive and culturally biased outlook is that it confuses political development with political democratization. There are a number of authoritarian political regimes which by any standard (bureaucratization, governmental research, governmental expenditure, and so on) must be considered politically developed, although not democratic. Such political systems also exhibit a high degree of economic development. For analytic purposes, it is important to distinguish between political development and democratization. Political development refers to the degree to which the political system exhibits modern management methods, its degree of bureaucratization, governmental employment, and expenditure patterns. On the other hand, democratization refers to the degree to which the policy exhibits democratic procedures of governance. With this distinction in mind, research reports in this section deal with political development, while those in the next section deal with democratization. As the reader will quickly see, there is considerable confusion and lack of consensus about the meaning and operationalization of these terms.

If any consensus can be gleaned from analysts of political development, it seems to reside in concern for the prevailing structures in political systems. Among the research reports in this section, this is most apparent in the two factor analysis of Banks and Gregg, and in Snow's scalogram analysis. In all three precis of research, the data relied upon are those collected by Banks and Textor (1963) and reported in *A Cross-Polity Survey* (Cambridge: MIT Press). In the Banks and Textor volume, information on 73 characteristics of countries was collected and coded. Sixteen of these characteristics are ecological, and the remaining are political and social. Such attributes as modernity of the bureaucracy, political neutrality of the military, level of articulation of political goals by associational groups, and the level of governmental stability were coded on ordinal scales. Thus, for example, the variable "modernity of bureaucracy" was categorized into modern bureaucracies, semi-modern bureaucracies, post-colonial transitional bureaucracies, and traditional bureaucracies. Data on each of the political variables were classified in this manner. On some variables, simple dichotomies were used; on others, five and six categories were employed.

Ordinal variables of this sort are not an ideal way of measuring variables. Ordinal variables allow for few statistical advantages, and furthermore are often reductions of interval data, which, if reported, can be very useful in testing hypotheses. However, at the same time, ordinal scales represent an extremely valuable first step in achieving good interval measures of variables. The preliminary quantification by Banks and Textor and the speculative analyses which uncover interesting relationships, although with crude data and measurement, further enable more refined efforts to explore relationships between social and economic development and political development.

In the first research report by Banks and Gregg, an R-factor analysis was performed on 68 variables, which the authors call attributes, of political systems. The effort of this quantitative analysis was to determine which

Introduction: *Studies in Political Development*

attributes tend to cluster with other attributes. In the second report, Banks and Gregg used a Q-factor analysis to determine which countries tend to cluster together on the 68 variables. Although many questions can be raised about the adequacy of these analyses, such as the appropriateness of the data, the violation of the assumptions of factor analysis and the particular factoring techniques selected, some interesting results are revealed from the authors' analyses. Of primary interest is that the variables in the R-factor analysis tend to cluster with respect to areal groupings. That is, the attributes normally assigned to Western democracies cluster together, those assigned to Eastern European political systems cluster together, and so on. This areal clustering is further evidenced in the Q-factor analysis in which countries tend to go together by geographical groupings. These areal groupings, if indeed they reflect empirical realities, tend to provide some evidence for the lack of comparability among regions, and the need for analysis within regions as well as across regions.

However, the tight areal groupings often used in the configurative approach to comparative politics are not entirely confirmed by Banks and Gregg. Those nations that contribute most to the polyarchic factor are all Western European-type systems, but there are significant loadings associated with other nations from diverse regions. The factors denoted by the centrist and personalist rubrics also show some geographical mix. What the Banks and Gregg analyses point to is that both intraregional and interregional analyses are necessary for understanding political systems and their development.

Peter Snow, in his research report "Scalogram Analysis of Political Development," specifically focuses on political development in Latin America. Using a set of twenty variables from *A Cross-Polity Survey*, Snow suggests that there is a pattern to political development whereby certain attributes of political systems develop before other attributes. The Guttman scalogram technique is uniquely suited to Snow's proposition, and the fit of the data to the hypothesized pattern is convincing evidence of the unidimensional nature of political development and its apparently progressive character. As Snow points out, this attribute may be characteristic of Latin American countries rather than of developing nations generally. This is hardly a random sample of developing nations, but it offers extremely interesting findings for the determination of just what is characteristic of a continuum of political development.

Adelman and Morris, in their factor analysis of data collected on 74 developing countries, provide a further discussion of the relationships between social, economic, and political development. The data consist of a broad selection of these variables. The clusterings of variables that emerge from the Adelman and Morris analysis reinforce the commonly held assumptions that certain political and social characteristics covary with economic development, as measured by GNP per capita. Thus, the authors find a strong positive relationship between GNP per capita and the social and cultural changes which accompany urbanization and industrialization. A lesser, but still moderately strong association, is found between competitive political institutions and economic development.

These findings of the Adelman and Morris research point to the previously discussed fallacy that there is some kind of natural association between economic growth and democratization. To be sure, Adelman and Morris find some evidence of such patterning, but the factor in which competitiveness is found only accounts for 18.5 percent of the variation in GNP per capita, while characteristics accompanying urbanization and industrialization account for an impressive 51.5 percent of the variation in GNP per capita. As Adelman and Morris demonstrate, the relationship between economic development and democratization is something different from the relationship between economic development and political modernization.

In addition to the matrix with data from all 74 nations, Adelman and Morris display factor analyses for areal groupings—Africa, the near East and Far East, and Latin America. In each of these three groups, the pattern found in the overall analysis is supported, in that indicators of social and cultural aspects of urbanization and industrialization continue to be highly associated with economic development. Interesting regional differences emerge, however, when the indicators of democratization are associated with economic development. For the African countries, almost no relationship is found, but, for the other two regions, the indicators of democratization account for about 22 percent of the variation in economic development. Also, Adelman and Morris find substantial differences in the clusterings of the social and political variables for the areal groups. The Adelman and Morris analysis points out that for countries in different areal groupings the relationships between social, economic, and political development differ considerably. In addition, the Adelman and Morris research points to the need for both cross-national analyses within areal groupings and across areal groupings.

The above analyses have focused generally upon interrelationships among various indicators of economic and social development, and political development. Benjamin and Kautsky examine another phenomenon of political development. The authors suggest that Communist parties can be viewed as modernizing agents and thus hypothesize that there is a curvilinear relationship between economic development and the strength of Communist parties, that nations in a transitional stage of development will experience increasing strength of Communist parties as economic development advances, but that this relationship falls off abruptly as the countries become more fully industrialized. In testing their propositions, Benjamin and Kautsky construct a set of simple indices so that nations can be grouped and scored on a variety of variables. Thus, the measure of Communist party strength uses data estimating the number of members of the Communist party in each country and then collapses these data into nine groups. Of the three independent variables, agricultural population as a percentage of the total population and per capita GNP are collapsed into four groups, while a rating for societal types is collapsed into five groups. Mean levels of Communist party membership are calculated and graphed within each of the four groups of economic development, within each of the four groups of economic development, and within each of the five groups of societal types. As presented, the findings clearly substantiate the authors' hypothesis.

There are problems, however, with the procedures used by Benjamin and Kautsky to analyze their data. Calculation of mean scores may obscure a wide range within each grouping on the independent variable. This difficulty may not be so great a hazard when the number of cases in each group is fairly sizable, but when the number is quite small, knowledge of the range is crucial to the interpretation of findings. This difficulty is exemplified by examining the results of the relationships between societal types and strength of the Communist party. For example, the authors' hypothesis suggests that Type IV countries should have the highest number of Communist party members and that there should be a sharp drop-off in Type V nations. This is certainly the case when the mean scores in each group are used. However, the small number of cases in Type IV makes one curious as to the range in country scores in this group, and it is indeed wide. Finland is scored 5; France, 8; Greece, 4; Italy, 9; and Spain is scored 1. With both the maximum and minimum scores within this grouping, questions have to be raised as to the strength of the authors' findings. Even with this methodological weakness, the authors' findings are strongly suggestive of the relationship between economic development and Communist party movements.

A second reservation can be raised in the Benjamin and Kautsky use of the index of Communist party strength. By using simple aggregate totals of Communist party memberships, rather than some standardized measure such as membership as a proportion of population or of voting age population, or the like, the authors do not have entirely comparable data. For example, Iraq's 15,000 members are certainly more significant a portion of the population than India's 135,000 but Iraq is given a rating of 3 and India is rated 8. Although the authors appropriately discard an index of Communist party membership as a proportion of the working age population because of the noncomparable effects of modernization on this measure, some standardized measure would seem more appropriate than the raw total numbers.

Benjamin and Kautsky present some important findings for understanding the relationship between economic development and the strength of mass political parties. With some refinement of method and data, further analyses of this relationship would seem important. The authors present a more refined hypothesis than those found in Banks and Gregg or Adelman and Morris, and their hypothesis, as well as others suggested by the authors, are worthy of further analysis.

As with most areas of cross-national research, quantitative analysis into the nature of political development, its consequences and accompanying phenomena is a preliminary explanatory stage. Inevitably, inadequacies are readily apparent. There is probably no more efficient way, however, to become aware of these inadequacies in measuring instruments and data analysis than to thoroughly examine the present studies and to ask questions based upon what has already been learned about political development.

12 Dimensions of Political Systems: Factor Analysis of A Cross-Polity Survey

PHILLIP M. GREGG and ARTHUR S. BANKS

Since the publication of David Easton's *The Political System* (1953) it has become increasingly common for political scientists to speculate as to the basic factors which may be common to all political systems and which, in their varying manifestations, determine the unique styles of political behavior within each. Efforts to identify the basic political phenomena and their complex relationships have generated a variety of cross-national conceptual schemes and propositions. Some authors speak of structural and functional requisites, some refer to equilibrium conditions for system maintenance.[1] Others, employing more traditional concepts, refer to power, legitimacy, ideology, instability, consensus, influence, and bargaining. Regardless of the form these efforts assume, they all posit the existence of factors or dimensions which are common to all political systems.[2] Such attempts at cross-national theory raise two questions. If basic dimensions can be said to underlie the complex behavior within political systems, how can the dimensions be identified? And, what set of concepts have the greatest empirical relevance for describing the dimensions?

The Empirical Search for Basic "Dimensions"

This kind of theory construction and these questions are not a unique outgrowth of political science. Psychologists began grappling with similar problems sixty years ago. Anthropologists, sociologists, economists and political scientists, who are plagued by more complex units of study, have been struggling along behind.

Authors' Note: We are indebted to Professor Karl F. Schuessler for commenting on an earlier draft of this paper.

Reprinted from *The American Political Science Review*. Volume LIX, pages 555–578, by permission of the authors and the publisher. Copyright © 1965. The American Political Science Association.

What is unique to political science is the near absence of systematic empirical tests of the many propositions about basic dimensions. In addition to entertaining such propositions, the other social sciences have begun testing them. The psychologists, led initially by Spearman and later by Thurstone, have developed a statistical technique, factor analysis, for testing hypotheses as to the basic dimensions of intelligence and personality.[3] In discussing the particular relevance of factor analysis for identifying basic dimensions and organizing concepts in the social sciences, Thurstone (1947: 55–56) says:

> A factor problem starts with the hope or conviction that a certain domain is not so chaotic as it looks.... If no promising hypothesis is available, one can represent the domain as adequately as possible in terms of a set of measurements of numerical indices and proceed with a factorial experiment. The analysis might reveal an underlying order which would be of great assistance in formulating the scientific concepts covering the particular domain....
>
> The exploratory nature of factor analysis is often not understood. Factor analysis has its principal usefulness at the border line of science. It is naturally superseded by rational formulations in terms of the science involved. Factor analysis is useful, especially in those domains where basic and fruitful concepts are essentially lacking and where crucial experiments have been difficult to conceive.

In spite of this ground work by psychologists the broader potential of the method was largely ignored until 1949, and even then a psychologist led the way. In a seminal article, the psychologist Cattell (1949: 443–469) adapted the technique to the measurement of common dimensions of cultural organization. Subsequently, Berry (1961: 110–119 and 1960: 78–107) introduced geographers and economists to factor analysis.[4]

Rummel's 1963 study (reprinted in this volume, Chapter 3) "Dimensions of Conflict Behavior Within and Between Nations," was the first cross-national application of the technique in political science. A year earlier, Schubert (1962: 90–107) had published a factor analysis of Supreme Court voting patterns. More recently, Alker (1964: 642–657) has published a similar analysis of voting in the UN General Assembly. Both Rummel and Russett are currently conducting factor analyses which in part replicate Cattell's measurement of the dimensions of cultural organization within nations.

Even though a growing number of political scientists are employing factor analysis, none have used the technique to address the questions: "What are the basic dimensions of political systems and what concepts best describe them?" One major obstacle has been a lack of variables with which to tap the phenomena of political institutions across all nations. Publication of *A Cross-Polity Survey* (Banks and Textor, 1963) represented, in part, an effort to remedy this deficiency.[5]

The *Survey* data are particularly relevant to questions about the common dimensions of political systems and their organizing concepts because the variables operationalize many of the concepts and categories used in recent attempts at cross-national theory. The authors (Banks and Textor, 1963: 6) after canvassing the existing literature, "attempted to select and adopt—experimentally at least—every possible raw characteristic that gave promise of being workable and analytically powerful."

The Research Purpose

Given a relevant domain of data and an appropriate statistical technique, this paper seeks to answer the following questions:

(1) What factors emerge when the *Survey* data are factor analyzed?
(2) What dimensions can be inferred from these factors?
(3) What relevance have these dimensions for cross-national study?
(4) What specific propositions about conflict behavior are suggested by the findings?

The first question is straightforward and is answered with the factorial results. The second question is answered by inferring from the factors the existence of dimensions or "latent variables" which give rise to the intercorrelation of variables within the independent clusters.

The third question is more complex and requires elaboration. Once a dimension is identified and named, the label used becomes a concept which is operationalized by the factor. In this sense the labels are highly significant concepts, for theoretical purposes, because of their lawful (statistical) relationships with all the other variables included. Thus the interrelationships among all the variables are explained by their relationships to a limited number of concepts. In other words, the factor labels comprise a set of concepts with high generalizing power for cross-national study.

The fourth question is answered by examining the factorial results for the relationships of the conflict variables with the factors.

The Data

The present study is based on a factor analysis of the political component of *A Cross-Polity Survey*. The input data comprise 68 variables, all but five of which were derived from the 57 polychotomous characteristics of the *Survey*.[6] We omitted 16 *Survey* characteristics of an essentially ecological character, since we wished to analyze relationships *within* the political domain itself, rather than *between* the political system and its environment.[7]

In addition to the 16 nonpolitical characteristics, three additional characteristics, 41 (Party System: Qualitative), 47 (Vertical Power Distribution), and 56 (Character of Legal System), were deleted from the factor analysis for distributional reasons.

Of the remaining 38 *Survey* characteristics, 27 were ordinal-scaled and 11 were nominal-scaled. Each nominal-scaled characteristic was "decomposed" according to its attribute components, as may be seen in Table 1.[8]

Rotated Factor Matrix

	I	II	III	IV	V	VI	VII	h²
1. East European Areal Grouping (1)	−.58	.22	.26	−.06	.36	.00	−.24	.64
2. Advanced Western Areal Grouping (1)	.45	.25	.66	−.13	−.11	−.17	−.01	.76
3. Latin American Areal Grouping (1)	.21	.31	−.59	−.49	.17	.12	−.14	.78
4. Asian Areal Grouping (1)	−.16	.13	−.24	.55	−.06	.22	.00	.46
5. African Areal Grouping (1)	−.05	−.90	.02	−.05	−.10	.06	−.16	.86
6. North African, Middle Eastern Areal Grouping (1)	−.06	.17	−.08	.31	−.20	−.25	.50	.49
7. Freedom of the Press (13)	.80	−.22	.17	−.17	.08	.13	−.13	.79
8. Date of Independence (19)	.06	.66	.29	−.36	−.33	−.05	−.27	.83
9. Westernization (20)	.32	.60	.50	−.30	.16	−.12	−.13	.86
10. Ex-British Dependency (21)	.27	.14	.35	.69	.01	−.01	−.14	.71
11. Ex-French Dependency (21)	−.39	−.51	.10	−.13	−.15	.04	.49	.70
12. Ex-Spanish Dependency (21)	.10	.54	−.47	−.71	.09	−.01	−.24	1.08
13. Early European Political Modernization (22)	.37	.17	.45	.07	−.19	.06	−.06	.42
14. Later European Political Modernization (22)	−.04	.46	−.07	−.67	.32	−.16	−.22	.85
15. Non-European Political Modernization (22)	−.17	.21	−.02	.12	−.50	.15	−.13	.38
16. Developed Tutelary Political Modernization (22)	−.09	.14	−.26	.70	.06	.01	.39	.73
17. Undeveloped Tutelary Political Modernization (22)	−.01	−.93	.01	−.11	.03	.07	−.05	.89
18. Political Modernization—Periodization (23)	.03	.76	.30	−.10	.16	−.15	.18	.75
19. Developmental Ideological Orientation (24)	.00	−.83	−.25	−.02	.12	.07	.29	.86
20. Conventional Ideological Orientation (24)	.73	.46	.29	−.20	.02	−.01	−.10	.87
21. System Style (25)	−.74	.11	.13	.14	.37	.14	.19	.79
22. Constitutional Regime (26)	.93	.02	.11	−.08	.28	.04	.05	.96
23. Authoritarian Regime (26)	−.32	−.18	−.36	.13	−.70	−.06	.04	.77
24. Totalitarian Regime (26)	−.81	.21	.26	−.07	.39	.05	−.18	.96
25. Governmental Stability (27)	.15	.10	.89	−.01	.01	.07	−.03	.83
26. Representativeness of Regime (28)	.85	.15	.05	.02	.27	−.02	−.08	.83
27. Electoral System (29)	.94	.22	−.01	.12	.04	−.08	−.15	.98
28. Freedom of Group Opposition (30)	.92	.16	−.04	.00	−.01	−.11	−.04	.89
29. Political Enculturation (31)	.33	.21	.54	−.08	.13	.22	−.02	.52
30. Sectionalism (32)	.02	−.09	−.07	.41	−.23	−.01	−.15	.26
31. Articulation by Associational Groups (33)	.63	.54	.27	−.13	.06	−.04	.09	.79
32. Articulation by Institutional Groups (34)	−.83	.01	−.36	.21	−.03	−.10	.02	.86
33. Articulation by Non-Associational Groups (35)	−.28	−.58	−.33	.52	−.24	.05	.06	.85
34. Articulation by Anomic Groups (36)	−.43	−.17	−.51	.35	−.16	−.08	−.10	.63
35. Articulation by Political Parties (37)	.68	.20	−.16	.00	.03	−.55	−.16	.85
36. Aggregation by Political Parties (38)	.06	−.10	.34	.12	.01	.82	.20	.85
37. Aggregation by Executive (39)	.19	−.48	.15	.00	.18	.46	.61	.90
38. Aggregation by Legislature (40)	.73	.38	.28	−.07	.08	−.32	.05	.87
39. One-Party System (41)	−.77	−.23	.26	−.14	.13	.23	.24	.86
40. One Party Dominant System (41)	.14	−.24	−.24	−.02	.08	.15	−.02	.16
41. Two-Party System (41)	.43	.20	.15	.17	.00	.50	−.19	.57
42. Multi-Party System (41)	.47	.22	−.18	−.09	.08	−.69	−.06	.78
43. Stability of Party System (43)	−.12	.14	.84	−.03	.19	.28	.08	.87
44. Personalismo (44)	.00	−.08	−.66	−.22	−.34	−.12	−.09	.63
45. Elitism (45)	−.70	.41	−.18	.03	−.17	−.01	−.41	.90
46. Charisma (46)	−.33	−.37	−.04	.20	−.21	.29	.44	.60
47. Horizontal Power Distribution (48)	.86	.29	.19	.02	.20	−.07	−.08	.92
48. Presidential System (49)	.01	−.26	−.59	−.47	−.03	.21	.21	.72
49. Parliamentary-Republican System (49)	.27	.04	.20	.13	.08	−.35	.15	.28
50. Parliamentary-Royalist System (49)	.47	.01	.28	.33	.01	.02	−.35	.53
51. Status of Legislature (50)	.87	.01	.29	.02	.10	−.01	.03	.84
52. Unicameral Legislature (51)	−.49	−.51	−.03	−.11	.28	−.19	.04	.63
53. Bicameral Legislature (51)	.49	.51	.03	.11	−.28	.19	−.04	.63
54. Status of Executive (52)	−.82	−.18	−.11	−.03	−.21	.14	.13	.80
55. Modern Bureaucracy (53)	.52	.22	.65	−.01	−.10	−.25	.06	.81
56. Semi-Modern Bureaucracy (53)	−.29	.54	−.46	−.10	.47	.22	.01	.87
57. Post-Colonial Transitional Bureaucracy (53)	.00	−.92	−.05	.01	.05	.00	−.06	.85
58. Traditional Bureaucracy (53)	−.22	.11	−.10	.21	−.80	−.02	−.04	.74
59. Military Interventive (54)	−.03	.18	−.60	−.06	−.15	−.28	.04	.50
60. Military Supportive (54)	−.77	.19	.16	.12	−.12	.00	−.08	.69
61. Military Neutral (54)	.73	−.32	.34	−.07	.21	.20	.05	.84
62. Role of Police (55)	−.75	−.06	−.45	−.11	−.16	−.11	.10	.84
63. Communist System (57)	−.71	.25	.26	.06	.40	.04	−.16	.82
64. System Stability	.20	.03	.82	−.09	−.02	.05	−.09	.74
65. Demonstrations	.24	.00	−.39	−.05	−.11	−.21	.06	.27
66. Domestic Killed	.05	−.06	−.62	.21	−.06	.06	−.01	.44
67. Expulsion of Ambassadors	−.06	.09	.03	−.12	.20	.00	.51	.32
68. Foreign Killed	.00	.01	−.33	.21	−.03	.06	.49	.40
Percent of Total Variance	24.6	13.5	13.2	6.4	5.4	4.7	4.3	72.0
Percent of Common Variance	34.1	18.7	18.3	8.9	7.4	6.6	6.0	100.0

In order to examine the relationship of conflict to other political phenomena, we included five non-*Survey* ordinal variables: System Stability, Demonstrations, Domestic Killed, Expulsion of Ambassadors, and Foreign Killed. All but the first of these are taken directly from Rummel's (1963) work in conflict behavior.

The System Stability variable is of a composite character. Standard scores were calculated for the domestic conflict factor scores appearing in Rummel, and then weighted on the basis of his figures for percent of common variance. Standard scores were also calculated for an "Executive Stability" index derived largely from data appearing in the *World Handbook of Political and Social Indicators* (Russett et al., 1964: 101–104). The latter scores were weighted on the basis of twice the mean of the weights assigned to the Rummel-based scores. The four weighted scores were then summed into a composite stability index which, for present purposes, was dichotomized into "high" and "low" components.

The range for each of the ordinal variables is either 2 or 3. The range for each nominal variable component (as it appears in Table 1) is, of course, 2.

The Statistical Technique: Factor Analysis

Technically speaking, factor analysis is "that branch of multivariate analysis which deals with the internal structure of matrices of covariances and correlations" (Lawley and Maxwell, 1963: 1). More simply, it is a technique by means of which a large number of variables may be clustered on the basis of their intercorrelations, each set of which is presumed to reflect a single dimension which is "causing" the association within the set of variables. In the context of the *Survey* data, the factors which emerge summarize the major components of variation among the 68 variables.

Scoring and Correlation Procedure. The first step in the factor analysis was to construct a correlation matrix of the *Survey* data. The original data were in the form of polychotomous characteristics. For this study they were collapsed into two and three place variables which were then correlated using the product moment coefficient. This procedure, which, in effect, consists of assigning interval values to noninterval data for correlation purposes, is not wholly orthodox. We adopted it on the pragmatic ground that it provides a measure of the relationships among the *Survey* variables from which the major clusters can be factored out.

The suitability of various scoring and correlation techniques in factor analysis has been extensively debated by the psychologists. Thurstone (1947: 66–67) advances the following argument corroborating our position:

> The factorial methods are sufficiently powerful that one can take considerable liberties with the raw scores without seriously affecting the results. If we take a factor analysis in which several fundamental and meaningful factors have been clearly identified, it would be instructive to subject the factor methods

to a severe test by radical changes in the original raw scores. . . . The correlation coefficients to be analyzed would then be markedly different from those used in the original analysis, but it seems quite likely that the same basic factors would be identified. This demonstration has not been made,* but it probably would be successful in showing the power of the factorial methods in isolating the underlying order among the test variables and the basic factors that determine the individual differences.[9]

In the context of the present study, this position is substantiated by correspondence between our factors and those identified by Berry (1960, 1961), Rummel (1963a), and Russett (1968) in three independent factor analyses. (See the section below, entitled "Interpreting and Naming the Factors.")

Factorial Procedure. The next step was to factor analyze the product moment correlation matrix. Unities were inserted in the principal diagonal of the matrix. The principal-factor (or principal-component) technique was selected over competing methods on the ground that it yields a mathematically unique solution in which the first factor accounts for the maximum amount of variance within the data, while each succeeding factor extracts the maximum of the remaining unexplained variance.[10]

In order to identify the most invariant factor structure, we rotated the principal-factor solution. Using the inflection point criterion for practical significance, we selected the first seven factors for rotation. Each of these factors accounted for more than 4.0 percent of the total variance, and the seven, when summed, accounted for 72.0 percent of the variance. The factors were rotated to an orthogonal and to an oblique solution using Kaiser's (1958: 187–200) varimax and Carroll's (1957: 1114–1115) oblimin biquartimin criteria respectively. The orthogonal solution best fulfilled the simple structure criteria and was selected for presentation.[11]

Interpreting and Naming the Factors. The interpretation and naming of the factors involve further methodological considerations. However, by including the entire population of nations in the factor analysis, we have avoided one issue. We are not faced with the problem of estimating the significance of inferences from a sample to a larger population.

One important consideration is whether to adopt the *descriptive* or the *inferential* approach in interpreting the meaning of the factors (Henrysson, 1960: 86–88). The former considers a factor to be a set of coefficients which conveys only descriptive information about the clustering of variables on a factor. The inferential school takes one step further and assumes that the factor indicates the presence of a basic dimension or "latent variable" which "causes" the array of variables along the factor. The composition of the variables loaded by the factor and the percent of total variance which the factor explains determine the appropriateness and strength of the inferential interpretation.

In the light of these criteria, we first employ the descriptive and then, when appropriate, the inferential approach for interpreting the *Survey* factors. Thus, in the discussion that follows, we first present the extreme clusters of each factor (all are bimodal) and interpret them descriptively as opposite types. We then consider what basic dimension might be inferred. When each variable's rank can be interpreted as representing more or less of a phenomenon common to all of the variables in the extremes, we label the factor with the appropriate ordinal concept. The inferences implied by the labels are, of course, weaker when the factors account for small portions of the total variance.

The next consideration is the *validity* of the factors. If our factors identify basic phenomena operating within political systems, they will also be delineated by other factor analyses. Even though no comparable political study has been completed, we found partial correspondence between our factors and those of independent studies by Rummel, Russett, and Berry. Rummel's (forthcoming) and Russett's (1968) factor analyses of social, economic, and political variables yielded the following five factors: "Economic Development," "Communism," "Intensive Agriculture" or "Density," "Size," and "Catholic Culture" or "Religion." These factors correspond to five of eleven which we calculated in an earlier factor analysis of the social and economic in addition to the political variables of the *Survey*. The remaining six factors closely resemble the political factors reported on below. Berry's study (1961) of economic data identified three factors ("Technology, Demography," and "Size"), which also correspond to factors calculated from the *Survey* data.

From this convergence, we conclude that the earlier *Survey* factors are valid measures of the dimensions suggested, including one that is political in character. More importantly, the earlier results encourage the expectation that future factorial studies will add to the validity of the political factors yielded by the present study.

A further consideration is raised by the communality value 1.08 for the variable "Ex-Spanish Dependency" in Table 1. This high communality (the normal range is zero to one) was caused by missing data.[12] We did not estimate values for missing data; therefore the number of cases entering into each correlation is not the same. As a consequence, the correlation matrix does not exhibit Gramian properties, and the variances and communalities in the factor matrix are slightly inflated. With this consideration in mind, we rely on the relative, rather than absolute, values of the factor loadings and communalities in interpreting the factors. Also, we adopt a high value, $\pm.50$, for identifying the significant variable loadings. This value is safely above the $\pm.30$ generally suggested by factor analysts.

Research Findings

Before examining Table 1 in detail, the single most important implication of the factor matrix should be noted, viz., that the *Survey* data are highly structured along factors largely independent of each other.

The seven factors account for 72 percent of the total variance among the 68 variables, i.e., an average of 72 percent of the variance of each variable. Of the 68 variables, only seven failed to be loaded higher than ±.50 by at least one factor, while only three were loaded higher than ±.50 by more than one factor. Hence, except for three overlapping variables, the solution employed yields mutually independent factors.

TABLE 2

Factor I: Access

Factor loading	Variable	Factor loading	Variable
.94	Electoral system		
.93	Constitutional regime		
.92	Group opposition		
.87	Status of legislature	−.58	East European areal grouping
.86	Horizontal power distribution	−.70	Elitism
.85	Representativeness of regime	−.71	Communist system
.80	Press freedom	−.74	System style
.53	Aggregation by legislature	−.75	Role of police
.73	Military neutral	−.77	One-party system
.73	Conventional ideological orientation	−.77	Military supportive
		−.81	Totalitarian regime
.68	Articulation by parties	−.82	Status of executive
.63	Articulation by associational groups	−.83	Articulation by Institutional groups
.52	Modern bureaucracy		

These findings indicate that the political phenomena measured by the data do not occur randomly from one polity to the next; they occur in highly associated patterns or dimensions. In other words, basic dimensions do underlie the complex behavior within political systems.

In the following sections these factors are interpreted and the dimensions are inferred. It must be remembered, when hypothesizing with regard to dimensions, that the inferences are made with varying degrees of confidence. The large proportions of total variance accounted for by each of the first three factors (24.6, 13.5, and 13.2 percent, support strong inferences. The smaller amount of variance explained by the last four factors (6.4, 5.4, 4.7, and 4.3 percent) sustain successively weaker inferences.

Factor I: Access. Table 2 displays the highly loaded variables comprising the extreme portions of Factor I, which accounts for a large portion, 24.6 percent, of the total variance. In examining these variables, the following dichotomies emerge: hierarchical as opposed to competitive bargaining processes; consolidated as opposed to distributed authority and force; executive and single-party politics as opposed to legislative and group politics; totalitarian restrictions as opposed to institutionalized openness of political channels. The dichotomies refer generally to restrictive as opposed to permissive institutions and interaction. Or, to use Truman's (1955: 264 ff.) concept, Factor I reflects *the degree of access to political channels.*

This conclusion is further substantiated when we examine the rank order of the areal groups on the factor (Table 3). The high loadings of the Western, Latin American, and East European groups correspond to documented fact.

TABLE 3

DISTRIBUTION OF AREAL GROUPING VARIABLES ALONG THE ACCESS FACTOR

Factor loading	Variable	Factor loading	Variable
.45	Advanced Western areal group	−.06	North African, Middle Eastern areal group
.21	Latin American areal group	−.16	Asian areal group
−.05	African areal group	−.58	East European areal group

The low loading of the African group reflects political channels which, due to their variety, absence, lack of differentiation, and newness are randomly rather than systematically distributed in terms of access. For similar reasons, the random distribution of North African and Middle Eastern nations is not surprising.

Specialists in political development, consensus, and conflict will note that these phenomena are not highly associated with degree of political access.

Factor I yields empirical evidence supporting the widespread use of measures of constitutionalism, authoritarianism, totalitarianism, and representation in comparative and theoretical work. In addition, the factor suggests a need for more precise measurement of the quantity and quality of restrictions imposed on competition for control of political channels.

Factor II: Differentiation. Table 4 rank orders the variables loaded heavily by Factor II, which accounts for 13.5 percent of the total variance. The extremes of the factor contrast late stages of modernization against undeveloped tutelary modernization, conventional against developmental ideology, semimodern against postcolonial bureaucracy, and aggregation by legislature against aggregation by executive. Note that the extremes do not contrast the westernized democracies with traditional monarchies. The factor does not, therefore, measure the full range of phenomena which could properly be interpreted as "political development." In the light of these findings, we interpret the factor to reflect a dimension of *differentiation of political institutions within former colonial dependencies.*

Factor II lends empirical support to the comparative and theoretical focus on measures of institutional differentiation and specialization within the ex-colonial nations. It also indicates the need to develop more sophisticated typologies than presently exist for the classification of transitional political systems. For example, the two polity groups most directly involved in the variable extremities of this factor (the Latin American and the African) are classified according to quite different sets of typological criteria in Almond

TABLE 4

Factor II: Differentiation

Factor loading	Variable	Factor loading	Variable
.76	Political modernization—periodization		
.66	Date of independence		
.60	Westernization	−.37	Charisma
.54	Articulation by associational groups	−.48	Aggregation by executive
		−.51	Ex-French dependency
.54	Semimodern bureaucracy	−.51	Unicameral legislature
.54	Ex-Spanish dependency	−.58	Articulation by nonassociational groups
.51	Bicameral legislature		
.46	Later European political modernization	−.83	Developmental ideological orientation
.46	Conventional ideological orientation	−.90	African areal grouping
		−.92	Post-colonial bureaucracy
.41	Elitism	−.93	Undeveloped tutelary political modernization
.38	Aggregation by legislature		

and Coleman (1960: 522–567). Thus, while the negative loadings might be regarded as according with one or more components of the "Almond-Shils" schema (e.g., "Tutelary Democracy" or "Terminal Colonial Dependency"), it is evident that no element of the same typology applies to the set of high positive loadings for Factor II.

The latter extreme loads characteristics of older ex-colonies whose political institutions have *at least in a structural sense* been substantially westernized. The other extreme loads characteristics of recently dependent territories which have yet to become accommodated to other than rudimentary institutions of self-government. While one might expect polities exhibiting high positive scores for this factor to be more democratic, more stable, and more consensual than those exhibiting high negative scores, variables indexing these phenomena are, by and large, conspicuous by their absence.

We hypothesize, therefore, that this factor measures what may be termed the political counterpart to social differentiation. This is to suggest that if a large number of variables indexing social structure had been included in the present study, a "social differentiation" factor would undoubtedly emerge and many of the high loading Factor II variables might also be expected to load heavily on such a factor.

Certain of the positive loading Factor II variables may also represent, or suggest, necessary (but not sufficient) conditions for a stable democratic political system in a highly differentiated social and economic *milieu*. Indeed, the presence of a moderate degree of elitism, when coupled with articulation by associational groups and legislative aggregation does not appear to be inconsistent with this hypothesis when viewed in the context of Kornhauser's (1959) theses as to the preconditions of democracy and totalitarianism, respectively.

TABLE 5

FACTOR III: CONSENSUS

Factor loading	Variable	Factor loading	Variable
.89	Government stability	−.51	Articulation by anomic groups
.84	Stability of party system		
.66	Advanced Western regional grouping	−.59	Latin American areal grouping
.65	Modern bureaucracy	−.59	Presidential legislative-executive structure
.54	Political enculturation		
.50	Westernization	−.60	Military interventive
	.	−.66	Domestic killed
	.	−.66	Personalismo
	.		

Factor III: Consensus. The extreme loading variables of Factor III, which accounts for 13.2 percent of the total variance, are presented in Table 5. Examination of the variables reveals the following dichotomies: personalistic party politics as opposed to party system stability; governmental stability as opposed to military intervention; overall system stability as opposed to domestic killed; political enculturation as opposed to articulation by anomic groups. These dichotomies reflect agreement as opposed to dissent with regard to the basic channels and institutions of political participation. Factor III seems to tap *the degree of consensus and cooperation among participants* as to the rules governing political activity. Note that the negative pole of the factor reflects not only dissent and opposition, but direct, physical conflict.

The rank order of the areal groups on the factor (Table 6) adds further substance to this interpretation. The positive loadings of the Western and East European nations are as expected. The low correlation of the African nations reflects a widespread lack of consensus as to the structure of political institutions in the area. However, this lack of consensus is not typically accompanied by a high incidence of open conflict (domestic killed and military intervention) between opposing groups. Lack of consensus in Latin American and

Asian countries, on the other hand, gives rise to open dissent, coups, and conflict. This contrast raises the question, "What are the forms and causes of open opposition when political consensus is absent within a nation?"

TABLE 6

DISTRIBUTION OF AREAL GROUPING VARIABLES ALONG THE CONSENSUS FACTOR

Factor loading	Variable	Factor loading	Variable
.66	Advanced Western areal grouping	−.08	North African, Middle Eastern areal grouping
.26	East European areal grouping	−.24	Asian areal grouping
.02	African areal grouping	−.59	Latin American areal grouping

TABLE 7

FACTOR IV: SECTIONALISM

Factor loading	Variable	Factor loading	Variable
.70	Developed tutelary political modernization	.	
.69	Ex-British dependency	.	
.55	Asian areal grouping	.	
.52	Articulation by nonassociational groups	−.36	Date of independence
		−.47	Presidential legislative-executive structure
.41	Sectionalism	−.49	Latin American areal grouping
.35	Articulation by anomic groups	−.67	Later European political modernization

The emergence of this dimension supports the comparative and theoretical use of concepts bearing on agreement, consensus, cooperation, dissent, opposition, and conflict. Most of these phenomena fall within that area of the discipline now focusing on political culture and attitudes. The findings suggest that in addition to measuring attitudes of consensus and dissent researchers should more systematically explore the overt behavior resulting from these attitudes.[13]

Factor III also serves to substantiate the usefulness of typologies delineating clusters of characteristics that contrast "stable" with "unstable" political systems.

Factor IV: Sectionalism. The fourth factor, accounting for 6.4 percent of the total variance, is only one-fourth as strong as the first and one-half as strong as the second and third, and therefore provides a weaker basis for

TABLE 8
Factor V: Legitimation

Factor loading	Variable	Factor loading	Variable
.47	Semimodern bureaucracy	.	
.40	Communist system	.	
.39	Totalitarian regime	.	
.37	System style	−.50	Non-European political modernization
.36	East European areal grouping	−.70	Authoritarian regime
.32	Later European political modernization	−.80	Traditional bureaucracy

TABLE 9
Distribution of Variables Reflecting Phenomena of Legitimation and Authority on the Legitimation Factor

Factor loading	Variable	Factor loading	Variable
.47	Semimodern bureaucracy	−.02	Conventional ideological orientation
.40	Communist regime	−.12	Military supportive
.39	Totalitarian regime	−.15	Military interventive
.37	System style	−.16	Role of police
.28	Constitutional system	−.17	Elitism
.27	Representativeness of regime	−.21	Charisma
.21	Military neutral	−.24	Articulation by nonassociational groups
.20	Horizontal power distribution	−.34	Personalismo
.12	Developmental ideological orientation	−.70	Authoritarian regime
		−.80	Traditional bureaucracy

TABLE 10
Factor VI: Interest

Factor loading	Variable	Factor loading	Variable
.82	Aggregation by political parties	−.32	Aggregation by legislature
.50	Two-party system	−.35	Parliamentary-Republican
.46	Aggregation by executive	−.55	Articulation by political parties
.		−.69	Multi-party system
.			
.			

inference. For this same reason, inferences based on factors five, six, and seven cannot be made with the high degree of confidence earlier expressed.

The extremes of the factor (see Table 7) contrast colonial developmental characteristics in much the same manner as does Factor II. An important difference is that the earlier set of ex-French, African characteristics is here replaced by an ex-British, Asian configuration. The extreme loading variables are, however, less amenable to interpretation than in the case of Factor II. The ex-British dependencies are, in certain respects, more "developed" than their ex-French counterparts, yet the internal developmental cleavages between social sectors are obviously more pronounced. This is reflected in the loadings of sectionalism and anomic group activity. For want of a better term, we therefore interpret this factor as tapping a specific *pattern of institutional differentiation occurring in a political system exhibiting high sectionalism.*

Factor V: Legitimation. The extremes of Factor V, as exhibited in Table 8, contrast totalitarian regimes against authoritarian regimes, semimodern bureaucracies against traditional bureaucracies, and later European political modernization against non-European political modernization.

Most of these variables reflect the source and distribution of authority within political systems. More specifically, they refer to *the means by which political authority is legitimized.* As demonstrated by the rank order of variables in Table 9, they can be construed as falling along a continuum between the classical Weberian ideal types of rational-legalistic legitimation and traditional legitimation. In examining the variable positions, the characteristics of rational and legalistic authority fall at one extreme, while the characteristics of traditional and charismatic authority occupy the other. (See, for example, Binder, 1962: 44-45.)

Factor VI: Interest. The extreme loading variables of Factor VI are exhibited in Table 10. In addition to contrasting two-party and multi-party systems, this factor identifies the role which political institutions assume in *patterns of interest circulation.* It should be stressed that this factor is typological in that it contrasts patterning rather than the amount of interest circulation. The Access factor, which contrasts systems with large numbers of interest articulation points against systems with few access institutions, measures the volume of interests processed by the system.

Also, it is significant that this factor does not measure all components of the Almond-Coleman (1960: 33 ff.) articulation-aggregation schema. It identifies only the distinctly political institutions for handling interests injected into the system, rather than the full range of interest bearing groups.

This factor highlights the importance of the channels of interest circulation in the political process. It also provides support for the generalizing power of typologies of party systems.

Factor VII: Leadership. Factor VII loads only 4.3 percent of the total variance and does not exhibit the pronounced bimodal configuration of the

Dimensions of Political Systems: Factor Analysis

others. The positive extreme of the factor loads variables which reflect *strong executive leadership in both domestic and foreign affairs.*

This dimension calls attention to the need for systematic studies of executive roles and leadership style in both comparison and theory. The random distribution of other leadership variables along this factor indicates the complexity of the phenomena in question. The relatively low strength of the factor indicates that its typological value is limited.

TABLE 11

FACTOR VII: LEADERSHIP

Factor loading	Variable	Factor loading	Variable
.61	Aggregation by executive	.44	Charisma
.51	Expulsion of ambassadors	.	
.50	North African, Middle Eastern areal grouping	.	
.49	Foreign killed	−.41	Elitism
.49	Ex-French dependency		

TABLE 12

VARIABLES LEAST EXPLAINED BY THE SEVEN FACTORS

Highest factor loading	Variable	Communality
−.24	One party dominant system	.16
.41	Sectionalism	.26
−.39	Demonstrations	.27
−.35	Parliamentary-Republican system	.28
(.51)	Expulsion of ambassadors	.32
(.55)	Non-European political modernization	.38
(.51)	Foreign killed	.40
.45	Early European political modernization	.42
(−.62)	Domestic killed	.44
(.55)	Asian areal grouping	.46
(.50)	North African, Middle Eastern areal grouping	.49

Unexplained Variables. The factor structure accounts for less than 50 percent of the communalities (h^2) of the variables exhibited in Table 12. However, as indicated by the factor loadings in parentheses, six of these variables correlate above .50 with one of the factors. In other words, at least one major source of variation for each of these six variables is identified by the factor matrix. We conclude, therefore, that only five exhibit variation substantially independent of the factors identified.

Of the regional groupings, the North African, Middle Eastern and the Asian display considerably less explained total variance than do the others. In short, political phenomena in these countries are not highly structured along the dimensions discovered. These areas may, of course, exhibit characteristics that structure themselves along other dimensions, possibly religious or cultural, that the present study is not designed to tap.

Conclusions: Relevance of the Findings for Cross-National Study

In the preceding sections, we have proposed the following answers for the first two research questions: the *Survey* data are highly correlated along a relatively limited number of factors; these factors provide evidence for inferring seven basic political dimensions—Access, Differentiation, Consensus, Sectionalism, Legitimation, Interest, and Leadership.

Theory and Research. The third question asks, "What is the relevance of these dimensions for cross-national study?" The dimensions have impact in the following areas: theory and research, comparison, and typology construction. First, they suggest a basic set of concepts around which *theory construction and research* should proceed. According to our findings the seven underlying dimensions are systematically related to ("cause") a wide variety of manifest political behavior. In this sense, the concepts naming the dimensions are theoretically significant; they are lawfully related to much political behavior and therefore can be used as basic concepts within a large body of interrelated generalizations. And this is the first step toward empirical theory. However, to facilitate their use in theory and research, the concepts need to be operationalized by simple definitions rather than by elusive factors. This is done by devising variables which correlate highly with each of the factors. If future factor analyses yield similar factors and a set of corresponding variables is devised, theoreticians and researchers will have advanced an enormous step toward an important goal—empirical theory.

Comparative Study. Second, the seven factors can be used as composite scales for *comparing political systems*.[14] For example, the political system of Great Britain has a higher score on Factor I (which measures the degree of political access) than does that of Poland.[15] By knowing the scores of a nation on all seven factors, we are in a position to make statistical predictions as to the probabilities with which phenomena measured by the 68 variables of Table 1 will occur within the political system in question. This capability seems especially useful with regard to phenomena indexed by variables such as government stability, articulation by anomic groups, stability of party system, military intervention, demonstrations, and the like.

Typology Construction. The findings have import in a third area of cross-national study—*typology construction*.[16] The latter approach seeks a middle ground between the powerful but scarce results of theory and the multitudinous but mundane yields of comparison. Instead of focusing on the

Dimensions of Political Systems: Factor Analysis

dimensions common to all systems, it involves the construction of a small set of categories which will adequately describe the *range* of relationships across a variety of systems. Generally, the elements of a typology are a set of definitions mixed with propositions, each of which is assumed to describe a cluster of phenomena that is highly recurrent (predictable) in each of the system types specified.

The usefulness (generalizing power) of a typology depends on the number of characteristics and political systems which it can explain. For example,

TABLE 13

MAJOR CLUSTER TYPES OF *Survey* VARIABLES

Survey factor	Loading	Cluster type
I	Positive	Polyarchic system
I	Negative	One-party totalitarian system
II	Positive	Westernized democratic system
II	Negative	Underdeveloped democratic system
III	Positive	Stable system
III	Negative	Unstable system
V	Negative	Traditional authoritarian system
VI	Positive	Two-party system
VI	Negative	Multi-party system
VII	Positive	Modernizing authoritarian system

Aristotle's three-type classificatory scheme (monarchy, aristocracy, democracy) seems to have described adequately all political systems of the classical Greek period with reference to a single set of characteristics having to do with authority structure. In a somewhat similar manner, Almond and Coleman's (1960: 33 ff.) basic typology (traditional, transitional, modern) is useful as a means of categorizing contemporary political systems with reference to a set of characteristics centering on specialization of political structure.

The objective of the approach is to develop the most parsimonious set of categories that will serve as the basis of generalization about the greatest number of political systems. Success depends on delineating the most frequently recurring types which are mutually independent and not simply disguised mutations. In this sense, the underlying assumptions and criteria of typology construction and factor analysis correspond. Both endeavor to delineate sets of variables which are highly associated across many cases. When only the highest loading variables on each factor are considered, they reflect a small cluster of phenomena occurring simultaneously in a specific set of nations. The simple structure criterion guarantees that the cluster and the set are mutually exclusive of all others along their respective factors. In this way, factor analysis utilizes systematic methods for identifying sets of variables that are analogous to typological constructs.

Therefore, the results of this factorial study provide information as to what clusters of characteristics will yield types of greatest inclusiveness and generalizing power. Table 13 displays the cluster types suggested by the *Survey* factors.[17]

These categories, inductively derived from the *Survey* data, provide confirmation for many types which political scientists currently employ. For example, the *Survey*-derived type, "One-party totalitarian system," exhibits the same characteristics that Friedrich and Brzezinski (1956: 9–10) label "Totalitarian Dictatorship." The types "Two-party system" and "Multiparty system" substantiate many of the propositions that Duverger (1963: 203 ff.) sets forth in his party system typology. The *Survey* types "Westernized democratic system," "Undeveloped democratic system," "Traditional authoritarian system," and "Modernizing authoritarian system" add support to Shils' and Almond's (Almond and Coleman, 1960: 53–55) types, "Political Democracy," "Tutelary Democracy," "Traditional Oligarchy," and "Modernizing Oligarchy." "Polyarchic system" encompasses most of the characteristics which Dahl (1956: 63 ff.) subsumes under the label "Polyarcal."

Conflict Propositions. The final research question posed asks, "What specific propositions about conflict in political systems are suggested by the findings?" Examination of the conflict variables (Demonstrations, Domestic killed, Expulsion of ambassadors, and Foreign killed) leads to the following propositions:

(1) The political dimension, *leadership*, which accounts for foreign conflict does not account for domestic conflict.

(2) The presence of strong executive *leadership* is frequently accompanied by both diplomatic and violent foreign conflict.

(3) *Access* to political channels, *differentiation* of political institutions, *sectionalism* within developing systems, kind of *legitimation*, and type of *interest* circulation tend to be unassociated with violent and diplomatic foreign conflict.

(4) The political dimension, *consensus*, which accounts for most of the domestic conflict does not account for diplomatic conflict, but is moderately associated with violent foreign conflict.

(5) An absence of political *consensus* is associated with violent domestic conflict.

(6) An absence of political *consensus* is moderately associated with nonviolent domestic conflict.

(7) The degree of *differentiation* of political institutions, kind of *legitimation*, and type of *leadership* tend to be unassociated with violent and nonviolent domestic conflict.

These propositions, in large measure, substantiate those advanced by Rummel (1963b [reprinted in this volume, Chapter 3]) and Tanter (1966 [reprinted in this volume, Chapter 4]) in their conflict research. In addition, they identify the two political phenomena (lack of consensus, strong executive leadership) which are most frequently associated with domestic and foreign conflict, respectively.

NOTES

1. For an attempt to integrate the structural and functional approaches with the systems approach, see Almond's introductory essay in Almond and Coleman (1960: 3-64).

2. The terms "factor" and "dimension" are here used as equivalent, nontechnical concepts. Henceforth the former will be employed in reference to the mathematical result (the columns of variables' loadings in the factor matrix) of the factor analytic calculations; the latter will refer to the phenomena of the real world which the factor delineates.

3. For a brief history of factor analysis, see Harman (1960: 3-11).

4. For a collateral, but less ambitious study by a sociologist, see Schnore (1961: 229-245).

5. A somewhat related effort is Russett et al., *World Handbook of Political and Social Indicators* (1964). The compilers of the *Handbook*, however, set themselves the task of assembling a large number of interval-scaled data series which are ecologically relevant to political research, but which are not, in the main, substantively political in character.

6. Since each of the *Survey* variables is discussed in the *Survey* itself, it seems unnecessary to provide a set of definitions for purposes of the present article. For those unfamiliar with the *Survey*, one variable that appears in Table 1 may, however, require specification. "System Style" refers to the degree of "mobilization" (to attain political or social objectives) present in the system.

7. In an earlier factor analysis involving all 57 polychotomous characteristics of the *Survey* and an eleven-factor solution, four nonpolitical factors ("Economic Development," "Size," "Population Density," and "Religion") emerged. The remaining seven factors closely resembled those reported on below. The four nonpolitical factors correspond to factors identified by Berry (1960, 1961), Rummel et al. (forthcoming) and Russett (1968).

8. The numbers in parentheses in Table 1 indicate the *Survey* raw characteristics from which the variables have been derived. Thus variables 22-24 are all derived from *Survey* Raw Characteristic 26 (Constitutional Status).

9. The asterisk refers to the following footnote in the revised edition of Thurstone's original work: "Since this chapter was written, the demonstration has been made, and is described in Chapter XV."

10. This technique is explained by Harman (1960) in Chapter 9, "Principal-Factor Solution."

11. Calculations were performed by the Indiana Research Computing Center's IBM 709. The MESA-3 program employed was developed by John B. Carroll at Harvard, coded by R. A. Sandsmark at Northwestern, and revised by Norman Swartz with the assistance of Gary Flint at Indiana.

12. Due to an artifact of coding procedure taken over directly from the *Survey*, the variable "Ex-Spanish Dependency" exhibits an unusually high missing data component. For this variable, in addition to normal missing data attrition, only

ex-colonial dependencies were assigned substantive codings, some 40 countries being regarded as "irrelevant" to the coding category.

13. Rummel has initiated an examination of "causes" of domestic conflict but has encountered a lack of relevant survey data. See Rummel (1963a). A useful pilot study in this regard is Almond and Verba (1963).

14. Russett (1968) develops a very useful method for applying the factors as comparative scales.

15. We have not actually calculated factor scores in order to compare nations on the factors. The loadings of the areal grouping variables do, of course, provide insight as to what nations might be expected to correlate most strongly with the various factors. However, the loadings of the areal grouping variables lose their meaning when the nations are quite heterogeneous with respect to the dimension that the factor taps. On this point, see Lawley and Maxwell (1963: 88-92).

16. For an excellent discussion of the methodological status of typologies in the social sciences, see the remarks of Hemple (1952: 65 ff.).

17. We have not named those factor clusters which are not readily interpreted or which duplicate other clusters.

REFERENCES

ALKER, JR., H.R. (1964) "Dimensions of conflict in the General Assembly." *American Political Science Review* 56 (March): 90-107.

ALMOND, G.A. and J.S. COLEMAN, Eds. (1960) *The Politics of the Developing Areas*. Princeton: Princeton University Press.

ALMOND, G.A. and S. VERBA (1963) *The Civic Culture*. Princeton: Princeton University Press.

BANKS, A.S. and R.B. TEXTOR (1963) *A Cross-Polity Survey*. Cambridge: MIT Press.

BERRY, B.J.L. (1960) "An inductive approach to the regionalization of economic development," Pp. 78-107 in N. Ginsberg, Ed., *Essays on Geography and Economic Development*. Chicago: University of Chicago Press.

— (1961) "Basic patterns of economic development." Pp. 110-119 in N. Ginsberg, Ed., *Atlas of Economic Development*. Chicago: University of Chicago Press.

BINDER, L. (1962) *Iran: Political Development in a Changing Society*. Berkeley: University of California Press.

CARROLL, J.B. (1957) "Biquartimin criterion for rotation to oblique simple structure in factor analysis." *Science* 126 (November 29): 1114-1115.

CATTELL, R.B. (1949) "The dimensions of cultural patterns for factorization of national characters." *Journal of Abnormal and Social Psychology* 44 (October): 443-469.

DAHL, R.A. (1956) *A Preface to Democratic Theory*. Chicago: University of Chicago Press.

DUVERGER, M. (1963) *Political Parties: Their Organization and Activity in the Modern State*. New York: John Wiley.

FRIEDRICH, C.J. and Z.K. BRZEZINSKI (1956) *Totalitarian Dictatorship and Autocracy*. Cambridge: Harvard University Press.

HARMAN, H.H. (1960) *Modern Factor Analysis*. Chicago: University of Chicago Press.

HEMPLE, C. G. (1952) "Symposium: problems of concept and theory formation in the social sciences." In *Science, Language and Human Rights*. Philadelphia: University of Pennsylvania Press.
HENRYSSON, S. (1960) *Applicability of Factor Analysis in the Behavioral Sciences*. Stockholm: Almquist & Wiksell.
KAISER, H.J. (1958) "The varimax criterion for analytic rotation in factor analysis." *Psychometrika* 23 (September): 187–200.
KORNHAUSER, W. (1959) *The Politics of Mass Society*. New York: Free Press.
LAWLEY, D.N. and A.E. MAXWELL (1963) *Factor Analysis as a Statistical Method*. London: Butterworth.
RUMMEL, R.J. (1963a) "Testing some possible predictors of conflict behavior within and between nations." *Proceedings of the Peace Research Society* 1.
— (1963b) "Dimensions of conflict behavior within and between nations." Pp. 1–50 in *General Systems Yearbook 8*. Reprinted in this volume, Chapter 3.
RUMMEL, R.J., H. GUETZKOW, J. SAWYER and R. TANTER (forthcoming) *Dimensions of Nations*.
RUSSETT, B.M. (1968) "Delineating international regions." Pp. 317–352 in J.D. Singer, Ed., *Quantitative International Politics: Insights and Evidence*. New York: Free Press.
RUSSETT, B.M. et al. (1964) *World Handbook of Political and Social Indicators*. New Haven: Yale University Press.
SCHNORE, L.F. (1961) "The Statistical measurement of urbanization and economic development." *Land Economics* 37 (August): 229–245.
SCHUBERT, G. (1962) "The 1960 term of the Supreme Court: a psychological analysis." *American Political Science Review* 56 (March): 90–107.
TANTER, R. (1966) "Dimensions of conflict behavior within and between nations, 1958–60." *Journal of Conflict Resolution* 10:41–64. Reprinted in this volume, Chapter 4.
THURSTONE, L.L. (1947) *Multiple Factor Analysis: A Development and Expansion of the Vectors of the Mind*. Chicago: University of Chicago Press.
TRUMAN, D.B. (1955) *The Governmental Process*. New York: Alfred A. Knopf.

13 Grouping Political Systems: Q-Factor Analysis of A Cross-Polity Survey

ARTHUR S. BANKS and PHILLIP M. GREGG

In a recent paper, "Delineating International Regions," Professor Bruce M. Russett (1965) surveys the literature dealing with criteria for intranational and international regionalization and finds it lacking in both substance and sophistication. He then advances, most persuasively, the case for factor analysis as a grouping or "regionalizing" technique.[1]

It is a commonplace that the results of any factor analytic undertaking are a function of the input data. Thus, despite the undisputed merits of Russett's study, the factors (determinants of groups) extracted do not define political regions, but regions demarcated primarily in terms of a set of social and economic variables drawn from the author's (1964) *World Handbook of Political and Social Indicators*.[2] For insight into the grouping of nations on the basis of their political characteristics, a somewhat different set of input variables is called for.

The present paper reports on a Q-factor analysis of the political component of *A Cross-Polity Survey* (Banks and Textor, 1963).[3] The analysis embraces the 115 independent nations of the *Survey*[4] and the 68 variables displayed in Table 1.

The difference between the Q-technique and the more commonly used R-technique is simply that the input data matrix is transposed so that "cases" (in this instance, nations) are grouped rather than variables. As Driver and Schuessler (1957: 659) put it, with reference to the analysis of ethnographic materials, "Q-technique is the correlation of the cultural inventories of a group of tribes; culture traits are counted. R-technique refers to the correlation of culture traits; tribes are counted."[5]

Reprinted from *The American Behavioral Scientist*, Volume IX, Number 3 (November, 1965), pages 3–5, with permission of the authors and the publisher. Copyright © 1965 Sage Publications, Inc.

TABLE 1

List of Variables

1. East European areal grouping (1)
2. Advanced Western areal grouping (1)
3. Latin American areal grouping (1)
4. Asian areal grouping (1)
5. African areal grouping (1)
6. North African, Middle Eastern areal grouping (1)
7. Freedom of the press (13)
8. Date of independence (19)
9. Westernization (20)
10. Ex-British dependency (21)
11. Ex-French dependency (21)
12. Ex-Spanish dependency (21)
13. Early European political modernization (22)
14. Later European political modernization (22)
15. Non-European political modernization (22)
16. Developed tutelary political modernization (22)
17. Undeveloped tutelary political modernization (22)
18. Political modernization—periodization (23)
19. Developmental ideological orientation (24)
20. Conventional ideological orientation (24)
21. System style (25)
22. Constitutional regime (26)
23. Authoritarian regime (26)
24. Totalitarian regime (26)
25. Governmental stability (27)
26. Representativeness of regime (28)
27. Electoral system (29)
28. Freedom of group opposition
29. Political enculturation (31)
30. Sectionalism (32)
31. Articulation by associational groups (33)
32. Articulation by institutional groups (34)
33. Articulation by nonassociational groups (35)
34. Articulation by anomic groups (36)
35. Articulation by political parties (37)
36. Aggregation by political parties (38)
37. Aggregation by executive (39)
38. Aggregation by legislature (40)
39. One-party system (41)
40. One party dominant system (41)
41. Two-party system (41)
42. Multi-party system (41)
43. Stability of party system (43)
44. Personalismo (44)
45. Elitism (45)
46. Charisma (46)
47. Horizontal power distribution (48)
48. Presidential system (49)
49. Parliamentary-Republican system (49)
50. Parliamentary-Royalist system (49)
51. Status of legislature (50)
52. Unicameral legislature (51)
53. Bicameral legislature (51)
54. Status of executive (52)
55. Modern bureaucracy (53)
56. Semi-modern bureaucracy (53)
57. Post-colonial transitional bureaucracy (53)
58. Traditional bureaucracy (53)
59. Military interventive (54)
60. Military supportive (54)
61. Military neutral (54)
62. Role of police (55)
63. Communist system (57)
64. System stability
65. Demonstrations
66. Domestic killed
67. Expulsion of ambassadors
68. Foreign killed

Of the 68 variables in Table 1, all but five were derived from *Survey* characteristics.[6] We omitted 16 *Survey* characteristics that are essentially non-political in nature. In addition, three political characteristics, 41 ("Party System: Qualitative"), 47 ("Vertical Power Distribution"), and 56 ("Character of Legal System") were deleted from the present analysis for distributional reasons.[7] On the other hand, five non-*Survey* variables were added: "System Stability," "Demonstrations," "Domestic Killed," "Expulsion of Ambassadors," and "Foreign Killed." All but the first of these are taken directly from Rummel's work in conflict behavior (1963 [reprinted in this volume, Chapter 3]).

The essentials of the factorial procedure employed are as follows. A correlation matrix was generated by inter-correlating the nations across the 68 *Survey* variables.[8] Unities were inserted in the principal diagonal of the correlation matrix as the initial estimates for the communalities. The matrix was factored using the principal-components method. Final communalities were calculated by Horst's modification of Hotelling's iterative technique. In order to insure a relatively invariant and replicable solution, the factor matrix was rotated to an orthogonal solution using Kaiser's (1958: 187–200) varimax criterion. On the basis of Kaiser's eigenvalue criteria (Kaiser, 1960; Cattell, 1952: 298) for statistical significance and the inflection point criterion for practical significance, the first five factors were selected for rotation. Each of these factors accounted for more than 5.0 percent of the total variance, and the five, when summed, accounted for 88.7 percent of the variance. The rotated factor matrix is presented in Table 2.[10]

Group I: Polyarchic

The nations loaded heavily by Factor I, which accounts for 29.4 percent of the total variance, are identified as comprising a *polyarchic* group. Virtually all of the nations correlating above .80 with this factor are economically developed, western nations. From this, one may perhaps conclude that there is a relationship between degree of polyarchy, on the one hand, and economic development and "westernization," respectively, on the other—at least within the rather broad category of nations normally regarded as "democratic."[11] The relatively low ranking of Gaullist France seems to be of a somewhat deviant character in this regard.

Two additional nations that appear in this group require brief comment. *Survey* coding for the Dominican Republic occurred shortly after the ouster of Trujillo and quite obviously overemphasized the democratic potential of the Bosch regime. The coding for South Africa, on the other hand, exhibits a high missing data component for many of the variables that might otherwise serve to limit its polyarchic rating.[12]

Group II: Elitist

The nations loaded heavily by Factor II, which accounts for 22.4 percent of the total variance, are largely African. The five non-African states are: Burma,

Cambodia, Indonesia, Pakistan, and the Republic of Vietnam. We identify this group as *elitist* in character, though in so doing we are perhaps guilty of using the term in a somewhat specialized sense. What we have in mind is that in all of the recently independent states of this group (none were independent prior to World War II), relatively small "modernizing elites" are attempting to bring about rapid and radical social change in the face of impressive cultural resistance of an essentially "parochial" character that remains as a carry-over from the colonial period.[13] Rather than "elitist," we might have used the term "segmental" to characterize this group, but the latter term has more of a social-structural connotation than we wished to invoke in the present, essentially *political* context.

Group III: Centrist

The nations loaded heavily by Factor III, which accounts for 19.8 percent of the total variance, are all politically *centrist* in character. All of the nations correlating above .80 with this factor are Communist states. Those loaded less heavily are a mixed group of totalitarian, semi-totalitarian, and authoritarian regimes.

Group IV: Personalist

The nations loaded heavily by Factor IV, which accounts for 11.4 percent of the total variance, are identified as constituting a *personalist* group. All of the Central American nations (with the exception of Costa Rica) are included. Also included are the following non-Latin states: Iraq, the Republic of Korea, Lebanon, Syria, and Thailand. We have called this a "personalist" group since the dominant political feature of most of the regimes in question (including the non-Latin) is a high degree of political personalism as the term is normally construed in the Latin American context. A possible alternative label might have been the somewhat unwieldy expression "sporadically authoritarian."

The inclusion of Haiti, Paraguay, and Thailand (all of which exhibit relatively high Factor III loadings) is perhaps questionable. These polities might well have been designated as "unclassifiable."

Group V: Traditional

Factor V accounts for only 5.8 percent of the total variance and only four countries are loaded heavily by it. Nonetheless, we interpret this factor as defining an embryonic *traditional* group. A number of other states that are normally regarded as quite traditionally oriented—states such as Afghanistan, Ethiopia, Jordan, and Libya—all exhibit strong *secondary* correlations with this factor. Many of these states also have fairly high missing data components, and we assume that more ample and more reliable data would probably have the effect of moving most of them into the traditional group.[14]

Nonetheless, the relative weakness of the factor and the composition of the group as it stands mitigate against drawing conclusions with any high degree of confidence in this case.

Conclusions

A Cross-Polity Survey was the first attempt to deal in a truly comparative manner with all of the major independent nations of the world across a large number of prime political variables susceptible of quantitative analysis. Certain of the individual codings and coding categories could (and most assuredly will) be improved upon in other studies and in future revisions of the *Survey* itself. The factors reported on in this paper are nonetheless intuitively suggestive and would appear to delineate significant components of difference among major political groupings of the contemporary world.

TABLE 2

ORTHOGONALLY ROTATED FACTOR MATRIX

	Factor				
	I	II	III	IV	V
Polyarchic					
Norway	−.924	.142	.235	.143	−.045
Luxembourg	−.920	.149	.210	.170	−.057
Ireland	−.919	.190	.238	.686	−.038
German F.R.	−.918	.205	.208	.107	−.070
Sweden	−.918	.151	.250	.148	−.040
Australia	−.917	.211	.246	.018	−.126
Netherlands	−.914	.152	.227	.121	−.145
Iceland	−.910	.182	.217	.179	−.027
Denmark	−.907	.171	.243	.145	−.010
New Zealand	−.906	.233	.251	.030	−.020
Austria	−.905	.192	.254	.092	−.009
Finland	−.901	.186	.218	.171	−.004
Switzerland	−.870	.163	.254	.133	−.271
Italy	−.859	.181	.214	.281	−.108
U.K.	−.857	.185	.291	.043	−.187
U.S.A.	−.855	.238	.268	.105	−.097
Canada	−.854	.261	.251	.036	−.236
Belgium	−.844	.224	.187	.180	−.239
Costa Rica	−.807	.272	.189	.383	.111
Uruguay	−.807	.169	.348	.277	−.128
Japan	−.789	.279	.258	.298	−.122
Jamaica	−.788	.421	.035	.244	−.150
Trinidad	−.771	.363	.045	.281	−.183
Greece	−.769	.251	.161	.397	.100
Israel	−.753	.344	.251	.153	−.125

TABLE 2 (Continued)

	Factor				
	I	II	III	IV	V
Polyarchic					
France	−.751	.300	.271	.258	−.028
Chile	−.741	.153	.159	.559	−.041
Dominican Rep.	−.738	.278	.129	.538	−.014
Philippines	−.729	.421	.249	.176	−.178
Turkey	−.716	.234	.272	.394	−.182
Colombia	−.656	.291	.284	.467	−.191
Mexico	−.650	.359	.429	.278	−.042
Malaya	−.636	.530	.097	.222	−.342
Venezuela	−.634	.319	.217	.560	.030
India	−.620	.522	.217	.245	−.243
Brazil	−.616	.241	.341	.491	−.253
Cyprus	−.593	.344	.323	.454	−.210
Libya	−.583	.409	.326	.122	−.423
Bolivia	−.573	.443	.185	.550	−.027
South Africa	−.551	.335	.414	.197	−.432
Morocco	−.548	.506	.368	.224	−.212
Ceylon	−.504	.401	.131	.462	−.441
Elitist					
Niger	−.313	.901	.192	.186	−.048
Central African Rep.	−.200	.888	.238	.215	−.005
Dahomey	−.209	.882	.300	.187	−.099
Gabon	−.209	.882	.300	.187	−.099
Upper Volta	−.307	.874	.250	.127	.008
Ivory Coast	−.216	.867	.401	.145	.034
Congo (Brazzaville)	−.261	.866	.236	.216	−.128
Mali	−.351	.862	.230	.180	−.079
Chad	−.353	.860	.296	.158	−.136
Senegal	−.241	.825	.454	.060	−.093
Togo	−.192	.820	.228	.233	−.306
Cameroun	−.439	.813	.127	.222	−.164
Tanganyika	−.397	.808	.339	.029	.000
Burundi	−.469	.799	.077	.131	−.079
Mauritania	−.358	.798	.320	.190	−.115
Rwanda	−.370	.774	.116	.290	−.185
Indonesia	−.139	.748	.327	.350	−.231
Guinea	−.177	.708	.619	.100	−.091
Ghana	−.154	.702	.579	.192	−.115
Congo (Leopoldville)	−.213	.682	.181	.369	−.454
Cambodia	−.188	.679	.471	.152	−.205
Malagasy Rep.	−.612	.634	.046	.123	−.315
Sierra Leone	−.562	.615	.070	.218	−.363
Somalia	−.400	.608	.188	.249	−.463

Grouping Political Systems: Q-Factor Analysis

TABLE 2 (CONTINUED)

	Factor				
	I	II	III	IV	V
Elitist					
Burma	−.187	.590	.411	.321	−.421
Tunisia	−.489	.577	.501	.045	.098
Vietnam Rep.	−.039	.569	.517	.381	−.205
Uganda	−.536	.556	.190	.236	−.492
Sudan	−.257	.554	.453	.302	−.394
Pakistan	−.131	.553	.475	.432	−.378
Centrist					
Bulgaria	−.295	.157	.901	.167	−.049
Albania	−.243	.246	.885	.140	−.110
Germany, E.	−.276	.157	.878	.177	.010
Hungary	−.363	.139	.863	.231	.069
Mongolia	−.179	.313	.861	.204	−.137
Czechoslovakia	−.306	.144	.860	.161	−.098
Korea, N.	−.176	.363	.853	.126	−.109
U.S.S.R.	−.319	.219	.845	.117	−.219
Rumania	−.333	.251	.843	.157	−.035
Poland	−.395	.211	.832	.179	−.013
Yugoslavia	−.327	.242	.822	.163	−.222
Spain	−.416	.173	.800	.234	−.166
Vietnam, N.	−.113	.468	.783	.050	−.125
Portugal	−.507	.043	.766	.186	−.066
China, P.R.	−.127	.385	.764	.280	−.168
Cuba	−.171	.290	.686	.669	.164
Algeria	−.309	.483	.678	.221	−.109
Afghanistan	−.297	.302	.639	.246	−.430
Saudi Arabia	−.265	.404	.628	.181	−.369
U.A.R.	−.265	.473	.616	.294	.061
Liberia	−.374	.382	.582	.158	−.321
Jordan	−.154	.346	.575	.333	−.525
Nepal	−.178	.428	.528	.409	−.381
Ethiopia	−.184	.429	.515	.384	−.399
Personalist					
Guatemala	−.399	.203	.383	.776	−.110
El Salvador	−.339	.285	.438	.683	−.128
Panama	−.587	.254	.201	.681	−.064
Peru	−.481	.228	.321	.681	−.273
Honduras	−.488	.290	.296	.673	−.119
Argentina	−.539	.157	.330	.662	−.067
Korea Rep.	−.198	.453	.418	.650	−.233
Syria	−.283	.456	.381	.645	−.323
Nicaragua	−.431	.247	.411	.640	−.158
Ecuador	−.536	.246	.281	.591	−.330

TABLE 2 (CONTINUED)

	Factor				
	I	II	III	IV	V
Personalist					
Lebanon	−.438	.386	.305	.589	−.276
Paraguay	−.316	.213	.573	.583	−.088
Iraq	−.152	.483	.338	.566	−.483
Haiti	−.258	.444	.508	.532	−.140
Thailand	−.213	.354	.480	.495	−.382
Traditional					
Yemen	−.201	.562	.396	.280	−.645
Nigeria	−.470	.508	.156	.224	−.579
Laos	−.069	.485	.368	.477	−.550
Iran	−.245	.383	.484	.403	−.495
% Tot. Var.	29.4	22.4	19.8	11.4	5.8
% Com. Var.	33.1	25.2	22.3	12.8	6.5

NOTES

1. A revised version of this paper is to appear in J. David Singer, Ed., *Empirical Studies in International Relations* (forthcoming).

2. See Russett et al. (1964) *World Handbook of Political and Social Indicators*. Despite the focus implied by the title, most of the data series in this collection are of limited *political* significance.

3. A somewhat cruder analysis, based on a non-factorial design and embracing *all CPS* variables is included in Banks (1964).

4. The only independent nations not included are China, Gambia, Mali, Western Samoa, Zambia, and Zanzibar (now part of Tanzania).

5. For an analysis of the *Survey* data based on the R-technique, see Gregg and Banks (1965 [reprinted in this volume, Chapter 12]).

6. The numbers in parentheses in Table 1 indicate the *Survey* raw characteristics (nominal and ordinal polychotomous variables) from which the present variables are derived. Thus Variables 10–12 of Table 1 are all derived from *Survey* Raw Characteristic 21 ("Former Colonial Ruler").

7. Less than ten percent of the 115 nations received substantive scores on these variables.

8. The calculating formula employed was Pearson's product moment correlation coefficient. When used to intercorrelate ordinal and nominal variables, as in the present study, the formula is the equivalent of Spearman's rank-order correlation, rho, and the phi coefficient, respectively. See Yule and Kendall (1950: 261, 271).

Calculations were performed by the Indiana Research Computing Center's IBM 709. The MESA-3 program employed was developed by John B. Carroll at Harvard, coded by R. A. Sandsmark at Northwestern, and revised by Norman Swartz with the assistance of Gary Flint at Indiana.

9. For a discussion of Hotelling's iterative technique, see Harman (1960: 154, ff.).

10. Russett (1965) employs a somewhat different factorial procedure. Instead of using the Q-technique, he factors a "distance" matrix based on summed factor scores for each nation. Professor Rummel has utilized this procedure at Yale in grouping 79 nations across a representative selection of *CPS* political variables with results that exhibit a high degree of correspondence with four of the five groups reported on here. Our Group II does not appear in Rummel's analysis because virtually all of the African nations were excluded.

11. Cf., Lipset (1959: 69–105) and the remarks by James S. Coleman, Almond and Coleman (1960: 536, ff.).

12. The computer program employed, unlike many similar programs, was designed to cope with the problem of missing data. It does so by permitting only correlations between substantive codings to enter into the factor analytic calculations. Where the missing data component is high (as is the case for a limited number of *CPS* nations), distortions can be introduced that are interpretable only by an examination of the original codings. In the case of South Africa, with its quite different policies toward the two major racial groups, many of the political variables were coded as "ambiguous" (a residual category) in the *Survey*. However, for certain variables, such as "Status of the [All-White] Legislature," relatively "polyarchic" substantive codings were entered.

13. The term "parochial" is Gabriel Almond's. See Almond and Verba (1963: 17, ff.).

14. In Rummel's factor analysis of ten *CPS* political variables, a traditional group emerged that included Afghanistan, Ethiopia, Iran, Jordan, Nepal, Saudi Arabia, Cambodia, Yemen, and Libya.

REFERENCES

ALMOND, G.A. and J.S. COLEMAN, Eds. (1960) *The Politics of the Developing Areas.* Princeton: Princeton University Press.

ALMOND, G.A. and S. VERBA (1963) *The Civic Culture.* Princeton: Princeton University Press.

BANKS, A.S. (1964) "A cross-polity survey: preliminary analysis." Paper delivered at the 1964 Annual Meeting of the American Political Science Association.

BANKS, A.S. and P.M. GREGG (1965) "Dimensions of political systems: factor analysis of *A Cross-Polity Survey.*" *American Political Science Review* 59 (September): 555–578. Reprinted in this Volume, Chapter 12.

BANKS, A.S. and R.B. TEXTOR (1963) *A Cross-Polity Survey.* Cambridge: MIT Press.

CATTELL, R.B. (1952) *Factor Analysis.* New York: Harper.

DRIVER, H.E. and K.F. SCHUESSLER (1957) "Factor analysis of ethnographic data." *American Anthropologist* 59 (August).

HARMAN, H.H. (1960) *Modern Factor Analysis.* Chicago: University of Chicago Press.

KAISER, H.F. (1960) "The application of electronic computers to factor analysis." *Educational and Psychological Measurement* 20: 141–151.

— (1958) "The varimax criterion for analytic rotation in factor analysis." *Psychometrika* 23 (September): 187–200.

LIPSET, S.M. (1959) "Some social requisites of democracy: economic development and political legitimacy." *American Political Science Review* 53 (March): 69–105.

RUMMEL, R.J. (1963) "Dimensions of conflict behavior within and between nations." Pp. 1–50 in *General Systems Yearbook 8*. Reprinted in this Volume, Chapter 3.

RUSSETT, B.M. (1968) "Delineating international regions." Pp. 317–352 in J.D. Singer, Ed., *Quantitative International Politics: Insights and Evidence*. New York: Free Press.

— (1965) "Delineating international regions." Carnegie IDRC Joint Study Group on Measurement Problems, Paper Number G60, Indiana University, February.

RUSSETT, B.M., H.R. ADLER, JR., K.W. DEUTSCH and H.D. LASSWELL (1964) *World Handbook of Political and Social Indicators*. New Haven: Yale University Press.

YULE, G.U. and M.G. KENDALL (1950) *An Introduction to the Theory of Statistics*. 14th ed. London: Charles Griffin.

14 A Scalogram Analysis of Political Development

PETER G. SNOW

At least 2,300 years ago, students of comparative politics began classifying different forms of government, and this endeavor is still very much in vogue; however, the criteria used to devise classificatory schemes have changed radically. Now instead of the constitutional structure of government, it is the means and the degree of political development that have become the major criteria for classification. This seldom defined concept of political development, in its simplest form, postulates the existence of three types of polity: traditional (or distinctly unmodern in form), modern (primarily North American and Western Europe), and transitional (those in the process of moving from the traditional to the modern type).

In many respects, this tripartite division is of no greater utility than the old unitary-federal and presidential-parliamentary dichotomies. It has become a useful tool of analysis only with the subdivision of the transitional class. Fortunately, in recent years a great deal of emphasis has been placed upon different patterns of development during this transitional process. Thus, for example, Milliken and Blackmer (1961: 74) speak of neotraditional, transitional and actively modernizing oligarchies; Apter (1963) of mobilization, reconciliation and modernizing systems; and Shils (1962), of political and tutelary democracies, and modernizing, totalitarian and traditional oligarchies. While these concepts are of some use in the analysis of different processes of political development, they still leave a great deal to be desired—if for no reason other than the fact that placement of polities in one class rather than in another is basically intuitive.[1]

The study of different types of developmental processes employed by transitional polities appears to have gone about as far as possible given the present tools of analysis. It would seem that in order to go beyond

---

Reprinted from *The American Behavioral Scientist*, Volume IX, Number 7 (March, 1966), pages 33–36, with permission of the author and the publisher. Copyright © 1966 Sage Publications, Inc.

semi-impressionistic studies it will be necessary to employ research techniques which differ fundamentally from those currently in use. One such tool, which appears to be readily adaptable to the study of political development, is scalogram analysis.

The purpose of this paper is to explain how the scalogram can be used in the study of the process of political development. To illustrate its use, twenty developmental characteristics are scaled against the independent polities of Latin America—the area of the world with which the author is the most familiar. The construction of this scalogram is described in some detail, not because it is *the* method to be used, but to allow others to judge its reliability by replication with other sets of polities or developmental characteristics.

MULTIDIMENSIONAL USE OF SCALOGRAM ANALYSIS

In the past, scalogram analysis has been used by sociologists, psychologists, and political scientists as a means of measuring attitudes, but only rarely for other purposes. Louis Guttman, who was largely responsible for the formulation and early development of scalogram analysis, has used it almost exclusively for attitudinal measurement. However, his definition of this tool as "a simple method for testing a series of qualitative items for unidimensionality" (Guttman, 1950a: 46) would not appear to bar its use in other areas. Indeed, Guttman (1950b: 88) also said that it is applicable "to any universe of qualitative data of any science, obtained by any means of observation."

Quite recently some anthropologists have turned to the Guttman scaling as a means of studying cultural evolution. For example, Carneiro (1962) has shown that eight culture traits scale perfectly for eight primitive tribes in South America.[2] Scalogram analysis has also been used by anthropologists and sociologists in studying the evolution of legal institutions (Schwartz and Miller, 1964), bureaucratic elements in non-industrial societies (Udy, 1958), and even community development (Young and Young, 1960).[3] It has not, however, been applied to the more general area of political development. It is entirely possible that scalogram analysis has not been used in this area because it would require a careful delineation of the various characteristics of the developmental process. Admittedly, data for all desired characteristics are not available, and thus the profile of development will not be ideal. However, it should be adequate for preliminary studies.

The advantages in the use of scalogram analysis to measure political development would appear to be far greater than the difficulties involved. First of all, the Guttman scaling will allow one to determine whether or not groups of nations share a developmental pattern (as so many assume without offering any evidence); and second, if the existence of such a pattern is established, that some scalogram can be used in the analysis of the developmental process itself. The scalogram will yield not only a rank ordering of the nations being studied, but also, an ordering of the characteristics used to measure their development. Nations may be ranked from the most to the least developed (or from modern to traditional). Each nation will have all the characteristics of the nations below it on the scale and may have additional ones as well. Similarly, developmental characteristics can be ranked as to frequency of occurrence—a characteristic will appear at least as often as those to its right (or left) on the scale, and perhaps more often. Also, given the nature of this ordering of characteristics, there exists at least the possibility that these characteristics may also be ordered in time.[4]

LATIN AMERICA–SAMPLE PROTOTYPE AREA

Before the actual construction of a scalogram of political development, it is necessary to decide upon the polities to be scaled and the characteristics to be used as a means of measuring development. Selection of polities is, of course, the easier of the two. Although it may be possible to fit all the world's polities into a single scale, an operation of such magnitude is not essential in a preliminary study such as this. One should be able to determine the usefulness of scalogram analysis as a means of studying political development by using a relatively small sample; thus only the independent polities of Latin America are scaled below.

Prerequisites to Scalogram Construction

In an effort to obtain as many developmental characteristics as possible, the fifty-seven "raw characteristics" used by Banks and Textor (1963) in *A Cross-Polity Survey* were examined.[5] Characteristics of a completely nonpolitical nature (size, population, linguistic homogeneity, and so forth) were eliminated, as were those obviously not discriminatory as far as the polities of Latin America are concerned (the character of the legal system, for example). Also eliminated were characteristics which did not appear to bear any relationship to political development (such as the differentiation between federal and unitary states, or between those with unicameral and bicameral legislatures). Thus only twenty of the fifty-seven raw characteristics were retained:

    (1) government stability
    (2) the representative character of the regime
    (3) freedom of group opposition
    (4) interest articulation by associational groups
    (5) interest articulation by institutional groups
    (6) interest articulation by nonassociational groups
    (7) interest articulation by anomic groups
    (8) interest articulation by political parties
    (9) interest aggregation by political parties
  (10) interest aggregation by the executive

(11) interest aggregation by the legislature
(12) stability of the party system
(13) type of political leadership
(14) horizontal power distribution
(15) current status of the legislature
(16) current status of the executive
(17) current electoral system
(18) freedom of the press
(19) character of the bureaucracy
(20) political participation by the military

Next, using Banks and Textor's evaluations of the Latin American nations, each of these characteristics was dichotomized. For example, Banks and Textor classify the representative character of a regime as (1) polyarchic, (2) limited polyarchic, (3) pseudopolyarchic, or (4) nonpolyarchic. In the construction of the scalogram the Latin American nations were divided into two groups: those with either polyarchic or limited polyarchic regimes, and those with pseudopolyarchic or nonpolyarchic regimes. Most of these characteristics were divided at the mid-point, that is, between the second and third of four classes. However, in some cases, this would have led to extreme marginals, and thus the cutting point was moved to assure several marginals as close as possible to fifty–fifty.[6] After this combining of categories, the following "finished characteristics" were scaled against the twenty Latin American nations:

(a) a modern bureaucracy
(b) a stable political party system
(c) a fully effective legislature
(d) significant interest aggregation by political parties
(e) a generally stable government since World War II
(f) at least moderate interest aggregation by the legislature
(g) no more than moderate interest articulation by institutional groups
(h) infrequent interest articulation by anomic groups
(i) at least moderate interest articulation by associational groups
(j) effective horizontal power distribution
(k) at least moderate interest aggregation by the executive
(l) political neutrality of the military
(m) limited or negligible interest articulation by nonassociational groups
(n) nonelitist or only moderately elitist political leadership
(o) the lack of executive dominance
(p) no more than occasional press censorship
(q) a competitive electoral system
(r) present regime of at least partly polyarchic character
(s) at least moderate interest articulation by political parties
(t) freedom of political organization for autonomous groups

A Scalogram of Political Development in Latin America

Nation	Scale type	Highly developed a b c d e f g h i j k l m n o p q r s t	Underdeveloped a b c d e f g h i j k l m n o p q r s t
Uruguay	18		O + + + + + + + + + + + + + + + + + + +
Chile	15		+ + + + + + + + + + + + + + + +
Costa Rica	14		+ + + + + + + + + + + + + + +
Dominican Rep.	11		+ + O + + + + + + + +
Mexico	10		+ + + + + + + + + +
Venezuela	10		+ O + + + + + + + +
Colombia	10		+ + + + + + + + + +
Bolivia	10		+ + + + + + + + + +
Argentina	8		+ + + + + + + +
Panama	8		+ + + + + + + +
Brazil	7		+ + + + + + +
Peru	7		+ + + + + + +
Ecuador	6		+ + + + + +
Honduras	4		+ + + +
Guatemala	2		O O + +
El Salvador	2		O O + +
Nicaragua	1		O O O +
Paraguay	1		O O O +
Cuba	0		
Haiti	0		

Errors: 0 1 0 1 1 0 0 0 1 5 1 1 0 2 0 1 1 0 0 3 0

CR = .95   CS = .79

Error Indication and Interpretation

With only eighteen errors occurring, these characteristics are clearly scalable as far as the nations of Latin America are concerned. The coefficient reproducibility (CR) is .95 and the coefficient scalability (CS) is .79. Of the eighteen errors, eleven are clustered in two areas. For example, the only nation with more than two errors is Mexico with seven errors. If one were to predict the nation least likely to follow the normal course of political development, Mexico would probably have been the choice. That nation is unique in at least one respect, for a full half-century it underwent fundamental social, economic, and political change as the result of a real revolution. Some might argue that Cuba and Bolivia should also appear as deviants on the scalogram since they too are in the process of revolution, but their revolutions are a relatively recent phenomenon. Certainly the degree of change in Bolivia since 1952 does not compare favorably with that of Mexico since 1910. In short, Mexico evidently is not scalable in terms of the characteristics chosen; that is, there are other important variables involved in its case—the most important is almost certainly its revolution.[7]

If Mexico were removed from the scalogram, four of the eleven errors would occur in a single characteristic—interest articulation by associational groups. It may be that this characteristic is simply not scalable, that in Latin America it is not a component of political development.[8] If the Latin American nations, minus Mexico, were scaled with the remaining characteristics, only seven errors are present. On such a scalogram the CR is .98 and the CS is .91, both extremely high.

As mentioned above, the scalogram gives an approximate ordering of nations according to their degree of political development, while at the same time ordering the characteristics used to measure that development. In the scalogram shown, the ranking of nations approximates that which a specialist in Latin American politics might devise intuitively.[9] The author would probably move Argentina up slightly and the Dominican Republic down. However, his evaluations of the various characteristics for these nations might differ sufficiently from those of Banks and Textor to allow the scalogram itself to take care of these shifts.

With regard to the ordering of characteristics, it will be noted that the removal of Mexico and characteristic (i) left only seven errors to mar an otherwise perfect scale. These errors involve: (1) ineffective horizontal power distribution in Brazil, (2) limited interest aggregation by the executive in Chile, (3) significant interest articulation by nonassociational groups in Bolivia, (4) the lack of freedom of the press in Venezuela, (5) infrequent interest articulation by anomic groups in Nicaragua, (6) limited interest articulation by political parties in the Dominican Republic, and (7) limited interest articulation by political parties in Costa Rica. (The ease with which such deviant cases may be identified is one of the major advantages of scalogram analysis.)

Each of these errors can probably be explained. For example, Venezuela has a rather strict press censorship. This in itself is not surprising because it is also true of seven other Latin American states. However, the scalogram indicates that no other nation in this area of the world which has a regime of at least partly polyarchic character, a competitive electoral system, and freedom of political organization, at the same time has strict press censorship. There should then be some peculiar reason for its existence in Venezuela. Students of Venezuelan politics might well explain this by pointing out that that nation is not committed to press censorship as such, but is forced to resort to it as a means of combatting subversion by Communists and Castroites.

Other deviant cases might be examined in much the same manner. None appears important as an isolated fact, yet each involves departure from a remarkably uniform pattern of political development, and each can probably be explained in terms of peculiar—and more likely than not, temporary—circumstances.

Advantages and Disadvantages of Scalogram Analysis

It must be pointed out that this method of scaling political development is by no means ideal. There are several problems; the most important stems from two factors: the type of data used here to measure political development and limitations inherent in scalogram analysis. With regard to the former, there are two major problems. Firstly, a great deal of the data are "soft" or judgmental rather than "hard" or factual; thus there is always the possibility that the judgments themselves are in error. Secondly, a more serious limitation is that these data are static. The "finished characteristics" in *A Cross-Polity Survey* were based upon the situation at one specific period, and thus one is in the uncomfortable position of analyzing a dynamic phenomenon with static data. These problems are typical of those confronting the social scientist who frequently must use data not readily susceptible to quantification. As reliable quantified data become more available, one will be able to have more confidence in studies such as this. This does not mean, however, that one should await the availability of absolutely perfect data.

Scalogram analysis, itself, also has some limitations. Firstly, it must be pointed out that while the scalogram demonstrates the unidimensionality of the characteristics used, at least in the case of the Latin American nations, it does not of necessity demonstrate the unidimensionality of the concept of political development—unless it can be assumed that these characteristics comprise an adequate index of this concept. This is something which must be determined by the individual, for there is no independent measure of validity. Secondly, Guttman scale types are not of equal interval. Thus the interval between scale types 7 and 8 may be larger, equal to, or smaller than the interval between scale types 10 and 11. Therefore one cannot assume that Honduras is half as well developed as Argentina, nor that there is the same difference in degree of development between Chile and Costa Rica as between Ecuador and Peru. Nevertheless, scalogram analysis still offers unique advantages:

(1) It can be used to demonstrate the existence of a pattern of political development shared by various nations.

(2) It can be used to rank nations according to their relative degrees of development.

(3) It can be used to rank developmental characteristics according to the frequency of their occurrence.

(4) It can be used to determine which nations depart from a general pattern of development, and the manner of this departure.

All this can be done in a *single* process. It is the contention of the author that such advantages more than compensate for the problems involved.

NOTES

1. One might ask, for example, why James Coleman (1960) places Indonesia in a "tutelary democracy" class and Thailand in a "modernizing oligarchy" class, when his table—Functional Specificity of Structure—shows that in both nations, there is over participation in the performance of governmental functions by the executive, bureaucracy, and army, but not by religious organizations or dominant parties. (The assignment of polities to various classes is far less arbitrary in Coleman's study than in almost any other study.)

2. See also the critique of this paper by Ward H. Goodenough in Goodenough (1963).

3. See also Young and Young (1962).

4. This is a point very much in dispute at this time. See Hawkins and Jackson (1957), Udy (1962), Udy (1965), and Schwartz (1965).

5. As might be expected, this work does not include every desired characteristic. As the authors explain on page 6, "some of the characteristics that we would like to have used were discarded for conceptual reasons, and others, because adequate data for a sufficient number of polities proved unavailable." Within this limitation, they have selected and adapted "every possible raw characteristic that gave promise of being workable and analytically powerful."

6. While it is true that combining of categories may have the tendency to raise artificially the coefficient of reproducibility, this is not the case with the coefficient of scalability, which also has been computed for the scalogram presented here. See Menzel (1953).

7. One might put forward the hypothesis that political development in Latin America has, on the whole, been relatively random in nature, and that the development pattern in Mexico, on the other hand, has been quite rigorously planned (at least for the past several years); thus, Mexico's deviation on the scalogram.

8. Or, it might be that interest articulation to associational groups needs to be measured in some manner different from that employed by Banks and Textor (1963).

9. See Fitzgibbon and Johnson (1961). Fitzgibbon asked specialists on Latin America to rank the twenty nations of that area (excellent, good, average, poor, or

insignificant) in respect to 15 criteria "which had an apparent relationship to the sum total of democratic attainment. . . ." (Several of these criteria approximate closely the characteristics used here as a measure of political development.) The rank order coefficient of correlation between the scalogram ranking and that of Fitzgibbon and Johnson is .72; the only serious disagreement is in the position of the Dominican Republic. If the Dominican Republic were removed from consideration, rho would be .84.

REFERENCES

APTER, D.E. (1963) "Systems, process and politics of economic development." Pp. 135-158 in B.F. Hoselitz and W.E. Moore, Eds., *Industrialization and Society.* s' Gravenhage: Mouton.

BANKS, A.S. and R.B. TEXTOR (1963) *A Cross-Polity Survey.* Cambridge: MIT Press.

CARNEIRO, R. (1962) "Scale analysis as an instrument for the study of cultural evolution." *Southwestern Journal of Anthropology* 17: 149-169.

COLEMAN, J. (1960) "The political systems of developing areas." Pp. 564-565 in *Politics of the Developing Areas.* Princeton: Princeton University Press.

FITZGIBBON, R.H. and K.F. JOHNSON (1961) "Measurement of Latin American political change." *American Political Science Review* 55 (September): 515-526.

GOODENOUGH, W.H. (1963) "Some applications of Guttman Scale Analysis to ethnography and culture theory." *Southwestern Journal of Anthropology* 19 (Autumn): 235-250.

GUTTMAN, L. (1950a) "The problem of attitude and opinion measurement." In S.A. Stouffer et al., Eds., *Measurement and Prediction*, Vol. IV of Studies in Social Psychology in World War II. Princeton: Princeton University Press.

— (1950b) "The basis of scalogram analysis." In S.A. Stouffer et al., Eds., *Measurement and Prediction*, Vol. IV of Studies in Social Psychology in World War II. Princeton: Princeton University Press.

HAWKINS, N.G. and J.K. JACKSON (1957) "Scale analysis and the prediction of the life process." *American Sociological Review* 22 (October): 579-591.

MENZEL, H. (1953) "A new coefficient for scalogram analysis." *Public Opinion Quarterly* 17 (Summer): 268-280.

MILLIKEN, M.F. and D.L.M. BLACKMER, Eds. (1961) *The Emerging Nations.* Boston: Little, Brown.

SCHWARTZ, R.D. and J.C. MILLER (1964) "Legal evolution and societal complexity." *American Journal of Sociology* 70 (September): 159-169.

SCHWARTZ, R.D. (1965) "Reply." *American Journal of Sociology* 70 (March): 627-628.

SHILS, E. (1962) *Political Development in New States.* s' Gravenhage: Mouton.

UDY, S.H., JR. (1958) "Bureaucratic elements in organizations: some research findings." *American Sociological Review* 23 (August): 415-418.

— (1962) "Administrative rationality, social setting, and organizational development." *American Journal of Sociology* 58 (November): 299-308.

— (1965) "Dynamic inferences from static data." *American Journal of Sociology* 70 (March): 625-627.

YOUNG, F.W. and R.C. YOUNG (1960) "Social integration and change in twenty-four Mexican villages." *Economic Development and Cultural Change* 8 (July): 366–377.

YOUNG, F.W. and R.W. YOUNG (1962) "The sequence and direction of community growth: a cross-cultural generalization." *Rural Sociology* 27 (December): 374–386.

15 A Factor Analysis of the Interrelationship Between Social and Political Variables and per capita Gross National Product

IRMA ADELMAN and CYNTHIA TAFT MORRIS

The interdependence of economic growth and sociopolitical change is generally recognized by social scientists. Development economists in particular, are aware that key economic functions used in analyzing advanced economies may take quite different forms in less-developed countries for reasons which are largely political, social and institutional (see, for example, Hoselitz, 1957: 28–41 and Higgins, 1963: 141–251 esp. 178–182). However, efforts to extend growth analyses to include noneconomic factors are hampered by the absence of empirical knowledge about the manner in which they operate.

The best method for studying the interaction of economic and noneconomic forces in development would clearly be joint research by interdisciplinary teams of social scientists. However, few noneconomists have shown interest in comparative *empirical* investigation of the process of economic growth.[1] It may be desirable, therefore, for development economists to take the initiative in pursuing and stimulating empirical research into the complex interrelationships determining the course of development.

Authors' Note: We are grateful to H. B. Chenery for making this study possible. We are indebted to David Cole, Clarence Gulick, Joan Nelson and Alan Strout for helpful comments and suggestions at various stages of this investigation. A large number of regional and country experts at the Agency for International Development and the Department of State were extremely helpful in the classification of individual countries with respect to the various social and political indicators included in the study. Final responsibility for both the country classifications and the results of the study rests, of course, with the authors.

Reprinted from the *Quarterly Journal of Economics*, Volume LXXIX, pages 555–578, by permission of the authors and the publisher. Copyright © 1965 by the President and Fellows of Harvard College.

The current analysis of sociopolitical and institutional influences upon development is a modest attempt to gain more precise empirical knowledge about the extent and nature of interdependence of economic and noneconomic aspects of the development process. Such an analysis, undertaken by economists, may serve two purposes. First, it may suggest hypotheses relating noneconomic to economic variables which are both suitable for testing by more intensive analyses and relevant to the central concerns of development economics. Second, it may underscore the need felt by economists for more exact knowledge about the interrelationships of the development process and thus stimulate joint research efforts by economists and members of other disciplines.

More specifically, an attempt is made in this paper to gain some semiquantitative insights into the interaction of various types of social and political change with the level of economic development. For this purpose, the techniques of factor analysis[2] are applied to per capita income and to a large number of indexes representing the social and political structure of 74 less-developed countries in the period 1957–62. Purely economic variables (other than income per head) have been omitted in order to analyze the nature of the interdependence between broad levels of economic development and the transformation of sociopolitical institutions and cultural values associated with industrialization and urbanization.

The results of the analysis show that a remarkably high percentage of intercountry variations in the levels of economic development (66 percent) are associated with differences in noneconomic characteristics. Thus it would appear that it is just as reasonable to look at underdevelopment as a social and political phenomenon as it is to analyze it in terms of intercountry differences in economic structure. That is not to say, of course, that economic forces do not play a significant role in accounting for cross-country variations in dynamic economic performance, especially once the take-off stage has been reached. Nor should the relationships found be interpreted in a causal sense. The results of the factor analysis neither demonstrate that economic growth is caused by sociopolitical transformations nor indicate that variations in development levels determine patterns of social and political change. Rather they suggest the existence of a systematic pattern of interaction among mutually interdependent economic, social and political forces, all of which combine to generate a unified complex of change in the style of life of a community.

Choice of Social and Political Variables

Since factor analysis can use as data inputs a relatively large number of intercorrelated variables, a broad selection of indicators of the social and political structure of 74 less-developed countries during the period 1957–62 was included in our study of differences in levels of economic development.

The social characteristics included were selected to depict important aspects of the social changes associated with urbanization and industrialization, such as the modernization of communication, education and outlook. The choice of political indicators for our study was designed to summarize leading aspects of the growth of modern nation states. In addition, several characteristics represent the quality and orientation of political administration and leadership and the importance of key interest groups within a nation.[3]

The complete list of the social and political characteristics included in the final version of the factor analysis is as follows: (1) per capita GNP, (2) size of the traditional agricultural sector, (3) character of the basic social organization, (4) extent of literacy, (5) extent of mass communication, (6) degree of cultural and ethnic homogeneity, (7) significance of an indigenous middle class, (8) degree of modernization of outlook, (9) extent of social mobility, (10) effectiveness of democratic institutions, (11) degree of freedom of political opposition and the press, (12) degree of factionalization of political parties, (13) basis of the political party system, (14) strength of the labor movement, (15) political strength of the military, (16) degree of administrative efficiency, (17) degree of centralization of political power, (18) strength of the traditional elite, (19) extent of nationalism and sense of national unity, (20) degree of commitment of leadership to economic development, (21) extent of government participation in economic activity, (22) degree of social tension, and (23) extent of stability of the political system.

Definition of Variables and Method of Classification

A description of the classification scheme for each sociopolitical indicator incorporated in the study is available from the authors, together with a list of the countries included in the sample. The discussion in this section will be merely illustrative.

The procedures used in defining indicators and in ranking countries differed somewhat for various types of country characteristics. Three different types were distinguished: (a) those for which classification could be based solely on published statistics; (a) those for which it was necessary to combine statistical and qualitative elements; and (c) those which were purely qualitative in nature.

With respect to indicators defined by published statistics, classification of countries was relatively simple. Four to six brackets were established into which countries were grouped. Where data permitted, gradations within categories were also differentiated. The classification scheme for the extent of literacy illustrates the methods used for this type of variable.

Sometimes more than one statistical series was used to describe a characteristic. For example, the variable describing the extent of mass communication is based upon a composite index of newspapers in circulation and radios in use. The principal categories were set in terms of newspapers in circulation and gradations within brackets based on radios in use or licensed.[4] To illustrate, the classification scheme for the B category of the extent of mass communication is as follows:

Classification	Case deciles of newspaper circulation	Case deciles of radios licensed or in use
B+	V	III or IV or V
B	V	VI
B−	VI	V or VI or VII
B−	VII	V

A second type of country characteristic is distinguished by a blend of important judgmental elements with statistical elements. The derivation of the variable describing the extent of social mobility illustrates the procedures employed for this type of characteristic. Since social mobility proved too broad a concept to be described by published statistics alone, two qualitative aspects of mobility, access to leadership elite and extent of ethnic barriers to advancement, were combined in this variable with a statistical measure of educational opportunity.

Four principal categories of social mobility were distinguished in the following manner. The fourth category was defined to include all countries with prohibitive racial or cultural barriers affecting important segments of the population; countries were assigned to this class on the basis of published country studies. Next, the third interval was distinguished on the basis of the extent of educational opportunity; this class comprised all countries not having prohibitive social barriers to mobility in which less than 25 percent of school-age children (5–19) were in school, since de facto social mobility is of necessity low where very few people have access to education.[5] Finally, the remaining countries with over 25 percent of school-age children (5–19) in school were distributed between the first and second categories according to access to membership in leadership elites.[6]

A third and important type of country characteristic included in our study was the purely judgmental one. Even for qualitative indicators, it proved possible to arrive at category descriptions which were sufficiently precise and inclusive to permit unambiguous classification of most countries. Cross-checks to preliminary classifications were obtained by consulting A.I.D. and other country experts and by referring to published country and regional studies.

The classification of countries according to extent of nationalism and senses of national unity illustrates the procedures followed with purely judgmental indicators. Three categories of countries were distinguished: (a) Countries characterized by intense nationalism and strong senses of national unity; (b) Countries having moderate degrees of nationalism and moderate senses of national unity; and (c) Countries in which there was little evidence of nationalism or national unity. A statement of category descriptions together with preliminary country classifications was circulated to some

30 A.I.D. regional experts with a request for corrections and suggestions.[7] It appeared from their comments that the proposed scheme did not distinguish sufficiently between the intensity of nationalism of the leaders and the overall sense of national unity. The final formulation therefore differentiated between two categories of intense nationalism, one for countries with intense nationalism and strong senses of national unity and another for those with intense nationalism and only moderate or limited senses of national unity.[8]

Once the classification of countries according to the various characteristics was complete, each of 74 less-developed countries had been given a letter score, A, A−, B+, B, etc., with respect to 22 social and political indicators.

Since the use of factor analysis requires that the variables be specified numerically, the final task in preparing data inputs was the assignment of scores to the letter classifications. The scale chosen was a simple linear one.[9] It is obvious, of course, that the choice of a numerical scale for qualitative indicators is arbitrary. However, the use of an arbitrary scale does not appear seriously to invalidate the results. For inasmuch as the raw material of factor analysis consists of the correlation matrix among the various social and political characteristics and correlation coefficients are unaffected by linear changes in scale, the results are invariant with respect to linear transformations of the scale used.

Several nonlinear changes in scale were also tried (such as a log transformation and the use of reciprocal), but it was found that the results of these transformations either yielded similar results or made less sense and varied more with changes in sample size than the simple linear scale chosen (see Thurstone, 1961: Chapter 2).

The Factor Analysis: Results and Interpretation

The results of the factor analysis are summarized in the matrix of common factor coefficients presented in Table I. Each entry a_{ij} of the matrix shows the importance of the influence of factor j upon sociopolitical indicator i. More specifically, the entries or "factor loadings" indicate the net correlation between each factor and the observed variables.

The interpretation of factor loadings may more easily be made in terms of the squares of the entries in the factor matrix. Each $(a_{ij})^2$ represents the proportion of the total unit variance of variable i which is explained by factor j, after allowing for the contributions of the other factors. If the first row of the table is examined, it can be seen that 41.5 percent of intercountry variations in per capita GNP are explained by Factor I, an additional 18.5 percent by Factor II, and another 4.8 percent by Factor III; the net contribution of Factor IV is only 1.4 percent.[10]

The right-hand column of the table gives the sum of the squared factor loadings, or the "communality" of each variable. The communality indicates the proportion of the total unit variance explained by all the common factors

TABLE I
Rotated Factor Matrix for Per Capita GNP Together with Twenty-two Social and Political Variables [1]
(74 Less-Developed Countries)

Political and Social Indicators	F_1	F_2	F_3	F_4	h_i^2 (R^2)
1. GNP Per Capita	.64	.43	−.22	.12	.661
2. Size of Traditional Agricultural Sector	−.83	−.32	.21	.03	.832
3. Character of Basic Social Organization	.86	.26	−.05	−.04	.819
4. Extent of Literacy	.83	.37	−.08	.09	.840
5. Extent of Mass Communication	.85	.34	−.08	.04	.843
6. Degree of Cultural and Ethnic Homogeneity	.72	−.30	.07	.17	.646
7. Significance of Indigenous Middle Class	.63	.31	−.40	.05	.658
8. Degree of Modernization of Outlook	.64	.46	−.33	.13	.753
9. Effectiveness of Democratic Institutions	.36	.79	−.17	.19	.815
10. Freedom of Political Opposition and Press	.27	.86	.04	.08	.829
11. Degree of Factionalization of Political Parties	.33	.78	.07	−.30	.810
12. Basis of Political Party System	.42	.68	−.06	−.11	.657
13. Strength of Labor Movement	.29	.71	−.34	.08	.715
14. Political Strength of the Military	.38	−.58	.29	−.36	.690
15. Degree of Administrative Efficiency	.30	.53	−.48	.20	.636
16. Degree of Centralization of Political Power	−.03	−.76	.20	−.07	.617
17. Extent of Social Mobility	.42	.14	−.55	.24	.549
18. Strength of Traditional Elite	.03	.15	.82	−.04	.700
19. Extent of Nationalism and Sense of National Unity	.61	−.05	−.57 [3]	−.01	.694
20. Extent of Leadership Commitment to Development	.11	.21	−.75	.29	.696
21. Extent of Government Participation in Economic Activity	.27	−.41	−.48	−.41	.638
22. Degree of Social Tension	−.23	.03	.08	−.84	.771
23. Extent of Stability of Political System	.04	.08	−.24	.86	.808

1. Boxes indicate the factor to which each variable has been assigned.
2. The rotation of the factor matrix is performed by the varimax system. See H. H. Harman, *Modern Factor Analysis, op. cit.*, pp. 158ff.
3. Since the loadings for the indicator of extent of nationalism are not significantly different in Factors I and III, this variable is assigned to that factor to which it is judged to have the closest affinity.

A Factor Analysis of Interrelationship

taken together and is thus analogous to R^2 in regression analysis. The communality of per capita GNP, for example, is:

$$(.64)^2+(.43)^2+(-22.)^2+(.12)^2 = .661.$$

That is to say, 66 percent of intercountry variations in per capita GNP are associated with the four common factors which are extracted from the 22 sociopolitical variables incorporated in our analysis. This is a striking result which might not be expected from an analysis which excludes economic factors from its explanatory variables.

The matrix of factor loadings, in addition to indicating the weight of each factor in explaining the observed variables, provides the basis for grouping the variables into common factors. Each variable may reasonably be assigned to that factor with which it shows the closest linear relationship, i.e., that factor in which it has the highest loading. Where loadings of a variable in two factors are very close, the variable has been assigned to the one with which it is judged to have the closest affinity.[11] Table I lists, first, indicators which have their highest loading in Factor I, then those with highest loadings in Factor II, III and IV successively. Boxes indicate the loading in that factor to which each indicator is assigned.

Once variables are assigned to common factors, the factors need to be "identified" by giving a reasonable explanation of the underlying forces which they may be interpreted to represent. To quote Thurstone (1961: 61), who pioneered the use of factor analysis in psychology:

> The derived variables are of scientific interest only insofar as they represent processes or parameters that involve the fundamental concepts of the science involved.

We shall, therefore, proceed to identify the factors which are specified in the results of our statistical analysis.

The First Factor. The characteristics having their highest loadings in Factor I are: size of the traditional sector, character of the basic social organization, extent of literacy, extent of mass communication, degree of cultural homogeneity, significance of an indigenous middle class, and degree of modernization. Thus, this factor obviously portrays the social and cultural changes accompanying urbanization and industrialization.

More specifically, Factor I may be interpreted to represent the processes of change in attitudes and institutions associated with the breakdown of traditional social organization. Social change may be viewed as taking place through the mechanism of differentiation and of integration of social structure (see Smelser, 1963: 32 ff.). Differentiation involves "the establishment of more specialized and autonomous social units" (Smelser, 1963: 33), integration is the process which coordinates and fuses the interactions of specialized social entities.

Three variables with high loadings in this factor depict the process of social differentiation: character of the basic social organization groups countries according to the degree of differentiation of nuclear family (the parent-children unit) from extended kinship, village and tribal complexes; size of the traditional sector measures the extent to which self-sufficient family-community economic units have broken up; and strength of an indigenous middle class indicates the importance of a specialized group whose economic activities are removed from traditional socioeconomic contexts.

The process of social integration is also portrayed by several variables. Improvements in mass communication media, increases in literacy and the growth of linguistic homogeneity may all be viewed as part of the evolution of modern mechanisms which tend to weld together relatively diversified social units.[12]

The final variable composing Factor I, degree of modernization, summarizes fundamental changes in sociocultural attitudes which typically accompany urbanization and industrialization. It is an over-all indicator of the extent to which attachments to traditionalism and traditional society have lost their strength.

None of the associations evident in Factor I is surprising. Thus we find that: (a) size of the traditional agricultural sector is negatively related to per capita GNP; (b) less specialized kinship forms—the tribe, the clan, and the extended family—tend to be found in countries with low per capita income; (c) level of education, extent of mass communication, and degree of linguistic homogeneity are positively correlated with average GNP; and (d) strength of an indigenous middle class and extent of modernization of outlook vary directly with per capita income.

The finding that levels of economic development are closely associated with degree of specialization and integration of social structure is a familiar one (see, for example, Moore, 1963: 229–368). The rationalization and specialization of economic roles reflected in the decline of traditional social organization and the rise of the middle class are essential concomitants to the creation of an institutional framework favorable to economic change. At the same time, improvements in communication and education and modernization of outlook both promote the integration of specialized social units and also contribute to an increase in receptivity to technical and organizational innovations which is essential to successful economic performance. In general, therefore, Factor I expresses the strong interaction between economic development and degree of rationalization of social behavior, values and institutions.

The Second Factor. The sociopolitical indicators with their highest loadings in Factor II are strength of democratic institutions, freedom of political opposition, degree of factionalization of political parties, basis of the political party system, strength of the labor movement, political strength of the military, degree of administrative efficiency, and degree of centralization of political power. These are all indicators which describe variations among countries in political systems.

In particular, the pattern of associations incorporated in Factor II is strongly suggestive of broad historical and contemporary differences between the political organization of the countries of Western Europe and the North Atlantic and those of the rest of the world. An increase in this factor may be interpreted to represent a movement along a scale which ranges from centralized authoritarian political forms to Western-type parliamentary systems. Such an interpretation is consistent with the particular juxtaposition of characteristics subsumed in the factor. Thus, a positive change in Factor II is composed of (a) increases in the effectiveness of democratic institutions, freedom of political opposition, factionalization of political parties, strength of the labor movement, and efficiency of public administration; (b) a movement from political parties emphasizing considerations of national unity toward those stressing ideological platforms; and (c) decreases in the strength of the military and in the extent of centralization. Historically, it is in Western Europe that a pattern of change occurred in which effective parliamentary institutions were associated with strong labor movements, weak political strength of the military and decentralization of political power. This factor, therefore, may be interpreted to represent the extent of political Westernization.

The coefficients resulting from the factor analysis indicate that a typically Western configuration of political traits is generally associated with higher average income. Thus, the variable representing the basis of party system shows that there exists a tendency for high-income nations to have ideologically based or personalistic multiparty systems rather than mass-directed one-party systems. By the same token, countries with high income also tend to have well established labor movements and politically weak military groups. Finally, higher degrees of administrative efficiency and greater decentralization of political power often accompany higher income per head.

The presence of a systematic association between political systems and income per person should not be interpreted from a causal point of view. In our opinion, it is neither direct evidence that the evolution of Western-type democracy brings about more rapid economic growth, nor direct support for the thesis that higher levels of economic development tend to produce more democratic systems. While either theory may be correct, no analysis of covariance (such as correlation study or factor analysis) can rigorously demonstrate which, if any, of the above hypotheses is valid. Indeed, in the present instance, it appears more plausible to us to ascribe the positive association between Factor II and per capita GNP to the existence of common forces which underlie both the transformations of social institutions which typically accompany economic development and the changes in political structure characteristic of the evolution of modern political systems. More specifically, the increased functional specialization and the evolution of new mechanisms for integrating society, which are both familiar concomitants of economic development, appear to be as basic to the Westernization of political structure[13] as they are to the social changes characterizing industrialization. In addition, fundamental to the processes of both socioeconomic and political change is a transformation of basic attitudes affecting the habits, beliefs and emotions of the individual members of society. It is this transformation of individual outlook which tends to generate not only the receptivity to technical change, enterprise and initiative which are crucial to economic growth, but also the acceptance of the breakdown of ascriptive traditional norms which is essential to the creation of political institutions which can incorporate continuing social and political change. We therefore favor a more eclectic, general equilibrium, point of view.

The Third Factor. Factor III (which accounts for 5 percent of total unit variance) is based upon five sociopolitical characteristics: strength of the traditional elite, extent of nationalism, degree of leadership commitment to development, extent of government participation in economic activity, and extent of social mobility.[14] The character of leadership and the nature of leadership strategies provide the common bond for these indicators.

At one end of the scale are leaders motivated by strong attachment to the preservation of traditional society. Access to these traditional leadership groups is limited to particular social, cultural or ethnic strata of the population. At the other end of the scale are intensely nationalistic leaderships committed to industrialization and to state direction of economic development. A movement along the scale thus implies a decline in the power of traditional elites and a rise in the strength of nationalistic "industrializing elites."[15]

The signs of the loadings in Factor III indicate a tendency for countries characterized by nationalistic industrializing leaderships and a weakening of the power of traditional elites to have higher average incomes. This positive association of leadership characteristics and income levels is not unexpected. It is well known, for example, that the break-up of control by landed elites over the agricultural surplus is an important precondition for the take-off stage of economic development. The significance for economic growth of the willingness and ability of governments to direct or attract this surplus and other resources into modern sectors is also frequently emphasized.[15] Finally, nationalist forces may accelerate economic advance by weakening regionally based premodern social structures and by focusing nationwide effort upon the tasks of economic, social and political modernization.[17] This tendency for nationalist forces to promote increasingly important central government economic activity has been emphasized by Clark Kerr (1960: 47) and his coauthors:

> While nationalism itself has no social philosophy, and is usually more pragmatic than ideological, it does predispose toward state-directed effort. Nationalism initially is negative—against the old order or the external enemy. This is enough of a platform to gain power but not to rule an economy. There may be no theory in advance as to how to proceed, but there must be a practice, a practice which will almost inevitably involve the state as the only available

mechanism for a great national effort. This tends to lead to the planned economy, to state or state-sponsored investment, to state-controlled labor organizations, to workers dependent on the state for economic benefits and political direction, to state guidance of the new industrialists, to state appeals for hard work and saving, and to a call for unity.

The small proportion of intercountry differences in per capita GNP associated with the variables summarized by Factor III is surprising. It arises in part because, while per capita GNP is an indicator of broad stage of economic development, the leadership characteristics are defined only with respect to the period 1957–62, rather than in terms of the country's entire historical experience. The leadership variables used in this study would undoubtedly be of greater relative importance in an explanation of recent short-term economic performance.

The Fourth Factor. An examination of Factor IV shows a positive relation between per capita GNP and social and political stability. This appears to reflect the fact that the absence of serious social tensions and of grave political instability is a prerequisite for sustained economic growth. This necessity for reasonable stability arises from the well-known interdependence of sociopolitical environment and incentives to save and to invest: the prevalence of tension and instability greatly increases the desire to hoard; an atmosphere of uncertainty tends to promote investment in real estate and commercial activities showing a quick return rather than in productive capital projects requiring longer periods of gestation; frequent changes in political leadership may have detrimental economic effects upon personal savings decisions and business investment activity; and finally, to attract foreign investment in the expansion of productive capacity requires that foreign entrepreneurs be assured of reasonably stable and secure domestic social and political conditions.

The quantitatively small impact of Factor IV results in part from the different time periods reflected in the indicator of development levels and in the stability variables. While per capita GNP is a rough index of a country's long-run achievement in developing its economy, the degrees of social and political stability, as defined in this study, refer to the recent short-run period, 1957–62. Another explanation of the weakness of the relationship between this factor and income per head is that two opposing forces are at work relating growth and stability. On the one hand, the breakdown of traditional social and political structures commonly accompanying the industrialization-urbanization process tends frequently to aggravate internal discontent and tensions, thereby creating a negative association between stability and changes in average income. On the other hand, acute and widespread uncertainty clearly tends to retard economic development, thus producing a long-run tendency for stability and growth to be positively interrelated.

Regional Differences in the Interrelationship Between Per Capita GNP and Social and Political Influences

One of the tests of the validity of a relationship is the consistency with which it appears in subsamples of the larger population analyzed. Tables II, III and IV present the rotated factor matrices for per capita GNP together with series of social and political variables for three regions: Africa (Table II), the Near East and Far East (Table III), and Latin America (Table IV).[18] It may immediately be seen that the over-all communality for per capita GNP in the three subsamples is even larger than for the full sample, ranging as it does from 71 to 80 percent. To obtain "explanation" of variance in the small samples which is as good or better than that found in the large sample is a rather unusual finding which tends to support the reliability of the full sample results.

In all three regional samples, the grouping of variables into (a) a factor representing the social aspects of industrialization, and (b) a factor (or factors) representing the extent of political Westernization is broadly similar. The principal differences in the small sample results lie, on the one hand, in variations in the relative weight of the political as distinct from the social factors and, on the other hand, in the grouping into factors of the leadership and stability variables. These differences and the reasons for them will be discussed in detail below.

Africa. The results of the factor analysis for Africa are very similar to those for the full sample. The grouping of variables into common factors is the same in all but two instances and the directions of the relationships to per capita income are the same within three of the four factors. The interpretation of the forces which Factors I, II and III represent, which was made in analyzing the full sample, appears to hold without important qualification for this subsample. Only Factor IV (representing the character of social and political stability) shows markedly different characteristics.

A principal distinctive feature of the African results is the very large percent of intercountry variations in levels of development explained by Factor I alone. In this region, intercountry differences in social structure and in degrees of modernization of education, communication and outlook account for more than three-quarters of cross-country variations in per capita GNP.[19] The explanation for this striking weight of social influences lies in the concentration in Africa of countries which are characterized by the predominance of preliterate communities. As emphasized by Rostow, an essential prerequisite for successful economic take-off is a social transformation characterized by the breakdown of traditionalism, the spread of literacy, increased communication and greater receptivity to modern ideas and techniques. The results of the regional analysis underscore the fact that most African nations are still in the pre-take-off stage of development in which traditional social structures create critical barriers to growth.

The degree of "explanation" offered by Factors II and III is negligible and

TABLE II
Rotated Factor Matrix for Per Capita GNP Together with Twenty Social and Political Variables [1]
(27 African Countries)

Political and Social Indicators	F_1	F_2	F_3	F_4	h_i^2 (R^2)
1. Per Capita GNP	−.88	.04	.02	.13	.800
2. Size of Traditional Agricultural Sector	.73	−.20	−.36	−.31	.796
3. Extent of Literacy	−.67	.43	.21	.21	.724
4. Extent of Mass Communication	−.93	.17	.01	−.17	.929
5. Degree of Modernization of Outlook	−.71	.22	.30	.36	.775
6. Effectiveness of Democratic Institutions	−.27	.83	−.14	.02	.776
7. Freedom of Political Opposition and Press	.08	.81	−.26	−.12	.739
8. Degree of Factionalization of Political Parties	−.24	.85	−.04	.33	.888
9. Basis of Political Party System	−.12	.64	−.30	.15	.532
10. Strength of Labor Movement	−.20	.75	.04	.02	.596
11. Degree of Administrative Efficiency	−.31	.56	.40	.18	.598
12. Degree of Centralization of Political Power	−.36	−.66	−.16	.08	.593
13. Strength of Traditional Elite	−.39	−.08	.75	.15	.745
14. Extent of Social Mobility	.15	.24	.47	−.43	.485
15. Extent of Nationalism and Sense of National Unity	−.22	−.26	.68	−.01	.576
16. Extent of Leadership Commitment to Development	−.22	−.07	.76	−.10	.639
17. Extent of Government Participation in Economic Activity	−.25	−.18	.51	.08	.357
18. Political Strength of the Military	−.43	−.33	−.01	.61	.675
19. Extent of Stability of Political System	.02	−.15	.19	−.83	.743
20. Degree of Social Tension	−.28	.17	−.04	.84	.817
21. Degree of Cultural and Ethnic Homogeneity	−.39	−.16	−.16	−.50	.456

1. Boxes indicate the factor to which each variable has been assigned.

TABLE III

ROTATED FACTOR MATRIX FOR PER CAPITA GNP TOGETHER WITH TWENTY-TWO SOCIAL AND POLITICAL VARIABLES [1]

(25 Near Eastern and Far Eastern Countries)

Political and Social Indicators	F_1	F_2	F_3	F_4	h_i^2 (R^2)
1. Per Capita GNP	.72	.47	−.14	−.03	.762
2. Size of Traditional Agricultural Sector	−.77 [2]	−.41	.17	−.29	.881
3. Character of Basic Social Organization	.58 [2]	.35	.04	.58	.793
4. Extent of Literacy	.64	.38	−.15	.29	.655
5. Extent of Mass Communication	.82	.33	−.03	.25	.850
6. Degree of Cultural and Ethnic Homogeneity	.79	−.43	−.11	−.15	.831
7. Significance of Indigenous Middle Class	.70	.32	−.09	.37	.747
8. Extent of Social Mobility	.77	−.03	−.16	.38	.765
9. Effectiveness of Democratic Institutions	.27	.85	−.26	.25	.926
10. Freedom of Political Opposition and Press	.31	.88	−.02	.25	.935
11. Degree of Factionalization of Political Parties	.28	.58	.32	.54	.800
12. Strength of Labor Movement	.28	.63	−.11	.39	.639
13. Political Strength of the Military	−.04	−.81	.14	−.08	.688
14. Degree of Centralization of Political Power	−.11	−.87	−.07	−.18	.810
15. Extent of Government Participation in Economic Activity	−.00	−.71	.18	.34	.654
16. Degree of Modernization of Outlook	.40	.52	−.52 [2]	.43	.882
17. Extent of Leadership Commitment to Development	.08	.09	−.73	.49	.781
18. Degree of Social Tension	−.23	.01	.81	.10	.714
19. Extent of Stability of Political System	−.01	.19	−.92	−.05	.883
20. Degree of Administrative Efficiency	.47	.33	−.50 [2]	.51	.851
21. Extent of Nationalism and Sense of National Unity	.48	−.19	−.48	.61	.871
22. Strength of Traditional Elite	−.51	−.13	.09	−.60	.650
23. Basis of Political Party System	.18	.52	.00	.60	.658

1. Boxes indicate the factor to which each variable has been assigned.
2. Variables having loadings which are nearly the same in two factors are assigned to that factor to which they are judged to have the closest affinity.

TABLE IV

ROTATED FACTOR MATRIX FOR PER CAPITA INCOME
TOGETHER WITH TWENTY-ONE SOCIAL AND POLITICAL VARIABLES [1]

(21 Latin American Countries)

Political and Social Indicators	F_1	F_2	F_3	F_4	h^2 (R^2)
1. Per Capita GNP	.62	.46	−.32	−.13	.706
2. Size of Traditional Agricultural Sector	−.81	−.29	.08	.08	.760
3. Extent of Literacy	.87	.24	−.09	.17	.856
4. Extent of Mass Communication	.71	.23	−.41	−.18	.761
5. Degree of Cultural and Ethnic Homogeneity	.80	−.26	.15	−.14	.753
6. Significance of Indigenous Middle Class	.59	.32	−.24	−.26	.581
7. Effectiveness of Democratic Institutions	.52	.68	−.27	−.02	.814
8. Strength of Labor Movement	.23	.79	−.08	−.28	.771
9. Political Strength of the Military	−.17	−.70	.24	.03	.577
10. Degree of Administrative Efficiency	.59	.60	−.38	−.04	.862
11. Degree of Centralization of Power	−.12	−.70	.31	.41	.770
12. Degree of Modernization of Outlook	.55	.70	−.05	−.20	.838
13. Extent of Social Mobility	.35	.74	.36	−.04	.808
14. Strength of Traditional Elite	−.07	−.87	−.22	.17	.841
15. Extent of Leadership Commitment to Development	.05	.83	−.27	−.03	.770
16. Extent of Stability of Political System	.52	.51 [2]	.15	.37	.688
17. Degree of Social Tension	−.37	−.46 [2]	−.26	−.48	.647
18. Freedom of Political Opposition and Press	.45	.27	−.72	.07	.799
19. Degree of Factionalization of Political Parties	.07	−.07	−.82	.05	.677
20. Basis of Political Party System	.00	.41	−.52	−.48	.671
21. Extent of Nationalism and Sense of National Unity	.30	.19	−.06	−.82	.808
22. Extent of Government Participation in Economic Activity	.02	.19	.19	−.78	.681

1. Boxes indicate the factor to which each variable has been assigned.
2. Variables having loadings which are nearly the same in two factors are assigned to that factor to which they are judged to have the closest affinity.

that contributed by Factor IV is less than 2 percent. This lack of a significant interrelationship between the political characteristics summarized in these three factors and per capita income is probably due to the fact that most African countries have not yet experienced the minimal transformations of social institutions required for successful Westernization of political forms.

The character of the stability factor (IV) is yet another distinctive feature of the African results. In this factor higher per capita GNP levels are accompanied by more serious social tensions, greater political instability, stronger military influence,[20] and less cultural homogeneity.[21] The negative association of short-run social and political stability and income levels in Africa probably arises in part because of the tensions and unrest created by the early stages of economic change during which traditional social structures and norms are being undermined and transformed.

Near East and Far East. The results of the factor analysis for the Near East and Far East strongly resemble the results for the 74 country sample. As before, Factor I is the most important factor associated with differences in development levels. The grouping in this factor of the extent of social mobility (which did not appear in the over-all sample) is a logical one, since Factor I has been interpreted to represent the social and cultural changes accompanying industrialization. As premodern social structures are broken down, individual movement between social classes, types of community and occupations becomes freer and facilitates the adaptation of skills to the requirements of economic change.

Factor II with one notable exception contains the same indicators of character and democracy of party system as in the over-all sample.[22] By contrast with the African subsample, this factor accounts for a significant percent of unit variance in income levels. This greater importance of forces of political Westernization probably occurs because in the Near East and Far East economic growth is less critically hindered by traditional social structures than it is in Africa.

Factor III in this sample groups together the two indicators of social and political stability with three variables characterizing central government administrations. Associated with higher per capita income levels are greater modernization of outlook, more leadership commitment to economic development, better administrative efficiency, less social tension and more stability of the political system. This particular pattern of associations is a reasonable one in view of the well-known long-run tendency for greater government efficiency and commitment to economic modernization to promote economic growth. The reason that these relationships between leadership and stability appear only in this sample may be due to the concentration of this subgroup of several higher-income countries in which social and political stability and fairly effective leadership date back a considerable number of years.

In Factor IV, higher per capita GNP is associated with more intense nationalism, weakened power of the traditional elite, and political party systems based on ideological and personalistic considerations rather than upon regional interests or mass-based appeals. The logic of these relationships is self-evident.[23] It should be noted, however, that the influence of these variables in explaining per capita income in the Near East and Far East is extremely small, if not negligible.

Latin America. The results of the factor analysis for Latin America display the most typically regional pattern of the three subsamples. While no important differences emerge in the composition and absolute weight of Factor I, the influences of political Westernization assume a distinctive regional aspect.

In Latin America, two factors, rather than one, represent the impact of Westernization. The first of these includes not only the effectiveness of democratic institutions, strength of the labor movement, degree of administrative efficiency and centralization of political power, as in the full sample, but also indicators of leadership characteristics[24] and of social and political stability. The fusion of these varied elements into a single factor is probably the outcome of the longer historical experience which Latin American countries have had with Westernizing influences.

The second of the political Westernization factors, which alone explains some 10 percent of the total unit variance of income per head, is composed of three indicators of the degree of articulation of political party systems (freedom of political opposition and the press, degree of factionalization, and predominant basis of political party systems). The separation of this subset of political variables into a separate factor emphasizes the fact that they represent more sophisticated forms of political articulation than the other political characteristics incorporated in Factor II of this subgroup. The significant positive association of GNP levels with this factor undoubtedly results from the close relationship between degree of political articulation and degree of urbanization and industrialization. To quote an expert (Blanksten, 1960: 477) on Latin American political development:

> It is typical of Latin America that, with the exception of the landowners and the Church, few interests arising in the rural areas are capable of making themselves heard in national politics. In the cities, however, interest groups form more readily and give voice to the demands of the urbanized sectors of the population. Similarly, new interests find organized expression in consequence of the processes of restratification, secularization, and commercialization.

Factor IV, which contributes insignificantly to the analysis, groups together more intense nationalism with greater government participation in economic activity. This association was also found in the over-all sample.[25]

Summary and Conclusion

In this paper the nature of the systematic interrelationship between income per head and various indicators of social and political structure was explored. In particular, an association was derived between per capita GNP and two aspects of sociopolitical change: the sociocultural concomitants of the industrialization-urbanization process (Factor I) and the Westernization of political institutions (Factor II). The relationship expressed in Factor I indicates a strong tendency for levels of economic development to be positively correlated with the extent of functional differentiation and integration of diverse social units. A similarly significant positive association is evident in Factor II between income levels and the degree of articulation and Westernization of political systems. In contrast, a rather weak relationship appears between broad levels of development and indicators summarizing the character of leadership and the degree of social and political stability in the past decade (Factors III and IV).

The results of the regional studies support the findings of the over-all analysis. In addition, they indicate that the role of the social aspects of the industrialization-urbanization process is overwhelmingly important for low income economies in which the absorptive capacity is sharply limited by the inhibiting nature of the social structure. As the barriers to industrialization imposed by the social institutions become weaker, the importance of the forces summarized in Factor I tends to decline. However, even among countries at higher stages of evolution, the social variables remain the most important element associated with intercountry differences in per capita GNP.

Another feature of the regional analyses is the systematic pattern of variation in the significance of the factor representing the forces of political Westernization. At the early stages, Factor II is of negligible importance; it assumes increasing relevance as social institutions become more adaptable to the requirements of economic growth. This association between more democratic and better articulated and integrated political systems, on the one hand, and levels of economic development, on the other, probably arises because both the ability to generate sustained economic growth and the evolution of more sophisticated political institutions require fundamental changes in mentality characteristic of Western thought patterns. The participant style of life typical of Western culture tends to generate a capacity to adapt existing institutional frameworks to continual economic and social change. This malleability of social structure is essential both to successful entrepreneurial activity and to effective political modernization.

In interpreting the results of this investigation, it is important to bear in mind that the relationships found between levels of economic development and differences in social and political structure are neither caused nor causal. Rather they reflect the interaction of an integrated system of institutional and behavioral change which underlies the process of economic development. As emphasized earlier by one of the authors (Adelman, 1961: 145):

> The phenomenon of underdevelopment must be understood ... in the context of the entire complex of interrelationships that characterize the economic and social life of the community.

The degree of intimate interrelationship found in this analysis between the economic and noneconomic concomitants of a country's historical evolution is rather surprising. It lends support to the views, long held by development economists, that, in the last analysis, the purely economic performance of a community is strongly conditioned by the social and political setting in which economic activity takes place. It would appear that the splitting off of *homo economicus* into a separate analytic entity, a common procedure since Adam Smith in theorizing about growth in advanced economies, is much less suited to countries which have not yet made the transition to self-sustained economic growth.

NOTES

1. There are, of course, excellent analytical and interpretive studies of development by political scientists and sociologists as well as a few studies by anthropologists. *A Cross-Polity Survey* (1964) by Banks and Textor classifies a large number of developed and less-developed countries with respect to a wide variety of political and economic "raw characteristics"; this study provides a considerable amount of data suitable for comparative analyses of political structure. The Yale Political Data Program under the direction of Karl Deutsch has also prepared numerous series of social and political data which can be utilized in comparative analyses of sociopolitical change; see, for instance, Russett et al., *World Handbook of Political and Social Indicators* (1964).

2. For a detailed treatment of the technique of factor analysis, see Harman (1960) and Thurstone (1961).

3. We were obliged at an early stage in classifying countries to reject several indicators which we found could not be formulated with sufficient concreteness to permit unambiguous country classifications. The importance of achievement motivation and social attitudes toward economic activity were indicators which appeared desirable a priori but which we were obliged to reject on this score.

4. These data are published in Russett et al., *World Handbook of Political and Social Indicators* (1964).

5. We used adjusted data on primary and secondary pupils published in Russett et al. (1964), for all countries but a few for which country experts considered that the published data were grossly in error.

6. The principal source of judgmental information used for this purpose was Banks and Textor, *A Cross-Polity Survey* (1964). The Banks and Textor raw characteristic deck became available prior to the publication of *A Cross-Polity Survey*, when the classification of countries on the basis of published sources was underway. It provided basic information for four indicators and valuable cross-checks for ten others.

7. Our use of the suggestions of regional experts may require some comment. Where more than one expert made corrections of an individual country classification which were consistent with respect to direction and degree, these were accepted without further study. Where corrections were consistent with respect to direction but differed somewhat in degree, a rough average of the corrections was made. Where corrections showed marked inconsistency and differences,

an attempt was made to reformulate the categories in an effort to obtain more consistent classification of individual countries.

8. Detailed descriptions of these categories are available from the authors.

9. The linear scale used ranged from 1 to 100, assigning a score of 90 to the highest letter classification, A, and a score of 10 to the lowest letter classification of each characteristic (C, D, E, or F). We then scored the intermediate letters at equidistant intervals between 10 and 90. Plus and minus classifications were not scored at equidistant intervals, but were scored in such a manner that the distance between the plus and minus of different adjacent categories was approximately double the difference between any given letter classification and its plus or minus. This procedure may be illustrated by the following scoring scheme for classifications ranging from A to C, and those ranging from A to D:

Letter classification	Numerical score	Letter classification	Numerical score	Letter classification	Numerical score
A+	100	C+	20	B	60
A	90	C	10	B−	54
A−	80	C−	1	C+	41
B+	60	A+	97	C	35
B	50	A	90	C−	29
B−	40	A−	83	D+	16
		B+	67	D	10
				D−	4

10. Slight differences between these values and the squares of the entries in Table I are due to rounding.

11. This is accepted procedure for combining variables into common factor groups. See, for example, Ferber and Verdoorn (1962: 105). Unfortunately, no tests for the significance of differences in factor loadings exist; however, it is evident that small differences in loadings cannot be considered significant.

12. Emil Durkheim (1949: 41) has pointed out with special emphasis that the increasing division of labor and growing social heterogeneity which accompany industrialization require the creation of new mechanisms for integrating societies.

13. In this connection, J. S. Coleman (1960: 532) writes: "The most general characteristic of [a modern political system] is the relatively high degree of differentiation, explicitness, and functional distinctiveness of political and governmental structures, each of which tends to perform, for the political system as a whole, a regulatory role for the respective political and authoritative functions."

14. The reason for the high loading of the indicator of extent of social mobility in the factor which groups together leadership characteristics is that an important element in the definition of this indicator is the degree of openness or access to membership in the leadership elite.

15. The concept of an industrializing elite is discussed in Kerr et al. (1960: chapter 2).

16. On these points see Rostow (1960: chapter 3).

17. Nationalism may, of course, hinder economic growth if it seriously hampers the contributions to development of foreign investment and entrepreneurial activity.

18. Variables showing little variation within a region (as indicated by regional standard deviation less than one-third of the regional mean) have been eliminated from the regional subsample. The indicator of basic social organization was omitted on this score from the African and Latin American samples. Also omitted from the African sample was the indicator of an indigenous middle class. One country, Israel, was dropped from its subsample because its per capita GNP represented an extreme value for that sample which could have distorted the results of the analysis.

19. As noted above, the indicators of character of basic social organization and of the significance of an indigenous middle class, both associated with Factor I in the full sample, were omitted from the African subsample.

20. The reason for the inclusion in this factor of the political strength of the military is obvious, since increases in political tensions are frequently generated by military coups.

21. A test run of the African subsample omitting South Africa indicated that the presence of the indicator of cultural homogeneity in the stability factor results from the fact that South Africa, the African country with the highest average income and highest score with respect to degree of social tension, is also characterized by marked cultural heterogeneity. When South Africa is omitted from the sample, the indicator of cultural homogeneity is grouped in Factor I as in the full sample.

22. The exception is that the indicator of government participation in economic activity is associated with this factor rather than with the leadership factor; also, it is negatively rather than positively related to income levels. The explanation for this pattern of associations appears to lie in the particular composition of this subsample. At one end of the scale in this sample are several countries (among them, Greece, Japan and Lebanon) which have experienced fairly lengthy periods of indigenously directed Westernization and modernization (with little if any Western colonial rule); these countries have been able to raise their per capita incomes above the average for their regions with important reliance upon private indigenous activity. At the other end of the scale in the sample are several lower-income countries such as Afghanistan, Iran and Cambodia, in which indigenous non-Western religious beliefs and traditions have historically tended to pervade the entire social, political and economic structure; in these countries governments have tended to hamper severely both indigenous and foreign private enterprise.

23. See p. 340 above for the discussion of the third factor for the full sample.

24. The extent of social mobility and strength of the traditional elite, included in this factor, are indicators which express degree of access to leadership groups. The degree of modernization of outlook and the extent of leadership commitment to economic development indicate modernization of leadership.

25. For a discussion of the rationale of this association, see particularly the discussion of the second factor, pp. 338–340, in the full sample.

REFERENCES

ADELMAN, I. (1961) *Theories of Economic Growth and Development.* Stanford: Stanford University Press.

BANKS, A.S. and R.B. TEXTOR (1964) *A Cross-Polity Survey.* Cambridge: MIT Press.

BLANKSTEN, G.I. (1960) "The politics of Latin America." In G.A. Almond and J.S. Coleman, Eds., *The Politics of the Developing Areas*. Princeton: Princeton University Press.

COLEMAN, J.S. (1960) "The political systems of the developing areas." In G.A. Almond and J.S. Coleman, Eds., *The Politics of the Developing Areas*. Princeton: Princeton University Press.

DURKHEIM, E. (1949) *The Division of Labor in Society*. New York: Free Press.

FERBER, R. and P.J. VERDOORN (1962) *Research Methods in Economics and Business*. New York: Macmillan.

HARMAN, H.H. (1960) *Modern Factor Analysis*. Chicago: University of Chicago Press.

HIGGINS, B. (1963) "An economist's view." Pp. 141–251 in *Social Aspects of Economic Development in Latin America*, II. UNESCO.

HOSELITZ, B.F. (1957) "Noneconomic factors in economic development." *American Economic Review* 47 (May): 28–41.

KERR, C. et al. (1960) *Industrialism and the Industrial Man*. Cambridge: Harvard University Press.

MOORE, W.E. (1963) "Industrialization and social change." Pp. 229–368 in B.F. Hoselitz and W.E. Moore, Eds., *Industrialization and Society*. UNESCO.

ROSTOW, W.W. (1960) *The Stages of Economic Growth*. London: Cambridge University Press.

RUSSETT, B.M. et al. (1964) *World Handbook of Political and Social Indicators*. New Haven: Yale University Press.

SMELSER, N. (1963) "Mechanisms of change and adjustments to change." In B.F. Hoselitz and W.E. Moore, Eds., *Industrialization and Society*. UNESCO.

THURSTONE, L.L. (1961) *Multiple Factor Analysis*. Chicago: University of Chicago Press.

16 Communism and Economic Development

ROGER W. BENJAMIN and JOHN H. KAUTSKY

One of the major efforts of students of comparative politics in recent years has been directed at establishing, more or less systematically, relationships between economic development and political change. Much of the literature in this area, perhaps because of its stated or unstated value and policy orientation, has been concerned with the conditions and the prospects for democracy. In the present article, we attempt to correlate economic development with another phenomenon of political change, that of Communism and, more specifically, the strength of Communist parties.

We begin with the hypothesis that the relationship between economic development and Communist party strength is curvilinear.[1] In underdeveloped countries—and these included all Communist-ruled countries at the time the Communist party came to power except East Germany and the Czech sections of Czechoslovakia—Communist parties may be regarded as merely one variety of the modernizing movements that evolved in these countries in response to the impact of Western industrialism.[2] Where no or virtually no modernizing movements have as yet developed, because there has been relatively little impact of Western industrialism and little economic development, there should, then, be no or practically no Communist parties. As economic development proceeds, modernizing movements, and hence also Communist parties, are composed largely of intellectuals and are therefore small. With the further progress of economic development and consequent social mobilization,[3] however, these movements may grow, sometimes to considerable size, as they attract support not only from more intellectuals, but also from

---

Authors' Note: The authors are indebted to their colleague at Washington University, John Sprague, for advice on statistical matters. Financial support of the Washington University Computing Facilities through National Science Foundation Grant G-22296 is also gratefully acknowledged.

Reprinted from *The American Political Science Review*, Volume LXII, pages 110–123, by permission of the authors and the publisher. Copyright © 1968 The American Political Science Association.

incipient and growing labor movements, from urban middle strata, and, more rarely, from peasants.

In the now industrially more advanced countries, where economic development came from within rather than without, Communist parties historically grew out of anarchosyndicalist or socialist movements representing some intellectuals and large numbers of workers more or less alienated from and hostile to their societies and governments. Where, in these countries, economic development is relatively backward (though more advanced than in any of the underdeveloped countries just mentioned) and workers find themselves in a minority in a largely anti-labor society, Communist parties can be expected to be strong. It is at this level of economic development that they reach their greatest strength, especially since they represent not only sizable labor movements and intellectuals in sympathy with them, but also draw support

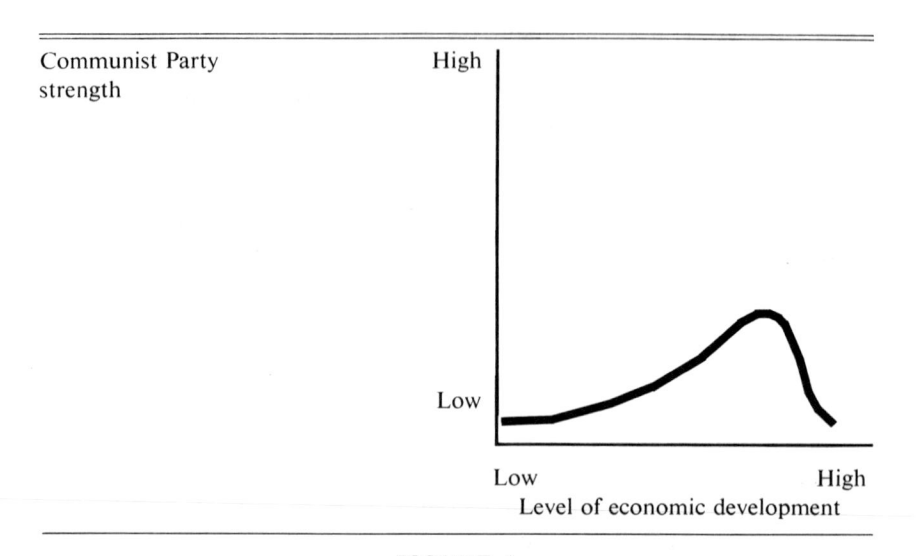

FIGURE 1

PREDICTED RELATIONSHIP BETWEEN LEVEL OF ECONOMIC DEVELOPMENT AND COMMUNIST PARTY STRENGTH

from small peasants and the middle strata of shopkeepers and artisans, still numerous, but feeling threatened by industrialization. As economic development proceeds, however, these latter groups are absorbed by the advanced industrial economy, either to disappear or be converted into farmers or small businessmen, and workers become integrated into the society and are no longer alienated. With high economic development, then, Communist party strength may be expected to be very low.

In the interpretation of our findings we shall draw some further distinctions between types of societies at various levels of economic development and

The Evidence

Figure 1 presents graphically the relationship we predict between Communist party strength and level of economic development. We hypothesize that Communist party strength is lowest at the lowest stage of economic development, rises gradually with economic development, crests at a fairly high level of such development, and declines sharply with the highest level.

We have three potential measures of Communist party strength, our dependent variable: estimated membership of the Communist party, membership of the Communist party, as a percentage of the working-age population, and percent of total vote cast for the Communist party in national elections. There are difficulties with each of these, which finally limited our selection principally to one—estimated membership of the Communist party (see Appendix A).[4] To be sure, that measure does not show Communist membership as a percentage of the total population of the country, but the significance of that proportion is dubious, especially in traditional societies where modernization is just beginning and where the politically active strata of the society are small. We should really know what proportion of these active strata the Communist party membership constitutes, but no such data are available.

Percent of the vote given to the Communist party in national elections might be superior to the other measures in some respects, but here also data limitations make use of this measure impractical. Above all, there are no national elections or only one-party elections in many countries, or Communist parties do not participate in elections, or published election results are unreliable or not subject to comparison. Membership of the Communist party as a percentage of the total working-age population (see Appendix A) removes some of the possible limitations found in the Communist party membership indicator. It is used only as a check on the latter measure to allow the amount of congruence between the two indicators to be computed. All that we are willing and able to assert is that our measures of Communist party membership provide at least strong partial indicators of Communist party strength.

On economic development, our independent variable, we took data and measures from Banks and Textor, *A Cross-Polity Survey* (1963). Six commonly used indices of economic development were selected from the Banks and Textor code (see Appendix B):

(1) level of urbanization
(2) agricultural population as a percentage of the total population
(3) gross national product
(4) per capita gross national product
(5) status of economic development
(6) international financial status

Three screening procedures eliminated all but our sample of 91 countries (see Appendix A for the country listing). First, all countries were eliminated for which we had no estimates of Communist party membership. Secondly, since Communist strength is obviously affected by different factors in Communist-ruled countries than in non-Communist ones and is hence not comparable, we omitted all Communist-ruled countries from our sample. Thirdly, only countries on which *A Cross-Polity Survey* contains data were selected.

To test the hypothesized relationship between Communist party strength and level of economic development, contingency coefficients,[5] frequency distributions and percentages were computed comparing our measures of

TABLE 1

Communist Party Membership	High	9	1		1	
		8	1	1	1	
		7				
		6				
		5		2		1
		4		2	2	1
		3	1	2	2	2
		2	1	2	2	
	Low	1	40	17	6	3
			over 66%	34–66%	16–33%	under 16%
			Agricultural Population as Per Cent of Population			
Index Mean			1.41	2.04	2.93	2.57

Communist party strength—party membership and party membership as a percentage of the working-age population—to the six measures of economic development presented above. If our hypothesis is correct, the countries should be spread along the predicted path, as in Figure 1 above, when the dependent variable, Communist party membership, is compared to the measures of economic development.

First, to view the reliability between the two measures of Communist party strength, the mean and range for the contingency coefficients relating the two Communist party strength indicators and the six economic development measures are presented. The mean contingency coefficient between Communist party membership and the economic development measures is .59, whereas it reaches .55 when Communist party membership as a percentage of the working-age population and the economic development measures are related. The range of the contingency coefficients between Communist party membership and the economic development measures is from .47 to .70, and .53 to .67 between the economic development measures and Communist party membership as a percentage of the working-age population.

Two representative measures of economic development, per capita gross national product (contingency coefficient .60) and agricultural population as percent of total population (c.c. .51), were selected to present the results of the analysis. To put the data in convenient form, an index was constructed for the purpose of evaluating the shape of the plotted relationship between economic development measures and Communist party membership. Table 1 is an example of a raw table out of which the index was constructed.

The index for Communist party membership is simply a 9-point scale which corresponds to the coded categories for Communist party membership shown in Appendix B. The frequencies in each cell were multiplied by the rank in the scale, and the mean for each total category was computed by dividing the result of the multiplication by the column frequency.

Figures 2 and 3 demonstrate the closeness with which the relationship of our economic development measures to Communist party membership agrees with our hypothesized relationship presented in Figure 1.

Interpretation

Our evidence shows, then, that a definite curvilinear relationship exists between degree of economic development and Communist party strength. A correlation, however, is not an explanation; rather, it requires one. Since our initial hypothesis has been corroborated, we may now present a somewhat more refined version of it as our explanation, or at least interpretation, of the relationship we have established.

Even though all Communist parties profess to adhere to the same well-codified ideology, to accept the same organizational model and to pursue the same ultimate goal, and all have, until a few years ago, looked for inspiration, guidance, and support to the Soviet government, we suggest that Communist parties in different types of societies aggregate different interests.[6] We shall now briefly describe five roughly distinguishable types of societies and in each identify the major interests, if any, aggregated by the Communist party.

As stated earlier, we regard Communist parties in underdeveloped countries as modernizing movements. Both their elites and their mass following, if any, are drawn from the same social strata as those of non-Communist modernizing or so-called nationalist movements (see, for example, North, 1952), and their goals are similar and may be summed up in the interrelated demands for political and economic independence from the West, rapid industrialization, and land reform. Indeed, in the past two decades, many policies of the two movements have become more and more alike, the formerly sharp distinctions between Communist and non-Communist modernizers with respect to the symbols they have employed have become more and more blurred, and in the last few years even the distinct organizational character of Communist parties has been breaking down.[7]

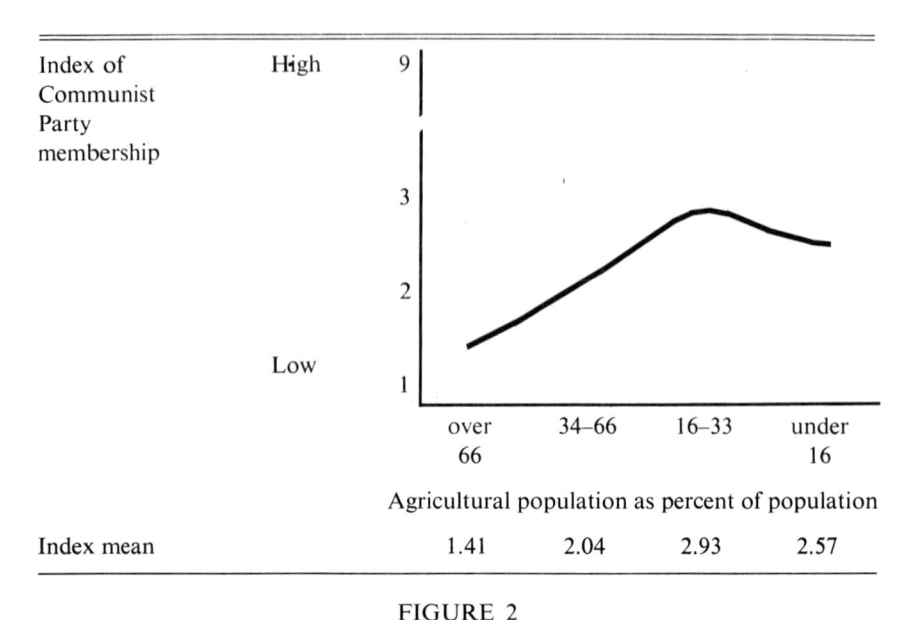

Index of Communist Party membership					
	High	9			
		3			
		2			
	Low	1			
			over 66	34–66	16–33	under 16
			Agricultural population as percent of population			
Index mean			1.41	2.04	2.93	2.57

FIGURE 2

COMMUNIST PARTY MEMBERSHIP AND AGRICULTURAL POPULATION
AS PERCENT OF POPULATION

The anti-colonial and anti-traditional modernizing movements with their characteristic love-hate attitude toward the West (which Communism shared with the others from its beginnings in Russia) are clearly a response to the impact of Western industrialism on traditional societies. The first type of society we must distinguish, then, is one in which this impact has so far been so slight as to elicit little or no response in the form of modernizing movements. Since the interests the Communist parties aggregate in underdeveloped countries are here virtually or entirely nonexistent, it is not surprising that Communist party strength in countries at the lowest level of economic development is, as we found it to be, near or at zero. Among countries to be included in our Societal Type I are Afghanistan, Saudi Arabia, Libya, Ethiopia, Liberia and some of the most backward former French colonies in West and Equatorial Africa.

In societies in the early stages of economic development (Type II), modernizing movements are composed mainly of intellectuals, that is, of those relatively few natives who, usually in the course of acquiring an advanced education by Western standards, whether at home or abroad, have absorbed the Western-industrial values of the desirability of material progress

Communism and Economic Development 359

and abundance, of growing social equality and political participation. In their industrially backward environments, they become anti-colonial revolutionaries favoring industrialization, and where applicable, land reform. Among these intellectuals may be those who think of themselves as Communists, whether

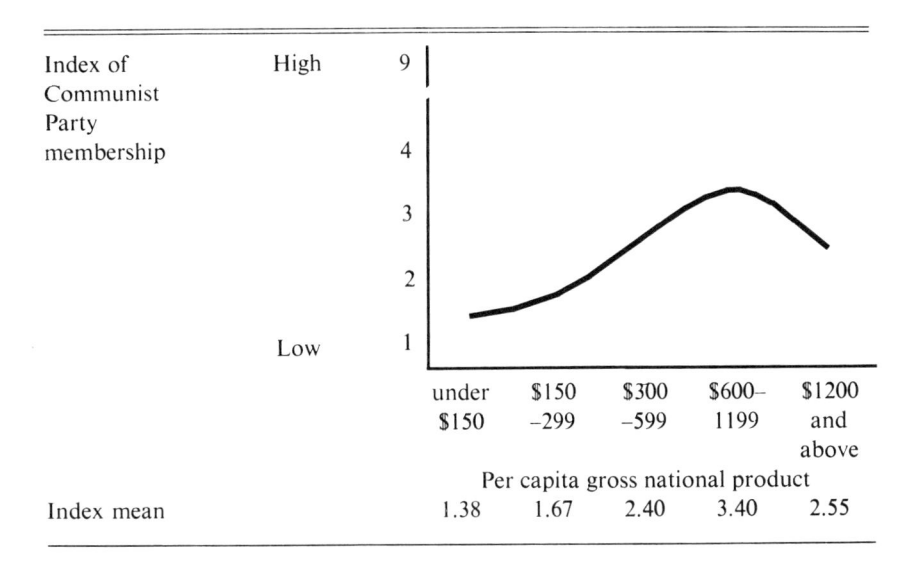

Index of Communist Party membership	High	9					
		4					
		3					
		2					
	Low	1					
			under $150	$150 –299	$300 –599	$600– 1199	$1200 and above
			\multicolumn{5}{c}{Per capita gross national product}
Index mean			1.38	1.67	2.40	3.40	2.55

FIGURE 3

COMMUNIST PARTY MEMBERSHIP AND PER CAPITA GROSS NATIONAL PRODUCT

they are organized in parties or not, and whatever relation of affiliation or rivalry to other modernizing movements they may have. Since modernizing movements are small in this type of society and Communists account generally for only a fraction of them, Communist parties, if they are organized at all, are very small at this level of economic development. Among countries included in Societal Type II are many in Africa and the Middle East not included in Type I as well as some of the least developed countries of Central and South America.

If economic development proceeds (in Societal Type III), at first under the influence of economic colonialism and then perhaps under regimes of revolutionary intellectuals, labor movements of plantation workers and miners, transportation and factory workers may emerge. They are led by intellectuals and furnish a more or less substantial mass base for their modernizing movements—Communist or non-Communist or both. Thus, in India, some trade unions are close to the Congress, others to the Communists; in Indonesia most unions were, until the coup of 1965, Communist-led; in Tunisia they are non-Communist "Nationalist"; in Cuba, in pre-Castro days, some were Communist-controlled; in Argentina most have been Peronist.

Advancing economic development may also threaten the old urban middle class of artisans and shopkeepers who may then become politicized and provide some strength for the anti-colonial movement. And in some instances, where intellectuals are driven out of the cities, they may turn to the peasants, whose traditional village communities may be disintegrating under the impact of economic development, and may organize them to support the modernizing movement, again whether it be Communist or non-Communist. Thus, in China, peasant guerrilla warfare was Communist, in Algeria non-Communist "nationalist," in Vietnam it may be both.

Communist party strength varies widely in countries in Societal Type III. In some, where what mass movements have been developed have come under the leadership of non-Communist intellectuals, the Communist party may be non-existent, as in Ghana and Guinea, or small, as in Egypt (where it dissolved itself in 1965) and in Turkey. In others, however, where the Communist party has organized mass support, especially among workers and peasants, as in India and, above all, until 1965, in Indonesia, it can become a very sizable party. Among underdeveloped countries (other than Communist-ruled ones) it is in those in Societal Type III, i.e., those with the relatively highest economic development, that Communist parties attain their greatest membership strength.

The modernizing movements, Communist or non-Communist, may or may not actually advance their society to the status of industrial ones. If they do, they in effect destroy themselves and are replaced in power either by a combination of other groups, e.g., labor and business groups, or by a technical-managerial intelligentsia. Such an intelligentsia may, then, constitute another type of Communist party that appears where an underdeveloped Communist-ruled country becomes rapidly industrialized. This has happened in Russia beginning under Stalin and is probably happening in Eastern Europe and possibly in China now. Since we are excluding Communist-ruled countries from our comparative survey, we mention this type of society here only parenthetically. There is no need to assume, however, that the replacement of revolutionary intellectuals by managerial-technical intellectuals cannot also take place in non-Communist underdeveloped countries, as may be the case in Mexico. One can assume that the Communist party in such countries should be weak, since a non-Communist one will perform its functions as the organization representing the technical-managerial intelligentsia.

Our first three societal types are found in countries to which economic development has come from without, under the impact of Western industrialism. They represent roughly three levels of economic development and, on the whole, one can expect that the greater the Western impact and economic development the more support there is for the anti-colonial modernizing movement and the better the chance for a big Communist party.

Countries where economic development took place indigenously, too, may be subdivided by the degree to which such development has progressed.

In some of them (Type IV), as compared to the most advanced countries, industrialization came late and slowly and has still not penetrated the entire economy. In such societies, Communist parties express the protests of people drawn chiefly from three strata, two of them large enough to provide mass support for Communism. The principal one is industrial labor, a class that remains a minority in the population and whose trade unions are both numerically and organizationally weak as compared to their counterparts in more advanced countries. Confronting a seemingly permanent strong anti-labor majority of both industrial and preindustrial propertied groups, many workers are alienated, turn their backs on their society and political system, and look for some kind of radical change. This attitude was expressed in the anarcho-syndicalist tradition at the turn of the century, to which Communism has fallen heir.

The second major stratum consists of propertyless or propertied but relatively poor small peasants and of the old middle class of shopkeepers and artisans, groups still very numerous in the non-industrialized regions of the country. They feel threatened by the advances of big industry and big commercial organizations and can thus be attracted by either the Fascists' or the Communists' anti-capitalist posture. Many are ideologically still preoccupied with their ancient fight against the Old Regime and its present-day remnants in the Church, the army and the bureaucracy, and the old revolutionary tradition is hence still alive among them. Since the Communists have inherited much of this, too, such members of the peasantry and old middle class may support the Communist party.

The third stratum from which the Communists draw some strength are the intellectuals. They, too, are frequently deeply attached to the revolutionary tradition, whose ideology their predecessors did so much to fashion. Also, they tend ideologically to associate themselves, often due to a sense of guilt, with the underprivileged proletariat.

Since industrialization has progressed relatively slowly, at least until recently, the groups mentioned above and the social and economic order against which they protest have been subject to little change. Protest has become a permanent feature of the political landscape and so has the vehicle of that protest, the Communist party. The party is thus not only large but also very stable in the support it enjoys and in its organizational structure. It is deeply entrenched in the trade unions and in many social organizations as well as the organs of local government in both industrial and rural areas and thus, paradoxically, becomes a well established and, indeed, widely respected part of the society it professes to reject.

This description, obviously, applies most nearly to France and Italy. In the underdeveloped southern regions of Italy, however, the Communist party may function in part as a modernizing movement, especially as the organizer of a peasantry demanding land reform. With advancing industrialization in Spain, it is conceivable that the formerly anarcho-syndicalist workers and poor peasants may turn to the Communist party there. And possibly the Communist parties of Greece and Finland, too, serve functions of interest aggregation similar to those of France and Italy. It is in countries of Societal Type IV, the "less developed advanced" countries of Europe, especially France and Italy, that Communist parties attain their greatest strength, because the interests they represent in these societies are numerically very large.

Quite a few now more advanced industrialized countries (Type V) share the traditional past of France of a feudal-aristocratic society. As industry grew in their hierarchical environments, workers reacted in large numbers by adhering to class-conscious socialist movements. Historically, the Communist

Societal types				
	over 66	34–66	16–33	under 16
Contingency coefficient .72	Agricultural population as percent of population			
Index mean	1.80	2.96	4.43	4.71

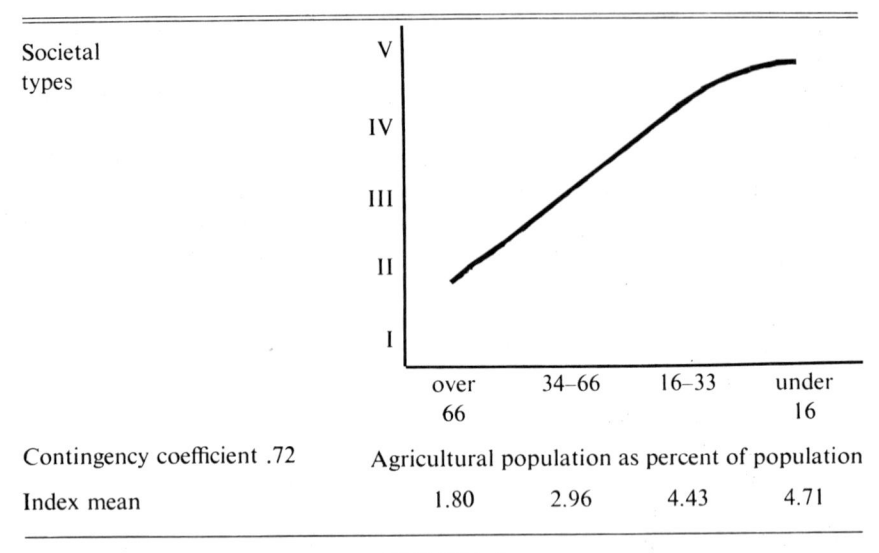

FIGURE 4

THE SOCIETAL TYPES AND AGRICULTURAL POPULATION AS PERCENT OF POPULATION

parties of these countries originated from these movements and they have maintained some strength among radical workers and especially intellectuals in sympathy with them. However, unlike many workers of France and Italy, most of the workers in these advanced countries are not alienated. Through their economic and political power, they have become integrated into their societies and have come to share their growing wealth. As a result, workers, and intellectuals ideologically attached to the labor movement, have turned to socialist labor parties, leaving only insignificant Communist parties to exist on the fringe of the labor movement. As the socialist labor movement is now rapidly losing its radicalism and class consciousness and labor parties are making the corresponding political adjustments, a few workers and particularly some intellectuals deeply attached to the crusading socialist tradition, may yet move over to the Communist parties. Whatever slight gain may accrue to them from that source is likely to be more than offset, however, by losses due to death and defection among old-line adherents for whom the new society produces no replacements. Britain (and perhaps also Australia), Sweden and Denmark and probably Norway, Belgium and the Netherlands, Germany and Austria, and, to a large extent, Japan, all fit into this Societal Type V. In these highly industrialized countries,[8] then, Communist parties must be expected to be very weak.

Some other societies that developed advanced industry from within, but have no significant traditional aristocratic background, need not be sharply distinguished from the last-mentioned category for our purposes here. As industrial labor grew in them, it developed class consciousness or a socialist tradition only exceptionally among some groups of recent immigrants not yet fully adjusted to their new environment and especially among isolated groups of workers, like miners and lumbermen in syndicalist organizations.[9] It was from these sources that the Communists received some initial support in these societies, but they were destined to disappear by absorption. What little is left of Communist strength can hardly be explained in terms of any major social group or movement. It would seem to consist largely of individuals who joined the party in response to needs arising out of personal maladjustment. The United States and Canada are major examples of such societies, though Switzerland, too, and, to some extent, Australia and Norway would seem to fit into this category (which we include in Societal Type V).

Societal Types, Economic Development, and Communist Party Membership

We have now interpreted the relationship between economic development and Communist party strength, which we demonstrated earlier, in terms of different functions performed by Communist parties in different types of societies. We have allocated each non-Communist-ruled country for which adequate data are available to one of our five societal types (see Appendix C). In applying the criteria of the five societal types outlined above, we have made frankly qualitative judgments. Since the criteria are by no means sharply defined, there are many borderline cases in which these judgments have, no doubt, been somewhat arbitrary and are subject to disagreement.

As a check on our allocation of countries to societal types and thus on our interpretation of the curvilinear relationship between economic development and Communist party strength, we related our five societal types both to economic development and to Communist party membership.

To establish whether our societal types measures are highly associated with Banks and Textor (1963) indicators of economic development, we computed a five-point index in a manner similar to that used in the index for Figures 2 and 3 above. Figures 4 and 5 report linear relationships and contingency coefficients at a level which allows us to assume close correspondence between our measures of economic development and our societal types.

Finally, Figure 6 relates the five societal types to Communist party membership. The curve is closely congruent to those in Figures 2 and 3, above, which related Communist party membership to two different measures of economic development.

Societal types: V, IV, III, II, I

Per capita gross national product: under $150, $150–299, $300–599, $600–1199, $1200 and above

Contingency coefficient .74

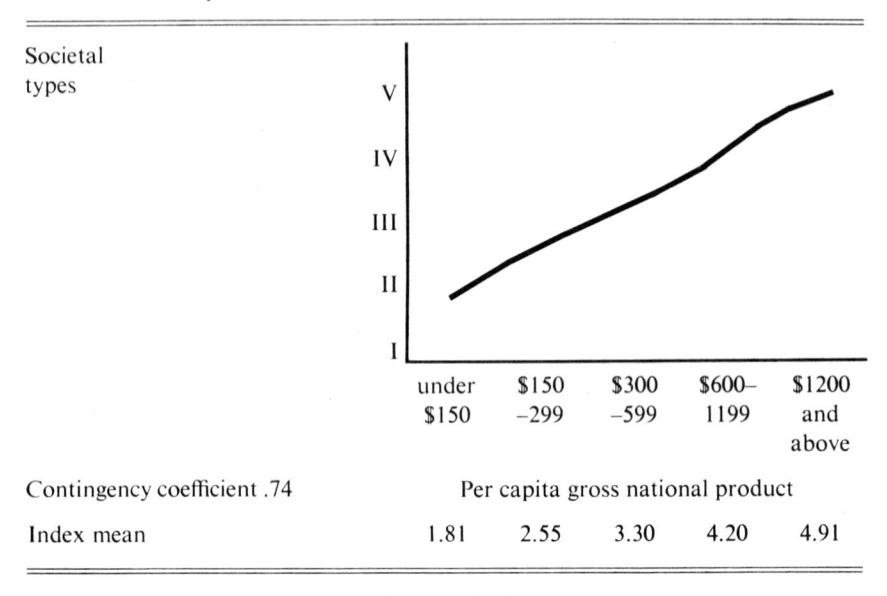

Index mean: 1.81, 2.55, 3.30, 4.20, 4.91

FIGURE 5

THE SOCIETAL TYPES AND PER CAPITA GROSS NATIONAL PRODUCT

Conclusion

Our evidence shows that Communist party membership strength differs with different levels of economic development and our interpretation of this relationship suggests that Communist parties perform different functions, especially with respect to interest aggregation, in different types of societies. Though they have all borne the same name, Communist parties are not all alike. On the other hand, this also suggests that their Communist character, however it may be defined, does not make them unique but leaves them functionally comparable not so much with each other as with other parties and movements, especially those that perform similar functions in similar social and political environments.

It follows further that comparative analysis of Communist parties may best proceed within similar types of societies or societies grouped at similar stages of economic development. If Communist parties are to be compared using countries from different societal types or different levels of economic development, care has to be taken to provide control devices to hold the social and economic development factors constant so as to preclude actually comparing stages of economic development or modernization rather than Communist parties.

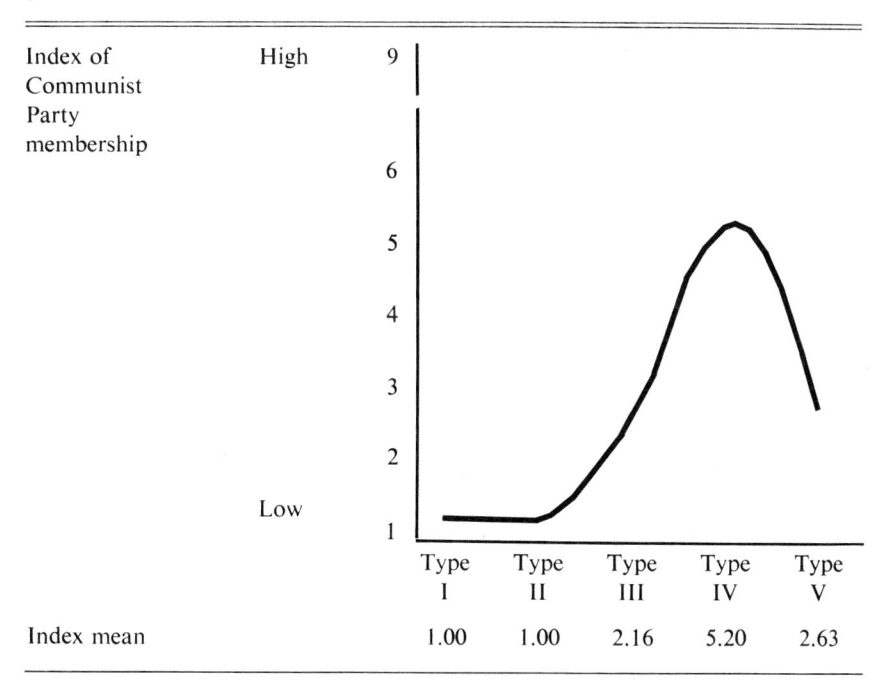

Index of Communist Party membership							
	High	9					
		6					
		5					
		4					
		3					
		2					
	Low	1					
			Type I	Type II	Type III	Type IV	Type V
Index mean			1.00	1.00	2.16	5.20	2.63

FIGURE 6

COMMUNIST PARTY MEMBERSHIP AND SOCIETAL TYPES

As the study of comparative politics has, in recent years, moved from the analysis of individual countries toward a truly comparative approach, there has been a growing awareness among political scientists of the need to integrate the analysis of the politics of the Soviet Union and of other Communist-ruled countries with the study of comparative politics.[10] Economists have for some time applied the same concepts regarding economic development to Communist and non-Communist societies, but it has been historians who have first pointed to some similarities in the political processes accompanying economic development in Communist and non-Communist countries,[11] while political scientists have been relatively slow to study Soviet and Communist politics as a form of the politics of development.[12]

As the Soviet Union has moved from the ill-defined status of a "developing" country to that of a developed one, efforts at comparison with other industrially advanced societies have been made. Economists have noted uniformities in the industrialization process with respect to managers and workers (see, for example, Kerr et al., 1960); sociologists have pointed to the evolution of similar individual values, including a consumer ethic (see especially Inkeles and Bauer, 1959); and more recently two political scientists have undertaken a bold pioneering effort to compare certain aspects of the political systems of the Soviet Union and the United States (see Brzezinski and Huntington, 1964).

Now that political systems ruled by Communist parties are beginning to be drawn into the purview of comparison both with underdeveloped and advanced non-Communist systems and it is thus being recognized that the element of Communism does not render these systems unique, the time may be ripe for a comparison of non-ruling Communist parties with non-Communist parties and movements. It is our hope that our research, reported here, may help open the way to such a further development of the study of comparative politics.

APPENDIX A. ALPHABETICAL LIST OF COUNTRIES AND THEIR COMMUNIST PARTY MEMBERSHIP

Country	C.P. Membership[a]	C.P. Membership as percent of working age population[b]	Country	C.P. Membership[a]	C.P. Membership as percent of working age population[b]
Afghanistan	No known members	.000	Iran	1,500	.015
			Iraq	15,000	.474
Australia	5,000	.078	Ireland	100	.006
Austria	35,000	.760	Israel	2,000	.156
Belgium	11,000	.186	Italy	1,350,000	4.190
Bolivia	6,500	N.A.	Ivory Coast	Nil	.000
Brazil	31,000	N.A.	Jamaica	Nil	.000
Burma	5,000	N.A.	Japan	120,000	.200
Burundi	Nil	.000	Jordan	500	N.A.
Cambodia	100	.004	Laos	100	N.A.
Cameroun	Nil	.000	Lebanon	3,000	N.A.
Canada	3,500	.033	Liberia	Nil	.000
Central African Rep.	Nil	.000	Libya	Nil	.000
Ceylon	1,900	.040	Luxemburg	500	.221
Chad	Nil	.000	Malaysia	2,000	.060
Chile	27,500	.650	Mali	Nil	.000
Colombia	13,000	N.A.	Mauritania	Nil	.000
Congo (Brazzaville)	Nil	.000	Mexico	50,000	.275
Congo (Leopoldville)	Very small	N.A.	Morocco	1,250	.017
Costa Rica	300	.051	Nepal	3,500	N.A.
Cyprus	10,000	3.243	Netherlands	12,000	.169
Dahomey	Nil	.000	New Zealand	500	.039
Denmark	5,000	.170	Nicaragua	250	.031
Ecuador	2,500	N.A.	Niger	Nil	.000
El Salvador	200	.023	Nigeria	Less than 100	N.A.
Ethiopia	Nil	.000	Norway	4,500	.199
Finland	40,000	1.441	Pakistan	3,000	.007
France	260,000	.905	Panama	400	.070
Gabon	Nil	.000	Paraguay	5,000	.600
Germany, Fed. Rep.	50,000	.138	Peru	8,500	.180
Ghana	Nil	.000	Philippines	1,800	.013
Greece	20,000	.366	Portugal	2,000	.035
Guatemala	1,300	N.A.	Rwanda	Nil	.000
Guinea	Nil	.000	Saudi Arabia	Negligible	N.A.
Honduras	2,400	.261	Senegal	Nil	.000
Iceland	1,000	.999	Sierra Leone	Nil	.000
India	135,000	.055	Somalia	Nil	.000
Indonesia	2,000,000	3.800	Spain	5,000	.025

Communism and Economic Development

APPENDIX A (CONTINUED)

Country	C.P. Membership[a]	C.P. Membership as percent of working age population[b]	Country	C.P. Membership[a]	C.P. Membership as percent of working age population[b]
Sudan	2,500	.382	United Arab Rep.	1,000	N.A.
Sweden	20,000	.402	United Kingdom	34,372 (claimed)	.114
Switzerland	Less than 6,000	.167			
Syria	4,000	.190	United States	12,000 (claimed)	.007
Tanganyika	Nil	.000			
Togo	Nil	.000	Upper Volta	Nil	.000
Trinidad	Very small	N.A.	Uruguay	10,000	.600
Turkey	1,000	.007	Venezuela	30,000	.760
Uganda	Nil	.000	Yemen	Negligible	N.A.

[a] Source: U.S. Department of State (1965).

[b] Calculated from working-age (15–64) population figures obtained from *United Nations Statistical Yearbook* (New York: United Nations Statistical Office, 1963).

APPENDIX B. CODE

The following measures and categories were used in our research.[13]

(1) Membership of Communist parties:

1. 5,000 and below
2. 5,001– 10,000
3. 10,001– 20,000
4. 20,001– 35,000
5. 35,001– 50,000
6. 50,001– 75,000
7. 75,001– 100,000
8. 100,001–1,000,000
9. 1,000,001 and above
10. N.A.

(2) Membership of Communist party as percent of working age population:

0. .25 and below
1. .26–.50
2. .51–1.0
3. 1.1–5
4. N.A.

APPENDIX B (CONTINUED)

(3) Level of urbanization
  1. High (20 percent or more of population in cities of 20,000 or more and 12.5 percent or more of population in cities of 100,000 or more)
  2. Low (less than 20 percent of population in cities of 20,000 or more and less than 12.5 percent of population in cities of 100,000 or more)
  3. Ambiguous
  4. Unascertained

(4) Agricultural population as percent of total population:
  1. High (over 66 percent)
  2. Medium (34–66 percent)
  3. Low (16–33 percent)
  4. Very low (under 16 percent)
  9. Unascertained

(5) Gross national product:
  1. Very high ($125 billion and above)
  2. High ($25–124.9 billion)
  3. Medium ($5–24.9 billion)
  4. Low ($1–4.9 billion)
  5. Very low (under $1 billion)

(6) Per capita gross national product:
  1. Very high ($1200 and above)
  2. High ($600–1199)
  3. Medium ($300–599)
  4. Low ($150–299)
  5. Very low (under $150)

(7) Status of economic development:
  1. Developed (self-sustaining economic growth; GNP per capita over $600)
  2. Intermediate (sustained and near self-sustaining economic growth)
  3. Underdeveloped (reasonable prospect of attaining sustained economic growth by the mid-1970s)
  4. Very underdeveloped (little or no prospect of attaining sustained economic growth within the foreseeable future)
  8. Ambiguous

(8) International financial status:
  1. Very high (UN assessment of 10 percent of above)
  2. High (UN assessment of 1.50–9.99 percent)
  3. Medium (UN assessment of 0.25–1.49 percent)
  4. Low (UN assessment of 0.05–0.25 percent)
  5. Very low (minimum UN assessment of 0.04 percent)
  9. Unascertained

APPENDIX C. COUNTRIES BY SOCIETAL TYPES

Type I
Afghanistan
Burundi
Cambodia
Central African Rep.
Chad
Dahomey
Ethiopia
Gabon
Ivory Coast
Laos
Liberia
Libya
Mali
Maritania
Nicaragua
Niger
Saudi Arabia
Sierra Leone
Togo
Upper Volta

Type II
Cameroun
Congo (Brazzaville)
Congo (Leopoldville)
El Salvador
Honduras
Iran
Jordan
Malaysia
Nepal
Nigeria
Panama
Paraguay
Rwanda
Senegal
Somalia
Syria
Tanganyika
Uganda
Yemen

Type III
Bolivia
Brazil
Burma
Ceylon
Chile
Colombia
Costa Rica
Cyprus
Ecuador
Ghana
Guatemala
Guinea
India
Indonesia
Iraq
Ireland
Israel
Jamaica
Lebanon
Mexico
Morocco
Pakistan
Peru
Philippines
Portugal
Sudan
Trinidad
Turkey
United Arab Rep.
Uruguay
Venezuela

Type IV
Finland
France
Greece
Italy
Spain

Type V
Australia
Austria
Belgium
Canada
Denmark
German Federal Rep.
Iceland
Japan
Luxembourg
Netherlands
New Zealand
Norway
Sweden
Switzerland
United Kingdom
United States

NOTES

1. The interesting research note by Marsh and Parish, "Modernization and Communism: A Re-Test of Lipset's Hypotheses" (1965), establishes that Communist party strength is not inversely related to economic development, as had been suggested by Lipset (1960). Whereas Marsh and Parish attempt a critical evaluation of existing theoretical propositions, we are attempting to utilize evidence for the purpose of hypothesis testing.

2. This interpretation of Communism rests on the analysis of one of the present authors, Kautsky, "An Essay in the Politics of Development," in Kautsky (1962).

3. The concept of social mobilization is developed by Deutsch (1961).

4. Data on estimated membership of Communist parties and on Communist party percentage of total votes cast in national elections appear in U.S. Depart-

ment of State, Bureau of Intelligence and Research, *World Strength of the Communist Party Organizations* (January 1965). See pp. 1–5 of this report for a discussion of the reliability of the data. It goes without saying that Communist party membership figures are likely, for most parties, to be neither precise nor reliable. The State Department report itself states (p. 4): "The reader is reminded ... that although the best usable sources have been consulted, communist membership figures are very difficult to obtain and are not subject to verification." Indeed, in the case of illegal Communist parties and especially of "fronts," "crypto-Communist" and divided parties, it may even be difficult to define "the" Communist party. We are, nevertheless using the State Department's 1965 estimates as the best membership figures available and feel that, for our purposes, they are adequate. Examination of the 1966 report, which became available only after our analysis was completed, indicates relatively little change in State Department estimates of world Communist party membership. Membership figures for the Communist Party of the United States, which are not given by the State Department, were obtained from *The New York Times*, June 22, 1966, Section 3, p. 1.

5. The contingency coefficient is appropriate for tests of association for nominal and ordinal categories and non-linear relationships.

6. Our typology of Communist parties is not dissimilar from that developed by Almond, as expanded by Burks. Gabriel A. Almond, *The Appeals of Communism* (1954), distinguished between the sectarian or deviational parties of the advanced Western industrial countries and the mass proletarian parties of France and Italy. R. V. Burks, *The Dynamics of Communism in Eastern Europe* (1961), adds a third category of national and anti-Western Communist parties to be found in underdeveloped countries, including those of Eastern Europe.

7. For evidence, see Kautsky, "Soviet Policy in the Underdeveloped Countries," in Kautsky (1968), and works cited there.

8. Agriculture is not necessarily insignificant in these countries, but their peasants—now more accurately described as farmers—are thoroughly integrated into the industrial system with respect both to what they produce and what they consume.

9. On the relationship between labor radicalism and social isolation, see Lipset (1960: 232–236, 248–252).

10. See Skilling (1960); an unpublished address by Gabriel A. Almond to the Conference on Soviet and Communist Studies at the annual meeting of the American Political Science Association, September 10, 1964; Skilling (1965); Skilling (1966); Tucker (1967); Meyer (1967); Kautsky, "Communism and the Comparative Study of Development," in Kautsky (1968: 13–17).

11. For example, Seton-Watson, "Twentieth Century Revolutions" (1951), and the same author's *Neither War Nor Peace* (1960); Daniels, *The Nature of Communism* (1962); von Laue, *Why Lenin? Why Stalin? A Reappraisal of the Russian Revolution, 1900–1930* (1964).

12. For an attempt by one of the present authors, see Kautsky (1968 and 1962). Communist and nationalist single-party systems in underdeveloped countries are, along with Fascist ones, compared as "three species of a single political genus" by Tucker (1961).

13. The economic development measures are taken from Banks and Textor (1963) where explanations of the measures are provided.

REFERENCES

ALMOND, G.A. (1954) *The Appeals of Communism.* Princeton: Princeton University Press.
BANKS, A.S. and R.B. TEXTOR (1963) *A Cross-Polity Survey.* Cambridge: MIT Press.
BRZEZINSKI, Z.K. and S.P. HUNTINGTON (1964) *Political Power: USA/USSR.* New York: Viking Press.
BURKS, R.V. (1961) *The Dynamics of Communism in Eastern Europe.* Princeton: Princeton University Press.
DANIELS, R.C. (1962) *The Nature of Communism.* New York: Random House.
DEUTSCH, K.W. (1961) "Social mobilization and political development." *American Political Science Review* 55: 493–514.
INKELES, A. and R.A. BAUER (1959) *The Soviet Citizen: Daily Life in a Totalitarian Society.* Cambridge: Harvard University Press.
KAUTSKY, J.H. (1968) *Communism and the Politics of Development: Nationalism and Communism.* New York: John Wiley.
— (1962) "An essay in the politics of development." In J.H. Kautsky, Ed., *Political Change in Underdeveloped Countries.* New York: John Wiley.
KERR, C. et al. (1960) *Industrialism and Industrial Man: The Problems of Labor and Management in Economic Growth.* Cambridge: Harvard University Press.
LAUE, T. VON (1964) *Why Lenin? Why Stalin? A Reappraisal of the Russian Revolution, 1900–1930.* Philadelphia: Lippincott.
LIPSET, S.M. (1960) *Political Man.* Garden City: Doubleday.
MARSH, R.M. and W.L. PARISH (1965) "Modernization and communism: a re-test of Lipset's hypothesis." *American Sociological Review* 30: 934–942.
MEYER, A.G. (1967) "The comparative study of communist political systems." *Slavic Review* 26 (March): 3–12.
NORTH, R.C. (1952) *Kuomintang and Chinese Communist Elites.* Stanford: Stanford University Press.
SETON-WATSON, H. (1960) *Neither War Nor Peace.* New York: Frederick A. Praeger.
— (1951) "Twentieth century revolutions." *The Political Quarterly* 22 (July–September): 251–265.
SKILLING, H.G. (1966) "Interest groups and communist politics." *World Politics* 18 (April): 435–451.
— (1965) "Soviet and American politics: the dialectic of opposites." *Canadian Journal of Economics and Political Science* 31 (May): 273–280.
— (1960) "Soviet and communist politics: a comparative approach." *The Journal of Politics* 22: 300–313.
TUCKER, R.C. (1967) "On the comparative study of communism." *World Politics* 19 (January): 242–257.
— (1961) "Towards a comparative politics of movement-regimes." *American Political Science Review* 55 (June): 281–289.
U.S. Department of State, Bureau of Intelligence and Research (1965) *World Strength of the Communist Party Organizations.* Washington, D.C.: U.S. Government Printing Office, January.

Part IV

STUDIES ON DEMOCRATIZATION

17 Introduction: Studies on Democratization

JOHN V. GILLESPIE

If not the most central concern for political scientists, democracy—and the conditions under which it will flourish—is one of the most consistent themes of both contemporary and traditional political science. In recent years, social scientists have used the cross-national approach to study democracy, quantitatively, as well as the development of political system attributes that can be labeled democratic. Many methodological and theoretical difficulties beset the cross-national study of democracy and the conditions that give rise to democratic political development. Each research report contained in this section takes a slightly different view on these theoretical and methodological questions. Also, each in its own way raises methodological and theoretical questions about the cross-national study of democracy.

The first and foremost problem in the study of democratization and its conditions is the problem of definition and measurement. To some degree, this difficulty stems from the lack of theoretical consensus on the meaning of the term "democracy," but it is also a problem of operationalizing conceptual definitions of democracy into comparable measures holding across political systems. Further, the problem of definition and measurement surrounds the selection of indicators of democracy to assess the degree to which a given political system, in fact, exhibits democratic attributes. Also, we must be conceptually clear as to how the concept of democratization differs in meaning from such similar concepts as political development, political stability, and political integration.

Democracy as a concept used by political and social scientists is often confused with the concept of democratization. The term democracy refers to a certain state of affairs, governmental institutions, and political processes. The term democratization, although of similar empirical referent, refers to the processes over time through which political systems acquire democratic attributes, rather than to that state of affairs that can be labeled as democratic in nature. By use of the term democratization, we mean to ask the question: "Under what conditions can we expect to find democratic attributes of political systems?" Furthermore, political systems experiencing democratization may not be at the present or even in the future "democratic." Likewise, democratic political systems may not be experiencing further democratization, or the process through which democratic attributes are acquired. Hence, democratic systems may not be experiencing democratization, and democratizing systems may not be democratic.

The term democratization refers to a process which occurs over time. Democracy is a state of affairs at a given moment in time. Generally, we measure democratization by the change from one time period to the next on some scale or index of democracy. That is, democratization is measured by the change in the score for some country describing its level of democracy at a given time period, to the same score at the next time period, and so forth. Hence, when the term democratization is used, we are referring to democratic change over time; whereas with the use of the term democracy we mean a particular state of affairs, whether within a progressive or regressive period of democratization.

The conceptual distinction between democracy and democratization is only one of a group of distinctions which have to be made. Obviously, there are important and significant differences between the notions of political development and democratization, yet this distinction has not always been maintained. Not all developed countries are democratic, and more importantly, not all political development is democratic in nature. By the term political development, we refer to the processes through which political systems adopt modern methods of management, bureaucratic procedures, research on government and governance, and so forth. By democratization, we mean the processes through which political systems acquire democratic forms of rule and procedures of governance. Obviously, the indicators that one might select for the study of political development are quite different from those that a researcher would choose to study democratization. Democratization does not necessarily imply that a political system is undergoing political development, and likewise, political development does not necessarily imply that a political system is undergoing democratization. Theoretically at least, without any explanation of a relationship between democratization and development, all combinations between democratization and development should be possible. The question of any relationship between these two concepts is an empirical one, to be solved by theoretical discourse and subsequent empirical research.

Not only are the meanings of the terms democratization and development different, but also the indicators that the researcher selects to quantify these variables are different. In measuring political development we look for such political indicators as the size of the governmental bureaucracy, the proportion of the governmental budget provided for administrative personnel, the number of governmental agencies, the specialization of tasks assigned to governmental employees, and so on. In measuring democracy and democratization, such indicators as the degree of competitiveness in elections and in the legislature, the extent of suffrage, and the degree of censorship are used. For political development to be theoretically independent from democratization, not only must the conceptual distinctions be made between the two terms, but also the indicators selected in the measurement of one variable cannot be used in the measurement of the other variable. To say that the indicators selected are theoretically independent does not imply that with replicable empirical research the observed relationships between the two variables— development and democratization—cannot be described. By theoretical independence, we mean that the values assigned to one variable do not necessarily imply the values assigned to the other variable. Hence, to achieve this theoretical independence the indicators assigned as measures of democratization cannot be used as measures of political development.

Not only is it important to distinguish clearly between political development and democratization, but it is also important to keep in mind the conceptual differences between political stability and democracy. Although it may be empirically true (and some sound theoretical arguments could be made to this effect) that for a political system to maintain itself as a democracy, it must remain stable. It is not, however, necessarily the case that there is a relationship between the notions of political stability and democracy. Keeping such notions as political development, political stability, and democratization analytically separate allows the researcher to describe empirically the relationships between these phenomena, and to test hypotheses concerning how the variables are related.

The measurement of democratization not only involves definition and selection of indicators, but involves also the combining of indicators into summary scores for each country. The problem that arises is by what procedure are the multiple indicators of democracy and democratization to be reduced into single scores for each political system. It is difficult to say that each indicator of democracy is just as important as every other indicator, and indeed, under differing conditions, the same indicator may be of differing importance. For example, competitive elections may be more important as an indicator of democracy than the extent of suffrage. Hence, in combining indicators into some summary measure of democracy, we would want to weight more heavily the competitiveness of elections rather than the extent of suffrage. Likewise, under conditions of competitive elections, the existence of a legislative opposition may be less important to a measure of democracy than the extent of suffrage, or perhaps, for some notions of democracy, the relative importance of these indicators may be reversed if suffrage is limited to only a small proportion of the population. Since some indicators are more important than others in measuring democracy, and since the conditions under which the certain indicators are exhibited may be important in constructing an overall measure of democracy and democratization, methodological problems arise in combining the indicators into single scores for each country. These methodological problems involve the selection of weights, the selection of statistical routines for reduction of data, and the like. In any analysis it is important that the procedures used to reduce data and to construct measures are compatible with the theoretical conceptualization of the variables, so that the findings of the research are not artifacts of the data reduction methods employed, but are truly reflections of the relationships between the variables that the researcher is examining.

There is no one quick and easy solution to the problem of assigning weights to indicators or to the selection of statistical routines for the reduction of data. Similarly, there is no simple solution to the selection of indicators to be included in some summary measure of democracy and democratization. Only through replication and extensive analysis can we begin to tell what indicators and which data reductions are the most useful. Indeed, there may be several differing ways of measuring democracy and democratization which are useful in cross-national research. Those measures that are the most productive in the formulation of generalizations explaining democracy and democratization are those that are the most productive to cross-national research and the eventual formulation of laws about the conditions under which political systems are likely to exhibit democratic political attributes.

Each research report contained in this section takes somewhat of a different strategy in measuring democracy and democratization. Russell Fitzgibbon, in his research report, attempts to measure democratic political development in Latin America by consulting specialists on Latin American politics. Each specialist was asked to rank the Latin American republics on a series of attributes which Fitzgibbon takes as indicators of democracy. Each specialist was asked to consider the degree to which he thought each Latin American country exhibited the attributes. As Fitzgibbon notes, there are numerous methodological problems associated with measuring democracy by polling a team of experts. As Fitzgibbon points out, he is actually measuring the attitudes and informed opinions of selected specialists on Latin American politics, more so than measuring democracy in Latin America per se. Further, although Fitzgibbon does provide some evidence of disagreement among his panel of experts following his methods, it is difficult to ascertain the degree to which the results are artifacts of disagreement among the specialists or are functions of their consensus as to the degree of democratic achievement in Latin America. One might also disagree with the indicators that Fitzgibbon provides for the panel of experts. Some indicators, Fitzgibbon claims, are preconditions for democratic political development, while others are attributes of democracy. Mixing the preconditions and the attributes into a single summary score does not tell us anything about the relationship between the conditions and democratic achievement itself.

The use of a team of experts to measure democracy imposes many methodological constraints. First, the experts may well be biased by certain cultural perspectives, their information or lack thereof on given countries, as well as by current events, which may have little lasting significance. Further, each expert may use differing criteria and may assign differing interpretations to the meanings of the attributes on which they ranked the Latin American republics. Even with these methodological constraints, the Fitzgibbon research does arrive at several interesting conclusions. Comparing the rankings by the panel of judges (the composition changes over time), Fitzgibbon finds that there are changing perceptions about Latin American democratic political development over time. Hence, although some countries are consistently ranked high on democracy and some are consistently low, there is considerable fluctuation over time. As the author notes, it seems that for Latin America, democratization is not a consistent upward or downward movement, at least as assessed by specialists. Flanigan and Fogelman, in their attempt to measure democratization, using similar, although not identical indicators, and for a longer time period and for a larger set of countries, substantiate this finding. As the Flanigan and Fogelman analysis demonstrates, political systems tend to exhibit democratic attributes at certain junctures, but at other points, they seem to slide away from democratic achievement. The important, although tentative, conclusion of these analyses is that democratization is not a simple process of growth over time, but that it involves fluctuations that are important for an understanding of democratic development.

Feierabend and Feierabend in their research report attempt to analyze the relationship between political stability, systemic frustration, political coerciveness and permissiveness, concepts similar to authoritarianism and democracy. To measure the degree to which political systems are permissive (coercive), the researchers have placed countries into categories based on a set of criteria. Although the Feierabend and Feierabend analysis might be challenged on the particular categorical decisions made, it does point to some propositions worthy of further investigation. The relationships that the Feierabends find between political stability, systemic frustration, and political permissiveness are not simple linear relationships, but involve curvilinear distinctions. Although the Feierabend analysis does not permit exact determination of the shape of the curvilinearity, it does provide some insights for further testing of propositions relating political stability and systemic frustration to democratization.

Whereas the Fitzgibbon and Flanigan and Fogelman analyses are logitudinal, that is, they cover a time span, the Feierabend and Feierabend analysis is cross-sectional, that is, it deals with a given time period by comparing among groups of nations. Flanigan and Fogelman present some rather convincing evidence, denoting the weaknesses with the cross-sectional approach. The Flanigan and Fogelman analyses demonstrate that for given historical periods, the cross-sectional analysis yields differing patterns. Hence, they argue that only by use of the longitudinal approach can the true empirical relationships between the conditions of democratization and the variable itself be revealed.

The Flanigan and Fogelman scheme for measuring democratization is similar to that employed by the Feierabends. The primary difference is that the Feierabends have categorized political systems based on a set of criteria describing each level of coerciveness. Flanigan and Fogelman have attempted to score political systems on a set of attributes and, then, with a weighting system, have combined their scores to achieve a democratization score. Although both schemes for measuring democracy and democratization might be challenged, especially on the criteria used and the distinctions made between the political systems, in both analyses, the authors are well aware of the methodological problems imposed by their measuring devices.

Yet another measure of democratization is found in the research reports of Cnudde and McCrone and Cutright. Cnudde and McCrone and Cutright rely on the earlier measure of democratic political development developed by Cutright (1963). This measure involves the determination of democratic attributes of political systems, and then the weighting of these attributes to arrive at a summary score for each political system. As with Flanigan's and Fogelman's index of democratization, Cutright's index is open to the same methodological questions. Simply, why were the particular weights selected? Why the particular set of indicators rather than some other set of indicators? Although these questions might not seem to be integral to the research, to have valid measures of democracy and democratization, it is important that we know what we are measuring and that the procedures used for constructing the measure are providing what we think they are providing. By replicating research using other measures, we can begin to assess the degree to which measurement differences make for differences in conclusions. We can further determine the degree to which differing measuring instruments involving differing notion of democratization yield different findings, and hence have some insight as to where theoretical and operational ambiguities lie.

The McCrone and Cnudde analysis is an expansion on Cutright's early analysis of democratic political development (Cutright, 1963). McCrone and Cnudde attempt to find the best causal fit among three conditions of democratization in an effort to build some theoretical basis relating conditions of democracy to democratic political development. Although questions can be raised about the statistical routine employed by the authors, the McCrone and Cnudde analysis does provide some interesting insights into the relationships between urbanization, education, communications development, and democratic political development. The authors identify a causal sequence leading from urbanization to education to communication to democratic political development. Such analyses as that performed by Cnudde and McCrone allow us to examine a range of possible explanations of democratization and provide statistical criteria for verification, and hence are of extreme value in the development of theories of democratic political development.

Cutright's research reports focus on specific components of democratization, namely the equality of income distribution and the development of social welfare programs. Although it can be argued, depending on one's perspective as to what the term democracy means, that income equality and developed social welfare programs are not necessarily attributes of democratic political systems, Cutright does provide evidence demonstrating positive relationships between democratic political development and the achievement of developed social security programs and income equality. Hence, in this sense, these attributes of political systems are indeed closely linked with democratization, if not an important component of it.

In Cutright's analyses problems do arise with the use of the statistical methods. For example, the forced correlation analysis in Cutright's attempt to relate the GINI index of income inequality to a variety of systems attributes can be questioned on its appropriateness to the particular theoretical problem under investigation. Also, the reliance on mean values in Cutright's analysis of income inequality does not take into consideration the entire range of data, especially with the high degree of variance in standard deviation scores. In his analysis of the development of national social security programs, Cutright faces a similar problem with the use of mean scores. However, even with these methodological problems, Cutright's analyses yield some very significant findings. They demonstrate that democratization is a complex phenomena, and that it is tightly linked to a wide variety of social and economic variables. Further, his analyses suggest more refined efforts in taking attributes of democracy rather than democracy as a single composite variable in his attempts to explain democratic political development.

Each of the studies contained in this section take differing views and approaches to the problems of measuring democratization and its conditions. However, without exception, the authors call for more refined and precise methods to measure democratic political development, as well as further efforts to analyze the conditions under which democracy will flourish and democratization will take place.

REFERENCE

CUTRIGHT, P. (1963) "National political development: measurement and analysis." *American Sociological Review* 28: 253-264.

18 Measuring Democratic Change in Latin America

RUSSELL H. FITZGIBBON

The continuing struggle between democracy and various forms of totalitarianism for control of men's minds and actions does not, as time passes, lose either intensity or interest. The conflict is focused and dramatized by the nature of international politics in what we earlier referred to as a bipolarized world. The sharpness of the competition makes it important, even imperative, that we study, as carefully and thoroughly as may be, not only the form and philosophy of one or another system of political control but also the component elements of different types, how and why they change, and what trends may be deduced from as penetrating analysis as is possible.

We like to think that the United States is a democratic country, perhaps "the great exemplar of the democratic way of life and government." At times the claims become even more grandiose and perfervid. And yet, a hundred miles south of Florida a highly vocal Latin American spokesman—probably more vocal than logical—maintains that democracy in the United States is a sham and a pretense. Fidel Castro holds that Cuba provides the genuine illustration of democracy in the hemisphere and that progress toward democratic goals is more viable and significant by far in his country than in ours. Such is the semantic value of the word "democracy."

In perhaps oversimple fashion, most persons in the United States would be willing to define democracy in Lincoln's homely phrase, "government by

---

Author's Note: The author gratefully acknowledges grants from the Senate Committee on Research, University of California, Santa Barbara, and assistance of various sorts from Dr. Charles Wolf, Jr., RAND Corporation; Professors Glenn J. Culler, David Gold, Marvin Marcus, and J. Harold McBeth, University of California, Santa Barbara; Professor Paul G. Hoel, University of California, Los Angeles; and Mr. Gordon Zenk, Defense Research Corporation. Much of his greatest indebtedness, however, is to Mr. William F. Royer, his research assistant, who worked with sustained imagination, perceptiveness, and enthusiasm above and beyond the call of his all too inadequate pay checks.

Reprinted from *Journal of Politics*, Volume 29 (February, 1967), pages 129–166, by permission of the author and the publisher.

the people." More thoughtful ones add some elementary corollaries: majority control but respect for minority rights, a spirit of compromise, self-discipline and criticism, fair play and tolerance, emphasis on law rather than personalities. Castro, if he were willing to acknowledge a Lincolnian debt at all, would doubtless want to use a contiguous phrase, "government for the people." Many *latinos* share his view. It is only a change of preposition but it can make great difference in how we proceed from there.

The average North American is likely to put great stress on the suffrage and the supremacy of the sovereign voter, especially since the concept of "one man, one vote" has become judicially exalted. The average Latin American, on the other hand, views the problem differently. He is much more apt to equate democratic government with a regime which brings social justice or economic betterment or both to a large segment of the population. In other words, he is thinking more in terms of social and economic than of political democracy. The interrelationship among all of them is at times lost on him.

In some degree, the Latin American attitude resembles that of the American West in Andrew Jackson's day. But we must not commit the fallacy of assuming that contemporary Latin America is necessarily made in the image of the United States of a century and a quarter ago. There are important qualifications. Two basic ones suggest themselves: the differing nature of the social structures in the two areas and the vastly greater ease of communication in the second half of the twentieth over the mid-nineteenth century.

Much of the colonization and expansion of the United States was made in a spirit of protest, of revolution. It was Pennsylvania Quaker or Maryland Catholic protest against religious restrictions in England. It was Massachusetts Puritan protest against the social and economic limitations in the mother country. It was Roger Williams' Rhode Island protest against the harshness of Massachusetts Bay's Puritanism. It was trans-Appalachian protest against the growing lack of opportunity in the older Atlantic seaboard. All of this made for a deeply ingrained spirit of independence and individualism.

The establishment of what became the eighteen Spanish American republics was far more in a framework of regimentation and control. Social organization was more stratified and social mobility less possible than in the English colonies. The sanctity of authority and an almost total inability to compromise, whether in the government, the Church, or the social process, were accepted well nigh unquestioningly. This situation carried over into the independent period and made for an interrelationship of groups and forces which would have been almost unrecognizable in the United States at a comparable time.

An eminent Peruvian, Francisco García Calderón (1913: 369), wrote half a century ago describing Spanish America's political problem as of early independence:

> Each party supports a leader, an interest, a dogma; on the one side a man beholds his own party, the missionaries of truth and culture; the others are his

enemies, mercenary and corrupt. Each group believes that it seeks to retain the supremacy in the name of disinterested virtue and patriotism. For the gang in possession of power, the revolutionaries are malefactors; for the latter the ruling party are merely a government of thieves and tyrants. There are gods of good and evil, as in the Oriental theogonies. Educated in the Roman Church, [Latin] Americans bring into politics the absolution of religious dogmas; they have no conception of toleration. The dominant party prefers to annihilate its adversaries, to realize the complete unanimity of the nation; the hatred of one's opponent is the first duty of the prominent politician.

Social revolution ultimately broke this static and primitive situation. If we except Haiti, it came first in Uruguay and Mexico, then in varying degree in half a dozen other Latin American states, most recently and dramatically in Cuba. None of these Revolutions—and for movement as broad and basic as they were, the word should be capitalized—was aimed fundamentally or primarily at the concept of equality of voting (even though a long-standing slogan of the Mexican Revolution was *sufragio efectivo—no reelección*). They did point toward the goal that Juan José Ciudadano must have a better life: improved health and more to eat, a chance at jobs and education and self-respect, roads, hospitals, factories. An effective vote as an objective played only an incidental part. The question inevitably arises, how are such changes to be achieved if not by an irresistible grass-roots demand? The Latin answer has often been that it must be by gift from a Leader.

What usually emerges from crisis, then, is the charismatic and haloed *jefe, caudillo, lider, presidente, general,* or Moses under some other title who will point, almost always dramatically, to the imminence of arrival at the promised land under his leadership. Cuba's Castro is a near-perfect example. It is logical that the Leader will probably not be especially interested in seeing that the underprivileged get the prosaic blessing of being able periodically to mark a piece of paper called a ballot. If the concept of government by the consent of the governed catches on, it may breed the revolutionary thought (or counter-revolutionary, depending on the point of view) that the people rule and that the Leader is dispensable. Hence the emphasis on social and economic rather than political democracy.

In more than one instance, the channel for achieving this brand of democracy is likely to be the force-dominated Revolution, quite possibly led by someone liberally endowed with the aura of charisma. For at least three reasons, the channel is less apt to be the customary political expression with which we are familiar: in many places, that machinery is not now effectively implemented; many *latinos* distrust its efficacy or honesty; most of the countries where the change might be expected are seriously lacking in integration.

But, as time goes on in such present or potential revolutionary situations, at least the façade of occidental democracy seems inevitable, whether the area be mid-Africa or mid-America. Mid-Asia presents a different prospect because in that area the Iron-Bamboo Curtain rather effectively precludes any significant penetration by such insidious democratic ideas as bills of rights, periodic free elections, respect for representative institutions, and the like. It is not merely that the prestige of democratic forms is so high, regardless of the definition of democracy, that its paraphernalia are adopted or imitated. More substantial reasons also point toward a gradual and ultimate merging of political with economic and social democratizing. One such factor is the seemingly inevitable Latin American realization that as people are given dignity and self-esteem—face, as it were—they can and should become masters of their political fate rather than merely the beneficiaries of social and economic largess. They will then want a more effective vote and the framework of political democracy. Uruguay is a case in point. Another factor is the inevitably greater impact of economic forces, cast in an occidental mold, whether in the public or the private sector, which will in all likelihood—barring complete Communist regimes—point toward implementation through traditional western political forms and channels. Mexico provides an illustration.

In any event, not only the nature of the change but also the measurement of it assumes increasing importance as time passes. The present author became interested in the problem—and the measurement—more than twenty years ago and in consequence undertook surveys among Latin Americanists knowledgeable about the politics of the area. The surveys began in 1945 and have been repeated at five-year intervals. They now provide a study in depth of the course and rapidity of change of various components of democracy in the Latin American scene. It should be stressed that this is change and achievement as seen by a group of specialists who have long observed and weighed Latin American political phenomena. Their evaluations are informed but, of course, subjective. It should also be underlined that the surveying techniques used were not those of a "Gallup poll" in which carefully selected random groups of laymen participating in a social process are asked for opinions; the progressively larger number of respondents taking part in the five surveys have been chosen as highly qualified experts who are observers of, not participants in, the process of change.

Analyses of earlier surveys have previously been published in article form (Fitzgibbon, 1951, 1956a, 1956b; Fitzgibbon and Johnson, 1961). They have attracted widespread attention and interest, mostly favorable. It is true that in a critical review of Howard Cline's *Mexico: Revolution to Evolution, 1940-1960*, Lesley B. Simpson (1963: 296) referred to "Russell Fitzgibbon's astonishing attempt to measure (by IBM computer) the progress of democracy in Latin America." It must be concluded, alas, that the adjective in the quotation was meant to be pejorative rather than complimentary. This author stands in awe of Professor Simpson's erudition; his staccato, impressionistic, and eminently readable *Many Mexicos* has deservedly become a classic. At the same time, it is respectfully submitted that he just may have missed the point of the successive surveys. On the other hand, several authors have commented in recent volumes (Davis, 1958: 91-92, 237, 294-295; Gomez, 1960: 92-93;

Lieuwen, 1961: 57; Scott, 1959: 301–302; Stokes, 1959: 511–513) on the methods and problems involved in the surveys, and Professors John D. Martz (1965: 113–129) and Robert D. Tomasek (1966: 4–22) reprinted the 1961 article, cited above, in collections of readings. At least three professional papers (Wolf, 1965a, 1965b; Marvick, 1962) were tied directly to the 1960 analysis and in 1963 the RAND Corporation organized a seminar, participated in by about a dozen staff members and the present writer, to discuss problems and techniques involved in the surveys.

It was necessary initially to decide whether to rely for measurement on objective data derived from census-type or other statistical materials or, on the other hand, to tap the expertise of experienced students of the Latin American scene. The decision was made for the latter alternative. Both approaches have their respective advantages. Reliance on statistical data as a base would seem to assure elimination of all subjective or emotional considerations and to presume mechanical efficiency and accuracy; it would ostensibly mean use of quantifiable or "hard" data rather than judgmental or "soft" variables. But there are difficulties: for one thing, applicability of the data to the problem must first be determined, often a subordinate problem of considerable complexity in itself. Furthermore, there is seemingly firm evidence that in at least one or two Latin American states the governmentally published "census-type" information has at times been "doctored" to present a more favorable national picture of one or another aspect. Use of the area specialists as a source of evaluations does open the door to subjective applications of the various criteria. Furthermore, the breadth, depth, and recency of the information on which respondents base their subjective and perhaps unconscious reactions will vary greatly. A considerable panel of respondents will run the gamut from very "liberal" to quite "conservative" points of view. But, granting such handicaps, the overall assessments made by specialists are likely to introduce desirable nuances and balances which are impossible in the use of cold statistical information, even of the most accurate sort.[1]

It is interesting, of course, to set one approach off against the other, and that is attempted in part later in the present paper.

The surveying method itself was relatively simple. In the first place, fifteen criteria contributing, directly or indirectly, to the state of democracy in a given Latin American country were devised (see Figure 1). Some of them, it is obvious, are preconditions of democracy, others are contemporary manifestations of it, still others are products of it; some can be characterized as political in nature, others as administrative, economic, social, or cultural. An admixture of this kind might initially seem open to criticism, especially inasmuch as the criteria were not arranged as the characterizations in the preceding sentence suggest. The main reason for the choice of criteria was that these particular measurements appeared to the writer to include the important conditioning and reflective components of the total picture of viable democracy in the Latin American context. The arrangement seemed to be a logical one, progressing from the very elemental factor of basic education and seminal socio-economic conditions, through conditions directly contributory to a democratic process, such as freedom of speech, press, etc. (necessary for meaningful campaigning), honest elections, and free party organization and

Comments:

Your Name

Date Mailed Back

Continue on reverse if necessary*

your Familiarity Level

	Argentina	Bolivia	Brazil	Chile	Colombia	Costa Rica	Cuba	Dom. Rep.	Ecuador	El Salvador	Guatemala	Haiti	Honduras	Mexico	Nicaragua	Panama	Paraguay	Peru	Uruguay	Venezuela	(leave blank)
1. Educational level	232	99	161	211	173	228	192	122	115	135	111	57	111	183	119	156	97	131	232	178	
2. Standard of living	217	85	158	177	156	201	144	121	109	139	118	58	114	177	122	148	105	130	213	177	
3. Internal unity	177	113	175	217	161	235	178	137	117	150	122	86	129	214	138	156	128	136	229	184	
4. Political maturity	200	112	184	230	184	243	151	115	115	140	117	58	119	214	122	139	96	146	230	183	
5. Freedom from foreign domin.	230	149	215	219	236	223	85	157	184	176	162	174	164	236	163	128	152	193	229	189	
6. Freedom of press, etc.	225	130	192	244	218	245	59	146	165	169	143	60	137	206	134	184	86	200	246	212	
7. Free elections	193	121	157	243	204	247	56	116	131	155	130	57	122	190	107	181	71	182	246	230	
8. Party organization	187	121	172	238	200	234	70	119	133	154	131	61	123	175	113	177	82	188	237	218	
9. Judiciary	199	116	154	225	201	230	63	123	145	146	129	61	125	187	117	156	89	169	227	187	
10. Governmental funds	182	109	152	204	179	217	131	123	135	150	130	59	125	179	125	136	108	157	205	185	
11. Social legislation	187	148	164	206	168	215	173	126	128	153	129	65	119	209	119	146	102	156	226	198	
12. Civilian supremacy	145	106	131	241	198	247	115	111	110	129	105	84	108	235	106	172	70	152	245	188	
13. Ecclesiastical freedom	211	199	223	228	157	229	186	170	150	174	174	155	171	219	175	199	162	158	243	217	
14. Government administration	183	101	161	205	179	209	127	115	127	142	123	64	117	188	128	147	106	157	207	180	
15. Local government	177	102	159	190	167	212	86	111	118	140	130	60	113	172	114	141	91	149	201	174	
(leave blank)																					
	A	Bo	Br	Ch	Co	CR	Cu	DR	Ec	ES	G	Ha	Ho	M	N	Pa	Pr	Pu	U	V	

FIGURE 1

activity, to more refined products of such a development, such as scientifically evolved public administration and intelligently organized local government.

It seemed important to devise such criteria in the light of the total Latin American culture. To apply the standards and critiques of mature Western political societies to the developing states of Latin America would be roughly analogous to using a skilled machinist's fine precision tools for construction of a garage workbench. To use uncritically the definitions, approaches, and measurements that would be useful in studying conditions in, say Canada, the Netherlands, Norway, or the United States, would, as applied to Latin America (or various other parts of the world) suggest only a pathological or distorted situation.[2] This is not a matter of drawing invidious contrast but simply one of trying to fit norms of measurement to the thing to be measured.

Once the criteria were phrased, it appeared desirable to weight them, inasmuch as they would obviously have differing degrees of impact in conditioning the resultant total evaluations. Freedom and honesty of elections in a given country would surely be of greater significance than, say, the influence (now largely historical) of ecclesiastical pressures on politics. As they finally evolved, the criteria used, with the weighting for each criterion given in parentheses, were as follows:

1. An educational level sufficient to give the political processes some substance and vitality (weighting of 1).
2. A fairly adequate standard of living (1).
3. A sense of internal unity and national cohesion (1).
4. Belief by the people in their individual political dignity and maturity (1).
5. Absence of foreign domination (1).
6. Freedom of the press, speech, assembly, radio, etc. (1½).
7. Free and competitive elections—honestly counted votes (2).
8. Freedom of party organization; genuine and effective party opposition in the legislature; legislative scrutiny of the executive branch (1½).
9. An independent judiciary—respect for its decisions (1).
10. Public awareness of accountability for the collection and expenditure of public funds (1).
11. Intelligent attitude toward social legislation—the vitality of such legislation as applied (1).
12. Civilian supremacy over the military (1½).
13. Reasonable freedom of political life from the impact of ecclesiastical controls (½).
14. Attitude toward and development of technical, scientific, and honest governmental administration (1).
15. Intelligent and sympathetic administration of whatever local self-government prevails (1).

Were the surveys being started *de novo*, it is quite possible that the author would select, organize, phrase, or arrange the criteria somewhat differently. (Friends have suggested, probably entirely correctly, that others might have been included, different weightings given, etc.) But, for the sake of comparability of successive analyses, it has seemed desirable to retain the criteria in their original form with the same weightings.

Brief explanatory paragraphs amplified each of the criteria as circulated among the respondents and attempted to establish a reasonable uniformity of approach to evaluations. Respondents were asked to express their evaluations for each state on each criterion in letter terms, A through E, signifying respectively a judgment of excellent, good, average, poor, or insignificant (virtually no) democratic achievement in respect to the particular state and criterion. Respondents were also asked to provide self-ratings of their presumed "familiarity level" with respect to each state and each criterion in terms of "great" (familiarity), "moderate," or "little." Evaluation sheets (see

TABLE 1
Raw Scores by States

	1945 POINTS	1945 RANK	1950 POINTS	1950 RANK	1955 POINTS	1955 RANK	1960 POINTS	1960 RANK	1965 POINTS	1965 RANK
Argentina	628	5	536	8	499½	8	704½	4	662	6
Bolivia	308	18	334	17	374½	15	439	16	401	17
Brazil	481½	11	605	5	633	5	648½	7	574½	8
Chile	712½	3	732½	2	713	3	741½	3	755	3
Colombia	683½	4	597½	6	507	6	651½	6	638½	7
Costa Rica	730	2	702½	3	746	2	768	2	781½*	1½*
Cuba	590½	6	659	4	504	7	452	15	381	18
Domin. Rep.	301	19	320½	19	307	19	315	18	426	14
Ecuador	379½	14	474	9	487	10	556½	10	448	12
El Salvador	411½	13	424	14	461½	11	508½	12	510½	11
Guatemala	416	12	472½	10	393½	14	483½	13	437	13
Haiti	330½	16	329	18	367	17	309½	19	248	20
Honduras	328	17	379	15	418½	12	452½	14	423½	15
Mexico	545½	7	569½	7	639½	4	664	5	674	4
Nicaragua	345½	15	354	16	329½	18	370½	17	420	16
Panama	528	8	471	11	498	9	519½	11	542½	10
Paraguay	289	20	293½	20	291½	20	284	20	331	19
Peru	494	10	428	13	369½	16	562½	9	556	9
Uruguay	772	1	788½	1	820	1	785	1	781½*	1½*
Venezuela	504	9	451	12	397	13	611½	8	665	5

*Tie

Figure 1) were distributed among the respondents with this presumptuous request for 335 judgments: on fifteen criteria for each of twenty states and on familiarity levels for fifteen criteria and twenty states.[3] Respondents cooperated most generously.

Once the evaluation sheets were all in hand, analysis proceeded with the aid of an electronic computer at almost all points.[4] Evaluations, as well as criteria, were assigned numerical values. A judgment of A in a given cell was given a value of five points, one of B a value of four points, and so on to one point for an E. Considering the varying weights of the criteria ($\frac{1}{2}$ to 2) it was thus possible for a respondent to give a state a maximum evaluation of eighty-five points (all A's) or a minimum rating of seventeen (all E's). A necessary first step was compilation of original or "raw" scores for the several states, determined simply by adding cell evaluations, with proper regard for weightings of criteria. Raw scores for the several states in the five surveys, 1945 to 1965, inclusive, are shown in Table 1. In Figure 1, raw-score totals, by state and criterion for the 1965 survey, have been added to the reproduction of the evaluation form.

Use of the raw scores permits a crude determination of how the respondents collectively view the course of Latin American democracy over twenty years. Total raw scores (with appropriate division for the latest three surveys to account for the larger numbers of participants) were: 1945: 9,763$\frac{1}{2}$; 1950: 9,943; 1955: 9,760; 1960: 10,827$\frac{1}{2}$; 1965: 10,656$\frac{1}{2}$. The fluctuations are a rough indication of shifts in the democratic weathervane over the years. The considerable jump in 1960 is probably to be accounted for by what Tad Szulc aptly used as a book title, "The Twilight of the Tyrants" (Perón, Somoza, Rojas Pinilla, Pérez Jiménez, for example), during the preceding half decade. The consensus appeared to be that by 1965 the state of democracy had slightly worsened from its 1960 condition.

Certain statistical difficulties are inherent, however, in the use of raw scores. Scores ranged through several hundred points and minima and maxima were widely separated.[5] One respondent is inclined to view the foibles and failures of the Latin American political process leniently, another will see them harshly; their respective evaluations, in consequence, will be high and low. Conveniently, the raw-score totals in each survey straddled 1,000 points. It seemed desirable, therefore, to adjust or "normalize" evaluations by allotting each respondent 1,000 points for all states and recalculating individual state scores on the basis of that uniform total. Such a statistical adjustment resulted in a change of totals for each state but, except possibly in cases of very close evaluations, relative rankings would remain the same.[6] Later parts of the present analysis are based on adjusted scores. Omitting fractions (which are statistically insignificant), adjusted scores are shown in Table 2 and, graphically, in Figure 2.

In addition to recording the adjusted-point score and the rank order for each state in the first two columns of each survey's data, as shown in Table 2,

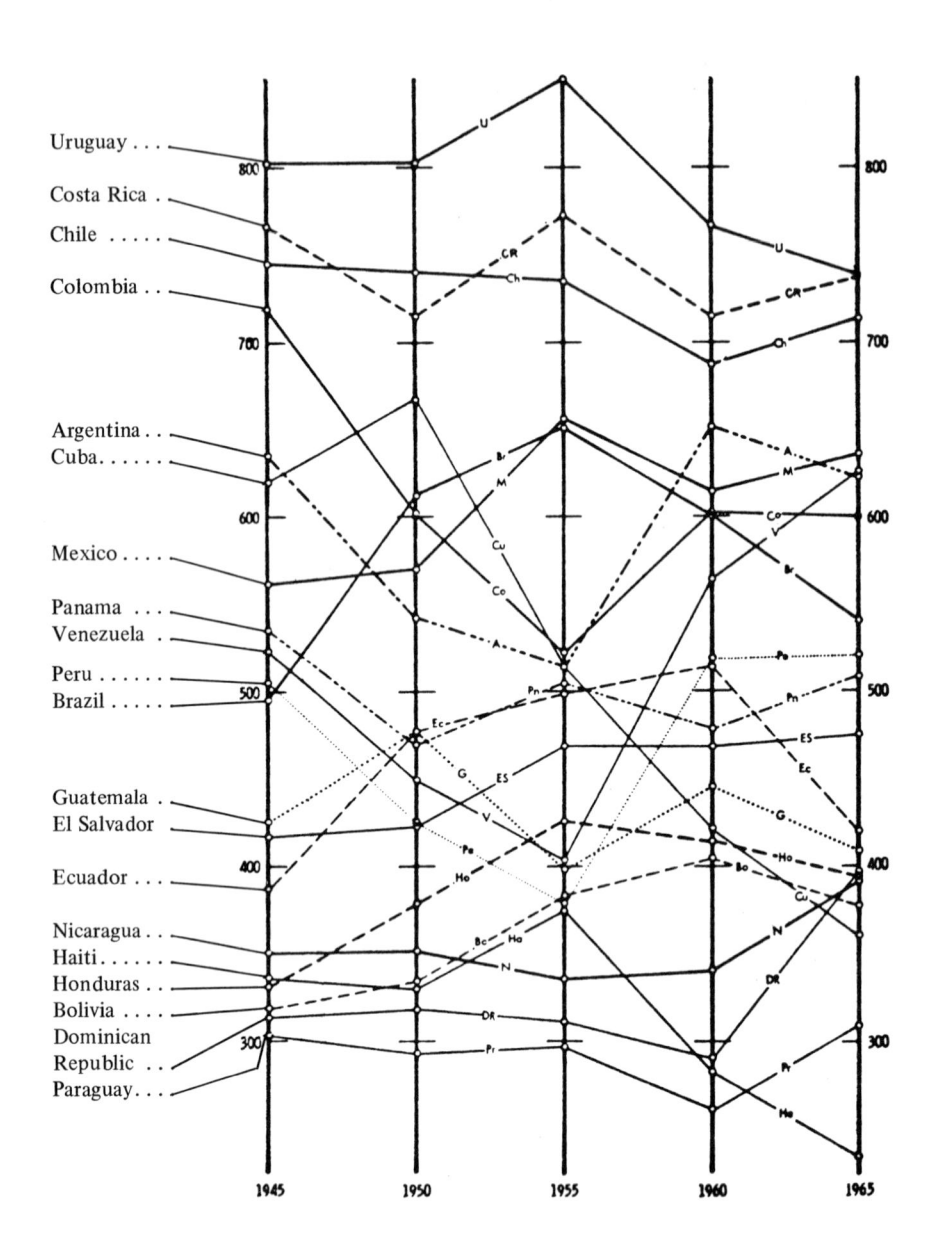

FIGURE 2

TABLE 2
ADJUSTED SCORES BY STATES

	Points	1945 Rank	%	Points	1950 Rank	%	Points	1955 Rank	%	Points	1960 Rank	%	Points	1965 Rank	%
Argentina	634	5	63.9	542	8	53.3	513*	7½*	47.8*	652	4	78.0	622	6	71.7
Bolivia	315	18	19.2	335	17	23.4	384	15	29.5	406	16	39.2	377	17	33.6
Brazil	495	11	44.4	612	5	63.4	651	5	67.4	600	7	69.2	539	8	58.8
Chile	745	3	79.4	740	2	81.9	735	3	79.3	688	3	83.7	713	3	85.8
Colombia	718	4	75.6	602	6	62.0	524	6	49.4	602	6	70.1	599	7	68.1
Costa Rica	765	2	82.2	713	3	78.0	773	2	84.7	713	2	90.8	737	2	89.6
Cuba	619	6	61.8	667	4	71.4	513*	7½*	47.8*	422	14	41.7	361	18	31.1
Domin. Rep.	310	19	18.5	318	19	20.9	312	19	19.3	290	18	20.9	396	14	36.6
Ecuador	387	14	29.3	479	9	44.2	498	10	45.7	514	10	56.2	419	12	40.1
El Salvador	417	13	33.5	422	14	36.0	469	11	41.6	468	12	49.0	476	11	49.0
Guatemala	426	12	34.7	478	10	44.1	398	14	31.5	445	13	45.3	408	13	38.4
Haiti	336	16	22.1	331	18	22.8	375	17	28.2	283	19	19.7	233	20	11.2
Honduras	331	17	21.4	378	15	29.6	426	12	35.5	414	15	40.4	395	15	36.4
Mexico	562	7	53.8	570	7	57.4	657	4	68.2	613	5	71.9	635	4	73.7
Nicaragua	349	15	23.9	351	16	25.7	336	18	22.7	341	17	28.9	392	16	35.9
Panama	537	8	50.3	468	11	42.6	505	9	46.7	478	11	50.6	508	10	54.0
Paraguay	304	20	17.6	293	20	17.3	297	20	17.1	261	20	16.3	308	19	22.9
Peru	505	10	45.8	425	13	36.4	378	16	28.7	518	9	56.9	520	9	55.8
Uruguay	804	1	87.7	804	1	91.2	850	1	95.6	767	1	96.2	738	1	89.7
Venezuela	518	9	47.6	448	12	39.7	404	13	32.3	564	8	64.1	625	5	72.1

*Tie

TABLE 3
PERCENTAGE AND POINT CHANGES BY STATES, 1945-65

	% Change 1945-50	% Change 1950-55	% Change 1955-60	% Change 1960-65	% Change 1945-65	Maximum Point Shift	Net Point Shift 1945-65
Argentina	−10.6	− 5.5	+30.2	− 6.3	+ 7.8	139	− 12
Bolivia	+ 4.2	+ 6.1	+ 9.7	− 5.6	+14.4	91	+ 62
Brazil	+19.0	+ 4.0	+ 1.8	−10.4	+14.4	156	+ 44
Chile	+ 2.5	− 2.6	+ 4.4	+ 2.1	+ 6.4	57	− 32
Colombia	−13.6	−12.6	+20.7	− 2.0	− 7.5	194	−119
Costa Rica	− 4.2	+ 6.7	+ 6.1	− 1.2	+ 7.4	60	− 28
Cuba	+ 9.6	−23.6	− 6.1	−10.6	−30.7	306	−258
Domin. Rep.	+ 2.4	− 1.6	+ 1.6	+15.7	+18.1	106	+ 86
Ecuador	+14.9	+ 1.5	+10.5	−16.1	+10.8	127	+ 32
El Salvador	+ 2.5	+ 5.6	+ 7.4	0.0	+15.5	59	+ 59
Guatemala	+ 9.4	−12.6	+13.8	− 6.9	+ 3.7	80	− 18
Haiti	+ .7	+ 5.4	− 8.5	− 8.5	−10.9	142	−103
Honduras	+ 8.2	+ 5.9	+ 4.9	− 4.0	+15.0	95	+ 64
Mexico	+ 3.6	+10.8	+ 3.7	+ 1.8	+19.9	95	+ 73
Nicaragua	+ 1.8	− 3.0	+ 6.2	+ 7.0	+12.0	56	+ 43
Panama	+ 7.7	+ 4.1	+ 3.9	+ 3.4	+ 3.7	69	− 29
Paraguay	− .3	− .2	− .8	+ 6.6	+ 6.3	47	+ 4
Peru	− 9.4	− 7.7	+28.2	− 1.1	+10.0	142	+ 15
Uruguay	+ 3.5	+ 4.4	+ .6	− 6.5	+ 2.0	112	+ 66
Venezuela	− 7.9	− 7.4	+31.8	+ 8.0	+24.5	221	+107

the third column indicates the percentage position of each state in each survey. Utility of this calculation flows from the fact that, although the rank-order indicates an even distribution from first-ranked to last, this is not really the case, as is seen from distributions in the first column for each survey. In the 1965 results, for example, "1" and "2" are as far removed from each other as "3" and "4," but in points Uruguay and Costa Rica are separated by one though Chile and Mexico are distant from each other by seventy-eight points. Percentages are those of the spread between lowest and highest possible scores in each survey. If raw scores were to be used, the variation would be that between 170 and 850, but, in view of the adjustment of state scores, minima and maxima also need to be adjusted.[7] Using the minimum possible score in each survey as 0 percent and the maximum as 100 percent, appropriate distribution of adjusted point scores can be calculated, as shown in the third column for each survey. Especially for the 1960 survey but in a few instances in earlier surveys, a seeming anomaly can be noted by comparing the second and third columns. In the case of six states in the 1960 survey, the rank position declined from that of 1955 but the percentage increased. The explanation lies in the considerably higher total scores allotted by respondents in 1960 over those assigned in 1955.

The first four columns of Table 3 (derived from Table 2) indicate percentage changes by states for successive quinquennia of the surveys. The fifth column combines these and shows the net percentage change over twenty years. The sixth column reflects maximum point shifts by states through the five surveys, and the last column indicates the net point change between first and fifth surveys, i.e., between 1945 and 1965.

Even a cursory examination of Table 2 reveals the tendency of certain states to remain in relatively the same ranking in successive surveys. This is illustrated in a different way by determination of the respective numbers of evaluations of excellent, good, average, poor, and insignificant (A through E) allotted the several states in total on the five surveys. The sixty-one respondents participating in from one to five surveys gave each state a total of 1,950 evaluations (in chronological order for the five surveys, they were 150, 150, 300, 600, and 750). If a given state had received from every respondent in each survey an evaluation of B, it then would have had 1,950 B's and no other evaluations. The actual distribution is reflected in Table 4. Figures in parentheses indicate distribution for the 1965 survey alone.

Nearly as large a number of possibilities—1,500—was presented by the five surveys for total concentration of evaluations or partial or complete distribution by the respondents. In other words, all respondents could evaluate a given criterion as applied to a particular state as poor, or, on the other hand, their evaluations could wholly or partially cover the range from excellent to insignificant. The calculation is a test of how like-minded the respondents are; the answer is: they are not. Table 5 indicates the nature of the spread or concentration of evaluations in the respective surveys (with statistics for

TABLE 4
Distribution of Evaluation by States

	Excellent	Good	Average	Poor	Insignificant
Argentina	558 (216)	767 (302)	407 (193)	130 (39)	88 (0)
Bolivia	46 (17)	202 (75)	538 (220)	772 (320)	392 (118)
Brazil	310 (97)	713 (249)	723 (303)	177 (91)	27 (10)
Chile	874 (380)	805 (279)	250 (88)	20 (3)	1 (0)
Colombia	328 (123)	773 (315)	680 (263)	142 (48)	27 (1)
Costa Rica	1009 (446)	783 (272)	152 (32)	6 (0)	0 (0)
Cuba	208 (81)	450 (114)	514 (131)	363 (143)	415 (281)
Domin. Rep.	48 (17)	178 (78)	517 (283)	595 (294)	612 (78)
Ecuador	75 (20)	337 (81)	825 (316)	580 (277)	133 (56)
El Salvador	92 (43)	347 (131)	881 (381)	526 (179)	104 (16)
Guatemala	58 (18)	218 (73)	769 (293)	761 (326)	144 (40)
Haiti	34 (20)	107 (35)	276 (50)	578 (125)	955 (520)
Honduras	49 (11)	164 (67)	718 (291)	790 (320)	229 (61)
Mexico	463 (215)	837 (326)	525 (186)	99 (22)	26 (1)
Nicaragua	41 (22)	145 (70)	594 (268)	799 (320)	371 (70)
Panama	129 (53)	449 (185)	861 (354)	425 (141)	86 (17)
Paraguay	22 (14)	90 (45)	305 (150)	769 (306)	764 (235)
Peru	135 (71)	386 (178)	865 (354)	444 (138)	120 (9)
Uruguay	1272 (473)	586 (226)	85 (48)	7 (3)	0 (0)
Venezuela	267 (156)	667 (357)	692 (212)	221 (25)	103 (0)

TABLE 5
CONCENTRATION OR SPREAD IN EVALUATION, BY STATES

	1	2	3	4	5
Argentina	0 (0)	11 (0)	28 (7)	30 (8)	6 (0)
Bolivia	0 (0)	6 (0)	29 (4)	29 (7)	11 (4)
Brazil	0 (0)	6 (0)	33 (3)	28 (7)	8 (5)
Chile	0 (0)	15 (0)	47 (12)	12 (3)	1 (0)
Colombia	0 (0)	10 (0)	29 (4)	30 (10)	6 (1)
Costa Rica	0 (0)	27 (7)	45 (8)	3 (0)	0 (0)
Cuba	1 (0)	8 (0)	23 (4)	24 (4)	19 (7)
Dominican Republic	2 (0)	12 (0)	19 (0)	25 (8)	17 (7)
Ecuador	0 (0)	1 (0)	24 (1)	39 (11)	11 (3)
El Salvador	0 (0)	0 (0)	12 (1)	46 (9)	17 (5)
Guatemala	0 (0)	3 (0)	26 (0)	31 (11)	15 (4)
Haiti	0 (0)	12 (3)	33 (6)	21 (2)	9 (4)
Honduras	0 (0)	0 (0)	24 (1)	38 (13)	13 (1)
Mexico	0 (0)	3 (0)	33 (9)	29 (5)	10 (1)
Nicaragua	0 (0)	3 (0)	25 (0)	36 (9)	11 (6)
Panama	0 (0)	0 (0)	16 (1)	37 (6)	22 (8)
Paraguay	0 (0)	9 (0)	38 (1)	19 (9)	9 (5)
Peru	0 (0)	4 (0)	25 (1)	40 (11)	6 (3)
Uruguay	4 (0)	36 (1)	29 (12)	6 (2)	0 (0)
Venezuela	0 (0)	1 (0)	24 (5)	44 (10)	6 (0)

TABLE 6

CRITERIA	1945 POINTS	1945 RANK	1950 POINTS	1950 RANK	CHANGE IN POINTS, 1945-50	1955 POINTS	1955 RANK
Educational level	521	15	586	6	+65	562	8
Standard of living	525	13	563	11	+38	559	9
Internal unity	623	4	639	3	+16	627	3
Political maturity	561	8	576	8	+15	582	6
Lack of foreign domination	659	2	669	2	+10	686	2
Freedom of speech, etc.	650	3	609	5	−41	605	5
Free elections	552	9	538	15	−14	541	12
Free party organization	546	10	548	14	+ 2	533	14
Judicial independence	574	5	581	7	+ 7	547	10
Government funds	523	14	552	12	+29	544	11
Social legislation	562	7	622	4	+60	609	4
Civilian supremacy	567	6	568	10	+ 1	521	15
Lack of ecclesiastical control	732	1	717	1	−15	722	1
Government administration	539	12	569	9	+30	565	7
Local government	542	11	551	13	+ 9	540	13

* Tie

1965 alone given in parentheses). In 197 instances, a considerable majority of them in 1960 and 1965 because of the larger numbers of respondents, evaluations represented the whole gamut from A to E inclusive (Column 5). In only seven instances in the five surveys were all respondents agreed on their evaluations for a specific criterion applied to a given state (Column 1). All respondents were in accord in 1950 that civilian supremacy over the military in Cuba should be rated as good and that progress toward free elections in the Dominican Republic was insignificant; in 1955, all concurred in adjudging that freedom of party organization and operation in the Dominican Republic was insignificant and that Uruguay's position in regard to freedom of expression, freedom of elections, nature of party organization, and civilian supremacy should be rated excellent. No unanimity in evaluations was shown in 1945, 1960, or 1965.

Spread of evaluations over two, three, or four ratings, not necessarily contiguous (i.e., A and B; B and C; B, C, and D; etc.) reflected all the variation shown in Table 5. Like-mindedness was least with respect to (a) Panama, in which case twenty-two of the seventy-five evaluations reflected the complete range of ratings and thirty-seven more represented a spread over four possibilities, and (b) El Salvador, which showed a complete distribution of evaluations in seventeen instances and a spread over four ratings in forty-six other cases. Concurrence of viewpoint was most in evidence with regard to Uruguay,

CHANGES IN EVALUATIONS, BY CRITERIA, 1945-65

	1960			1965				
CHANGE IN POINTS,	POINTS	RANK	CHANGE IN POINTS, 1955-60	POINTS	RANK	CHANGE IN POINTS 1960-65	CHANGE IN POINTS 1945-65	% GAIN 1945-65
−24	590	13	+28	609	10	+19	+88	16.9
− 4	571	15	+12	573	14	+ 2	+48	9.1
−12	666	4	+39	636	4	−30	+13	2.1
+ 6	617	10	+35	621	8	+ 4	+60	10.7
+17	724	2	+38	729	2	+ 5	+70	10.6
− 4	689	3	+84	680	3	− 9	+30	4.6
+ 3	659	5	+118	628*	5½*	−31	+76	13.3
−15	630	7	+97	627	7	− 3	+81	14.8
−34	620	9	+73	615	9	− 5	+41	7.1
− 8	602	12	+58	597	12	− 5	+74	14.1
−13	629	8	+20	628*	5½*	− 1	+66	11.7
−47	632	6	+111	600	11	−32	+33	5.8
+ 5	739	1	+17	761	1	+22	+29	4.0
− 4	612	11	+47	594	13	−18	+55	10.2
−11	583	14	+43	561	15	−22	+19	3.5

Costa Rica, and Chile; it was doubtless not coincidence that those three were uniformly regarded as the most democratic of the Latin American states.

Analysis of the data is possible also with respect to the criteria used as well as the state involved. Any consensus revealed may give clues to the direction and tempo of shifts occurring among the various components of Latin American democracy. Table 6 reflects the points attained by each criterion in successive surveys, the corresponding ranks, and point changes for appropriate periods. The same data are shown graphically in Figure 3. Scrutiny of the shifts as seen by successive panels of specialists shows interesting trends that can now be backed up by measurable methods, although perhaps only gross deductions are justifiable at this stage.

Insofar as the cumulation of evaluations of excellent, good, etc., is concerned, it presumably stands to reason that such distribution, as it affects the criteria, would show less divergence than as applied to the states. The distribution for the five surveys is indicated in Table 7, with that for the fifth survey alone being shown in parentheses in each case. Concentration or spread of evaluations, as applied to criteria, is presented in Table 8, analogous to Table 5 affecting the states; 1965 survey results are indicated in parentheses. Implications of Table 8 are that respondents found disagreement easiest with respect to the state of internal unity and the absence or presence of foreign domination;

400　　　　　　　　　　　　　　　　STUDIES ON DEMOCRATIZATION

1. Freedom from ecclesiastical control .....
2. Lack of foreign domination
3. Freedom of speech, etc. ....
4. Internal unity ....
5. Judicial independence .....
6. Civilian supremacy ....
7. Social legislation ....
8. Political maturity ....
9. Free elections ....
10. Free party organization....
11. Local government ....
12. Government administration.
13. Standard of living ....
14. Government funds ......
15. Educational level ....

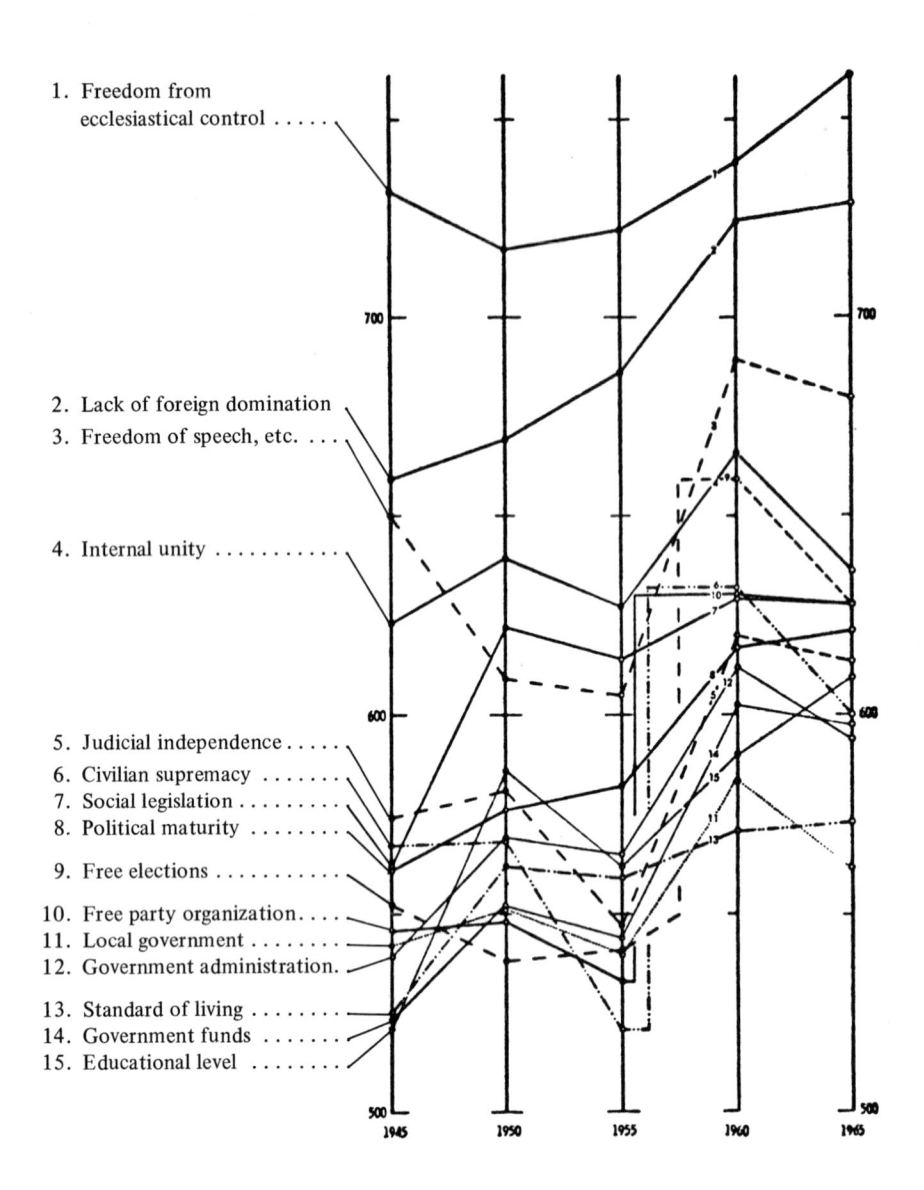

FIGURE 3

TABLE 7
DISTRIBUTION OF EVALUATIONS, BY CRITERIA

	EXCELLENT	GOOD	AVERAGE	POOR	INSIGNIFICANT
Educational level	342 (139)	496 (198)	742 (319)	692 (256)	328 (88)
Standard of living	136 (56)	548 (214)	918 (367)	734 (267)	264 (96)
Internal unity	391 (144)	668 (243)	824 (323)	547 (231)	170 (59)
Political maturity	377 (169)	548 (197)	737 (293)	651 (253)	287 (88)
Lack of foreign domination	652 (264)	756 (318)	695 (255)	384 (124)	113 (39)
Freedom of speech, etc.	688 (276)	560 (221)	589 (241)	415 (151)	348 (111)
Free elections	556 (234)	510 (186)	551 (228)	494 (191)	489 (161)
Free party organization	446 (182)	574 (245)	602 (241)	500 (188)	478 (144)
Judicial independence	367 (157)	610 (233)	675 (280)	556 (188)	392 (142)
Government funds	243 (94)	553 (224)	858 (357)	602 (224)	344 (101)
Social legislation	295 (117)	669 (269)	850 (331)	563 (202)	223 (81)
Civilian supremacy	481 (212)	474 (153)	589 (217)	583 (259)	473 (159)
Lack of ecclesiastical control	715 (320)	830 (296)	737 (275)	251 (89)	67 (20)
Government administration	175 (67)	672 (259)	893 (350)	577 (223)	283 (101)
Local government	154 (62)	538 (202)	917 (339)	655 (274)	336 (123)

TABLE 8

CONCENTRATION OR SPREAD IN EVALUATIONS, BY CRITERIA

	1	2	3	4	5
Educational level	0 (0)	20 (1)	52 (8)	28 (11)	0 (0)
Standard of living	0 (0)	21 (1)	50 (8)	29 (11)	0 (0)
Internal unity	0 (0)	6 (1)	25 (5)	41 (7)	28 (7)
Political maturity	0 (0)	18 (2)	30 (3)	42 (12)	10 (3)
Lack of foreign domination	0 (0)	5 (0)	29 (6)	39 (8)	27 (6)
Freedom of speech, etc.	1 (0)	17 (1)	38 (8)	34 (9)	10 (2)
Free elections	2 (0)	18 (1)	33 (6)	35 (8)	12 (5)
Free party organization	2 (0)	11 (2)	35 (1)	39 (13)	13 (4)
Judicial independence	0 (0)	6 (0)	40 (6)	40 (7)	14 (7)
Government funds	0 (0)	5 (0)	27 (3)	47 (7)	21 (10)
Social legislation	0 (0)	8 (0)	51 (5)	35 (12)	6 (3)
Civilian supremacy	2 (0)	16 (1)	31 (3)	36 (11)	15 (5)
Lack of ecclesiastical control	0 (0)	7 (1)	35 (6)	37 (8)	21 (5)
Government administration	0 (0)	6 (0)	40 (8)	45 (8)	9 (4)
Local government	0 (0)	3 (0)	45 (4)	41 (13)	11 (3)

the two criteria represented, respectively, complete spreads in twenty-eight and twenty-seven instances.

Development of a stereotypic point of view is apparently easier with regard to the states than it is respecting the criteria. As Tables 7 and 4 indicate, only one of the criteria, that on the lack of ecclesiastical influence, shows a disparity between the largest and smallest numbers of evaluations of more than 10:1. In the case of the states, such a ratio is exceeded in fifteen instances. It would seem a reasonable deduction that "images" generally held in common, whether favorable or unfavorable, are more easily formed with regard to the states than the criteria.

The question is also raised: how are the criteria interrelated, what is their correlation, what impact does one have on others? Intuitive answers are possible in some degree, but they are often unsatisfactory, even to the person who gives them: they leave the frustration of lack of proof of the "hunch." With only fifteen criteria involved in the present analysis, correlations could not be made with the impressiveness of those reached in the comprehensive Yale Political Data Program, for example, an operation that involved many scores of kinds of data. And yet, with the use of a chi-square formula, supplemented with determination of correlations, as given by the coefficient of contingency, a satisfactory measure of the interrelationship of the various criteria as seen by the respondents can be ascertained.[8] Values of the correlations are indicated in Table 9. The upper right diagonal half of the table gives the chi-square values for each pair of criteria; the lower left half gives corresponding values of the coefficient of contingency correlation. Criterion numbers, at top and side for columns and rows, are those identifying the criteria listed above.

TABLE 9
CORRELATIONS AMONG CRITERIA

Criteria	1	2	3	4	5	6	7	8	9	10	11	12	13	14	15
1		1362.3	926.8	1185.3	282.1	849.1	720.2	683.3	794.6	770.1	892.9	611.8	318.5	857.8	737.6
2	.759		875.7	1033.1	271.5	641.9	570.7	542.5	748.9	764.9	777.5	483.5	309.5	834.6	754.3
3	.694	.683		1330.2	280.2	550.4	533.0	572.3	531.0	627.4	685.2	614.0	407.7	715.2	598.3
4	.736	.713	.756		382.9	979.4	936.2	858.4	885.8	882.5	980.2	797.4	375.3	990.6	561.3
5	.469	.462	.468	.526		587.8	410.5	337.0	502.8	414.0	265.4	302.5	371.6	376.2	361.8
6	.678	.625	.596	.703	.608		1532.1	1351.3	1254.0	880.7	739.4	764.1	460.7	795.7	948.8
7	.647	.603	.590	.695	.539	.778		1650.9	1273.4	888.8	779.8	1055.6	403.9	867.2	888.7
8	.637	.593	.603	.680	.502	.758	.789		1159.6	835.0	709.2	854.5	325.5	794.6	849.0
9	.665	.654	.589	.685	.578	.746	.748	.733		1145.3	990.0	710.6	471.3	1130.3	1192.1
10	.660	.658	.621	.685	.541	.684	.686	.675	.731		1045.7	645.6	387.5	1214.0	1033.4
11	.687	.661	.638	.704	.458	.652	.662	.644	.705	.715		577.7	356.2	996.0	821.9
12	.616	.571	.617	.666	.482	.658	.717	.679	.645	.626	.605		293.8	703.2	619.4
13	.491	.486	.538	.522	.520	.562	.536	.496	.566	.528	.512	.477		332.3	351.5
14	.680	.674	.646	.705	.523	.666	.681	.665	.728	.740	.706	.643	.499		1426.7
15	.652	.656	.612	.700	.515	.698	.686	.678	.737	.713	.672	.618	.510	.767	
C averages	.648	.628	.618	.677	.513	.672	.668	.652	.679	.662	.640	.616	.517	.666	.658

High values in the lower half of the table indicate a high degree of correlation. Greatest correlation shown is that between freedom of elections and freedom of party organization and expression; the result is not unexpected, but the table reveals just how high the respondents feel the correlation is. Lowest degree of correlation is that between freedom from foreign domination and the nature of social legislation; these two criteria, the respondents believe, have little interaction on each other.

Averages for correlation values (C) are shown at the bottom of Table 9. Again, a high average indicates high correlation. Somewhat surprisingly, the greatest overall correlation is that of judicial independence with the other criteria. In order following it are: political maturity, freedom of expression, freedom of elections, governmental administration, attitude toward public funds, nature of local government, party organization, educational level, social legislation, standard of living, internal unity, civilian supremacy, freedom from ecclesiastical influence, and freedom from foreign domination. It should be stressed, however, that these are *averages* of correlations. Highest individual instances of correlation were between freedom of election and both freedom of party organization and of expression and between governmental administration and local government.

Continued caution about blind reliance on statistical determination of correlations is important. As was suggested in the published analysis of 1960 survey results (Fitzgibbon and Johnson, 1961),

> the size of the scores obtained in the chi-square analysis is no absolute basis for judgment. Rather, the scores act as a guide to further inquiry. The scores themselves are not nearly so important as the reason for their occurrence. If intuitive "hunches" about the analytical categories can be confirmed statistically, there is every reason to suggest their continued use. If the statistical procedures tend to contradict well based intuition then an additional analysis into latent structures and operative sub-variables may remove the contradiction or reveal errors in method.

Evaluation sheets sent to respondents for the 1960 and 1965 surveys included provision for indicating self-assessment as to the respondent's familiarity with both states and criteria (see Figure 1). From the beginning of the surveys, many respondents have protested that they were not qualified to pass judgment on certain criteria applied to particular states (the author, as a participant, it may be added, shares the feeling as it relates to himself). It was only the author's insistence, on the ground that statistical analysis required complete filling of the sheets, that ultimately elicited loyal, though reluctant, cooperation in some instances. Unfortunately, no analysis of the "familiarity level" assessments could be undertaken in 1960, but it has been done this time. The computer was programmed to make a relatively intricate digest of the influence of familiarity levels on evaluations, but it turned out that a simpler analysis was in reality more revealing.

TABLE 10

INFLUENCE OF FAMILIARITY LEVELS ON EVALUATIONS

STATES	LITTLE A+B	LITTLE D+E	GREAT A+B	GREAT D+E
Argentina	15	0	247	15
Bolivia	25	131	21	81
Brazil	34	9	167	38
Chile	15	0	302	2
Colombia	35	18	182	24
Costa Rica	97	0	244	0
Cuba	36	122	57	145
Dominican Republic	15	130	24	80
Ecuador	27	117	23	46
El Salvador	71	93	49	31
Guatemala	16	102	55	81
Haiti	20	275	5	53
Honduras	24	166	17	65
Mexico	0	0	348	17
Nicaragua	26	164	25	56
Panama	32	45	56	33
Paraguay	21	281	11	61
Peru	21	24	93	36
Uruguay	60	0	243	0
Venezuela	33	4	187	2
Totals	623	1,681	2,356	866

CRITERIA				
1	14	17	115	125
2	0	0	105	163
3	0	0	115	113
4	8	8	178	170
5	0	0	348	79
6	0	0	279	153
7	0	0	289	257
8	0	0	237	178
9	150	154	65	37
10	90	112	45	39
11	45	42	100	61
12	0	0	132	238
13	48	13	162	28
14	69	88	37	40
15	115	242	19	40
Totals	539	676	2,226	1,721

As a general conclusion, it may be asserted that those who tend to be less self-confident in their evaluations, i.e., the respondents who indicate "little" familiarity with a given state or criterion, are harsher or more unfavorable in their evaluations. Ones who are more confident of their acquaintance with particular states or criteria (who recorded "great" familiarity) look more favorably on achievement in the appropriate categories. Results, for 1965, are shown in Table 10. The first two columns of figures indicate the numbers of instances in which those who expressed *little* familiarity with the states or the criteria evaluated the one or the other as either excellent or good (A+B) or, on the other hand, poor or insignificant (D+E). The third and fourth columns show the same results on the part of respondents who expressed *great* familiarity with particular states or criteria. It will be noted that in all pairs of additions, for both states and criteria, the totals of unfavorable evaluations are substantially greater than the favorable ones from those who felt little familiarity, but that the reverse is true in all cases for those who consider themselves quite familiar with the states or criteria.

A related area of analysis involved determination, from the 1965 survey, of which states and which criteria appeared to be most familiar to the respondents. This, as shown in Table 11, required only a simple calculation. The first three columns of figures show, for both states and criteria, the numbers of respondents indicating, respectively, little, moderate, or great familiarity. These self-ratings are assigned, respectively, values of one, two, and three points per unit and totals are indicated in the fourth column; ranking then follows in the last column. As might be expected, neighboring Mexico is the state with which most respondents consider themselves familiar, then the ABC countries of South America, and least of all, Paraguay, Haiti, and Honduras. Similarly, respondents collectively regard themselves as most familiar with the criterion of freedom of elections, least so with the nature of local government.

It also seemed worthwhile to attempt to determine the relationship of respondents' professions or approach to Latin America as a factor in the sorts of evaluations they gave. With a sample of no more than fifty (respondents), it would be possible to use only relatively broad categories in order to have subgroups sufficiently large to be statistically significant. The only categories thus possible were (a) those engaged in academic pursuits and (b) all others. The "academics" and "nonacademics" numbered, respectively, thirty-six and fourteen. Identifications had to be somewhat arbitrary, inasmuch as in a few cases individuals straddled a professional fence or had had both kinds of careers at one time or another. The panel includes a small group engaged in journalism, several who formerly were in government service, and a very small number who, because of the diversity of their professional interests, would have to be labeled "miscellaneous"; in no case are these subgroups large enough to treat separately from a statistical standpoint. Had circumstances permitted, it would have been interesting and probably desirable to

TABLE 11

Familiarity with States and Criteria

States	Little	Moderate	Great	Points	Rank
Argentina	1	27	22	121	2½
Bolivia	14	27	9	95	13
Brazil	4	25	21	117	4
Chile	2	25	23	121	2½
Colombia	6	23	21	115	5
Costa Rica	7	26	17	110	8½
Cuba	13	21	16	103	10
Dominican Republic	17	23	10	93	14
Ecuador	17	24	9	92	15
El Salvador	22	19	9	87	17
Guatemala	13	23	14	101	11
Haiti	21	25	4	83	19
Honduras	23	18	9	86	18
Mexico	0	17	33	133	1
Nicaragua	20	22	8	88	16
Panama	10	31	9	99	12
Paraguay	25	19	6	81	20
Peru	5	30	15	110	8½
Uruguay	4	29	17	113	6
Venezuela	4	30	16	112	7

Criteria					
1	2	30	18	116	8½
2	0	29	21	121	7
3	0	34	16	116	8½
4	1	25	24	123	6
5	0	22	28	128	3
6	0	22	28	128	3
7	0	15	35	135	1
8	0	23	27	127	5
9	21	23	6	85	14
10	14	30	6	92	13
11	6	32	12	106	11
12	0	22	28	128	3
13	4	34	12	108	10
14	12	32	6	94	12
15	27	19	4	77	15

include a selection of Latin Americans among the respondents, though a few are included who (though United States citizens) are of Latin birth or ancestry.

The author would have guessed that those who dwelt in groves of academe would have been more lenient in judgment of Latin American political achievement and that the "hard-boiled" and "practical" men of affairs, in direct professional contact with Latin America, would have viewed the several

Comparison of Respondents' Indices, Academic and Non-Academic, 1965

MEANS
O = Overall: .94609
A = Academic: .97256
N = Non-academic: .87804
● Academic
■ Non-academic

Respondents' Rank Order

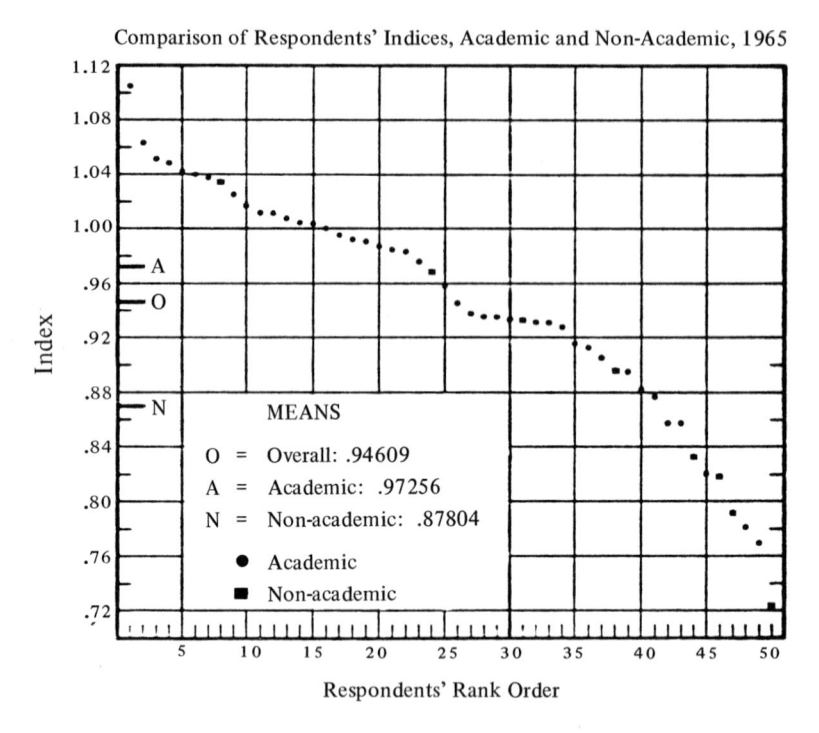

FIGURE 4

countries with more jaundiced eyes. That turned out decidedly not to be the case. The approach of the "eggheads" (to label them irreverently) was definitely the more rigorous. To determine the differentials at all accurately, it was necessary to calculate what, for want of a better term, can be called a "respondent index" for each survey participant. This was based on the total letter evaluations made by each respondent. They varied from a high of 1.10680 (most critical or rigorous) to a low of .72124 (most lenient or favorable).

Of the fourteen nonacademic participants, two came above the median point, twelve below it. Twenty-three of the academic respondents were above the median, thirteen below that point. Distribution is shown graphically in Figure 4. Perhaps there are deductions to be made from such distribution but the author shies away in timidity from making them.

The problem of comparing objective and subjective measurements, i.e., those making use of census-type data and, on the other hand, the evaluations of specialists, is complex and, at this stage of development of analyses, not entirely satisfactory or reliable. The Lipset (1959) and Almond-Coleman (1960) studies employed a limited number of indices of development. The precise relevance of those, or a larger number, to the aspects whose measurement is sought, is difficult to be assured of.

It seemed desirable, at any rate, to select as large a number of indices as could be found which presumptively contributed to improvement of the human situation in Latin America, on the assumption that that in turn would be conducive to democratic development. The relationship here is indirect and tenuous, but perhaps as good as can be devised, granted the reliance on objective data only. As a source of information, the *Statistical Abstract of Latin America* for 1963 was used.[9] The writer selected from it thirty-three indices over which human endeavor has some ability to control the results, and each with statistics for at least half of the Latin American states. They divided broadly into five categories: demographic, economic, social, cultural, and political. In some instances, indicated below by the characterization "reversed," a low figure reflects high achievement, e.g., for infant death rate or illiteracy.

The indices used were: *demographic:* (1) crude death rate (reversed); (2) infant death rate (reversed); (3) annual percentage increase in population (reversed); (4) life expectancy of males at birth; (5) urban population as a percentage of the total; *economic:* (6) percentage of economically active population in manufacturing; (7) per capita energy consumption; (8) motor vehicles per 1,000 persons; (9) miles of road per 1,000 square miles of area; (10) miles of railway per 1,000 square miles of area; (11) percentage of government receipts from direct taxes; (12) percentage of government receipts from customs (reversed); (13) annual per capita growth rate of GDP; (14) per capita share of national income in U.S. dollars; (15) per capita currency circulation in U.S. dollars; *social:* (16) number of persons per physician (reversed); (17) number of persons per hospital bed (reversed); (18) number of persons per dentist (reversed); (19) per capita daily caloric intake; (20) per capita production of quality meats; (21) per capita production of milk; (22) percentage of dwellings with electricity; (23) telephones per 1,000 persons; (24) percentage of government budget used for public health and welfare; *cultural:* (25) illiteracy (reversed); (26) school enrollment as percentage of school-age population; (27) per capita expenditures for education in U.S. dollars; (28) percentage of national income used for education; (29) percentage of central government budget used for education; (30) daily newspaper circulation per 1,000 persons; (31) per capita frequency of cinema attendance; (32) radio receivers per 1,000 persons; *political:* (33) percentage of population voting.

The best performance, either direct or reversed, was treated as 100 percent and other percentages calculated therefrom. Totals of percentages for each

TABLE 12

	No. of Indices Applicable	Total of Percentages	Average of Percentages	Objective Rank	Subjective Rank 1960	Subjective Rank 1965
Argentina	32	2,347	73	2	4	6
Bolivia	29	1,308	45	14	16	17
Brazil	30	1,437	48	10	7	8
Chile	31	1,954	63	5	3	3
Colombia	31	1,627	52	9	6	7
Costa Rica	30	1,695	56.5	7	2	2
Cuba	23	1,656	72.0	4	14	18
Domin. Rep.	24	948	40	18	18	14
Ecuador	30	1,232	41.1	16	10	12
El Salvador	28	1,320	47.1	12	12	11
Guatemala	32	1,311	41	17	13	13
Haiti	26	693	27	20	19	20
Honduras	28	989	35	19	15	15
Mexico	31	1,681	54	8	5	4
Nicaragua	23	1,056	46	13	17	16
Panama	28	1,585	56.6	6	11	10
Paraguay	23	1,021	44	15	20	19
Peru	29	1,372	47.3	11	9	9
Uruguay	17	1,253	74	1	1	1
Venezuela	31	2,240	72.3	3	8	5

state, for all indices for which information was available, were then determined and an average worked out (taking into account the varying number of indices applicable to each state). The detailed analyses were much too comprehensive to be reproduced here, although a summary is shown in Table 12. For comparison's sake, the specialists' state rankings in 1960 and 1965 (from Table 2) are included. Inasmuch as the time lag of reproduction of data in the *Statistical Abstract* is probably at least a year or two "after the fact," comparison of objective rankings with subjective rankings for 1960 is likely to be more valid than with those for 1965.

These views, however, purport to give total pictures of Latin America, either objective or subjective. And the pictures, assuming them to be photographs, are not, as it were, taken from the same angle. It would consequently be better, if possible, to get a more accurate comparison of objective and subjective measurements. Of the fifteen criteria used in these surveys, the first two—the educational level and the standard of living—are the ones which lend themselves best to comparison with the census-type data. For a more accurate comparison, then, the data included in Indices 25–29, as listed above, were compared with 1960 and 1965 evaluations on Criterion 1 (educational level) and the data in Indices 19–23 above with respective evaluations on Criterion 2 (standard of living). Results are shown in Table 13. It is not possible to compare objective and subjective percentages in the table, inasmuch as they were calculated differently; percentages do serve the purpose, however, of indicating relative differentials among states by either the objective or subjective measurement. Comparison of rank orders is possible and it indicates, especially insofar as the educational level is concerned, that little correlation exists between the objective and subjective approaches; correlation is somewhat better in respect to measurement of the standard of living, although considerable discrepancies are in evidence, particularly with regard to the Dominican Republic, Haiti, and one or two other states. The author trusts it is not merely rationalization which leads him to believe that the subjective measurements may be more accurate than the objective. It is, of course, very possible that the objective indices available did not give an accurate or complete profile of a given aspect of a state, but it is difficult to believe, for example, that Argentina would have no better than seventh or Uruguay ninth rank among Latin American states in respect to the educational level.

Overall conclusions to be drawn from surveys of this kind are, and perhaps will always have to be, tentative. As has been stressed repeatedly, it is not democratic achievement per se that is being measured, but rather attitudes regarding democratic achievement. This may be a distinction without a difference, but the distinction needs to be made. With that caveat, a number of deductions may be indicated. Three Latin American states, Uruguay, Costa Rica, and Chile, have uniformly occupied the first three rankings over a twenty-year period. Paraguay, Haiti, Nicaragua, and Bolivia have regularly been included among the lowest six states throughout five surveys; the

TABLE 13

	Educational Level								Standard of Living							
	Objective		Subjective						Objective		Subjective					
			1960		1965						1960		1965			
	%	Rank	%	Rank	%	Rank			%	Rank	%	Rank	%	Rank		
Argentina	62	7	99	3	99	2			91	2	100	1	100	1		
Bolivia	48	12	42	18	42	18			23	20	41	18	39	19		
Brazil	67	5	67	8	69	9			36	10	75	9	72	7½		
Chile	72	4	90	4	89	4			55.8	4	79	5	81	6		
Colombia	54	10	74.9	7	74	7			46	6	76	8	72	7½		
Costa Rica	77.6	3	100	1½	97	3			56.2	5	93	3	93	3		
Cuba	65	6	75.1	6	82	5			61	3	77	7	66	10		
Dominican Republic	47	14	52	13	52	13			24	19	68.2	10	55.7	14		
Ecuador	47.2	13	51	14	49	15			29	15	58	14	50	17		
El Salvador	41	17	59	11	59	11			32.4	11	63	12	64	11		
Guatemala	35	18	48	16	47	16½			28.7	16	53.5	16	54	15		
Haiti	22	20	29	20	24	20			30	13	31	20	26	20		
Honduras	41.6	16	44	17	47	16½			31.7	12	48	17	52	16		
Mexico	52	11	80	5	78	6			40	9	81	4	82	4½		
Nicaragua	34	19	49	15	51	14			28	17	54.1	15	56.3	13		
Panama	79	1	63	9	66	10			41	8	67.6	11	68	9		
Paraguay	58	8	34	19	41.5	19			29.5	14	41	19	48	18		
Peru	42.5	15	56	12	56	12			26	18	62	13	60	12		
Uruguay	55	9	100	1½	100	1			94	1	95	2	98	2		
Venezuela	78.4	2	62	10	73	8			45	7	78	6	82	4½		

Measuring Democratic Change in Latin America 413

Dominican Republic and Honduras were in that unenviable bottom half dozen four times each. No state has yet "cracked" the monopoly of the top three; Peru and Cuba have, once each, been in the lowest bracket, for which blame is probably due, respectively, to Odría and Castro. As is revealed by percentage measurements in Table 2, states show a tendency to "bunch" in the successive surveys. Such grouping is indicated in Table 14. Gaps between groups are in no case less than 5 percent.

TABLE 14

BUNCHING

1945	1950	1955	1960	1965
Uruguay	Uruguay	Uruguay	Uruguay	Uruguay
Costa Rica			Costa Rica	Costa Rica
Chile	Chile			Chile
Colombia		Costa Rica		
	Costa Rica	Chile	Chile	
	Cuba		Argentina	Mexico
Argentina		Mexico		Venezuela
Cuba	Brazil	Brazil	Mexico	Argentina
	Colombia		Colombia	Colombia
Mexico	Mexico	Colombia	Brazil	
Panama	Argentina	Argentina	Venezuela	Brazil
Venezuela		Cuba		Peru
Peru	Ecuador	Panama	Peru	Panama
Brazil	Guatemala	Ecuador	Ecuador	El Salvador
	Panama	El Salvador	Panama	
Guatemala	Venezuela		El Salvador	Ecuador
El Salvador	Peru	Honduras	Guatemala	Guatemala
Ecuador	El Salvador	Venezuela	Cuba	Dominican Rep.
		Guatemala	Honduras	Honduras
Nicaragua	Honduras	Bolivia	Bolivia	Nicaragua
Haiti	Nicaragua	Peru		Bolivia
Honduras	Bolivia	Haiti	Nicaragua	Cuba
Bolivia	Haiti			
Dominican Rep.	Dominican Rep.	Nicaragua	Dominican Rep.	Paraguay
Paraguay	Paraguay	Dominican Rep.	Haiti	
		Paraguay	Paraguay	Haiti

Greatest change in democratic ranking naturally takes place among the states that are consistently neither at the top nor the bottom. The plummeting of Cuba from fourth rank in 1950 to eighteenth in 1965 is most spectacular. Venezuela's improvement from twelfth rank in 1950 to fifth in 1965 is also significant.

With regard to conclusions to be drawn from scrutiny of the data involving the criteria, the immediate postwar half decade appeared to reflect improvement in the overall situation, especially with regard to such matters as the educational level, social legislation, and the standard of living. Conditions in the first half of the 1950s deteriorated, as one after another dictator consolidated a hold on power. The last half of the same decade witnessed a remarkable improvement, as one by one the *caudillos* fell from power, almost always violently. The quinquennium just past has written a balance sheet with both red- and black-ink entries. For the period of two decades, however, the respondents are of the opinion that progress has been general and in some ways remarkable. More than half of the criteria employed showed better than 10 percent improvement during the twenty years.

The nature of the political process in Latin America is subtle and fluid, as, indeed, it is everywhere. Latin America possesses enough of a common denominator to make analysis of changes in that whole community of states useful and perhaps significant. No one realizes better than the present writer that the approach and methodology used in the current series of surveys are subject to improvement. They do, however, provide an in-depth attitudinal and judgmental consensus by a panel of specialists whose expertise cannot be challenged (see for example Wolf, 1965b: 20). Presumably the technique could be extended to other areas, perhaps Africa and Asia, although the common denominator would doubtless be less substantial in both of those continents.

NOTES

1. The advantages and risks of the two approaches are well summarized in Marvick (1962: 5). See also, e.g. Lipset (1959: 69–105) and Almond and Coleman (1960: 532–576).

2. See, e.g. Almond (1956: 391–409). The dramatically different nature of the Latin American milieu from that in the United States is vividly analyzed in Alba (1965).

3. In the first two surveys ten persons participated each time; in the third survey, twenty, in the fourth, forty; and in the last one fifty. The list below identifies by superscript numbers the respective surveys participated in by each person: Robert J. Alexander[4-5] (Rutgers), Marvin Alisky[4-5] (Arizona State), Samuel F. Bemis[1-2] (Yale), George I. Blanksten[2-5] (Northwestern), Spruille Braden[4-5] (former Assistant Secretary of State), Frank R. Brandenburg[4-5] (Committee for Economic Development), Ben Burnett[5] (Whittier), James L. Busey[4-5] (Colorado), Ronald H. Chilcote[5] (California, Riverside), Howard Cline[4-5] (Director, Hispanic Foundation, Library of Congress), George G. Daniels[5] (*Time*), Harold E. Davis[3-5] (American), John C. Dreier[5] (Hopkins), Jules Dubois[3-5] (*Chicago Tribune*), Alex T. Edelmann[5] (Nebraska), Charles G. Fenwick[5] (former Director, Department of International Law and Organization, Pan American Union), Russell H. Fitzgibbon[1-5] (University of California, Santa Barbara), William Forbis[4] (*Time*), Jesús de Galíndez[3] (Columbia), Federico G. Gil[4-5] (North Carolina), Rosendo Gomez[4-5] (Arizona), Stephen S. Goodspeed[3-5] (California, Santa Barbara), Frances R. Grant[5] (Secretary General, Inter-American Association for Democracy and Freedom), Paul E. Hadley[4-5] (Southern California), Robert M. Hallett[3]

(*Christian Science Monitor*), Simon G. Hanson[5] (*Inter-American Economic Affairs*), Clarence H. Haring[1] (Harvard), Robert D. Hayton[5] (Hunter), Hubert C. Herring[1-5] (Claremont Graduate School), Henry F. Holland[4] (former Assistant Secretary of State), Preston E. James[4-5] (Syracuse), Betram B. Johansson[4-5] (*Christian Science Monitor*), Kenneth F. Johnson[5] (Colorado State), Miguel Jorrín[3-5] (New Mexico), Harry Kantor[3-5] (Florida), Merle Kling[4-5] (Washington, St. Louis), Leo B. Lott[4-5] (Ohio State), Austin F. Macdonald[1-4] (California, Berkeley), William Manger[4-5] (former Assistant Secretary General, Organization of American States), John D. Martz[5] (North Carolina), Herbert L. Matthews[4-5] (*New York Times*), J. Lloyd Mecham[1-5] (Texas), Edward G. Miller, Jr.[4-5] (former Assistant Secretary of State), Dana G. Munro[1-5] (Princeton), Harry B. Murkland[3-4] (*Newsweek*), Martin C. Needler[5] (Michigan), L. Vincent Padgett[4-5] (San Diego State), C. Neale Ronning[5] (Tulane), William L. Schurz[3-4] (American Institute of Foreign Trade), Robert E. Scott[3-5] (Illinois), K. H. Silvert[4-5] (Dartmouth), James H. Stebbins[4] (former Executive Vice President, W. R. Grace and Company), William S. Stokes[1-5] (Claremont Men's), Graham H. Stuart[1-2] (Stanford), Tad Szulc[5] (*New York Times*), Philip B. Taylor, Jr.[3-5] (Hopkins), Edward Tomlinson[5] (*Reader's Digest*), Martin B. Travis, Jr.[3-5] (State University of New York), Henry Wells[5] (Pennsylvania), Arthur P. Whitaker[1-5] (Pennsylvania), A. Curtis Wilgus[4-5] (Florida).

4. In a moment of whimsy, Mr. Royer programmed the computer to conclude its printouts of occasional data with a neatly typed "sir." In view of the increasing respect which he and the writer developed for the computer's abilities, it was perhaps only appropriate that the machine, too, should be somewhat respectful.

5. Minima and maxima in raw scores given by a single respondent in the five surveys were: 1945: 750 and 1,229½, a range of 479½; 1950: 798 and 1,184, a range of 386; 1955: 741½ and 1,186, a range of 441½; 1960: 911½ and 1,334½, a range of 423; 1965: 903½ and 1,386½, a range of 483.

6. Alteration of rankings as between raw and adjusted scores occurred in only one instance in the five surveys. Table 1 indicates that Costa Rica and Uruguay are tied in 1965 for first rank with 781½ points each. Actually, Costa Rica led by an infinitesimal margin. Total raw scores accumulated by Costa Rica and Uruguay were, respectively, 3,980½ and 3,907½. Inasmuch as the third, fourth, and fifth surveys involved larger numbers of respondents, it was necessary to divide their raw and adjusted scores by, respectively, two, four and five to make them comparable with results in the first two surveys. In the rounding necessary, this meant that the two states appeared to have identical raw scores in 1965. After adjustments were calculated, as indicated above, Uruguay took first rank with 738 points to 737 for Costa Rica.

7. Adjusted minima and maxima for the successive surveys were: 1945: 178 and 892; 1950: 173 and 865; 1955: 176 and 881; 1960: 158 and 792; 1965: 161 and 804.

8. A more complete description of the process of determining correlations as used in the 1960 surveys, is given in Fitzgibbon and Johnson (1961: 522-525).

9. The *Statistical Abstract of Latin America* for 1964 (copyright, 1965) was available but in some ways was less satisfactory than that for the preceding year. Many of the data are carried over unchanged from the 1963 issue and certain indices used in the 1963 issue are omitted from that for 1964.

REFERENCES

ALBA, V. (1965) *Alliance without Allies: The Mythology of Progress in Latin America.* New York: Frederick A. Praeger.

ALMOND, G.A. (1956) "Comparative political systems." *Journal of Politics* 18: 391–409.

ALMOND, G.A. and J.S. COLEMAN, Eds. (1960) *The Politics of the Developing Areas.* Princeton: Princeton University Press.

CALDERÓN, F.G. (1913) *Latin America: Its Rise and Progress.* London: T.F. Unwin.

DAVIS, H.E., Ed. (1958) *Government and Politics in Latin America.* New York: Ronald Press.

FITZGIBBON, R.H. (1956a) "How democratic is Latin America?" *Inter-American Economic Affairs* 9 (Spring): 65–77.

— (1956b) "A statistical evaluation of Latin-American democracy." *Western Political Quarterly* 9: 607–619.

— (1951) "Measurement of Latin-American political phenomena: a statistical experiment." *American Political Science Review* 45: 517–523.

FITZGIBBON, R.H. and K.F. JOHNSON (1961) "Measurement of Latin American political change." *American Political Science Review* 54: 515–526.

GOMEZ, R.A. (1960) *Government and Politics in Latin America.* New York: Random House.

Hispanic American Historical Review (1963) 43: 296.

LIEUWEN, E. (1961) *Arms and Politics in Latin America.* New York: Frederick A. Praeger.

LIPSET, S.M. (1959) "Some social requisites of democracy: economic development and political legitimacy." *American Political Science Review* 53: 69–105.

MARTZ, J.D., Ed. (1965) *The Dynamics of Change in Latin American Politics.* Englewood Cliffs: Prentice-Hall.

MARVICK, D. (1962) "A memorandum on Fitzgibbon's survey of Latin American specialists." Paper read before the American Sociological Association, Washington, D.C., August.

SCOTT, R.E. (1959) *Mexican Government in Transition.* Urbana: University of Illinois Press.

SIMPSON, L.B. (1963) Review. *Hispanic American Historical Review* 43: 295.

— (1941) *Many Mexicos.* New York: G.P. Putnam's Sons.

STOKES, W.S. (1959) *Latin American Politics.* New York: Crowell.

TOMASEK, R.D., Ed. (1966) *Latin American Politics: Studies of the Contemporary Scene.* Garden City: Doubleday.

WOLF, C., JR. (1965a) "The political effects of military programs: some indications from Latin America." *Orbit* 8: 871–893.

— (1965b) "The political effects of economic programs: some indications from Latin America." *Economic Development and Cultural Change* 14: 1–20.

19 The Relationship of Systemic Frustration, Political Coercion, and Political Instability: A Cross-National Analysis

IVO K. FEIERABEND and ROSALIND L. FEIERABEND

Within the last few years, conflict behavior within nations has been studied empirically and has been found to consist of a systematic set of events which can be analyzed, measured and even scaled. For example, internal conflict behavior, exemplified by such events as demonstrations, riots, coups d'etat, assassinations and others indicative of political unrest, has been determined empirically for specified periods of time within large samples of nations,[1] and the resultant data then subjected to factor analyses.[2] The success of these empirical approaches, and the patterning which they seem to indicate in the data, supports the view that internal conflict is not a random occurrence.

Furthermore, a scaling instrument has been devised to measure political instability which places the various manifestations of internal conflict behavior at different positions on a seven-point scale (see for example Feierabend and Feierabend, 1965: 17-19). The occurrence of instability behaviors within a polity is then noted and the country is assigned an instability score which represents the frequency of occurrence of instability events of different intensity weightings. In this way, the stability levels of the countries for which data have been collected may be estimated and compared with one another. This scaling has yielded stability profiles for eighty-four polities for both a seven-year period (1955-61, inclusive) and a fifteen-year period (1948-62).

Authors' Note: This is an abridged version of a paper prepared for delivery at the Annual Meeting of the American Psychological Association, New York City, September 2-6, 1966. The research for this paper was partially supported by a grant from the San Diego State College Foundation.

Reprinted by permission of the authors. Copyright © 1970 by Sage Publications, Inc.

If these analyses of internal conflict are valid, then it is obviously of interest to inquire into the possible correlates of political instability behavior. What factors or conditions may be uncovered which tend to covary with political unrest? Using the available measurable data on political instability, the second step of seeking correlates of political unrest is open to inquiry.

The first investigation of the correlates of political instability made by the authors (Feierabend, Feierabend and Nesvold, 1963) necessitated some theoretical basis from which to postulate relationships. Identifying internal conflict as systemic aggressive behavior,[3] the frustration-aggression hypothesis (Dollard et al., 1939) was brought to bear on the problem. Much has been written regarding the validity of this hypothesis since 1939 and many refinements in interpretation have been suggested.[4] Nevertheless, for the purpose of rough and preliminary investigation, the basic hypothesis as originally stated seemed applicable to the prediction of political instability, with only slight modification. Identifying political instability as a form of systemic aggression, the hypothesis was restated as follows:

Systemic aggression is a result of systemic frustration[5]

It remained, then, to identify and quantify sources of systemic frustration and to see whether or not they would covary with systemic aggression in the form of political instability behaviors. In breaking new ground, one must choose among a vast array of potential variables, hoping that a small sample thereof will yield some estimate of the true picture. In this respect, our first analyses were limited but sufficient to yield evidence of some consistent relationships.

The notion of systemic frustration was defined as including those situations in which large strata of the population experience expectations, needs or aspirations which remain unmatched by equivalent levels of satisfaction. This type of gap between need or demand and achievement may most easily be identified among the ecological variables of political systems, especially in the socio-economic sphere. Also, ecological data on the various nations of the world are most readily available through United Nations and other sources.[6] Hence, identifying one form of systemic frustration as the ratio of social want formation to social want satisfaction, it was predicted that those countries in which this ratio was large would be more stable politically, whereas those in which the ratio was small, and hence the gap between wants and satisfactions was large, would exhibit a higher level of political instability.[7]

In order to test this prediction, a frustration index was calculated based on eight socio-economic measures for which data were available for a large sample of nations for the seven-year period, 1948–55.[8] These eight indicators, GNP and caloric intake per capita, physicians, telephones, newspapers and radios per unit of population, literacy level, and level of urbanization, were combined in a ratio based on coded scores. The ratio pooled the coded scores on the first six indicators (GNP, caloric intake, physicians, telephones, newspapers and radios) and, considering the combined level on these six to be a rough indication of a country's socio-economic satisfaction level, divided that combined score by either coded literacy level or coded urbanization level, whichever was higher. Literacy and urbanization were thus interpreted as want formations, that is, as the two most likely media for exposure to economic aspirations through the demonstration effect of the modernization process.[9]

The relationship yielded by correlating this frustration index, based on the years 1948–55 to the political instability profile calculated for the time period 1955–61, was Pearson $r = .499$, for the sample of sixty-one nations for which data were available on all indices.[10] A contingency table dividing countries into high and low groups on both the frustration index and the political instability scale yielded a Chi Square of 30.5, with a probability level of less than .001. Thus this first attempt to identify countries frustrated in socio-economic terms showed a definite relationship between this type of frustration and political unrest.

A second type of frustration index, labeled the modernity index, was based on the same eight ecological indicators converted into standard scores and averaged (Nesvold, 1964: 34–44). The modernity index thus yielded a composite picture of a country's relative level of attainment on these eight aspects of socio-economic environment. This modernity index correlated with political instability at an even higher level than did the first frustration index. The Pearson r between modernity and instability was .625.

Finally, a third type of socio-economic frustration was explored which was based on a country's rate of change over time on various economic indicators. It was hypothesized that change is an unsettling, disruptive societal experience and thus the faster the rate at which a country improves its economic position, the more unstable it will be during the period of rapid change.[11] Only when a country reaches a sufficient level of modernity will it then tend toward political stability.

In order to test this hypothesis relating rate of change to political instability, data were collected on nine socio-economic indicators for a twenty-eight year time period, 1935–62. The nine indicators were those for which maximum data were available and showed considerable overlap with the eight used previously. These nine indicators were: national income, caloric intake per capita, cost of living, infant mortality rate, level of urbanization, primary and post-primary education, and radios per thousand population. A country's percentage rate of change score was calculated on each indicator (Conroe, 1965: 62–65) and then an overall rate of change score was determined based on all nine indicators combined.[12] This combined rate of change index based on the 1935–62 time period was then correlated to political stability score for the period 1955–61, and the resulting Pearson r was .647. Thus, indeed, countries changing the most rapidly toward improvement in ecological conditions exhibited the greatest instability and it was also evident from the data that those high-changing countries were predominantly the less modern, transitional, or under-developed nations. Modern polities were, by and large, low changers and relatively politically stable.

It was felt from these three studies, first, that empirical investigation of the correlates of political unrest was feasible, and, secondly, that a country's systemic frustration level, crudely translated in terms of ecological indicators, showed a definite relationship to its level of political instability.[13] Two patterns emerged: one, the modern, relatively stable and relatively satisfied country, no longer subject to rapid socio-economic change; the other, the relatively less satisfied country, experiencing rapid economic change and a high level of political instability.

With this picture in mind, a further question was raised which led to the additional study reported in this article. In this analysis we investigate the influence upon political stability level of the coerciveness-permissiveness dimension of political regimes. Political coerciveness may be identified with the variable of punishment in the frustration-aggression sequence, which acts as an inhibitor of the aggressive response. In the same fashion, the coerciveness of a political regime may serve to curb the overt expression of political unrest. The question raised then is, in what way is the coerciveness of political regimes related to political instability level?

The Relationship Between Political Instability and the Coerciveness and Permissiveness of National Political Systems

Conflict and frustration are bound to occur in the context of social action, yet aggression is not the uniform response. Other variables, in particular, restraints or inhibitions to aggression, must also be taken into account. In the original formulation of the frustration-aggression hypothesis, Dollard et al. (1939: 33) postulated that "the inhibition of any act of aggression varies directly with the strength of the punishment anticipated for its expression. Punishment was seen to play a dual role. On the one hand, as already stated, it could serve to inhibit the aggressive response. On the other hand, interference with aggressive behavior in the form of punishment also served to heighten frustration and thus acted as a further instigation to aggression. Punishment itself, then, was seen as acting both as a "negative sanction" and as a source of frustration. The authors suggested that the strength of the anticipated punishment determined whether or not it functioned successfully as an inhibitor of aggression. Maier (1949) on the other hand, has emphasized the importance of the level of frustration experienced rather than simply the adequacy of the penalties imposed. Certain aggressive behaviors are likely to occur during periods of intense stress regardless of the penalties entailed.

The relationship of strength of punishment to instigation to aggression is, in fact, curvilinear. Low levels of punishment do not serve as inhibitors; it is only high levels of punishment which are likely to result in anxiety and withdrawal. Punishment at mid-levels of intensity acts as a frustrator and elicits further aggression, maintaining an aggression-punishment-aggression sequence (Buss, 1961: 58).

In order to fit the notion of punishment into the systemic frustration-political instability sequence, it must be described in politically relevant terms. Punishment is equated with patterns of permissiveness and coerciveness of political regimes. Thus a permissive system, commonly identified with free, democratic states, will show greater tolerance for demonstrations of political unrest than will coercive systems, typically identified with tyrannous states.

The addition of the permissiveness-coerciveness variable to the systemic frustration-systemic aggression sequence leads to the following set of hypotheses:

> I. In the case of polities with permissive political regimes, there is a greater likelihood of political stability, the higher the level of socio-economic systemic satisfaction. Conversely, there is a greater likelihood of political instability, the higher the level of socio-economic systemic frustration.
>
> II. In the case of polities with coercive political regimes, there is a greater likelihood of political stability if coerciveness is sufficiently high to act as a deterrent to aggression. Conversely, there is a greater likelihood of political instability if coerciveness is at mid-level, not sufficient to act as a deterrent to aggression but sufficient to be a source of systematic frustration.
>
> III. Combining the variables of coerciveness of political regimes and socio-economic systemic frustration yields the following predictions:
>> A. The threshold level of coercion necessary to act as a deterrent to systematic aggression will be a function of the level of socio-economic systemic frustration. The greater the socio-economic systemic frustration, the higher the level of coerciveness necessary to act as a deterrent to aggression.
>> B. The greatest tendency to political instability will result from a high level of socio-economic systemic frustration in combination with mid-level coerciveness of political regime. This combination, in fact, pools two sources of systemic frustration, one socio-economic, the other political.
>
> IV. Finally, it is suggested that the coerciveness level of political regimes may be a function of, and possibly a response to the level of socio-economic systemic frustration. The higher the level of such systemic frustration, the higher the level of political coerciveness.

A curvilinear relationship is thus postulated between coercion and stability. Highly permissive and highly coercive governments should both tend to be stable, provided the countries with highly permissive governments are also those with relatively high levels of socio-economic systemic satisfaction. When coercion is not sufficiently strong, as in the authoritarian systems of transitional states, it will not be capable of preventing overt aggression and will further stimulate frustration. Political instability should then be greatest in these states of mid-level coerciveness. One previous test of this hypothesized curvilinear relationship between coerciveness and aggression was carried out by LeVine (1959). Limiting himself to African colonial systems, LeVine found that consistently repressive and consistently permissive colonial systems experienced the least amount of anti-European violence.

In order to test these hypotheses regarding the effect of political coercion upon political unrest, some method was needed to reduce the permissiveness-coerciveness variable to an empirical, measurable dimension. In defining political coerciveness, various authors and approaches were considered. The most useful definition was felt to result from taking both Bay and Oppenheim as a point of departure.[14] The following questions were asked as guidelines to assessing the political and social freedom present within a society:

1. To what degree are civil rights present and protected?
2. To what extent is political opposition tolerated and effective?
3. How democratic is the polity?[15]

These three questions might seem to be redundant, in that they refer to three aspects of political regimes in which a common policy is pursued in most modern western democracies. Conceptually, however, they are three distinct domains and, in less developed societies, at least, or in nineteenth century European political history, the three are not necessarily characterized by concomitance of policy.

The task of assigning a value to permissiveness-coerciveness was pursued by constructing an ordinal, six-point scale which rated countries from most permissive (scale position *1*) to most coercive (scale position *6*). The indicators appropriate to each rank position are given below:

Rating *Description of polity*
1 *Most permissive:*
civil rights present and protected; rights of political opposition protected, i.e., in press, parliament, party formation, etc.;
government elected at regularized intervals in fair, free elections;
public opinion effective in policy formation;
significant heads of government limited in power and duration of office;
legislative bodies effective participants in decision process;
judicial bodies independent and have regularized procedures;
tradition of structures mediating between individual and central government, e.g., strong local government, states' rights, etc.;
constitution representative of sectors and interests within population, respected yet not impossible to amend.

2 *Moderately permissive:*
civil rights protected by law with perhaps occasional attempts at infringement;
rights of political opposition usually protected, e.g., press occasionally reprimanded, or certain parties illegal;

government elected at periodic intervals in usually fair, free elections;
public opinion usually effective in policy formation;
significant head of government responsible to public or popular legislature yet may be more powerful or have greater ability to perpetuate his tenure in office;
legislative bodies usually participate in decision process;
judicial bodies adequately independent and regularized;
structures mediating between individual and central government moderately strong;
constitution representative, respected and procedures for amendment adequate.

3 *Slightly permissive:*
intermittent interference with protection of civil rights, e.g., press occasionally suspended or censored, states of siege occasional;
political opposition tolerated but generally ineffective, e.g., only one party effectively participates in decisions;
government elected at more or less periodic intervals in elections which are usually free;
public opinion occasionally effective in policy formation;
significant head of government not very responsible, e.g., is hereditary office, or appointive from within non-popular legislative branch;
significant head of government may possess rather extraordinary powers within an otherwise democratic polity, or has been able to perpetuate tenure in office by changing the constitution, etc.;
legislative bodies occasionally participate in decision process;
judicial bodies adequately independent but may not have entirely fixed procedures, e.g., existence of ad hoc bodies or "drumhead courts" or military tribunals;
structures mediating between individual and central government relatively weak;
constitution rather easily altered, or, the converse, is rather difficult to amend.

4 *Slightly coercive:*
regular infringement of civil rights, e.g., press regularly suspended or censored, or frequent states of siege;
political opposition severely limited or harassed, e.g., occasional suspension of all parties, or opposition leaders arrested;
government changes at arbitrary intervals set by party in power; elections often interfered with or manipulated;
alternation of civilian and military government;
significant head of government irresponsible or perpetual, i.e., unlimited by constitution, tradition, etc.;
judicial bodies often interfered with by executive or legislature;
few, and very weak, structures mediate between individual and central government;
constitution unrepresentative of society, occasionally suspended or disregarded.

5   *Moderately coercive:*
   civil rights respected in arbitrary fashion, e.g., trade unions illegal or press severely censored;
   political opposition unlikely but not impossible, e.g., parties outlawed most of the time;
   government perpetual, elections usually serve no democratic function;
   public opinion usually disregarded in policy formation;
   significant head of government irresponsible, unlimited in powers or tenure of office;
   legislative bodies ineffective in policy formation;
   judicial bodies dependent on executive or legislature;
   constitution often suspended or extremely difficult to amend.

6   *Most coercive:*
   civil rights nonexistent, i.e., entirely dependent on whim of government;
   political opposition impossible, e.g., no parties or autonomous associational groups exist, government penetrates all institutions of society;
   government perpetual, elections serve only showcase function;
   public opinion disregarded in policy formation;
   significant head of government has dictatorial and absolute powers;
   legislative bodies serve only to reiterate executive decisions, have no powers of their own;
   judicial bodies completely dependent;
   no intermediary structures or institutions exist between the individual and central government;
   constitution completely disregarded in practice, impossible to amend [Walton: (1965) 48–51].

These criteria were applied to the sample of eighty-four nations used in the three previous studies, in order to arrive at a judgmental rating of these polities on the six-point, permissiveness-coerciveness scale. Approximately five separate works on each nation were consulted before an overall judgment was made.[16] A reliability check on the judgmental procedure consisted in having a second rater judge a sample of the polities independently, using the same rating criteria and source materials. Agreement between the two raters was satisfactorily high.[17]

The resultant country profiles on the permissiveness-coerciveness dimension are given in Table 1. The equating of high permissiveness with democracy and high coercion with totalitarianism is obvious from the table. Almost all of the modern democracies fall at scale positions *1* and *2* (with the exception of Austria and France) and all of the totalitarian regimes of the communist bloc, without exception, may be found at scale position *6*.

Between these two extremes lie polities which experience varying degrees of coerciveness or permissiveness within the three aspects of political life considered in making the ratings.

TABLE 1
COERCIVE-PERMISSIVE SCALING OF NATIONAL POLITICAL SYSTEMS[a]

Country	Rank	Country	Rank
Australia	1	Cyprus	4
Canada	1	Ecuador	4
Denmark	1	El Salvador	4
Netherlands	1	Ghana	4
Norway	1	Guatemala	4
Sweden	1	Honduras	4
Switzerland	1	Indonesia	4
United Kingdom	1	Iran	4
United States	1	Iraq	4
		Jordan	4
Belgium	2	Laos	4
Costa Rica	2	Lebanon	4
Finland	2	Liberia	4
Iceland	2	Libya	4
Ireland	2	Peru	4
Israel	2	Sudan	4
Italy	2	Syria	4
Luxembourg	2	Thailand	4
Mexico	2	Tunisia	4
New Zealand	2		
West Germany	2	Afghanistan	5
Uruguay	2	Argentina	5
		Cuba	5
Austria	3	Egypt	5
Brazil	3	Ethiopia	5
Burma	3	Haiti	5
Cambodia	3	Korea	5
Ceylon	3	Morocco	5
Chile	3	Nicaragua	5
France	3	Paraguay	5
Greece	3	Portugal	5
India	3	Saudi Arabia	5
Japan	3	Spain	5
Malaya	3	Union of South Africa	5
Pakistan	3	Venezuela	5
Panama	3		
Philippines	3	Albania	6
Turkey	3	Bulgaria	6
		China	6
Bolivia	4	Czechoslovakia	6
Colombia	4		

[a] Based on data collected for the years 1948–60.

TABLE 1 (continued)

| | | | |
Country	Rank	Country	Rank
Dominican Republic	6	Romania	6
East Germany	6	Taiwan	6
Hungary	6	U.S.S.R.	6
Poland	6	Yugoslavia	6

This coerciveness-permissiveness profile finds considerable support in works by other authors interested in analyzing similar aspects of political regimes. Thus Coleman's (1960) distinction between Competitive, Semi-Competitive and Authoritarian systems, although it excludes the modern democracies, yields a very similar rating of those nations which it has in common with our sample of eighty-four.[18] Similarly, Lipset's (1960: 51, 53) distinctions between European and English-speaking stable democracies and European and English-speaking unstable democracies plus dictatorships, on the one hand, and Latin American democracies and unstable dictatorships and Latin American stable dictatorships, on the other hand, also bears a strong relationship to the ratings given in Table 1 for the forty-nine nations in common to the two studies.[19] Finally, the recent factor analysis of cross-national political variables by Gregg and Banks (reprinted in this volume, Chapter 12) also lends some support both to the criteria used in determining permissiveness-coerciveness level and to the ranks assigned the nations. Thus Factor I in the Gregg and Banks analysis, labeled the "Access" factor, shows high loadings on such aspects of democratic regimes as electoral system, constitutional regime, and group opposition. The regional group labeled "Advanced Western Areal Group" also shows high loadings on this factor. The components of Factor I seem very similar to the criteria used in determining coerciveness scale positions *1* and *2*.[20] Furthermore, totalitarian regimes have a very high negative loading on Factor I, and they also place at the opposite end of the coerciveness scale, at scale position *6*.

Thus the permissiveness-coerciveness profiles, based on the six-point rating scale, appear to have construct validity in terms of the criteria used to determine each scale position, to have some consensual validation and corroboration in related studies by other authors, and to be based on some degree of interrater reliability. What, then, is the result of introducing the permissiveness-coerciveness variable to the predictive systemic frustration-systemic aggression equation?

The first comparison made was between political stability level and coerciveness level for the sample of eighty-four nations. Ratings of stability, it will be remembered, are based on the years 1955–61, and coerciveness ratings

TABLE 2
Relationship Between Level of Coercion and Degree of Political Stability, 1955–61

Degree of political stability	Level of coercion — Permissive (1–2)	Mid-level coercive (3–4)	Coercive (5–6)	Total
Stability (000–328)	Australia, Canada, Costa Rica, Denmark, Finland, Iceland, Ireland, Israel, Luxembourg, Netherlands, New Zealand, Norway, Sweden, Switzerland, United Kingdom, United States, Uruguay, W. Germany — 18	Austria, Cambodia, Libya, Philippines, Tunisia — 5	Czechoslovakia, East Germany, Ethiopia, Portugal, Romania, Saudi Arabia, Taiwan — 7	30
Mid-level instability (329–499)	Belgium, Italy, Mexico — 3	Burma, Ceylon, Chile, Ecuador, El Salvador, France, Ghana, Greece, Iran, Japan, Liberia, Malaya, Pakistan, Panama, Jordan, Sudan, Thailand — 17	Afghanistan, Albania, Bulgaria, China, Dominican Rep., Egypt, Haiti, Morocco, Nicaragua, Paraguay, Poland, Spain, So. Africa, U.S.S.R., Yugoslavia — 15	35
Instability (500–699)	0	Bolivia, Brazil, Colombia, Cyprus, Guatemala, Honduras, Indonesia, India, Iraq, Laos, Lebanon, Peru, Syria, Turkey — 14	Argentina, Cuba, Hungary, Korea, Venezuela — 5	19
Total	21	36	27	84

Chi square = 38.37 $p < .001$

are based on the time period 1948–60. The results of this comparison are given in Table 2.

The first finding which emerges is the strong relationship between stability and coerciveness. The permissive countries are overwhelmingly stable, while the coercive countries tend toward mid-levels and high levels of political instability. The Chi Square calculated from this contingency table is 38.37, which is highly significant at less than the .001 level of probability. A product-moment correlation calculated between the variables of coercion and political instability is .409.

Examining the table in more detail, it may be seen that all countries ranked *1* on the coercion index are stable and that the three permissive countries which are moderately unstable all received a *2* coerciveness rating. This finding, that there are no permissive, unstable countries in the sample may be explained by the fact that the countries falling at scale position *1* (and, to some extent, at scale position *2*) on the coerciveness scale are also the modern democracies that are relatively satisfied in socio-economic terms on the frustration index calculated in a previous study. Thus permissiveness of regime appears to be another component of this particular stability pattern.

Looking at the coercive countries, the question arises, does the predicted curvilinearity of relationship obtain, such that the more highly coercive nations tend to be more stable politically than the nations at mid-levels of coercion? There is evidence in the table that highly coercive regimes show less tendency to extreme political instability, and somewhat more of a tendency to political stability, than do regimes at mid-level coerciveness. Also, countries at mid-level values of coerciveness tend to aggregate at both mid-level instability and extreme instability positions. Only five of thirty-six polities at mid-coerciveness level are politically stable.

This curvilinear tendency may be brought out more clearly in Table 3, which gives the number and proportion of countries which are politically stable and those which are politically unstable at each level of coerciveness. In Table 3, it may be seen that two-thirds of the countries at coercion level *6* tend to be stable and only one-third are unstable. For the countries at position *5*, however, these proportions are reversed: two-thirds of these countries are unstable and only one-third are stable. Furthermore, at scale position *4*, three-quarters of the countries are politically unstable. An *eta* calculated to assess the degree of curvilinearity in these data yields a relationship of .72, which is a significant improvement over the r of .409 ($F = 14.02$, $p < .001$). Thus the curvilinear hypothesis is supported by the data, with countries at mid-coerciveness levels showing a greater tendency to political instability than countries with highly coercive regimes. Looking again at the highly coercive countries in Table 2, it may also be seen that of the five countries (Argentina, Cuba, Hungary, Korea and Venezuela) which are rated both highly coercive and highly unstable politically—a combination which is contrary to prediction—only one, Hungary, was scaled at position *6* on the

TABLE 3

RELATIONSHIP BETWEEN LEVEL OF COERCION AND DEGREE OF POLITICAL STABILITY, 1955–61

	1 p	1 N	2 p	2 N	3 p	3 N	4 p	4 N	5 p	5 N	6 p	6 N	Total N
Stable (000–422)	1.00	9	.75	9	.40	6	.24	5	.33	5	.67	8	42
Unstable (423–699)	.00	0	.25	3	.60	9	.76	16	.67	10	.33	4	42
Total	1.00	9	1.00	12	1.00	15	1.00	21	1.00	15	1.00	12	84

coercion index. Hungary could thus be considered a truly deviant case. It is also interesting that aggression in this country was the result of a revolution following an ambiguously coercive governmental policy, the result of "de-Stalinization" of the Soviet bloc. Also, if one separates the countries in Table 2 at scale position 6 from those at position 5, it may be seen that more of the countries rated 6 are stable than are unstable, while all of the countries rated 5 are politically unstable.

These data, taken in combination, would seem to reveal another finding of this study, namely, that level 5 coerciveness is not sufficient to act as an inhibitor to aggression. It may be suggested that the coerciveness exhibited by authoritarian regimes classed at ordinal position 5 may serve as much as a source of frustration to the populace, thus promoting political aggression, as it serves to deter these acts of political instability. The finding may be indicative of a threshold level of political coerciveness necessary to achieve some degree of political stability in the face of systemic frustration. Nothing less than a full-fledged totalitarian regime seems sufficient, over time, to keep the populace from expressing dissatisfaction in high levels of systemic aggression; then only if totalitarianism is unambiguously pursued will it be successful. Hungary serves as an example of what may ensue from a temporary relaxation of totalitarian policy. However, it is also true that level 4 countries show an even greater tendency toward high levels of political instability than do countries at level 5. Hence the conclusion should perhaps be modified to say that interference with liberties without the imposition of an authoritarian regime simply adds to the level of frustration and hence also of aggression within the country, without imposing any apparent inhibition upon the expression of that aggression. Countries with authoritarian regimes (level 5) do curb the expression of political aggression somewhat, although certainly not sufficiently to eliminate high levels of such expression entirely.

TABLE 4
RELATIONSHIP BETWEEN LEVEL OF COERCION AND DEGREE OF SOCIO-ECONOMIC FRUSTRATION

Level of social frustration	Level of coercion			Total
	Permissive (1-2)	Mid-level coercive (3-4)	Coercive (5-6)	
Satisfaction (4.00-4.75)	Australia, Belgium, Canada, Denmark, Finland, Iceland, Ireland, Netherlands, New Zealand, Norway, Sweden, Switzerland, United Kingdom, United States, Uruguay, W. Germany — 16	France — 1	Argentina, Czechoslovakia, Morocco, Portugal, So. Africa — 5	22
Mid-level frustration (3.00-3.75)	Costa Rica, Israel, Italy, Mexico — 4	Austria, Brazil, Chile, Colombia, Cyprus, India, Indonesia, Iran, Japan, Lebanon, Pakistan, Panama, Tunisia, Turkey — 14	Bulgaria, Cuba, Haiti, Spain, Venezuela — 5	23
Frustration (1.50-2.75)	0	Bolivia, Ceylon, Ecuador, El Salvatore, Greece, Guatemala, Iraq, Peru, Philippines, Syria, Thailand — 11	Dominican Rep., Egypt, Korea, Nicaragua, Paraguay, Yugoslavia — 6	17
Total	20	26	16	62

Chi Square = 36.12 $p < .001$

The second relationship of interest to this study is that between the coerciveness level of political regimes and the degree of systemic frustration calculated in terms of socio-economic components. It was hypothesized above that level of coerciveness would covary with systemic frustration in such a way that the higher the frustration level, the greater the coerciveness of the political regime. Table 4 shows the relationship between these two variables for the sample of 62 nations for which data are available on both indexes.

Again, the pattern is very much the same as in Table 2. The permissive countries, in large measure, experience relative socio-economic satisfaction, as was anticipated in view of their high level of political stability. Frustrated countries, on the other hand, tend toward both mid-levels and high levels of coerciveness of regime. The Chi Square for this contingency table is again very high: 36.12, with a probability level of less than .001. The product-moment correlation between the two variables of coercion and systemic frustration is .57. Thus, in fact, the data support the notion that more coercive regimes tend to occur in countries experiencing socio-economic frustration.

It is interesting to note, however, and contrary to hypothesis, that there is also a tendency toward a high level of coerciveness of political regime in systemically satisfied countries. This reversal of tendency in the highly coercive countries suggests that some factor other than systemic frustration, measured in terms of ecological indicators, is also related to coerciveness of political regime. Thus, while it seems quite clear that permissiveness of regime does not occur unless the country experiences socio-economic satisfaction and is also politically stable, a high level of coerciveness may occur in relatively satisfied countries. Of the five countries which combine coerciveness with socio-economic satisfaction, three (Morocco, Argentina and the Union of South Africa) are subject to political instability, which may in some measure explain their coerciveness level.

A look at the relationship between modernity level and coerciveness of regime completes the picture. The sample of eighty-four nations was divided into three groups, designated modern, transitional and traditional,[21] and compared as to permissiveness and coerciveness of political regime. These results are given in Table 5.

Again, we find a clear-cut pattern combining modernity with permissiveness of regime. Furthermore, the table gives striking evidence, in corroboration of works on economic development, that coerciveness of regime is the norm in non-modern countries.[22] The Chi Square for this contingency table is 53.9, well beyond the .001 level of probability, and the product-moment correlation measuring the degree of relationship between these two variables is —.699. While both traditional and transitional countries tend toward coerciveness of regime, it is evident from Table 5 that the least modern countries (designated traditional) are more apt to fall at mid-levels of coerciveness than in the highly coercive category. Transitional states, however, which are also the most unstable group of countries in the sample, are almost evenly

TABLE 5
RELATIONSHIP BETWEEN LEVEL OF COERCION AND LEVEL OF MODERNITY

Level of modernity	Permissive (1–2)	Mid-level coercive (3–4)	Coercive (5–6)	Total
Modern (.34–2.54)	Australia, Canada, Belgium, Denmark, Finland, Iceland, Ireland, Israel, Luxembourg, Netherlands, New Zealand, Norway, Sweden, Switzerland, United Kingdom, United States, Uruguay, W. Germany — 18	Austria, France — 2	Argentina, Czechoslovakia, East Germany, U.S.S.R. — 4	24
Transitional (−.49–.24)	Costa Rica, Italy, Mexico — 3	Brazil, Ceylon, Chile, Colombia, Cyprus, Ecuador, El Salvador, Guatemala, Greece, Honduras, Japan, Lebanon, Panama, Peru, Syria, Thailand, Turkey, Tunisia — 18	Albania, Bulgaria, Cuba, Dominican Rep., Egypt, Korea, Nicaragua, Paraguay, Poland, Portugal, Romania, So. Africa, Venezuela, Yugoslavia — 16	37
Traditional (−1.62–−.50)	0	Bolivia, Burma, Cambodia, Ghana, Indonesia, India, Iraq, Jordan, Laos, Liberia, Libya, Malaya, Pakistan, Philippines, Sudan — 16	Afghanistan, China, Ethiopia, Haiti, Morocco, Saudi Arabia, Taiwan — 7	23
Total	21	36	27	84

Chi Square = 53.91 $p < .001$

divided between mid-levels and high levels of political coerciveness.

As a final analysis of the relationship between the three variables, political stability, systemic frustration and coerciveness of regime, an expanded table was constructed dividing the sixty-two nations for which scores were available on all indexes into those experiencing high, those experiencing medium and those subject to low levels of all three variables. Since the present study indicated that coerciveness level is curvilinearly related to level of political instability, countries are ordered in the table in such a way that those at mid-levels of coerciveness appear at the end of the coerciveness distribution (see Table 6).

Two syndromes appear in this table. The first indicates the strong relationship among high levels of ecological systematic satisfaction, permissiveness of political regime and political stability, typified in the modern industrial nations of the world. Of twenty-two stable polities, fifteen, or 68 percent, fit this pattern. The opposite syndrome, of the politically unstable polity, emerges more clearly in this expanded table than in the previous tables based on single indices. Of sixteen countries forming the most unstable group of nations, twelve, or 75 percent, experience a combination of two sources of systemic frustration: mid-level coerciveness of political regime and some degree of frustration having its source in socio-economic deprivations. No country in this highly unstable group is among the permissive countries of the world and only one nation, Argentina, is rated as satisfied in socio-economic terms. The four coercive countries which show a high level of political instability (Argentina, Cuba, South Korea and Venezuela) may perhaps be explained in that none of the four falls at coerciveness scale position 6, and coerciveness level 5 has not been found sufficient to act as an inhibitor of high levels of political aggression.

The third group of countries, exhibiting mid-levels of political instability, also show some combination of frustrations. Of twenty-four moderately unstable countries, ten, or 42 percent, experience a combination of mid-level coerciveness and socio-economic frustration. Another eight countries, or 33 percent of this sub-sample, are characterized by a high level of coerciveness of regime and some degree of socio-economic frustration. Thus, 75 percent of the mid-instability group shows some combination of these two sources of systemic frustration. Only one country, Belgium, is both permissive and satisfied and yet evidences mid-level political instability. Two countries, Italy and Mexico, show only one source of frustration: both experience mid-level socio-economic frustration but have permissive regimes.

Finally, it should perhaps be pointed out that the largest number of exceptions occurs in the case of the satisfied, permissive, politically stable syndrome. As may be seen in the table, there are stable countries in the world stemming from many other combinations of coerciveness and frustration levels, although they are certainly not as frequent as the permissive, satisfied combination. Absolutely in contradiction to the syndrome are the three countries, Austria, Tunisia and, especially, the Philippines, which remain

TABLE 6
Relationship Between Level of Coercion, Level of Socio-economic Frustration and Degree of Political Stability

Stability	Level of coercion, socio-economic frustration								
	Permissive, satisfied	Permissive, mid-level frustrated	Permissive, frustrated	Coercive, satisfied	Coercive, mid-level frustrated	Coercive, frustrated	Mid-level coercive, satisfied	Mid-level coercive, mid-level frustrated	Mid-level coercive, frustrated
	Australia Canada Denmark Finland Iceland Ireland Netherlands New Zealand Norway Sweden Switzerland U.K. U.S.A. Uruguay W. Germany	Israel Costa Rica		Czechoslovakia Portugal				Austria Tunisia	Philippines
	15	2	0	2	0	0	0	2	1

22

	Belgium	Mexico Italy	Morocco U.S. Africa	Bulgaria Haiti Spain	Egypt Dominican Rep. Nicaragua Paraguay Yugoslavia	France	Chile Iran Japan Pakistan Panama	Ceylon Greece Ecuador El Salvador Thailand	
Mid-level instability	1	2	0	2	5	1	5	5	24
			Argentina	Cuba Venezuela	Korea		Brazil Colombia Cyprus India Indonesia Lebanon	Bolivia Guatemala Iraq Peru Syria	
Instability	0	0	0	1	1	0	Turkey 7	5	16
	0	0	0	0	1	0	0		
Total	16	4	5	5	6	1	14	11	62

relatively politically stable despite a combination of mid-level coerciveness of regime and some degree of socio-economic frustration.

What may be concluded from this exploration of systemic variables? At the simplest level, it affords an empirical mapping of the state of the world in terms of variables of considerable interest to political and social scientists. The map which emerges is, in large measure, a corroboration of insights which have often been stated. The combination of modernity, permissiveness, socio-economic satisfaction and political stability, on the one hand, and low modernity, coerciveness, socio-economic frustration and political instability, on the other hand, entails the gross division between "have" and "have-not" nations of the globe. To this may be added the variable of rate of change explored in a previous study, which, when calculated in percentage terms, also correlates with modernity so that modern nations are low changers on ecological variables and non-modern nations are high changers.

The scaling techniques used in these empirical analyses, however, allow for more than a gross division among countries. By placing each country in its relative position on all scales, a more refined set of groupings and sub-groupings, exceptions and confirmations, are revealed. Also, it must be emphasized as a methodological point of considerable import that the scaling of each systemic variable was approached independently. Only after scaling was completed were patterns sought between systemic variables. Thus the map which emerges offers independent empirical support for many current notions regarding the interrelationships among democracy, economic development and political stability.

NOTES

1. Cross-national data of internal conflict behavior have been collected by Harry A. Eckstein, covering 113 nations for the time period 1946-59; by Rudolph J. Rummel, including 77 nations for the years 1955-57; by Raymond A. Tanter, including the same 77 nations for the years 1958-60 (see Chapter 4, this volume); and by Ivo K. Feierabend and Rosalind L. Feierabend, covering 84 nations for the years 1948-65. These data collections are available through the Inter-University Consortium for Political Research, Ann Arbor, Michigan.

2. Cf. Rudolph J. Rummel, Chapter 3, this volume and Chapter 2, this volume; Francis W. Hoole, 1964; Raymond Tanter, Chapter 4, this volume; and Ivo K. Feierabend, Rosalind L. Feierabend, and Norman G. Litell, 1966.

3. Specifically, it was defined as the degree or the amount of aggression directed by individuals or groups within the political system against other groups or against the complex of office-holders and individuals and groups associated with them. Or, conversely, as the amount of aggression directed by these office-holders against other individuals, groups or office-holders within the polity.

4. Some recent important works on the nature of aggression and its relation to frustration are those by Leonard Berkowitz (1965), (1962); Arnold H. Buss (1961); Elton B. McNeil (1959); and J. D. Carthy and F. J. Ebling (1964).

5. The frustration-aggression sequence was originally postulated in terms of individual behavior, although the adaptation of the sequence to the behavior of groups was envisaged by the authors. See, for example, the following statements: "Although frustration as such can occur only to an individual organism, any given frustrating condition may occur to several individuals simultaneously. In such a case, a 'group' is viewed distributively rather than as a collective thing" (Dollard et al., 1939: 13).

6. The most comprehensive compilations of such cross-national data, including a listing of data sources, may be found in Bruce M. Russett et al., *World Handbook of Political and Social Indicators* (1964); and in Arthur S. Banks and Robert B. Textor, *A Cross-Polity Survey* (1963).

7. Specifically, the hypothesis was: the higher (lower) the social want formation in any given society and the lower (higher) the social want satisfaction, the greater (the less) the systemic frustration and the greater (the lesser) the impulse to political instability. See Ivo K. Feierabend and Rosalind L. Feierabend, "Aggressive Behaviors Within Polities, 1948-1962: A Cross-National Study," Chapter 6, this volume.

8. See Betty A. Nesvold (1964: 34-44). This frustration index, based on a ratio between correlated indicators, each of which contains some error component, yields an attenuated correlation as compared with the modernity index also calculated from the same eight ecological indicators.

9. Two very relevant discussions of the effects of the modernization process on under-developed nations may be found in Karl W. Deutsch (1961) and Lerner (1958). The enormous and ever-growing literature on the processes of modernization cannot be encompassed here.

10. This time lag was deliberate: it was assumed that some lag would occur before social frustrations would make themselves felt in political aggressions.

11. Specifically, it was hypothesized: the faster (slower) the rate of change in the modernization process within any given society, the higher (the lower) the level of political instability within that society. See Feierabend and Feierabend, Chapter 6, this volume.

12. A later analysis of the effect of change in the socioeconomic sphere on the level of political instability can be found in Feierabend, Feierabend and Nesvold (1969).

13. The claim that such research is feasible depends not only on the availability of data but also on the question of the possible vitiating effects of error on the relationships determined. That the data contain an error component is undeniable. Russett et al. (1964) discuss the extent of such error in the *World Handbook* and make an attempt to estimate error margins for each ecological indicator. Rummel, using the method of factor analysis, has determined that such errors are not entirely random but beset primarily the under-developed countries and the totalitarian states. (See Rudolph J. Rummel, 1964.) On the other hand, also using the method of factor analysis, Rummel determined that there was minimal systematic error in the data collected on internal conflict behavior due to censorship and newsworthiness of country. (See Rummel, Chapter 3, this volume.) Gurr (1966) is making an attempt to correct for errors of reporting of some cross-national indicators. In view of the existence of some error component, the question of the effects of this error upon the validity of cross-national empirical research is crucial.

The view that the difficulties are not insurmountable is perhaps best expressed in Hayward R. Alker, Jr. (1968), and also Erwin K. Scheuch (1966). The very cogent discussion of the interpretation of error in the validation of hypotheses in Hubert M. Blalock, Jr. (1961) is especially relevant.

14. See Christian Bay (1958) and Felix E. Oppenheim (1961). Also relevant were the discussion of power in David B. Easton (1958) and the definition of coercion in Harold Lasswell and Abraham Kaplan (1950). Equally useful were Karl W. Deutsch (1963) and Gabriel A. Almond and James S. Coleman (1960).

15. An amplification of these questions may be found in Jennifer G. Walton (1965: 44–46). See also Feierabend, Feierabend and Nesvold (1969).

16. The complete bibliography may be found in Walton (1965: 98–148, Appendix B).

17. The correlation between the two sets of ratings for a small sample of nine countries chosen from all scale positions (in the estimation of the first rater) was $r = .88$. Projection onto the sample of 84 nations, using the Spearman-Brown formula, yields a corrected correlation of .985.

18. See James S. Coleman, "The Political Systems of the Developing Areas" (in Almond and Coleman, 1960: 538–44). A table comparing Coleman's classification with the positioning of the same countries on the six-point coerciveness scale yields the following degree of agreement:

COERCIVENESS-PERMISSIVENESS SCALE

	1	2	3	4	5	6	Totals
Competitive	0	3	7	1	1	0	12
Semi-competitive	0	1	2	9	2	0	14
Authoritarian	0	0	2	9	9	1	21

19. See Seymour Martin Lipset (1960: 51, 53). A table comparing Lipset's classification system with the six-point coerciveness-permissiveness scale shows the following extent of agreement:

COERCIVENESS-PERMISSIVENESS SCALE

	1	2	3	4	5	6	Totals
European and English-speaking stable democracies	9	4	0	0	0	0	13
European and English speaking unstable democracies and dictatorships	0	3	3	0	2	8	16
Latin American democracies and unstable dictatorships	0	3	2	1	1	0	7
Latin American stable dictatorships	0	0	1	6	5	1	13

20. Specifically, the variables with high loadings on Factor I are the following, with their loadings indicated in parentheses: Electoral System (.94); Constitutional Regime (.93); Group Opposition (.92); Status of Legislature (.87); Horizontal Power Distribution (.86); Representativeness of Regime (.85); Press Freedom (.80); Aggregation by Legislature (.73); Military Neutral (.73); Articulation by Parties (.68); Articulation by Associational Groups (.63); Modern Bureaucracy (.52)

21. The three groups were determined by taking the 24 highest-ranking countries on the modernity index to form the modern group, selecting 23 countries falling at the opposite end of the index to be the traditional group, and counting those countries lying in between these two as the transitional group. This modernity distribution, based on an average of 8 indicators, correlates very highly with the modernity ranking in Russett et al. (1964: 294–298) which is based on GNP alone. The rank-order correlation between the two is $R = .92$.

22. Many authors have noted this relationship. See, e.g. Lipset (1960); Coleman (1960); Hagan (1962); Cutright (1963); and de Schweinitz (1964).

REFERENCES

ALKER, H.R., JR. (1968) "Research possibilities using aggregate political and social data." In S. Rokkan, Ed., *Comparative Research Across Cultures and Nations*. Round Table Conference on Comparative Research. Paris and The Hague: Mouton.

ALMOND, G.A. and J.S. COLEMAN, Eds. (1960) *The Politics of the Developing Areas*. Princeton: Princeton University Press.

BANKS, A.S. and R.B. TEXTOR (1963) *A Cross-Polity Survey*. Cambridge: MIT Press.

BAY, C. (1958) *The Structure of Freedom*. Stanford: Stanford University Press.

BERKOWITZ, L. (1965) "The concept of aggressive drive: some additional considerations." In L. Berkowitz, Ed., *Advances in Experimental Social Psychology*. Vol. 2. New York: Academic Press.

— (1962) *Aggression: A Social Psychological Analysis*. New York: McGraw-Hill.

BLALOCK, H.M., JR. (1961) *Causal Inference in Nonexperimental Research*. Chapel Hill: University of North Carolina Press.

BUSS, A.H. (1961) *The Psychology of Aggression*. New York: John Wiley.

CARTHY, J.D. and F.J. EBLING, Eds. (1964) *The Natural History of Aggression*. New York: Academic Press.

COLEMAN, J.S. (1960) "The political systems of the developing areas." Pp. 538–544 in G.S. Almond and J.S. Coleman, Eds., *The Politics of the Developing Areas*. Princeton: Princeton University Press.

CONROE, W.W. (1965) "Cross-National Analysis of the Impact of Modernization upon Political Stability." Master's thesis, San Diego State College.

CUTRIGHT, P. (1963) "National political development: measurement and analysis." *American Sociological Review* 28: 253–264.

DE SCHWEINITZ, K. (1964) *Industrialization and Democracy*. New York: Free Press.

DEUTSCH, K.W. (1963) *The Nerves of Government*. New York: Free Press.

— (1961) "Social mobilization and political development." *American Political Science Review* 55: 493–514.

DOLLARD, J. et al. (1939) *Frustration and Aggression*. New Haven: Yale University Press.

EASTON, D.B. (1958) *The Political System: An Inquiry into the State of Political Science*. New York: Alfred A. Knopf.

FEIERABEND, I.K. and R.L. FEIERABEND (1965) *Cross-National Data Bank of Political Instability Events* (Code Index). Public Affairs Research Institute, San Diego State College.

FEIERABEND, I.K., R.L. FEIERABEND and N.G. LITELL (1966) "Dimensions of political unrest, 1948–1960: a factor analysis of cross-national data." Paper delivered at the Annual Meeting of the Western Political Science Association, Reno, March.

FEIERABEND, I.K., R.L. FEIERABEND and B.A. NESVOLD (1969) "Social change and political violence." Pp. 606–668 in H.D. Graham and T.R. Gurr, Eds., *Violence in America*. New York: New American Library.

— (1963) "Correlates of political stability." Paper presented at the Annual Meeting of the American Political Science Association, New York City, September.

GURR, T. (1966) *New Error-Compensated Measures for Comparing Nations*. Research Monograph No. 25, Princeton University Center of International Studies, May.

HAGAN, E.E. (1962) "A framework for analyzing economic and political change." Pp. 1–8 in R.E. Asher et al., Eds., *Development of the Emerging Countries: An Agenda for Research*. Washington, D.C.

HEMPEL, C.G. (1952) *Fundamentals of Concept Formation in Empirical Science*. Chicago: University of Chicago Press.

HOOLE, F.W. (1964) "Political Stability and Instability within Nations: A Cross-National Study." Master's thesis, San Diego State College.

LASSWELL, H. and A. KAPLAN (1950) *Power and Society: A Framework for Political Inquiry*. New Haven: Yale University Press.

LERNER, D. (1958) *The Passing of Traditional Society*. New York: Free Press.

LEVINE, R.A. (1959) "Anti-European violence in Africa: a comparative analysis." *Journal of Conflict Resolution* (December): 420–427.

LIPSET, S.M. (1960) *Political Man*. New York: Doubleday.

MCNEIL, E.B. (1959) "Psychology and aggression." *Journal of Conflict Resolution* 3: 195–293.

MAIER, N.R.F. (1949) *Frustration: The Study of Behavior Without a Goal*. New York: McGraw-Hill.

NESVOLD, B.A. (1964) "Modernity, Social Frustration and the Stability of Political Systems: A Cross-National Study." Master's thesis, San Diego State College.

OPPENHEIM, F.E. (1961) *Dimensions of Freedom*. New York: St. Martin's Press.

RUMMEL, R.J. (1964) "Dimensions of error in cross-national data in the mid-1950s." Dimensionality of Nations Project, Yale University (mimeo.).

RUSSETT, B.M. et al. (1964) *World Handbook of Political and Social Indicators*. New Haven: Yale University Press.

SCHEUCH, E.K. (1966) "Cross-national comparisons using aggregate data: some substantive and methodological problems." In R.L. Merritt and S. Rokkan, Eds., *Comparing Nations: The Uses of Quantitative Data in Cross-National Research*. New Haven: Yale University Press.

WALTON, J.G. (1965) "Correlates of Coerciveness and Permissiveness of National Political Systems: A Cross-National Study." Master's thesis, San Diego State College.

20 Patterns of Political Development and Democratization: A Quantitative Analysis

WILLIAM FLANIGAN and EDWIN FOGELMAN

One of the significant developments in the study of politics during the last decade has been the far-reaching extension of quantitative analysis. From international organization to constitutional law, virtually every field of study has been affected by the introduction of quantitative measures with accompanying statistical techniques. No doubt the ultimate value of this emphasis on quantification is still uncertain. But one thing seems clear: the potential value of quantitative analysis will be determined not only by abstract discussion, but by actual attempts to treat in quantitative terms significant topics in political research.

In this paper we propose to examine, through the use of varied quantitative measures, a central problem in political analysis: on the one hand, the relationships through time between socio-economic variables and, on the other hand, two basic political variables—political development and democratization. Interest in such relationships is hardly new. In this paper, however, we introduce measures and indices based on quantitative data that have not been used previously and that permit forms of analysis not otherwise applicable. The studies of Deutsch, Russett, Lipset, Banks and Textor, and others have made plain the possibilities of comparative quantitative analysis. Almost without exception, however, these studies are cross-sectional in focus rather than historical or longitudinal; that is, they employ data from the contemporary period to make comparisons among units at a particular point-in-time. But although many interesting problems can be investigated through cross-sectional analysis, there are other significant problems that can only be studied

---

This paper was originally presented before a panel at the 1967 annual meeting of The American Political Science Association in Chicago, September, 1967 and is reprinted by permission of the authors and the Association (copyright holder).

through longitudinal or time-series analysis. It is this neglected area of longitudinal quantitative analysis that we shall explore in this study.

The dearth of quantitative longitudinal studies dealing with such obviously dynamic problems as the patterns of political development, and democratization, has undoubtedly been due less to any question about the possible interest of such studies than to the absence of usable relevant data.

Some Disclaimers. Before turning to the main part of the paper, we feel it would be prudent to enter several disclaimers. In the first place, the political measures and indices we are using, as well as the data themselves, are being introduced here for the first time; we do not expect they will go entirely unchallenged. We recognize that the judgments and interpretations we were called upon to make at every step in the course of collecting the data and constructing the indices are not beyond reproach. Specialists in the politics of particular countries and areas may question judgments of fact; students of comparative politics generally may disagree with aspects of our indices or the way we have formulated certain problems for analysis; methodologists may question some of the statistical techniques we propose. We can only say that we welcome the helpful comments which will be forthcoming.

In the second place, our selection of countries as the units for analysis in this initial presentation is largely arbitrary. That is, no particular sampling principle guided our selection of the countries included in the archive at its present stage. We expect eventually to collect data in historical depth for all the countries of the world. Until then, practical limitations made necessary some restriction on the units we could include. Faced with a choice between covering a few areas of the world comprehensively or selecting at least some countries from all geographical areas, we adopted the latter alternative. The countries we included seem interesting to us for one reason or another, but no more systematic justification for our choices can be offered. The selection of countries is a mixture, and definitely not a sample. We have frequently regretted not selecting countries on the basis of availability of data or from more limited geographical areas. But we have consoled ourselves that we will include omitted countries in subsequent data collection.

Beyond the problem of selecting countries is the further difficulty of determining the time-span, when particular units are actually in existence. It is not always self-evident when specific countries come into existence and when they are transformed, fragmented, or otherwise disappear. Originally, we had intended to incorporate data on fragmented and integrated units, but we now view the entire problem of integration-disintegration as a separate major focus for further data collection. Under the circumstances, we have had, in many cases, to make judgments among several possible dates for both the beginning and the termination of a unit. For those countries that did not exist before 1800, we used the following time-periods:

        Argentina (1830–1960)   Canada (1860–1960)
        Burma (1880–1960)   Colombia (1830–1960)

Czechoslovakia (1920–60)
Germany (1870–1950)
Italy (1860–1960)

Nigeria (1910–60)
South Africa (1910–60)
Switzerland (1840–1960)

The time-spans for various countries are significant because they affect the number of data-points that can be used in the analysis. For this paper, we have arranged the data in terms of a single data-point for every country in each decade. The maximum of 16 decades as data-points is sufficient for simple descriptive purposes, but it becomes a troublesome limitation as more complex time-series analysis is introduced. When fewer decades are included, this difficulty obviously increases. Unavoidably, the use of a single data-point for each decade results in the omission of many annual or other sub-decade variations; moreover, to obtain a single point for any decade often requires some manipulation of the available data. In spite of these difficulties, the use of single decade data-points seems to be the most convenient basis for organizing the available data in view of the limitations of the data themselves during much of the nineteenth century.

Finally, this analysis is only the beginning in examining more fully the data available in the archive. We have in mind a number of further studies based on these data. We present this paper, therefore, not as the last word, but rather as a first step in political time-series analysis.

Our main purpose is to examine relationships through time between three socio-economic variables (urbanization, education, and economic development) and two basic political variables (political development and democratization). The first problem is to find appropriate measures for each of the political variables.

Political Development: An Index of Governmental Publications

Although the concept of political development is commonplace among students of comparative politics, there is notable disagreement concerning both the meaning of the concept and the indices that are appropriate for measuring levels of development. It seems, however, that one important aspect of political development is the extent to which a government is able to adopt the varied and complex policies that are demanded in every modern community. This ability to adopt complex policies we may term "administrative capacity." A basic premise in the analysis of political development is that not all political systems are equal in administrative capacity; not all governments are equally able to adopt the complex policies that are demanded by influential participants. The administrative capacity of a political system depends on a number of conditions, including the introduction of appropriate institutional structures, the presence of trained and motivated personnel, and the availability of relevant information on which policy-decisions can be based. The first two of these conditions have been discussed often by students of political development. A number of typologies have been constructed, based on the institutional characteristics of political systems at different levels of development. Although the institutional characteristics that are usually stressed in such typologies do not refer merely to the administrative capacity of a system, some of these characteristics have a direct connection with the relative ability of different systems to adopt complex policies. However, from the standpoint of quantitative analysis, a fundamental difficulty with such typologies is that the institutional characteristics they emphasize are never measured quantitatively. It would be unwarranted to say that institutional characteristics cannot be measured quantitatively; but the fact remains that leading typologists show little inclination toward quantitative measurement.

The most widely-used quantitative measures that bear on the administrative capacity of different political systems concern government employment and government revenues and expenditures. Compilations of political data regularly include figures on the number of government employees as a percentage of population or as a percentage of work force, as well as figures on government revenues and expenditures as a percentage of gross national product (GNP), or on the ratio of different types of government expenditures. We have collected considerable data of this kind in historical depth. The difficulty, however, aside from serious problems in finding such data over long periods, is that the suitability of these measures as indications of administrative capacity is somewhat doubtful. Perhaps more elaborate measures of patterns of government employment and expenditures would yield more satisfactory results. But more elaborate measures are not yet available, and our own attempts to find data for such measures have not been encouraging.

In place of the familiar measures of government employment, revenue, and expenditures, we suggest an alternative indicator of administrative capacity related to the availability within a political system of certain types of information. Specifically, we propose an index of governmental publications based on the volume and kinds of policy-relevant information that is published by the agencies of government. The underlying assumption is that the ability of a government to adopt complex policies is indicated by the volume and kinds of information that the government collects and publishes. Three kinds of information were selected as a basis for constructing the index: (1) census information, (2) reports on trade and commerce, and (3) government statistics. The volume of these types of information that a government publishes through the years is an indication of administrative capacity and a measure of political development.

In constructing the index, we counted the number of serial census reports, trade and commercial reports, and statistical reports published by our 29 governments from 1800 to 1960. The number of these serial publications in every decade was totaled as a score for each country in each decade. There are, however, certain limitations to the data. In the first place, the sources for these data should be government publications. Scores for each country should be computed directly from the publications issued by governmental agencies, but our limited resources made this procedure impossible. Instead, for the period 1800–1920, we counted the volumes of serial governmental publications in all United States libraries in the *List of Serial Publications of Foreign Governments*, and for the period 1920–60, we counted the volumes of serial governmental publications in selected British libraries in the *London Bibliography of the Social Sciences*. The use of these sources rather than the governmental publications introduces certain biases into the data, although the extent of these biases is uncertain. Probably, the publications of non-Western governments are underestimated, but more generally, we cannot be sure that the volume of publications for any country is completely accurate. For this reason, the index presented here is less reliable than we would like. We emphasize, however, that the sources of data for a more reliable index are accessible. With more time and funds, the relevant government publications can be examined directly, and a highly reliable index can certainly be constructed.[1]

In the second place, since the data for the index were obtained from two separate sources, it posed the problem of combining all of it into a single measure despite discrepancies in the figures reported in the two sources. To solve this difficulty, we obtained raw scores for two overlapping decades (1910–29), and on the basis of this overlap, we fitted the more recent data from the *London Bibliography* to the trend established from our main source, *Serial Publications*. A conversion ratio for each country was obtained by comparing the two scores for the overlapping decades, and this ratio was used to extrapolate scores from 1930 to 1950.

In the third place, we limited ourselves only to serial governmental publications rather than to total governmental publications, and we allowed a maximum score of 10 for each serial publication in each decade, even when the number of publications in the series was higher. Moreover, we took no account of differences in the size of publications in a particular series; a series of pamphlets was counted equally with a series of voluminous tomes. One result of these decisions is to depress the score for the more developed countries. Again, direct perusal of the relevant publications would enable us to construct a more sensitive and reliable index than has in fact been possible.

No extensive validation of this index was undertaken, but we do have governmental nonmilitary employment data for the United Kingdom and the United States over most of the 160 years. To the same degree, the proportion of the population in civilian government employment indicates the extent of development, and we would expect a high correlation with the index of governmental publications as another indicator of political development. In this instance, we find a simple correlation coefficient of .95 in each country, which gives as much support for the index as we could hope for at the present time. Adequate validation depends on better independent indicators than government employment, but we lack indicators at this time.

For this report all the countries have been grouped into four categories on

FIGURE 1

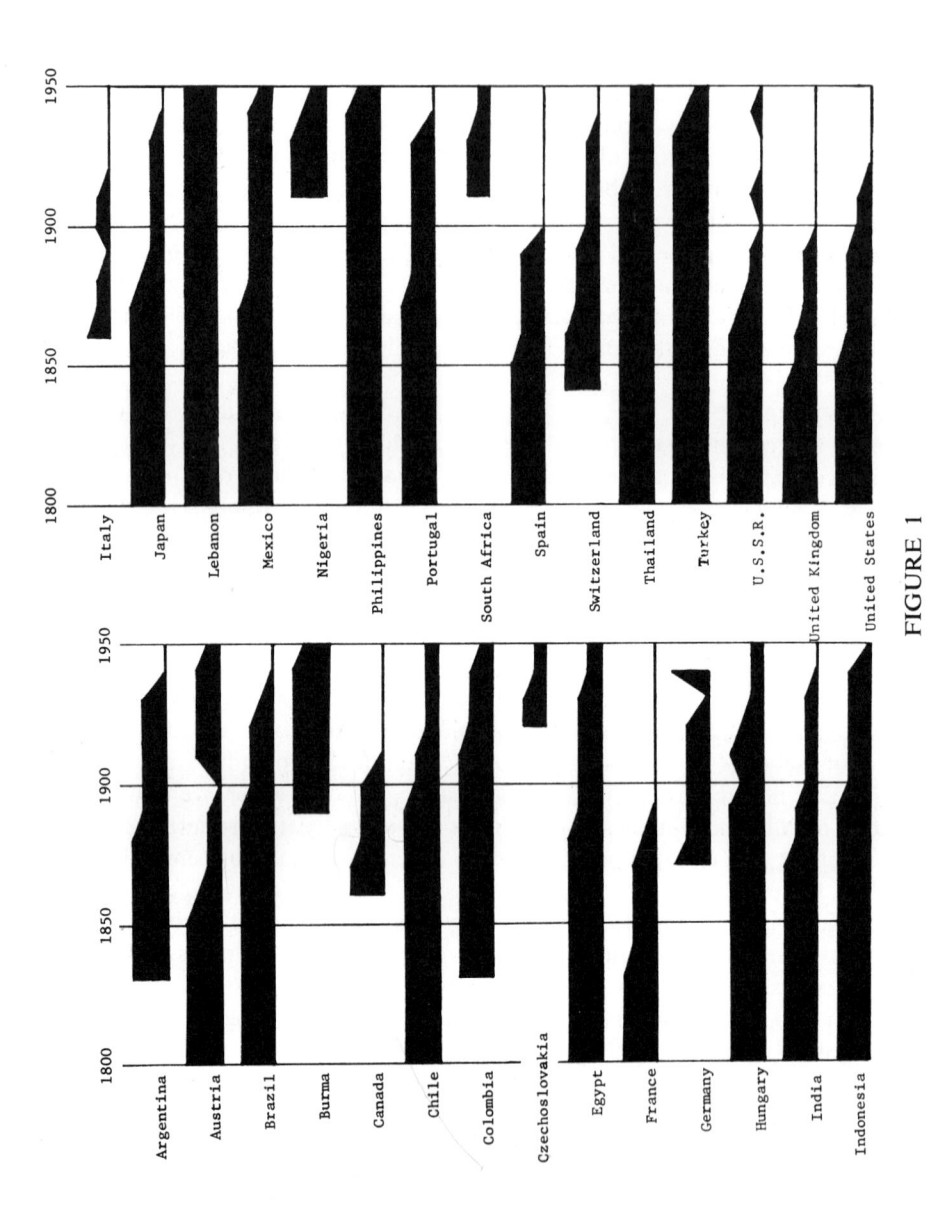

INDEX OF GOVERNMENTAL PUBLICATIONS

the basis of their scores on the index of governmental publications. Summary scores from 0 to 3 were assigned on the following basis:

Score	Range on the Index of Governmental Publications
0	1–50
1	51–150
2	151–250
3	251 and over

The patterns of change in political development, based on these summary scores, are shown in Figure 1.

The distributions shown in Figure 1 reveal four distinct patterns of change in political development.

Pattern A. One set of countries achieves an early high level of political development. These countries include Canada, U.K., U.S., France, Italy, U.S.S.R., and Spain. All maintain the highest level of development for at least four decades. With two exceptions, they show an early and gradual increase in political development. In the case of Italy, the pattern of development is somewhat uneven; the pattern for the U.S.S.R. is more abrupt as well as obviously uneven in the decades of the revolutions and World War II.

Pattern B. A second set of countries attains a high level of development in the mid-twentieth century. These countries include India, Japan, and Switzerland. All have moderately high levels of development throughout the twentieth century, but they reach the highest level only after World War II.

Pattern C. A third set of countries maintains a moderate level of development for a prolonged period, but they do not sustain the highest level of development. These countries include Argentina, Austria, Brazil, Chile, Colombia, Czechoslovakia, Egypt, Germany, Hungary, Indonesia, Mexico, Portugal, and South Africa. With three exceptions, the trend of development is smooth. Austria, Germany, and Hungary reveal uneven fluctuations in development associated with major political disruptions.

Pattern D. A fourth set of countries remains at a low level of political development with, at most, moderate increase in the mid-twentieth century. These countries include Burma, Lebanon, Nigeria, Philippines, Thailand, and Turkey.

Although there are important problems in generalizing the index of governmental publications as a measure of political development, the index seems to have sufficient face validity to warrant its use in examining interrelationships of political development, democratization, and socio-economic variables.

An Index of Democratization

Like political development, the concept of democratization has been defined in different ways by different scholars. But despite the variety of definitions, students of democracy tend to emphasize four basic characteristics as distinctive features of democratic political systems. These distinguishing characteristics are electoral or parliamentary succession, political competition, popular electoral participation, and absence of suppression. If measures could be devised for each of these characteristics, an index of democratization could be constructed, based on combinations of the four basic measures. In this section we shall introduce such an index and apply it to our 29 countries.

Democratic Succession

The practices through which political leaders succeed to the principal executive offices are a major aspect of every political system. To describe these practices, however, is not always easy, if only because there may be significant divergence between the formal practices and the actual practices of succession. In describing the processes of succession that are characteristic of democratic systems, we found it useful to identify a number of different combinations of formal and actual practices of succession that can prevail in any political system. This variety of formal and actual practices can be described as follows:

Formal practices	Actual practices
electoral or parliamentary: of chief executive official through a general election of through investiture by a legislature	electoral or parliamentary
	managed electoral or parliamentary: manipulation of electoral or parliamentary procedures through varied types of pressure, bribery, and so forth
parliamentary monarchy: selection through appointment by a monarch with legislative approval	parliamentary monarchy
institutional support: selection of the chief executive official by a specific group or organization, such as a party, military, or religious organization	institutional support: including in addition to selection by a party, military, or religious organization; succession as a result of popular uprising and other forms of usurpation
monarchy: selection through inheritance	monarchy
colonial: selection by a colonial power	colonial
no formal practice established: interim period in which there has been as yet no formalization of the process of succession	foreign imposition

Patterns of Political Development and Democratization 449

On the basis of this general typology of practices of succession, we constructed a summary measure for democratic succession to the chief executive offices in terms of the following code:

Index of democratic succession

0 democratic: formal succession through elections or parliamentary investiture and actual succession through elections or parliamentary investiture

1 semi-democratic: formal succession through elections or parliamentary investiture and actual succession through manipulation, institutional support, or other non-electoral practices

2 non-democratic: formal succession through non-electoral practices and actual succession through non-electoral practices

The use of this measure involves certain difficulties with a number of implications in assessing a system as democratic. To begin with, identification of the chief executive official is sometimes a matter of judgment. When alternative choices were possible, we selected the official or officials who seemed to us to occupy the most critical role in the making of policy. Secondly, decisions as to which practices are actually prevalent in a system can also be controversial. Especially in instances of institutional support or managed elections, it is not always easy to identify the actual means of succession. Thirdly, the measure discriminates against systems that are formally democratic, but in which actual succession occurs through controlled elections or manipulated parliamentary procedures. In this respect, the measure is biased against democratic scores. Moreover, this bias is reinforced by our decision to count the worst score for the decade. In other words, our scoring reflects the failure of democratic succession in a country rather than the typical pattern of succession in that country.

The measure of democratic succession applied to our 29 countries is shown in Figure 2. When a decade passes with no instance of succession, the practice of the previous decade is continued.

Competition

The second measure comprised within our overall index of democratization is a measure of political competition. There are many different ways in which political competition can be defined, described, and measured, but in a broad comparative and historical perspective, only rather simple measures seem feasible, at least for the time being. Our measure of political competition is based on two characteristics of the system: the presence in the system of legal opposition parties, and the presence of opposition in a regular, important

FIGURE 2

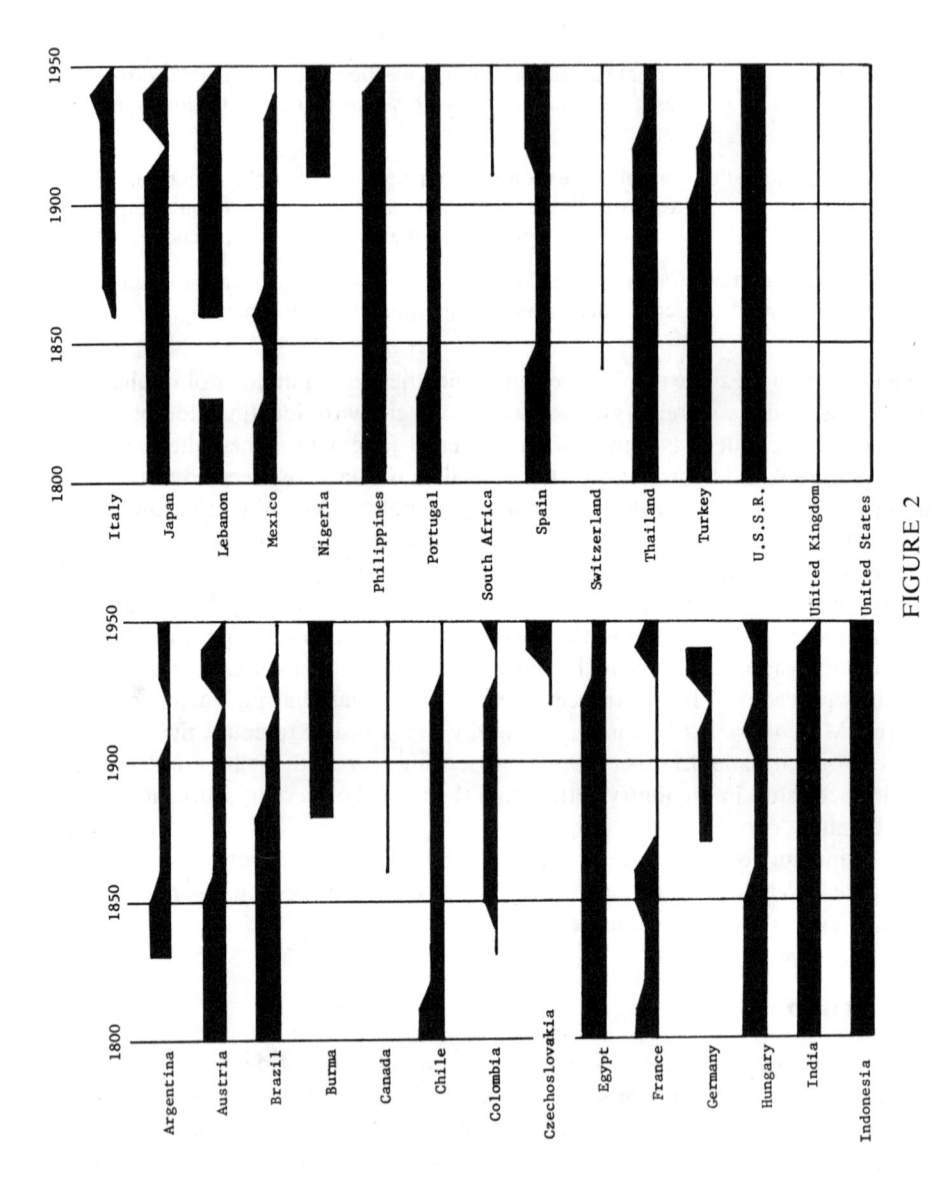

INDEX OF DEMOCRATIC SUCCESSION

elected legislature. Countries are scored in terms of the combination of these characteristics present in any decade, as follows:

Index of political competition

0 presence of legal opposition parties and opposition in a regular, important elected legislature
1 presence of either legal opposition parties or opposition in a regular, important elected legislature
2 presence of neither feature

Like the measure of democratic succession, the use of this measure of political competition has certain implications that should be noticed. In the first place, the presence of opposition parties is treated rather formally. A "party" is regarded as any group that identifies itself as such, and the presence of an opposition party is considered as a matter of legal status without regard to how effective the opposition party might be as a political organization. Secondly, identification of a regular, important elected legislature involves some controversial matters of judgment. By "regular," we mean that the legislature has not been convened only for a single or limited number of sessions, and that it has not been disrupted during the decade; by "important," we mean that the legislature either selects the chief executive or plays a major role in policy-making; by "elected," we mean that members of the legislature are selected by some broad electorate. The existence of these conditions is obviously, in many cases, a matter of judgment, especially in regard to whether or not a legislature should be regarded as "important." Thirdly, at least, in part, the measure of political competition was intended to discriminate between modern democratic and modern totalitarian systems, and it does serve this purpose well enough. However, it appears rather indiscriminate for developing systems in both the 19th and 20th centuries. The measure seems too generous in scoring systems, which quite early in their development, contain both forms of opposition—party opposition and legislative opposition. It appears that highly undeveloped, traditional regimes and highly developed, totalitarian regimes are most likely to suppress opposition. All other regimes are likely to permit at least token opposition.

The measure of political competition applied to our 29 countries is shown in Figure 3.

Popular Electoral Participation

A third characteristic of democratic systems is widespread popular participation in the electoral process. Actually, mass electoral participation is also characteristic of developed systems, as contrasted with democratic systems, so popular participation is not an indicator of democracy. To construct an index of democratization, a measure of electoral participation must be combined with the other measures we have been describing.

452　STUDIES ON DEMOCRATIZATION

FIGURE 3

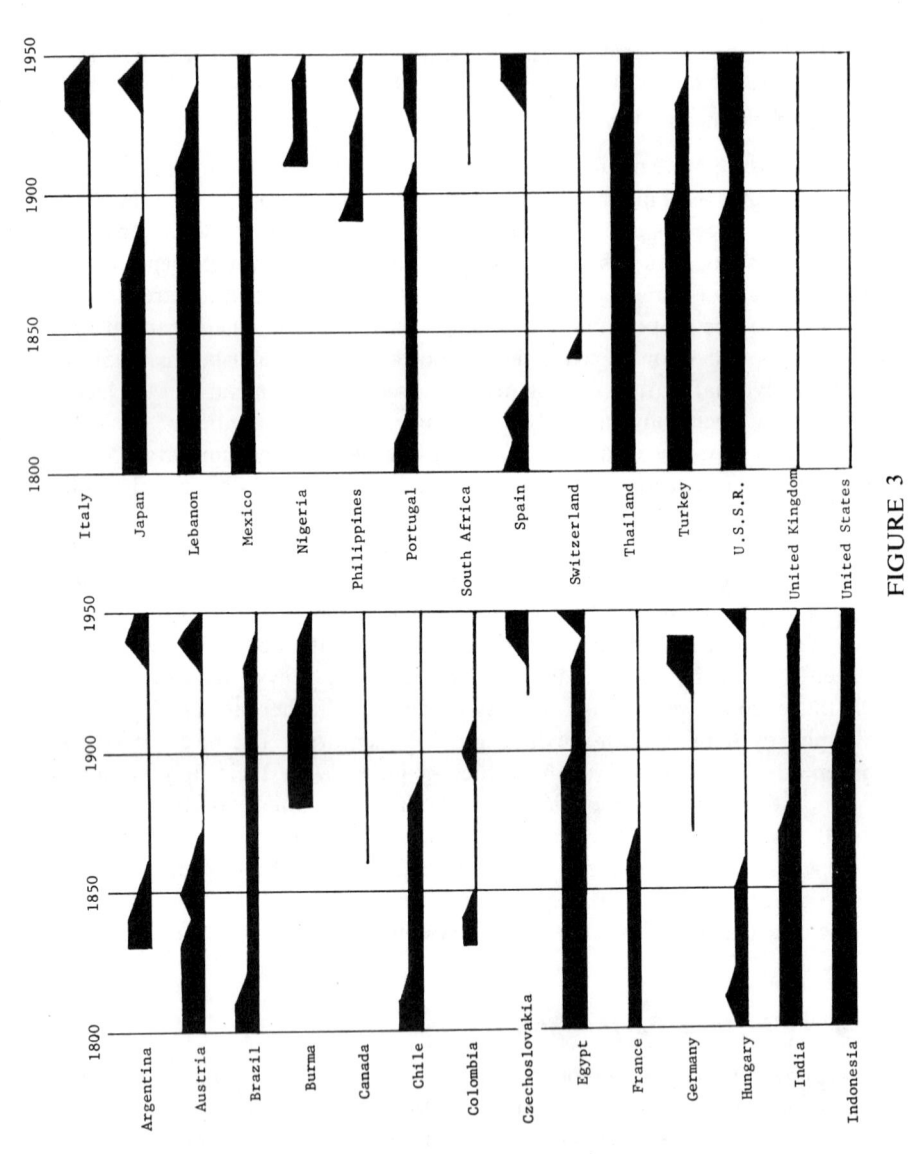

INDEX OF POLITICAL COMPETITION

Patterns of Political Development and Democratization

To measure electoral participation, we have recorded the type of suffrage prevalent in each decade in national elections for the legislature or the presidency, whichever elections were most important in the selection of the chief executive official. These types of suffrage were scored as follows:

0 national elections with universal suffrage (including universal male suffrage as well as minor suffrage requirements such as residence)
1 national elections with moderate restrictions on suffrage
2 national elections with severe restrictions on suffrage
3 no elections

Obviously, the distinction between "moderate" and "severe" restrictions on suffrage is partly a matter of judgment. Moreover, the measure, as a whole, refers to the effects of formal suffrage requirements rather than actual electoral participation. No doubt, there would have been advantages in using turnout as the indicator of electoral participation, but turnout data are extremely difficult to obtain for many countries. Some of the variation in scores for individual countries probably exaggerates fluctuation in actual participation, since the scores reflect on easing and tightening of suffrage requirements, which may have had relatively slight impact on turnout in the short run.

The measure of popular participation applied to our 29 countries is shown in Figure 4.

Absence of Suppression

The fourth characteristic of democratic systems is the absence of suppression directed against individuals, groups, or organizations that participate in the political process. To indicate the extent of suppression in a system, we have scored instances of suppressive acts in terms of both the degree of coercion and the selectivity of the acts. We assigned scores on the following basis:

Index of political suppression

0 no significant political suppression (may include the outlawing of a minor extremist party or media censorship)
1 selective coercive suppression (including individual and group arrests or executions as well as coercive measures against parties or other organizations)
2 widespread electoral suppression (applied to widespread coercion practiced during an election period against opposition individuals, groups, and organizations)
3 general repression (including colonial regimes, generally autocratic regimes, and foreign occupation)
4 civil war conditions
5 severe suppression (applied to police-state and totalitarian regimes)

454   STUDIES ON DEMOCRATIZATION

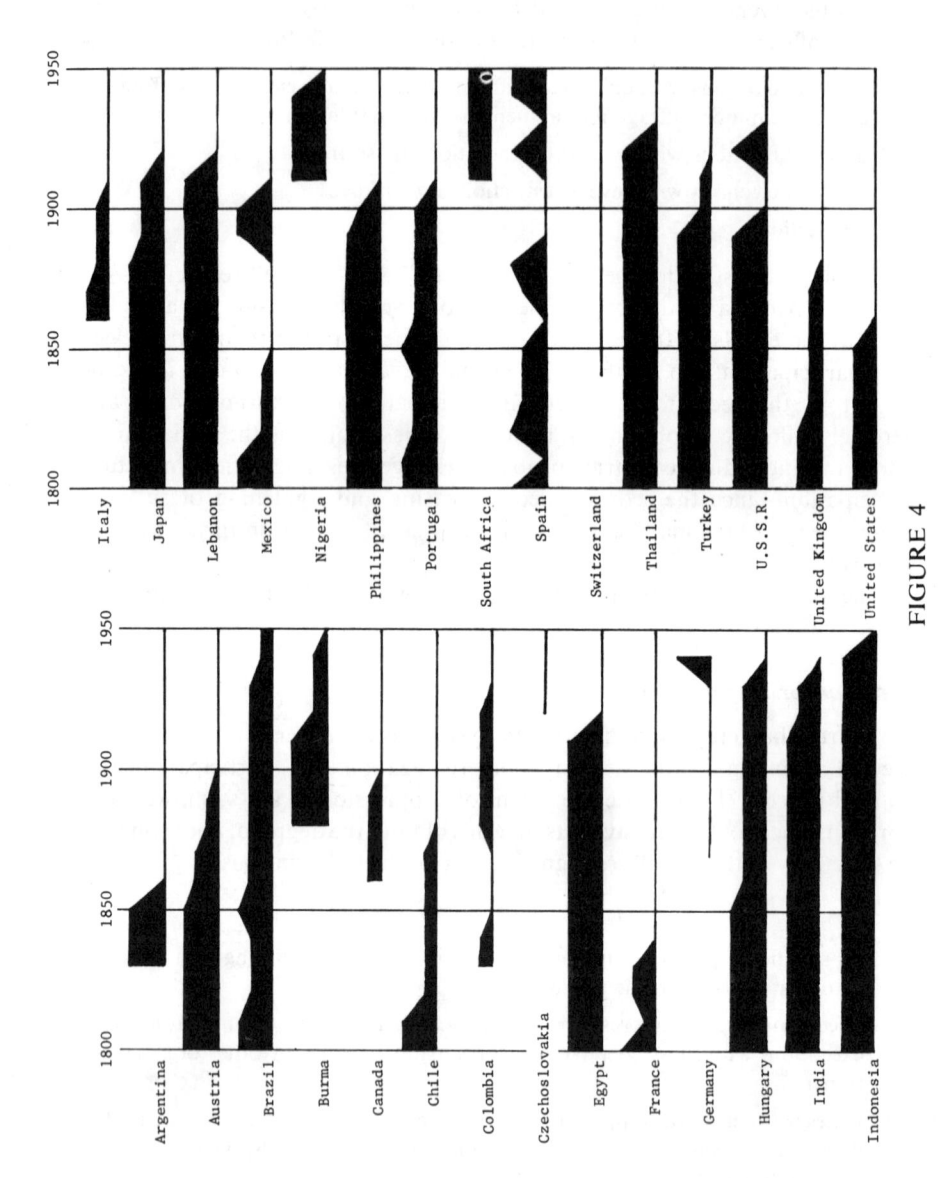

FIGURE 4
INDEX OF POPULAR ELECTORAL PARTICIPATION

Patterns of Political Development and Democratization 455

Since all regimes attempt to maintain order, we have not considered governmental responses to riots or uprisings as instances of suppression; rather, we have tried to record more general suppressive acts for each decade, so the measure is biased toward suppressive scores. Therefore, our measure again reflects the failures of democratic systems rather than their typical patterns. Several types of suppression are omitted in our measure. We have not recorded acts of suppression by local governmental units, when such acts were obviously distinct from the national unit nor have we recorded acts of suppression carried out by non-governmental organizations, although suppressive acts of this kind could be extremely significant under certain circumstances.

The measure of political suppression applied to our 29 countries is shown in Figure 5.

To construct a general index of democratization, we combined the four measures of democratic succession, political competition, popular participation, and political suppression into a single comprehensive measure. Scores were assigned to each country for every decade in terms of the following eight-point rankings:

Index of democratization

0 Succession = formal *and* actual succession through elections or parliamentary investitute
　Competition = presence of legal opposition parties *and* opposition in a regular, important elected legislature
　Participation = national elections with universal suffrage
　Suppression = no significant suppression

1 Succession = formally electoral, parliamentary or parliamentary monarchy—actual succession managed or institutional support
　Competition = same as for "0"
　Participation = any national election
　Suppression = no widespread electoral suppression, or worse

2 Succession = same as for "1"
　Competition = same as for "0"
　Participation = same as for "1"
　Suppression = no general repression, or worse

3 Succession = same as for "1"
　Competition = opposition in regular elected legislature
　Participation = same as for "1"
　Suppression = same as for "2"

4 Succession = same as for "1"
　Competition = opposition in any elected legislature
　Participation = same as for "1"
　Suppression = same as for "2"

456　　　　　　　　　　　　　　　　STUDIES ON DEMOCRATIZATION

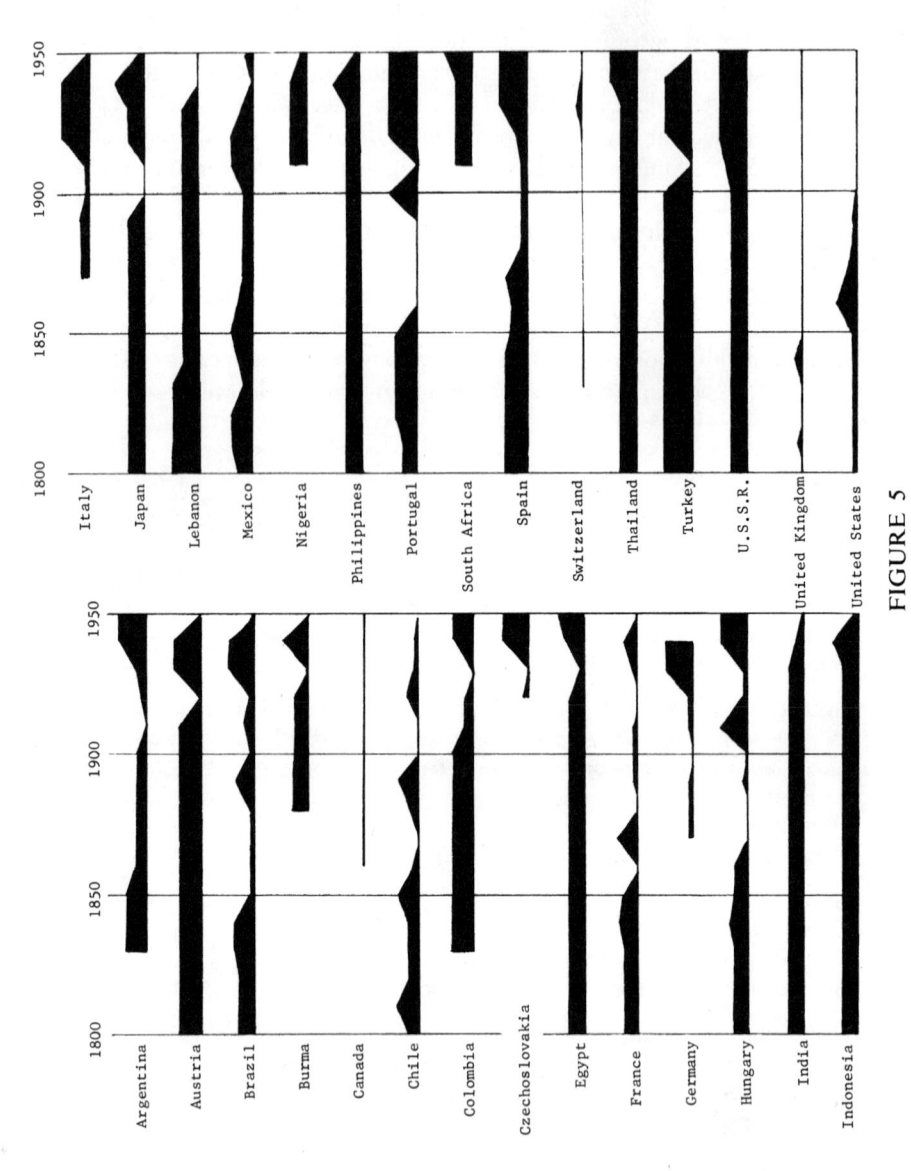

FIGURE 5
INDEX OF POLITICAL SUPPRESSION

5   Succession = legitimate succession including colonial and monarchical
    Competition = opposition in any elected legislature *or* legal opposition party
    Participation = same as for "1"
    Suppression   = same as for "2"
6   Succession = same as for "1"
    or
    Participation = same as for "1"
    or
    Competition = same as for "5"
7   All other combinations

The combination of four measures—competition, participation, suppression, and democratic succession—yields the ranking of democratization shown in Figure 6.

Inspection of Figure 6 reveals four patterns of democratization.

Pattern I. One set of countries remains consistently democratic virtually without interruption through the entire period. These countries are Canada, Switzerland, United Kingdom, and United States. The major departure from a consistently democratic pattern occurs in the United States during the decade of the Civil War. This results from the high suppression score for civil war conditions under our coding. The fact that only four countries are consistently democratic reflects the severity of our index of democratization. The requirements for political competition, including legal opposition parties and opposition in a regular important elected legislature, are sufficiently demanding to exclude most countries even during otherwise democratic decades.

Pattern II. A second set of countries remains moderately democratic for a number of decades without ever sustaining a consistently democratic regime. These countries include Argentina, Chile, France, Germany, Hungary, and Italy. All reveal some unevenness in patterns of democratization. With the exception of Chile, all have undergone one or more decades of highly undemocratic disruptions during their development.

Pattern III. A third set of countries is predominantly non-democratic with some interludes of at least moderate democracy. These countries include Austria, Brazil, Colombia, Czechoslovakia, Mexico, Portugal, and Spain. Despite considerable variation in specific patterns of democratization among these countries, all revert to highly undemocratic regimes following their most democratic interludes.

Pattern IV. A fourth set of countries remains consistently undemocratic throughout the entire period. These countries are Burma, Egypt, India, Indonesia, Japan, Lebanon, Nigeria, Philippines, South Africa, Thailand, Turkey, and U.S.S.R. The major departure from the consistently undemocratic pattern occurs after World War II, when India, Japan, Lebanon, the Philippines, and Turkey achieved relatively democratic regimes. Within the

458

FIGURE 6

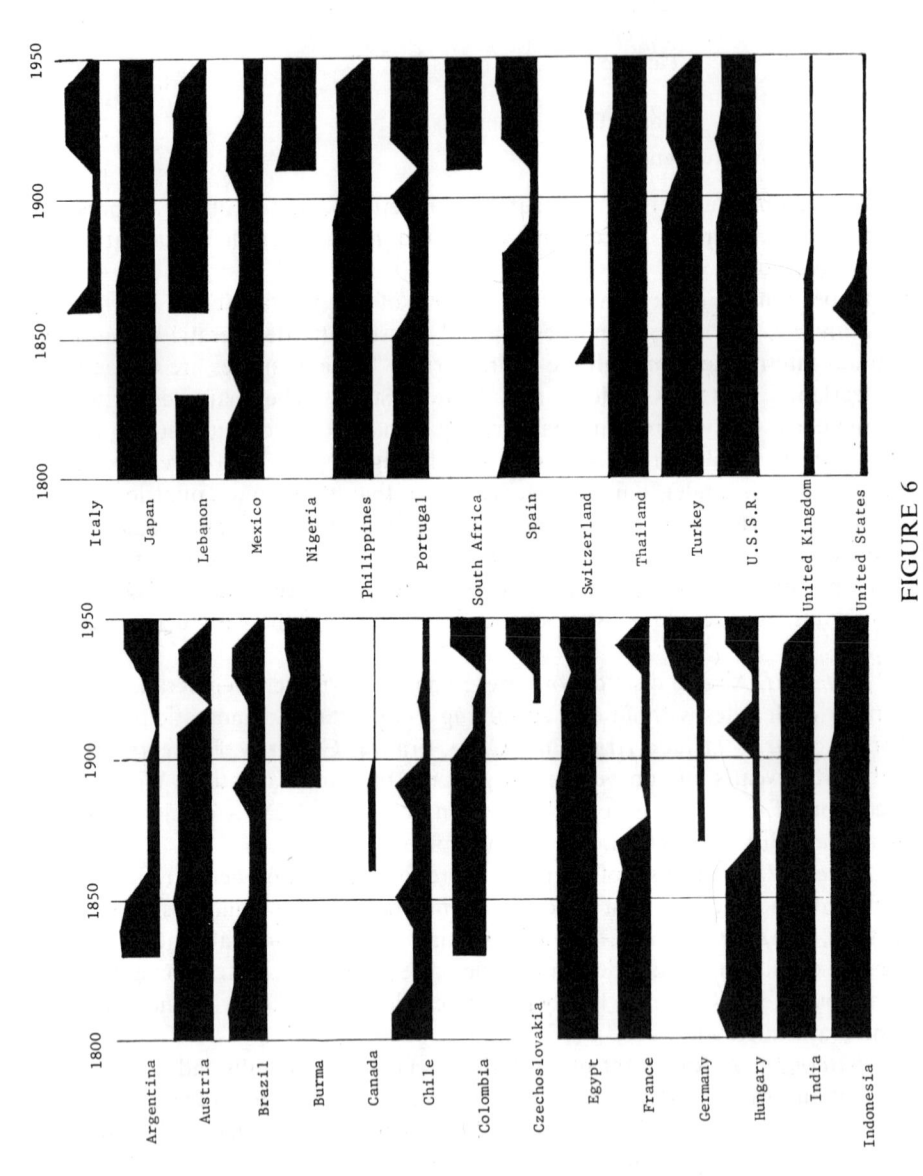

INDEX OF DEMOCRATIZATION

generally undemocratic pattern, three types of regimes can be distinguished: colonial regimes, for varying periods (Burma, Egypt, India, Indonesia, Lebanon, Nigeria, and Philippines); traditional authoritarian regimes, for varying periods (Egypt, Japan, Lebanon, Thailand, Turkey, Russia, and South Africa); and a modern totalitarian regime (U.S.S.R.).

No doubt, exception can be taken as to the specific scores for democratization assigned to particular countries in various decades. In part, such disagreements may reflect differences in judgment and interpretation. Beyond differences of judgment, however, our code does contain some implicit limitations. Scoring under the code ignores abortive attempts to establish democratic regimes (as in Russia in 1917 or during the European revolutions of 1848), as well as short-lived democratic regimes during a decade of severe suppression or undemocratic suppression (as in Japan in the 1920s). At the same time, other scores may exaggerate the extent of democratization through our effort to record periods of experience with some democratic institutions and practices under otherwise undemocratic conditions (as in Brazil and Mexico during the early decades). These implicit biases certainly affect our patterns of democratization to some degree, but whatever the effects may be, the general acceptability of the findings depends on face validity.

Social and Economic Variables

Since our main purpose is to examine relationships between political variables and socio-economic variables, we must now describe briefly the social and economic measures we propose to use in the analysis. In our archive, we have collected data for a rather wide range of social and economic variables. However, in this paper, we will employ only three of these variables: urbanization, education, and agricultural employment.

Urbanization

The simplest of the three measures is urbanization, which is defined as the proportion of the population in cities over 100,000. Population estimates are generally available for all 29 countries throughout the entire period of our study. During earlier periods, when the accuracy of population estimates is most questionable, considerable variations in urbanization figures are quite tolerable, since the proportion of population in cities over 100,000 is so small that large changes in proportions would not influence the overall trend.

The selection of 100,000 as a basis for estimating the population in urban areas was arbitrary, dictated by the greater availability of worldwide data on cities over 100,000 in several almanacs and yearbooks. For most countries, our data predates to 1800, or to a time when the unit has no cities over 100,000. However, there are several characteristics of the measure that should be noted. In countries with a small population, the growth of any city over the 100,000 mark causes the measure to jump markedly—the trend appears more jagged than the actual overall growth of the urban areas warrants. In countries with large populations, this is no problem. There is also difficulty in establishing comparability among units because of uncertainty in some data as to whether population figures for cities include the entire urban area or merely the central city.

Agricultural Employment

Agricultural employment is measured by the proportion of the labor force engaged in agriculture. Unfortunately, this measure appears subject to error, particularly in the early periods. During preindustrial and precommercial periods, estimates of the proportion of a country's labor force employed in various ways may be quite inaccurate. More accurate estimates generally are available only when industrialization is underway. Not only are estimates of the labor force in agriculture subject to error, but estimates of the total labor force are also open to question. Moreover, the reported estimates are not always strictly comparable either within a country or between countries, since practices change in estimating the labor force, particularly with respect to including women, counting rural populations, or counting all males as opposed only to employed males. Nevertheless, this measure remains the best single indicator we have of economic development for all our units over the whole time period.

Education

Our measure of education consists of the number of children in primary education as a proportion of total population. This rather curious way of measuring the level of education in a country is used because of its sensitivity during early periods of development. However, it is not as appropriate for more developed countries. In early periods, the measure accurately reflects the low level of investment in education as well as the gradual increase in this investment. But later, as the age distribution of the population shifts, it also responds to the proportional decline of primary school students in the entire population. The accuracy of estimates on primary education is probably fairly good, once a government begins reporting such information. However, there are problems with comparability from one unit to the next, especially since nongovernmental schools may be included or excluded in various patterns.

Political Development and Patterns of Democratization

Having introduced our principal measures and indices, we can now consider some relationships between the political variables and, also, between the political variables and the socio-economic variables. First, we will examine the relationships between democratization and political development. Then, we

Patterns of Political Development and Democratization 461

Governmental publications

Democratization	Continuous low development	Prolonged moderate development	Moderate to high development	Early high development
Consistently democratic			Switzerland	Canada United Kingdom United States
Moderately democratic		Argentina Chile Germany Hungary		France Italy
Predominantly undemocratic		Austria Brazil Colombia Czechoslovakia Portugal Mexico		Spain
Consistently undemocratic	Burma Lebanon Nigeria Philippines Thailand Turkey	Egypt Indonesia South Africa	India Japan	U.S.S.R.

FIGURE 7

INDEX OF DEMOCRATIZATION AND INDEX OF GOVERNMENTAL PUBLICATIONS

will consider social and economic patterns associated with various combinations of political change.

Figure 7 shows the distribution of countries according to democratization and political development. The categories in the figure are those described in our earlier discussion of the respective indices. We should stress that the variables we are considering are not cross-sectional summaries of democracy and development, but rather *patterns* of democratization and development through time. From Figure 7, we notice the high association of democratization and political development as indicated by the clustering of countries on or near the diagonal. Consistently democratic countries are likely to become highly developed, politically, while predominantly and consistently undemocratic countries are likely to remain at a low level of political development. In addition, the few extremely typical countries all appear in the lower right-hand corner of the figure; that is, although they have become highly developed, politically, they are predominantly or consistently undemocratic.

In no instance are consistently democratic countries less than highly developed. There is no instance of a country, remaining continuously undemocratic, displaying any pattern of democratization other than consistently undemocratic.

Although at first glance, the close association between political development and democratization may seem quite unremarkable, we should emphasize that in terms of how our measures are constructed this association is by no means self-evident. Many measures of political development do coincide at important points with measures of democracy, but this is not at all true here. It would be equally plausible to find that politically developed countries, as measured by our index of governmental publications, are mostly autocratic. Indeed a significant body of democratic theory holds that just such a relationship might be expected. In other words, the finding that political development and democratization are so closely associated invites further examination; it is not an obvious conclusion.

To pursue further the connection between development and democratization, we can consider relationships between each of these political variables and the social and economic variables of urbanization, education, and agricultural employment. If we examine relationships between political development and the three social and economic variables (Figure 8), we find, as the overall tendency, that on the average, countries with long periods at high levels of political development (Group A) are the most urbanized, the least involved in agriculture, and with the highest levels of education.[2] Countries that remain at the lowest level of political development (Group D) reveal the opposite tendencies, when all the countries are averaged. Figure 8 shows the average of each social and economic characteristic for all our countries grouped according to level of governmental publications.

Besides demonstrating the strong connection between political development and urbanization, agricultural employment, and education at the highest and lowest levels of development, Figure 8 also shows that countries at the middle levels of development (Groups B and C) are rather indistinguishable on the social and economic variables. The close correspondence in the distributions of Groups B and C reveals, however, one consistent pattern: during the last decades of the 19th century, countries in Group B (India, Japan, and Switzerland) are less developed, socially and economically, than countries in Group C; but countries in Group B overtake those in Group C around the turn of the century, and they remain until the present at slightly higher levels of urbanization and economic development.

If we turn now to democratization, we find that countries with different patterns of democratization over the last 160 years have quite distinct social and economic characteristics for the same period. The findings are generally similar to those for political development, but the relationships between democratization and social and economic variables are more striking. As Figure 9 shows, consistently democratic countries have smaller proportions

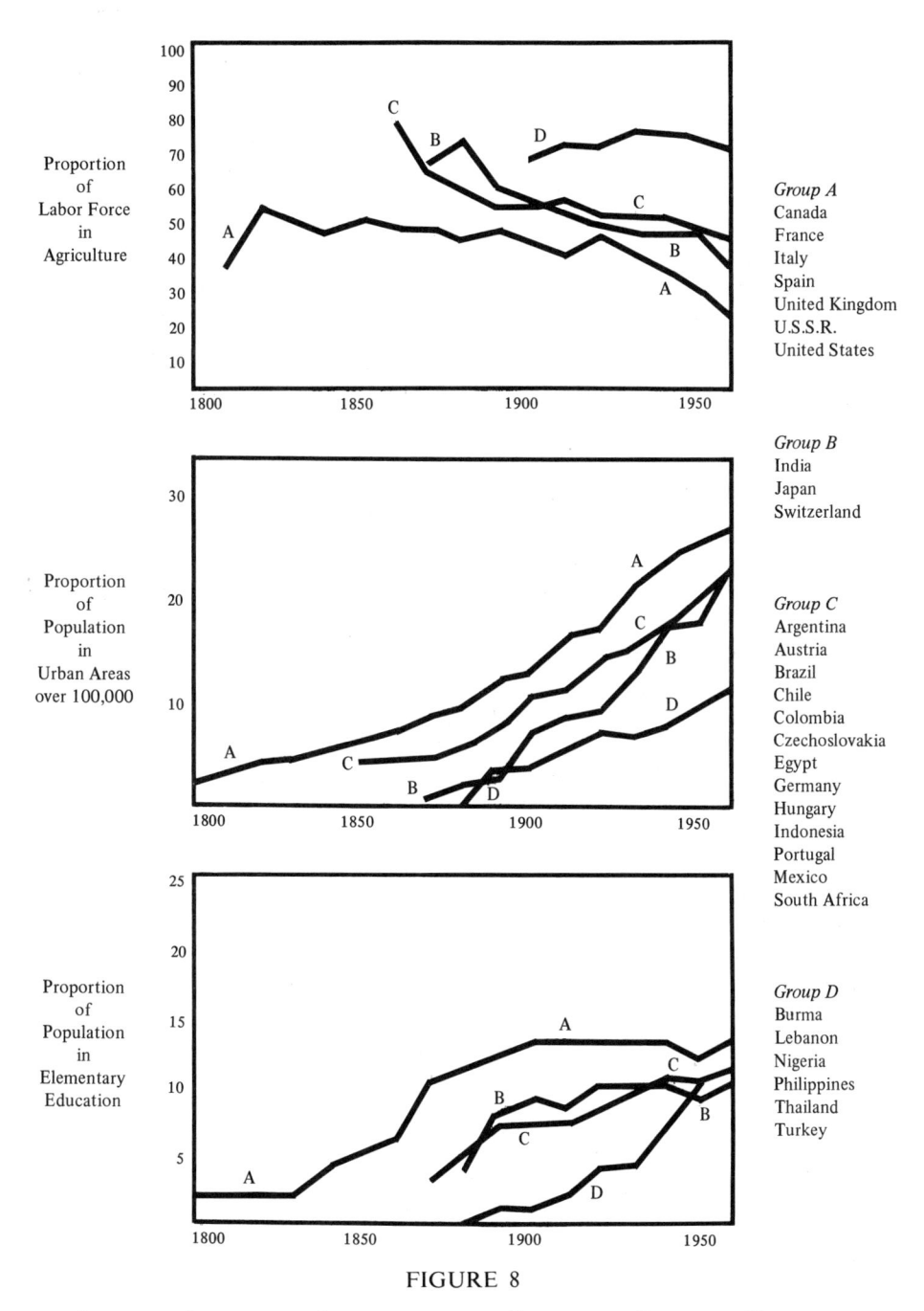

Patterns of Political Development and Democratization 463

FIGURE 8

INDEX OF GOVERNMENT PUBLICATIONS AND SOCIAL AND ECONOMIC VARIABLES

Group A
Canada
France
Italy
Spain
United Kingdom
U.S.S.R.
United States

Group B
India
Japan
Switzerland

Group C
Argentina
Austria
Brazil
Chile
Colombia
Czechoslovakia
Egypt
Germany
Hungary
Indonesia
Portugal
Mexico
South Africa

Group D
Burma
Lebanon
Nigeria
Philippines
Thailand
Turkey

of their labor forces in agriculture, are more urbanized, and have higher proportions of the population in elementary schools. The consistently undemocratic countries show the opposite tendency, with high levels of employment in agriculture throughout, relatively little urbanization until quite recently, and low levels of education until the last two decades. On all three variables, the moderately democratic patterns (Group II) fall clearly between the consistently democratic countries and the predominantly undemocratic.

So far, the relationships between the individual political variables and the social and economic variables are not unexpected. A more significant inquiry, however, concerns the relationship between the social and economic variables and the two political variables examined jointly, as they are arrayed in Figure 7. In Figure 10, we have arranged the countries according to their interrelated patterns of development and democratization, and for each grouping we show the average level of agricultural employment. This configuration enables us to examine the relationships between economic development and each political variable, controlling for the other political variable.

Since the agricultural variable was directly related to democratization and development viewed separately, we would expect the overall relationships to persist also within the cells of Figure 10. There is a steady decline in agricultural employment as we move from lower left to upper right along the diagonal. Within the consistently undemocratic category, there is some tendency for lower proportions of agricultural employment in agriculture to be associated with higher levels of political development. At the three higher levels of democratization, no differences in the agricultural variable appear in association with development. Within the development categories, however, in all cases agricultural employment is associated with the pattern of democratization. In other words, the less agricultural countries enjoy longer periods of democracy regardless of their level of political development, and the more agricultural countries are undemocratic regardless of their level of political development—keeping in mind, that among all our countries, there are no cases in which democratic patterns are associated with low levels of political development. Assessed in this impressionistic manner, the association between political development and level of agricultural employment nearly disappears when we control for democratization; that is, the association between democratization and agricultural employment is stronger than between political development and agricultural employment. The association between political development and agricultural employment can be viewed largely as a result of the high association between democratization and development.

Another interesting pattern among the socio-economic variables to which we ought to draw attention is the relationship between urbanization and the combination of democratization and development. In general, levels of urbanization increase along the diagonal from lower left to upper right as should be expected. However, the deviant cases—low in democratization, but high in development—reveal an overall low level of urbanization with a rapid

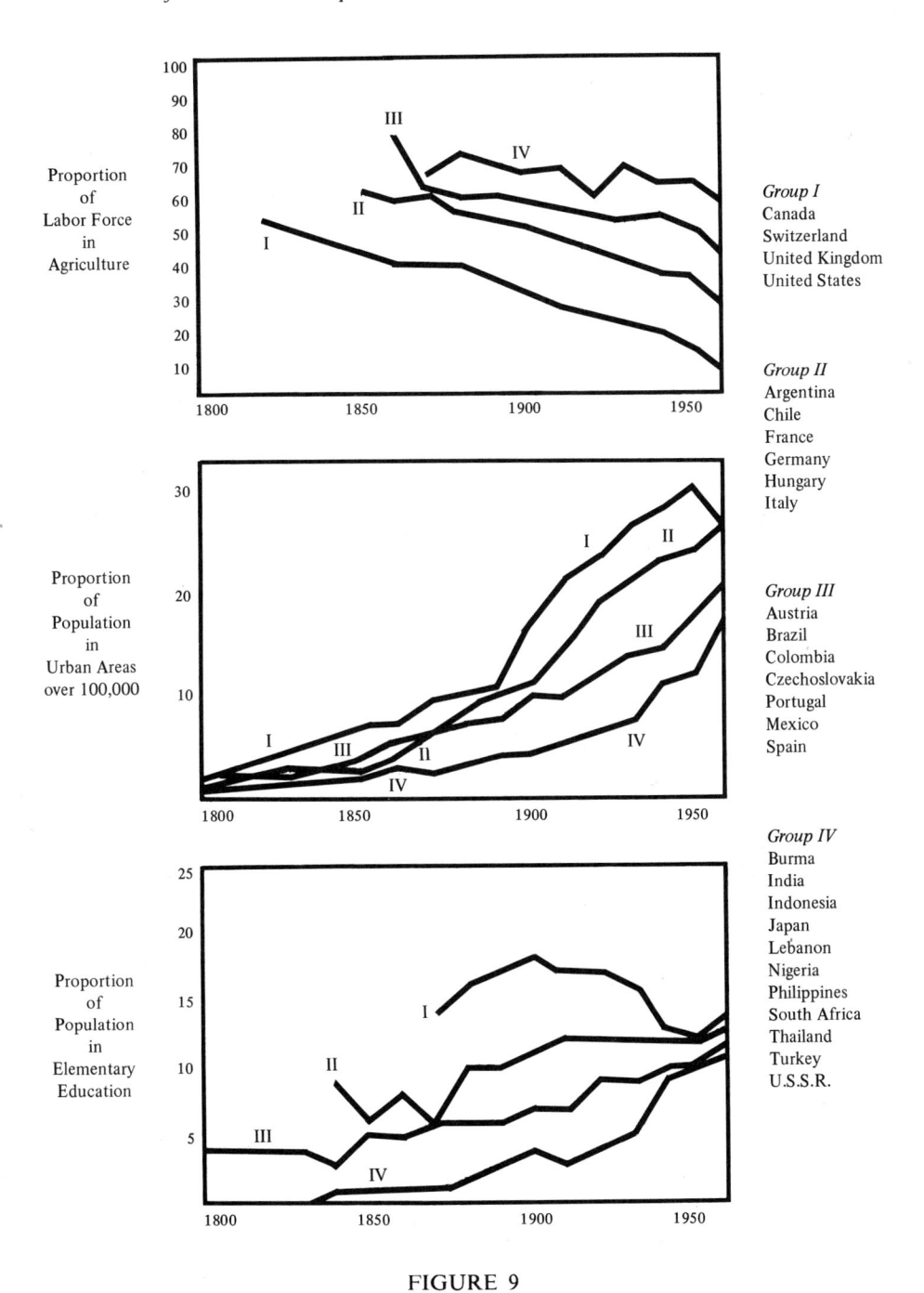

Patterns of Political Development and Democratization

FIGURE 9

INDEX OF DEMOCRATIZATION AND SOCIAL AND ECONOMIC VARIABLES

Group I
Canada
Switzerland
United Kingdom
United States

Group II
Argentina
Chile
France
Germany
Hungary
Italy

Group III
Austria
Brazil
Colombia
Czechoslovakia
Portugal
Mexico
Spain

Group IV
Burma
India
Indonesia
Japan
Lebanon
Nigeria
Philippines
South Africa
Thailand
Turkey
U.S.S.R.

rate of increase during recent decades. All other countries show a moderate increase in urbanization throughout the period, but these deviant cases are undergoing urbanization at an atypically rapid rate. This characteristic, which suggests accelerated social change within these countries, is also reflected in another way in the education data. Here these same deviant countries show some extraordinary increases in education during one or two decades at about the same time as the rapid increase in urbanization.

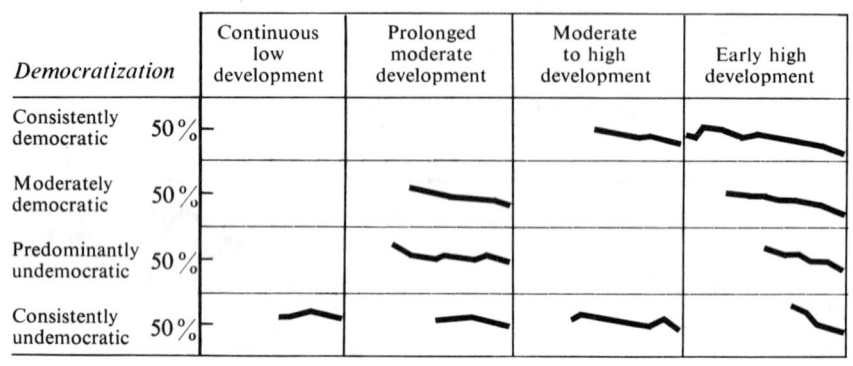

Governmental publications

Democratization	Continuous low development	Prolonged moderate development	Moderate to high development	Early high development
Consistently democratic 50%			⁀⁀	⁀⁀⁀
Moderately democratic 50%		⁀⁀		⁀⁀
Predominantly undemocratic 50%		⁀⁀		⁀⁀
Consistently undemocratic 50%	⁀	⁀	⁀⁀	⁀⁀
	1850 1900 1950	1850 1900 1950	1850 1900 1950	1850 1900 1950

FIGURE 10

INDEX OF DEMOCRATIZATION AND INDEX OF GOVERNMENTAL PUBLICATIONS AND THE PROPORTION OF LABOR FORCE IN AGRICULTURE

The apparent dominance in a crude statistical sense of democratization over development suggests a further topic for consideration: the sequential ordering of these two political variables over time. Many of our countries remain throughout the entire period in a relatively undemocratic and undeveloped condition. But, if we confine ourselves to those countries that have sustained relatively long periods of democracy and relatively prolonged periods of high political development, we notice two quite distinct temporal patterns. A comparison of patterns of political development (Figure 1) and patterns of democratization (Figure 6) shows, on the one hand, that the four countries that are consistently democratic (Canada, Switzerland, U.K., and U.S.) *do not become even moderately developed until at least 50 years after the introduction of democracy.* On the other hand, the two "moderately democratic" countries (France and Italy) that show a more uneven and less consistent pattern of democratization achieve a relatively high level of political development at the same time democracy is introduced. Reference to the relationships between the political variables and the social and economic variables (Figure 10) shows that all six countries enjoyed high levels of economic development throughout their periods of democratization and development, so that on the basis of an examination of these variables, it appears that differences in timing between the advent of democracy and the advent of political development are highly significant for the success of democratic regimes. During the past century and a half, countries that did not succeed in establishing democratic regimes well before they became politically developed had difficulty sustaining their democratic systems. In other words, the sequence of political development and democratization, as contrasted with relationships between the levels of political development and democratization, is a critical factor in sustained democratic rule. This suggests a rather pessimistic implication: undemocratic countries that achieve a high level of political development are not likely subsequently to establish successful democratic regimes.

The conclusion that sustained democratic rule is not dependent on prior or simultaneous political development raises another general problem: the conditions under which democratic regimes flourish or flounder along different points in time. Since the time at which democratization occurs in a country seems to affect profoundly the country's future political course, we are led to ask why the introduction of democratic practices is successful sometimes, but unsuccessful other times. Under some conditions, once democratic regimes are introduced, they can be maintained without interruption for decades, or, in a few instances, for over a century; while under other conditions, attempts to establish democratic regimes prove abortive or short-lived. Undoubtedly, the relative success or failure of democratization depends on a large number of variables in complex interrelationships. To identify these variables and their interrelationships is far beyond the scope of this paper. But a beginning can be made by isolating at least a few of the conditions that seem to accompany successful democratization.

In order to identify the conditions under which democratic regimes persist through time, first of all, we grouped our countries on the basis of the number of consecutive decades during which the country experienced democratic rule. If a country underwent more than one interrupted period of democracy, each such period was recorded separately. A country was considered democratic if it received a score of "0," "1," or "2" on our index of democratization. If a regime met the criterion of democratization but lasted less than a decade, it was included under the heading "less than two decades of democracy." Then, we distributed the countries in each group in terms of two variables: agricultural employment, which is our principal measure of economic development, and the presence for some length of time of what we call "participatory institutions." Since we have not mentioned participatory institutions before, we shall describe briefly what they include.

The basis for our measure of participatory institutions is the presence or absence of certain distinctive institutions through which political participation is carried on in all modern systems. These institutions are political parties, regular elected legislatures, and elections with universal suffrage. We have constructed an index based on the number of these institutions that are present in any decade. It must be emphasized that participatory institutions, as we are discussing them here, are not equivalent to the institutions of democracy. The presence of even a single political party counts in our index of participatory institutions, but systems in which only one party is legal do not qualify as democratic; the presence of an elected regular legislature also counts as an instance of participatory institutions, but elected legislatures in which there is no opposition or which play an unimportant role in policy-making are not indicative of democracy. The presence of elections with universal suffrage is recorded among participatory institutions, but such elections carried on without political competition are not instances of democracy. In other words, although both participatory institutions as well as democratization are connected with political participation, the forms of participation that characterize democracy are sufficiently distinctive so separate indices of democratization and participatory institutions can be readily devised. Actually, we will hypothesize that the presence of participatory institutions for some length of time prior to the introduction of democracy is a necessary but not sufficient condition for sustained democratization.

In general, we want to examine the connection between the persistence of democracy in a country and (1) the level of economic development in the country (measured by percent of agricultural employment), as well as (2) the length of time during which the country has prior experience with a particular set of political institutions. Specifically, we will show the connection between the persistence of democracy and (1) 50 percent or less employment in agriculture, as well as (2) two decades or more experience with at least two participatory institutions. (That is, any two of the three institutions described: political parties, a regular elected legislature, and elections with universal suffrage.) If at least two participatory institutions were present in a country for at least two decades prior to the advent of democracy, the country is grouped in one category. If fewer than two participatory institutions were present in a country during the two decades prior to the advent of democracy, the country is grouped in a second category. The result of this distribution of countries in terms of both percentage of agricultural employment and presence of participatory institutions is shown in Figure 11.

A number of conclusions are apparent from Figure 11. First, there is an obvious connection between the persistence of democracy in a country and the level of economic development at the advent of democracy. In four out of five cases (or six out of eight cases if we include Switzerland, U.K., and U.S.), countries with six or more decades of democracy had 50 percent or less agricultural employment at the beginning of the democratic period. The significance of participatory institutions for this group of countries is more difficult to assess because so many of the countries fall in the "inappropriate" category for this variable. A country is placed in the inappropriate category for one of two reasons: either it did not exist as a unit prior to the advent of democratization (Canada, Czechoslovakia, Germany, Italy, and Switzerland), or else the advent of democracy predates 1800, and therefore lies outside our time-period (U.K. and U.S.). The U.K. and the U.S. can be included within the analysis simply by extending the time-period, and in this respect, they pose no special difficulties. However, the other inappropriate countries do involve special problems. In order to include these countries in the analysis, we must go back to a period in which the country does not exist as an integrated unit, so that any further observations of these countries requires an examination of the characteristics of subnational units as well as the process through which these units become integrated. We might look, for example, at the role of dominant "core" areas in the process of integration and identify the varied patterns by which integration is achieved. Actually, we do intend in the near future to investigate the relationships among democratization, political development, and integration with special attention to the role of these core areas. But such a study is beyond the scope of our present data.

From Figure 11 we learn also that countries in which democratic regimes do not survive more than three decades have either over 50 percent agricultural employment or suffer major foreign intervention, which undermines or openly destroys their democratic governments. The experience with participatory institutions among democracies that do not survive three decades is more mixed. To be sure, most of the democratic regimes that did not persist, but that had extended experience with these institutions were disrupted from outside. But several democratic failures in countries, where the presence of participatory institutions was extensive, cannot be explained by outside intervention—specifically, Spain (before World War I), Japan (during the 1920s), and Turkey (after World War II).

The other deviant cases in Figure 11 are Argentina, Hungary, and Italy in the late 19th and early 20th centuries, when a moderate level of democracy persisted rather a long time in association with high agricultural employment and limited experience with participatory institutions. But these countries also involve problems connected with the role of core areas in their development. Further examination of these cases would again entail a consideration of the political experiences and social and economic characteristics of subnational core areas.

The limited number of appropriate cases in Figure 11 reduces confidence in the conclusions derived from this figure. However, if we ignore those instances in which democratic regimes were short-lived as the result of outside intervention, there is a strong tendency for economically developed countries to sustain democratic rule, and for predominantly agricultural countries to undergo only brief and unsuccessful periods of democracy. Furthermore, among countries that do not sustain democracy for more than three decades, those with extended prior periods of participatory institutions are, without exception, predominantly agricultural. In other words, there is a tendency for

FIGURE 11

DURATION OF DEMOCRACY ACCORDING TO THE PROPORTION OF LABOR FORCE IN AGRICULTURE AND PARTICIPATORY INSTITUTIONS

Duration of democratic regimes

Proportion of labor force in agriculture	Less than two decades	Two or three decades	Four or five decades	Six or more decades	Current attempts
50 percent or over	Portugal (1910) Burma (1930, 1940) Brazil (1950) Japan (1920) Turkey (1940)	Colombia (1910) Spain (1890) Hungary (1920)	Hungary (1870) Italy (1870)	Argentina (1860)	India Lebanon Philippines
Less than 50 percent	Austria (1920) Czechoslovakia (1940) France (1940) Spain (1930)			Canada (1860) Chile (1900) France (1880) Germany (1870)	Austria Italy Japan
Inappropriate[a]				Switzerland (1890–58%) U.K. (1800–37%) U.S. (1800–72%)	

Participatory institutions					
Limited experience	Portugal (1910) Burma (1930, 1940) Brazil (1950)	Colombia (1910)	Hungary (1870)	Argentina (1860)	
Extended experience	Japan (1920) Turkey (1940) Austria (1920) Czechoslovakia (1940) France (1940) Spain (1930)	Spain (1890) Hungary (1920)		Chile (1900) France (1880)	Austria India Italy Lebanon Japan Philippines
Inappropriate[a]		Czechoslovakia (1920)	Italy (1870)	Canada (1860) Germany (1870) Switzerland (1840) U.K. (1800) U.S. (1800)	

[a] This category includes cases which for one reason or another could not be scored at advent of democracy.

extended prior experience with participatory institutions to be a necessary, but not sufficient condition of sustained democratization.

Summary

In this paper we have touched upon a number of topics concerning patterns of political development, patterns of democratization, and the social and economic conditions that accompany these patterns. The discussion proceeded through several steps. First, we were able to show that political development and democratization are strongly associated with each other, in that all consistently democratic countries achieved early high levels of political development. We were also able to show that both patterns of political development and patterns of democratization are associated with distinctive levels and patterns of urbanization, education, and agricultural employment. It appeared, further, that the association between political development and particular social and economic conditions was mainly a reflection of the strong connection between political development and democratization. This led us to consider the relationship between political development and democratization in terms of the sequence in which the respective patterns occur. We found that among consistently democratic countries high levels of political development do not precede or accompany democratization, but invariably appear many decades later. This finding seems to have important implications for the prospects of democracy throughout the presently developing areas of the world. Recognizing that a high level of political development need not accompany democracy—or may indeed impede democratization—we attempted to identify some of the conditions that do account for the success of democratization some times and the failure of democratization other times. We examined two variables that may be associated with prolonged democratic rule: level of economic development and the presence of a particular set of political institutions, which we called participatory institutions. We found that two conditions for sustained democratic rule over long periods appear to be a high level of economic development at the time of democratization and extended prior experience with these participatory institutions.

We emphasize that all our discussions and findings are preliminary. The limited number of cases, the gross nature of the data, and the simplicity of the analysis permit only the most tentative conclusions. At this point, we are satisfied if we have been able to illustrate some interesting possibilities for quantitative political analysis and to identify some important hypotheses for further investigation.

NOTES

1. Scores for the United States were obtained from the Department of Commerce Index of Publications and from counting, exhaustively, the number of relevant publications. None of our sources contained enough listings for Lebanon to

compute an index. From 1900 to 1929, the Philippines was scored from the Catalogue of the Library of Congress, since publications for the Philippines were not listed in Serial Publications.

2. Averaging has important weaknesses in this application. Since the number of cases varies greatly from group to group and from decade to decade, the reliability of the figures varies considerably. Moreover, the averages conceal a rather wide range of deviation, although the ranges overlap at relatively few points. Obviously, averaging does not provide a "best fitting" curve, and subsequent analysis must move in that direction. In subsequent studies, the manipulation of these variables will proceed on a country-by-country basis, probably through regression analysis, as the means for reaching summary comparisons and interpretations. Obviously none of the basic problems will disappear through this approach, but at least the difficulties will be more explicit.

21 Patterns of Democratic Development: An Historical Comparative Analysis

WILLIAM FLANIGAN and EDWIN FOGELMAN

The conditions under which democratic systems flourish or fail have been a problem for analysis ever since the time of Aristotle. In recent decades, the subject has received renewed attention, partly because, since World War II, so many attempts have been made in all parts of the world to introduce or revive democratic regimes, and partly because new types of analyses give promise of significant novel conclusions. Among these new types of analyses are those involving the application of statistical techniques to quantitative comparative data on the social and political characteristics of many countries. This paper is a contribution to such efforts. It is an attempt to examine patterns of democratic development through an analysis of longitudinal comparative data on 44 countries from 1800 to 1960.[1]

Our general purpose in this paper is to identify the patterns of social and economic conditions associated with successful and unsuccessful attempts to introduce and maintain democratic systems through time. In order to do this, we shall follow these procedures: (1) Describe the incidence of democracy in 44 countries during the past 160 years in relation to prevailing levels of urbanization and agricultural employment. (2) Examine the social and economic characteristics of decades in which attempts to introduce democracy have resulted in varying degrees of success or failure. (3) Show correlations through

---

Authors' Note: In the preparation of the data and tables for this paper we have had the invaluable aid of Richard Pride, formerly our principal graduate research assistant and now on the faculty at Vanderbilt University; Cheryl Christenson, formerly our principal undergraduate research assistant and now a fellow at MIT; and Suzanne Couillard, our current principal undergraduate research assistant. Financial support for the archive, since its inception, has been provided by the University of Minnesota's Office of International Programs under a grant from the Ford Foundation.

This paper was originally presented before a panel at the 1968 annual meeting of The American Political Science Association in Washington, D.C., September 3–7, 1968 and is reprinted by permission of the authors and the Association (copyright holder).

time between the extent of democracy and changes in urbanization and agricultural employment within particular countries. (4) Suggest some patterns of related social, economic, and political conditions associated with democratic development.

Most of the analysis concerns relationships among three major variables: democracy, urbanization, and agricultural employment. For this analysis, we have assigned each country a single score for each decade on each of the three variables, although the procedures of decade scoring introduce biases and are insensitive to shorter term variation.

Our measure of democracy is an eight-point index based on varying combinations of four basic characteristics of a political system: form of selection of the chief executive, political competition, popular elections, and degree of political suppression.[2]

Our two major nonpolitical variables are urbanization and agricultural employment.

Urbanization

Urbanization is defined as the proportion of the population in cities over 100,000. Population estimates are generally available for all 44 countries throughout the entire period of our study. During earlier periods, when the accuracy of population estimates is most questionable, considerable variations in urbanization figures are quite tolerable, since the proportion of population in cities over 100,000 is so small that large changes in proportions would not influence the overall trend.

The selection of 100,000 as a basis for estimating the population in urban areas was arbitrary, dictated by the greater availability of world-wide data on cities over 100,000. For all countries our data predate to 1800, or to a point where the unit has no cities over 100,000. There are, however, several characteristics of the measure that should be noted. In countries with a small population, the growth of any city over the 100,000 mark causes the measure to jump markedly—the trend appears more jagged than the actual overall growth of the urban areas warrant. In countries with large populations, this is no problem. There is also the difficulty in establishing comparability among units because of uncertainty in some data as to whether population figures for cities include the entire urban area or merely the central city.

Agricultural Employment

Agricultural employment is measured by the proportion of the labor force engaged in agriculture. Unfortunately, this measure appears subject to error, particularly in the early periods. During preindustrial and precommercial periods, estimates of the proportion of a country's labor force employed in various ways may be quite inaccurate. More accurate estimates generally are available only when industrialization is underway. Not only are estimates of the labor force in agriculture subject to error, but estimates of the total labor force are also open to question. Moreover, the reported estimates are not always strictly comparable either within a country or between countries, since practices change in estimating the labor force, particularly with respect to including women, counting rural populations, or counting all males as opposed only to employed males. Nevertheless, this measure remains the best single indicator we have of economic development for all our units over the whole time period.

TABLE 1

The Proportion of Democratic[a] Decades from 1800 to 1959 According to Levels of Agricultural Employment and According to Levels of Urbanization[b]

Proportion of labor force employed in agriculture	Ratio	Proportion	Proportion of total population in cities over 100,000	Ratio	Proportion
60%+	13/332	.04	0–5%	12/282	.04
50–59%	10/49	.20	6–10%	23/96	.24
40–49%	21/54	.39	11–15%	19/55	.35
30–39%	26/45	.58	16–20%	16/39	.41
20–29%	32/37	.86	21–25%	19/23	.83
0–19%	15/23	.65	26%+	28/45	.62

[a] Democracy is defined in this and the following tables as a score of "0," "1," or "2" on the Index of Democracy for a decade. For the presentation of relationships with demographic variables we have ignored the German occupation of Belgium, Denmark, France, Netherlands, and Norway and given them the score they would have otherwise had. This has a very slight impact on the findings but it seemed unwarranted to reduce the apparent relationships because of a brief disruption wholly unrelated to demographic variables.

[b] There are a number of decades with missing data on agricultural employment where we could not assume (as we otherwise would) that the figure was well over 60 percent. In order not to complicate subsequent integration of the sets of data, we eliminated all decades with missing data from all distributions. This has the impact of making the top three categories in these distributions appear to have a slightly higher rate of democracy than they would with complete data.

I

To begin, we shall first of all describe the incidence of democracy at varying levels of urbanization and agricultural employment. We want to determine the likelihood that democratic systems are present at differing levels of urbanization, agricultural employment, and combined urbanization and agricultural employment. In order to do so, we will indicate, for different levels of urbanization and agricultural employment, the total number of decades that all 44 countries have been at these levels from 1800 to 1960, and also the total number of decades that democracy has been present at each of these levels. This will enable us to determine the amount of time that democracy has been present at different levels of urbanization and agricultural employment as a proportion of the total amount of time that countries have existed at these levels or the percentage of decades during which democracy has been present at each level. Throughout this section, "democracy" is defined as a country with a score of 0, 1, or 2 on the Index of Democracy.

Table 1 shows the proportion and percentages of democratic decades to total number of decades at six different levels of urbanization and agricultural employment. From Table 1 we see, as expected, that democracy is much less likely to occur at very low levels of urbanization than at higher levels, and at very high levels of agricultural employment than at lower levels. With urbanization of 5 percent or less, democracy occurs in only 4 percent of the decades, and this small likelihood of democracy is exactly the same with 60 percent or more of the work force employed in agriculture. As urbanization increases or agricultural employment decreases, the likelihood of democracy improves by very comparable degrees with each variable. With urbanization of 11 to 15 percent, democracy occurs in 35 percent of the decades; with agricultural employment of 40 to 49 percent, democracy occurs in 39 percent of the decades. Only in the next range, urbanization 16 to 20 percent, agricultural employment 30 to 39 percent, is there a significant difference in the incidence of democracy. At this range of urbanization, 41 percent of the decades are democratic; but with agricultural employment of 30 to 39 percent, 58 percent of the decades are democratic. Actually, of course, changes in the ranges for the different levels of the two variables would alter these percentages, and since the ranges were chosen quite arbitrarily, no great significance attaches to the comparability or lack of comparability of the percentages in any particular cells. The table, however, does confirm a generally similar relationship between democracy and either urbanization or level of agricultural employment.

But one aspect of Table 1 is perhaps less expected. Although democracy is unlikely to be present at low levels of urbanization or high levels of agricultural employment, and although, up to a point, the likelihood of democracy increases steadily with higher urbanization or lower agricultural employment, it is not likely that democracy continues to improve directly as urbanization increases or agricultural employment decreases. On the contrary, there is a marked decline in the incidence of democracy, both at the highest levels of urbanization or at the lowest levels of agricultural employment. The greatest proportion of democratic decades occurs not at these highest and lowest levels, but at the preceding levels. With urbanization in our highest category—26 percent or more—democracy occurs in 62 percent of the decades; but with urbanization of 21 to 25 percent, the percentage of democratic decades increases to 83 percent. Similarly, with agricultural employment of 0 to 19 percent, 65 percent of the decades are democratic; but with agricultural employment of 0 to 9 percent, the figure increases to 86 percent. The increase in percentages is identical for both variables, which gives added confidence in the finding. Again, changes in the ranges would alter the percentages, and too great importance cannot be attached to the specific ranges we are using. But the basic observation remains: the relationship between the incidence of democracy and either increased urbanization or reduced agricultural employment is not linear. Once conditions of urbanization and agricultural employment reach a certain level, the direction of the relationship alters. Instead of continuing to improve, the likelihood of democracy at the highest levels of urbanization or the lowest level of agricultural employment declines significantly.

In Table 1 the incidence of democracy at different levels of urbanization and employment is described separately for each variable; that is, we can say something about the likely occurrence of democracy at varied levels of either urbanization or agricultural employment. It is also interesting to examine the incidence of democracy in relation to both urbanization and agricultural employment in various combinations. This information is shown in Table 2.

TABLE 2

THE PROPORTION OF DEMOCRATIC DECADES FROM 1800–1959 ACCORDING TO LEVELS OF AGRICULTURAL EMPLOYMENT AND URBANIZATION

Agricultural employment	Urbanization		
	0–5%	6–15%	16%+
50%+	8/260 .03	15/106 .14	0/17 .00
30–49%	3/15 .20	22/41 .54	23/45 .51
0–29%	1/1	3/9	44/51 .86

Each cell indicates the proportion and percentage of decades of democracy over the total number of decades during which countries have been at varying levels of both urbanization and agricultural employment from 1800 to 1960. (Note that the ranges of levels of urbanization and agricultural employment are defined differently in Tables 1 and 2, so the figures in the cells of the respective tables are not strictly comparable.) From this table we can see the likelihood of democracy at different combined levels of the two variables. The information provides some important additions to the results suggested in Table 1.

It becomes clear from Table 2 that neither urbanization alone nor decline in agricultural employment alone is strongly associated with the incidence of democracy; rather, it is the combination of these conditions that is most highly associated with democracy. In other words, higher urbanization by itself or lower agricultural employment by itself is much less likely to accompany democracy than the two conditions together. This is particularly evident with respect to urbanization. The small number of cases of low agricultural employment combined with low or moderate urbanization makes generalization

TABLE 3

THE PROPORTION OF DEMOCRATIC DECADES FROM 1800–49 ACCORDING TO AGRICULTURAL EMPLOYMENT AND URBANIZATION

Agricultural employment	Urbanization		
	0–5%	6–15%	16%+
50%+	5/114 .04	/3	
30–49%	/5	3/4	
0–29%			2/2

about these cases doubtful. But cases of high urbanization combined with high or moderate levels of agricultural employment are sufficiently numerous to justify some conclusions. It is striking that there are no decades at all of successful democracy under conditions of high urbanization combined with

TABLE 4

THE PROPORTION OF DEMOCRATIC DECADES FROM 1850–99 ACCORDING TO AGRICULTURAL EMPLOYMENT AND URBANIZATION

Agricultural employment	Urbanization		
	0–5%	6–15%	16%+
50%+	3/94 .03	7/35 .20	/3
30–49%	3/10 .30	5/15 .33	2/6
0–29%			5/5

high agricultural employment. Under conditions of high urbanization combined with moderate levels of agricultural employment, about half the decades have periods of democracy. When high urbanization occurs together with low levels of agricultural employment, the incidence of democracy increases again. It would seem that a high degree of urbanization is not conducive to

TABLE 5

THE PROPORTION OF DEMOCRATIC DECADES FROM 1900–59 ACCORDING TO AGRICULTURAL EMPLOYMENT AND URBANIZATION

Agricultural employment	Urbanization		
	0–5%	6–15%	16%+
50%+	/52 .00	8/68 .12	/14 .00
30–49%		14/22 .64	21/39 .54
0–29%	1/1	3/9	37/44 .84

successful democracy unless the urbanization is accompanied by low levels of employment in agriculture.

These relationships between democracy and conditions of urbanization and agricultural employment can be explored further by distributing the cases in Table 2 into several different categories. We can, for example, distribute the cases according to different time-periods, to see whether the same relationships hold in the first half of the nineteenth century, the second half of the nineteenth century, and the twentieth century. We can also distribute the cases according to regions, to see whether the same relationships hold true in Western Europe and in South America.

The distributions, according to time-periods, are shown in Tables 3, 4, and 5. We see in Table 3 that, during the first half of the nineteenth century, so few of our countries had moved out of conditions of low urbanization and high agricultural employment that any generalization about these cases is extremely hazardous. Nevertheless, the overall tendency found in Table 2 is reinforced. The combination of low urbanization and high agricultural employment is most unpromising for democracy. Increased urbanization alone or decline in agricultural employment alone does not seem conducive to the maintenance of democracy. Only the two conditions together are associated with successful democratic systems. These general conclusions are further illustrated during the period from 1850 to 1899. In Table 4, we begin to get combinations of conditions not found in the earlier period. Again, however, the likelihood of democracy under conditions of either moderate urbanization alone or moderate agricultural employment alone, as well as the two conditions in combination, remains low compared to the sharp increase in this likelihood, when high urbanization and low agricultural employment occur together. Indeed, considering only the few cases in the lower right-hand cells of both Tables 3 and 4, we can say that, during the nineteenth century, there was a perfect association between the incidence of democracy and the combined conditions of high urbanization plus low agricultural employment.

The largest number of cases and the most varied combination of conditions are found in the twentieth century. These cases dominate the overall totals in Table 2, so that the percentages in Tables 2 and 5 are very similar. Comparing Table 5 with Tables 3 and 4, we see that the pattern of relationships between democracy and our two nonpolitical variables becomes more complex: the former perfect association in the lower right-hand cells disappears. Clearly, the twentieth century provides the most numerous, varied, and unexpected cases. Some further distribution to throw additional light on these cases seems desirable.

Tables 6 and 7 contain the twentieth century cases distributed between South American countries and Western Europe. (Note that countries in other regions are also included in Table 5, so the totals in Table 5 are greater than the sum of cases in Tables 6 and 7.) A comparison of Tables 6 and 7 reveals a number of basic similarities between conditions in South America and

Western Europe, and some important differences. Both South American and European countries show a very small likelihood of democracy under conditions of high agricultural employment, regardless of degree of urbanization. In both sets of countries the only decades of democracy under conditions of high agricultural employment occur in combination with moderate urbanization. There are no decades of democracy in either table when high agricultural employment is combined with either low urbanization or high urbanization.

TABLE 6

THE PROPORTION OF DEMOCRATIC DECADES IN SOUTH AMERICAN COUNTRIES FROM 1900–59 ACCORDING TO AGRICULTURAL EMPLOYMENT AND URBANIZATION

Agricultural employment	Urbanization		
	0–5%	6–15%	16%+
50%+	/20 .00	2/23 .09	/4
30–49%		/1	6/12 .50
0–29%			/4

We also see that, when a moderate level of agricultural employment is combined with high urbanization, chances of democracy are about the same in both tables. In these respects, the experience with democracy in both regions is similar. However, in two other respects, the patterns of relationships in the two tables are significantly different. In Western Europe a considerable number of decades (19) occur under conditions of moderate agricultural employment combined with moderate urbanization, and a substantial proportion of these decades (63 percent) are democratic. In South America, however, there is only one decade in this category. In other words, a combination of conditions, which in European countries is rather strongly associated with successful democracy, is almost completely absent in the experience of South American countries. South American countries simply do not provide at least

TABLE 7

THE PROPORTION OF DEMOCRATIC DECADES IN EUROPEAN COUNTRIES FROM 1900–59 ACCORDING TO AGRICULTURAL EMPLOYMENT AND URBANIZATION

Agricultural employment	Urbanization		
	0–5%	6–15%	16%+
50%+	/4	3/16 .19	/4
30–49%		12/19 .63	10/18 .56
0–29%		2/8	21/24 .88

one combination of social and economic conditions that elsewhere has accompanied democracy to a significant degree. A second significant difference in the two tables concerns the effects of low agricultural employment combined with high urbanization. In European countries, this combination of conditions (represented in the lower right-hand cell) has provided the most likely environment for successful democracy—83 percent of the decades in this category have been democratic; but in South America not one decade of democracy appears in this category, although it is also true that there are few decades in this cell altogether. The combination of conditions which throughout the nineteenth century is consistently associated with democracy and which in twentieth century Europe continues most highly associated with democracy produces in South America not one decade of democracy. Clearly, some further analysis is required.

II

So far, we have focused on the social and economic conditions associated with the presence of democracy for entire decades. The findings tell us something about the conditions that accompany ongoing democratic regimes; in other words, they tell us something about the conditions that sustain democratic regimes once democracy has been established. But there are also important questions concerning the social and economic conditions that accompany attempts to initiate democracy. It would be interesting to learn not only about the conditions that sustain democracy, but also about the conditions that are likely to accompany a successful launching of democracy. We have tentatively concluded that to a high degree successful democratic regimes are associated with low agricultural employment and considerable urbanization. We turn now to investigate the conditions associated with success or failure in attempts to introduce democracy.

The immediate objective will be to determine some of the social and economic characteristics of those critical decades in which attempts to establish democracy are made. By "attempt to establish democracy," we mean a situation in which the chief executive is selected at least once through a parliamentary or electoral mechanism, where previously succession had been nondemocratic. Consistent with the earlier discussion, a "successful" attempt to establish democracy is an attempt followed by the existence of democracy, as indicated by a score of 0, 1, 2, on the Index of Democracy on all four characteristics described above for two decades or more.[3]

By these definitions, we have been able to locate 74 attempts to establish democracy in our 44 countries from 1800 to 1960. All of these attempts were immediately successful. Both the unsuccessful attempts and the successful attempts are distributed quite unevenly among countries and over time. About three-fourths of all attempts have been made in the twentieth century, and about half the successes have come in this century. Thus, the chances of success have been less in recent decades compared to the nineteenth century. About half of all attempts took place in South American countries, although very few successful attempts are found there. Over one-third of the attempts occurred in Europe, and about half of the successes are found there. The question is: "Under what conditions are these attempts made, and under what conditions do they result in success or failure?"

TABLE 8

THE DISTRIBUTION OF ATTEMPTS TO ESTABLISH DEMOCRATIC REGIMES FROM 1800–1959 ACCORDING TO AGRICULTURAL EMPLOYMENT AND URBANIZATION

Agricultural employment		Urbanization 0–5%	6%+	Total
50%+	Immediately successful democracies for two or more decades	10%	10%	10%
	Immediately unsuccessful	60	40	48
	Initially inconclusive	30	50	42
	n =	20	30	50
0–49%	Immediately successful democracies for two or more decades		30%	29%
	Immediately unsuccessful		22	21
	Initially inconclusive	1	48	50
	n =	1	23	24
Total	Immediately successful democracies for two or more decades	10%	19%	16%
	Immediately unsuccessful	57	32	39
	Initially inconclusive	33	49	45
	n =	21	53	74

Table 8 describes the combined conditions of urbanization and agricultural employment that were prevalent when all these attempts were made. It also distributes immediately successful and unsuccessful attempts according to the same conditions, as well as several types of attempts that were or are inconclusive, initially, and could not be assigned to either of the other categories. Looking only at the marginals, it is clear that very few successful attempts to introduce democracy occur at either low levels of urbanization or high levels of agricultural employment, although numerous attempts are found under all combinations of conditions except low urbanization and low agricultural employment. The absence of attempts under the latter condition is, in part, an artifact of the dimensions used in the table, and an alteration of the division on urbanization would both increase the number of cases in this category and reveal a fairly high rate of success. Not only is the absolute number of successful attempts very small under conditions of low urbanization or high agricultural employment, but the ratio of successful attempts to unsuccessful attempts is also adverse except under conditions of combined

TABLE 9

THE DISTRIBUTION OF ATTEMPTS TO ESTABLISH DEMOCRATIC REGIMES FROM 1900–59 ACCORDING TO AGRICULTURAL EMPLOYMENT AND URBANIZATION

Agricultural employment		Urbanization		
		0–5%	6%+	Total
50%+	Immediately successful democracies for two or more decades	8%		3%
	Immediately unsuccessful	67	48%	54
	Initially inconclusive	25	52	43
	n =	12	23	35
0–49%	Immediately successful democracies for two or more decades		24%	24%
	Immediately unsuccessful		24	24
	Initially inconclusive		52	52
	n =		21	21
Total	Immediately successful democracies for two or more decades	8%	11%	11%
	Immediately unsuccessful	67	36	43
	Initially inconclusive	25	53	46
	n =	12	44	56

high urbanization and low agricultural employment. Even under these most favorable conditions, the likelihood of immediate success is only .30, and shifting the dimensions of the table produces no significant improvement. In other words, there is apparently no simple combination of urbanization and agricultural employment that produces a high rate of success in attempts to establish democracy.

Table 8 contains no probabilities as high as those in Tables 1 and 2. Thus, it is extremely likely that countries that are experiencing high urbanization combined with low agricultural employment will also be democratic. But under these same conditions, countries that are not democratic have only a

TABLE 10

Successes and Failures in Establishing Democratic Regimes for at Least Two Decades According to Rate of Change in Urbanization and Agricultural Employment and Prior Civil Strife for Countries High on Urbanization and Low on Agricultural Employment

	Change in urbanization[a]	Change in agricultural employment	Civil strife[b]
Successes:			
Netherlands 1860	4	0	
France 1870	3	7	+
Norway 1880	4	0	
Australia 1900	4	0	
Denmark 1900	3	5	
Czechoslovakia 1920	4	1	
Chile 1930	4	1	+
Sweden 1930	5	13	
Total	3.88	3.88	2/8
Failures:			
France 1870	3	7	+
Venezuela 1900	2	5	+
Argentina 1930	7	12	
Spain 1930	7	5	+
Venezuela 1930	2	20	+
Uruguay 1930	10	6	+
Czechoslovakia 1940	4	3	+
Uruguay 1940	8	8	+
Venezuela 1940	9	12	
France 1950	1	11	+
Total	5.30	8.90	8/10

[a] These rates of change are the absolute percentage change over a two decade period surrounding the attempt.

[b] This indicates the presence of coups d'etat, civil wars, rebellions, and foreign military occupation.

30 percent chance to maintain democracy after an attempt to introduce it. The likelihood of success in such attempts decreases further in the twentieth century. In Table 9, attempts to introduce democracy are examined separately for the twentieth century. Generally, similar results are obtained for the twentieth century as for the entire period from 1800 to 1960. But the rate of success even under the most favorable conditions declines. In the twentieth century, more and more countries have become urbanized and industrialized,

and countries under these conditions are likely to be democratic (Table 5). There is, however, less likelihood in recent decades for attempts to initiate democracy under these conditions to be successful.

One category of countries that attempted to introduce democracy following World War II does not fit into this scheme. These countries had only one full decade of successful democracy by 1959. If Austria, Italy, and Japan are all added as "successes" in Table 8, the rate of success in the lower right hand cell increases to slightly less than 50 percent.[4]

The presence in the lower right-hand cell of Table 8 of a number of cases of both successful and unsuccessful attempts to introduce democracy enables us to extend the analysis by examining some additional conditions associated with success or failure beyond levels of urbanization and agricultural employment. One such condition is the prevailing rates of change in these variables. The general hypothesis would be that the success or failure of attempts to introduce democracy are related not only to existing levels of urbanization and agricultural employment, but also to prevailing rates of change in these variables at the time of the attempt.

In order to examine this hypothesis, we first noted the levels of urbanization and agricultural employment in the decades immediately preceding and following the decade, when an attempt to introduce democracy was made. By connecting these points, we were able to estimate the rates of change in each variable during the critical decade. Then, we compared the average rates of change in urbanization and agricultural employment associated with successful or unsuccessful attempts. This information is presented in Table 10. Comparing the average rates of change for each variable in successful and unsuccessful attempts, we find some significant contrasts between the two sets of cases. For both urbanization and agricultural employment, the average rates of change during the 20-year period surrounding attempts to introduce democracy are noticeably lower in the successful attempts. In other words, successful attempts to introduce democracy are accompanied by more moderate change in urbanization and agricultural employment, while unsuccessful attempts are accompanied by more rapid change. Especially with respect to agricultural employment, the contrast in rates of change is striking: the average rate of change in agricultural employment associated with successful attempts to introduce democracy is less than half the rate with unsuccessful attempts. That is, less than 3.5 percent for successful attempts compared to almost 9 percent for unsuccessful attempts.

Assuming that the relative rates of change in our two major variables are rough indicators of the general extent of social and economic stability in any period, and recognizing the marked difference in these rates for the two sets of countries, we were led to inquire further whether success or failure in attempts to introduce democracy might not also be associated with different degrees of political stability during the critical decades. To assess the relative degrees of political stability, we used a simple measure of the incidence of political violence: countries were considered politically unstable if, during the 20 years preceding an attempt to introduce democracy, there occurred at least one coup d'etat, civil war, rebellion, or military occupation by a foreign power. The results of this simple scoring are also shown in Table 10. Again, the difference between the two sets of countries is striking. Of 8 successful attempts to introduce democracy, only 2 were preceded by significant political violence, while out of 11 unsuccessful attempts, 9 were preceded by such violence.

In introducing prevailing rates of change in urbanization and agricultural employment, as well as extent of political violence as relevant variables in examining the likely success or failure of attempts to initiate democracy, we are suggesting a connection between the establishment of democracy and conditions of social, economic, and political stability. Obviously, such a connection cannot be confirmed through the very incomplete analysis provided here. But on the basis even of this incomplete analysis, it appears that the prospects for successfully launching a democratic regime are markedly lower under conditions of rapid change and preceding political violence than under conditions of moderate change and relative political calm.

The failures of democracy we have been examining are failures in attempts to introduce democracy. There are also failures that occur after democracy has already been established for a decade or more. Since there is a general trend toward greater urbanization and economic development in all countries, failures of established democracies are likely to occur under conditions that are increasingly favorable to the maintenance of democracy. This is indeed the case of the ten instances of failure in the 44 countries since 1800. Only Colombia's, in 1940, occurred under relatively low levels of urbanization and high levels of agricultural employment. Actually, the major factor in the disruption of established democracies was the military occupation of European countries by Germany during World War II—half the failures are in this category. The remaining failures occurred in countries with only one or two decades of democratic experience. In other words, democracies that survived more than two decades were displaced only through outside intervention. Moreover, unlike the immediately unsuccessful attempts to introduce democracy described above, the disruptions of established democracies do not reveal exceptional levels of violence in the decades preceding their overthrow. That is, three out of five of these showed little prior social and political unrest. Further refinements would permit the investigation of more short-lived democratic regimes and would doubtless yield cases deviating from this simple analysis.

III

So far, we have been discussing the likelihood of success or failure of attempts to introduce and maintain democracy in 44 countries in relation to

Patterns of Democratic Development

prevailing social and economic conditions at particular points in time. The cases under discussion have occurred at various decades from 1800 to 1960, but the analysis itself has been cross-sectional rather than longitudinal or serial. That is, we have been concerned with the degree of association among several variables in given decades, without attempting to observe the relationships among these variables through successive decades in given countries. Yet there are severe limitations in attempting to explain the incidence of democracy through cross-sectional analysis. These limitations, some of which

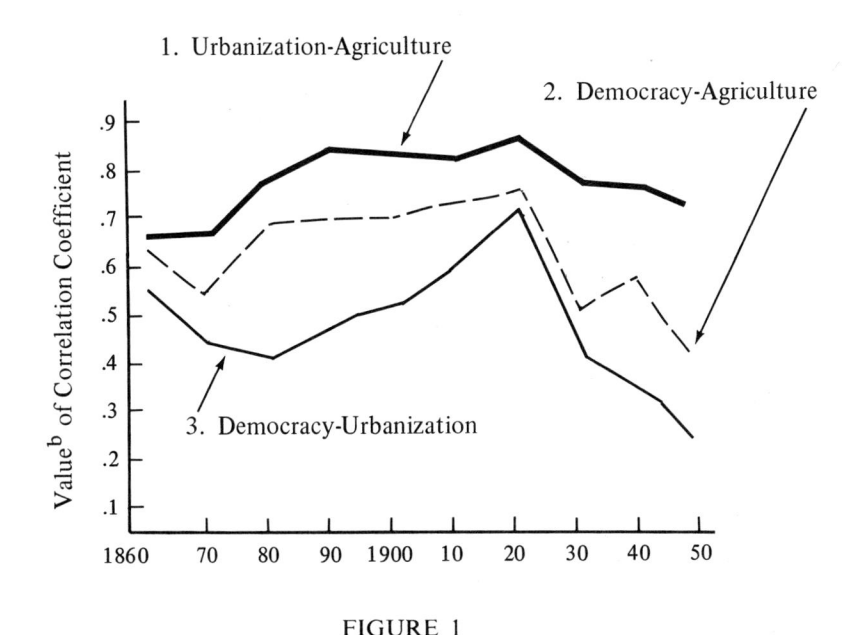

FIGURE 1

CROSS-SECTIONAL CORRELATIONS DECADE BY DECADE FROM 1860 TO 1950[a]

[a] These product moment correlations were computed with data from 33 countries; the omissions represent countries with missing data during the period. Countries occupied by Germany during World War II were coded without regard for that interruption. Since the Index of Democracy does not qualify as an interval measure, we computed these relationships with Kendall's Tau[b] and the same general pattern obtains but with consistently lower values for all correlations.

[b] The signs of the coefficients have been disregarded in this figure in order to focus attention only on their varying magnitude.

we shall explore briefly in this section, lead us to believe that satisfactory answers to the problems posed at the outset—Under what conditions do democratic systems flourish or fail, and under what conditions are attempts to introduce democracy successful or not?—can only be found through time-series analysis.

One way to approach the distinction between cross-sectional and serial analysis is to compare the correlations between democracy and our nonpolitical variables for all countries, decade-by-decade, with the correlations among these variables across all the decades, country-by-country. The question is: To what extent do the cross-sectional correlations and the serial correlations lead to similar conclusions about the relationships among democracy, urbanization, and agricultural employment? To answer this question, we have computed three sets of cross-sectional correlations for all decades from 1860 to 1950. These are simple product moment correlations between urbanization and agricultural employment, democracy and urbanization, and democracy and agricultural employment. The results of these correlations are shown in Figure 1. Line 1 in the figure represents the changing correlations between urbanization and agricultural employment, decade-by-decade; line 2 represents the changing correlations between democracy and agricultural employment, decade-by-decade; and line 3 represents the changing correlations between democracy and urbanization, decade-by-decade.

Several conclusions are apparent from Figure 1. First of all, the strength of correlations between each pair of variables differs in successive decades, sometimes very considerably. The relationship between urbanization and agricultural employment is always strong, yet even this relationship varies from low values under .7 to well over .8. Variation in the strength of the cross-sectional correlations in the other two sets is much more pronounced. Correlations between democracy and urbanization vary from .4 to .7; correlations between democracy and agricultural employment vary from .5 to .7. These variations mean, simply, that the discovery of a strong correlation between democracy and agricultural employment through cross-sectional analysis in any particular time-period provides no assurance that the observed relationship will, in fact, persist through time. The strength of the observed relationship may only reflect conditions in that particular time-period; the next period may reveal a quite different relationship. Nor is there any way to determine from the cross-sectional analysis whether the observed relationship is increasing in strength or decreasing, yet the variations found in Figure 1 suggest that this question of the direction of change in the strength of the correlations is significant. Looking at Figure 1, it becomes apparent that one problem for the analyst is to explain those variations in the strength of successive correlations, which are simply neglected in cross-sectional analysis.

A second observation from Figure 1 is that the relationship between the correlations of different sets of variables also changes through time, so that alternative correlations which are similar in explanatory power in one decade are divergent in other decades. Every decade reveals the same order in the strength of the correlations: that is, in every decade the correlation between urbanization and agricultural employment is strongest, the correlation between democracy and agricultural employment is next in strength, and the correlation between democracy and urbanization is weakest. But at the same time, there is great variation in the closeness of the three correlations from decade to decade.

Patterns of Democratic Development 491

For present purposes, the crux of the distinction between cross-sectional and serial correlations lies in the question of whether the same order and magnitude of correlations among a particular set of variables that are revealed through cross-sectional analysis obtain also in serial analysis. In other words, do the expected relationships between democracy and urbanization—expected on the basis of a cross-sectional analysis of these relationships—in fact, hold true, when these same relationships are examined

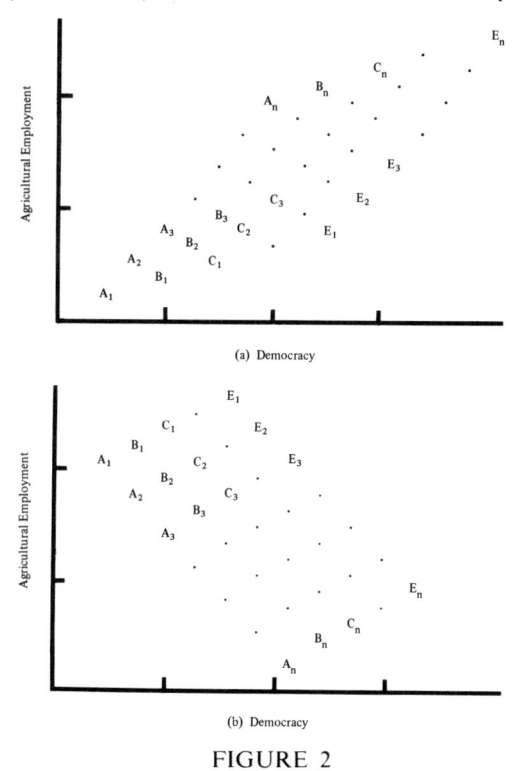

FIGURE 2

HYPOTHETICAL DISTRIBUTION OF DATA OVER TIME FOR SEVERAL COUNTRIES

through time? It must be noted that, in principle, there is no necessary reason why they should. It is quite easy to devise two sets of cases that diametrically oppose correlations in serial analysis. Figures 2a and 2b present such hypothetical sets of observations. Each figure contains hypothetical observations on countries A, B, ..., E, where A_1 is the first decade observation in country A, A_2 the second decade observation, and so on. The array of observations in Figure 2a would yield a perfect positive correlation for each decade examined, cross-sectionally, as well as a set of perfect positive serial correlations for each country. The array of observation in Figure 2b would also yield a perfect positive correlation for each decade examined cross-sectionally. But unlike the previous figure, the observations in Figure 2b would actually yield perfect negative serial correlations within each country. The identical cross-sectional correlations obtained in the two figures are accompanied in each instance by diametrically opposed serial correlations.

The possibility of such a contradiction between the findings of cross-sectional and serial analysis raises a serious question as to which analysis is preferable for particular purposes. There are also other characteristics

TABLE 11

TIME SERIES CORRELATIONS FOR COUNTRIES WITH SOME
VARIATION ON ALL THREE DIMENSIONS, 1860–1950

	Urbanization-democracy	Agricultural employment-democracy
Expected pattern:		
Austria	−.41	.59
Italy	−.12	.42
United Kingdom	−.67	.83
Uruguay	−.19	.49
Compatible pattern:		
Canada	−.85	.82
Japan	−.57	.54
Netherlands	−.81	.81
Sweden	−.92	.92
United States	−.74	.75
Unexpected pattern:		
Denmark	−.81	.62
Finland	−.78	.55
France	−.55	.39
Norway	−.88	.47
Russia	−.68	.49
Deviant pattern:		
Argentina	.42	−.38
Hungary	.28	−.42
Portugal	.76	−.63
Spain	.46	−.31
Venezuela	.30	−.35

of the two types of analyses that should be noted in this connection. Some countries remain thoroughly agricultural throughout the entire period, with no measurable variation in agricultural employment. This means a zero serial correlation between democracy and agricultural employment, although in each decade, these countries aid observations which contribute to strong cross-sectional correlations between these variables. In addition, some countries reveal no variation in democracy. They are uniformly high or uniformly low and the impact is the same; no serial correlations result, but in all cases the observations contribute to strong cross-sectional correlations.

Despite these complications it is still plausible to expect that the serial correlations will follow the same pattern as the cross-sectional correlations. In some countries this is indeed the case as shown in Table 11. All countries with substantial variation on all three variables yield strong serial correlations between urbanization and agricultural employment. Other expected serial relationships also appear: in several countries the correlation between democracy and agricultural employment is stronger than between democracy and urbanization; in another group of countries, the serial correlations between democracy and agricultural employment and between democracy and urbanization have about equal values. However, there is a sizable number of countries with higher coefficients of correlation for democracy and urbanization than for democracy and agricultural employment. In other words, the relative value of the correlations expected on the basis of cross-sectional analysis does not hold in the serial analysis. These countries are Denmark, Finland, France, Norway, and Russia.

Another expected relationship is that the correlation between democracy and urbanization is negative, while the correlation between democracy and agricultural employment is positive. For most countries these relationships hold in our serial analysis. Again, however, it happens that for one group of countries, even the signs of the coefficients are reversed. That is, the serial correlations between democracy and urbanization are positive, while those between democracy and agricultural employment are negative. These countries are Argentina, Hungary, Portugal, Spain, and Venezuela. Thus, in comparing the results of cross-sectional and serial analysis we find within our selection of countries a full range of consistent and contradictory correlations.

The main reason for stressing the distinction between cross-sectional and serial analysis is to emphasize the different types of explanations or predictions that are possible from each form of analysis. Granted that we are interested in the likelihood of the introduction and persistence of democracy in particular countries at different periods of time: the most important information for such a study must come from a longitudinal analysis of relationships within those particular countries rather than a cross-sectional analysis that groups all countries into an array of similar and dissimilar cases. To be sure, cross-sectional analysis yields information of the distribution of countries in relation to each other; it explores how democratic one country is in relation to others at particular points in time. But if we want to know the likelihood that any one country will become more or less democratic, only longitudinal analysis of that country will suffice.

IV

The limitations of cross-sectional analysis have led us to consider an alternative form of analysis which will describe more adequately the complex variety of conditions that are associated with the success or failure of democracy in particular countries. We would suggest an analysis in terms of patterns of development; patterns consisting of successive phases through which countries pass together with probabilities in each phase of alternative political events and outcomes, which in turn affect the direction of further change and the probability of further alternative outcomes. To elaborate and apply this analysis is beyond the scope of the present paper. However, in this concluding section, we will attempt at least to illustrate the general form of such an analysis.

The actual patterns of development that will appear from an analysis of modern democracy will certainly include the effects of other important variables besides those we have been considering in this paper. But for purposes of illustration, we will continue to use only our two major variables of urbanization and agricultural employment. Using these two variables, we

	Urbanization				Common Patterns
Agricultural employment	0–5%	6–15%	16%		
50%+	A	G	J	I	A – B – C
30–49%	D	B	H	II	A – D – E – C
				IIIA	A – G – H – C
0–29%	F	E	C	IIIB	A – G – B – C

FIGURE 3

COMBINATIONS OF URBANIZATION AND AGRICULTURAL EMPLOYMENT AND THEIR PATTERNS

will suggest a simple scheme for identifying patterns of democratic development, including probabilities that democracy will be introduced or sustained during successive phases within a particular pattern.

Figure 3 presents the brief set of possible patterns to be considered. Each pattern can be visualized as extending over time in successive phases of varying duration, as illustrated in Figure 4. The initial and terminal phases of the pattern are of indefinite duration, but other phases can be assigned specific time-periods. The limits of the phases are defined in terms of the prevailing combined levels of urbanization and agricultural employment. A country moves through successive phases as it crosses thresholds from one level of urbanization and agricultural employment to another. At each successive phase of the pattern, and at particular points within any phase, it should be possible to assign probabilities to various political events and to introduce additional conditions that affect those probabilities.

Patterns of Democratic Development

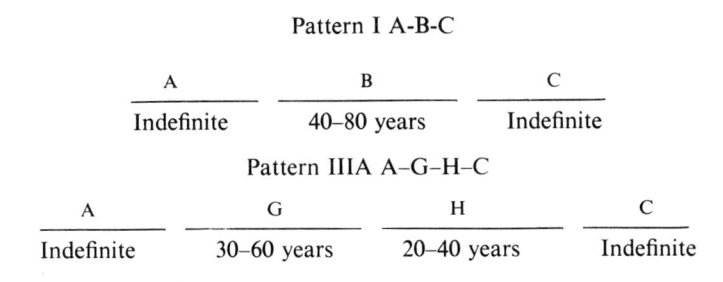

```
                Pattern I A-B-C

      A                 B                 C
  ─────────      ───────────────     ──────────
  Indefinite      40–80 years        Indefinite

              Pattern IIIA A-G-H-C

   A              G              H              C
─────────   ─────────────   ─────────────   ──────────
Indefinite   30–60 years    20–40 years    Indefinite
```

FIGURE 4

HYPOTHETICAL TIME PERIODS IN PATTERN SEQUENCES

The political events we are considering here include attempts to introduce democracy in a country, the success or failure of these attempts, and the maintenance of democracy over a number of decades. The analysis of patterns of development should yield probabilities concerning the likelihood of any of these events occurring at various points within the pattern. For example, Figure 5 shows a portion of a hypothetical pattern IIIA. The four boxes

	A	G	H	C
Probability of: sustaining an existing democracy	.20	.60	.30	.90
establishing a new democracy	.05	.25	.20	.40

FIGURE 5

HYPOTHETICAL PROBABILITIES IN PHASES OF PATTERN A-G-H-C

show the probability of sustaining a democratic regime (top cell of each box) and the probability of launching such a regime (bottom cell) in successive phases within the pattern. The hypothetical probabilities show that during Phase G the chances of either sustaining or launching a democratic regime continue to improve, but then, as a country moves to phase H, these chances decline sharply. In all phases, a country is much more likely to sustain an ongoing democracy than successfully to initiate democracy.

The problem now is to cull from the findings in the preceding section of the paper appropriate data to place within the framework of such an analysis of developmental patterns. Since the discussion is intended to be only illustrative, we will confine our attention to a single pattern rather than examine the whole set of patterns that can in fact be found.

Table 12 is an attempt to determine the actual probabilities of various political events and outcomes at different phases in pattern A-G-H-C (pattern IIIA in Figure 3).

The probabilities should be read as follows:

Countries in phase A are almost certain to remain undemocratic (the data say "certain"), and attempts to establish democracy are rather infrequent (about once every ten decades).

Countries in phase G are extremely likely to remain undemocratic, although attempts to introduce democracy are made somewhat more often (once every five decades) and are occasionally successful (one successful attempt in five). Although the numbers are small, once a democracy is successfully established in this phase, it appears likely to endure.

TABLE 12

THE PROBABILITIES OF CHANGE AND STABILITY IN PATTERN A-G-H-C

PHASE	A		G		H		C	
Sustaining democracy where already democratic			4/5		6/8		9/9	
Remaining undemocratic where already undemocratic	177/177	1.00	72/80	.90	11/15	.73	4/4	
Frequency of attempts per decade to establish democracy	16/177	.09	22/80	.28	5/15	.33	1/4	
Attempts immediately successful for at least one decade	1/16	.06	4/22	.18	2/5		0/1	

In phase H, undemocratic countries are still likely to remain undemocratic (.78), but attempts to introduce democracy are made quite often (about every other decade) and have about a fifty-fifty chance of success for at least one decade. Established democracies appear somewhat vulnerable, with only a slightly better than fifty-fifty chance of sustaining themselves from one decade to the next.

In phase C, it is extremely likely that established democracies will endure. In this phase there are relatively few undemocratic countries, but these are likely to remain undemocratic, and attempts to introduce democracy are not so frequent (once every three decades).

We stress again that the analysis throughout this paper has been tentative and illustrative. Many additions and refinements are necessary before the analysis of developmental patterns can be offered confidently as a framework for the study of political change. But even the tentative findings from this preliminary effort seem to warrant continued attempts to elaborate this form of analysis.

NOTES

1. The countries include the following:

Argentina	Denmark	Lebanon	Spain
Australia	Ecuador	Mexico	Sweden
Austria	Egypt	Netherlands	Switzerland
Belgium	Finland	New Zealand	Thailand
Bolivia	France	Nigeria	Turkey
Brazil	Germany	Norway	U.S.S.R.
Burma	Hungary	Paraguay	United Kingdom
Canada	India	Peru	United States
Chile	Indonesia	Philippines	Uruguay
Colombia	Italy	Portugal	
Czechoslovakia	Japan	South Africa	

2. The measure of democracy used in this paper is a slight variation of the measure employed in the previous paper—Eds.

3. This is a rather restrictive definition, which limits "attempts" to circumstances where considerable success is attained. All such efforts toward change in a democratic direction, which do not succeed in changing chief executives, more or less, democratically, are excluded, so we have, obviously, greatly underestimated what would, by other definitions, count as attempts. This also means that we overestimate the chances of success, since our definition overlooks only unsuccessful attempts.

4. The six countries in question are Austria, Brazil, India, Italy, Japan, and the Philippines. Only one of these democratic attempts, Brazil, has failed to date. Like Brazil, India and the Philippines are relatively underdeveloped, economically, and unurbanized; that is, they are in cells of the table suggesting little chance of success. For this analysis, we have ignored the World War II interruption in the otherwise stable democracies of Denmark, the Netherlands, and Norway.

22 Toward a Communications Theory of Democratic Political Development: A Causal Model

DONALD J. McCRONE and CHARLES F. CNUDDE

The construction of an empirical theory of democratic political development is dependent on the formulation of causal propositions which are generalizations of the developmental process. To date, several essential steps in the process of constructing such a theory have been taken. First, concept formation and clarification by students of political development has led to an emphasis upon political democracy as one of the dependent variables for the field.[1] Second, the gathering and publication of quantitative indicators of social, economic, cultural, and political phenomena provide a firm basis for subsequent empirical inquiry (see Russett et al., 1964). Finally, correlational analysis has identified numerous variables which are closely associated with the development of democratic political institutions (see Cutright, 1963).

The next major task is the formulation and testing of empirical models of democratic political development which provide a basis for inferring causal relationships by distinguishing between spurious correlations and indirect and direct effects.[2] The accomplishment of this task would enable us to derive explanatory propositions concerning the process of democratic political development.

The purpose of this essay is to suggest the combined utility of two similar theory-building techniques in the accomplishment of this task and to take a modest step in the direction of constructing an empirical model of democratic political development.

Concepts of Political Development

Seymour Martin Lipset (1959) explicitly adopts democratic political development as his dependent variable. He defines political democracy as:

Reprinted from *The American Political Science Review*, Volume LXI, pages 72–80, by permission of the authors and the publisher. Copyright © 1967 The American Political Science Association.

a political system which supplies regular constitutional opportunities for changing the governing officials. It is a social mechanism for the resolution of the problems of societal decision-making among conflicting interest groups which permits the largest to choose among alternative contenders for political office [Lipset, 1959: 71].

For Lipset, this definition of democracy implies three key specific conditions: first, one set of political leaders who occupy official governing positions; second, one or more sets of competing leaders who do not occupy governing positions, but who act as a loyal opposition; third, widespread acceptance of a "political formula" which specifies the legitimate political institutions for the society (political parties, free press, etc.) and legitimizes democratic political competition (Lipset, 1959: 71). European and English-speaking nations are classified as stable democracies or unstable democracies and dictatorships on the basis of whether they fulfilled these specific conditions in the period since World War I. Lipset (1959: 73-74) also adds the condition that there be an absence of Communist or Fascist parties (i.e., political movements opposed to the democratic "political formula") garnering more than twenty percent of the vote in the last twenty-five years.[3]

Lipset's measurement of political democracy unfortunately has severe limitations. His "all-or-nothing" requirement transforms political democracy from a continuous variable into an attribute. Theoretically, democracy may be most usefully conceived of as a continuum. A political system is not democratic or nondemocratic—democracy is not present or absent—rather a political system is more or less democratic. Moreover, even if democracy were best conceived to be an attribute, the problem of selecting nonarbitrary cutpoints would still present severe problems.[4] Finally, a dichotomous dependent variable places strains on the power of the statistical techniques that may be applied.

Philips Cutright (1963) on the other hand, attempts to define political development in terms which do not rely explicitly on liberal democratic standards.

The degree of political development of a nation can be defined by the degree of complexity and specialization of its national political institutions [Cutright, 1963: 571].

Nevertheless, a careful examination of Cutright's (1963: 574) political development scoring procedure indicates a reliance on the same standards utilized by Lipset. In fact, Cutright's measurement procedure is an excellent operationalization of Lipset's concept of political democracy. Points are assigned to a political system on the basis of one set of officials in office, one or more sets of political leaders out of office, and reliance on political parties and free elections as the legitimate political institutions for the society.[5] The virtue of the Cutright measure is that it transforms Lipset's democratic attribute into a continuous variable, thereby avoiding the problems cited above. Pending further refinements in this field, democratic political development may best be conceptualized in Lipset's terms and measured by Cutright's procedures.[6]

Both Lipset and Cutright have established correlations between socio-economic factors and democratic political development. Lipset (1959) finds that indices of *wealth* (per capita income, thousands of persons per doctor, and persons per motor vehicle), *communication* (telephones, radios, and newspaper copies per thousand persons), *industrialization* (percentages of males in agriculture and per capita energy consumed), *education* (percentage literate, and primary, post-primary, and higher education enrollment per thousand persons), and *urbanization* (percent in cities over 20,000, 100,000, and in metropolitan areas) are all strongly related to political democracy.[7]

Cutright (1963: 577) using product-moment correlation analysis, identifies indices of *communication* (summed T scores of newspaper readers, newsprint consumption, volume of domestic mail, and number of telephones per capita), *urbanization* (T score of the proportion of the population in cities over 100,000), *education* (combined T scores of literacy and number of students per 100,000 in institutions of higher education), and *agriculture* (T score of the proportion of the economically active labor force employed in agriculture) as being closely associated with political development.

Regardless of the imaginativeness and utility of these studies, they do not constitute theoretical formulations of the process of democratic political development. They remain studies of the correlates of democratic political development.

Communications Development Model

Communications development suggests itself as a variable around which a theory of the process of democratic political development might be constructed for several reasons.[8] First, both normative and empirical theory point to communications as a prerequisite to a successfully operating political democracy. Normative thinking gives communications networks the role of providing an informed citizenry, while more empirical scholarship sees communications as integrative, producing the social cohesion necessary to prevent disintegration in the face of democratic policy conflict.[9] Second, Cutright (1963:577) finds that communications development is by far the strongest socio-economic correlate of political development. Third, the most ambitious attempt at a theoretical formulation of the process of democratic political development views communications development as the final prerequisite for a successfully functioning democratic political system (Lerner, 1958).

Lerner theorizes that the process of democratic political development (which he defines as the "crowning institution of the participant society") is the consequence of a developmental sequence beginning with urbanization.

> The secular evolution of a participant society appears to involve a regular sequence of three phases. Urbanization comes first, for cities alone have developed the complex of skills and resources which characterize the modern

industrial economy. Within this urban matrix develop both of the attributes which distinguish the next two phases—literacy and media growth. There is a close reciprocal relationship between these, for the literate develop the media which in turn spread literacy. But, literacy performs the key function in the second phase. The capacity to read, at first acquired by relatively few people, equips them to perform the varied tasks required in the modernizing society. Not until the third phase, when the elaborate technology of industrial development is fairly well advanced, does a society begin to produce newspapers, radio networks, and motion pictures on a massive scale. This, in turn, accelerates the spread of literacy. Out of this interaction develop those institutions of participation (e.g. voting) which we find in all advanced modern societies [Lerner, 1958: 60].

$$U \longrightarrow E \longrightarrow C \longrightarrow D$$

FIGURE 1

INITIAL CONCEPTION OF DEMOCRATIC POLITICAL DEVELOPMENT AS A DEVELOPMENTAL SEQUENCE.

(U-Urbanization, E-Education, C-Communications, D-Democratic political development.)

Lerner's thesis is not satisfactorily confirmed by his data, but his conceptualization of political development as a developmental sequence provides a basis for a causal formulation of the process of democratic political development.

Figure 1 represents our initial causal model based on the conception of democratic political development as a developmental sequence. This four-variable causal model is, of course, only one of a whole family of logically alternative models utilizing the same four variables. A means for testing the adequacy of this particular causal model and for eliminating alternative models is clearly needed.

Testing the Model

Two interrelated theory-building techniques are applied in this study in an effort to eliminate logical alternative models and to provide a basis for inferring the adequacy of the postulated model of democratic political development. First, Simon-Blalock causal model analysis (Blalock, 1964; also see Simon, 1954) is utilized because it enables us

> to make causal *inferences* concerning the adequacy of causal models, at least in the sense that we can proceed by eliminating inadequate models that make predictions that are not consistent with the data [Blalock, 1964: 62].

Prediction equations based on the correlation coefficients between variables are computed for each alternative model. Models that make prediction equations inconsistent with the actual relationships between the variables in the system are rejected (Blalock, 1964: 60-94).

Second, path coefficients are computed for the causal model that is inferred by use of the Simon-Blalock technique. In causal analysis, we are primarily concerned with changes in the dependent variable(s) which are produced by changes in the independent variable(s). The correlation coefficients used in the Simon-Blalock prediction equations only measure the goodness of fit around the regression line. Path coefficients which may be viewed as being analogous to beta weight(s), are used because they measure changes in the dependent variable produced by standardized changes in the independent variable (see Wright, 1921).

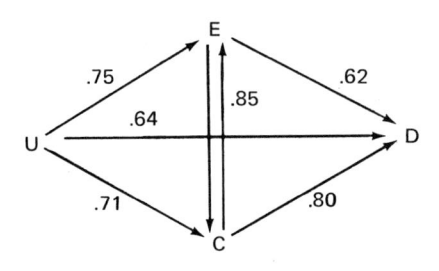

```
              E
         .75 ↗ ↑ ↖ .62
            ╱ .85 ╲
         .64       
       U ←─────────→ D
            ╲     ╱
         .71 ╲   ╱ .80
              ↓ ↓
               C
```

FIGURE 2

SEVEN LOGICALLY POSSIBLE CAUSAL PATHS BETWEEN THE FOUR VARIABLES, INCLUDING CORRELATION COEFFICIENTS.

The data to be utilized in this study consist of Cutright's (1963: 577) previously published intercorrelations computed from four aggregate indicators for seventy-six nations. The four variables are urbanization, education, communication, and political development.

Prior to the analysis of alternative causal models, several fundamental assumptions on which this analysis is based must be explicitly set forth. First, political development is assumed to be the dependent variable and urbanization is conceived not to be dependent on any other variable in the system. Second, relationships between the variables in the system are assumed to be additive and linear. Third, other causes of each of the four variables are assumed to be uncorrelated with the other variables in the system. And fourth, it is necessary to assume uni-directional causation.

Unfortunately, assumptions of this nature are usually left implicit. Yet whenever correlational analysis is attempted with the assumption of which are independent and dependent variables, these other assumptions logically follow. The techniques to be applied in this paper merely make the assumptions more explicit. However, this state of affairs should not obscure the basic similarity between making causal inferences from a variety of techniques, whether they be correlation coefficients, regression coefficients, path coefficients, or the Simon-Blalock technique.[10]

Perhaps the least satisfying of these assumptions is that of uni-directional causation. While several respectable hypotheses involving reciprocal effects could be constructed, they would considerably complicate the analysis. We will therefore tentatively exclude such possibilities here. In a subsequent analysis we will attempt to evaluate these possible reciprocal relationships with a technique devised by one of the authors (see Cnudde, 1966b).

Figure 2 shows the seven logically possible causal relationships between the four variables in the model under the assumptions as set forth above.

Alternative Causal Models

Restricting our attention to the first half of the democratic political development model (the relationships between U, E, and C), Figure 3 notes three

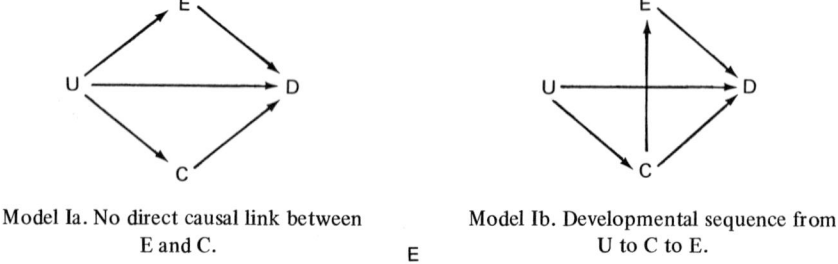

Model Ia. No direct causal link between E and C.

Model Ib. Developmental sequence from U to C to E.

Model Ic. Developmental sequence from U to E to C.

FIGURE 3

ALTERNATIVE CAUSAL MODELS—FIRST HALF.

logically alternative causal relationships. Model Ia predicts that the relationship between E and C is spurious due to the causal effects of U on both variables. If Model Ia were to fit the data, both educational and communications development would be inferred to be the common consequence of the rise of urbanization with no causal link between education and communication. Model Ib, on the other hand, predicts that the developmental sequence from U to C to E interprets the relationship between U and E. If the prediction equations for Model Ib were correct, urbanization would be seen as producing the spread of communications which would, in turn, produce widespread growth in literacy and education levels. The spread of mass media would be inferred to be a prerequisite to the spread of mass education, rather than the

Toward a Communications Theory of Democratic Political Development 505

reverse. Model Ic, based on our original model, predicts that the causal links proceed from U to E to C and account for the original relationship between U and C. The success of Model Ic in predicting the actual relationships between these three variables would confirm the notion that urbanization is the prerequisite to the widespread growth of literacy and education. The consequent educational development would then provide the mass public necessary for the growth of the mass media of communication.

The prediction equations for Ia, Ib, and Ic in Table 1 show the Simon-Blalock test of each of these alternative models. Clearly, the excellence of the fit between the predicted and actual correlations for Model Ic, as opposed to the results for Ia and Ib, provides a basis for eliminating the latter two alternatives and inferring that the direction of causation is indeed from urbanization to education to communication.

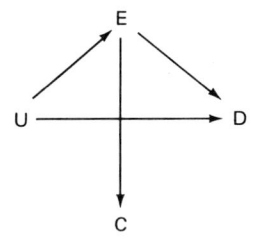

Model IIa. No direct causal link between C and D.

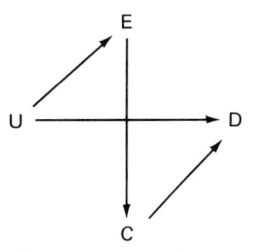

Model IIb. Developmental sequence from E to C to D.

FIGURE 4

ALTERNATIVE CAUSAL MODELS—SECOND HALF.

Turning our attention to the second half of the democratic political development model (the relationships between E, C, and D), Figure 4 indicates that only two logically alternative causal models can be posited. This is due to the fact that we have already inferred the direction of causation between E and C from Model Ic. Model IIa predicts that the relationship between C and D is spurious due to common causation by E. If this model were to fit the data, education, not communication, would be confirmed as the final prerequisite to a successfully functioning political democracy. Model IIb posits a developmental sequence from E to C to D as interpreting the original correlation between E and D. If this model is confirmed, communications development will be seen to be the final link in the chain of causation. The spread of mass education creates an informed public that supports the growth of a system of mass communication which penetrates and integrates the society thereby laying the basis for democratic political competition.

Table 2 shows the prediction equations for Models IIa and IIb. These prediction equations confirm the inference that the relationship between education and democratic political development is an indirect one through communications.

TABLE 1

PREDICTION EQUATIONS AND DEGREE OF FIT FOR MODELS OF DEMOCRATIC POLITICAL DEVELOPMENT–FIRST HALF

		Predictions		Degree of Fit	
	Models	Predicted		Actual	Difference
Ia	rUErUC = rEC	(.75)(.71) = .53		.85	.32
Ib	rUCrCE = rUE	(.71)(.85) = .60		.75	.15
Ic	rUErEC = rUC	(.75)(.85) = .64		.71	.07

TABLE 2

PREDICTION EQUATIONS AND DEGREE OF FIT FOR MODELS OF DEMOCRATIC POLITICAL DEVELOPMENT–SECOND HALF

		Predictions		Degree of Fit	
	Models	Predicted		Actual	Difference
IIa	rECrED = rCD	(.85)(.62) = .53		.80	.27
IIb	rECrCD = rED	(.85)(.80) = .68		.62	.06

TABLE 3

PREDICTION EQUATION AND DEGREE OF FIT FOR A MODEL OF DEMOCRATIC POLITICAL DEVELOPMENT–FINAL LINK

		Predictions		Degree of Fit	
	Model	Predicted		Actual	Difference
III	rUErECrCD = rUD	(.75)(.85)(.80) = .51		.64	.13

TABLE 4

SIMULTANEOUS EQUATIONS AND PATH COEFFICIENTS FOR THE CAUSAL MODEL IN FIGURE 6

Path	Equation	Path Coefficient
a	bUE+rUE = 0	.75
b	bEC+rEC = 0	.85
c	bCD+rCD = 0	.80
d	bUD+(bCD XrUC)+rUD = 0	.07

One final link, the direct original relationship between U and D, remains to be tested. A final logically possible model would postulate that the developmental sequence from U to E to C to D accounts for the entire relationship between U and D. If Model III were to be confirmed, the inference would be that there is no direct relationship between U and D. Figure 5 and Table 3 illustrate and test this possible alternative respectively. The relatively poor fit (over .10 difference) indicates that Model III can be rejected and the direct link between U and D should be maintained.

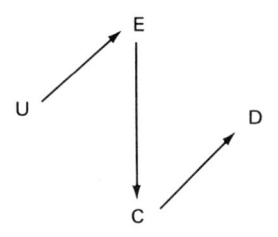

FIGURE 5

MODEL III–DEVELOPMENTAL SEQUENCE FROM U TO E TO C TO D.

Before settling on the final system of causal relationships indicated by use of the Simon-Blalock technique, let us briefly evaluate the direct effects of each of the remaining paths through the computation of path coefficients. The correlation coefficients utilized in the Simon-Blalock analysis, it should be recalled, only measure the degree of association between variables. We found above, for example, that the association between U and D is maintained even when the effect of the path from U to E to C to D was taken into account. Correlation coefficients, however, do not measure the amount of change in the dependent variable which is associated with changes in the independent variable. Our primary concern at this stage is with the measurement of changes in the dependent variable produced by changes in the independent variable path coefficients, therefore, are utilized because they measure the amount of *change* in the dependent variable produced by *standardized changes* in the independent variable.

Figure 6 shows two paths from U to D remain in associational terms. First, there is the developmental sequence from U to D with three links—U to E, E to C, and C to D. Second, there is the direct link between U and D. Path coefficients for each of these links in the causal model of democratic political development are computed in Table 4.

An examination of the path coefficients placed on each link in Figure 6 indicates that the overwhelmingly important causal links in the process of democratic political development are contained in the developmental sequence from U to E to C to D. The direct effect of urbanization on democratic political development (as indicated by the use of a broken line) is negligible.

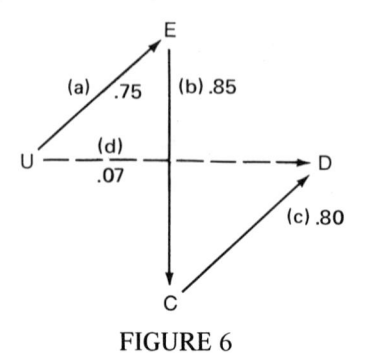

```
                    E
                    ↑
           (a)  /.75  | (b) .85
               /      |
          U --(d)-----+-----→ D
               .07    |       ↗
                      |      (c) .80
                      |    /
                      ↓
                      C
```

FIGURE 6

A CAUSAL MODEL OF DEMOCRATIC POLITICAL DEVELOPMENT INCLUDING PATH COEFFICIENTS.

The remarkable correspondence between this empirically derived causal model of democratic political development and the original causal model postulated in Figure 1 is clear.

Conclusion

This causal model, because it represents the beginnings of a parsimonious theory of, rather than mere correlates of, the process of democratic political development enables us to derive a series of empirical propositions concerning this crucial process.

  1. Democratic political development occurs when mass communications permeates society.

  Education affects democratic political development by contributing to the growth of mass communication, therefore:

  2. Mass communications occurs when literacy and educational levels rise in society.

  Urbanization affects democratic political development primarily by increasing educational levels, which then increase mass communications, therefore:

  3. Education and literacy development occur in urbanizing societies.

This causal model, then, is a series of interrelated causal propositions which link urbanization through a developmental sequence to democratic political development.

Since the causal relationships specified in the model are not perfect, the model and the propositions derived therefrom are probabilistic in nature. The r^2 between U and E (.56), E and C (.72), and C and D (.64) leave a significant proportion of the variance unexplained. For this reason, deviant cases (in terms of the model) can be found. Basically, there are two kinds of deviant cases. First, there are those cases where the nation is "overdeveloped" in one of the variables included in the model. For example, Cutright (1963: 577–581) discusses nations with a relatively low level of communications development which are defined as being relatively highly developed politically. In this case, the democratic political system does not have sufficient communications development to maintain the regime. In terms of our model, this nation is likely to experience severe difficulty in maintaining democratic political competition and may even collapse. The dangers of attempting to impose a democratic regime on socio-economically underdeveloped nations in the post-World War II world are indicated by this type of analysis.

Stepping further back in the chain of causation, we may also find nations which are experiencing communications revolutions, but without prior developments in urbanization and education. In this case, disruption of the regime may occur because the citizenry has not been prepared for the sudden exposure and communications development may bring social disintegration, rather than social cohesion. The examination of such deviant cases may give us insight into other factors that produce changes in these four variables and bring such disruptions. Moreover, we may also ascertain the explanatory power of the model by examining the reliability of predictions about disruption based on these discontinuities.

The second type of deviant case is the nation that has fulfilled the requirements for development, in terms of the model, yet fails to maintain a democratic regime. Germany, for example, would seem to have fulfilled the prerequisites for a democratic regime long before the present Federal Republic. Nevertheless, Germany has experienced severe difficulty in establishing and maintaining a democratic regime in the twentieth century. Apparently, the developmental sequence can be disrupted by influences outside the model. Cutright (1963: 580) for example, examines the impact of foreign invasion and war on political development. He finds that such events seem to intervene to upset the normal sequence of events. The examination of this type of deviant case and of time series data may subject our propositions to further tests. For example, the effect of urban growth over time may be quite different from that of variations in urbanization at one point in time. In general, additional research should shed light on other variables that might be included in a more complete model of the process of political development.[11]

A major virtue of this form of causal model analysis is its capacity to elaborate and extend the model by the inclusion of new variables. This type of elaboration may take two forms. First, when variables outside the system are identified and hypothesized to be causal variables in the process of democratic political development, they can be explicitly introduced into the model. The introduction and testing of such variables provides a test of both the causal nature of the specified variable and the adequacy of the existing model. As additional causal variables are identified and included, the model of democratic political development will begin to match the complexity of the phenomenon it seeks to explain.

A second form of elaboration is the introduction and testing of new dependent variables. In this manner, we can gauge the effects of democratic political development. By the introduction of measures of welfare, education, and military expenditures into the model, we can measure the effects of both democratic political systems and the causal factors in development on public policy. More specifically, answers might be obtained to these questions: what is the independent effect of democratic politics on welfare expenditures? What are the effects of education on welfare expenditures? Are the effects of education interpreted through political development? Answers to questions such as these require the testing of several alternative models including welfare expenditures as a new variable.

In a previous study, on an unrelated substantive matter, the authors have expressed the belief that

> in regard to the subject of theory building in political science, the cumulative nature of empirical model building needs to be stressed. By explicit articulation of the model of constituency influence and emphasis on establishing empirical relationships, the Miller-Stokes study provides a basis for further development. The application of new techniques and the possible inclusion of new variables is thereby facilitated [Cnudde and McCrone, 1966: 72].

We can only hope that this particular causal model of the process of democratic political development may also facilitate the elaboration and testing of models of development by the application of new techniques and the inclusion of new variables. In this manner, a cumulative body of development theory may arise.

NOTES

1. For an interesting discussion of this material as well as important findings on factors which relate to democracy, see Lipset (1959).

2. For an example of this type of model testing in political science, see Cnudde and McCrone (1966).

3. Latin American political systems are classified somewhat differently, but still dichotomously.

4. For the pitfalls involved in choosing cutpoints, see Blalock (1964).

5. See Cutright (1963: 574). Scores may vary from 0 to 66 based on a total of three for each of twenty-two years (1940-61).

6. Of course political scientists' interest in democracy includes more than the existence and maintenance of democratic institutions. Two lines of further refinements have relied upon system-level democratic "behaviors" to make additional distinctions among political systems with democratic institutions. One of these developments deals with Dahl's (1956) concept of polyarchy, the other with political equality. While extremely meaningful, these concepts require much ingenuity to operationalize, especially on a cross-national level. For the concept of polyarchy see Dahl (1956: 84). For operational measures of the concept see Neubauer (1967),

and Alker (1965). For an operational measure of political equality within the United States, see Cnudde (1966a).

7. See Lipset (1959: 76-77). He relies on means and ranges to establish the relationships.

8. For theoretical contributions which indicate the central role of communications systems in more general types of political developments, see Pye (1963).

9. For the relationship between communication and civic cooperation at the individual level in nations which vary in the degree to which democracy is successfully institutionalized, see Almond and Verba (1963: 378-381).

10. Social scientists are becoming increasingly aware of the similarities in the logic of these techniques. Boudon (1965) for example, subsumes them all under a more general formulation which he calls "dependence analysis."

11. Clearly, there is no incompatibility between Cutright's technique of using the prediction equation based on the regression line and this type of causal analysis. In fact, Cutright's technique applied at each stage of the developmental process would effectively isolate the deviant cases at each stage. His present research on historical trends in political development should also shed light on the adequacy of this causal model. See Cutright (1963: 577-581) for a discussion of Cutright's techniques and research.

REFERENCES

ALKER, H.R. (1965) "Causal inference and political analysis." Pp. 7-43 in J.L. Bernd, Ed., *Mathematical Applications in Political Science*. Dallas: Southern Methodist University Press.

ALMOND, G.A. and S. VERBA (1963) *The Civic Culture: Political Attitudes and Democracy in Five Nations*. Princeton: Princeton University Press.

BLALOCK, H.M. (1964) *Causal Inferences in Nonexperimental Research*. Chapel Hill: University of North Carolina Press.

BOUDON, R. (1965) "A method of linear causal analysis: dependence analysis." *American Sociological Review* 30: 365-374.

CNUDDE, C.F. (1966a) Consensus, "Rules of the Game" and Democratic Politics: The Case of Race Politics in the South. Ph.D. dissertation, Department of Political Science, University of North Carolina.

— (1966b) "Legislative behavior and citizen characteristics: problems in theory and method." Paper presented at the Midwest Conference of Political Scientists, Chicago, April 29.

CNUDDE, C.F. and D.J. MCCRONE (1966) "The linkage between constituency attitudes and congressional voting behavior: a causal model." *American Political Science Review* 60: 66-72.

CUTRIGHT, P. (1963) "National political development." Pp. 569-582 in N. Polsby et al., Eds., *Politics and Social Life*. Boston: Houghton Mifflin.

DAHL, R.A. (1956) *A Preface to Democratic Theory*. Chicago: University of Chicago Press.

DEUTSCH, K.W. (1964) "Communication theory and political integration." Pp. 46-74 in P.E. Jacob and J.V. Toscano, Eds., *The Integration of Political Communities*. Philadelphia: Lippincott.

— (1963) *The Nerves of Government*. New York: Free Press.

LERNER, D. (1958) *The Passing of Traditional Society*. New York: Free Press.
LIPSETT, S.M. (1959) "Some social requisites of democracy." *American Political Science Review* 53: 69–105.
NEUBAUER, D. (1967) "Some conditions of democracy." *American Political Science Review* 61: 1002–1009.
PYE, L.W., Ed. (1963) *Communications and Political Development*. Princeton: Princeton University Press.
RUSSETT, B.M. et al. (1964) *World Handbook of Political and Social Indicators*. New Haven: Yale University Press.
SIMON, H.W. (1954) "Spurious correlations: a causal interpretation." *Journal of the American Statistical Association* 49: 467–479.
WRIGHT, S. (1921) "Correlation and causation." *Journal of Agricultural Research* 20: 557–585.

23 Inequality: A Cross-National Analysis

PHILLIPS CUTRIGHT

Lenski's synthesis of the "functionalist" and "conflict" theories of the distribution of rewards in societies has cleared the way for empirical research.[1] His theory of social stratification is concerned with the distribution of material rewards and the socio-economic and political conditions that account for differences in the way the "distributive process" allocates the nation's product.

Both the functionalist's view of inequality as the product of society's needs, and the conflict theorist's view of inequality as the product of power group conflict, are rejected as incomplete. Lenski accords importance to the functionalist position when he considers societies that do not create a surplus product, but he turns chiefly to the conflict theorist for explanations of inequality in societies at higher levels of economic development. Societies that develop a surplus product are said to allocate that product largely in terms of the distribution of power within the society. The size of the surplus product is largely determined by the level of technology which, in turn, is the prime factor affecting the forms of political and social organization which distribute power within societies.

The purpose of this paper is to fit empirical indicators to Lenski's conceptual scheme and to test his model. We will also test additional variables that may provide us with an explanation of the variation in the degree of income inequality among the nations of the world.

Concepts and Indicators

A. The Dependent Variable. An ingenious measure that allows us to compare the degree of intersectorial income inequality for a large number of

---

Author's Note: My thanks to J. Romaninsky and K. McClelland for assistance, to E. A. Weinstein and R. L. Gorsuch for statistical advice, and to Vanderbilt University for financial support. G. Lenski contributed a helpful criticism of an early draft.

Reprinted from *The American Sociological Review*, Volume 32, pages 562–578, by permission of the author and the publisher. Copyright © 1967 American Sociological Association.

nations has been developed by Kuznets. This measure compares the degree to which "worker participation income" in eight sectors of the economy is equal or unequal.[2] The degree of inequality in the distribution of worker participation income among industry sectors is the dependent variable. We are not, at this point, able to provide a comprehensive measure of income inequality that would take into account all sources of income, the acts of government to redistribute income through transfer payments, or the effects of living arrangements on equality.[3] We are, however, able to measure the degree of intersectorial income inequality.

The percent of the total domestic product produced by each sector and the percent of the total labor force in each sector is computed. The industry sectors are ordered in terms of the level of worker participation income. If the percent of the labor force in the sector equals the percent of the national product produced by the sector, there is no intersectorial income inequality; if it is not the same, inequality exists. The Lorenz coefficient is used by economists to measure the degree of inequality in income distributions.[4] An example using Denmark is shown in Figure 1.

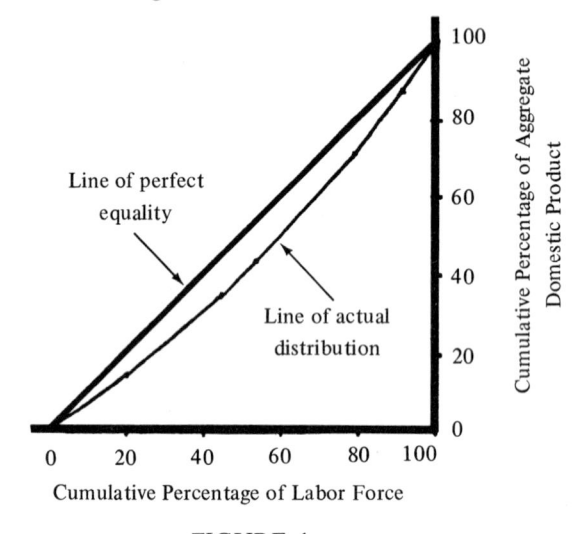

FIGURE 1

Lorenz Curve for Worker Participation Income: Denmark, 1955

The area between the line of perfect equality and the actual distribution line, as a percent of the total area below the line of perfect equality, is given by the Lorenz coefficient. The line of actual distribution is drawn by ordering the eight sectors in terms of average worker participation income, and, starting with the sector with the lowest worker income, plotting the percent of the labor force in that sector against the percent of the national product it produced. In Denmark, the service sector had the lowest average income; about

20 percent of the labor force was in the service sector but it produced only 14 percent of the national product. This gives us the first point below the line of perfect equality. The next sector's labor force and domestic product (agriculture in this case) is *cumulated* with the first sector, and the resulting two figures provide the second point, and so on. The measure is *not* sensitive to extreme deviations in worker income when these deviations apply to a small proportion of the labor force.[5] It is a statistic that can take on values from about zero to about one hundred (after omitting the decimal point) and can be used in correlation-regression analysis. For this distribution, the Lorenz coefficient is 13; 13 percent of the area beneath the line of the perfect equality is enclosed by the sagging line of the actual distribution.[6] In the forty-four non-Communist nations in this study, the Lorenz coefficients vary from five (Belgium) to fifty-eight (Belgian Congo, Leopoldville). The measure of inequality for non-Communist nations is for the early 1950s (eight Communist nations having been measured in 1959), and all independent variables are fitted, where possible, to the appropriate time period.

B. *Independent Variables.* Lenski's generalized scheme to explain differences in "the nature of the distributive system" applies to all types of societies. Five types are described: hunting and gathering, simple horticultural, advanced horticultural, agrarian, and industrial. If the five types of societies are ordered as above, the degree of inequality rises from a very low point in hunting and gathering societies to an apex in agrarian societies, followed by a decline as industrialization takes over.[7]

1. Level of economic development and the size of the surplus. Lenski's (1966) explanation of the reversal of a historical trend is apparently unique. For the agrarian and industrial nations in this study, we should find that the higher the level of economic development, the lower the inequality. This hypothesis stems more from scattered empirical facts assembled by Lenski than from his general theory. The increasing level of economic development across the first four types of societies was associated with increasing inequality. Lenski's explanation of the reversal of this trend rests on two changes: (1) the absolute size of the economic surplus, and (2) changes in the distribution of power. As the level of economic development increases, the higher level of technology and declining fertility create a surplus.

The forms of social and political organization that affect the distribution of power also change. So long as the economy is unable to produce a large surplus, the political and economic elite can enforce inequality to ensure the existence of a surplus and their own position of privilege.[8] Populations in industrialized societies will demand equal distribution of the society's product, and, because the amount of the surplus is so vast, the elite can afford to give up some of the surplus and allow the masses to rise above the subsistence level. Societies with high levels of economic development will have an elite willing to make concessions and a population demanding equality. If economic growth is maintained, the elite can continue to take an ever increasing *absolute* (but not relative) share of the wealth produced by the economy.

Two types of empirical indicators are suggested by this discussion. The first is the size of the surplus product, which can be measured by an Economic Development Index.[9] The second type of indicator would measure changes in the size of the surplus over a particular time period preceding the measurement of inequality. This could be expressed in relative terms (percent growth of GNP per capita between two time periods) or in absolute terms (the dollar added value in GNP growth per capita between two time periods). Unfortunately, available data do not allow the use of either indicator because measures covering the appropriate time periods do not exist. This loss is not as great as one might think, since the level of economic development would be almost perfectly correlated with the size of the absolute surplus if the relative rate of per capita growth in GNP were constant. A rough measure of the absolute rate of cumulation of the surplus during the 1950s does, in fact, correlate nearly as well with our index of inequality as does the Economic Development Index.[10] The level of economic development is empirically a better measure of the size of the surplus than either the absolute or the relative rate of recent economic changes. The Economic Development Index is obviously a superior measure of technology. It was retained as our indicator of the size of the surplus *and* the level of technology.

2. Political institutions and the distribution of power. In Lenski's (1966) theory, both "political organization" and the degree of "constitutionalization" are said to affect the degree of inequality. Political structures that facilitate access by the masses to the elite will decrease inequality. High levels of "constitutionalization" will decrease inequality because the power of the many to organize against the few will be guaranteed. Constitutionalization in industrial societies may be measured by the extent to which the society has extended the modern concept of "citizenship" to all segments of the population, and thus identified human as opposed to property rights as the basis of the distributive process. To the extent that citizenship is broadly accepted, the elite will be forced to respond to the claims of the non-elite classes for a greater share of the national product. As political structures increasingly incorporate this modern concept of "citizenship," governments will enter the distributive process and counteract the self-interest of the economic elite.[11]

Our measure of "political organization" and "constitutionalization" is the Political Representativeness Index. This index is constructed by allocating a number of points to each nation during each year in which it had a certain type of legislature and chief executive during the 1945–54 period.[12] The index measures the extent to which the government is likely to be under effective pressure to take the demands of the non-elite population into account.[13]

3. Farm Rental and the propertied class. Lenski (1966) suggests that in lower GNP nations the power of the "propertied class" will be positively

Inequality: A Cross-National Analysis 517

related to the degree of inequality.[14] One indicator of its power is the proportion of all farms which are rented. We hypothesized that in lower GNP nations, high Farm Rental would indicate high vulnerability of the agricultural population to exploitation by large landowners. The degree of inequality would be large in nations where the size of the agricultural population is large *and* Farm Rental is high. In high GNP nations (with their smaller agricultural labor force), the mechanization of agriculture has transformed the meaning of this variable.

In this stratum, we hypothesized that Farm Rental would be negatively related to inequality since the higher the proportion of farms that are rented, the greater will be agricultural income relative to non-agricultural income. Therefore, in the high GNP stratum, Farm Rental is an indicator of technology in agriculture, and may be entered in the correlation analysis prior to certain other variables. Farm Rental data were available for non-Communist high and middle GNP nations, but no information was available for a number of low GNP nations. Farm Rental is not, of course, relevant for Communist nations.

Economic and Security Decisions. Lenski's model allows for "unknown" factors that may affect the degree of inequality. It seems appropriate to investigate *external* as well as *internal* factors that may influence the distribution of the national product. Two external factors are considered: the allocation of funds to military use, and the dependence of the nation on foreign trade. One internal factor—the level of capital formation—is added. The common characteristic of these three variables is that they are subject to conscious decisions and are, in part, a response by decision makers to forces beyond their immediate control. The effect that these variables may have upon the degree of inequality within the nation should be seen as a "latent," not a "manifest" function. The rationale for inclusion of each variable follows.

4. Military Participation Ratio. The proportion of males 15–64 in military service (the Military Participation Ratio) is used as a measure of the economic drain imposed by military activities. This measure is closely associated with the proportion of the nation's GNP which is devoted to defense expenditures.[15] However, among the poor non-Communist nations in our sample, the infusion of large amounts of foreign military aid decreases the usefulness of defense expenditures as a measure of the drain of military spending on the nation's economy. Furthermore, defense expenditure data were not available for seven of the eight Communist nations.

We did not expect that a large mass army would be related to lower inequality in a developed industrial society.[16] The existence of large modern armies requires a vast expenditure of money that could otherwise be allocated more efficiently to speed the rate of economic progress and decrease inequality.[17] We reasoned that the Military Participation Ratio would be positively related to inequality in high GNP nations. We were uncertain about the relationship across all types of nations or in the middle and lower GNP strata.

5. Dependence of the nation on foreign trade. Our second indicator of a nation's relationship to other nations is the value of exports and imports as a percent of GNP.[18] This variable fits logically into Lenski's discussion of the distribution of power and inequality, but it is not mentioned in his theory.

Inequality should be greater in poor nations than in rich nations because poor nations dependent on foreign trade are vulnerable to the economic power of richer nations. Within the lower GNP stratum, those nations dependent on foreign trade should have greater inequality because the exchange process is in the hands of a powerful elite who should prosper relative to the powerless non-elite who produce raw materials. We hypothesized that lower GNP nations would show a positive relation between Foreign Trade and inequality, while high GNP nations would not be affected because the commercial sector's power would be countered by the power of producers of the exchanged products.

6. Level of Gross Domestic Capital Formation. The powerful negative relation between Gross Domestic Capital Formation as a percent of GNP and private consumption suggests that, in the short run, the diversion of funds from private consumption to Capital Formation (regardless of who determines the level of Capital Formation) should increase inequality.[19] The higher the Capital Formation, the smaller the surplus to be distributed. If Lenski's theory is correct, and the power relations among groups in societies are the basic determinants of variation in the distribution of the society's product, it follows that funds for Capital Formation should be drained away from the relatively powerless. Since these are the same people who are at the bottom of the income distribution, the loss of consumable income to these groups (particularly farmers and the urban poor) should be relatively greater than the loss of consumable income to groups with greater power. High levels of Capital Formation should be associated with high inequality.[20]

7. Size of the powerless labor force. In most nations, the income of the agricultural labor force is lower than the income of people in urban areas.[21] Those in the mass agricultural labor force have been the last to gain literacy, political power, and organizational skills. It is likely that by the time they acquire the skills long before gained by urban populations, their numbers will have diminished, and those who remain in agriculture will still be relatively powerless. The larger the size of this "vulnerable" population, the greater will be the degree of inequality in a nation. It is not possible to deduce whether inequality associated with the size of the agricultural labor force is the result solely of the distribution of power, or simply the result of economic outcomes associated with the generally low value the market assigns to the agricultural product. The truth probably lies somewhere in between.[22] The powerlessness of the agricultural labor force refers to a lack of control over the price of agricultural goods, and a lack of political power that would counteract free market factors.[23] Low reward for agricultural labor is only partially explained

by the abundance of this type of labor and "low" productivity. Rural populations lack the educational skills, economic power, and political organization necessary to counteract the claims of the better organized and more powerful urban sectors.[24]

Strategy for the Analysis

The analysis will first consider the relationship of the independent variables with our measure of inequality in forty-four non-Communist nations. The second phase of the analysis will group these nations into three strata according to their level of GNP per capita. Eight Communist nations will make up a fourth stratum. Stratification of the non-Communist nations according to the level of GNP per capita allows us to investigate hypotheses concerning the different ways certain independent variables will affect inequality in different types of nations.

Surplus product per capita	Distribution of power
Economic Development Index, negative in and across all strata; Farm Rental, negative in high GNP stratum	Political Representativeness Index, negative in and across all strata; Farm Rental, positive in lower GNP strata

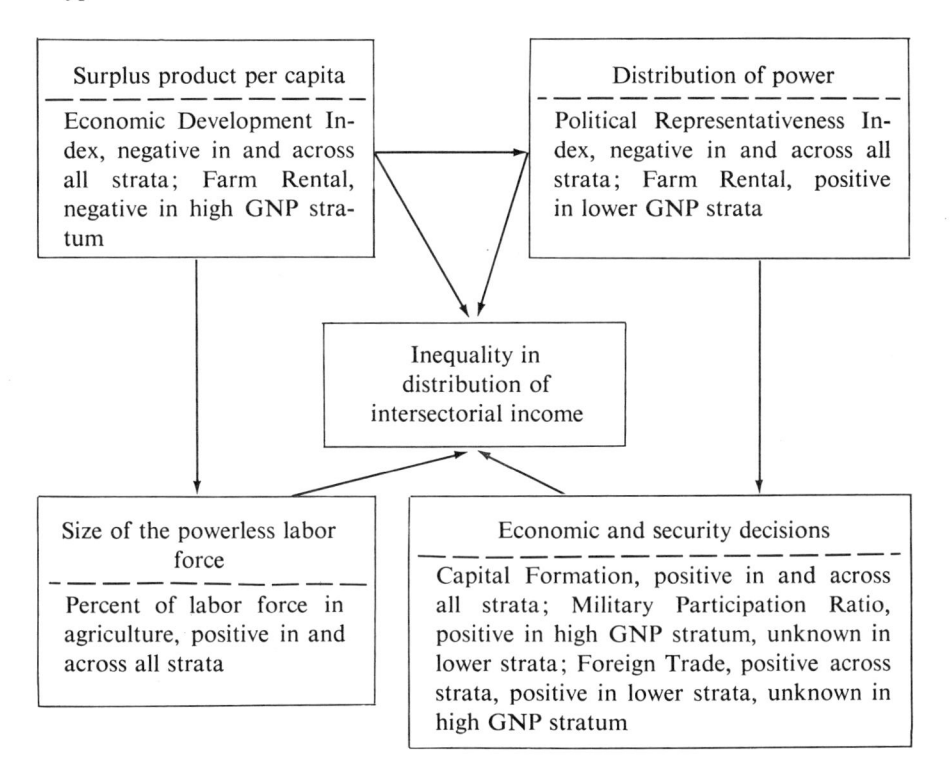

Inequality in distribution of intersectorial income

Size of the powerless labor force	Economic and security decisions
Percent of labor force in agriculture, positive in and across all strata	Capital Formation, positive in and across all strata; Military Participation Ratio, positive in high GNP stratum, unknown in lower strata; Foreign Trade, positive across strata, positive in lower strata, unknown in high GNP stratum

FIGURE 2

CONCEPTUAL SCHEME AND EMPIRICAL INDICATORS

Note: "Positive" means that as an independent variable increases, inequality will also increase; "negative" means that as an independent variable increases, inequality will decrease.

In both phases of the analysis, a "forced" multiple correlation analysis will be used. This type of multiple correlation analysis differs from the conventional type in that the analyst does not allow the independent variables to "compete" freely for their share of the variance. The analyst specifies the order in which independent variables are entered and reports the amount of explained variance which is accounted for by each successive independent variable.[25]

Figure 2 summarizes the conceptual scheme and expected relationship of each indicator to inequality. The order in which variables enter a forced multiple correlation analysis is determined by postulating causal priorities among variables. Figure 2 shows the direction of causality with arrows. The rise in the surplus product has a direct effect on inequality; but it also has an indirect effect because it forces changes in a nation's political institutions and alters the distribution of power. To make a conservative test of the effect of variation in political institutions (or the power of the propertied class in lower GNP nations), one would want first to remove the variance in inequality that is associated with variation in the size of the surplus product. Therefore, the Economic Development Index is entered first. The Political Representativeness Index (along with Farm Rental in lower GNP nations) is entered after removing the effects of the Economic Development Index. The order of the remaining variables was determined by our opinion that "Economic and Security Decisions" should be considered prior to the size of the agricultural labor force. Economic and Security Decisions are made within the framework of the nation's level of economic and political development, and the association of these latter two factors with inequality should be removed prior to entering the Decision variables. Furthermore, the size of the agricultural labor force is not likely to affect decisions on national security or the economy (assuming that economic and political factors are controlled), and should be entered last.[26] The problem of how one orders the decision variables themselves will be discussed below.

Analysis of Non-Communist Nations

An analysis of nations at widely different levels of economic and political development is necessary if one is to test empirically the two major constructs in Lenski's (1966) theory. Table 1 presents an analysis of the forty-four non-Communist nations. The approximate dates for each variable are given, along with their means and standard deviations. We also show the percentage of total variation in our inequality measure that is associated with each indicator, given the order of its appearance in the forced correlation analysis. When entered first, the Economic Development Index accounts for 27 percent of the variation; the addition of the Political Representativeness Index adds 14 percent.[27] The three variables measuring current economic and national security efforts contribute very little. All together they add only 6 percent.

TABLE 1. MEANS, STANDARD DEVIATIONS, AND PERCENT OF VARIANCE IN INEQUALITY EXPLAINED BY INDEPENDENT VARIABLES IN A GIVEN ORDER: 44 NON-COMMUNIST NATIONS

Independent Variable and Date	Mean	Standard Deviation	Percent of Variance	Sign[b]
Economic Development Index, 1953–1955	209.0	34.9	27[a]	—
Political Representativeness Index, 1945–1954	50.1	9.6	14[a]	—
Foreign Trade, 1955	39.1	18.1	4[a]	+
Military Participation Ratio, 1959	1.4	1.8	1	—
Capital Formation, 1950–1959	19.0	6.1	1	+
Agricultural Labor Force, 1951	41.1	22.0	17[a]	+
			64	

Note: The measure of inequality was taken for 1951 and has a mean of 19.1 and a standard deviation of 11.2. The variable "Farm Rental" was not included because of missing data in the lowest GNP stratum.

[a] $P<.05$, one-tailed test.

[b] A positive sign indicates that as the value of the independent variable increases, the measure of inequality also increases. It is taken from the sign of the beta weight for the variable at the time it is introduced into the analysis.

We also note that Lenski's (1966) view that the size of the agricultural labor force will be related to inequality is confirmed. Even after we control for economic development and four additional variables, knowledge of the size of the agricultural labor force allows us to account for an additional 17 percent of the variation. A total of 64 percent of the variation is accounted for.

The results support Lenski's contention that the size of the surplus and the distribution of power bear an important relation to the degree of inequality in modern nations. Because of the 0.69 intercorrelation between our economic and political variables, and the -0.63 zero order correlation of the Political Representativeness Index with inequality, as compared to the -0.52 correlation between the Economic Development Index and inequality, alternative methods of dividing the explained variance between our economic and political variables would result in allocating a larger share of the explained variance in inequality to the Political Representativeness Index. Also, given the pattern of high correlations between the Economic Development Index and other modernization factors not considered here, one might want to redefine, to some degree, the importance one puts on the level of economic development in reducing inequality.

Although the broad outlines of the major factors related to inequality seem relatively clear, our conceptual scheme contains a number of important qualifications concerning the effect of certain variables on inequality in nations at different levels of economic development. If our conceptual scheme is correct, we would expect that stratification of this heterogeneous group of forty-four nations would *increase* the total variance explained (in spite of the loss of prediction we might expect when we drop the Economic Development Index and, in the high GNP stratum, the Political Representativeness Index as well). We expect that the indicators of Economic and Security Decisions will improve our explanation of the variation of inequality within a stratum because interactions among variables are different within the different strata. Also, variables like the Military Participation Ratio and Farm Rental (not included in Table 1 because of missing data) will be available, and will work in opposite directions within different strata. If this is the case, it follows that when nations are put into "homogeneous strata" these previously suppressed effects will appear.

We begin our analysis with the stratum of nineteen nations, none of which had a per capita GNP above $299 in 1957, move next to nations with a per capita GNP between $300–799, then to those with over $800 per capita GNP.[28] Our fourth stratum includes eight Communist nations. This stratum is homogeneous with respect to political structure, but it contains nations at varying levels of economic development. (The relationship of the Economic Development Index to inequality within this stratum provides a small replication of our analysis of the forty-four non-Communist nations.)

Analysis of Inequality in Low GNP Nations

Nations in this group vary from about $75 to $290 per capita GNP. Variation in the Economic Development Index is not, however, strongly related to inequality.[29] (The correlation is -0.18.) The Economic Development Index was, therefore, omitted. Variation within the stratum on the Political Representativeness Index is, however, powerfully related to inequality, and Table 2 reveals that 20 percent of the variation in inequality can be assigned to national differences on the Political Representativeness Index. The only two "decision"

TABLE 2. MEANS, STANDARD DEVIATIONS, AND PERCENT OF VARIANCE IN INEQUALITY EXPLAINED BY INDEPENDENT VARIABLES IN A GIVEN ORDER: 19 LOW GNP NATIONS

Independent Variable	Mean	Standard Deviation	Percent of Variance	Sign
Panel A				
Political Representativeness Index	43.2	7.1	20*	—
Foreign Trade	33.6	17.6	14*	+
Capital Formation	15.6	5.2	28*	+
Agricultural Labor Force	61.6	12.7	23*	+
			85	
Panel B				
Political Representativeness Index	43.2	7.1	20*	—
Capital Formation	15.6	5.2	40*	+
Foreign Trade	33.6	17.6	2	+
Agricultural Labor Force	61.6	12.7	23*	+
			85	

Note: The measure of inequality has a mean of 26.1 and a standard deviation of 11.9. Farm Rental data were missing for several nations, and the distribution of the Military Participation Ratio did not allow its use in correlation analysis for this stratum.

*$P<.05$, one-tailed test.

variables on which we have data contribute an additional 42 percent to the explained variance. Comparison of the explained variance in Panel A and Panel B shows clearly that the order in which Foreign Trade and Capital Formation are entered will alter our view of the relative importance of these two variables. These two variables are intercorrelated (0.44), and Capital Formation has a higher zero order correlation with inequality (0.74) than does Foreign Trade (0.52). Until we know more about the causal relationship between Foreign Trade and Capital Formation in this type of nation, there seems to be no reason to prefer one order to the other. Also, in this stratum, Capital Formation has only a 0.41 correlation with growth in per capita GNP (using 1950–59 data for both variables), and this may heighten the effect of Capital Formation on inequality. The importance of Capital Formation might be further reduced if additional variables, e.g., Farm Rental or the Military Participation Ratio, were available.

One should not, of course, conclude that a nation should cut back either capital investment or foreign trade. Nations must have capital investment if they are to grow, and they must also trade if they are to reach higher levels of economic development. One can conclude, however, that certain economic decisions will have the latent function of increasing inequality in the short run. On the other hand, if these same actions lead to economic development, the long run effect will be to decrease inequality.

Finally, we should note that the size of the agricultural labor force in these low GNP nations is positively related to inequality. This relationship will not reappear in the next two strata. It may appear here because we did not have data on Farm Rental, or a good measure of military expenditures in this stratum. These variables have powerful relationships to inequality in the middle and high GNP levels, and when entered, they eliminate the independent effect of the size of the agricultural labor force on inequality. On the other hand, there may be important qualitative differences between strata in the relation of the size of the agricultural labor force to inequality.

Analysis of the Middle GNP Stratum

Within the group of nations with a per capita GNP between $300–799 a year, there was no correlation between the Economic Development Index and inequality. Table 3 shows the results of our analysis. In the first arrangement, we follow the conceptual scheme, allowing the Political Representativeness Index to enter first and Farm Rental second, conceiving of Farm Rental in this stratum as an indicator of the distribution of power specific to the agricultural sector. (The average nation in this stratum had 34 percent of its labor force in agriculture.) The Political Representativeness Index accounts for 34 percent of the variation, while Farm Rental adds 13 percent to the explained variance. Even with a control on the former, we find that nations high on Farm Rental have high inequality. There is no correlation between the size of the agricultural labor force and Farm Rental; Farm Rental is negatively related

TABLE 3. MEANS, STANDARD DEVIATIONS, AND PERCENT OF VARIANCE IN INEQUALITY EXPLAINED BY INDEPENDENT VARIABLES IN A GIVEN ORDER: 13 MIDDLE GNP NATIONS

Independent Variable	Mean	Standard Deviation	Percent of Variance	Sign
Panel A				
Political Representativeness Index	51.6	8.2	34[a]	—
Farm Rental	12.4	9.0	13	+
Foreign Trade	42.9	15.9	16[a]	+
Military Participation Ratio	1.1	1.3	7	—
Capital Formation	20.9	5.7	2	—
			72	
Panel B				
Political Representativeness Index	51.6	8.2	34[a]	—
Military Participation Ratio	1.1	1.3	12	—
Farm Rental	12.4	9.0	12	+
Foreign Trade	42.9	15.9	12[a]	+
Capital Formation	20.9	5.7	2	—
			72	

Note: The measure of inequality has a mean of 15.2 and a standard deviation of 8.5. The percent of the labor force in agriculture added nothing to the explained variance when inserted either before or after Capital Formation in Panel A.

[a] $P<.05$, one-tailed test.

to the Political Representativeness Index (-0.32), and Foreign Trade (-0.24). Nations high on Foreign Trade are also high on inequality; this variable accounts for an additional 16 percent of the variance. The Military Participation ratio adds another 7 percent to the explained variance, and the sign indicates that in these middle GNP nations, the higher the Military Participation Ratio, the lower the inequality. This finding is in accord with Lenski's (1966) discussion of military participation in underdeveloped societies. Finally Capital Formation accounts for only 2 percent of the variance, and the sign is opposite to our prediction. This stratum is, however, the only non-Communist stratum in which Capital Formation and Annual Growth in per capita GNP are closely associated (0.60), and this may account for the anomaly. Placing Capital Formation after Farm Rental, or even in the first position, yields nearly the same result. Finally, the size of the agricultural labor force does not add even 1 percent to the explained variation.

An alternative arrangement that puts Foreign Trade to a more severe test is shown in Panel B of Table 3. Placing the Military Participation Ratio in the second position increases its share of explained variance from 7 to 12 percent, while moving Foreign Trade from third to fourth position decreases its share from 16 to 12 percent.[30] Farm Rental continues to account for about the same amount of variance, regardless of its position.

Analysis of High GNP Nations. Nations with per capita GNP above $800 a year have, as a group, less inequality than lower GNP nations. Lorenz coefficients, however, vary from twenty-two (France) to five (Belgium). In this stratum, variation in the Economic Development Index is slightly related to inequality (−0.25), but the amount of variance explained by it is relatively small, and it is omitted from our analysis. There is no meaningful difference among these nations in their Political Representativeness Index scores, and this variable can also be dropped. Our conceptual scheme suggested that Farm Rental could be used as an indicator of the level of technology in the agricultural sector, since we expected that high Farm Rental would be associated with high capital investment in agriculture and high productivity relative to the non-agricultural sectors. The ordering of variables in Panel A of Table 4 adopts this view. Farm Rental is negatively related to inequality and accounts for 16 percent of the variance when entered first. We expected that a high Military Participation Ratio would result in high inequality in this stratum

TABLE 4. MEANS, STANDARD DEVIATIONS, AND PERCENT OF VARIANCE IN INEQUALITY EXPLAINED BY INDEPENDENT VARIABLES IN A GIVEN ORDER: 12 HIGH GNP NATIONS

Independent Variable	Mean	Standard Deviation	Percent of Variance	Sign
Panel A				
Farm Rental	24.7	18.5	16	−
Military Participation Ratio	1.6	0.7	47[a]	+
Capital Formation	22.4	5.0	26[a]	+
Foreign Trade	43.0	20.1	9[a]	+
			98	
Panel B				
Military Participation Ratio	1.6	0.7	33[a]	+
Farm Rental	24.7	18.5	30[a]	−
Foreign Trade	43.7	18.7	20[a]	+
Capital Formation	26.8	16.6	15[a]	+
			98	

Note: The measure of inequality has a mean of 12.4 and a standard deviation of 4.9.
[a] $P<.05$, one-tailed test.

because of the drain of high defense expenditures on a developed economy. Variation in the Military Participation Ratio is, in fact, powerfully related to inequality—some 47 percent of the explained variance is linked to it after the variance associated with Farm Rental is removed. Capital Formation is positively associated with inequality and adds another 26 percent to the explained variation. (Capital Formation has a 0.05 correlation with annual per capita GNP growth in this stratum.) Nations with high levels of Foreign Trade have higher inequality, and this variable adds 9 percent to the explained variance.

Panel B of Table 4 reveals rather dramatic changes in the accounting power of each variable when their order is changed. If one assigns the Military Participation Ratio to the first position, we find that it accounts for "only" 33 percent of the variation, in contrast to 47 percent when it was entered after Farm Rental. The two have an intercorrelation of 0.23. Farm Rental jumps its "take" of the explained variance from 16 to 30 percent when entered second. Panel B of Table 4 also reveals the effect of Foreign Trade in depressing the amount of variation assumed by Capital Formation when it is entered prior to Capital Formation instead of after it. In this new order, Foreign Trade appears to dominate Capital Formation. The two variables share an intercorrelation of 0.20. Capital Formation is a powerful variable in this stratum, although its zero order correlation with inequality was only 0.35. Our uncertainty concerning the causal order among these variables would suggest that Capital Formation and Foreign Trade be retained in future studies.

The most parsimonious set of independent variables is the Military Participation Ratio, Farm Rental and Capital Formation. Regardless of their order, they will account for 89 percent of the variation in inequality within this stratum. This analysis suggests one major alteration in the conceptual scheme: it appears that high levels of Foreign Trade are associated with higher levels of inequality within *all* three strata.[31]

Analysis of Communist Nations

Communist nations have identical Political Representativeness Index scores, and we have no alternative measure of differences in the distribution of power within these nations. In Communist nations, variation in the level of the Economic Development Index is powerfully related to inequality. In Table 5, two alternative orders are shown. Panel A, conforming to our conceptual scheme, enters the Economic Development Index first, and shows that 68

TABLE 5. MEANS, STANDARD DEVIATIONS, AND PERCENT OF VARIANCE IN INEQUALITY EXPLAINED BY INDEPENDENT VARIABLES IN A GIVEN ORDER: 8 COMMUNIST NATIONS

Independent Variable and Date	Mean	Standard Deviation	Percent of Variance	Sign
Panel A				
Economic Development Index, 1953–1955	230.6	22.8	68*	—
Military Participation Ratio, 1959	2.2	0.9	14*	+
Agricultural Labor Force, 1959	47.5	18.2	15*	+
			97	
Panel B				
Military Participation Ratio	2.2	0.9	45*	+
Economic Development Index	230.6	22.8	37*	—
Agricultural Labor Force	47.5	18.2	15*	+
			97	

Note: The measure of inequality refers to 1959 and has a mean of 33.7 and a standard deviation of 8.4. This measure is similar to, but not directly comparable with, the measure for non-Communist nations. Kuznets, *op. cit.*, 1963, discusses differences in Communist and non-Communist national accounting practices that result in comparable inequality measures within, but not across, Communist and non-Communist countries.

*$P<.05$, one-tailed test.

percent of the variation in inequality is linked to variation in the Economic Development Index. As economic development increases, inequality decreases. Controlling for the Economic Development Index, we find that Communist nations with a high Military Participation Ratio, have high inequality, while the addition of data on the size of the agricultural labor force virtually exhausts the unexplained variation. In Panel B of Table 5, we enter the Military Participation Ratio first, and see that it accounts for 45 percent of the variance, while the Economic Development Index adds 37 percent when it is in second position. It is instructive to compare these results with those shown in Table 4. In that table, we were dealing with nations that are, by and large, the other half of the "cold war." Comparison of the two tables indicates that in both sets, those nations with heavy and continuing cold war defense expenditures (measured by the Military Participation Ratio) are nations with high inequality, regardless of whether or not we first remove the variance in inequality that is associated with the Economic Development Index.

Unfortunately, we do not have an indicator for Communist nations that would allow us to insert a variable like Farm Rental, nor do we have Foreign Trade data for all Communist nations. Examination of the relationship of Capital Formation to inequality in Communist nations revealed no association; this may be explained by noting the 0.93 correlation in this stratum between Capital Formation and annual per capita GNP growth, and assuming that annual growth is effectively cancelling out the expected effects of Capital Formation on inequality.

Errors of Prediction Using Separate Strata and All Nations

One may use the accuracy of prediction as a criterion for deciding whether or not a single regression equation for all nations is preferable to separate equations for several strata. Table 6 lists the nations by strata. It shows the Lorenz coefficient (decimal point omitted) for each, and the direction and size of the error of two predictions—the first based on all forty-four non-Communist nations and the second using selected variables for each stratum. Comparison of the two columns reveals that prediction is greatly improved if a separate analysis of each stratum is used.

Stratification on the basis of GNP per capita effectively controls the variation in inequality that is associated with the Economic Development Index in the three non-Communist strata, and with the Political Representativeness Index in the high GNP and the Communist strata as well. Smaller errors of prediction using regression equations that omit these important variables should not be construed as evidence against Lenski's model, since the Economic Development Index and the Political Representativeness Index are significant variables in predicting inequality across strata.

One might expect that decreasing the number of nations while retaining a large number of independent variables will decrease the errors of prediction.

TABLE 6

INEQUALITY SCORES AND ERRORS OF PREDICTION: NON-COMMUNIST COUNTRIES CLASSIFIED BY PER CAPITA GNP, AND COMMUNIST COUNTRIES

Stratum and country	Inequality Score (Lorenz coefficient)	Across-strata error	Within-stratum error	Stratum and country	Inequality score (Lorenz coefficient)	Across-strata error	Within-stratum error
High GNP				**Low GNP**			
Australia	8	0.1	−3.2	Algeria	39	0.2	0.5
Belgium	5	−4.7	0.8	Belgian Congo (L.)	58	15.9	−0.8
Canada	12	−4.6	−0.7	Brazil	29	9.9	6.6
Denmark	13	1.3	2.0	Ceylon	14	−10.4	−6.1
France	22	9.4	0.1	Colombia	12	−4.6	−6.9
Great Britain	6	1.7	−1.5	Ecuador	20	4.0	−0.3
Luxembourg	15	−4.1	0.7	Egypt	18	−6.0	−0.4
Netherlands	15	3.2	1.7	El Salvador	29	2.8	6.9
New Zealand	11	−1.5	1.4	Honduras	27	−5.6	−7.1
Norway	19	7.1	0.5	India	21	−4.7	−0.7
United States	12	−0.1	−2.2	Morocco	41	4.2	8.3
West Germany	11	2.4	0.5	Pakistan	17	−12.9	−4.1
				Peru	45	19.0	1.8
Mean error		3.35	1.27	Philippines	16	1.0	5.3
Middle GNP				Portugal	19	−3.1	0.0
				Spain	12	−6.4	5.7
Argentina	20	6.5	−4.9	Taiwan	18	0.9	0.2
Austria	14	4.2	0.6	Thailand	34	2.6	1.9
Chile	23	9.3	7.4	Turkey	21	−0.8	−0.1
Costa Rica	5	−18.9	−10.6				
Finland	9	−7.7	1.1	Mean error		6.06	3.40
Greece	10	−5.6	−1.3				
Ireland	6	−8.4	−3.6	**Communist**			
Israel	6	−2.5	−0.5	Bulgaria	41		−1.8
Italy	15	1.1	−0.2	Czechoslovakia	27		−0.0
Jamaica	30	1.4	2.5	East Germany	19		−0.5
Japan	9	2.1	0.4	Hungary	28		−1.5
Panama	21	1.8	7.9	Poland	36		2.1
Venezuela	30	0.8	1.2	Romania	41		0.7
				U.S.S.R.	35		1.3
Mean error		5.40	3.24	Yugoslavia	43		−0.2
				Mean error			1.01

Note: "Across-strata errors" are based on a regression using as independent variables the Political Representativeness Index, Economic Development Index, Foreign Trade, and Agricultural Labor Force. "Within-stratum errors" are based on regressions using Capital Formation, Military Participation Ratio, and Farm Rental in the High GNP stratum; Foreign Trade, Political Representativeness Index, Military Participation Ratio, and Farm Rental in the middle GNP stratum; Agricultural Labor Force, Foreign Trade, Capital Formation, and Political Representativeness Index in the low GNP stratum; Economic Development Index, Military Participation Ratio, and Agricultural Labor Force in the Communist stratum. A positive error means that the nation had higher inequality, i.e., a higher Lorenz coefficient, than was predicted; a negative error means that the nation had less inequality than was predicted. Communist nations could not be included in the across-strata regression because their inequality scores were not comparable to those for the non-Communist nations.

Our stratification procedure, however, effectively controlled for one (or two) of the important variables identified in the across-strata analysis, and did not add previously unexamined variables to the within-stratum analysis. The fact that within-stratum prediction is superior to across-strata prediction is testimony to the effect that across-strata relationships have in cancelling our correlations, rather than being a spurious artifact related to decreasing degrees of freedom. Our significance tests take the latter problem into account. One could further reduce the number of independent variables used for within-stratum prediction and *still* have superior prediction.[33]

Discussion

Our analysis leads us to qualify the conceptual scheme offered by Lenski (1966) and ourself. Table 1 revealed that 64 percent of the variance in inequality among the forty-four non-Communist nations could be accounted for by our indicators. In that analysis, the size of the surplus product, the distribution of power and the size of the powerless labor force were relatively powerful predictors, while our measures of economic and security decisions were not. However, the errors of prediction using this model are much greater than the errors of prediction obtained if the nations are broken into strata. When stratified according to their level of per capita GNP, we account for about 85 percent of the variance in the lowest GNP stratum, 70 percent in the middle stratum, and over 90 percent in the high GNP stratum. Over 90 percent of the variance in the Communist stratum was related to three predictors.

Although the stratification procedure generally controlled the variation in inequality related to the size of the surplus product (and, in two strata, variation in political structure as well), it allowed Farm Rental to enter and confirm its expected relationship to inequality in the middle and high GNP strata. The Military Participation Ratio also worked as we expected in the high GNP stratum and in Communist nations, and conformed to Lenski's expectations in middle GNP stratum. Foreign Trade worked, as we expected, in the low and middle GNP strata, but had the same effect in the high GNP stratum where we did not expect it to be related to inequality. Except for the low and possibly the high GNP stratum, Capital Formation was found to be a relatively weak variable, and we offered two possible explanations for this, while reserving a final judgment pending further research.

Although different "causes" of inequality are only partially illuminated by our analysis, it seems clear that investigators will obtain different results depending on the type of nation they study and their choice of a causal model. It also appears that the "functionalist" view of inequality (from a macro point of view at least) is supported by our analysis of the latent functions of certain economic and security decisions, while the conflict theorist is supported by our consistent finding that the distribution of power is an important predictor of inequality across all strata and within both strata in which there were differences on the Political Representativeness Index. Finally, the economist may be heartened that his interpretation of inequality as a function of the level of economic development also received solid empirical support.

NOTES

1. See Lenski (1966). One statement of the functionalist position is Davis (1949: 366–378). The debate generated by an earlier article (Davis and Moore, 1945: 242–249) has been long and occasionally bitter, largely because the theory was not subject to empirical testing. The conflict view finds expression in Dahrendorf (1959); Mills (1956); and Kolko (1962).

2. Worker participation income is computed by dividing the number of workers in a sector into the value of the product produced by that sector. This might better be called "per worker product," but we follow Kuznets' terminology. See Kuznets (1963: 70–71). The eight sectors are services; agriculture; mining; construction; manufacturing; commerce; transportation; communications; electricity and gas. Names of the nations in this study are given in Table 6. Lorenz coefficients on four high GNP nations were calculated and added to the eight high GNP nations in Kuznets' study. In a few nations, less than eight sectors are used. For sources of data used to compute the Lorenz coefficients, see Kuznets (1963). Measurement error is introduced because of national differences in the accuracy of labor force statistics, as well as varying practices determining the inclusion or exclusion of unpaid family workers and other classes of workers to a given industrial sector. Also, national definitions measuring the product of a given industrial sector vary. We would expect, therefore, that measurement error in the dependent variable will be relatively high, but studies replicating this one with later data will show higher correlations than those reported in this paper.

3. Transfer payments and living arrangements act to equalize the distribution of income in the total population since transfer payments go primarily to low income groups, and persons not in the labor force cluster around high earners. See Morgan et al. (1962: 315), and Kuznets (1963: 6, Table 2). The determinants of national level of transfer payments in forty nations have been reported in Cutright (1967). He reports that transfer payments are greatest in the same nations (high GNP nations) that have low intersectorial income; transfers further equalize the distribution of income in those nations.

4. A simplified method of computing the Lorenz coefficient is given in Morgan (1962: 281–282). Further discussion of the properties of the Lorenz coefficient and its relation to alternative statistics is reported in Alker and Russett (1966: 349–372).

5. Efforts to describe the degree of inequality in income distributions using the "top one percent" (or a similar small group) of earners or wealth holders fail to consider the distribution of income to the total population. Since our concern here is with the distribution of income to the entire labor force, the Lorenz coefficient based on the total labor force is preferable to alternative indicators of the concentration of wealth in small groups in the society.

6. The measure does not take into account inequality within sectors. The Lorenz coefficients are lower than those that would be found if individual incomes were ordered into deciles and a Lorenz coefficient were calculated. However, Kuznets (1963: 19–22), using limited data and economic theory, argues persuasively that nations ordered by the degree of inequality on intersectorial income will have

much the same order as nations ordered by individual earner measures of inequality. Romaninsky (1966) reports that the correlation between Lorenz coefficients computed from intersectorial or individual income distributions (using 1949 and 1953 United States data from the forty-eight states) is 0.82. This is powerful validation of Kuznets' theory, and strengthens our use of intersectorial inequality scores in place of (unavailable) inequality data based on individuals.

7. In the analysis below, we stratify nations according to their level of GNP per capita. High GNP nations are clearly in the later stages of industrialization. Lenski has suggested that nations in the middle GNP stratum are in the early industrialization stage while the low GNP stratum is largely agrarian. He would predict diminishing equality with increasing levels of GNP per capita. The mean of the Lorenz coefficient is 26 in the low GNP stratum, 15 in the middle and 12 in the high GNP stratum, providing a rough confirmation of his theoretical statement. Lenski's conclusion also is supported by the theoretical and empirical work of several economists. See Kravis (1960: 408–416); Oshima (1962: 439–445) and Kuznets (1963: 58–69).

8. This view of the positive contribution of elites to economic development in pre-industrial societies supports the "functionalist" view of inequality, but empirical evidence is missing. A similar positive perspective on inequality and saving and investment by the moneyed elites of industrial nations could be advanced, but Lenski does not take this step.

9. The Economic Development Index was constructed by T-scoring the nations of the world on their mid-1950 level of per capita energy consumption, income converted to U.S. dollars per capita, steel consumption, and number of motor vehicles per capita. For each nation, the four T scores were added to provide a single measure of economic development. (See Edwards, 1954, for a discussion of T-scoring.) Deviations in raw data from a normal distribution are usually corrected by T-scoring. For a single variable, the mean of a T-scored distribution will be 50 and the standard deviation will be 10. The Economic Development Index correlated 0.97 (using the forty-four non-Communist nations in this study) with 1957 GNP (log scale) per capita, an alternative single indicator of economic development.

10. Data from Russett et al. (1954: 160–161). Annual rates of GNP percentage growth during the 1950s were applied to 1957 per capita GNP data (also in Russett) to get an estimate of recent absolute change in the size of the surplus in this decade.

11. Raymond Breton (1966) has identified eight types of government activities that may help to explain inequality.

12. A detailed description of the Political Representativeness Index is given in Cutright (reprinted in this volume, Chapter 24). Most of the weight in the index comes from the characteristics of the nation's parliament and the type of chief executive. For example, for each year the nation's lower or only chamber of the national parliament had minority party representation of at least 30 percent, and the members achieved office through competitive elections, the nation received 2 points. If the minority party had less than 20 percent of the seats, the nation received only one point. If there was no parliament it received no points. If the chief executive was selected by a party or parliament or directly elected by the people under conditions indicating a free and competitive party system, the nation received an additional one and one-half points, while if it had a junta it received only one-half point. No points were given if the nation had an hereditary ruler, or if the

nation was occupied by a foreign power during a given year. Several additional gradations in scoring the parliament and chief executive are outlined in Cutright (reprinted in this volume, Chapter 24). The total raw scores for Communist and non-Communist nations during 1945-54 were comulated, and the resulting distribution was *T*-scored.

13. Lenski notes that the operation of the free market without government intervention would lead industrial nations to increasing levels of inequality. Therefore, the role of government is crucial in understanding the reversal of the historical trend of increasing inequality associated with economic development.

14. Farm Rental data are from Russett et al. (1954: 241-242) and usually are close to 1950. Farm Rental might legitimately be used in conjunction with the Political Representativeness Index as a measure of the distribution of power in society. This will be taken up in the text below. The relation of land ownership to political instability is discussed in Russett (1964: 442-454).

15. Data are from Russett et al. (1954: 77-78) and are for the late 1950s. He reports a correlation of 0.68 for 75 nations, but notes that the reliability of the expenditure data for some lower GNP nations is questionable. The highly skewed distribution of the Military Participation Ratio in low GNP nations forced its exclusion from our analysis of that stratum.

16. Lenski concluded that high military participation would be related to low inequality in agrarian societies but he was uncertain about the relationship in industrial societies. He cites the work of Andrzejewski (1954) on pre-industrial societies, and notes that the dependence of the modern state on a mass army hastened the extension of universal male suffrage and, therefore, altered the distribution of power in modern societies. Mass suffrage, and its resultant political institutions have been with us for some time however, and there is little reason to think that the Military Participation Ratio will continue to have the same effect on equality it once did. The dependence of the elite on a mass army, is, nonetheless, one of the conditions of modern elite existence, and should not be overlooked in examining the conditions that help explain the stability of representative political institutions.

17. See Melman (1966) for numerous examples of the negative effects of continuing high defense expenditures on the United States economy.

18. Data are from Deutsch and Russett (1963: 19) and apply to 1955. The correlation of Foreign Trade and the size of the population (log scale) for 81 nations is -0.69. See Russett et al. (1954: 264). An analysis of the effect of colonial status in raising the level of Foreign Trade, and the importance of population size in creating a home market that can support an industrialized economy, is given in Deutsch, Bliss and Eckstein (1962: 353-366). Their discussion suggests that some of the relationship of Foreign Trade to inequality should properly be allocated to population size. Colonial status is included in the Political Representativeness Index. Missing data forced us to omit Foreign Trade in the analysis of Communist nations. In our data, the Foreign Trade against population size (log scale) correlations are -0.61 for all non-Communist nations, -0.56, -0.50, and -0.69 in the low, middle and high strata, respectively. Foreign Trade is always superior to population size (log scale) as a predictor.

19. Data on Gross Domestic Capital Formation are from Russett et al. (1954: 168-169) and are an average of 1950-59 figures. Russett reports a -0.77 correla-

tion for 62 nations between Capital Formation and private consumption. The correlation using our 44 non-Communist nations was −0.67; it was −0.64 in the high GNP nations, −0.86 and −0.90 in the middle and low GNP nations, and −0.66 among the Communist states. Russett notes that the probable error range for this variable may be as high as 15 or 20 percent in some nations. For most nations, the value of residential and other domestic (non-military) construction, machinery and other equipment and inventories as a percent of GNP will give the percent of GNP that Gross Domestic Capital Formation comprises. Capital Formation data precede the measurement of inequality only in the Communist nations, where inequality was measured in 1959. In non-Communist nations, we assume that the level of Capital Formation during the 1950s was about the same as the level immediately preceding 1951, the date of measurement of inequality. This may not be too absurd an assumption. See Kuznets (1962: part II, Appendix Table 4, pp. 72–74). Financing of Gross Domestic Capital Formation is, for the most part, not from foreign sources. See Kuznets (1960: part II, Table 19, p. 70).

20. The association of Capital Formation and inequality will be moderated by the effect of Capital Formation on economic growth. Russett et al. (1954: 277) reports a 0.57 correlation for 58 nations. Nations experiencing high rates of growth should also be nations with full employment, and workers will transfer from low-paying sectors to better-paying sectors. Shifts of this type will reduce intersectorial inequality. Where there is a strong association between Capital Formation and economic growth, the relationship between Capital Formation and inequality should be low. The correlation between rate of economic growth in the 1950s and Capital Formation in that period is only 0.18 in our non-Communist nations; it is 0.05, 0.60, and 0.41 in high, middle and low strata, and 0.93 in the Communist strata. If a strong association between growth and Capital Formation cancels out the relationship of Capital Formation to inequality, we would, therefore, expect this effect in the Communist and the middle GNP strata. This expectation is supported by the within-stratum analysis. See Tables 2 through 5. Capital Formation does not work across strata, in spite of its low correlation with growth. This may be related to curvilinearity in the relationship of economic growth and Capital Formation. Curvilinearity is partially controlled by the stratification procedure.

21. A. Stinchcombe, in an unpublished paper, notes that for 60 nations his measure of urban and rural income shows the agricultural sector receiving from 72 percent (in nations with small agricultural populations) to about 40 percent (nations with high agricultural populations) the income of urban sectors. A figure similar to his can be calculated by subtracting the percent of the gross domestic product originating in agriculture from the percent of the labor force in agriculture. The difference indicates the size of the rural-urban income gap. See Russett et al. (1954: 173–179) for the data. Our measure of the size of the agricultural labor force is from Kuznets (1963: 24, 70–71).

22. It is interesting that the low income of agricultural workers in poor nations is thought to be the result of low productivity, while the low income of agricultural workers in rich nations is said to result from high productivity. An examination of "deviant" nations (for example, New Zealand and Ceylon) in which the value of agricultural products is high relative to the size of the agricultural labor force, might illuminate this problem.

23. The drive to industrialization necessarily involves accumulation of a surplus that takes the form of Capital Formation. Internal funds for Capital Formation must, in underdeveloped nations, come largely out of the agricultural sector.

24. If we think of inequality as a measure of differences in the level of living of sub-groups in a population, we should also note that the same standard of living can be maintained by a rural population with less money income than an urban population needs. In the United States, the value of home grown food is estimated to add some 30 percent to the money income rural families have available for food. See Orshansky (1965: 10). Following this reasoning, people dependent on the agricultural sector could have a lower income than the non-agricultural sectors but still enjoy the same level of living, provided they were able and willing to produce much of their own food.

25. See Blalock (1964: 61-94). Rigid application of a formal model to these data is undesirable because the small case base will yield relatively unstable correlations, and the risk of rejecting a hypothesis should be minimized. Alternative models are shown, therefore, when appropriate.

26. If a direct measure of the size of the surplus product (our Economic Development Index) were not available, one might want to use a labor force variable like percent in agriculture as an indicator of variation in technology and the surplus product. Although the percent in agriculture is correlated -0.89 with the Economic Development Index in the 44 nations (and -0.68, -0.52, and -0.27 in low, medium and high GNP strata, respectively), we feel justified in treating agriculture as an indicator of the powerlessness of the population rather than an indicator of the size of the surplus product, since the variance in inequality linked to the Economic Development Index is removed first. If agriculture were entered first, one would be removing variation in inequality related *both* to agriculture's relationship to the size of the surplus product and to its power as an indicator of the size of the powerless population. This view is supported by the finding that the zero-order correlation of inequality with agriculture is always stronger (within and across strata) than is the correlation of inequality with the Economic Development Index.

27. The statistical significance of the first variable to enter can be judged using standard significance tests for product moment correlations. To ease the burden of interpreting the tables, the F ratio for the variable entered first was computed, and the significance level is reported, using the same notation followed for the second and higher order variables. For the F test with zero order correlations, see Walker and Lev (1953: 470). The significance of successive higher order variables can be assessed with the F ratio:

$$F = \frac{(R^2_A - R^2_B)/(m_A - m_B)}{(1 - R^2_A)/(N - m_A)}$$

where N is the number of observations, m_A and m_B the numbers of predictors in the A solution and B solution, R^2_A is the coefficient of determination using m_A predictors, and R^2_B is the coefficient of determination using $m_A - 1$ predictors. The F table is entered with 1 degree of freedom in the numerator and $N - m_A$ degrees of freedom in the denominator. See Winer (1962: 642-647) for F table with F at 0.10 level. For the formula, see Bottenberg and Ward (1963). When the direction of the relationship has been predicted, it is appropriate to use F at the 0.10 level in setting the limits to establish significance at the 0.05 level, if the sign of the beta weights (see Tables 1–5) is in accord with our hypotheses. The 0.10 level is not acceptable if the sign is not in the predicted direction.

28. See Russett et al. (1954: 293–303) for a similar definition of cut-off points used in determining the stages of economic development.

29. Since GNP (log scale) is correlated 0.97 with the Economic Development Index, we would expect that stratification on the basis of GNP would reduce the correlation of economic development with inequality. Still, the strata are far from homogeneous on GNP, and some correlation should remain. It is worth noting that if agriculture is simply another indicator of the size of the surplus product, "controlling" the level of economic development should also control the relationship of agricultural with inequality. This is not the case. In the high GNP stratum, the correlations of the agriculture labor force and the Economic Development Index with inequality are 0.82 and −0.25 respectively; in the middle stratum they are 0.34 and 0.05, while in the low GNP group the correlations are 0.65 and −0.18. This systematic difference is, we believe, due to the effect of the powerlessness of the agricultural labor force (and the relationship of agriculture with the decision variables and our political index) rather than to its superiority to the Economic Development Index as an indicator of technology.

30. It is a mistake to think that it is always "harder" for a variable to explain variance when it is near the bottom of a list. The accounting power of some variables will appear only *after* the effects of other independent variables are removed. See Table 3, for example.

31. Further study of the relation of domestic market size, population size, and Foreign Trade within strata is needed to clarify this effect. See note 17.

32. Communist nations have a high percent of their labor force in agriculture (see Table 5) while having a remarkably low birth rate. See Tietze (1964: 119–125). Seven of the eight Communist nations are in the middle GNP range and one is in the lowest stratum. Control over the birth rate may help account for the strong association (0.93) in this stratum between Capital Formation and annual economic growth.

33. The standard error of the errors of prediction will equal the standard deviation of the dependent variable when the independent variables are uncorrelated with the dependent variable. Therefore, the *total* errors of prediction across strata will be larger than the total error of the three within-stratum predictions if the stratification procedure decreases the standard deviation of the dependent variable. The standard deviation of inequality is *higher* in the low GNP stratum than it is for all forty-four nations. More important, our comparisons of the mean errors in Table 6 are within-stratum, not the total across strata.

REFERENCES

ALKER, H. and B. RUSSETT (1966) "Indices for comparing inequality." Pp. 349–372 in R. Merrit and S. Rokkan, Eds., *Comparing Nations*. New Haven: Yale University Press.

ANDRZEJEWSKI, S. (1954) *Military Organization and Society*. London: Routledge & Kegan Paul.

BLALOCK, H. (1964) *Causal Inferences in Nonexperimental Research*. Chapel Hill: University of North Carolina Press.

BOTTENBERG, A. and J.A. WARD (1963) *Applied Multiple Linear Regression*. Technical Documentary Report, PRL-TDR-63-6. Washington, D.C.: Office of Technical Services, Department of Commerce.

BRETON, R. (1966) "Ethnic factors in predicting the shape of stratification systems." Department of Social Relations, Johns Hopkins University (mimeo.).

CUTRIGHT, P. (1967) "Income distribution: a cross-national analysis." *Social Forces:* 180–189.

DAHRENDORF, R. (1959) *Class and Class Conflict in Industrial Society*. Stanford: Stanford University Press.

DAVIS, K. (1949) *Human Society*. New York: Macmillan.

DAVIS, K. and W. MOORE (1945) "Some principles of stratification." *American Sociological Review* 10 (April): 242–249.

DEUTSCH, K. and B. RUSSETT (1963) "International trade and political independence." *The American Behavioral Scientist* 6 (March).

DEUTSCH, K., C. BLISS and A. ECKSTEIN (1962) "Population, sovereignty and the shape of foreign trade." *Economic Development and Cultural Change* 10 (July): 353–366.

EDWARDS, A. (1954) *Statistical Methods for the Behavioral Sciences*. New York: Holt, Rinehart & Winston.

KOLKO, G. (1962) *Wealth and Power in America*. New York: Frederick A. Praeger.

KRAVIS, I. (1960) "International differences in the distribution of income." *Review of Economics and Statistics* 42 (November): 408–416.

KUZNETS, S. (1963) "Quantitative aspects of the economic growth of nations: VIII. The distribution of income by size." *Economic Development and Cultural Change* 11, No. 2, Part II (January).

— (1962) "Quantitative aspects of the economic growth of nations: VII. The share and structure of consumption." *Economic Development and Cultural Change* 10 (January).

— (1960) "Quantitative aspects of the economic growth of nations: V. Capital formation proportions." *Economic Development and Cultural Change* 8 (July).

LENSKI, G. (1966) *Power and Privilege: A Theory of Stratification*. New York: McGraw-Hill.

MELMAN, S. (1966) *Our Depleted Society*. New York: Dell Publishing.

MILLS, C.W. (1956) *The Power Elite*. New York: Oxford University Press.

MORGAN, J. (1962) "The anatomy of income distribution." *Review of Economics and Statistics* 44 (August): 281–282.

MORGAN, J., et al. (1962) *Income and Wealth in the United States*. New York: McGraw-Hill.

ORSHANSKY, M. (1965) "Who's who among the poor." *Social Security Bulletin* 28 (July).

OSHIMA, H. (1962) "The international comparison of size distribution of family incomes with special reference to Asia." *Review of Economics and Statistics* 44 (November): 439–445.

ROMANINSKY, J. (1966) "Comparison of intersectorial and individual income inequality." Vanderbilt University (mimeo.).

RUSSETT, B. (1964) "Inequality and instability: the relation of land tenure to politics." *World Politics* 16 (April): 442–454.

RUSSETT, B., et al. (1954) *World Handbook of Political and Social Indicators.* New Haven: Yale University Press.
TIETZE, C. (1964) "The demographic significance of legal abortion in eastern Europe." *Demography* 1, No. 1: 119–125.
WALKER, H. and J. LEV (1953) *Statistical Inference.* New York: Henry Holt.
WINER, J. (1962) *Statistical Principles in Experimental Design.* New York: McGraw-Hill.

24 Political Structure, Economic Development, and National Social Security Programs

PHILLIPS CUTRIGHT

Comparative sociological studies of political systems in modern nations have, in recent years, experienced impressive theoretical development. Attention has been focused on the "functional prerequisites" for political democracies, the structural conditions generating political stability or instability in "democratic" states, and the value structures necessary for a democratic order.[1] A number of excellent studies of political stability in non-democratic nations exist, but when more than one nation is studied, the comparison is usually limited to somewhat similar underdeveloped nations. When comparisons between democratic and non-democratic nations are made, the number of observations (nations) is severely limited by the absence of scales and indexes relevant to the analytical variables guiding the analysis (see Simpson, 1964: 21-25).

Elsewhere the author has developed and tested a scale of the complexity of national political organization.[2] The development of similar scales that would increase the number of nations in comparative studies and serve to aid in the selection of a few nations to fit the requirements of special studies is clearly a desirable goal. One aspect of this article is the development of a scale that can be applied to nations throughout the world. It measures the development of national programs to provide populations with insurance against severe loss of income under stated conditions, that is, the general level of social security development in the nations of the world. Because such national programs are an output of government activity, the analytical value would seem to go beyond the concrete phenomena directly measured. The scale can be used as a yardstick against which governments with varying characteristics can be compared.[3] It may allow one to measure, for example, one aspect of

---

Author's Note: My thanks to E. Palmore for criticism and helpful suggestions.

Reprinted from *The American Journal of Sociology*, Volume 70, pages 537-548, by permission of the author and the publisher. Copyright © 1967 University of Chicago Press.

what democratic governments *do* that may distinguish them from non-democratic governments.[4]

In this paper we develop an index of the general level of social security in different nations that is a direct consequence of one kind of government activity (i.e., legislation or government order). We then analyze the relationship of this index to an index measuring the political representativeness of nations and to other indicators of economic and social development. The general purpose of the analysis is to assess the importance of representativeness in governmental organization to the social security and welfare of national populations. Our working hypothesis is that governments in nations whose political structures tend to allow for greater accessibility to the people of the governing elite will act to provide greater social security for their populations than that provided by governments whose rulers are less accessible to the demands of the population. The theoretical contribution of this analysis is toward an application of the construct of representativeness (or accessibility) to actual government activity.

Measuring National Social Security

Perhaps one of the more striking developments of the twentieth century has been the effort by national governments to protect that portion of the population that is, for one reason or another, not in the employed labor force. National social-insurance programs, initiated in Europe near the end of the nineteenth century, first dealt with the problem of income loss resulting from industrial work injury, a problem that was greatly intensified by the expansion of industrial activity. As urbanization and industrialization (and their social and political correlates) continued, social-insurance programs covering other types of risks—sickness, old age, unemployment—began to appear.

Although there exists some detailed information on the extent of coverage or the level of benefits provided by various national social-insurance schemes, these data are available for only a few nations. In a study that concentrated on the economic correlates of certain social-insurance programs, Henry Aaron was able to locate adequate detailed data on twenty-two nations—all economically well developed—and subjected these data to an intensive multiple-regression dummy variable analysis (see Aaron, 1963). These data on program coverage and benefit levels showed that the most powerful explanatory variables were (1) years of experience with the program (number of decades since its initiation) and (2) various indicators of national economic development. If one knows how long a nation has had certain programs and what its level of economic development is, then one can assess how the nation will rank in coverage and benefit levels relative to the remaining twenty-one nations in the sample. (The homogeneous economic and political character of the nations in Aaron's study should be noted. Correlations are often low within homogeneous groups; the present instance is an exception to this rule.) Aaron suggests that the relationships among his variables may not be the same in

Political Structure: Social Security Programs 541

less-developed nations; but the question is not whether the regression is the same but whether Aaron's detailed study can be applied to a slightly different type of analysis that will allow us to get around the problem of lack of detailed program data in many nations. If number of years' experience with a program is highly correlated with the total expenditures, benefit levels, and coverage of a program, then the number of years can be used as an indicator of the level of program development.

However, the lack of detailed and comparable data on social security programs is not the only stumbling block in the way of international comparisons. We have also to establish that what we call social security programs are conceptually related. The fact that custom and administrative usage have grouped different types of programs under a common label (social security) is not proof that these programs are interrelated and form a continuum along which nations may be placed in order from high to low social security development. The first task is to offer some evidence that we can talk about the social security development of nations because a definite pattern of program occurrence or non-occurrence exists among the nations of the world.

Patterns of Social Security Program Development

There are five major types of social security programs.[5] Of the seventy-six nations outside Africa[6] that had achieved independent political status by 1960, seventy-one had begun work-injury programs, fifty-eight had sickness and/or maternity programs, fifty-six had programs grouped under old-age, invalidism, and death, forty had some type of family allowance plan, and twenty-seven had unemployment-insurance programs. This frequency distribution does not, in itself, tell us that a nation with an unemployment program is necessarily more or less advanced toward a social-insurance goal than is a nation with only a work-injury program. There are several ways to approach this question, but perhaps the simplest is with the Guttman scale.[7] If several discrete items, in this case the five types of social-insurance and benefit programs, form a Guttman scale, we can say that the scale is measuring an underlying dimension along which each of the items may be placed in a known order, and that a given combination of items (i.e., social-insurance programs) represents a higher place along a continuum of social-insurance development than some alternative combination.

The five major types of social security programs do form a Guttman scale. A nation can have between zero and five programs, and we have six possible perfect-scale types with varying combinations of programs. Twenty-two nations in our sample are in the first perfect-scale type, having all five programs, while the second type contains thirteen nations lacking only unemployment insurance. It is interesting that seven of these thirteen nations were Soviet Russia and its satellites. A third perfect-scale type contains the twelve nations that had neither unemployment nor family allowances, but did have the three other programs. The five nations in the fourth scale type lack, in addition to unemployment and family-allowances programs, a program to provide for the aged, invalidism, and/or death. They have both work-injury and sickness programs. In the fifth scale type are six nations with work-injury programs only, and the final scale type contains five nations with no programs at all. Thus sixty-three of the seventy-six countries are in perfect-scale types. It is worth noting that, had we included African nations, the sixth scale type would have had many more nations, with a resulting increase in the coefficient of reproducibility (CR) to about .98. However, even without this group the CR is .966, considerably above the usually acceptable level of .90.

Because the items do form a Guttman scale, these scale types may be used to rank order the nations of the world according to the extent to which they have developed a social-insurance program. The scale does not necessarily tell us whether a nation in scale type 1 has a better or more comprehensive old-age program than a nation in scale type 2, but it does indicate that the general social security coverage of the population outside the employed labor force is better in scale type 1 than in scale type 2, 3, and so on.

A Cumulative Measure of the Years of Social-Insurance Program Experience

Because the programs form a Guttman scale, it is possible to apply a measure that distinguishes more than six levels of social security development. The measure is, simply, the years of experience with social-insurance programs for each of the seventy-six nations for the period 1934–60. This statistic is similar to that used by Aaron for well-developed nations, and from the above analysis it appears applicable to less-developed nations as well.

An index of a nation's social insurance program experience (SIPE) can be computed by totaling the number of years from 1934 through 1960 that the nation had a given type of program in operation. For each of the five programs, a score of from 0 to 27 is possible. A score of 27 on each program would yield a maximum SIPE score of 135.[8]

The following analysis concentrates on the relationship of SIPE scores to various aspects of national political and economic life. The final section focuses on a social-insurance completion index and relates scores on this index to political and economic levels and changes from 1928 to 1960.

SIPE scores are one possible index of the responsiveness of governments to the needs of the governed. A nation that lacks work-injury or old age insurance programs may or may not have the economic base capable of supporting such programs, but the extent to which governments initiate and improve insurance programs may reflect much more than the operation of an automatic and economically triggered mechanism.

Nevertheless, it is also the case that the ability of a government to begin a program is closely related to the nation's level of social and economic development. The SIPE scores of the seventy-six nations have been correlated with 1960 indexes of energy consumption, urbanization, literacy, and political representativeness (PRI),[9] and the full matrix of product-moment correlations is shown in Table 1.

TABLE 1

ZERO-ORDER CORRELATION MATRIX OF ENERGY CONSUMPTION, URBANIZATION, LITERACY, POLITICAL REPRESENTATIVENESS, AND YEARS OF SOCIAL-INSURANCE PROGRAM EXPERIENCE, 1960*

	Urbanization	Literacy	PRT	SIPE
Energy consumption	72	81	61	90
Urbanization		64	58	58
Literacy			76	83
PRI				74

* All variables except SIPE have been T-scored; $N = 76$.
Source Data for energy consumption, urbanization, and literacy are taken from the U.N. *Demographic Yearbook* and the U.N. *Statistical Yearbook*. The primary source for political data is the *Political Handbook of the World: Parliaments, Parties and Press* (New York: Harper & Bros. [for the Council on Foreign Relations], annual publication 1928-62).

The highest correlation is between energy consumption and SIPE. This correlation of .90 accounts by itself for 81 percent of the variation around the mean SIPE score. It is much higher than the correlation of energy consumption with PRI, literacy, or urbanization. Further, it is considerably higher than the zero-order relationship between literacy and SIPE. This indicates that the level of economic development has a powerful role in determining the level of social-insurance development, and that we must control for level of economic development as measured by energy consumption as well as for level of political development in any analysis of the amount of change in social-insurance programs from the 1930s through the early 1960s.

The high correlations between social security development and energy consumption or political representativeness do not mean, however, that urbanization and the literacy level of the population are not also important correlates of social security development. Quite the opposite is true. In general, nations with high levels of SIPE also have high literacy rates and tend to be highly urbanized. Nations with low levels of urbanization or literacy have less-developed social security programs as well as lower levels of energy consumption and political representativeness.

Although this analysis centers on the relationship of economic development and PRI, it should not be assumed that a change in one or both of these variables alone would be sufficient (although it might be necessary) to produce changes in social security. Changes in the levels of literacy and urbanization of the population usually occur concomitantly with changes in PRI or energy consumption. It would appear that the probability of an increase in the level of social-insurance development is greatest when all four variables are rising. This view is compatible with the proposition that changes in major institutional areas of the society do not proceed far without reacting on each other as well as on lesser aspects of life. Institutions are interdependent. The matrix of correlations is evidence in support of this hypothesis—at the level of national social systems.

In the following section we test the hypothesis that the levels of economic development and PRI will have independent and joint effects on SIPE. Economic development was selected because of its high correlation with SIPE and political development because it is central to analysis.

Analysis of National Differences in Years of Social-Insurance Program Experience

Table 2 presents the mean SIPE scores for nations at five levels of economic development—as measured by energy consumption—and four levels of political development in 1930. The mean social-insurance experience of these nations and the number of nations is shown.

TABLE 2

MEAN YEARS OF SOCIAL-INSURANCE PROGRAM EXPERIENCE BY MEAN 1930-60 ENERGY CONSUMPTION AND 1930 LEVEL OF POLITICAL REPRESENTATIVENESS*

MEAN ENERGY CONSUMPTION 1930-60	1930 PRI†				
	Dependent Nations	Below Mean	Above Mean	Highest Nations	Row Mean
I.............	99 (1)	101 (2)	114 (4)	116 (14)	114 (21)
II............	25 (3)	93 (4)	100 (5)	102 (3)	83 (15)
III...........	36 (1)	88 (4)	62 (5)	54 (2)	67 (12)
IV...........	30 (8)	44 (9)	54 (1)	....	39 (18)
V............	18 (5)	7 (4)	63 (1)	....	18 (10)
Column mean..	30 (18)	59 (23)	86 (16)	107 (19)	70

* Nations are placed into energy consumption levels according to their *T*-score. Groups I and II are above the mean of 50; Groups III, IV, and V are below the mean. Groups I and V contain nations that were more than 1 standard deviation from the mean.
† Number in parentheses = *N*.

In the upper left-hand cell is a single nation with 99 cumulative years of program experience and immediately below it are three nations with a mean of 25 years' experience. (The reader may prefer to collapse cells having only one case with adjacent cells before comparing individual cells with column means.) The mean SIPE scores associated with each level of economic development are in the "row mean" column. The twenty-one nations with the highest level of economic development had an average of 114 years of cumulative social-insurance program experience from 1934 through 1960. Nations in the second highest group had an average of eighty-three years' experience while the ten nations at the lowest level had an average of only eighteen years' experience. The same pattern of decreasing length of program experience is found within each column. We may conclude that the level of economic development is related to SIPE; statistical control for political development does not remove the positive association between the two.

The mean SIPE scores associated with each level of 1930 PRI are in the bottom row of Table 2. The scores show a steady gain with increasing PRI levels. The eighteen nations with dependent political status in 1930 have a mean score of thirty years compared to 107 years for the nineteen nations with the highest PRI scores. This pattern of larger SIPE scores with higher PRI levels holds at the first, second, and fourth levels of economic development. The third level does not fit the general pattern—this "deviant" row may explain why the correlation between PRI and SIPE was "only" 74—and the association in the lowest economic level is also of dubious strength.

Controlling first for one and then for the other variable, then, we see that each is related to the SIPE scores. We should note that the ten nations at the lowest level of economic development have considerably lower SIPE scores than the nations at the highest level of development. For these nations, it is level of economic development rather than level of political development that determines the level of social-insurance program experience. In terms of causal sequence, it appears that before positive change in political structure can bring about positive change in social-insurance program development, a nation must have experienced some economic growth.

Table 2 supports our working hypothesis. In general, governments in nations with more representative political structures have provided greater social security coverage to their populations. Among self-governing nations there is a nearly uniform increase in government social security activities from one level of representativeness to the next. However, nations with the highest PRI scores—those we would normally call "democratic"—do not really differ qualitatively from those nations of parallel economic development that are in the next lowest PRI group. This finding will be discussed at the conclusion of this paper.

In the next section the idea that changes in political structure are associated with changes in years of social-insurance experience will be tested.

Changes in Years of Social-Insurance Program Experience and Changes in PRI

Table 3 shows the relationship between changes in political representativeness and changes in SIPE. Since the amount of change in PRI is strongly associated with initial level of PRI (as seen in the disproportionately high gains made by the initially lowest PRI group), it is important to control for 1930 PRI level;

level of economic development is not controlled. Nations are ranked in each column according to the size of their gain or loss in political representativeness between 1930 and 1960. Reading down the columns, a near-perfect correlation can be seen between changes in PRI and changes in SIPE. Even within the initially highest PRI group, the twelve nations whose political structure

TABLE 3

Mean Change in Social-Insurance Program Experience, 1934–60, and Size of Change in Political Representativeness Index, 1930–60*

| Ranked PRI Change Interval | 1930 PRI ||||||||||||
| | Dependent (N = 18) ||| Below Mean† (N = 20) ||| Above Mean† (N = 15) ||| Highest† (N = 17) |||
	PRI Gain	N	SIPE Gain	PRI Gain	N	SIPE Gain	PRI Gain	N	SIPE Gain	PRI Gain	N	SIPE Gain
Largest	23	3	63	13	4	97	7	6	114	0	12	121
Second	16	6	31	5	7	56	3	3	70	0	3‡	81
Third	11	4	22	3	3	20	−2	3	66	−8	2	76
Fourth	6	5	14	0	6	49	−5	3	65	§	§	§

* Controlled for PRI.
† Soviet satellites (Albania, Bulgaria, Hungary, Poland, Romania, and Czechoslovakia) are omitted from this table as scoring of PRI changes excluded those caused by external domination. They are included in all other tables.
‡ These three nations began and ended the period with the highest PRI scores, but were unstable during the period.
§ No. cases.

remained perfectly stable throughout the period had an average gain of 121 years of experience; the three that ended at the same level as they began but experienced instability in between (Japan, Uruguay, and Costa Rica) had an average increase of eighty-one; and the two that declined in political representativeness (Canada and Colombia) had a gain of only seventy-six years.

We might note that SIPE gains also are strongly associated with initial PRI level. The largest gains in social insurance are found in nations that began the time period with a maximum political-representativeness score. Reading across the rows in Table 3, within each PRI-change interval there is a positive association (slightly reversed in only one case) between 1930 PRI level and SIPE gains.

A Non-Cumulative Measure of Social-Insurance Development

An alternative measure of social-insurance development in a nation is, for some purposes, more satisfactory. Instead of using a cumulative measure of years of program experience, we can examine the political situation surrounding major changes in a nation's social-insurance programs (i.e., each time a new program is launched). An index can then be developed to measure the extent to which a nation is moving toward social-insurance program completion (SIPC). Completion is used here to mean that a nation has begun to tackle the needs associated with the five basic types of social security programs, and not to refer to the extent of coverage of the population by any or all programs. Some examples of how the SIPC index is constructed follow.

If a nation had three programs in 1928, it can introduce only two additional programs. Assume that such a country experiences a positive political change in 1932 and in 1934 adds one program. Between 1932 and 1934 no political changes occur. A score of 50 (i.e., 50 percent of the total change possible in social-insurance program coverage) is awarded to that specific 1932 political change. If, however, the nation experiences a positive change in 1932 and a negative change in 1933 and adds a social-insurance program in 1934, the positive 1932 political change receives a score of zero, and the negative 1933 change a score of 50. The social-insurance-program completion index is, therefore, a measure of the amount of social-insurance change associated with each change in PRI.[10] The mean SIPC change per nation is calculated in the following manner. For positive and negative PRI changes (computed separately), if a nation has more than one change, the sum of the SIPC index scores associated with these changes is divided by the number of changes. Next, the average SIPC scores for each nation are summed and divided by the number of nations to get the mean SIPC change per nation. For nations with no PRI changes, the mean SIPC change per nation is merely the sum of the nations' SIPC scores divided by the number of nations.

It was suggested earlier that social-insurance programs may represent a measure of the responsiveness of government to the social needs of the population. If so, we would expect not only that social-insurance development would be associated with a *high level* of political representativeness but also that a *positive change* in political representativeness would be *followed* by an increase in social-insurance program coverage. The gain in SIPC index should be larger in association with positive political changes than with negative political changes.

Table 4 presents the results of an analysis of SIPC changes associated with political changes of both types. In the time covered, a total of ninety-eight positive political changes and an average increase in SIPC of twenty-two are found. In the same period, there were seventy negative changes with an increase in SIPC of eleven per negative change; a net gain of eleven points is associated with each positive change.

A slightly different statistic which allows us to consider SIPC changes in nations experiencing *no* political change between 1928 and 1960 is the mean SIPC change per nation. Table 4 shows that fifty-six nations experienced a positive political change, forty-one had negative changes, and sixteen experienced no change. A net advantage of nearly twenty points per nation goes to countries with positive rather than negative changes, but a still larger

SIPC increase of eighty-seven is found among nations that had no political change at all. These stable nations are nearly all at the highest level of economic and political development, a condition favorable to maximum SIPC changes.

TABLE 4

SIPC INDEX GAINS ASSOCIATED WITH POSITIVE, NEGATIVE, AND NO CHANGES IN PRI

Direction of PRI Change	Mean SIPC Change* per PRI Change	Mean SIPC Change per Nation
Positive.........	22 (98)	38 (56)
Negative.........	11 (70)	20 (41)
No change	Not applicable	87 (16)

* Numbers in parentheses are the number of PRI changes and the number of nations.

Table 5 controls for the level of economic development and shows the amount of social-insurance program-completion change associated in any economic level with either positive or negative political changes or with stable political systems.

At the highest level of energy consumption there were five nations that experienced positive political changes with an average social-insurance index increase of eighty, while seven nations that experienced negative changes had an increase of only seventeen per nation. The thirteen nations with completely stable political structures had an increase of ninety-two. At the second level of energy consumption there is no difference in the amount of social-insurance program-coverage gains between countries with positive or negative change, but the two nations (Finland and Italy) with stable PRI experience have a gain of seventy-five. The third level of economic development again shows the expected pattern with a score of forty-seven associated with positive political change compared to a score of twenty-three associated with negative change. In like fashion, the fourth energy-consumption level reveals an increase of thirty-nine associated with positive change and only eleven with negative change, while the single nation with stable government (Saudi Arabia) had an increase of forty. At the lowest level of development, the ten nations with positive increases had an average of only seven in social-insurance program completion. There were very few cases of negative change and no cases of stable governments in this category. Part of the reason for the small number of negative changes is that nations at this level of economic development have minimal PRI scores to begin with and thus have little room to decrease.

If we look down the columns in Table 5, we see some irregularities in the pattern associated with positive and negative PRI changes—there is not a perfectly steady decline in the size of the score from one energy-consumption level to the next.[11]

TABLE 5

SIPC INDEX GAINS PER NATION ASSOCIATED WITH POSITIVE, NEGATIVE, AND NO CHANGES IN PRI*

Energy Consumption Level and Type of Political Change	Mean SIPC Index Change per Nation Following Each PRI Change			No. of Nations	Net No. of Nations
Level I:					
Positive............	80	....	....	5	8
Negative...........	....	17	....	7	
No PRI change......	....	....	92	13	13
Level II:					
Positive............	35	....	....	13	13
Negative...........	....	35	....	9	
No PRI change......	....	....	75	2	2
Level III:†					
Positive............	47	....	....	10	11
Negative...........	....	23	....	8	
Level IV:					
Positive............	39	....	....	18	18
Negative...........	....	11	....	17‡	
No PRI change......	....	....	40	1	1
Level V:†					
Positive............	7	....	....	10	10
Negative...........	....	....	....	(4)§	

* Level of energy consumption controlled.
† Levels III and V had no nations without at least one PRI change between 1928 and 1960.
‡ Includes four cases from lowest level.
§ Combined with negative group in Level IV.

Regardless of the method used, the conclusion seems clear enough: Nations at very high levels of economic development are able to take advantage of stable government or positive political change, and they are likely to move toward completing the normal pattern of social-insurance programs. Social security growth is less likely to follow a negative PRI change than a positive change at *any* level of economic development. Again it is seen that nations with the lowest level of economic development are not introducing social insurance programs even when they have a positive PRI change. On the one hand, this reinforces the earlier conclusion that for these nations a rise in the level of the economy must precede the introduction of social-insurance programs. On the other hand, a positive change in political representativeness will tend to induce economically more-developed nations to introduce new social security programs.

Discussion

An index (SIPE) measuring the general level of social security protection legislated or otherwise directed by the national government was developed. The SIPE index was closely related (.90) to the level of economic development, literacy (.83), and to a lesser extent (.58) urbanization. The .74 correlation of the SIPE index with the Political Representativeness Index (PRI) was found, after further analysis, to be related to variation in the SIPE index when the level of economic development was controlled.

The effect of different levels of political representativeness on the development of national social security programs varied with the level of economic development enjoyed by the nation. In nations with very low economic development, the push for social security development has, in most cases, yet to begin, despite the presence in this group of several different levels of political representativeness. This finding was interpreted in terms of the necessity of certain technological and bureaucratic prerequisites for successful introduction of social-insurance schemes. However, nations that have this capability (Levels I through IV) do not always exercise it. Within the mid-range of economic development (III and IV), the level of PRI was not powerfully related to SIPE. Nations in the upper two economic-development strata not only had high SIPE scores but within each stratum SIPE was positively related to PRI. In general, the political condition that was most strongly related to low levels of social security development was colonial or quasicolonial status. With few exceptions (especially that of Iceland) little was done by occupying powers to institute social security programs. The difference between being politically dependent and being politically self-governing appears (Table 2) critical to the early development of social security programs. Once political independence is achieved, the degree to which the national government becomes more and more representative is also related to how rapidly the government acts to introduce national social security programs. This is most clearly demonstrated at the higher levels of economic development. In a separate analysis that controlled for the 1930 PRI level and ranked the 1930–60 PRI change against 1934–60 gains in SIPE, the size of PRI changes was positively related to SIPE gains.

A second index (SIPC) of government activity in the social security field was devised. A score was computed that measured the degree to which any new program instituted by a nation moved that nation closer to complete program coverage. Analysis of these scores revealed that social-insurance completion followed more upon positive political changes than upon negative political changes, whatever the level of economic development. Also, the few nations that enjoyed stable political structures had larger social security completion scores than did unstable nations.

If we are willing to speak of nations with the highest PRI scores as being democratic and of nations with lower scores as something less than democratic, we can engage the question of whether people living in a democracy enjoy levels of social security protection that are not provided to populations in other political systems. The analysis indicated that only a small difference could be found between nations at the very highest PRI level and a second group of nations above the mean on PRI. Further, at the upper levels of economic development even nations below the mean on PRI had SIPE scores close to those of the democratic nations.

The evidence presented in this paper supports the idea that national political, economic, and social systems are interdependent. Changes in the complexity of organization in one sphere are followed by changes in organization in other areas. The specific activities that engage the attention of national governments are not independent of the general level of development. Quite the contrary is true. In spite of very great differences among nations in ideological orientation as well as in type of political organization, we found that actual activities of government in the social security field were strongly related to the complexity of social organization in economic, social, and political institutions. Nations with high levels of economic development but with less than "perfect" (i.e., democratic) political systems had government activities highly similar to those undertaken by democratic governments. Further comparative studies of government activities in other areas of social life will aid in understanding this conclusion. One might see the activities of government as intimately related to the problem of maintaining motivation and order in societies as well as being a response to the democratically organized demands of the population. A government can act without being told what to do. The scholar operating within a democratic context (and especially that of the United States) may tend to view government activities as being dependent upon the demands of secondary groups. A major but tentative conclusion that can be drawn from this study of government activity is that it need not await the petition of secondary groups. The role (or even the existence) of politically relevant secondary groups in guiding government decisions in many of the nations included in this study is modest.

In many nations we would conclude that the introduction of social security measures is a response by government to changes in the economic and social order that is not strongly affected by some degree of departure from ideal democratic organizational forms. Similar levels of social security coverage are found in nations whose governments are thought to act in response to the popular will as occur in nations whose governments are thought to act with less regard to public demands. It appears that the level of social security in a nation is a response to deeper strains affecting the organization of society. Governments may ignore human needs, but there are rather tight limits on the extent to which they may ignore organizational requirements.

APPENDIX A.
YEARS OF SOCIAL-INSURANCE PROGRAM EXPERIENCE, 1934–60, BY NATION

Nation	Years	Nation	Years
Afghanistan	15	Japan	88
Albania	53	Jordan	6
Argentina	75	Laos	0
Australia	118	Lebanon	36
Austria	121	Luxembourg	122
Belgium	135	Malaya	37
Bolivia	54	Mexico	65
Brazil	101	Mongolia	0
Bulgaria	100	Nepal	0
Burma	34	Netherlands	130
Cambodia	27	New Zealand	131
Canada	106	Nicaragua	39
Ceylon	52	Norway	121
Chile	129	Pakistan	27
China	37	Panama	67
Colombia	46	Paraguay	63
Costa Rica	62	Peru	77
Cuba	81	Philippines	41
Czechoslovakia	97	Poland	95
Denmark	117	Portugal	100
Dominican Republic	55	Romania	98
Ecuador	86	Russia	98
Finland	96	Salvador	39
France	135	Saudi Arabia	28
Germany	115	South Korea	0
Great Britain	124	Spain	131
Greece	100	Sweden	122
Guatemala	30	Switzerland	104
Haiti	10	Syria	29
Honduras	9	Thailand	5
Hungary	104	Turkey	44
Iceland	99	United States	95
India	49	Uruguay	92
Indonesia	26	Venezuela	48
Iran	40	Vietnam	31
Iraq	40	Yemen	0
Ireland	125	Yugoslavia	115
Israel	45		
Italy	133		

APPENDIX B.
POLITICAL STRUCTURE POINT SYSTEM

The index used to measure differences among national political structures is computed according to a point system. Parliament and the executive branch of government are scored as follows.

A. Parliament scoring

2 points if the largest party has less than 70 percent of the seats in the lower or only chamber and achieved the seats through elections.

$1\frac{1}{2}$ points if the largest party has 70 percent or more but the second party has at least 20 percent.

1 point if the largest party has 70 percent or more and the second party has less than 20 percent.

$\frac{1}{2}$ point if the largest grouping in parliament is over 70 percent with the second less than 20 *and* they do not represent parties selected by election but are appointed to represent trade, commerce, ethnic, or other interests. Includes Fascist and Communist party systems.

No points if there is no parliament, if a former parliament is dissolved during year by coup or revolt, if it is a "constituent assembly," or if the nation still has colonial status.

B. Executive scoring

$1\frac{1}{2}$ points for each year under a chief executive who was selected by a party or parliament under conditions meeting the 70 and 20 percent rule.

$1\frac{1}{2}$ points if the chief executive is elected directly by the people in a competitive election held at the usual time, regardless of the 70–20 rule.

1 point when the chief executive is selected by a party that is a sustaining force (has existed for 5 years as a party in parliament), but the party composition (is not a multiparty system) violates the 70–20 rule.

1 point when the executive is selected by a party in a system that fails to observe the usual election time or goes outside the rules for having an election or has a non-competitive election or fails the 70 percent rule.

$\frac{1}{2}$ point for junta, clique, non-party selection of leaders, or when existing leaders remain in power beyond the regular time.

No points to independent nations with hereditary rulers having chief executive power.

No points to nations with dependent colonial status or occupied by a foreign power.

In order to maintain a distinction between dependent and independent nations, $\frac{1}{2}$ point was added to the over-all raw PRI score of each independent nation, while colonial or dependent nations received a score of zero.

It was possible for a nation to achieve from 0 to 4 points each year. A mean yearly PRI score was computed for each of the following four time periods: 1928–34; 1935–44; 1945–54; 1955–61, and a total of 304 scores (four for each of the seventy-six nations) was amassed and *T*-scored. The four distributions were T-scored separately as well. (A simple technique for computing the T-score is given in Edwards [1954]. For a single variable, T-scoring the raw data will yield a distribution with a mean of 50 and a standard deviation of 10.)

NOTES

1. Kornhauser (1959) in particular gives a detailed discussion of the concept of "representativeness" and democratic pluralism. Alford (1963) examines longitudinal data bearing on the relations between political parties and the social structure of five democracies. Lipset (1964) develops a framework for analyzing the value patterns that support democratic government.

2. See Cutright (1963: 253-264). That study also argues the case for scales rather than crude qualitative categories in international studies. See Appendix B for a description of the revised political representativeness index used in this study.

3. An inventory of municipal services in Bristol, England, and Seattle, Washington, revealed remarkable similarities "even in two cities where the governmental power is based on different philosophies. In Bristol the Labor (socialist) party holds political dominance with its leaders in almost all key legislative positions. In Seattle, a conservative local government rules (Republican). Yet each city has almost the same amount of municipal ownerships and control" (see Form and York, 1960: 501).

4. There has been relatively little systematic work on the consequences for national populations of living under more or less representative governments. Studies of this sort often compare only totalitarian and democratic governments, highlighting the impact of government activity on the expression of individual freedoms.

Unfortunately, an inventory of the activities of national governments, or even a conceptual scheme to aid in their classification, is not at hand. Comparative studies of the outputs of national governments are limited by the lack of scales of those activities, and relatively little attention has been given to classification of the activities. Available indicators of government activities are not, however, being fully exploited. Thus, studies using measures of education, health, or demographic conditions do not examine these phenomena as though they were related to government activity. For example, we are more likely to see a certain level of education as a requisite for democratic government than to view government activity as vital for the development of national education levels.

5. All data pertaining to social security programs are taken from U.S. Department of Health, Education, and Welfare, Social Security Administration (1961). Discussion of the characteristics of each type of program can be found in that document.

6. This part of the analysis is based on research initially focused on the correlates of political development, which for statistical reasons omitted all African nations in order to avoid spuriously high correlations. The seventy-six nations are listed in Appendix A.

7. See Stouffer et al. (1950: 60-90). For a more recent explication of Guttman scaling see Edwards (1957: 172-198).

8. SIPE scores for each of the seventy-six nations are shown in Appendix A. Data on political structure are available for as early as 1928, and that time is used

in analyzing the introduction of new social-insurance programs later in this paper. The base year for computing the years of program experience is 1934 rather than 1928, however. This is the product of error, not design. However, if 1928 had been used, there would be little difference beyond adding five points to the range of the scale; the relationships with other variables would remain the same.

9. See Appendix B.

10. One feature of the SIPC index that should be considered in future work is the correlation between economic and political development and the size of the score awarded to a single program change. Since nations at high development levels will also be more likely to have had several programs by 1928, they will also receive "extra" credit when they introduce their next program. Whether it is more difficult for a nation to launch its first than its last program is not the issue here. Comparison of the results using this index as opposed to another is a matter for investigation rather than for debate. Although it might be expected that larger scores would be associated with the economically and politically more-developed nations, this does not justify assuming that high scores should be associated with positive rather than with negative political changes. Controls for economic-development levels will also be introduced to reduce the spurious association between large scores and high economic-development scores.

11. An alternative method of computing SIPC change per political change rather than per nation provides a somewhat more consistent table when broken down in the same way as Table 5. At each level of energy consumption the average SIPC index change following each PRI positive change is larger than for negative PRI changes. The pattern of decline in SIPC change associated with decreasing energy consumption is also consistent for both positive and negative PRI change.

REFERENCES

AARON, H. (1963) Social Security in an Expanding Economy. Ph.D. dissertation, Harvard University.

ALFORD, R.R. (1963) *Party and Society: The Anglo-American Democracies.* Chicago: Rand McNally.

CUTRIGHT, P. (1963) "National political development: measurement and analysis." *American Sociological Review* 28 (April): 253–264.

EDWARDS, A. (1957) *Techniques of Attitude Scale Construction.* New York: Appleton-Century-Crofts.

— (1954) *Statistical Methods for the Behavioral Sciences.* New York: Holt, Rinehart & Winston.

FORM, W.H. and D. YORK (1960) *Industry, Labor and Community.* New York: Harper.

KORNHAUSER, W. (1959) *The Politics of Mass Society.* New York: Free Press.

LIPSET, S.M. (1964) "Democracy and the social system." In H. Eckstein, Ed., *Internal War: Problems and Approaches.* New York: Free Press.

SIMPSON, D. (1964) "The congruence of political, social and economic development." *International Development Review* 6 (June): 21–25.

STOUFFER, S.A., et al. (1950) *Measurement and Prediction.* Princeton: Princeton University Press.

U.S. Department of Health, Education and Welfare, Social Security Administration (1961) *Social Security Programs throughout the World, 1961.* Washington, D.C.: Government Printing Office.

SELECTIVE BIBLIOGRAPHY

I. GENERAL AND THEORETICAL WORKS

ALKER, H.R. (1966) "The comparison of aggregate political and social data: potentialities and problems." *Social Science Information:* 63–80.
— (1966) "The long road to international relations theory: problems of statistical nonadditivity." *World Politics:* 623–655.
ALMOND, G.A. (1965) "A developmental approach to political systems." *World Politics:* 183–215.
ALMOND, G.A. and G.B. POWELL (1966) *Comparative Politics: A Developmental Approach.* Boston: Little, Brown.
BERKOWITZ, L. (1962) *Aggression: A Social Psychological Analysis.* New York: McGraw-Hill.
BOULDING, K.E. (1962) *Conflict and Defense: A General Theory.* New York: Harper & Row.
BUCKLEY, W., Ed. (1968) *Modern Systems Research for the Behavioral Scientist.* Chicago: Aldine.
BUSS, A.H. (1961) *The Psychology of Aggression.* New York: John Wiley.
CANTRIL, H. (1941) *The Psychology of Social Movements.* New York: John Wiley.
CNUDDE, C.F. and D.E. NEUBAUER, Eds. (1969) *Empirical Democratic Theory.* Chicago: Markham.
COSER, L.A. (1956) *The Functions of Social Conflict.* New York: Free Press.
DEUTSCH, K.W. (1963) *The Nerves of Government.* New York: Free Press.
— (1960) "Toward an inventory of basic trends and patterns in comparative and international politics." *American Political Science Review:* 34–57.
DEUTSCH, K.W. and W.J. FOLTZ, Eds. (1966) *Nation-Building.* New York: Atherton.
EASTON, D. (1965) *A Systems Analysis of Political Life.* New York: John Wiley.
ECKSTEIN, H. (1969) "Authority relations and governmental performance: a theoretical framework." *Comparative Political Studies* 2: 269–325.
FARRELL, R.B., Ed. (1968) *Approaches to Comparative and International Relations.* Evanston: Northwestern University Press.
GALTUNG, J. (1964) "A structural theory of aggression." *Journal of Peace Research:* 116–118.
GURR, T.R. (1968) "Psychological factors in civil violence." *World Politics:* 245–278.
— (1970) *Why Men Rebel.* Princeton: Princeton University Press.
HAGEN, E. (1962) *On the Theory of Social Change.* Homewood, Ill.: Dorsey.
HIRSCHMAN, A.O. (1958) *The Strategy of Economic Development.* New Haven: Yale University Press.
HOLT, R.T. and J.E. TURNER (1966) *The Political Basis of Economic Development.* Princeton: Van Nostrand.

HUNTINGTON, S.P. (1968) *Political Order in Changing Societies.* New Haven: Yale University Press.
KALLEBERG, A.L. (1966) "The logic of comparison: a methodological note on the comparative study of political systems." *World Politics:* 69–82.
KAPLAN, M.A. (1969) *Macropolitics.* Chicago: Aldine.
—, Ed. (1968) *New Approaches to International Politics.* New York: St. Martin's Press.
— (1957) *System and Process in International Politics.* New York: John Wiley.
KNORR, K. and S. VERBA, Eds. (1961) *The International System: Theoretical Essays.* Princeton: Princeton University Press.
KORNHAUSER, W. (1959) *The Politics of Mass Society.* New York: Free Press.
LERNER, D. (1958) *The Passing of Traditional Society.* New York: Free Press.
LIPSET, S.M. (1960) *Political Man.* Garden City: Doubleday.
MCPHEE, W.N. (1963) *Formal Theories of Mass Behavior.* New York: Free Press.
MERRITT, RICHARD L. and STEIN ROKKAN, Eds. (1966) *Comparing Nations.* New Haven: Yale University Press.
MIDLARSKY, M. and R. TANTER (1967) "Toward a theory of political instability in Latin America." *Journal of Peace Research:* 209–227.
MILLIKEN, M.F. and D.L.M. BLACKMER, Eds. (1961) *The Emerging Nations.* Boston: Little, Brown.
MILNOR, A.J. (1969) *Elections and Political Stability.* Boston: Little, Brown.
MUELLER, J.E., Ed. (1969) *Approaches to Measurement in International Relations.* New York: Appleton-Century-Crofts.
NAROLL, R. (1965) "Galton's problem: the logic of cross-cultural research." *Social Research:* 428–451.
NEEDLER, M.C. (1968) *Political Development in Latin America: Instability, Violence, and Evolutionary Change.* New York: Random House.
NETTL, J.P. (1966) *Political Mobilization.* New York: Basic Books.
NIEBURG, H.L. (1969) *Political Violence.* New York: St. Martin's Press.
NILSON, S.S. (1967) "Measurement and models in the study of stability." *World Politics:* 1–30.
OLSON, M. (1965) *The Logic of Collective Action.* Cambridge: Harvard University Press.
PRZEWORSKI, A. and H. TEUNE (1966–67) "Equivalence in cross-national research." *Public Opinion Quarterly:* 551–568.
PYE, L.W. (1966) *Aspects of Political Development.* Boston: Little, Brown.
RETZLAFF, R.H. (1965) "The use of aggregate data in comparative political analysis." *Journal of Politics:* 797–817.
RIDKER, R.G. (1962) "Discontent and economic growth." *Economic Development and Cultural Change:* 1–15.
ROSENAU, J.N., Ed. (1969) *Linkage Politics.* New York: Free Press.
RUMMEL, R.J. (1965) "A field theory of social action and of political conflict within nations." *General Systems Yearbook:* 10.
RUSTOW, D.A. (1967) *A World of Nations: Problems of Political Modernization.* Washington: Brookings Institution.
SCHELLING, T.C. (1960) *The Strategy of Conflict.* Cambridge: Harvard University Press.
SHELDON, E.B. and W.E. MOORE, Eds. (1968) *Indicators of Social Change.* New York: Russell Sage Foundation.

SHERIF, M. and C.W. SHERIF, Eds. (1969) *Interdisciplinary Relationships in the Social Sciences.* Chicago: Aldine.
SINGER, J.D., Ed. (1968) *Quantitative International Politics: Insights and Evidence.* New York: Free Press.
SJOBERG, G. (1955) "The comparative method in the social sciences." *Philosophy of Science:* 106–117.
SOROKIN, P. (1937) *Social and Cultural Dynamics.* New York: American Book.
WISEMAN, H.V. (1966) *Political Systems.* New York: Frederick A. Praeger.

II. METHODOLOGICAL WORKS

ALKER, H.R. (1966) "Causal inference and political analysis." Pp. 3–43 in Bernd, J.L., Ed., *Mathematical Applications in Political Science.* Vol. 2. Dallas: Southern Methodist University Press.
— (1965) *Mathematics and Politics.* New York: Macmillan.
ANDERSON, T.W. (1958) *Introduction to Multivariate Statistical Analysis.* New York: John Wiley.
ANDO, A., F.M. FISHER and H.A. SIMON (1963) *Essays on the Structure of Social Science Models.* Cambridge: MIT Press.
BERND, J.L., Ed. (1964, 1965, 1967) *Mathematical Applications in Political Science.* Vol. 1 and 2. Dallas: Southern Methodist University Press. Vol. 3, Charlottesville: University of Virginia Press.
BLALOCK, H. (1967) "Causal inference, closed populations and measures of association." *American Political Science Review:* 130–136.
— (1964) *Causal Inferences in Nonexperimental Research.* Chapel Hill: University of North Carolina Press.
— (1963) "Making causal inferences for unmeasured variables from correlations among indicators." *American Journal of Sociology:* 53–62.
— (1969) *Theory Construction.* Englewood Cliffs: Prentice-Hall.
BLALOCK, H. and A.B. BLALOCK, Eds. (1968) *Methodology in Social Research.* New York: McGraw-Hill.
BORGATTA, E.F., Ed. (1969) *Sociological Methodology.* San Francisco: Jossey-Bass.
BORKO, H., Ed. (1962) *Computer Applications in the Behavioral Sciences.* Englewood Cliffs: Prentice-Hall.
BOUDON, R. (1965) "A method of linear causal analysis: dependency analysis." *American Sociological Review:* 365–374.
CAMPBELL, D.T. and D.W. FISKE (1959) "Convergent and discriminant validation by the multitrait-multimethod matrix." *Psychological Bulletin:* 81–105.
CAMPBELL, D.T. and J.C. STANLEY (1966) *Experimental and Quasi-Experimental Designs for Research.* Chicago: Rand McNally.
CARROLL, J.B. (1957) "Biquartimin criterion for rotation to oblique simple structure in factor analysis." *Science:* 1114–1115.
CATTELL, R. (1952) *Factor Analysis.* New York: Harper.
CHRIST, C.F. (1966) *Econometric Models and Methods.* New York: John Wiley.
COLEMAN, J.S. (1964) *Introduction to Mathematical Sociology.* New York: Free Press.
COOMBS, C.H. (1964) *A Theory of Data.* New York: John Wiley.
DUNCAN, O.D. (1966) "Path analysis: sociological examples." *American Journal of Sociology:* 1–16.

EDWARDS, A. (1957) *Techniques of Attitude Scale Construction.* New York: Appleton-Century-Crofts.
EZEKIEL, M. and K.A. FOX (1959) *Methods of Correlation and Regression Analysis.* 3rd ed. New York: John Wiley.
FARRAR, D.E. and R.R. GLAUBER (1967) "Multicollinearity in regression analysis: the problem revisited." *Review of Economics and Statistics:* 92–107.
FISHER, F.M. (1966) *The Identification Problem in Econometrics.* New York: McGraw-Hill.
FORBES, H.D. and E.R. TUFTE (1968) "A note of caution in causal modelling." *American Political Science Review:* 1258–1264.
FRANK, R.E. (1966) "Uses of transformations." *Journal of Marketing Research:* 247–253.
GURR, T.R. (1966) *New Error-Compensated Measures for Comparing Nations.* Princeton: Princeton University Center of International Studies.
GUTTMAN, L. (1950) "The basis for scalogram analysis." In Stouffer, S.A. et al., Eds., *Studies in Social Psychology in World War II, Measurement and Prediction.* Vol. IV. Princeton: Princeton University Press.
HAGGARD, E.A. (1958) *Intraclass Correlation and the Analysis of Variance.* New York: Dryden Press.
HARMON, HARRY H. (1960) *Modern Factor Analysis.* Chicago: University of Chicago Press.
HARRIS, E.W., Ed. (1963) *Problems in Measuring Change.* Madison: University of Wisconsin Press.
HOLT, R.T. and J.E. TURNER, Eds. (1970) *The Methodology of Comparative Research.* New York: Free Press.
JOHNSTON, J. (1963) *Econometric Methods.* New York: McGraw-Hill.
KEMPTHORNE, O. et al. (1954) *Statistics and Mathematics in Biology.* Ames: Iowa State College Press.
KENDALL, M.G. (1962) *Rank Correlation Methods.* 3rd ed. New York: Hafner.
LAWLEY, D.N. and A.E. MAXWELL (1963) *Factor Analysis as a Statistical Method.* London: Butterworths.
LAZARSFELD, P.F. and N.W. HENRY (1968) *Latent Structure Analysis.* Boston: Houghton Mifflin.
PRZEWORSKI, A. and H. TEUNE (1969) *The Logic of Comparative Social Inquiry.* New York: John Wiley.
RUMMEL, R.J. (1967) "Understanding factor analysis." *Journal of Conflict Resolution:* 444–480.
SIMON, H.A. (1957) *Models of Man.* New York: John Wiley.
STROTZ, R.H. and H.A. WOLD (1960) "Recursive versus nonrecursive systems." *Econometrica:* 417–427.
THURSTON, L. (1960) *Multiple Factor Analysis.* Chicago: University of Chicago Press.
TILLY, C. and J. RULE (1965) *Measuring Political Upheaval.* Princeton: Princeton University Center of International Studies.
TORGERSON, W.S. (1958) *Theory and Methods of Scaling.* New York: John Wiley.
TUFTE, E.R. (1969) "Improving data analysis in political science." *World Politics:* 641–654.
WEBB, E.J., D.T. CAMPBELL, R.D. SCHWARTZ and L. SECHREST (1966) *Unobtrusive Measures: Nonreactive Research in the Social Sciences.* Chicago: Rand McNally.

Wold, H. and L. Jureen (1953) *Demand Analysis.* New York: John Wiley.
Wright, S. (1921) "Correlation and causation." *Journal of Agricultural Research* 20: 557–585.
— (1960) "Path coefficients and path regressions: alternate or complementary concepts?" *Biometrics:* 189–202.
— (1934) "The method of path coefficients." *Annals of Mathematical Statistics:* 161–215.
— (1960) "The treatment of reciprocal interaction, with or without lag, in path analysis." *Biometrics:* 423–445.

III. RESEARCH STUDIES

Adelman, I. (1967) *Society, Politics and Economic Development: A Quantitative Approach.* Baltimore: Johns Hopkins.
Angell, R.C. (1964) "Social values of Soviet and American elites: content analysis of elite media." *Journal of Conflict Resolution:* 330–385, 415–523.
Apter, D. (1965) *The Politics of Modernization.* Chicago: University of Chicago Press.
Banks, A.S. and R.B. Textor (1963) *A Cross-Polity Survey.* Cambridge: MIT Press.
Buchanan, W. and H. Cantril (1953) *How Nations See Each Other.* Urbana: University of Illinois.
Cantril, H. (1965) *The Pattern of Human Concerns.* New Brunswick: Rutgers University.
Cantril, H. and L.A. Free (1962) "Hopes and fears for self and country." *American Behavioral Scientist* [Special Supplement of Vol. 6, No. 2]: 3–30.
Cattel, R. and R. Gorsuch (1965) "The definition and measurement of national morale and morality." *Journal of Social Psychology:* 77–96.
Cutright, P. (1967) "Income distribution: a cross-national analysis." *Social Forces:* 180–189.
— (1963) "National political development: measurement and analysis." *American Sociological Review:* 253–264.
— (1968) "Occupational inheritance: a cross-national analysis." *American Journal of Sociology:* 400–416.
DeSchweinitz, K. (1964) *Industrialization and Democracy.* New York: Free Press.
Deutsch, K.W. (1961) "Social mobilization and political development." *American Political Science Review:* 493–514.
— (1960) "Toward an inventory of basic trends and patterns in comparative and international politics." *American Political Science Review:* 34–57.
DiPalma, G. (1970) *Apathy and Participation: Mass Politics in Western Society.* New York: Free Press.
Dogan, M. and S. Rokkan, Eds. (1969) *Quantitative Ecological Analysis in the Social Sciences.* Cambridge: MIT Press.
Duff, E.A. and J.F. McCamant (1968) "Measuring social and political requirements for system stability in Latin America." *American Political Science Review:* 1125–1143.
Eckstein, H., Ed. (1964) *Internal War.* New York: Free Press.

EMERSON, R. (1966) "Nationalism and political development." Pp. 157–173 in Finkle, J.L. and R.W. Gable, Eds., *Political Development and Social Change*. New York: John Wiley.

FEIERABEND, I.K., R.L. FEIERABEND et al. (1965) *Cross-National Data Bank of Political Instability Events*. San Diego: Public Affairs Research Institute.

FISHMAN, J.A. et al. (1968) *Language Problems of Developing Nations*. New York: John Wiley.

GINSBERG, N. (1961) *Atlas of Economic Development*. Chicago: University of Chicago Press.

GRAHAM, H.D. and T.R. GURR, Eds. (1969) *Violence in America: Historical and Comparative Perspectives*. New York: Frederick A. Praeger.

HUNTINGTON, S.P. (1965) "Political development and political decay." *World Politics*: 386–430.

JOHNSON, C. (1964) *Revolution and the Social System*. Stanford: The Hoover Institution on War, Revolution and Peace.

KELMAN, H.C., Ed. (1965) *International Behavior: A Social-Psychological Analysis*. New York: Holt, Rinehart & Winston.

LEITES, N. and C. WOLF, JR. (1970) *Rebellion and Authority*. Chicago: Markham.

LERNER, D. (1957) "Communication systems and social systems: a statistical exploration in history and policy." *Behavioral Science*: 266–275.

LERNER, D. and W. SCHRAMM, Eds. (1967) *Communication and Change in the Developing Countries*. Honolulu: East-West Center.

LEVINE, R.A. (1959) "Anti-European violence in Africa: a comparative analysis." *Journal of Conflict Resolution*: 420–429.

MCCLELLAND, D.C. (1961) *The Achieving Society*. Princeton: Van Nostrand.

MARSH, R.M. and W.L. PARISH (1965) "Modernization and communism: a re-test of Lipset's hypothesis." *American Sociological Review*: 934–942.

NEEDLER, M.C. (1966) "Political development and military intervention in Latin America." *American Political Science Review*: 616–626.

— (1968) "Political development and socioeconomic development: the case of Latin America." *American Political Science Review*: 889–897.

NEUBAUER, D. (1967) "Some conditions of democracy." *American Political Science Review*: 1002–1009.

NIXON, R.B. (1965) "Freedom in the world's press: a fresh appraisal with new data." *Journalism Quarterly*: 3–14.

OLSEN, M.E. (1968) "Multivariate analysis of national political development." *American Sociological Review*: 699–712.

PUTNAM, R.D. (1967) "Toward explaining military intervention in Latin American politics." *World Politics*: 83–110.

RUMMEL, R.J. (1966) "A foreign conflict behavior code sheet." *World Politics*: 283–296.

— (1969) "Indicators of cross-national and international patterns." *American Political Science Review*: 127–147.

RUSSETT, B.M. (1964) "Inequality and instability: the relation of land tenure and politics." *World Politics*: 442–454.

— (1965) *Trends in World Politics*. New York: Macmillan.

— et al. (1968) "National political units in the twentieth century: a standardized list." *American Political Science Review*: 932–951.

Selective Bibliography 563

RUSSETT, B.M. et al. (1964) *World Handbook of Political and Social Indicators.* New Haven: Yale University Press.
SEBALD, H. (1962) "Studying national character through comparative content analysis." *Social Forces:* 318-322.
SILVERT, K. (1961) *The Conflict Society: Reaction and Resolution in Latin America.* New Orleans: Hauser Press.
TANTER, R. (1965) "Dimensions of conflict behavior within and between nations, 1955-60." *Peace Research Society Papers* 3.
WOLF, C. (1965) "The political effects of economic programs: some indications from Latin America." *Economic Development and Cultural Change:* 1-20.

IV. MISCELLANEOUS

Monographs and Occasional Papers on cross-national research are published in the following centers:

DIMENSIONALITY OF NATIONS PROJECT, University of Hawaii, Honolulu, Hawaii.
CENTER OF INTERNATIONAL STUDIES, Woodrow Wilson School of Public and International Affairs, Princeton University, Princeton, New Jersey.
STUDIES IN INTERNATIONAL CONFLICT AND INTEGRATION, Stanford University, Stanford, California.
CENTER FOR COMPARATIVE POLITICAL RESEARCH, State University of New York at Binghamton, Binghamton, New York.

Also of interest are two series published by Sage Publications, Beverly Hills, California:

STUDIES IN COMPARATIVE INTERNATIONAL DEVELOPMENT, edited by Irving Louis Horowitz.
SAGE PROFESSIONAL PAPERS IN COMPARATIVE POLITICS, edited by Harry Eckstein and Ted Robert Gurr.

ABOUT THE EDITORS

JOHN V. GILLESPIE is Assistant Professor of Political Science at Indiana University. He has been working with Dina A. Zinnes and Jonathon Wilkenfeld on a series of research projects in comparative foreign policy. Dr. Gillespie is the co-author of *Comparative Politics Laboratory* (1970) as well as author and co-author of several articles and professional papers. He has been the recipient of National Science Foundation research support.

BETTY A. NESVOLD is Associate Professor of Political Science at San Diego State College. She has been working with Ivo K. and Rosalind L. Feierabend on a research project sponsored by the National Science Foundation which investigates the attributes and correlates of political aggression as it occurs in nations. She has served as consultant to the National Commission on the Causes and Prevention of Violence (Eisenhower Commission), and has co-authored several articles analyzing political violence.

ABOUT THE AUTHORS

IRMA ADELMAN received her Ph.D. from the University of California, Berkeley, and is currently a Professor of Economics at Northwestern University. Mrs. Adelman is a consultant to the Agency for International Development, The International Bank for Reconstruction and Development and to the Government of Korea on technical aspects of development planning. Among her major publications are: *Theories of Economic Growth and Development*, Stanford University Press (1961); *The Theory and Design of Economic Development* (with Erik Thorbecke), Johns Hopkins Press (1966); and *Society, Politics and Economic Development—A Quantitative Approach* (with Cynthia Taft Morris), Johns Hopkins Press (1967). Numerous of her articles have appeared in the professional journals.

ARTHUR S. BANKS is Associate Professor and Director of the Center for Comparative Political Research at the State University of New York at Binghamton. He is the author (with Robert B. Textor) of *A Cross-Polity Survey* (1963) and various professional papers and articles. He has taught at the University of New Hampshire, the University of Massachusetts, and Indiana University. He is currently engaged in a study of multivariate analysis of cross-national time-series data.

ROGER W. BENJAMIN is Assistant Professor of Political Science at the University of Minnesota. He has done research in the area of cross-national analysis and is the author of articles and professional papers in this area. His special interests are in the Chinese and Japanese political systems.

D. P. BWY is Assistant Professor of Political Science at the University of Hawaii. He has been a research associate of the Oak Ridge National Laboratory (Behavioral Studies Group) and of the Civil Violence Research Center at Case Western Reserve University. One primary focus of his research has been "social conflict," and he has presented papers before meetings of the American Political Science Association, the American Psychological Association, the Midwest Political Science Association, and the Western Political Science Association. Mr. Bwy has contributed to the *American Behavioral Scientist*, *Latin American Research Review*, *Behavioral Science*, and several readers on "revolution" and cross-national studies. He is the author of *Social Conflict: A Keyword-in-Context Bibliography on the Literature of the Developing Areas* (1967), and *Patterns of Conflict in Latin America*, Charles Merrill Publishers (forthcoming).

PHILLIPS CUTRIGHT is on the staff of the Center for Urban Studies, Massachusetts Institute of Technology, Cambridge. He is compiling a study, with Omer Galle, of changing illegitimacy rates within 25 nations from 1947–65, and a companion study of trends in eight nations over a longer period of time. His most recent work is an analysis of the impact of military service on civilian earnings.

DENNIS DAVIS received a B.A. degree from St. Olaf College in Social-Psychology. He is currently a Ph.D. candidate in Journalism and Mass Communications at the University of Minnesota, where he holds the position of Research Assistant. His areas of special interest include research on the effects of mass communications and the relationship of communication systems development to other areas of national development.

IVO K. FEIERABEND is Professor of Political Science and his wife, ROSALIND L. FEIERABEND, is Professor of Psychology at San Diego State College, California. They are co-directors (with Betty A. Nesvold) of a research project, Systemic Conditions of Political Aggression, supported by the National Science Foundation. The Feierabends have served as consultants to the National Commission on the Causes and Prevention of Violence (Eisenhower Commission). They have authored numerous articles on comparative political violence. A book on political aggression is forthcoming, as well as a reader in the area of political violence (co-edited with Ted R. Gurr). The Feierabends' joint research on violence was awarded the 1966 Socio-Psychological Prize of the American Association for the Advancement of Science.

RUSSELL H. FITZGIBBON is Professor of Political Science at the University of California, Santa Barbara. He has written numerous articles on Latin American government and politics. His books include *Uruguay: Portrait of a Democracy* (1954); *Latin America, Past and Present* (1946); and a recent study published by the University of California, *The Academic Senate of the University of California*.

WILLIAM H. FLANIGAN is Director of the Political Behavior Laboratory and Associate Professor of Political Science at the University of Minnesota. He is author of *Political Behavior of the American Electorate* (1969), co-author of *Political Behavior Laboratory* (1969), and co-author of numerous articles and professional papers. Professor Flanigan is co-director (with Edwin Fogelman) of the Minnesota Political Data Archive Project, which is an attempt to collect cross-national historical data on political systems.

EDWIN FOGELMAN is Professor of Political Science at the University of Minnesota. He is co-author of *Comparative Politics Laboratory* (1970) as well as a frequent contributor to professional journals. Professor Fogelman is co-director (with William Flanigan) of the Minnesota Political Data Archive Project and has been instrumental in the development of laboratory teaching methods in political science.

About the Authors

PHILLIP M. GREGG is Assistant Professor of Political Science at the University of Michigan. He has published articles on cross-national research and international relations. His current research interest is the organization of the American public economy.

TED ROBERT GURR is Associate Professor of Political Science at Northwestern University and Associate Director of the Workshop of Comparative Politics at Princeton University (1966–70). His general research interests are the applications of social theory and empirical techniques to the analysis of sociopolitical problems, currently including the comparative study of civil strife, social authority patterns, and governmental performance. Among his publications are *Why Men Rebel*, Princeton University Press (1969), and a number of monographs and articles. He co-edited and contributed to *Violence in America: Historical and Comparative Perspectives*, a report to the National Commission on the Causes and Prevention of Violence (Bantam, Praeger, 1969).

JOHN H. KAUTSKY is Professor of Political Science at Washington University, St. Louis. He is the author of *Moscow and the Communist Party of India* (1956), "An Essay in the Politics of Development" in a volume edited by him on *Political Change in Underdeveloped Countries* (1962), *Communism and the Politics of Development* (1968), a forthcoming book on *Politics in Traditional Societies*, and numerous articles on Communism and on the politics of development.

KURT KENT was granted his B.A. by the University of Minnesota and his M.A. by the University of Iowa, both in journalism. He is now a candidate for the Ph.D. at the University of Minnesota School of Journalism and Mass Communication, where he holds the position of Research Fellow. Fields of special interest include international communication, communication and development, and research methods.

F. GERALD KLINE holds the degree of Ph.D. in Mass Communications and is presently Director of the Research Division and Assistant Professor in the School of Journalism and Mass Communications at the University of Minnesota. His areas of special interest include theory and methods in mass communications research and problems in cross-cultural research.

R. J. RUMMEL is a Professor of Political Science and the Director of the Dimensionality of Nations Project, Department of Political Science, University of Hawaii. He has taught at Yale and Indiana Universities and received his Ph.D. from Northwestern University in 1963. He has written *Applied Factor Analysis* and *Dimensions of Nations*, in addition to numerous articles on cross-national research, international relations, and conflict. Currently, he is involved in developing a mathematical theory of international relations linking the behavior of nations, including conflict behavior, to their geographic, social, economic, and political-military distances.

CHARLES L. RUTTENBERG is an Assistant Professor of Government, School of Government and Public Administration, at American University. He co-authored an article on the study of the legal process for a special issue of the *American Behavioral Scientist* on that subject which he co-ordinated. His current research interests are in the area of science-government relations, particularly the political interest group activity of scientists.

PETER G. SNOW is Associate Professor of Political Science and Chairman of the Committee on Latin American Studies at the University of Iowa. He is the author of *Argentine Radicalism* (1965) and the forthcoming *Political Forces in Argentina*, and the editor of *Government and Politics in Latin America: A Reader* (1967). His articles on Argentine politics have appeared in the *American Political Science Review, Midwest Journal of Political Science, Journal of Inter-American Studies, Parliamentary Affairs, Revista Española de Opinión Pública,* and *Ciencias Políticas y Sociales.* At present he is working on a book tentatively entitled *The Political Role of the Argentine Judiciary.*

RAYMOND TANTER, Associate Professor of Political Science at the University of Michigan, Ann Arbor, has taught at Northwestern and Stanford Universities, and served as Deputy Director, Behavioral Sciences, Advanced Research Projects Agency, Department of Defense. He has received grants from the National Science, Ford, and Carnegie Foundations. He has written articles in the fields of international relations and political development.

NAME INDEX

Aaron, H., 540, 541, 555
Aberle, D.F., 213n, 214
Adams, J.S., 213n, 214
Adelman, I., 285, 286, 287, 348, 351, 561, 565
Alba, V., 414n, 416
Alexander, R.J., 123, 138, 414n
Alford, R.R., 554n, 555
Alisky, M., 414n
Alker, H.R., 25n, 26, 247n, 248, 252, 255, 258, 261, 265, 266, 276n, 277, 290, 308, 438n, 439, 511, 511n, 530n, 535, 557, 559
Almond, G.A., 25n, 26, 119, 133, 138, 141, 143, 151, 164, 177, 186, 298, 302, 305, 306, 307n, 308, 308n, 319, 319n, 351, 370n, 371, 371n, 409, 414n, 416, 438n, 439, 511, 511n, 557
Anderson, T.W., 559
Ando, A., 559
Andrews, F.M., 258, 276n, 278
Andrzejewski, S., 532n, 535
Angell, R.C., 561
Apter, D.E., 321, 329, 561

Baker, B.E., 276, 276n
Baker, F.B., 276n, 277
Banks, A.S., 25n, 26, 141, 142, 164, 165, 181, 183, 185, 186, 193, 213n, 214, 246n, 248, 253, 254, 256, 276n, 277, 284, 285, 287, 290, 308, 311, 318n, 319, 323, 324, 328n, 329, 349, 351, 355, 363, 371, 371n, 426, 437n, 439, 441, 561, 565
Bauer, R.A., 369, 371
Bay, C., 422, 438n
Bechtoldt, H.P., 50, 83
Bemis, S.F., 414n
Benjamin, R.W., 286, 287, 565
Berkowitz, L., 142, 163n, 164, 214, 220, 245n, 248, 436n, 439, 557
Bernard, J., 50, 83
Bernd, J.L., 277, 559
Berry, B.J.L., 50, 83, 194, 214n, 214, 290, 294, 295, 307n, 308
Binder, L., 302n, 308
Black, M., 252, 277
Blackmer, D.L.M., 321, 329, 558
Blalock, A.B., 559

Blalock, H.M., 221, 247n, 248, 255, 258, 262, 276n, 277, 438n, 439, 502, 510n, 511, 534n, 535, 559
Blanksten, G.I., 113n, 114, 138, 347, 351, 414n
Bliss, C., 532n, 536
Borgatta, E.F., 49, 83, 559
Borko, H., 559
Bottenberg, A., 536
Boudon, R., 258, 277, 511, 511n, 559
Boulding, K.E., 248, 557
Braden, S., 414n
Brandenburg, F.R., 414n
Breton, R., 531n, 536
Breul, H., 83, 164
Brodbeck, M., 25n, 26, 253, 276n, 277
Brzezinski, Z.K., 306, 308, 369, 371
Buchanan, W., 561
Buchatzsch, E.J., 83, 83n
Buckley, W., 557
Burks, R.V., 370n, 371
Busey, J.L., 414n
Buss, A.H., 142, 164, 421, 436n, 439, 557
Bwy, D.P., 31, 32, 33, 189, 214, 219, 248, 251, 252, 260, 277, 565

Calderón, F.G., 384, 416
Campbell, D.T., 124, 136n, 138, 179, 186, 258, 260, 276n, 277, 278, 559, 560
Cantril, H., 141, 151, 164, 213n, 214, 557, 561
Carneiro, R., 322, 329
Carr, L.J., 51, 83
Carroll, J.B., 82n, 83, 294, 307n, 308, 559
Carthy, J.D., 436n, 439
Cattell, R., 25n, 26, 50, 56, 57, 58, 60, 76, 80, 81n, 82n, 83, 109n, 111, 141, 164, 290, 308, 313, 319, 559, 561
Chadwick, R., 39n, 47n
Cherney, H.B., 331n
Chilcote, R.H., 414n
Child, I.L., 144, 166
Christ, C.F., 559
Christenson, C., 475n
Cline, H., 386, 414n
Cnudde, C.F., 252, 255, 258, 276n, 278, 380, 504, 510, 510n, 511, 511n, 557

569

Colby, K.M., 252, 277
Cole, D., 331n
Coleman, J.S., 25n, 26, 119, 138, 143, 164, 177, 186, 260, 277, 298, 302, 305, 306, 307n, 308, 319, 319n, 328n, 329, 350n, 352, 409, 414n, 416, 426, 438n, 439, 439n, 557, 559
Collier, R.O., Jr., 276n, 277
Comrey, A.L., 82n
Conroe, W.R., 141, 156–163, 419, 439
Coombs, C., 198, 214, 559
Coser, L.A., 50, 83, 101, 102, 108n, 111, 248, 557
Cottrell, L.S., 83
Couillard, S., 475n
Culler, G.J., 383n
Cutright, P., 13, 25n, 26, 113n, 114, 134n, 138, 149, 164, 181, 183, 185, 186, 380, 381, 439, 439n, 499ff, 503, 509, 510n, 511, 511n, 536, 554n, 555, 561, 566

Dahl, R.A., 308, 510n, 511, 511n
Dahrendorf, R., 430n, 536
Daniels, G.G., 414n
Daniels, R.C., 371, 371n
Davies, J.C., 141, 164
Davis, D., 36, 566
Davis, H.E., 137n, 386, 416
Davis, K., 530n, 536
DeSchweinitz, K., 439, 439n, 561
Deutsch, K.W., 13, 25n, 26, 141, 143, 149, 151, 164, 349n, 370n, 371, 437n, 438n, 439, 441, 511, 532n, 536, 557, 561
Diamant, A., 25n
Dimensionality of Nations Project, 76, 81, 104, 144
DiPalma, G., 561
Dogan, M., 561
Dollard, J., 142, 164, 418, 420, 437n, 439
Doob, L.W., 151, 164
Dreier, J.C., 414n
Driver, H.E., 311, 319
Dubois, J., 414n
Duff, E.A., 561
Duncan, O.D., 258, 262, 264, 277, 559
Durkheim, E., 350n, 352
Duverger, M., 308

Easton, D., 143, 164, 289, 438n, 439, 557
Ebling, F.J., 436n
Eckstein, A., 532n, 536
Eckstein, H., 25n, 26, 40, 44, 46, 47, 48, 56, 57, 80, 83, 109n, 111, 120, 135n, 138, 141, 147, 163n, 164, 199, 217n, 231, 248, 436n, 557, 561, 563
Edelmann, A.T., 414n
Edwards, A.L., 86, 111, 536, 555, 560

Emerson, R., 276n, 277, 562
Ezekiel, M., 72, 81n, 83, 110n, 111, 560

Farrar, D.E., 560
Farrell, R.B., 557
Feierabend, I.K., 25n, 26, 31–33, 141, 144, 147, 164, 165, 167, 185n, 186, 189, 199, 248, 253, 254, 277, 379, 380, 417, 418, 436n, 437n, 438n, 439, 440, 562, 566
Feierabend, R.L., 25n, 26, 31–33, 141, 144, 147, 164, 165, 167, 185n, 186, 189, 199, 248, 253, 254, 277, 379, 380, 417, 418, 436n, 437n, 438n, 439, 440, 562, 566
Feigl, H., 252, 277
Fenwick, C.G., 414n
Ferber, R., 350n, 352
Finkle, J.L., 562
Fisher, F.M., 559, 560
Fishman, J.A., 562
Fiske, D.W., 179, 186, 559
Fitzgibbon, R.H., 113n, 124, 129, 130, 133, 134, 137n, 138, 141, 165, 328n, 329, 378, 386, 404, 414n, 416, 566
Flanigan, W., 25n, 167n, 379, 380, 566
Flint, G., 307n
Fogelman, E., 25n, 379, 380, 566
Forbes, H.D., 247n, 248, 560
Forbis, W., 414n
Form, W.H., 555
Fox, K.A., 72, 81n, 83, 110n, 111, 560
Frank, R.E., 255, 277, 560
Free, L.A., 141, 164, 561
Friedrich, C.J., 306, 308
Fruchter, B., 37, 37n, 59, 82n, 84, 136n, 138

Gable, R.W., 562
Gage, N.L., 258
Galíndez, J. de, 414n
Galtung, J., 213n, 214, 557
Gellner, E., 25n, 26
Gillespie, J.V., 557
Ginsberg, N., 50, 84, 308, 562
Glauber, R.R., 560
Godfrey, E.P., 49, 84
Gold, D., 383n
Gomez, R.A., 386, 414n, 416
Goodenough, W.H., 328n, 329
Goodspeed, S.S., 414n
Gorsuch, R., 561
Graham, H.D., 215, 562
Grant, F.R., 414n
Gregg, P.M., 141, 165, 181, 183, 185, 186, 193, 213n, 214, 284, 285, 287, 318n, 319, 426, 567
Guetzkow, H., 85n, 104, 111
Gulick, C., 331n
Gurr, T.R., 31, 34, 35, 36, 143, 165, 192n, 213n, 215, 217, 218, 219, 220, 245n, 246n,

Name Index

Gurr, T.R.—*contd.*
247n, 248n, 248, 440, 557, 560, 562, 563, 567
Guttman, L., 37, 37n, 168, 169, 186, 322, 560

Haas, E.B., 82n, 83n, 84, 86, 87, 104, 111, 141, 165
Hadley, P.E., 414n
Hagan, E.E., 439n, 440, 557
Haggard, E.A., 95, 111, 560
Hagood, M.J., 121
Hallett, R.M., 414n
Hanson, S.G., 415n
Hardyck, C.D., 276, 276n
Haring, C.H., 415n
Harman, H.H., 37, 37n, 47n, 48, 60, 81n, 82n, 84, 111, 307n, 308, 319, 319n, 349, 352, 560
Harris, E.W., 560
Hartman, H.P., 83, 164
Hartman, G.W., 219, 249
Hawkins, N.G., 328n, 329
Hayton, R.D., 415n
Hecksher, G., 25n, 26
Hempel, C.G., 308, 308n, 440
Henry, N.W., 566
Henrysson, S., 82n, 294
Herring, H.C., 415n
Higgins, B., 331, 352
Hirschman, A.O., 563
Hobbs, M., 85n
Hoel, P.G., 383n
Hofstaetter, P.R., 50, 84
Holland, H.F., 415n
Holt, R.T., 25n, 26, 563, 560
Hoole, F.W., 141, 142, 144–149, 163n, 165, 436n, 440
Horowitz, I.L., 569
Hoselitz, B.F., 331, 352
Hotelling, H., 138, 313, 319n
Human Relations Area Files, 25n
Huntington, S.P., 87, 102, 110n, 111, 219, 248, 369, 371, 558, 562
Hurley, J.R., 82n, 84

Inkeles, A., 141, 151, 165, 369, 371

Jackson, J.K., 328n, 329
James, P.E., 415n
Jennings, E., 136n, 138
Johnson, C., 213n, 215, 219, 248, 562
Johnson, K.F., 137n, 138, 141, 165, 328n, 329, 386, 404, 415n, 416
Johnston, J.O., 269, 277, 560
Jonassen, C.T., 49, 84
Jorrin, M., 415n
Jureen, L., 258, 561

Kaiser, H.F., 60, 84, 111, 136n, 138, 294, 309, 313, 319
Kalleberg, A.L., 558
Kantor, H., 415n
Kaplan, A., 438n, 440
Kaplan, M.A., 558
Katz, D., 86, 87, 111
Kautsky, J.H., 286, 287, 370n, 371, 371n, 567
Kelman, H.C., 562
Kempthorne, O., 566
Kendall, M.G., 318n, 320, 566
Kent, K., 36, 567
Kerlinger, F., 37, 37n
Kerr, C., 340, 350n, 352, 365, 371
Kline, F.G., 36, 260, 567
Kling, M., 113, 114, 138, 141, 165, 415n
Knorr, K., 558
Kolko, G., 530n, 536
Kornhauser, W., 219, 249, 299, 554n, 555, 558
Krantz, D.H., 276n, 277
Kravis, I., 531n, 536
Kregarman, J., 220
Kuznets, S., 25n, 26, 530n, 531n, 532n, 536

Laboritz, S., 276n, 278
Lasswell, H.D., 143, 165, 438n, 440
Lave, T.V., 371
Lawley, D.N., 293, 308n, 560
Lazarsfeld, P.F., 258, 278, 560
Leites, N., 562
Lenski, G., 513, 513n, 515ff, 530n, 531n, 532n, 536
Lerner, D., 141, 149, 150, 151, 165, 252, 260, 276n, 278, 437n, 440, 501, 502, 558, 562
Lev, J., 537
LeVine, R.A., 137n, 138, 141, 165, 440, 562
Levonian, E., 82n
Lichtheim, G., 214n, 215
Lieuwen, E., 387, 416
Lingoes, J.C., 270, 278
Lipset, S.M., 25n, 26, 129, 134n, 138, 141, 165, 319n, 320, 370n, 371n, 372, 409, 414n, 416, 426, 438n, 439, 439n, 440, 441, 499f, 510n, 511n, 512, 554n, 555, 558
Litell, N.G., 142, 144–149, 165, 436n, 440
Lott, L.B., 415n
Luce, D.R., 276n, 278

McBeth, J.H., 383n
McCamant, J.F., 561
McClelland, D.C., 55, 84, 141, 165, 181, 183–185, 186, 562
McClelland, K., 513n
McCrone, D.J., 252, 255, 258, 276n, 278, 380, 510, 510n, 511
McFarland, D.D., 270, 278

McKenna, J.G., 87, 103, 111
McNeil, E.B., 142, 165, 436n, 440
McPhee, W.N., 558
Macdonald, A.F., 415n
Mack, R.W., 51, 84
Maier, N.R.F., 142, 165, 420, 440
Mandeville, G.K., 276n, 277
Manger, W., 415n
Marcus, M., 383n
Marsh, R.M., 370n, 372, 562
Martz, J.D., 387, 415n, 416
Marvick, D., 387, 414n, 416
Massey, J., 185n
Matthews, H.L., 415n
Maxwell, A.E., 293, 308n, 309, 560
Mecham, J.L., 415n
Melman, S., 532n, 536
Menzel, H., 328n, 329
Merelman, R.M., 220, 249
Merritt, R.L., 25n, 26, 141, 165, 253, 254, 278, 535, 558
Merton, R.K., 143, 165
Mestas, A. de, 115, 138
Meyer, A.G., 371n, 372
Midlarsky, M., 189, 215, 558
Miller, E.G., Jr., 415n
Miller, J.C., 322, 329
Milliken, M.F., 321, 329, 558
Millis, W., 63, 84
Mills, C.W., 530n, 536
Milnor, A.J., 564
Moore, W.E., 338, 352, 530n, 564
Morgan, J., 530n, 536
Morgenthau, H., 78, 84
Morris, C., 49, 285, 286, 287
Mosier, C.I., 81n, 84
Mueller, J.E., 558
Munro, D.G., 415n
Murdock, G.P., 25n, 26, 144, 165
Murkland, H.B., 415n
Myers, A.E., 255, 278

Naegele, K., 166
Naroll, R., 25n, 26, 27, 558
Needler, M.C., 415n, 558, 562
Nelson, J., 331n
Nesvold, B.A., 31, 33–35, 141, 144–155, 165, 166, 186, 253, 278, 418, 419, 437n, 438n, 440, 564
Nettl, J.P., 558
Neubauer, D.E., 511n, 512, 557, 562
Nieburg, H.L., 558
Nilson, S.S., 558
Nixon, R.B., 249, 276n, 278, 562
North, R.C., 214n, 215, 372

Olsen, M.E., 562
Olson, M., 558

Oppenheim, F.E., 422, 438n, 440
Orshansky, M., 534n, 536
Oshima, H., 531n, 536

Paige, G., 104, 112
Padgett, L.V., 415n
Palmore, E., 539n
Parish, W.L., 370n, 372, 562
Parsons, T., 143, 166, 213n, 215
Pastore, N., 220
Payne, J., 113, 138
Pelz, D.C., 258, 276n, 278
Peres, S.H., 49
Petrinovich, L.F., 276n, 278
Pitts, J., 166
Powell, G.B., 557
Powell, J.D., 137n
Prager, J., 217n
Price, D.O., 121
Pride, R., 475n
Pruitt, D., 85n
Przeworski, A., 558, 560
Putnam, R.D., 562
Pye, L.W., 278, 511n, 512, 558

Rambo, A.T., 123, 138
Retzlaff, R.H., 25n, 27, 558
Rhodes, E.C., 50, 84
Richardson, L.F., 55, 56, 57, 77, 80, 84, 103, 109n, 110n, 111
Ridker, R.G., 558
Riggs, F., 85n
Robinson, E.A., 95, 111
Robinson, W.S., 256, 278
Rokkan, S., 25n, 26, 141, 165, 166, 253, 254, 278, 439, 535, 558, 561
Romaninsky, J., 513n, 531n, 536
Ronning, C.N., 415n
Rosecrance, R., 86, 87, 111
Rosenau, J.N., 558
Ross, A.M., 219, 249
Rostow, W.W., 342, 350n, 352
Royer, W.F., 383n, 415n
Rozelle, R.M., 258, 260, 278
Ruggels, L., 260, 276n, 278
Rule, J., 222, 249, 560
Rummel, R.J., 31, 32, 33, 37, 37n, 40, 42, 47n, 48, 48n, 85, 87, 88, 89, 98, 102, 104, 109n, 110n, 111, 113n, 122, 131, 135n, 138, 142, 147, 148, 163n, 166, 179, 180, 185n, 186, 194, 199, 214n, 215, 221, 222, 245n, 246n, 249, 290, 293, 294, 295, 307n, 308n, 309, 313, 319n, 320, 436n, 437n, 440, 558, 560, 562, 567
Russett, B.M., 25n, 27, 137n, 138, 141, 142, 163n, 166, 189, 193, 199, 213n, 215, 217n, 222, 249, 253, 254, 278, 290, 293, 294, 295, 307n, 308n, 309, 311, 318n, 319n, 320, 349n, 352, 437n, 439, 439n, 440,

Name Index

Russett, B.M.—*contd.*
441, 499, 512, 530n, 531n, 532n, 533n, 535, 535n, 536, 537, 562, 563
Rostow, D.A., 558
Ruttenberg, C., 35, 217n, 218, 219, 220, 246n, 248, 568

Sandsmark, R.A., 307
Sawyer, J., 104, 111
Schelling, T.C., 249, 558
Scheuch, E.K., 438n, 440
Schnore, L.R., 50, 84, 307n, 309
Schramm, W., 260, 276n, 278, 562
Schubert, G., 49, 84, 290, 309
Schuessler, K.F., 289n, 311, 319
Schurz, W.L., 415n
Schwartz, R.D., 322, 328n, 329, 560
Scott, R.E., 387, 415n, 416
Sebald, H., 562
Sechrest, L., 560
Seton-Watson, H., 371n, 372
Shannon, L., 25n, 27
Sheldon, E.B., 558
Sherif, C.W., 559
Sherif, M., 102, 112, 559
Shils, E.A., 143, 166, 306, 321, 329
Sidman, M., 55, 84, 86, 87, 108n, 112
Silvert, K., 113, 121, 134n, 136n, 138, 415n, 562
Simmel, G., 101, 102, 108n, 112
Simon, H.A., 255, 258, 278, 502, 512, 559, 560
Simpson, D., 539, 555
Simpson, L.B., 386
Singer, J.D., 85n, 141, 166, 318, 599
Sjoberg, G., 559
Skilling, H.G., 371n, 372
Small, M., 141, 166
Smelser, N., 213n, 215, 337, 352
Snow, P., 284, 285, 568
Snyder, R.C., 51, 84, 104, 112
Sorokin, P., 87, 103, 112, 195, 215, 559
Spearman, C., 290
Sprague, J., 353n
Stanley, J.C., 124, 138, 276n, 559
Stebbins, J.H., 415n
Stevens, C.D., 276, 278
Stinchcombe, A., 533n
Stokes, D.E., 185n
Stokes, W.S., 113, 114, 138, 387, 415n, 416
Strotz, R.H., 560
Strout, A., 331n
Stuart, G.H., 415n
Suits, D.B., 269, 278
Swartz, N., 307n
Szulc, T., 391, 415n

Tanter, R.A., 31, 32, 33, 39n, 42, 44, 45, 47n, 48, 104, 111, 113n, 119, 120, 122, 131, 135n, 138, 142, 146, 149, 166, 185, 186, 199, 215, 217n, 221, 222, 246n, 247n, 249, 309, 436n, 558, 562, 568
Taylor, P.B., Jr., 415n
Terwilliger, J.S., 255, 278
Teune, H., 558, 560
Textor, R.B., 25n, 26, 141, 142, 164, 186, 213n, 214, 246n, 248, 253, 254, 256, 276n, 277, 284, 290, 308, 311, 319, 323, 324, 328n, 329, 349, 351, 355, 363, 371, 371n, 437n, 439, 441, 561
Thrupp, S., 213n
Thurstone, L.L., 60, 82n, 84, 116, 134n, 138, 290, 293, 309, 337, 349, 352, 560
Tietze, C., 535n, 537
Tilly, C., 222, 249, 560
Tomasek, R.D., 387, 416
Tomlinson, E., 415n
Torgerson, W.S., 560
Travis, M.B., Jr., 415n
Truman, D.B., 297, 309
Tucker, L.R., 255, 278
Tucker, R.C., 371n, 372
Tufte, E.R., 247n, 248, 560
Tukey, J.W., 276n, 278
Turner, J.E., 25n, 26, 557, 560
Turner, M.E., 276n, 278
Tversky, A., 276n, 278

Udy, S.H., Jr., 322, 328n, 329

Vanden Helm, R., 247n
Verba, S., 133, 141, 151, 164, 308, 308n, 319, 319n, 511, 511n, 558
Verdoorn, P.J., 350n, 352

Walker, H., 537
Walton, J.G., 141, 166, 219, 249, 422–424, 438n, 440
Ward, J.A., 536
Wasserspring, L., 217n
Watkins, J.W.N., 25n, 27
Webb, E.J., 560
Wells, H., 415n
Whitaker, A.P., 415n
Whiting, A.S., 82n, 83n, 84, 86, 87, 104, 111
Whiting, J.W., 144, 166
Wilgus, A.C., 415n
Wilks, S.S., 121, 138
Winer, J., 537
Wiseman, H.V., 559
Wold, H.A., 258, 279, 560, 561
Wolf, C., Jr., 383n, 387, 414, 416, 562, 563
Wolins, L., 276n, 279
Wood, R.C., 49, 84
Worchel, P., 220

Wright, Q., 50, 84, 86, 87, 112
Wright, S., 258, 261, 276n, 279, 503, 512, 561

Yale Political Data Program, 13, 25n, 144, 349n, 402
Yates, A.J., 188, 215, 245n, 249
Yee, A.H., 258, 279
York, D., 555
Young, F.W., 322, 328n, 330
Young, R.C., 322, 328n, 330
Yule, G.U., 318n, 320

Zeizel, H., 276n, 279
Zenk, G., 383n
Zinnes, D., 39n
Zolberg, A.R., 213n, 215

SUBJECT INDEX

Aggregate data, 18, 36, 251–279, passim
Anomic Violence Index, 122, 123, 136n

Cause, as process, 253, 272, 273; and analysis of aggregate data, 251–279, passim
Censorship scale, 54
Charismatic leader, 385
Civil strife, 217–249; and relative deprivation, 218; definition of, 221
Coding criteria, 32, 34
Comparability, 20–21
Configurative approach, 14–18, passim; and cross-national approach, 14–18; weaknesses of, 15–16
Conflict behavior types, 31, 32, 39, 306, 307; dimensions of, 39–47 49–84, 85–113; measures of, 40, 45, 46, 51–53, 106–108; interpersonal and intergroup, 50; threats in, 75, 76
Consensual validation, 144, 168–169
Cross-national approach indicators, 18, 20, 31, 35; index stability, 189; data, attributes of, 18–21, passim; data, comparability of, 20, 21; data, missing, 19, 23, 26; data, reliability of, 18–21; data, stability of, 55, 74, 80
Cross-sectional analysis, 23, 488–493

Data reduction, 22
Democracy, problems of definition and measurement, 375–381, passim, 446ff

Error, 53–55, 61, 88–89, 326–327
Explanation, 16–18; emergentist, 16, 17; reductionist, 16, 17; different approaches to, 35

Frustration-aggression theory, 35, 142, 143, 149, 187–189, 195, 218–220, 418–420; and political instability, 142, 420; and want formation, 150, 151; and want satisfaction, 150, 151

Galton's problem, 24, 25n
Group cohesion, 102

Index of democratization, 446f; of frustration, 35; stability, 189
Inequality, 513–537, passim
Integration, national, 442

Longitudinal analysis, 23, 488–493

Measurement, 21, 31–34, passim; selection of indicators, 21, 22; reduction of multiple indicators, 21, 22; relation to theoretical and operational definitions, 22; of political instability, 31–34; of cooperation, 75; of civil violence, 196–198, 200, 217–249, passim; of deprivation, 223–228; of democracy and democratization, 375–381, passim, 441–473, passim

Nation, definition of, 251
National social security, measures of, 540f

Organized violence index, 122, 123, 136n

Political development, status of concept, 283–288, passim, 327, 375, 376, 499ff; longitudinal research designs in, 23; use of scalogram analysis in study of, 321–330, passim
Political instability, 113–139, 142–163; and frustration-aggression theory, 142, 417–436, passim
Political legitimacy, 129, 130, 133

Reliability, 18–20, 87–88
Replication of research, 21, 22, 32, 55, 75, 85–87, 377
Relative deprivation, 218, 221, passim
Research design, 23; cross-sectional, 23, 488–493; longitudinal, 23, 25n, 441, 442, 488–493
Revolution, use of term, 114, 115

Sampling, problems in cross-national research, 23, 24, 36

575

Statistical techniques, conjoint measurement analysis, 269, 270; dummy variable analysis, 269; error, measurement, 255; error, random, 53, 54, 55, 61, 255; error, systematic, 53, 54, 55, 75, 80, 88; factor analysis, 32, 33, 39, 49, 50, 53, 55, 58–60, 62, 65, 72, 76, 89, 109, 110, 116–118, 134n, 135n, 290, 293–295; independence problems, 23, 24; intraclass correlations, 93, 95; multi-collinearity, problems of, 25; multiple regression analysis, 49, 65, 66, 72, 97, 98, 110; Q-factor analysis, 311–320, passim; Scalogram analysis, 34, 78, 167–186, passim, 285, 321–330, passim, 541; step-wise regression analysis, 35, 201, 207; time lag regression, 99; transformations, 57, 255

Unit-of-analysis set, 14, 24, 36; independence of elements in, 23, 24

Validity, 33–34, 144, 167–169

Violence, types, 32, 33, 119–123, 167–186; unequivocal acts of, 40; equivocal acts of, 40; extended, 40; anomic, 119–134, passim; organized, 119–134, passim; civil, 187–215